Patterns of Government

PATTERNS
OF
GOVERNMENT

*The Major Political Systems
of Europe*

SAMUEL H. BEER *and* ADAM B. ULAM
Harvard University

HERBERT J. SPIRO
Amherst College

HARRY ECKSTEIN *and* NICHOLAS WAHL
Princeton University

under the editorship of
SAMUEL H. BEER *and* ADAM B. ULAM

Second Edition, Revised and Enlarged

RANDOM HOUSE 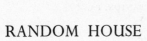 NEW YORK

Preface to Revised Edition

In the first edition of this book, the authors stressed the study of politics as a scientific discipline. They recognized that the scientific approach had made considerable progress in recent years and were convinced that the new ideas should not be confined to the learned journal and the graduate seminar, but should be shared with undergraduates. They knew that such a design would make unusual demands upon the student. But they also believed that the college students of today—to whose rising ability and better preparation teachers throughout the country testify—were themselves impatient of easy texts and ready for more rigorous analysis.

The reception of the first edition has confirmed the authors' belief that there is a need for such a book. Comment and criticism from colleagues all over the country have been very helpful in the work of revision. Errors of fact have been corrected and some of the original interpretations have been reconsidered. Considerable illustrative material has been added and the studies of the various systems have been brought up to date. The authors, however, have been encouraged to retain the same basic approach.

We characterize this approach as "scientific." This does not mean that political science—or any social science—can progress by mechanically imitating what is presumed to be the procedure of some natural science. A method of inquiry needs to be adapted to its subject matter. That being understood, the stress on scientific method performs the useful function of keeping in the foreground of attention certain major tasks of political analysis. These tasks are discussed in Part One, which tries to show how the present book fits into the political scientist's general program of inquiry.

In adapting their method to the subject matter of political science, the authors have been impressed by the utility of "systems analysis." One purpose of Part One is to explain this approach—the theory of the political system. In the following sections, the authors put the theory to work, analysing respectively the political systems of Great Britain, France, Germany and the Soviet Union. The principal changes in this edition have been made in the section on France: the actual practice of de Gaulle's Republic is fully treated, and at the same time, this particular pattern of government is set in the context of French political development. It is presented as an expression of the "administrative tradition" in French political culture. The forces which today, as in the past, work against governmental effectiveness are examined, the forms they took under the Third and Fourth Republics being continually related to their modes of expression under the Fifth. Dr. Wahl's interpretation of the basic forces and problems of the French system remains fundamentally the same as in the first edition.

One result of the systems approach is that the subdivisions of a particular country's account do not necessarily coincide with a discussion of each of the separate legal institutions of that country's government. The chapters in one section may take up separately the executive, the legislative, and the civil service, as is usually done in textbooks on government. But they will also depart from that outline, if necessary, in order to focus on real factors of power or major processes of decision-making. Yet if the authors have followed the logic of systems analysis, they have by no means disdained the conventional virtues of the introductory text. They have made a liberal use of history. They have described, often in detail, elements of formal structure, such as electoral laws and constitutional principles. They have also devoted a great deal of space to the social and economic forces impinging on a given political system. Indeed, the systems approach, by stressing the functioning of the political system in the social system as a whole, directs attention to such interaction of political and non-political forces.

Each account is factual, but is selective in its use of facts. Each is concerned with a certain problem, and evidence is mustered only insofar as it is relevant to this problem. This is sound scientific procedure. It means, of course, that some practices and institutions normally discussed in a textbook are passed over, while others are given relatively more attention.

What are these problems around which the authors have organized their accounts? Is there a single problem common to all? While each author has been free to emphasize the questions of greatest importance to the system with which he deals, certain common concerns can be traced through the whole book. Each author is centrally concerned with the problem of stability and development. How well has the system stood the test of time? What are the forces that keep it working and maintain its characteristic patterns? What are those that tend to disrupt these patterns or draw them on toward new forms? And while the authors have not tried to predict, they have permitted themselves to raise the further question: What are the major possibilities for the future?

Because they view the political system as performing a function in the social system as a whole, the authors are also concerned throughout with the effectiveness of each system. Certain questions therefore recur. For example: How effective is the system as a means of identifying and solving problems confronting its society? Has the system adapted, developing new patterns or reconciling old and incompatible ones, in such a way as to maintain or enhance its power for constructive action? Have basic values of the system—which in one system may be democratic and in another dictatorial—been so institutionalized as to hinder or to help effective government?

This book originally grew out of discussions among colleagues, all at that time engaged in teaching and research at Harvard. We had asked whether it might not be possible to write a textbook that not only had the "facts," but also presented them with a degree of sophistication. So we talked, we argued, we wrote memoranda. Together we considered both the general approach of the book and how it might be used in the analysis of particular systems. These analyses were guided by our common outlook; in turn this outlook was developed in the light of the particular country accounts. We did not reach perfect agreement. Nor did we present our views as final and unquestionable. What we said in the first edition and what we say in this revision can be critized, modified, refined, and developed. The student should not look to this book—or to any work of political science for "the word." Political science is not a fixed body of certain truths, but a developing discipline in which all propositions are subject to revision in the light of new evidence and more imaginative and rigorous analysis. There is no more essential trait of scientific inquiry.

For this as for any textbook, acknowledgments due are legion. While all the authors have done original research in their respective fields, in the writing of this book they are greatly indebted as well to the work of others. In the select bibliographies, they have tried to acknowledge these large debts. On behalf of all the authors, the editors would also like again to thank friends and colleagues for their many helpful comments on the first edition.

SAMUEL H. BEER
ADAM B. ULAM

Cambridge, Mass.
July, 1962

Contents

PART TWO   THE BRITISH POLITICAL SYSTEM

Contents

PART FOUR   THE GERMAN POLITICAL SYSTEM

Contents

List of Tables

and Figures

Part One

THE ANALYSIS
OF POLITICAL
SYSTEMS

---

by Samuel H. Beer

[I]

A Science of Politics?

To call the study of government and politics political science may seem a little pretentious. Consider the other subjects that come to mind when we speak of "science"—physics, chemistry, biology, and so on. What claim can our subject make to belong in this company? Can political science hope to be really "scientific"? Would we not do better to imitate the caution of the British who prefer the term, "political studies"?

A science is more than a branch of study. It is more than an organized body of knowledge. It is a branch of study in which knowledge is organized around empirically confirmed general laws. The discovery of such laws is a principal object of scientific inquiry. We think, for instance, of the Newtonian laws of motion in physics, or of the laws of chemistry associated with the kinetic theory of gases.

To be sure, no one today would say that such generalizations hold true with absolute certainty. The most richly confirmed and long-accepted laws of physical science remain hypotheses, and, as the history of science shows, may be superseded by new explanatory hypotheses more adequate to the evidence. But even with such a proviso, where are the general laws of political behavior? If we have not found them, it is not for lack of prolonged study. From the days of the ancient Greeks men of talent and sometimes of genius have applied their minds to the understanding of political affairs. We cannot excuse the modesty of our achievement by alleging that our branch of study is "young."

Not lack of effort, not "youth," but the nature of our material may be the source of the trouble. That material is man. Our study is concerned with the political aspect of men's relations with one another. And it can be powerfully argued—this argument, of course, applies to all the social sciences—that no reliable laws of human relations can be established because of the nature of the individual human being. Man is a thinking animal. He can invent new forms of behavior to achieve old ends; he can imagine new ends, new social and political values, to which he can commit his energies. "I myself believe," Toynbee wrote recently, "that, in human affairs, something that we may well call 'creativity' . . . is perpetually at work, and that this is constantly producing novelties that have not only not been predicted but have been intrinsically unpredictable."[1] If so, how can our explanations of human behavior achieve even the status of hypothetical laws?

Argument over this question can generate a good deal of heat. For points of ethical theory may be raised. Defenders of the value and worth of the individual human being, for instance, may rest their case on the presumption that each person *has* such creative powers. To deny creativity may therefore appear to them as an attack upon individuality. On the other hand, the political scientist will be loathe to save this ethical theory if the future of his study as a scientific discipline is to be denied.

Of course, it is absurd to think that the political scientist himself will have no ethical concerns. No doubt he is interested in the truth for its own sake and takes a purely scholarly delight in the pursuit of the elusive laws of politics. At the same time, the problems he chooses to investigate and the kinds of behavior that he thinks worth studying will be chosen in the light of some standard of what is important. His sense of what is important and worth investigating cannot help but be influenced by his ethical concerns. And if—like the authors of this book—he gives a high value to individuality, the premises of his ethics and his science may seem to be in conflict.

The first thing to be said is that the question whether a science of politics is possible can be answered only by inquiry. If we want to know how far we can go in establishing reliable explanatory hypotheses about political behavior, we can find out only by making the attempt. That attempt will be prolonged and complex. It must be carried out in a scientific spirit and according to scientific method.

The conviction of many political scientists today is that, in spite of the long history of "political studies," that attempt has not been made. Yet they share a feeling of modest, but genuine, confidence. They do not anticipate the imminent appearance of the Newton or Einstein of the discipline. They are not bemused by the physical sciences, whose universality and precision the social sciences cannot plausibly hope to rival.

---

[1] Arnold Toynbee, A *Study of History; Vol. XII: Reconsiderations* (London, 1961), p. 16, n. 6.

They certainly do not think that "scientific method" is some kind of mysterious intellectual machine into which the dull and unimaginative researcher can feed "data" and obtain "laws." They do believe, however, that we are gaining a clearer understanding of how scientific method can be used in the study of political behavior and they see a growing commitment in the discipline to the persistent and systematic use of that method.

The authors of this book approach their work in this spirit. They have not tried to write a comprehensive study of political science. You will not find in its final pages the culminating statement of a system of confirmed general laws of political behavior. Only too often the ambition to leap from brief, but global, inquiry to a definitive theory has been the undoing of would-be political scientists. Yet the kind of inquiry undertaken in this book can contribute to the development of a systematic and empirically tested body of knowledge.

What is the nature of this contribution? How do studies such as these fit in with the larger attempt to put the study of politics on a more scientific basis? What is the place of this book in the "program" of political science? To answer these questions is also to say something about scientific method and the main tasks of political science. We can examine these tasks under four headings: description, classification, explanation, and confirmation.

Description

Let us begin with a few reflections derived from common sense and common experience. If we ask, for instance, whether human behavior is predictable, common sense will probably answer "no—and yes." No two people are exactly alike; nor are any two families or homes or business firms. Our first response is to affirm novelty. At the same time, common sense affirms uniformity, regularity, and recurrence. No one could succeed in carrying out his day's work unless he could rely implicitly on massive uniformity in the behavior of other people. Fire engines come when you pull the alarm; secretaries answer when the phone rings; cars stop when the traffic lights turn red. None of these generalizations holds with absolute certainty. But in the experience of nearly all readers of this book, they hold with a very high degree of probability. These examples, of course, are commonplace, if not trivial, and the patterns on which each of us relies in daily life include far more complex, subtle, and important relationships—uniformities of action by employers and employees, friends and enemies, members of a family, persons in authority, various types of groups, and so on. Daily activity, indeed, survival, would be impossible if one could not rely upon such massive uniformity in social action.

Our common-sense knowledge of the society in which we live comprises a system of generalized expectations about such patterns. Whatever a more sophisticated inquiry may ultimately determine about the element of unpredictable novelty in human affairs—how great it is or whether it exists at all—we are enough encouraged by these impressions of everyday experience to proceed with the study of social science. In so doing we are simply developing systematically what common sense has already begun. Because there are patterns of social action, a first task of social science is to describe them. Because there are patterns of government, a first task of political science is descriptive generalization.

The primary purpose of this book is such description. Like the historian, the political scientist will observe and describe particular events—for instance, the fall of some cabinet in the history of the Third French Republic. But, unlike the historian, *the political scientist looks at any particular event in order to see whether it is an instance of some recurring pattern*. From observing the fall of a particular French cabinet, he goes on to examine the fall of other cabinets under the Third and Fourth Republics. He will hope to arrive at a generalized description of the making and unmaking of governments in those two Republican regimes.

In short, the political scientist observes particular, concrete events. But he looks at such events in order to find similarities on which to base his descriptive generalizations.

In the light of the grand objectives of political science, we may be inclined to speak slightingly of "mere" description. But we should not underestimate its importance. A great deal of vital inquiry—and not a little controversy—centers around such questions. What is the real power of the Presidency in the American system? How democratic is Gaullist France? Is Soviet Russia still correctly characterized as "totalitarian"? Political science rightly and necessarily devotes much effort to developing and answering questions such as these.

Nor should we underestimate the difficulties of accurate and sophisticated description. When describing the relations of the executive and legislature in modern British government, for instance, all writers would agree that the Cabinet is "dominant." They mean by this, among other things, that again and again when the Cabinet proposes to the House of Commons some measure of legislation, expenditure, taxation, or foreign policy, the House votes its approval, insisting on little or no modification. Understandably, some writers have referred to this pattern as "Cabinet dictatorship," characterizing the role of the House of Commons as little more than that of an electoral college. But such a description, as Dr. Eckstein points out, omits a subtle interplay of influence on several levels between the Cabinet and the House—for instance, the pressure that

M.P.s can exert through the political parties and the recognition by party leaders that they cannot too deeply affront the sentiments or interests of their followers. To describe the pattern of power between the Cabinet and the House of Commons, the political scientist must abstract from the particular acts of different prime ministers, cabinets, and M.P.s over a period of years. If he is to describe this pattern correctly and adequately, he needs an intimate knowledge of the concrete material of political history and a sensitivity to the nuances of human relationships. The pattern of "Cabinet dominance" in British government cannot be caught in some simple phrase—it is complex, subtle, and anything but obvious at first glance.

Not the least of our difficulties comes from the fact that the character of a political act (or any social act) depends very much upon what the individuals involved take it to mean. The act does not consist simply of certain overt, physical behavior by one or more individuals. It also includes the meaning that these people attribute to that physical behavior. When, for instance, a citizen of a country on election day goes to a polling place and makes a mark on a ballot, he and the other persons involved have a certain understanding of what this behavior means: he is "voting." What he thinks and feels the act of voting to be is an inseparable part of his act; this meaning may vary from one country to another and even among the voters of a single country.

Dr. Eckstein and Dr. Wahl, for instance, take pains to distinguish what the act of voting means in Britain and in France. On the whole, to vote in Britain for a House of Commons candidate is to express a choice not for a personal representative in the legislature but rather for a team of party leaders who are committed to a program and prepared to form a government. Such an attitude is an important part of the facts. It helps explain, for instance, the strong party cohesion in the House of Commons. For, given this attitude among the mass of the electorate, the M.P. who may be tempted to break party discipline realizes that his personal popularity, his ability, and his concern for the interests of the district will count for little if voters conclude that they cannot trust him to support the leadership of a party. If we are looking for the causes of the great power of British party leaders over their followers in the legislature, we cannot fail to include this distinctive intellectual and moral outlook on voting among the British electorate.

Patterns of government cannot be accurately described unless we show what meaning they have to the participants in the acts from which we generalize. This is one reason why the authors have given such heavy emphasis to "political culture," a term that will be defined and illustrated in Chapter 3. To mention it here is relevant because it refers to those basic attitudes toward government that are involved in the various patterns of action of a political system. If we have a grasp of these basic attitudes, it is much easier to identify the meanings that members of the system give to particular acts and patterns. Yet these matters of thought and feeling are far from easy to discern and describe correctly. Indeed, they are the stuff which poets and novelists continually struggle to articulate. The social scientist needs to cultivate the sensitivity of the humanist, as well as the rigor of the scientist.

Classification

When a number of systems have been described, it is logical then to classify them. So, for instance, if we were dealing with all the governments of modern Europe, we might find that we could put them in two broad classes, "democracies" and "dictatorships," and that within each of these classes various subclasses could be further distinguished. In this manner classification would follow as the next stage of political analysis after description. Yet our actual procedure is more complicated. For the political scientist cannot begin to describe unless he has some rudimentary scheme of classification already in mind. He will not simply "look at the facts." He will bring to his examination various notions that direct his attention to certain kinds of political structures and processes and to the possible relationships between them. In political analysis description and classification go hand in hand and, although in any particular piece of work greater stress may be given to one, each is indispensable to the other. A scheme of classification helps us recognize the various patterns of a particular system. In turn, the patterns we have found in particular systems help fill out our schemes of classification.

What we might call the common-sense political science of any educated man provides some elements of such a scheme. Our language is rich in nouns and verbs that refer to different types of political entities and relationships: "empire," "nation," "tribe"; "party," "faction," "coalition"; "voting," "law-making," "administering"; "power," "influence," "authority." The meanings of such words are, so to speak, the eyes of the mind through which we look at and reflect on politics and government. This array of concepts and terms helps the political scientist recognize and give a name to patterns in his material. Thus, for instance, in western countries, he distinguishes "democratic" from "nondemocratic" patterns; in the Soviet system, he recognizes what has often been called an "empire" and speaks of Soviet "imperialism"; in the developing countries he identifies certain goverments as "tribal" rather than "national." The political scientist seeks to make more precise the meanings of these common-sense terms. Moreover, as the discipline progresses, he also develops a more technical and specialized vocabulary. So, for instance, in recent years the concept of "totalitarianism" has been elaborated.

But description also presupposes a more fundamental category of classification. The political scientist must have some conception of what he means by "political"—some means of distinguishing political from nonpolitical events and patterns. Whether he is engaged in the direct observation of field work or in the study of documentary sources, the raw data confronting him will be relevant to many branches of study as well as to political science. The economist or the sociologist, for instance, will be looking for structures and relationships different from those that interest the political scientist. Each will find different patterns in the behavior of the same set of people—the economist, for instance, finding a pattern in the distribution of goods, the sociologist in the allocation of social status. Each is abstracting from the same concrete reality, selecting only those aspects that are of concern to his branch of study. This may seem to do violence to a reality that is at once social, economic, and political—and indeed also physical, chemical, biological, and psychological. Yet we could not hope to make progress if we sought to describe and understand all aspects of this undivided reality at once. All knowledge is selective, and specialization is necessary if any branch of study is to make progress.

Where does the political scientist get the standard that guides him in making this selection? How does he define the "political"? He may, of course, have no clearly defined standard but be content with knowing that certain things and activities, for example, "voting," "parties," "law-making," and "public administration," constitute the type of patterns for which he is looking. This approach to politics may work well sometimes but its weaknesses are many. There have been political regimes in which there was neither voting nor parties, as there have been regimes in which there was neither law-making nor public administration. We need so to define our subject matter as to enable us to identify the political not only in modern democracies, but also in modern dictatorships, in the traditionalist societies of developing countries, and in the predemocratic regimes of ancient and medieval times.

The need for such a definition of the subject matter of political science has been felt by the authors, who have tried to meet it with their concept of the "political system." This concept is a guide to description in that it defines in broad terms the kinds of structures and processes for which we are looking and enables us to distinguish what is political from what is nonpolitical. At the same time it is the foundation for schemes of classification. It states the common properties of a category of social entities—namely, "political systems"—within which class one may distinguish various subclasses—the various types of political systems. To develop such schemes of classification is an important task of political science.

I say "schemes" advisedly, for there is no single, definitive scheme of classification of political systems. It we look at those described in this book, for instance, the distinction that probably first springs to mind is that between "democracy" and "dictatorship." Under the latter heading we should place Soviet Russia and under the former the three Western governments. This classification is based on the distribution of power in the four systems. Keeping power structure as our principle of differentiation, we could distinguish further subclasses under each heading. In each of the three democracies, we find at the present time a "dominant executive," a characteristic that would set them off from the "weak executive" systems of the Third and Fourth Republics in France. Differences of party system might lead to a further division of the "dominant executive democracies" into those with a strongly organized opposition party—as in Britain and Germany—and those without—as in de Gaulle's France. Proceeding in this way, we could elaborate a scheme of classification based on the pattern of power (which, as we shall see later, is one of the main elements into which the present authors analyze a political system).

But power is only one of many principles of differentiation that could be used to construct a scheme of classification. The political scientist might be concerned primarily not with the distribution of power, but with the goals and purposes that are being advocated in various systems. He might therefore distinguish between systems where these goals and purposes are highly ideological and those where they are pragmatic. From these he could set up subclasses according to whether there were one, few, or many schools of political thought. Or he might base his scheme on some particular political philosophy—for example, "individualism" versus "collectivism"—and attempt to fit various systems into it. In any such scheme his main principle of differentiation would be not the pattern of power but what is called in this book the "pattern of interests."

In these illustrations, I have dealt with some broad aspect of a political system as a whole. But classification may, of course, be concerned only with a particular part or process. The student of political parties may wish to develop a scheme of classification for party systems or for party structures. Electoral systems, administrative machinery, legislative structures, and executive-legislative relations are other obvious headings for such schemes. Looking at executive-legislative power relations, for instance, the political scientist may wish to distinguish the "presidential" from the "parliamentary" models. And within the latter type, he will classify some executive-legislative relations as "cabinet government," others as "*régime d'assemblée."* Still others, for lack of an appropriate general term, he may characterize by referring to a well-known example—for instance, "the French type of parliamentary government."

Such schemes of classification—whether of parts or of wholes—are used by the political scientist. The richer and more developed these schemes, the greater are his chances of successfully recognizing and accurately describing the patterns in the political reality. This is not to say that he will invariably find familiar patterns. One reason for comparing different systems, or phases of the same system, is to identify new patterns that can be used to expand his schemes of classification. His existing theory must not, and need not, blind him to these possibilities. He may, for instance, begin his study of French parliamentary government with the British model in mind—it is almost a tradition among political scientists to do so. But the result of his comparative study will be to provide him with another model of parliamentary government in addition to that of cabinet government. Description thus forwards the task of classification.

Description and classification are intellectually demanding and, when well done, intellectually rewarding. They are valuable in their own right as achievements of a scientific discipline. But they also are steps in realizing the more ambitious aims of explanation and confirmation. Suppose, for instance, that, as in our previous illustration, we have classified a number of systems according to power structure, grouping some of these as dominant executive democracies. We are now in a position to ask and to attempt to answer various interesting questions. We may ask: What are the effects in a democratic system of a dominant executive? What are the reasons (or causes) for such an executive in various democratic systems? By examining the democratic systems classed as having dominant executives, we may find correlations that suggest a plausible hypothesis. By observing contrasts with democratic systems classed as having weak executives, we may find this hypothesis strengthened or we may be obliged to reject or modify it. Thus classification leads naturally into our further and more ambitious tasks.

Explanation

Description and classification are valuable, but they may seem not to be concerned with the vital problem of change. In a fundamental sense this is false. The reality with which the political scientist is concerned, and from which he starts, is process. The basic facts he deals with are events, acts, happenings. He describes the pattern of Stalinist dictatorship, for instance. But we must always remember that the pattern so described is abstracted from events: decisions of the dictator, acts of repression, responses of Communist Party members, and the like. The political scientist abstracts from these events to describe the pattern. In the political reality of Stalin's Russia there was no inert "thing" that was his dictatorship, but only this complex of human action and interaction. In this sense the political scientist is always concerned with change.

On the other hand, this underlying reality of process is compatible with there being stability in patterns. The Stalinist dictatorship was a set of patterns that persisted for some time: here is stability. When the more relaxed system of Khrushchev appeared there was a change of pattern. Similarly, there was change of pattern when, suddenly, the Fourth Republic gave way to the Republic of de Gaulle, or when, gradually, the welfare state modified the power structure of British government. Confronted with these facts, the political scientist tries to find out what caused the change. He wants to know why the old broke down and the new arose. From describing and classifying patterns, he turns to explaining changes of pattern.

This does not mean that explanation is concerned only with change. It is equally concerned with stability of pattern. The political scientist wants to know what caused the old pattern to persist and what causes the new to continue. Indeed, he can hardly explain why the new arose without at the same time understanding what had maintained the old. The conditions that account for the persistence of pattern in one context will, if they emerge in another context where a different pattern prevails, bring about change in that pattern. Whatever we may learn in the way of explanation may be useful in understanding either change or stability.

The purpose of this book is primarily description and secondarily classification. Yet we could hardly avoid venturing into the field of explanation. The term "explanation" has no single, exclusive meaning. What do we mean by it in the present context and how does it differ from description?

To explain, in the sense used here, has something to do with finding out the causes of an event or pattern. We commonly feel that we have explained a thing when we have identified the conditions that produce, or account for, or lead to it. Again, I can illustrate by referring to common sense.

Common sense embraces, as we have remarked, a body of knowledge about the patterns of social behavior in our everyday surroundings. It also includes explanations of why these patterns exist and why they may break off. Along with description and classification, explanation is part of what we might call the "microsociology" of everyday life. Consider how often you have had a conversation with friends that followed some such form as this: Why, you ask, does a certain person act the way he does? Or why does a certain practice prevail among some circle of persons? After a brief discussion, someone modestly steps forward and confesses that he

In citing these examples I have tried not to summarize the whole of Dr. Ulam's system of explanation but simply to illustrate how a political scientist, even when primarily concerned with description of certain patterns and the changes in them, may also offer general explanatory hypotheses. In Dr. Ulam's analysis these hypotheses form a fairly elaborate and logically connected body of statements. If we wish to designate such an intellectual construction as an explanatory theory, we can say that in the concluding paragraph of Chapter 26 Dr. Ulam in summary sketches a theory of "both the development and the potential decline of a totalitarian state."[8] He has derived this theory largely from, and has used it in explaining, the course of events in Russia. But as he suggests, it sheds light on certain types of change in any totalitarian state.

Dr. Ulam is concerned mainly with explaining change. It is to stability—persistence of pattern—that Dr. Eckstein addresses himself, although he is also interested in the modifications that have been introduced in the era of the welfare state in Britain. Again, I shall try not to summarize his work, but only to illustrate how in the course of description he also suggests explanatory hypotheses. One persisting pattern that he traces in modern British government is that subtle and complex relationship between the executive on the one hand and the legislature on the other, which we may refer to as cabinet dominance. In explaining this pattern, a causal condition to which he gives great stress is the British conception of authority. This is not to say that Dr. Eckstein is referring to some particular entity, unanalyzed and peculiarly British, for his explanation. On the contrary, he describes this complex political attitude in general terms, stressing especially its integration of predemocratic and democratic values. Although he finds it operating continually in the political evaluations and interpretations of a substantial number of the British people, there is nothing intrinsic in this attitude that prevents it from being held by other people at other times and places. Like the "two-party system," it is a pattern that, although rare, is still intrinsically repeatable in other contexts. In Dr. Eckstein's analysis it figures as an important, although not the sole, cause of cabinet dominance. But his analysis implies that in any political system, if such a conception of authority prevails (along with the parliamentary form and certain other conditions), the cabinet will have similarly large powers.

Like Dr. Eckstein, Drs. Wahl and Spiro lay great stress on the causal role of basic political attitudes, and in analyzing this influence in their respective accounts suggest hypotheses with general import. In the French conception of authority, for instance, Dr. Wahl finds both predemocratic

[8] See below, p. 744.

knows the answer. The real reason, he says, is to be found in certain circumstances of upbringing or social environment. Conditions of that kind, he concludes, always lead to such behavior.

Now the man with the answer might not be ready to claim that he had discovered a "law" of social behavior. Yet the form of his reply reflects the common, and perhaps inevitable, attempt of our minds to find general statements that assert that certain specified conditions will lead to certain results. It is understood, of course, that by "law" we mean not a rule that holds with absolute certainty but rather a hypothesis that in some degree has been confirmed. Given that understanding, we can say that *we have explained a certain act or pattern when we have found a law, holding for any time or place, which states that certain specified conditions will be followed by the act or pattern in question.* Popper writes that "to give a causal explanation of a certain *specific event* means deducing a statement describing this event from two kinds of premises: from some *universal Laws*, and from some singular or specific statements which we may call the *specific initial conditions*."[2] This conception of explanation merely states more precisely what common sense daily attempts.

In political science, the *descriptive generalization* refers to an observed pattern in some more or less limited region of time and space. On the other hand, the *explanatory generalization* is a hypothesis, cast in universal form, that states the causes or conditions accounting for such a pattern.

The descriptive generalization reports what has been observed in a number of instances, many or few. It does not explain any of these instances, which are merely illustrations. If we say that in the United States there is a presidential election every four years, this does not explain why there was an election in 1960; that event is rather an instance or illustration of the general statement. The same applies to our description of Cabinet dominance in modern British government, or of the dictatorship of Stalin, or of the prevalence of formalism in contemporary German attitudes toward politics. Nor need such a description be confined to one country. We similarly generalize when we say, for instance, that in each of the four political systems analyzed in this book we find a bureaucratic structure of administration. What is common to such statements is that they refer to (sum up or enumerate) the traits of a certain limited number of instances. In the examples we have cited there is a reference to a particular country, or to several countries, in a certain period of time.

In contrast, *the explanatory generalization tries to break away from this limited reference and to state a sequence or relationship that holds in an indefinite number of instances,* that is, wherever the initial conditions may

[2] Karl Popper, *The Poverty of Historicism* (London, 1957), p. 122.

be fulfilled. It sheds the reference to particulars, such as "British," "German," "Stalin," "modern," and confines itself to general terms. By a purely linguistic change, we could, to be sure, convert the generalizations just cited from descriptive into explanatory form. We could say, for instance, that wherever in executive-legislative relations we find a cabinet responsible to the legislature, the proposals of that cabinet will be substantially accepted by the legislature. In form this is an explanation of a pattern of legislative compliance where the specified conditions are fulfilled. Even the slightest acquaintance with parliamentary government in several countries, however, shows it to be false in fact. The political analyst will put his assertions in explanatory form only when he has reason to believe that they may well have general validity.

How far do the authors of this book go toward suggesting such explanatory hypotheses? Dr. Ulam's account will serve for illustration. He offers a dynamic analysis of three major shifts in the patterns of Russian government—the establishment of Communism, the transition to the Stalinist dictatorship, and the softening or relaxation of the regime under Khrushchev.

To explain the first of these events would lead one into a full-scale analysis of the conditions that brought about the Russian Revolution. Dr. Ulam concentrates rather on one critical question: "What caused Marxism *as a political movement* to be born in the context, not of a fully industrialized society and of democratic institutions, but of the initial stages of industrialization and of semi-feudal political institutions?"[3] His explanation, you will note, while directed at events in Russia, takes a general form. He writes, for instance:

> In a society undergoing the transition from the agricultural to the industrial order, Marxism offers the lower classes an effective and appealing exposition of their grievances and frustrations. . . . In a society where the mass of inhabitants are denied the right of participation in politics, and where the birth pangs of industrialism are in evidence, Marxism appeals both to the past, in denouncing the evils of factory discipline and the wage system, and to the future, in promising that in a socialist society industrialism will bring with it democracy and abundance.[4]

These generalizations are not confined to a description of events in Russia. They are rather an hypothesis that purports to explain why a certain kind of doctrine (designated as "Marxism," but described in general terms) will be widely accepted under certain specified social and economic conditions. So framed, this generalization can be tested against

3 See below, p. 601.
4 See below, pp. 601-602.

the experience of other countries in the early stages of industrializati Such testing—to be discussed under "Confirmation"—does not co within the scope of this book. But Dr. Ulam has done precisely this other works, elaborating his analysis of events in Russia and applying to some of the developing countries of the non-Western world tod

Likewise, in giving his account of how Stalinist totalitarianism fastened on Russian society in the name of industrialization, Dr. U not only narrates the sequence of events, but also puts his narratio such a way as to suggest a generalized explanation for transitions of kind. He gives some stress, for instance, to the causal role of Ma ideology, in particular its premise that a Communist regime can su only if it is founded on a large class of urban workers. Confronte backward Russia and its huge mass of peasants, the Soviet leaders, indeed Communists of all factions, were impelled by this belief to en on the prolonged and intensive drive to industrialize and socializ whole economy. "Being by temperament as well as by conviction Mar writes Dr. Ulam, "the Soviet leaders, whether led by Stalin, Trots Zinoviev, were bound in the long run to insist on a full-scale indu ization and socialization of the country."[6] As this sentence indicate its assertion of what any convinced Marxist was "bound" to do in situation, Dr. Ulam's account treats such temperamental and intel commitment not simply as the particular attitude of certain person certain historical time, but as a state of mind that could be repea other contexts and that, therefore, in conjunction with the other con he describes, would have similar consequences. He is suggesting, ir an explanatory generalization.

In explaining the third major transition, the shift to the new and more liberalized patterns of Khrushchev's regime, Dr. Ulam at great importance to the new social forces produced by a highly indus economy. He points out that the new managerial and technical far from being fanatic ideologues, have aspirations not dissimil those of similar classes in the West. Given the power of these which is derived from their technical ability and vital function system, some relaxing of totalitarian control was virtually in "What makes the present system different," he writes, "is that th been economic and social changes in Russia that impinge upon t and that make a return to full-fledged Stalinism impractical. . . . and industrialized U.S.S.R. cannot be ruled by sheer despotism ar as was Russia in the thirties."[7]

5 Adam B. Ulam, *The Unfinished Revolution: An Essay on the Sources of I Marxism and Communism* (New York, 1960).
6 See below, p. 630.
7 See below, pp. 696 and 722.

and democratic elements—the "administrative" and the "representative" traditions. Unlike similar elements in British attitudes, however, they are not integrated in what he calls a "theory of mixed government," but are so defined in people's minds as to be radically in conflict. Given such conflict in political attitudes and given also the emergence of opposing interest groups, such as those produced by the uneven development of the French economy, there will very probably result—so runs Dr. Wahl's argument—a frequent and abrupt change of regime, such as we find in French political history.

A major problem for Dr. Spiro is the instability of pattern in German politics—perhaps even greater than that of French politics. Like Dr. Wahl he finds a principal cause in the character of German political culture, but the explanation he offers is put in general terms, giving it relevance to other contexts. The fault—to put it very briefly—is that German political attitudes legitimize obedience mainly on the basis of the policies and goals being pursued by a regime. Conversely, the Germans lay little stress on the importance of "constitutionalism," that is, the legitimacy that comes from having followed established procedures in decision-making. "As a result," he writes, "when catastrophe befell the Germans—or they brought it on themselves—they had no home-grown rules for the settlement of quarrels that are always more numerous in adversity than in good fortune.[9]

Throughout this book, the reader will find explanatory hypotheses, sometimes more, sometimes less completely stated. To state them explicitly and fully would change the character—and increase the length—of the book, whose main concern is description. Such full and explicit statement, however, would be necessary if we were to proceed to the next state of political analysis, confirmation.

Confirmation

By confirmation is meant first of all testing explanatory hypotheses in a number of contexts. Let us suppose that, as has been done in many instances in this book, the political scientist has developed a hypothesis to explain some pattern that he has found in a particular political system. Having stated explicitly the initial conditions that appear to him to be the cause of the pattern, he looks for other contexts in which these conditions also appear. The larger the number of instances in which the pattern in question follows from the specified conditions, the more acceptable is the hypothesis.

We never achieve, it may be repeated, absolute certainty. Even our

[9] See below, p. 587.

most widely confirmed explanations remain hypothetical. Experience with explanatory hypotheses of natural as well as social science prompts this caution, since again and again new evidence has obliged us to give up or modify explanations that appeared to be irrefutably established. Yet without going further into the problem of induction—"the despair of philosophy" according to Whitehead—we can content ourselves with observing that it is only rational to rely upon the more rather than the less confirmed hypothesis.

Confirmation strengthens our acceptance of an explanation. But, of course, we may find that the initial conditions are not followed by the expected consequence—the hypothesis may be falsified, not confirmed. Such failures may be disappointing, but in the development of political science they are as interesting and important as success. For the repeated study of instances that bear out a hypothesis adds little to our understanding. The experiment yielding negative results, however, may be an opportunity for deepening our explanatory knowledge.

The attempt so to use an instance of falsification has its dangers. Above all, it may tempt the analyst to try to "save his hypothesis" by adding new initial conditions. This procedure does not really save the original hypothesis and at best achieves a narrower—though more correct—understanding.

Suppose, for example, that he begins with the hypothesis that an electoral system based on proportional representation will lead to a splintering of political parties, a suggestion that seems highly plausible in the light of the experience of the Weimar Republic in Germany and of France under the Fourth Republic. As he tests this hypothesis against the facts of other political systems, he finds that in many countries—such as Sweden and Ireland—the expected pattern of party splintering does not appear. He then tries to save his hypothesis by adding to the initial conditions. He has found, let us say, that proportional representation has been compatible with large parties in countries where there is a relatively small population or a single important issue dividing the electorate. He therefore modifies his hypothesis to read that, where there is proportional representation, *and* a relatively large population, *and* more than one important issue, there will be splintering.

This new hypothesis does not, it is obvious, save the original explanation that it is proportional representation alone that leads to splintering. For the "cause" in any explanation is the whole situation constituted by *all* the initial conditions. The enlarged hypothesis, however, can be considered more acceptable since it contains the two original cases (Weimar Germany and Fourth Republic France) and is not falsified by the cases that forced modification of the original hypothesis. Confirmation in only two instances, it is obvious, does not lend the hypothesis any great validity. Before taking this explanation very seriously we should want to find other instances in which the initial conditions required by the enlarged hypothesis are present. But such testing will be more difficult, because there will be fewer instances in which the initial conditions are found. The enlarged hypothesis will be more acceptable, but less general.

Most explanatory hypotheses in political science—and generally in the social sciences—are complex. They suppose not one, but several initial conditions; they are "multivariant." When the analyst begins with a "univariant" hypothesis that attributes causal efficacy to one condition, the testing of this hypothesis in other contexts may be useful by revealing to him that his original explanation is oversimplified and must be enlarged. In this way failures of confirmation may contribute to the better grounding of our explanations.

At the same time, we should keep in mind that it is our hope to reduce the complexity and raise the generality of our hypotheses. The more general hypothesis can be tested in more instances; in this sense it has a higher empirical content. And if confirmed, it is more useful to the effort of political science in developing a body of explanatory theory.

For example, Dr. Ulam's ideas about the influence of a doctrine such as Marxism on an industrializing society have explanatory force in a number of contexts in addition to Soviet Russia. If, however, we could arrive at confirmed knowledge of the influence of Marxist-type doctrine on *any* political and social circumstances, we would have a more general "law" of political behavior and a statement that could be tested in other contexts than merely those of early industrial countries.

Now, Dr. Ulam does suggest a more general hypothesis. When he discusses the Marxist belief that "any socialist party must be based on a mass of industrial proletarians,"[10] he stresses the influence of this belief on the behavior of Marxists generally. It is this attitude, flowing from Marxism, that largely accounts for the commitment to industrialization in the Stalinist period. At the same time, Dr. Ulam has stated a hypothesis that can be tested by a study of Marxist attitudes not only in backward countries but also in advanced industrialized countries. For he is saying that Marxists anywhere will be strongly committed to the creation of a party dependent upon the proletariat of an industrialized economy.

From this generalization some less general hypotheses can be deduced. One is the original hypothesis in question, i.e., that in backward countries Marxism produces a commitment to industrialization. The confirmation of the more general hypothesis will strengthen the acceptability of that

---

[10] See below, p. 630.

original hypothesis. Moreover, other deductions, that would not have occurred otherwise to the political scientist, may also be suggested. In this way general theory may raise questions for research by implying more particular hypotheses. A large body of confirmed explanatory theory is especially useful since it will be rich in such implications. Hypotheses may be derived from the study of one or more cases, that is, inductively, as when, for instance, the political scientist examines several systems that have been grouped together in a scheme of classification. But if we are to appreciate the role of theory in research, we must also recognize that new insights, new questions and hypotheses, may also be derived from theory, that is, deductively.

These comments on confirmation—regarding testing and development of hypotheses—take us well beyond the scope of this book. But they should help show how a volume such as this has its place in the broad program of political science. Description, classification, explanation, and confirmation refer to procedures of analysis, each of which has a value in itself. But they also fit together in the common effort to discover general laws of political behavior.[11]

---

[11] In this brief discussion of method, I have not referred to "comparative politics" or "comparative government." The terms are unfortunate, as they suggest that comparison is an operation confined to some limited field of political science. But as this discussion should have made clear, comparison—the study of more than one instance or case—is constantly used by the political scientist. In describing a pattern he compares many particular events in order to generalize. In classifying structures or systems, he will similarly make comparisons. He may derive explanatory hypotheses from the study of more than one case and, obviously, in testing and developing hypotheses he will examine cases that are similar in certain respects, in order to see whether they are also alike in others. Comparison is used not only between political systems but also within the limits of a system and between different stages of a system. Its methods are common to all the main procedures of the discipline.

[2]

The Concept of
a Political System

What is "politics" or "government"? These terms have their common-sense meanings. But defining our subject matter is not the task of merely making explicit what is already implicit in common usage and common sense. The ordinary understanding of what is meant by the political is far from unambiguous. Is "administration" a part? We usually differentiate it from "politics." Indeed, we seem to feel that "politics" and "government" themselves are distinguishable.

The nature of our subject matter is not obvious. Its definition must be frequently reconsidered and developed in the light of inquiry. We want a definition that is useful—useful in the sense that it gives promise of leading us toward a growing body of explanatory theory about human behavior and useful also in the sense that the behavior it identifies is not trivial, but important to enduring human concerns.

From such considerations has emerged the increasing use of the concept of the political system. This concept is part of a broad way of looking at all social behavior. From that perspective, the political system is a structure that performs a certain function for a society. In the fewest possible words: that function is to make *legitimate policy decisions*.

Let us consider briefly what this means. A political system includes an arrangement for making decisions. This we will readily admit. But it does not suffice to distinguish the political system from other non-political structures or systems. An economic system based on the free market, for instance, also makes decisions: by means of it, resources are allocated among various branches of production, the prices paid for goods and services are determined, and income is distrubuted among business units and individuals. What then is distinctive about the decision-making of the political system? We cannot find it in the *manner* in which these decisions are made, since the array of political regimes exhibited in history displays bewildering variety. It is more helpful to look at the *nature* of the decisions themselves. They are in the first place decisions on policy; that is, they define for the society courses of action directed at more or less clearly conceived goals. Moreover, these decisions have legitimacy: to some extent, members of the society accept them as being in conformity with their conceptions of authority and purpose. The rather technical meanings given these terms "authority" and "purpose" will be explained in Chapter 3. Perhaps the essential point can be conveyed by saying that political decisions do not rest entirely and exclusively upon force. They also are accepted and obeyed because they are felt to be justified by certain standards shared by both those who command and those who obey.

The political system, in short, produces a certain "output" for the society: legitimate policy decisions. The goals at which these decisions aim may be precise and programmatic, or only vague and general. They may be accepted readily or reluctantly, by many or by few. But to call them policy decisions is to stress that they do have consequences for the society, and to note their legitimacy is to draw attention to the main characteristic that makes them political. Through the political system goals for the society are defined and carried out by legitimate policy decisions.[1]

A Structural-Functional Definition

The concept of the political system has been developed as part of a larger outlook on social behavior as a whole—the "structural-functional" approach. A few words about this approach will help clarify and justify the concept.

The concept in question lays stress on the relation of the political to society. It characterizes a certain structure—that is, the arrangements by which legitimate policy decisions are made—but with an eye to its function in the whole context of social behavior. Indeed, no society can survive or develop, we might plausibly assert, unless it has a political system performing such a function; that is, we might hold that a political system is a "functional requisite" of a society. Going further, we could say that there

---

[1] In this discussion I have broadened the usual meaning of "legitimate" and "legitimacy." Usually political scientists say that a command or decision is legitimate if it is in accord with the prevailing conception of authority. As I explain in Chapter 3, I hold that the political values of a society will be concerned with purpose as well as authority and that the acceptance of decisions is affected by both sorts of criteria.

are other necessary functions that must be performed by other systems or structures, if a society is to have more than a brief and unstable existence. For example, we could say that any society must have some regular arrangement for producing and distributing material goods and services, that is, an economic system. Perhaps also it must have some way of allocating social status, that is, a system of social stratification.

So far as we succeed in identifying these functional requisites of any society, we may arrive at a scheme of definitions characterizing certain structures and their respective functions. This scheme would identify the subject matter of some of the main social sciences, with the various subsystems performing these functions. In this scheme the political system would appear as that subsystem performing the distinctive function of making legitimate policy decisions, or, to use a shorter expression, the function of "goal-attainment," for the society of which it is a part.

If we are to use this definition we must take care that it does not lead us to assert or presume too much. To say that any society must have a political system seems safe enough. We are not likely to find a society that has no politics and government, that is, one which is, in the literal sense of the word, an "anarchy." Yet to say that any society must have a political system if it is to survive is not to presume that every political system will actually promote the survival of its society. It is only too possible that a political system may perform its function in such a way as to lead to the decay or even the dissolution of the social order. It may be blind to great dangers or neglectful of great opportunities. Unintentionally it may be the author of fatality. The effectiveness of a regime, or a type of regime, in short, is a matter for hypothesis and testing. A virtue of the structural-functional approach is that it focuses attention on this question, one that is central to the concerns of the authors of this book.

Nor should we let our definition blind us to differences of degree. We may often find in a particular political system a very ragged performance. A problem may be recognized, but for various reasons—because of violent disagreement over means, because of intense distrust, because of the rivalry of power-seekers—a relevant decision may fail to emerge: the system may tend to immobility. Again, there may be such conflict of political values in the society that, even when decisions are made, they are felt as binding by and given acceptance among only one section of the society.

Our basic concept leads to questions rather than answers: How fully does a particular system conform to the definition? How effectively does this system promote the survival and development of its society?

So understood, the concept of the political system will, we hope, lead us to identify fully and adequately what is political in any society. We should not discover instances which we recognize as political or governmental but which this definition does not include. The concept should give us the broadest possible base for the tasks of description, classification, explanation, and confirmation. Two points concerning its comprehensiveness, however, need to be clarified.

First, is not this definition of politics and government guilty of what we might call an "interventionist" bias? Does it not suggest that the proper role of government is to be continually intervening in society, meddling with problems that might better be left to the judgment of private individuals? Such an implication, of course, cannot be drawn from it. It does imply that a political system will be concerned with identifying problems and making policy to deal with them. But this does not exclude by any means a policy of very limited intervention. Our definition, for instance, is quite compatible with a policy of *laissez faire* in economic matters. For *laissez faire* is a form of government action—to enforce contracts, prevent fraud, prohibit conspiracies in restraint of trade, and so on. Under it, intervention is limited by the conviction that the free market will best serve a certain kind of social and economic order. But *laissez faire* is as much a policy as would be the decision to plan economic life in detail. Our definition of a political system is sufficiently comprehensive to include political systems with either sort of policy.

A more serious objection is that the definition has a "rationalist" bias. It looks on politics and government as instrumental. It regards political activities as being not ends in themselves but means to reach certain goals. That surely is substantially correct with regard to most modern governments of Europe or America, and certainly with regard to the four systems examined in this book. But if we look back in history, we may question whether the political system is always so exclusively instrumentalist.

There have been regimes, for instance, in which an exact and rigid tradition controlled what was done and how it was done. The regime enforced a system of law. But this law, far from being regarded as something that men could make and unmake as a means of "solving problems," was held to be an unchangeable code sanctified by custom and perhaps also by the gods. To enforce this code, as to obey it, was something intrinsically good according to the traditionalist ethic of the society. If the code was thought to be divine, the acts of governing were conceived as morally imperative, regardless perhaps of their consequences for the society in this world. *Fiat justitia ruat coelum.*

Is not our definition of what is political and of the political system too narrow, too rationalist and modern, to include such cases? The question has more than historical interest. For today in many parts of the world there are societies and regimes still strongly traditionalist, and it would gravely hamper comparative analysis if our concept of the subject matter of political science failed to identify what is political in these regimes.

In the first place, we should observe that even in such regimes government has its instrumental aspect. Even if the major imperative is to please ancestors by copying them, the acts of carrying out ancestral laws are a means to this broad objective. But secondly and more important, our functional view of the political system does not require that the members of the system themselves take such an instrumentalist view. A set of arrangements can have the effect of helping or hindering the survival of a society even though the members of the society do not recognize this effect. For example, a code of law based on vengeance may develop without any thought of the consequences for the society's survival. Yet such a code—if, for instance, it serves to hold in check violence between individuals and clans—will promote the society's survival regardless of what members of the society may think of the meaning and purpose of the code. In short, the political scientist may identify and analyze the consequences of a political system for its society whether or not these consequences are intended or recognized by the members of the society themselves.

The Meaning of "System"

Our concept of the political system finds the political in a structure performing a certain function for a society. It also states something about this structure when it refers to it as a "system." What do we mean by this term and why do we use it?

The idea of a system has been taken over from biological theory and adapted by some social scientists to the study of their subject matter. In biological theory it has been given a fairly complex and technical meaning. The principal point of interest to the political scientist is the emphasis the concept gives to interdependence. That there is such interdependence in a living organism is fairly easy to perceive. Indeed, in common speech when we say some entity or process is "organic" we mean at least that its various parts are interdependent and mutually conditioning. "Life science," a distinguished biologist-philosopher has recently written, "is a single fabric of interconnected facts and concepts in which, as in all dynamic networks, the strength and structure of every portion depend significantly on the conditions of all others. Thus, even additions and alterations in a limited sector will of necessity rebound on the whole system and light shed on any part will penetrate and illuminate the rest."[2]

Not all subject matters can be usefully studied from this point of view.

---

[2] Paul Weiss, "Deformities as Cues to Understanding of Form," *Perspectives in Biology and Medicine*, Vol. 4, No. 2 (Winter, 1961) p. 149.

Some perhaps should be regarded as "mechanisms" rather than "systems." In a mechanism the various parts or sectors are not pervasively and continuously interdependent as in a system. Any particular sector can, therefore, be studied with little concern for its effects on other sectors, or for the effect of other sectors upon it. When studying a system, on the other hand, the analyst must be continually alert to such mutual interaction and one of his principal concerns will be to trace and explain the patterns arising from it.

Whether to regard a subject matter as system or mechanism is again a question to be settled by inquiry. To define political behavior as a system is, like our other basic concepts, hypothetical. Our present knowledge suggests that there is a high degree of interdependence among the various sectors or elements of our subject matter. Hence, the system approach promises to be useful by directing our attention to an important kind of pattern. Only by inquiry do we learn what these patterns of interaction are, or, indeed, that there is such interaction.

By system we mean at least a high degree of interdependence. But some theorists have taken the concept to mean more than that. In particular, they have taken it to mean such a mutual conditioning that the pattern of the whole system tends to maintain itself in the face of any disturbing force. The developing organism, one biological theorist has written, "possesses in each of its temporal slices an exceptional condition towards which the system tends, and towards which it tends to return after disturbance."[3] Similarly, some social scientists have suggested that there is in any political system a tendency to self-maintenance of pattern. This tendency, of course, is not thought of as a result of some nonempirical force above and beyond the political system. Its source is to be sought in the way each of the sectors interacts with the others to produce and maintain the pattern of the whole.

This hypothesis of a self-maintaining tendency is one of the most interesting elaborations of system theory. With regard to the four studies of this book, it is perhaps most plausible as applied to British politics. In Dr. Eckstein's analysis the main patterns of the system do indeed seem to interact with one another in such a way as to maintain each in its existing form. In Britain during the past decade or more, for instance, there has been a great decline of ideological conflict and little innovation of major issues in the field of domestic policy. This consensus in the interests and purposes pursued in the political arena has undoubtedly been promoted by the highly bureaucratic structure of power, not only in govern-

---

[3] Ludwig von Bertalanffy, *Modern Theories of Development: an Introduction to Theoretical Biology*, trans. by J. G. Woodger (London, 1933), p. 185.

ment, but also in parties and interest groups. Similarly, the policies carried out by government have tended to support first this consensus and second this bureaucratization of power—for example, (1) by easing the economic insecurities from which ideological conflict might arise and (2) by a policy of economic management that requires the cooperation of sectional economic interests. In this way three sectors of the system—the patterns of interest, power, and policy—tend to be mutually supporting. Disturbances in any one pattern may occur, such as the attempt to radicalize certain political issues, but the weight of the system as a whole tends to iron out these disturbances and restore the previous equilibrium. This is not to say that there has been no development in the system; Dr. Eckstein shows how the policies of the welfare state have affected the power structure as well as other aspects of the system. As in the growth and decay of an organism, a self-maintaining tendency at any stage does not rule out development from one stage to another.

The French case is also suggestive. Dr. Wahl believes that over a long period a set of mutually reinforcing patterns has tended to maintain certain basic traits of French politics. Through many regimes and under very different constitutions, there have persisted a highly centralized bureaucracy, a fragmentation of parties and interest groups, and a policy-making process marked by instability, incoherence, and ineffectiveness. For the maintenance of these patterns, Dr. Wahl holds largely responsible the political culture of France, in particular its deep and unresolved fissures between the "administrative" and "representative" traditions. De Gaulle's Republic is an attempt to reform some of these patterns. But, as Dr. Wahl points out, in spite of the great new concentration of formal authority in the executive, the old forces making for instability and incoherence are still powerfully active. In his concluding chapter he considers the various alternatives for the future. We might summarize these by asking whether De Gaulle's experiment will prove to be merely a "disturbance" followed by a reassertion of the old patterns, or a permanent and fundamental reform, marking a new stage in the development of the French political system.

The Main Variables

The concept of the political system directs our attention toward the process by which legitimate policy decisions are made in a society. The concept implies that the elements of this process will be interdependent. But what are the variables—the elements that vary in character from one system to another, or, within a system, from one moment of time to another? What are the basic elements—the main variables—of any political system?

In our common-sense reflections on government, we think in terms of the familiar—which for most present readers means the American system. When we assent to the proposition that the elements of a political system are interdependent, very probably the images that run through our heads are those of Congress, the presidency, the electorate, the Federal bureaucracy, and so on. And we give tentative assent because we recognize how the acts of any of these elements tend to have effects that spread throughout the system.

Clearly we cannot take these familiar institutions as the main variables of any political system. Nor would it do to adopt some scheme such as "the democratic electorate," "the party system," "the representative legislature," "the responsible executive." This scheme would apply to the American and European democracies. It would be misleading or useless if we tried to follow it in describing and analyzing the political systems of many countries in the non-Western world today, not to mention premodern regimes in Western history. Obviously the scheme of legislature-executive-party system could only confuse and distort the study of Soviet Russia. To be sure, there is in Russia an organization—the Communist party—that calls itself a "party." But this is an instrument of control for the dictatorship rather than what the West calls a party. The Supreme Soviet is called the legislature, but it would be a waste of time to give this body the kind of attention we give to, say, the British House of Commons. The scheme of variables, in short, must be such that it can be found in any political system. Only if it retains its high level of generality can the concept of the political system keep its high degree of usefulness.

The fact that we are concerned with human action may suggest a sufficiently general and quite simple scheme. Two elements of any human act are the *end* being pursued and the *means* used to reach it. A third element is the *consequence*—the outcome of the whole process. By analogy, we may apply this analysis of the acts of the individual to the process of policy-making. The analogy, we hasten to add, cannot be strict. The state, as has often been shown, is not a person. Yet a political system is like a personality system. In the language of sociology both are "action systems." In both, means are used to pursue goals, and results of some sort are achieved.

In the action taken by an individual, the means employed constitute the individual's power: they are the instruments that endow him with the ability to do more or less successfully what he intends. The ends at which he aims constitute his interests: they are the goals for whose achievement he exercises his power. Similarly, in the political system we distinguish the *pattern of power*—that array of means by which decisions may be influenced —and the *pattern of interests*—the set of goals that various individuals or groups are pursuing. The consequences of the interplay of power and interests are the decisions—the *pattern of policy*.

To theoretical and empirical reasons for using this scheme of variables, common sense adds its support. One could argue—and some political scientists do—that power is the central concept of our discipline and that the pattern of power is the sole heading under which we should classify and analyze our material. How are decisions made and who has influence on them? What are the means that are used in the exercise of such influence? From what sources do influential individuals or groups draw their ability to affect decisions? These certainly are questions that can be asked of any political system and that any political scientist will ask.

But surely he will be properly interested not only in *how* decisions are made but also in *what* decisions are made. He will be concerned with purpose as well as power. The struggle for power is one main subject of our study. No doubt, in certain situations some men seek power for its own sake. Yet many also seek power in order to use it for the sake of some further goal. What does this group—this pressure group, faction, or party —hope to achieve? In what ways are they trying to change government policy? What are the sources—in economic structure, social position, and ideological currents—of their aspirations and interests? These too are questions that common sense regards as political. A political system, as in the case of Soviet Russia, may not have a system of parties. But it is bound to include individuals and groups that are seeking to promote or prevent the adoption of certain policies. Dr. Ulam recalls, for instance, the peasants' desperate resistance to collectivization and describes the recent struggle in the Party Presidium over the production of more or fewer consumers' goods. The pattern of interests as well as the pattern of power is a legitimate part of our subject matter.

As with the interplay of means and ends, interests and power interact to produce certain consequences, the pattern of policy. Policy consists of decisions. Any particular policy—collectivization in Russia, the National Health Service in Britain, industrial regulation in Germany—emerges from a series of decisions. The political scientist is concerned with these decisions at each stage and how they affect the next stage of decision. The final outcome is the pattern of policy. This pattern has emerged from the interaction of interests and power. But also, as we shall see, it directly and indirectly conditions those other patterns.

A fourth variable to which the authors of this book attach particular importance is the *pattern of political culture*. Like the other variables, this concept will be discussed at some length in the next chapter. Here we can suggest its place in the scheme as a whole. Again, perhaps the analogy with the act of the individual is helpful. When a person acts to solve some particular problem, his decisions are made against a broad background of knowledge and values. He will have certain notions of what it is worthwhile to spend time and energy on, as well as notions of certain ethical limits that he ought not to overstep. He will look at the situation in the light of his practical knowledge, comparing the immediate obstacles and oppor- tunities facing him with the consequences of a certain line of action for other of his objectives. This broad background of attitudes will strongly influence what particular goals he decides to pursue and how he goes about working for them. If we want to understand why he makes particular choices and particular decisions, we need to get some idea of this back- ground of thought and emotion.

Similarly, in a political system, the basic political attitudes of its mem- bers will be an important influence on what is done—and not done. These attitudes will condition the interests and goals being pursued, the means that are adopted to reach them, and the acceptance—or rejection—of decisions by members of the system. As cultural background they will have great bearing upon the fortunes of the political system: whether it is stable or unstable; whether it is capable of orderly and gradual development or is caught in paralyzing stalemate; whether the struggle for power is kept within bounds or bursts forth in self-destroying excess.

These four patterns—political culture, power, interests, and policy—are the main variables in our concept of the political system. They exclude nothing that common sense recognizes as political and they are defined at a level general enough to be found in any political system.

Moreover, these four variables seem to be interdependent in the sense that a change in one pattern will have effects on the others. How great these effects may be and what character they may take are, of course, questions to be determined by research. Likewise, the analysis of a particular system will no doubt reveal interactions within a single pattern. A change in the party sector of the power pattern, for instance, will very probably affect the interest group pattern. For any particular system, or type of system, we may be able to distinguish subordinate sectors of the patterns. We might, for instance, find it useful to distinguish the pattern of foreign policy from the pattern of domestic policy and to examine their interrelations. Our scheme, far from preventing, actually encourages further elaboration.

This scheme enables us to study the political system as such, describing its various elements and analyzing their interrelations. In the political proc- ess so defined we have a distinctive field of study for political science. It has its patterns, different from those of other social sciences. From their description we may hope to develop explanatory hypotheses that are dis- tinctively political. In this sense, political science, like the political process, has a certain autonomy. That is to say, it cannot be reduced to, or explained away by, the concepts and laws of economics, social psychology, or other social sciences. It is a field of study in its own right.

At the same time, the autonomy of our discipline, as of the political process itself, is not complete. Political science (like any social science) cannot be treated as an isolated branch of study, because the political system is not isolated from the rest of society. Society also is a "system," not a "mechanism." The present scheme of analysis also has value in that *it continually directs attention to the relations of the political system with the other subsystems of society*. The stress on policy, for instance, leads naturally to consideration of the consequences of the political system for the society—its functioning for the society's stability or development. The patterns of political culture, power, and interest suggest major ways in which some disturbing force (for good or ill) may enter the political system. Economic changes resulting in a new distribution of wealth, for instance, may radically alter the power pattern. Revolutions in religious or scientific outlook may introduce new perspectives into political culture. While in this book, therefore, we have concentrated on describing patterns of government, we have by no means neglected their setting in the nonpolitical context.

[3]

The Four Variables
of a Political System

Political Culture

In political science, as in any social science, we begin with individuals—actual men and women going about the business of politics. The unit that is the individual is unique. There is something about it that makes it unlike any other. This distinctive something may be so striking and powerful that we call it genius; or it may be one of the amiable peculiarities that enable us to tell one friend from another. But for all their individuality, people also have much in common. They share a common human nature—certain emotional drives, intellectual capacities, and moral tendencies. As we find it in any particular society, however, this common human nature expresses itself in certain values, beliefs, and emotional attitudes, which, with greater or lesser modification, are passed on by instruction or imitation from one generation to the next. These we call the culture of the society.

Certain aspects of the general culture of a society are especially concerned with *how government ought to be conducted and what* it should *try to do.* This sector of culture we call political culture. As with the general culture of a society, the principal components of the political culture are *values*, *beliefs*, and *emotional attitudes.* In turn, within each of these we can distinguish between elements that emphasize means and those that emphasize ends—between *conceptions of authority* and *conceptions of purpose.*

POLITICAL VALUES: CONCEPTIONS OF AUTHORITY

What do we mean by a conception of authority? There is nothing abstruse or difficult about the idea and we can readily illustrate it from our everyday knowledge of our own country. In the United States certain general notions of how our government ought to be conducted are spread fairly widely throughout society. This does not mean that most people have retained from their high school civics course an exact idea of the constitutional powers and relations of Federal and state governments, or of Congress, the Presidency, and the Supreme Court. But the great bulk of Americans do share certain political ideals: that there should be elections at stated intervals for legislative and various executive offices, that elected officials should have the determining voice in making laws and public policy, that power should be divided between states and nation and at each level among various branches. We say that in general people believe that our system ought to be democratic, federal, and constitutional —although many might not use these words or be able to define them. These words, however, refer to elements of the American political tradition. With notable exceptions—such as the Civil War—this tradition has been shared by most people in this country. And in the light of it, the analyst of our political system today can explain much of the behavior of voters, officeholders, parties, and other groups. Thinking of this tradition as a present and living influence on our political behavior, we refer to it as the political culture of the American system.

Looking more closely at this tradition, we see that one major part consists of certain standards, certain norms, of *how* decisions ought to be made and carried out. It is concerned with means, rather than ends: with the methods and procedures by which decisions are made rather than the contents or purposes of decisions. These norms define, for instance, how officeholders should be chosen and the procedures they should follow in making policy. The decisions of an officeholder chosen in a rigged election or of a legislature bought up by bribery may be obeyed, but—so far as the public knows the facts—these decisions will tend to lack the moral sanction attaching to decisions that have been properly made by properly chosen officials. Quite apart from whether the policy is good or bad, people want also to know whether it was made in the right—the authoritative— way. Such procedural norms comprise our conception of authority, and because we believe that by and large these norms are followed when policy decisions are made we accept these decisions as having authority.

It is of the essence that these norms have moral force. Authority is a moral quality making commands issued in accord with its norms morally binding upon those accepting these norms. It is one reason for obedience. Authority, however, is only one of various factors that may account for obedience. Physical force cannot be wholly left out of account. Indeed, in some political systems—for example, Russian-occupied Hungary —obedience is rendered primarily out of fear of physical violence and other forms of coercion. But even in these cases we may well find that the ruling group itself—such as the elite of the Communist Party—is bound together by an ideology that includes a conception of how this group itself is to be governed. In his account of the Soviet system, Dr. Ulam examines this problem, showing how the Leninist doctrine of the role of the Communist Party and its governing bodies has developed into a conception of authority accepted by wide sectors of the Soviet elite. Whatever we may say about the relations of the Soviet ruling classes with the rest of the nation, we cannot credit force alone with the acceptance of decisions within these ruling classes themselves. They accept the dictatorship in some measure because they hold it to be legitimate.

Sheer habit and unthinking custom will normally also be a powerful support of a regime. So also will the dictates of self-interest: to find your own welfare bound up with a certain system of government is a reason for supporting that system, although it is hardly sufficient alone to explain why men endure all the burdens that government commonly inflicts on them. But beyond such further supporting factors—force, custom, self-interest—a widely shared conception of authority will enhance the stability of a political system.

Common knowledge of our own country illustrates what we mean by the term. The Soviet example reminds us how radically other people's ideals of authority may differ from our own. The primitive tribe, the Greek *polis*, the Roman Empire, the medieval *regnum*, the modern nation-state, the totalitarian dictatorship—all suggest the enormous variety we may find in political cultures and in people's ways of conceiving the rights and duties of rulers and ruled. In some systems authority is highly personal and traditionalist, legitimate power being vested in certain families and rigidly restricted in its manner of exercise by unchangeable custom. In contrast, our own and most modern Western systems vest authority in an impersonal structure of bodies and procedures, defined in general terms and distinguishing sharply between the person and the office he holds. Sometimes we find consensus within a system. But the values embodied in a political culture and expressed in its norms are not always harmonious with one another: we think, for instance, of the unsolved conflict of the Middle Ages over the respective authority of the temporal and spiritual powers.

In the study of these various ideals of authority and the conflicts within political cultures, the history of political philosophy may be a great help:

Plato for Greece, Cicero for Rome, Hooker for Tudor England, John Locke for early America, Lenin for Soviet Russia. But as these illustrations immediately suggest, political philosophers are often not entirely accurate guides to the really operative ideal or ideals of authority in a political system. The noblest speculations may be of little use to our inquiry. For what we are concerned with are the cultural forces that actually guide and shape the choices of people in everyday political life.

Our inquiry is into operative ideals. It follows that we cannot be satisfied with merely legal definitions. The constitutional laws and conventions of a system will often be a helpful guide to the conception (or conceptions) of authority of that system. But what we are interested in, so to speak, lies behind these laws and conventions. It may go beyond them; it may even be in conflict with them. As we shall have occasion to point out from time to time in the course of this book, constitutional law—the law laying down the frame of government—does not have the same status and function in each system. In any particular case we cannot presume without inquiry that it faithfully portrays the dominant conception of authority.

The American example itself shows how far the norms of authority may go beyond the requirements formally imposed by law. Our democratic ideal, for instance, requires that major decisions be made only after opportunity for wide discussion and criticism. If, therefore, a legislative majority uses its power to stifle debate and prevent adequate discussion in the assembly, we feel that it has acted improperly, even though legally. We like to think that electoral contests are determined in some degree by rational discussion of candidates and issues—we speak of them as "debates." Hence, we feel that the influence of money on elections may at some point become excessive. Indeed, it is because we first believe this influence to be improper that we take up the question of making a law to restrict it. Putting the matter briefly, we may say that the American ideal of authority requires that, on the whole, decisions should be made only after free and rational debate by people sincerely aiming at the common good. This ideal is expressed partly—but only partly—in law. Much of it is a matter of political ethics, externally sanctioned only by the diffuse rewards and penalties of public esteem.

Conceptions of authority differ not only from place to place, but also from time to time within the history of the same community. We speak of *the* American conception of authority, and no doubt in some respects that conception is the same today as in 1776. Yet in others it has profoundly changed. In the beginning we were not, as a people, committed to democracy. The extent of the suffrage was for long an issue of our politics—and with regard to the right of Negroes to vote in the Deep South it is still an issue today. Or to take a matter of lesser importance:

we know that the founders of this country regarded political parties with suspicion and hostility. Madison spoke of them as "factions" and, while he did not think they could be eliminated from politics, he sought means to nullify their effects. In time Americans came to take a more tolerant view and today they regard political parties as legitimate and valuable parts of the governmental process. British attitudes have gone through a similar evolution. Indeed, the common view in Britain today gives to parties far greater importance than they enjoy in the United States. We still entertain a certain suspicion of party—"independence" in a voter or in a Congressman is to be praised—and would regard as "bossism" the centralized control and discipline that the British tolerate and expect. To them two tightly knit and strongly led parties are indispensable to meaningful elections and the proper conduct of government. In these contrasting attitudes toward party we find an important difference in the ideals of authority of the two countries—a contrast, it hardly need be said, that makes a great difference to the ways the two political systems actually work.

POLITICAL VALUES: CONCEPTIONS OF PURPOSE

Rarely, if ever, will people accept a conception of authority without also entertaining some idea of what that authority is to be used for. Our ordinary use of the term "constitution" suggests this fact: a constitution is taken to mean, on the one hand, the structure by which authoritative decisions are made and executed and, on the other, an indication of what purposes these decisions are to serve. In our own political tradition, these purposes include such objects as the preservation of private property, freedom of speech, defense against external enemies—the preamble to the Federal constitution gives a familiar enumeration.

To put the matter broadly, we may say that the political culture of the United States includes both procedural and substantive values. It includes standards setting out the broad procedures that are to govern the way policy is made and executed—our ideal of authority. At the same time it includes certain notions of the common good with which the substance of public policy should be in accord. Like our conception of authority, these ideals of common purpose have moral force. Policy that we believe to be in accord with these ideals will receive support for this reason as well as for reasons of self-interest and custom; and government action cannot for long radically violate these values without endangering the stability of our system. This does not mean that all Americans are perfectly agreed upon the proper scope and subject of government action. The stakes for which parties and politicians contend in "the great game of politics" are often high. Still the figure of speech is apt: American politics is not war, but a game, hedged in and moderated by massive consensus on means and ends.

Like conceptions of authority, the common purposes of political systems range through many different possibilities. The drive for booty of warrior kingdoms; the traditional social values of the *ancien régime*; the mission of empire of Victorian Britain; the millenary hopes of revolutionary governments—these too were purposes that the members of these political systems accepted in greater or lesser degree and that the actions of governments—tribal, royal, aristocratic, or popular—were expected to serve.

Finally, we must stress that the presence of consensus on common purpose at any time in the history of a political system by no means excludes the possibility of change and development of such conceptions of common purpose as of authority. Our own history illustrates the point. Like our ideas of the proper extent of the suffrage, our ideas of the proper objects of government policy have altered. We have decided, through civil war, that we no longer would accept the maintenance of Negro slavery as an element in our national purpose. Other changes have been less violent. The general expectation today that government is responsible for maintaining a high level of employment marks a substantial change in our notion of the proper goals of public policy. The consensus on *laissez faire* of a few decades ago has shifted to a new consensus that includes a limited acceptance of the welfare state. In Britain, as Dr. Eckstein shows, a more radical shift in this direction has taken place. In both cases, the development in political culture, while avoiding violence, passed through a state of sharp conflict before reaching a new consensus.

In describing the conceptions of authority and purpose of a system, how far should we go toward including particular institutions and policies? How abstract or generalized will such conceptions be? To this there can be no single answer. The values of the traditionalist system are highly particular. In both procedure and substance they lean on the past for standards of what is proper and legitimate. And these standards form not a generalized, but an exact, particular image of the past. The reigning values are embedded in rigid and specific practice; hence, to change even what we might regard as a detail is to threaten a violation of common ideals. On the other hand, in rationalist systems, values are more general, admitting different interpretations and divergent applications to specific cases. This is an important fact when we examine the conditions that permit political conflict to take place without danger to the survival of a system. Where values take a more generalized form, different interpretations will legitimately and indeed inevitably arise. Yet the conflicts that result need not disrupt consensus on the fundamentals of the system.

By and large such a generalizing and rationalizing of political values is a necessary condition for the emergence of modern democratic parties. Because American political values, for instance, are of this sort, two parties can differ over such questions as the powers of the President or the level of farm price supports while agreeing on the fundamentals of American constitutional democracy. Even in times of far sharper political strife—as during the New Deal period—a plane on which consensus prevailed could be found in the American system. Dr. Eckstein maintains that the same has been true in Britain, even when we find "capitalism" and "socialism" in conflict.

Perhaps in some systems the distinction between conceptions of authority and conceptions of purpose is hardly worth making. In the traditionalist system, for instance, the very idea that laws can be deliberately "made" is alien. Laws rather are "declared" on the basis of what has always been done and accepted in the past. The ideal of procedure itself rigidly restricts the substance of law. But in the more rationalistic system, there is a greater likelihood that procedural standards may be satisfied only at the cost of substantive ones—or vice versa. In constitutional governments during wartime, for instance, there may be a strain between the need for rapid and forceful government action and the expectation that the authoritative but slow-moving procedures of the system will be respected. A similar problem may arise in peacetime, as Dr. Eckstein brings out in his discussion of British policy since World War II. New policies were adopted, but old and accepted modes of procedure made it difficult to devise new machinery of government appropriate to the new policies.

Problems such as these are likely to arise in the strongly "constitutionalist" systems in which the dominant political values give high priority to established procedures. Other political cultures may place so great a stress upon purpose that the norms of procedure cannot stand against the needs of policy. To such a trait of German political culture, Dr. Spiro very largely attributes the instability of German politics. Similarly, in Soviet Russia power has been legitimized mainly in terms of some compelling national purpose rather than through regular and accepted procedures of decision. Lenin's notion of "democratic centralism," while providing a foundation for dictatorship, did retain some vestiges of democratic control within the Communist Party. But, perhaps from the very start of the Soviet regime, the drive to industrialize and to banish Russian backwardness has had a far higher priority, as a national purpose, than "democratic centralism." Thus the pre-eminence of the economic drive contributed to the erosion of the remnants of democratic control that Lenin's doctrine had allowed.

Belief Systems

So far we have spoken of conceptions of authority and purpose as if they included only values, i.e., standards of right and wrong in political conduct and definitions of good and bad in the goals of public policy. But as the discussion must have suggested, these conceptions include not only values about what "ought" to be, but also beliefs about what "is"; not only normative propositions, but also existential propositions. Closely linked with the values of authority and purpose we find beliefs about the actual behavior of men and societies.

We can illustrate the distinction and the connection by looking at the democratic ideal as it is conceived in America and Western Europe. This ideal includes certain norms, such as that the adult population of a country has the right and duty to take part in political discussion and electoral decisions. But this ideal also includes the *belief* that ordinary people, on the whole, have the capacity to take part in politics with some degree of rationality. To say that most men are rational is not the same as saying that they ought to have the vote. Yet both are essentials of the democratic conception of authority. And if, for instance, it became widely believed that most voters were not rational, adherence to the democratic norm would be severely shaken. The democratic ideal includes both the norm of wide popular participation and the belief in the rationality of the common man.

Similarly, conceptions of purpose have a normative and an existential side. The ideal of *laissez faire*, for instance, was supported by an elaborate ethical theory inhibiting governments from interfering with private property and freedom of contract. John Locke gave this ethical theory a classic statement that was echoed by other writers in the eighteenth and nineteenth centuries. But support for *laissez faire* also derived from the economic theory that we think of as originating with Adam Smith. In its own terms this economic theory was primarily descriptive and analytical, not ethical. Yet as a demonstration that the wealth of the nation would be increased by a hands-off policy, it lent powerful support to the prohibitions of the Lockean ethic. Again, in the decline of the ideal of *laissez faire* we may distinguish these two aspects. As Dr. Eckstein shows, the welfare state in Britain has been advocated and justified on the grounds of ethical theories that broke with the rugged individualism of the nineteenth century. But its growth and acceptance was also immensely forwarded by the Keynesian "revolution" in economics. Today in Britain government intervention to maintain employment is accepted not only on ethical grounds, but also on the grounds of the new Keynesian economic beliefs that have spread widely through British society.

Of what use is this distinction to political analysis? One use is that it often helps us to see what is at issue in political conflicts. What at first sight looks like a clash of values may turn out on closer inspection to be mainly a disagreement over the facts. In the debates over the extension of the franchise in America and Europe in the early nineteenth century, for instance, both sides often agreed that in principle all men subject to a government ought to have the right to participate in it. Some of those who accepted this principle, however, rejected manhood suffrage and defended a property qualification for voting on practical grounds. They contended that in practice men without property could not be trusted to respect the property of others, or, what might be still worse, would be overly subject to the influence of wealth. Macaulay argued much along these lines in opposition to a democratic suffrage in Britain, although he granted that his argument did not apply with the same force in America. Apart from unspoken reasons that participants in the controversy may have entertained, the dispute was essentially a matter of fact: What is your view of human nature, and especially your view of the tendencies of unpropertied men in Britain or America at a particular time? Similarly, the controversies today over more or less government intervention in the economy are only in part conflicts between opposing ethical principles—such as "human rights" versus "property rights." Much of the difference lies in differing views of the long-run effects of government intervention. The controversy is not so much over the "rights" of property as over the question whether government control is actually "the road to serfdom."

Where political conflict is essentially one of values, a reconciliation by rational argument is far more difficult. However, if the issue is a question of fact, there is hope that an appeal to the evidence and to the reasoned outcome of factual inquiry may bring together the parties in conflict. Such a conciliating function is not a primary role of the political scientist, but the distinction between value and belief suggests a hypothesis that may help him understand change and development. Without trying to state the proposition as a general rule, we may say that in modern Western societies belief systems seem to be more easily subject to change than do value systems. Not only science in the technical sense, but also systematic thought and research in general have become widespread activities, highly institutionalized and continually producing and spreading new knowledge. Moreover, the members of these societies have grown accustomed to accept and act on such new knowledge—consider, for example, the swift impact new medical discoveries such as polio vaccine have had on behavior. At times, of course, new knowledge may affect important values in the political culture. It may undermine old beliefs on which old values depend, causing severe tensions as individuals and groups accept the new beliefs, yet cling to old values. Ultimately, the force of the new beliefs may compel an adaptation of values. Racial discrimination, for instance, has depended in part upon a belief that certain races were inferior. Since biology has exploded this belief, people accustomed to accepting new knowledge validated by science can no longer entertain it. In time we may hope the old norms of racial discrimination will be altered by the new beliefs.

Distinguishing beliefs from values also helps the student of politics to identify ways in which the political culture of a system is related to the general culture of the society. Ideas that do not appear at first glance to have relevance to politics may be intimately connected with it through the belief systems of the political culture. Christian theology is not primarily concerned with political man. Yet its various forms, within both the Catholic and Protestant traditions, have frequently provided the foundation for political beliefs. We think, for instance, of the role of Calvinism in the contending political theories and civil wars of Europe in the sixteenth and seventeenth centuries. Likewise, the democratic ideal, especially in the form in which it spread throughout Europe in the late eighteenth and early nineteenth centuries, appeared as the political expression of the large and complex system of thought elaborated by the philosophers of the Enlightenment and was intimately associated with beliefs in progress, science, and human perfectibility. In general, the beliefs and values of a political culture are aspects of a world-outlook in the development of which we may find the origins of changes in the patterns of the political system.

While it is right to make the distinction, it is hardly less important to recognize how hard it may be to separate values from beliefs in the actual course of inquiry. In some elements of political culture the two may seem inextricably intertwined. *Laissez-faire* economics—to return to a former example—was on its face a "value-free" analysis of how an economy actually would operate. Yet no one can read the classical economists of the nineteenth century without sensing the potent judgments of what was right in conduct and what was desirable as goals of policy. The very overriding concern with the increase in national wealth reflected such a judgment of value. A different concern—say, with noneconomic goals and conditions—would have led to a quite different social analysis.

Often sociologists use the term "ideology" to refer to belief systems that have such a bias derived from value-judgments. One of the most striking examples of ideology in this sense is Marxism-Leninism. This system of thought purports to be an objective, indeed a scientific, description and analysis of the development of society. Yet, obviously, the whole corpus of these writings is loaded with moral exhortation. Hence, the political culture of the ruling classes of Soviet Russia has a dual aspect. On the one hand, it is Marxism-Leninism as a system of belief that interprets the course of world history, specifically laying down as a matter of fact that Russian society will be led through the present stage of socialism by the Communist Party acting as the vanguard of the proletariat. In itself this belief does not state what "ought" to happen or what anyone "ought" to do. Yet, in fact, Marxist-Leninist ideology in Soviet Russia today embraces political values endowing the Communist leaders with authority and their policies with the sanction of common purpose.

EMOTIONAL ATTITUDES AND SYMBOLISM

One of Edmund Burke's lasting insights was his perception that a purely intellectual and ethical commitment to a theory of government is not enough to ensure political stability. He condemned the "barbarous philosophy" of the French Revolution because in it "nothing is left which engages the affections on the part of the commonwealth." Yet, he contended, without such a basis in emotion, the laws of a country are weakly founded, being "supported only by their own terrors, and by the concern which each individual may find in them from his own private speculation or can spare to them from his own private interests." Sharply aware of the role of emotional forces in politics, political scientists today would agree with Burke's emphasis and would stress the symbols and symbolic acts by which emotions favorable or hostile to a system are excited and by which leaders seek to manipulate the behavior of the masses. These symbols we may call *expressive symbols* in order to indicate the fact that they refer to emotional attitudes and feelings. Symbols may also, of course, refer to political values and beliefs—they may be evaluative and cognitive as well as expressive. But what we are interested in here is the symbolism that gets at the emotional side of politics. The role of the political emotions in the stability of a system can hardly be exaggerated: we think of the deep, unreasoning ties of nationalism and the support they lend to the common values and beliefs of a polity.

Underlying this subject is a general problem of social psychology—the problem of motivation. In particular there is the question of how values are geared into motives—how ideas of what is worthwhile as an object of individual achievement as well as ideas of moral rights and duties can themselves become needs enlisting the energies of the human organism. Sociologists and social psychologists discuss this problem as part of the complex process of "socialization" through which in earliest childhood the basic values of a culture are transferred to the motivation of individuals. We are concerned here with a related process by which political values are strengthened and reinforced by expressive symbolism.

Obvious examples of expressive symbols in politics are flags, anthems, national monuments, and the like. Persons too may become symbols. The British monarch is the key figure in the ceremonial institutions of Britain, symbolizing and keeping alive those predemocratic attitudes that Dr. Eckstein finds to be of central importance in British government. Party leaders—totalitarian or democratic—may perform similar functions, like the legends of a people's history, speaking to the emotions and continually re-creating the attitudes from which political action flows.

The particular things or persons that become symbolic, however, need to be seen in the context of action in which they are used. We recognize the function of public ceremony in strengthening political solidarity— occasions such as the Fourth of July in the United States, Bastille Day in France, a coronation or opening of Parliament in Britain, as well as the mass demonstrations of the Soviet May Day, or the Nuremberg rallies under the Nazis. On such occasions emotional commitment to a regime may be, so to speak, acted out and at the same time revived and rein- forced. While external objects, such as flags and monuments, will be used symbolically, the essential symbolism lies in the collective action of the people as they take part in the ceremony. Such action will not, of course, always be favorable to the regime. Parties as well as regimes have their particular symbolisms and if they are revolutionary, their gatherings and acts of symbolism will express this fact—we think, for instance, of the clenched fist salute of the Communists.

Such special occasions when action is wholly or largely ceremonial are normally only a small part of the expressive symbolism of a political sys- tem. Throughout the whole vast process of everyday politics, action has an expressive as well as an instrumental aspect and we need to consider this emotional side of political action and discourse if we are to under- stand the forces making for the stability or development of a system. When, for instance, a member rises in his place in the House of Commons and puts his question to a Minister at Question Time, he is seeking, say, to bring out some error of administration or to show the superiority of his party's position or to demonstrate his own dialectical ability. This is the instrumental aspect of his action. At the same time, however, this act of participation expresses an attitude toward the House, an attitude of ac- ceptance and identification. Apart from its instrumental effects, the daily participation of members expresses and heightens their emotional com- mitment to the system, strengthening their trust in one another and also the hold of the system over them.

It is essential, of course, that these acts conform to "the House of Com- mons manner." Speakers must be at least ostensibly courteous; the tone of discourse must be conversational, not oratorical; and the whole style of behavior and speech must conform not only to the rules of procedure of the House, but also to a complex and largely unspoken set of conventions, pro- ducing the "tone and temper" of the proceedings which Dr. Eckstein em- phasizes. This style is no insignificant aspect of the political process. Unspoken though its criteria may be, they constitute a rigorous discipline and perform an important function. It is a rule of rhetoric that style must fit content if there is to be effective communication. The same holds for political speech. How can you, for instance, call for a revolution and echo the cries of a distressed proletariat when you are standing in a back row without a table to pound or a tribunal from which to orate and are bound to speak of your class-enemy as "the Right Honorable gentleman"—and all in the tone of drawing-room conversation? You could, of course, say the words of such a message, but restricted by such a style how could you make it reach the emotions of your audience in Parliament or outside? It is no wonder that, as Aneurin Bevan remarked, the House of Commons "softens the acerbities of class feeling."

If political action is to be effective, if it is to get results among those to whom it is directed, it must arouse emotions appropriate to the conduct it aims to produce. But the style of British politics, not only in the House of Commons, but also generally, is not likely to touch off revolutionary zeal. On the contrary, it is a style conforming to the sedate and tolerant gradualism affirmed in the values and beliefs of British political culture. This does not mean that the style of British politics prevents an appeal to the emotions, but rather that it severely limits the range of emotions that can be effectively reached, restricting them to attitudes that support the generally accepted frame of authority and purpose. This limitation, effected through the system of expressive symbolism, thus protects the emotional foundations of the political system and is one source of its great strength.

Another way of making the same general point is to look at expressive symbolism from the point of view of political propaganda. In Britain, as in any other country, a political leader may manipulate the behavior and opinions of people by an appeal to certain emotions, inducing them to take actions that they would not have taken if they had merely considered the sober meaning of his words. Yet the common symbolism of British politics sets severe limits on what propaganda can accomplish by such an appeal. Some other systems are less fortunate. The revolutionary tradition in France, for instance, has perpetuated among many Frenchmen a certain predisposition to respond to the appeal of the political extremist. A receptive audience, a personal manner, a style of discourse, even certain key words—all are provided by that tradition, ready at hand for a Thorez or a Poujade. The division in French political culture that Dr. Wahl analyzes is not only a conflict between two sets of ideas and beliefs; it is also a conflict on the plane of emotions—and for that reason, all the more serious.

Nor will we always find that dominant emotions are perfectly matched with the explicit values and beliefs of a political system. Attitudes inherited from a long authoritarian past may impede the operation of a democratic system, even though most of its members sincerely accept the democratic ideal. If so, the manner and style of politics in the system may tell us more about the emotional forces at work than the explicit declarations of politicians and people. Germany under the Weimar Republic would provide interesting material for an analysis along these lines. Even today, in the democratic and liberal Bonn regime, the style of German politics, as Dr. Spiro portrays it, suggests an emotional preference for judicial and administrative methods of settling disputes and an aversion to the informal and pragmatic methods common in the older democracies. In these attitudes we may find the lingering effects of the practices and values of the *Rechtsstaat* of the old bureaucratic days of the Bismarckian Empire.

We have previously speculated on whether values or beliefs are more easily changed. How would we answer the same question with regard to the political emotions? Clearly, there is no brief and general answer. But the question is worth raising, since it is plausible to think that ideas, values, and emotions do not necessarily change at the same rate. In some circumstances, an appeal for action can be so directed to certain emotions that people will act contrary to the settled dictates of their own good sense and moral principles. Mob action, provides many examples. And again and again the history of the totalitarian demagogues of this century illustrates how the political action of masses of people can be controlled by "the deliberate manipulation of sub-conscious, non-rational inference," to use Graham Wallas's phrase. We can well believe that many Germans who became Nazis took the decisive step in becoming followers of Hitler under the compulsion of powerful emotions whose intellectual and moral meaning they did not understand, and that only afterward and in time did they adapt their beliefs and values to the Nazi system. Such cases as these—mob action and totalitarian self-surrender—are close to pathological. Rather more common and understandable would be the sequence in which ideas change first, then values, then finally and last, basic emotions. People often become intellectually and even morally convinced of the desirability of new institutions or new policies, and yet find that they can only gradually conquer their emotional attachment to the old ways. This is the order of change we might well expect if we started from Burkean premises.

The Pattern of Power

How are political decisions really made? What influences actually determine the choice of leaders, the making of policy, and the way it is carried out? What interests motivate the various groups attempting to win power?

What actually are the goals that they are trying to reach through government? Political culture does not tell the whole story. The political scientist may have a good grasp of the dominant values and beliefs of a system and yet be unable to answer such questions. Conceptions of authority and purpose will condition the pattern of power and the pattern of interests, but other influences will also play a part. If we want to get at political realities—"who gets what, when, and how"—we must examine these influences and their relations to political ideals.

A DEFINITION OF POWER

Let us look at the question of power. First, a definition: One person exercises power over another when he intentionally acts in such a manner as to affect in a predictable way the action of the other. This definition may appear either too narrow or too broad. It might be thought too narrow since it excludes cases in which persons affect others without realizing or intending the effects of their action. The acts of an individual continually set in motion trains of consequence of which he is not aware. Around the everyday behavior of any of us there is a penumbra of "unconscious power" lying outside the focus of our attention. Quite unwittingly we may make a friend or an enemy, bestow a benefit or frustrate a hope. Indeed, such influences may not only lie outside the focus of our attention; they may be so complex and devious as to escape our comprehension, even if we tried to understand them. Yet in a sense such influence is a kind of power that the individual might come to recognize and use. Continually our knowledge of social relations shows us more about such unanticipated consequences of individual and group behavior—in the relations of parent and child, of participants in economic life, of speakers and listeners in opinion formation. And frequently such knowledge reveals power relations that had not been suspected before and new forms of power that may be exercised for good or ill in the future. As we shall see later, this whole sphere of unanticipated consequences is of major concern to the political scientist.

It is more likely, however, that our definition will appear to be too broad. It states that there is power where a person—or a group—by an intended act brings about an intended result in the action of another. He may do this by the use of some sort of sanction—by an inducement, such as a bribe or other favor, or by the threat of a deprivation, such as a blow or withdrawal of esteem. Some might prefer to restrict the definition of power to influence supported by sanctions. This would exclude compliance resulting from manipulation or "mere" influence—as when, for instance, a newspaper or political orator sways public opinion by rational persuasion or an appeal to the emotions. If you wish to stress this distinction, you will say that what we call "the pattern of power" ought to be called "the pattern of power and influence." We have chosen the shorter phrase. And in actual political life, the two kinds of operation usually go together. Candidates mingle promises of benefits with "glad-handing"; pressure groups work on legislators both by threats of electoral retaliation and by appeals to sentiment.

Power in society takes many forms. An obvious one is wealth—every day each of us exercises this form of power by paying money in return for goods and services. Other familiar forms are physical strength, social status, education, moral character, personal magnetism, and military, legal or managerial skill. Often we may be able to trace the power of an individual over others to one or more such factors, his "power base." And similarly with groups: Dr. Eckstein, for instance, points out the principal power base of each of various groups within the Labour Party—in the case of the Fabians, brains; in the case of the constituency parties, political activism; in the case of the trade unions, money. Normally, of course, the power base of a group will be a complex of several factors.

To speak thus of the power base does not mean that power is something that the individual or group simply "has." Power is relational. The influence that one person has over another depends not only on the power-holder, but also on the person he influences. The situation of the person influenced will certainly make a difference. The poor man will probably be more subject to the influence of money than the rich; the unarmed man more subject to the influence of force than the armed. Moreover, the interests and general psychological equipment of the person to be influenced will affect the outcome. The martyr will not be swayed by threats of violence, the dunce by appeals to reason, the atheist by promises of heavenly bliss. While these are examples of special individual traits, they also suggest how the culture of society will profoundly condition the forms of power that may arise within it.

Authority is a form of power. To have won office according to the approved procedures of the political culture gives the officeholder a certain power—that is, it enables him by acting in a certain way to affect predictably the behavior of others. The American legislator, for example, makes laws with majority approval of his colleagues in both houses and with executive approval. Apart from other reasons, these laws meet with compliance because the bulk of the people accept the ideal of authority according to whose norms the officeholders have been chosen and the laws enacted. Indeed, in a democratic system, each of the people also has his minuscule ration of authority—above all, the vote—through which he too may exercise influence. When, in speaking of democratic systems, we say that size is one element in the power of a group, we are referring primarily to power based on this form of authority—the right to vote.

It hardly need be said that the holders of such power (i.e., authority) can profoundly affect the distribution of other forms of power in the society—as, for instance, by the redistribution of wealth or by schemes for public education. *Conversely, the possibility is raised that the holders of other forms of power may use them to influence or win authority.* It is because in any political system this possibility will in some degree be realized, that in political analysis we must distinguish the pattern of power. One general factor determining that pattern will be the power—other than authority—of groups in the political arena. Where we find that a group has considerable influence, we shall want to see how far this is explained by such reasons as the quality of its organization and leadership, and the level of wealth, social status, and relevant skills of its members. In American politics, for instance, we should expect that, other things being equal, a relatively poor group would be at a disadvantage in competition with a more wealthy one. On the other hand, greater skill in organization may be able to offset this disadvantage. The pattern of power will be determined by the distribution of such forms of power as well as by the distribution of authority.

Asking such questions may help us particularly when we try to identify and explain changes in the pattern of political power. Take, for instance, the increase in wealth of the industrial middle classes in Europe in the nineteenth century or the rise of trade union organization in recent generations. Such changes in the balance of "nonauthoritative" power will almost certainly affect the pattern of political power. On occasion this balance of power may come into radical conflict with the dominant ideal of authority and the legal institutions expressing it—as in France before the Revolution of 1789 or in Britain before the Reform Act of 1832. The balance of power in this sense cannot be left out of account when we seek to explain the stability or instability of a pattern of political power.

AUTHORITY AND POWER

What is the function of conceptions of authority? This depends on the extent to which a political culture is divided or united. So far as there is consensus, the conception of authority will have a stabilizing effect, guiding and integrating the relations of groups in their struggle for political power. In the first place, we must remember that a conception of authority in some degree confers effective power. Therefore, despite the shift in the balance of other forms of power, certain constants remain in the pattern of political power. Although a group in a democratic system may suffer a decline in some elements of its power (wealth, for example), its various political rights, particularly the right to vote, limit the extent to which its effective political power may fall. Similarly, in an aristocratic system, a rise in the level of wealth and education of the nonaristocratic classes is almost certain to affect the pattern of political power. Yet the aristocratic classes—quite apart from other foundations of power—will retain some significant influence because of their position as the repositories of authority.

Equally important, the way in which groups use their nonauthoritative power will be shaped and limited by the conception of authority. One reason decisions are accepted is that they are believed to have been made in the prescribed way. If a group is itself to enjoy the benefits of authoritative decisions, it can hardly afford to undermine the basis on which the power of such decisions rests. Hence, in influencing decisions it must conform—or at least appear to conform—to the norms of authority. Nor should we think of this conformity as merely external and "insincere." Political values are operative ideals precisely because they become "internalized." To the extent that they do, the norms of authority will be self-enforcing. For instance, when groups in a democratic polity do not resort to bribery, the reasons certainly include not only fear of consequences, but also the self-imposed ethical restraints of the democratic ideal itself.

In general, then, the conception of authority provides a framework of decision-making that defines within broad limits what power various participants shall have and how they shall proceed in making decisions. Not its least important function is to determine when a result—i.e., a decision —has been reached. Consider, for instance, the function of the norm of majority rule. According to this norm, when the majority of the people— or of the legislature or council—has declared for a certain outcome, a decision has been made. Without some such common norm, the struggle to influence government action could go on indefinitely without a decision being reached. In this sense, a conception of authority has an integrating effect upon the struggle for power.

But what if we find not consensus but dissensus on authority? The differing status of public law will illustrate the effects of political culture in the two cases. Where there is consensus, a principal expression of the common ideal of authority will be the basic legal framework of government. By this we mean the laws of its constitution and possibly also certain other important rules, such as those embodying the fundamentals of the electoral system and of parialmentary procedure. This aspect of a political system, although sometimes called "formal," is no insignificant force in the shaping of the pattern of political power. In the American system, our right to vote depends in the first instance upon the law. Whatever we may find out about the other sources of the power of a group and about the informal procedures by which it influences government, the actual power it wields in political struggle normally depends in very great degree upon this right. And this right—the law defining and establishing the power to vote—in turn is supported not only by special legal sanctions but also by a massive consensus throughout the society. According to Dr. Eckstein the same is true of the British system.

When we turn to France, however, we find a divided culture and an entirely different status for public law. An old and sound interpretation identifies two main opposing currents in the French tradition of authority, one representative, the other authoritarian. Following Dr. Wahl's account, we can carry further this familiar view of *les deux Frances*—the Red and the Black—and show how these two clusters of political values have become identified respectively with the legislature and the administration. From time to time, different classes and groups have tended toward one or the other of the traditions and accordingly have viewed one governmental structure with favor, the other with hostility. As a result of this fissure in political culture, Frenchmen for generations have found it virtually impossible to establish a basic legal framework—a constitution—that enjoys the whole-hearted support of the major segments of the people. The basic institutions of self-government of the Third and Fourth Republics rested not on consensus, but rather on a compromise among dissident groups, none of which was strong enough to get the constitution it really wanted.

Compromise, of course, is a feature of all constitution-making, and not even the British or American consensus extends to all details. But in the French case, the differences go much deeper than details or matters of mere degree. As a result the basic legal framework of the French polity has never had that direct and congruent relation with a single, unified conception of authority such as is enjoyed by the British constitution. Indeed, the constitutional laws governing the relations between executive and parliament in France have often resembled the terms of a treaty between opposing nations rather than the expression of a common view of government. As the seventy years of the Third Republic demonstrated, such a system can survive—although deeply afflicted by immobilism, weak and short-lived ministries, and, from time to time, ominous threats from Left or Right.

What of the Soviet "constitution"? Its status and function are very different indeed from the status and function of the constitutions of the three other systems. To call it a "constitution" is an extreme of Pickwickian language. Its rules are not laws in any ordinary sense of the word. Of course, they cannot be enforced by legal procedures and sanctions—such as an appeal to the courts—but that is often true of constitutional laws in the free countries. But when legal sanctions are lacking in free countries, constitutional rules are supported by other sanctions. Attempts to change radically the "rules of the game" would be resisted by an exercise of power, of which economic power—such as the power to strike—is only one of the more obvious examples. In comparison, the Russian constitution is simply so many words, having no relevance to the actual pattern of power.

Yet, as Dr. Ulam argues, the case is not quite so simple. Without these words the actual pattern of power would not be exactly the same. To some Soviet leaders and some indeterminate number of Soviet citizens, their system really is democratic. The words of the Soviet constitution state these values and thereby strengthen the effective power of the dictatorship. The proceedings of such bodies as the Supreme Soviet are functional as a kind of ceremony. Instrumentally insignificant, they express the belief, not entirely extinguished among Russians, that their system should and does express the "real" will of the masses.

The Supreme Soviet is controlled from outside, real power resting principally with the higher organs of the Communist Party. Yet the Communist leaders can secure compliance with their decisions on policy in some degree because they operate this "dumb show" of the Supreme Soviet from time to time. Some shred of authority attaches to its proceedings. As Dr. Ulam suggests, this raises an interesting, if distant, possibility. In a crisis, the "balance" upon which the power of the present leaders depends might shift in favor of other groups among the Soviet elites—the army or the managers, for example. In such a case, the Supreme Soviet might become a significant focus of decision-making—as at the overthrow of Mussolini the Grand Council of Fascist Italy, until then a "paper" body like the Supreme Soviet, sprang into life. This does not mean that the Supreme Soviet would become genuinely democratic. It might become, however, a body in which the representatives of various elites sealed the bargains in which they agreed to tolerate one another and according to which they would rule the country. All this, of course, is highly speculative. But it suggests what would have to happen before the present constitution could become a major determinant of the actual pattern of political power in Russia.

The Pattern of Interests

Analysis of the relations of political groups cannot be conducted solely in terms of power. We must also examine their interests—what they are trying to use power for. On the plane of political culture, we have distinguished authority from purpose. Similarly, on the plane of political action we must consider not only the pattern of power, but also the pattern of interests. Obviously, the pattern of power itself—say, the alliances and hostilities among groups—cannot be understood unless we look into the interests entertained by participants. Nor, as we have seen, can we understand the power base of a group or individual without taking into account the interests of those influenced.

A DEFINITION OF INTEREST

Interest is a slippery term and we need at the start to clear up certain ambiguities. One is the tendency to take "interest" as meaning "self-interest." For instance, when people talk about the activities of "interest groups" in politics, it is often with an overtone of disapproval, as if the goals of these groups were necessarily in conflict with the common good or with moral standards. That is not the meaning attached to the term in the present discussion. *By interest we mean here simply a disposition to act to achieve some goal.* Such a disposition has two sides. One is emotional—the felt need that gives the push or drive leading to action. But rarely is such a need entirely blind and undirected: associated with it is a cognitive aspect—some notion of the object or state of affairs that answers to the felt need. Even in an infant, the brute feeling of hunger soon becomes connected with some understanding of the object that will satisfy hunger; accordingly the infant tries to control his acts in such a way as to achieve this object. In the case of adults this cognitive side will be involved with a fairly complicated set of ideas about the nature of the thing desired and how it can be reached.

It is true, of course, that for child or adult, for the individual alone or in a group, achieving the desired state means satisfying the underlying emotional need and thus enjoying a feeling of psychological satisfaction. Looking at the emotional side of interests, therefore, we may say that in this limited sense all interests are "selfish"—and that there is a grain of truth in the Utilitarians' "law of universal selfishness." However, when we look at the cognitive side of interests—the goals to which they are directed —we see the distinction that common sense makes by means of the terms "selfish" and "unselfish." One interest aims at a benefit to the actor. Another aims at a benefit to others. This is an important distinction in political behavior. Yet each kind of motive is called an interest, as we have defined the term here. An interest, defined as such, includes a disposition to promote the relief of the poor as well as a disposition to pursue success, profits, or material luxury for oneself.

Perhaps it should also be noted that an interest may be positive or negative. As we use the term here, an interest may be a disposition to bring about a certain state of affairs; or it may be a disposition to prevent or do away with a certain state of affairs. We think of everyday efforts to acquire some useful object or to avoid or relieve pain. And certainly we need to make our definition of interest broad enough to include the fact that the groups active in politics are as often concerned with blocking some act of government or eliminating some existing condition as they are with promoting government action or setting up a government service helpful to themselves.

What in general are the factors that create and shape interests? Certain ones, obviously, are founded upon needs inherent in the human organism—the need for food, for example. No doubt there are others that have a psychological rather than a biological nature. The whole question of "inherent needs" is, and long has been, surrounded by controversy; it is essentially the problem of the "instincts." Fortunately we need not solve the problem to carry on political and social inquiry. For we do at least know that the interests we find in society and in politics have been profoundly shaped and directed by social experience. And we can with some success track down the contribution that society has made to forming these interests.

The very situation in which an individual finds himself will play no small part in directing his interests to one set of goals rather than another. A people's tastes in food will be shaped by the products available in the environment. The ambitions of politicians will be molded by the opportunities and barriers that confront them—by the existence of few or many elective officers, a parliamentary or presidential form of government, a multiparty or two-party system. Likewise in economic life, the profit "motive" itself is not an inherent psychological drive, but rather an interest shaped by the opportunities of a free enterprise system.

Along with the social situation, the general culture of a society will condition interests. Among the most important of these cultural influences will be the prevailing belief systems—in the sense in which we have used this term above. Interests are directed toward certain goals, but what people believe about the way they can most efficiently achieve their goals will have a real effect in shaping the goals themselves. When we think of the various things we wish to achieve—or avoid—we do not think of them apart from one another. Hunger leads us to eat, but what particular food we eat will be affected by our beliefs about the kinds of food that promote health. In this way, our goals tend to be interdependent. We may reject something we desire because we believe it to be incompatible with something we desire even more. Thus our beliefs about the relationships of goals will affect what goals we embody in our interests.

The role of belief systems is particularly striking when we consider the complex interests that groups pursue in modern politics. In the case of labor, farm, and employers groups, for instance, beliefs about how the economic system actually works will profoundly affect the interests the groups press for through political action. The American farmer's interest in high price-supports depends upon certain beliefs about the effects government action will have on farm income and on the general health of the economy. If most farmers believed—as some do—that such intervention menaces the farmer's freedom and will ultimately hurt his pocketbook, the interests that farmers pursue in American politics would be very different from what they currently are. There is in this sense a strong element of "theory" in the interests of even the most hard-headed and practical pressure groups.

Hardly separable is the conditioning influence of values. Some values—sometimes called "appreciative" values—define the goals that are worthwhile achieving for oneself. A moment ago we mentioned the "profit motive." Generally in Western society in modern times the achievement of pecuniary success in a free market has been a goal of intense interest for many people. This interest depends not only upon the economic situation, but also upon an "ethic" that leads us to attach prestige to such success and to take gratification in achieving it. This goal has had far less importance in other times and other places where entirely different values have directed self-interest. In Western civilization saintly discipline and the chivalric virtues once far outranked pecuniary or professional success as models for personal ambition. Political power itself has a value and prestige that vary from one political culture to another. As compared with the businessman, the politician has a higher standing in Britain than in the United States. The essential trait of appreciative values is that they shape our notions of self-interest. They have an important function in relating self-interest to another class of values that we may call moral values.

As distinguished from appreciative values, the characteristic of moral values is that they lay down the rights and duties of individuals and groups toward one another. Typically the function of moral standards is to define not objects of self-interest, but rather an order of relationships to which self-interest must be subject. The contents of moral codes vary as widely as do other elements of culture. Some lay a heavy burden of obligation on members of the community in relation to one another, erecting an elaborate system of rights and duties around various classes and ranks, each with its special responsibilities and legitimate demands toward the rest. Others conceive of society as composed of equal individuals, each with the same limited rights and duties.

Could a society survive without a moral code, the motives of its members being guided solely by self-interest? Some philosophers have thought so. Indeed, this would seem to be a major premise of the Utilitarian school. Their argument in brief was that, although all men are creatures of self-interest, they can live together in peace and good order, if they will only take a sufficiently intelligent view of their long-run advantage. Hence a stable society and political system could be founded upon enlightened self-interest. As has often been pointed out, however, the Utilitarians made an important assumption, namely that the character of the various goals that are pursued are such as to make possible a natural harmony of interests. This, we hardly need say, is a very dubious assumption. Empirically, it appears that social and political stability cannot be explained as a result of any such natural harmony: in a stable order we find some common moral code in terms of which the conflicts inevitable in any society can be harmonized to some degree.

Yet, much as we need to stress the function of a common moral code, we must also recognize the importance of the particular goals that are pursued as objects of self-interest. Here the function of appreciative values is crucial. The point can be illustrated from British experience in recent years. Along with the development of the welfare state has gone a certain reshaping of moral values. In general there has been a redefinition of the rights and duties of individuals and groups—particularly in relation to private property—and of the role of government as an instrument of these new moral standards. At the same time appreciative values have moved away from the standards of the era of vigorous capitalism and the goals of self-interest have been accordingly modified. While capitalistic acquisitiveness has declined, the evaluation of and interest in economic security has risen. Such a change in the goals of self-interest is complementary to the new moral and political values of the welfare state. For the sake of the stability of the political system, this is fortunate. Otherwise, the strain between new moral values and old interests might be excessive.

COMMON PURPOSE AND INTERESTS

We have been considering the relation of interests to the social situation and to culture in general. Let us look more closely at the role of political culture. The values and beliefs that are relevant are principally those of common purpose. Common purpose values are a class of moral values, since they are concerned with the rights and duties of individuals and groups. Their special character, however, comes from the fact that they define the role of government in relation to these rights and duties. They are the standards we follow when we decide that a certain condition is a problem *for* government—that government ought to do something to help one group or to hinder certain kinds of action or to direct some sphere of social action along certain lines. The problems that government tries to solve are not simply "given," confronting the political system, so to speak, from outside. There was a time, for instance, when unemployment was not a problem for government because interference with the economy lay outside commonly accepted notions of national purpose. Whether a certain condition is felt to be a problem will depend both on the objective situation and on the cultural perspective from which it is viewed. A problem may therefore arise because of a change in the situation, or because of a developing conception of common purpose.

The principal point to be made here is simple. It is that *interests are normally asserted as demands for policy only when they are felt to be justified by some conception of common purpose.* This is fairly easy to see when we consider interest groups that advocate some benefit for others. Such groups normally justify their demands by an appeal to the obligation of government to protect or enforce certain rights and duties, an appeal that more or less explicitly involves a view of common purpose. Advocates of legislation to restrict child labor, for example, pointed out the benefits to the community that would flow from protecting the health of growing children. But we must observe that groups urging action primarily favorable to themselves also show with greater or lesser sincerity some justification of their demand in terms of a view of the common good. When American farmers demand action to protect farm prices, they argue that this policy is based on the government's obligation to protect certain groups against undue economic hardship. Moreover, they contend that it will promote the health of the economy in general by maintaining the purchasing power of an important group of buyers. The demand for a benefit for themselves is intimately linked with a view of the whole American economy.

Such views of common purpose can be highly instrumental in bringing into the political arena interests that, without these views, might remain nonpolitical. A broad example will illustrate the point. We all recognize how economic development may reshape the pattern of interests of a political system. Consider the rise of socialism and social reform in Europe during the past three quarters of a century. We cannot understand these changes in the pattern of interests in European political systems unless we look at the new wants that sprang from the growth of an industrial economy. But, as the history of the nineteenth century shows, such wants may be felt, and felt acutely, and yet not be asserted as demands on government, unless they are also believed to be justified by some conception of common purpose. People may endure the deprivations of unemployment, poor housing, and inadequate medical care, and yet make no significant demand for government action because they consider such intervention neither proper nor efficacious. Those affected may, of course, try to improve their lot in other ways. But in the absence of some view of common purpose legitimizing government action, they will remain aloof from politics. To a considerable extent this was the case in many European countries during the heyday of *laissez faire*. In mid-Victorian Britain, for instance, even the trade unions accepted the orthodoxy of Liberalism and made remarkably few demands on government, stressing instead their function as "friendly societies" in relieving the ills of their working-class members.

It follows that, if we are to understand how the wants industrialization created eventually developed into the swelling demands for the welfare state, we must look beyond economic development alone. We must also consider the new views of the responsibility of the state and of the nature of the economy that provided ready justifications for new political demands. Not only economic conditions, but also—as Dr. Eckstein shows— the break with the political values of rugged individualism prepared the way for the massive government intervention that has taken place in recent decades.

New ideas of a proper and attainable standard of living can have as radical an impact on the pattern of interests as an industrial revolution. Today such ideas are sweeping over Asia, Africa, and Latin America as part of a world-wide "revolution of rising expectations." Moreover, they are being introduced into the developing countries in the context of new political values and beliefs. The idea of a higher standard of living has not spread to these continents as part of the doctrine of *laissez faire*. On the contrary, it has been spread in the context of theories of the welfare state, socialism, and communism—all of which, however much they differ on certain vital issues, make the satisfaction of this interest a primary duty of government. Conceptions of common purpose have given a fierce, political impetus to the new interests rising out of a cultural revolution.

This impressive role for political values and beliefs is not confined to systems that enjoy consensus. When new ideas of the proper goals of policy arise in or are imported into a political culture, they may deeply divide it and put severe, even revolutionary, strains on the system. Consensus on common purpose, on the other hand, like consensus on authority, will be a force making for political stability. Such general agreement on the broad objectives of government and its role in society is, as Dr. Eckstein points out, a principal reason for the fruitful and pragmatic politics of the British system. The principal interests asserted in British politics are shaped by the same basic view of government's role and responsibility and of the general scheme of priorities in the light of which conflicts should be settled. Given these common premises, interests can be adjusted and differences compromised without deep offense to the sense of justice of contending parties.

SPECIAL-INTEREST AND GENERAL-INTEREST GROUPS

Common sense suggests that some groups may be more, some less, concerned with the common good—that, in terms of the goals they pursue, some are more selfish, some less. Is this distinction of importance to political analysis? Psychology distinguishes between ego and superego functions; sociology between self-oriented and collectivity-oriented action. Political science should also be encouraged to examine the surmise of common sense.

The distinction is sometimes stated as that between special-interest groups and general-interest groups. The goal of the special-interest group is primarily a benefit to itself; that of the general-interest group primarily a benefit to others. This is a familiar distinction of everyday experience. But in the light of our previous discussion one qualification immediately springs to mind. The special-interest group, while putting primary stress on a benefit to itself, will also in the normal case be motivated by a view of common purpose—a theory of justification for its demand. This expression of political values may set the group in conflict with other groups. Or it may provide common premises that help it reconcile its goals with those of others. In either case, this operative ideal—the view of the common good in terms of which the group justifies its demand for benefits—is geared to the motivation of the members of the group, and so, strictly speaking, is part of its interest. In short, the criterion of the special-interest group is not exclusive, but only relatively greater, concern with benefits for itself. Similarly, the general-interest group, while concerned primarily with others, will also normally think of its action as benefiting itself. Pure altruism, like pure egoism, may occur, but neither seems to provide a model that often fits the interest groups we know.

How can the political scientist use the distinction between the two types of groups? How does this difference in motive make a difference to the structure and behavior of groups? Several possibilities come to mind. One is that the general-interest group is likely to be more "permeable" than the special-interest group. To belong to it you need not be someone who will benefit particularly from its activities, but rather a person concerned with certain values. For this reason such groups are sometimes called "open-ended." The special-interest group, on the other hand, in seeking to build up its membership will have, so to speak, a "ready-made" clientele, its potential membership being more clearly delimited and more easily identifiable than that of the general-interest group.

Another possibility is that the special-interest group will show greater perseverance and intensity than the general-interest group. We can readily think of examples of general-interest groups—those passionately committed to an "ideology" or a "crusade"—that have shown perseverance and intensity far greater than the ordinary special-interest group. Still, it is a common experience for the "reform" group, after a burst of idealistic activity, to subside, lose members, and break up, while the group based solidly on a program of self-interested benefits continues to maintain its membership and press its demands. In municipal politics this is often the fate of the "do-gooders" as compared with the "machine."

The different emphases in motivation will tend to have consequences for the structure and behavior of groups. But these consequences will also depend upon other factors in the situation. The degree of dissensus will be one such factor. Where a political culture is radically divided, these divergencies in values provide foci for the formation of opposing general-interest groups. If that happens, there is real danger that such groups will tend to exacerbate further the conflicts of goals among self-oriented groups. It is quite true that self-oriented groups will already in some degree reflect the divisions in the culture. Dr. Wahl takes this fact into account by classifying pressure groups as well as parties under the main ideological divisions of French politics. This peculiar cultural context is one reason why pressure groups in France and Britain, with similar economic bases, have different political goals. The self-interest of such groups, as we have seen, will be shaped by the political values to which they are committed. Moreover—and this is the main point being emphasized here—the stress on ideology by some French parties (which in terms of our present discussion are general-interest groups) still further intensifies the conflicts among self-oriented groups.

In a context of consensus, there may well be an opposite tendency. So far as the general-interest group puts its emphasis on values that are part of a generally accepted culture, its function will be to lessen the conflicts of self-oriented groups. British political parties perform some such function. Between them there are significant disagreements on values and beliefs. But the many basic views and sentiments they share make them a powerful force for cohesion in the polity. Frequently, self-oriented groups in British society find themselves in sharp conflict over opposing goals. When one of the major parties intervenes in such a situation, it is in a position to promote a solution reflecting generally shared premises and priorities.

The Pattern of Policy

When we study the interplay of power and interests, we ask the question: How and why was the decision made? When we study the pattern of policy we ask: What was decided? From the making of the decision, we turn to its outcome. But the decision as a product is not an inert thing. It is part of a further stage of political or social process. So, from asking what was decided, we go on to ask what are the consequences of this decision in those further stages. While the patterns of power and interest focus attention on the origins and emergence of decisions, the pattern of policy focuses attention on its content and consequences.

A Definition of Policy

This is not to say, however, that any of these patterns is confined to certain stages of the decision process. In some systems, we can distinguish various stages—for instance, the steps by which a problem is recognized, solutions are proposed, a broad choice is made, and finally a fully determinate decision is produced. At each stage power and interests interact. In the usual Western democratic system, for example, the study of the patterns of power and interest will be much concerned with political parties, pressure groups, legislative bodies, and the chief executive. But the action of the civil and military bureaucracy cannot be excluded. Certainly in the three democratic systems we examine in this book, bureaucrats have a large measure of power. This power may arise from the discretion that has been left them to make more determinate the broad decisions of the legislature, or from the influence that their expert knowledge gives them when they advise their superiors. Whatever its source, to say that the bureaucrat has power is to say that we cannot draw a line between those persons who make decisions and those who merely carry them out. The distinction between "policy-making" and "administration" is only relative. Nor can we assume that the civil servant—or judge, general, or policeman—is entirely "neutral" in his interests and goals. He will have views of what is good for society, not to mention the usual motives of ambition and self-interest. As he uses his power to give concrete form to the policies of his government, his purposes—broad or narrow, orthodox or heretical—will influence his action. The patterns of power and interest are aspects of the decision process at all stages.

Policy emerges from a broad background of decisions, in which process it acquires a morally binding quality—becomes "legitimate"—insofar as it conforms to the procedural and substantive values of the system. In modern systems, a policy is normally made determinate and concrete by the administrative and judicial organs of the system and sometimes also by the participation of private individuals or groups. In Great Britain, for instance, the act of 1946 setting up the National Health Service was a basic decision of policy. But the decision process is rarely, if ever, confined to such a single event or moment in time. In the case of this policy, it extends back to include at least the electorate's choice of the Labour Party in the election of 1945. It extends forward to include the shaping of the Health Service as it was put into effect and operated by the decisions of civil servants, hospital boards, individual doctors, and others. The product of this process is the pattern of policy. At this point, so to speak, the society is confronted with the "output" of the political system.

When he describes the pattern of policy, the political scientist asks, "What was decided?" But since he is also interested in causal interdependence, he will further ask, "What are the consequences of this particular policy—or of this set of policies?" This question may take a broad or a narrow form. In its broad form, it is the question of how the political system functions for the society's stability or development—how effective it is as an instrument for identifying and solving problems. In its narrow form the question is, "How does this policy, or set of policies, affect the political system itself?" This question also may take the political scientist beyond the bounds of the political system as he looks into the indirect effects of policy. But his concern is still primarily political.

Recent agricultural policy in Britain will serve for illustration. This policy has committed the government to providing "guaranteed prices and assured markets" for various farm products. Originating during World War II when the government took steps to increase home farm production, it has been carried out by means of a program of subsidies annually negotiated by the government with representatives of the farmers. In the past two decades British farmers have enjoyed unprecedented prosperity, the effect in no small part of this farm program. Now, to assess such effects of policy on the economy takes the political scientist into the field of the economist. The venture is unavoidable. Certainly we do not need to argue the point that what happens in the economic system will have some impact—possibly a great impact—on the political system. This does not mean, however, that the concern of the political scientist with economic affairs is the same as that of the economist. The political scientist is interested in tracing out the economic effects of policy only insofar as they have further effects on the political system. For example, the main pressure group among British farmers—the National Farmers Union— has more than doubled its membership since prewar days, and one modest, but not insignificant, reason for this increase has been the simple fact that in recent years farmers have had far more money. Being richer, the Union can now afford a large staff of experts and publicity men and, not least important, a full-time, paid president—all instruments that have made it a more formidable power in British politics.

The example is very simple and by no means exhausts the indirect political effects of British farm policy. It serves to illustrate, however, how government policy itself, through its effect on the economy, can bring about a shift in the balance of power in the political system. As Dr. Eckstein shows, the whole vast set of programs of the welfare state through its economic and social effects is reshaping the pattern of power in Britain.

POLICY, POWER, AND INTERESTS

But such indirect effects of policy will affect the pattern of interests as well as power. In the history of a political interest group, for instance, we often find that its demands are weak and confused until a relevant government program has been set up. The existence of such a program gives sharper definition to the interests it favors and in turn intensifies and clarifies the demands of the favored group. Before World War II—to turn again to the British farmers—the National Farmers Union included only about half the farmers of Britain and was concerned mainly with keeping up the price of home-grown products by means of producer-controlled marketing boards. During and after the war, as we have seen, government policy took a radically new direction and the farmers were given a position of importance in the administration of policy. From its new role in the annual negotiation of the subsidy, the Union has gained in power and prestige. Equally important, the new policy has given the Union a new definition of its goals. Hence, in recent years the Union's principal effort has been to maintain, and if possible increase, the government guarantees for the various farm products.

The impact of policy may also be directly felt by the political system. Consider Dr. Eckstein's analysis of the effect of the welfare state on the traditional machinery of government in Britain. These new programs of social security, farm subsidies, the health service, housing, and so on have immensely expanded the scope and complexity of policy. Far more major decisions and far more decisions involving intricate consequences and technical knowledge must be made than ever before. As a result, Ministers have not been able to maintain the same degree of control over the whole apparatus that they once had, so that some power has shifted from Ministers to civil servants. At the same time, representatives of interest groups—such as the farmers—have become more closely associated with government departments in the administration of the new programs, thereby gaining considerable influence over the course of policy. Hence as compared with Ministers, the bureaucrats—whether the public bureaucrats of government departments or the private bureaucrats of interest-group organizations—have gained in effective power and there has occurred, in Dr. Eckstein's phrase, a certain "pluralization" in this sector of the pattern of power.

In most Western political systems changes of this sort in patterns of policy in recent decades have had similar effects on patterns of power. Even in Russia, where power is highly centralized, it has been hard to establish effective control over the vast activities of government. In consequence, as Dr. Ulam shows, there has at times been a shift of some degree of power from the central elites to lower levels of the bureaucracy— only to be followed by an attempt to reassert strict central control.

Thus within the political system policy may affect power. But the flow of consequences may also be in the other direction. If Britain has carried out a more massive program of government intervention than France or

Germany, one reason surely lies in the fact that it has cabinet government based on a tight two-party system. These elements in the British pattern of power provide the foundations for the coherent policy-making and co-ordinated control of administration without which large-scale government intervention will be self-defeating and ineffective. Indeed, one might argue that the British system of strict party government under "programmatic" parties encourages the assertion of demands for more services and more active intervention. Government is an effective way of getting things done; hence, groups readily turn to it for the satisfaction of their interests. Conversely, weak and incoherent government discourages demands. Thus the pattern of power may affect the pattern of interests.

The object of this discussion of the pattern of policy has been, primarily, to clarify its meaning for the purpose of description. But I have also tried to indicate how one might examine its causal interdependence with the other patterns of a political system—suggesting, for instance, that British welfare programs have changed the distribution of political power and have shaped and crystallized political demands; that strong and effective cabinet government has encouraged the assertion of new interests; and that new programs have shifted and pluralized certain sectors of the power structure. These suggestions remain tentative, but they provide the starting point for further inquiry. Stripped of their reference to the particular context in which they have been stated—that is, the government of Britain—they can be restated, in more or less complex form, as explanatory hypotheses. One could then go on to test and develop them in the light of the experience not only of the British, but also of other political systems.

Intention and Situation

The stress given to values and beliefs in this Introduction may seem to commit the authors to a kind of cultural determinism. We do indeed mean to say that the political culture—and of course the general culture—of a society will have great effect on the behavior of individuals and groups and on the way the political system works. The basic values and beliefs of a people will tend to shape their institutions, so that when we find a change in their institutions it is plausible to look for the reason in a preceding change in political culture—just as when an individual acts differently it is plausible to seek the reason in a preceding change of intention. But this is not the only direction in which the inquirer should look. When trying to understand a change in behavior or institutions, we must make an analysis not only of intentions, but also of the situation. In tracing out the lines of cause and effect, we find that some are intentional, while others are situational.

SITUATIONAL COMPULSIONS

When we are looking for the causes of human action there are, broadly, two ways we can put our questions. One is to ask what the person set out to do—what was his intention or end-in-view. The other is to ask what the situation "forced" him to do—what circumstances he was obliged to adapt to and how this affected what he did. Rarely will the way be so smooth that a man need not adapt his intentions to the situation. The same holds of a society. We presume that the broad purposes of a community, as embodied in its religious and ethical values, make a deep imprint on its history. But we also recognize the influence—sometimes almost amounting to compulsion—that is exerted by physical environment. And a familiar theme of history is how climate, geography, and resources have shaped the development of institutions.

Physical environment is not the only compelling circumstance. The social environment itself—man-made institutions and patterns of action—may as powerfully condition behavior as geography or climate. Economic institutions are perhaps the most familiar example. We need not accept the extreme view that the mode of production wholly determines the shape of social action in all other spheres, but we can hardly deny that it will greatly affect the form taken by family life, the class system, government, and even religious and artistic activity. An underdeveloped economy in which the mass of the people are sunk in poverty, while a small minority enjoy great wealth, will be a poor foundation for a genuinely democratic regime. A primitive system of communications alone will tend to limit severely the area within which there can be general and active participation in government. This consequence is not intentional. It does not flow from a deliberate design to sabotage a democratic regime; we may even presume that people are doing their best to make the communications system as efficient as possible. The effect, nevertheless, is to limit and shape the possibilities in the political sphere.

Within the political system, as we have seen, the patterns of power, interest, and policy will condition one another in a similar way. When in Britain, for instance, the expansion of the scope of policy shifted some power from Ministers to civil servants, this was not an intended consequence of the welfare state. It was not one of the aims of the reformers, nor can it be regarded as a direct reflection of the values of British political culture. Quite the contrary. But in spite of their preferences, Ministers were faced with conditions that made it impossible to maintain the close and effective control they had exercised in the past. Given the fact that the new programs were being carried out, the shift of power resulted from the situation, not from anyone's intention. It was, so to speak, an un-planned consequence of planning.

Not only between the basic patterns of a political system, but also within one pattern, the action of individuals or groups will be conditioned by the situation. The pattern of power in Britain, including as it does cabinet government and a tight two-party system, will shape pressure-group activity along quite different lines from those prevailing in the United States. Hence, although a British and an American pressure group may have much the same goals of public policy, they will adopt different tactics. Along with the group's ends-in-view, the compulsions of the situation shape its pattern of action.

That politicians, pressure groups, and parties must adapt their conduct to circumstances is a commonplace—indeed it is part of what is meant by the maxim that "politics is the art of the possible." Yet it needs to be stressed in order to guard against the easy temptation to explain political action solely in terms of the immediate intentions or long-run values and beliefs of the actors. Within the arena of the day-to-day struggle of groups; among the basic patterns of the political system; between the political system itself and other spheres of social action, the lines of unintended consequence may lead to results far different from anything hoped for or expected by individuals or groups.

International as well as domestic politics illustrates the point. In trying to explain a war between two nations, we may set out to discover which had designs of aggression. This line of inquiry may be fruitful, as Nazi and Soviet behavior have shown. The revolutionary character of their values and beliefs is a major source of their respective imperialisms. Yet we also know—and if we do not Hobbes can teach us—that war may occur even though both parties to it are sincerely seeking only to defend them-selves. One nation, knowing that wars do occur and that national defense is a necessity, strengthens its armaments and alliances. The other, alarmed by these steps, takes similar ones—which confirm the initial fears of the first nation and lead to further preparation. Finally, although each nation has sought only security, the logic of the classic armaments race leads to war. It is the situation—in particular, the existence of separate, sovereign states—as much as the intentions of the nations, that has determined the course of events.

A look at the French system will help clarify what we mean by situa-tional analysis and why it is important. Consider two uniformities in the pattern of power of that system under the Third and Fourth Republics: that elections to the legislature were held about every four or five years; and that ministries fell on the average about every six months. The first of these resulted from the explicit provisions of a law which, in broad outline, was understood and approved by the bulk of the French people. In short, it was intentional. To say this, of course, does not end the analysis, but it is a sound, if obvious, first step. In explaining government instability, however, we could not start from such a generally accepted intention among the French people or French politicians. No one planned the instability of governments during the Third and Fourth Republics. Deputies and party groups did not have as a set purpose the frequent fall of governments. Yet each party group in pursuing quite other purposes brought about that result. The reason, we say, is to be looked for in the French multiparty system. Given such a system, instability will follow: it is an unintended consequence of the party situation.

In that situation governments had to be based on coalitions and no group joining a government was able to realize all or even most of its program. At the same time it was confronted with the fact that there were other party groups outside the coalition that were competing for similar electoral support but that were unimpeded by the frustrations of coalition government. Hence, some groups in the government would be strongly tempted to break away and restore their competitive position by reasserting the whole of their demands—that is, in the French phrase, to resort to a *cure d'opposition*. The intentions of the groups were the "normal" ones of a political party: to win a share of power, put their men in office, enact their programs, maintain and expand their electoral support. But when these intentions were followed in the situation we have described, certain groups found it necessary to withdraw their support. Conceivably, in some cases, they did not know they would bring down the government; that, at any rate, was not the end they were seeking. The end they did seek, however—the maintenance of electoral support—could not be achieved if they remained in frustrating coalition with other party groups. Over a period of time, since the same party situation prevailed, similar compulsions operated and similar decisions were made; hence, a characteristic uniformity of the French pattern of power under the Third and Fourth Republics —the frequent fall of governments.

Effect on Values and Beliefs

The analysis of intentions—whether the basic values and beliefs of political culture or the immediate aims and interests of groups—cannot suffice. The institutions that men deliberately create, like the tactics they pursue in political battle, may produce patterns and consequences that no person or group has intended or perhaps even foreseen. Sometimes institutions turn upon their creators with impersonal coercions that defeat the very purposes they were designed to serve. Then men, the creators, are driven along by the things they created in a course they never planned, and that may not only frustrate their original intentions, but also reshape these intentions to fit the new model of action. Thus, unplanned and unintended development may remake political style, tactics, ambitions, and ideals, reaching perhaps to the deepest levels of political culture. We have stressed the role of values and beliefs in shaping political behavior. Here we stress that unplanned and unintended patterns of behavior may themselves sometimes remake values and beliefs.

Consider again the case of France. If there was one purpose on which the bulk of Frenchmen were united at the Liberation, it was that the political patterns of the Third Republic should not be restored. Dr. Wahl describes these patterns—multipartism, instability of governments, immobilism. While at the birth of the Fourth Republic the French soon found that they could not agree on a radical remodeling of their system, they created some new institutions and parties and there was certainly a new spirit—"the spirit of the Resistance." Yet, in spite of the wishes of most of the actors on the scene, as Dr. Wahl goes on to show, the old system soon reappeared and along with it much of the old and despised spirit of the declining days of the Third Republic. The crusading, reformist politicians of the Liberation gradually adapted themselves, taking on the attitudes and traits of the politicians of prewar days. As the French themselves remarked, *"Le système bouffe les hommes"* ("The system gobbles up the men").

In no sense does the sociological principle expressed in this maxim apply only to democracies. Its irony is only heightened when we turn to Soviet Russia. Surely it would seem that in this mighty dictatorship, where political power is total and wholly centralized, the men in command could avert or control the compulsions of circumstance. Yet they are equally the creatures of their system. A principal theme of Dr. Ulam's analysis is that the success of the dictatorship in performing its major task, the industrialization of Russia, has created conditions and attitudes that make difficult, if not impossible, the continuance of a dictatorship of the Stalinist variety. But if the present dictators cannot go backward, neither can they safely go forward: to relax their coercions at home or in the satellite countries is to raise demands and strengthen forces that threaten the whole basis of their power. They are all-powerful, yet at the same time pressed relentlessly by circumstances that their system itself created.

Nor have their personal characters and motivations been untouched by these compulsions. The system, so to speak, selects the types of personality that can rise to power, as Dr. Ulam points out in his discussion of the prominence of the *apparatchik*. Moreover, by the kinds of action that the system continually involves, it leads men to accept and indeed to prefer these kinds of action. The personalities of the dictators are in no small part creations of the system they presumably command.

Cases such as these, where values and beliefs are remade by the development of unintended patterns, bring home the need to consider both situational and intentional factors. Having made the point, we may strike a more hopeful note. For, of course, the two sorts of factors may also work in harmony. As Dr. Eckstein points out, it is central to the British conception of authority that government is bipolar; that is, that a predominant authority of initiative and decision shall be in the hands of a central body, nowadays the government, which conducts its business subject to the constant criticism and influence of an opposing body, nowadays principally the opposition. In the British system, this ancient principle can be more easily realized because there are two major, disciplined parties. And if somehow many parties were to arise, the familiar and approved pattern of politics in terms of government versus opposition could be maintained only with great difficulty. As the British system now operates, however, any maverick group or individual tempted to follow the ways of multipartism is massively discouraged by the near monopoly of political power possessed by the two major parties. The compulsions of the party situation work in the same direction as basic political values and beliefs.

Of course, we must add, in Britain as in other countries, "the system" has its inevitable effects on the personalities and styles of its members. The new M.P. may at first find it distasteful invariably to troop into the division lobby at a signal from his chiefs and regardless of his personal opinions. In time, however, he comes not only to accept this odd division of opinion on all questions into only two sides, but even to feel that it is right and natural. Daily behavior, as well as parliamentary tradition, gently but firmly makes him a "House of Commons man."

Patterns of government may arise from situational or from intentional factors—usually, indeed, from both. The authors of this book are centrally concerned with the way in which intention and situation may interact to create patterns of political action. Environment shapes man and man shapes his environment. This is true of political man in his political environment, as of man in general.

Part Two

THE BRITISH
POLITICAL
SYSTEM

by Harry Eckstein

I SUPPOSE there are some folk who enjoy speaking in the House of Commons, and rise without a doubt or tremor. It is impossible to tell: for everyone must leap to his feet with the same alacrity if he is to catch [the Speaker's] eye. . . .

There is, of course, almost every possible ingredient of unease in that place. An after-dinner speaker or a platform speaker may reasonably expect to have the attention of most of his audience. They are in front of him, and they cannot easily get away. He has a table, or desk, for his notes and papers. Even the "front-bencher" commands the length of the House and can use the Dispatch Box for his notes and papers—and thumping fist, if necessary. The back-bencher, clutching his notes, is like a lonely man standing up in the middle of a public meeting. His audience is all round him, some in front, some behind, some above him, some below—. . . . An interruption, a sneer, an ironical laugh, may hit him from any quarter. And, if he rounds upon the interruptor to the southwest, or the sneerer to the east, he may be reminded that he must address his remarks to the Chair, which lies north.

More, unless he is very good, or fairly important—and even if he is—his audience is moving and changing all the time. Members, good friends, it may be, receive urgent telephone messages or "green cards," bow to the Speaker, and march out as he approaches his principal, or only, joke. The Minister whom he hopes to convert, or intends to shatter with a deadly jest, is relieved by another Minister and goes out for a cup of tea, just before the unanswerable argument or the crushing quip is reached. The Front Opposition Bench, in the same way, are constantly coming and going. There is a procession of Members to the Table, putting down Questions and getting advice from the Clerks. Others go up to the Speaker and engage him in conversation. There is movement everywhere. It is like making a speech in a beehive. And those who remain motionless are not necessarily attentive, or even silent. Ministers and Whips must confer upon the course of the debate, check facts and figures, read documents about something quite different. A Member will come in with a resolution or an amendment to another Bill, to which he is seeking signatures. He goes from friend to friend, and there is a whispered colloquy with each. . . . Behind the orator may be one of those Members who have the habit of muttering a running commentary—"Quite right, too"—"Not with this Government"—"They're *Afraid*"—quite friendly, maybe, but maddening. Then there are the professional interruptors, who, if they do not like the speaker or the speech, make it their business to snap at him from time to time—"Nonsense!" "Rubbish!" . . . and so on . . .

Here is perhaps the fundamental cause of alarm. Whatever jokes may be made about it, the House of Commons is a formidable body, drawn from every class and corner. They may not all be philosophers or senior wranglers, which is just as well; but you could mention hardly any subject, they say, without some Member shyly coming forward and confessing that he knows all about it.

—A. P. Herbert, *Independent Member**

---

* Copyright, 1950, by A. P. Herbert. Reprinted by permission of the author, Doubleday and Company, A. P. Watt and Son, and Methuen and Company.

[4]

The Sources of Leadership
and Democracy in Britain

The Effectiveness of British Government

British government, as a comparison with the other systems treated in this book will indicate, is unique. Of all these systems, the British alone lacks a written constitution. Only in Britain has there existed an enduring and genuine political consensus, that is, a broad and spontaneous agreement on what is authoritative in government: how the rulers are to be selected, laws made, and the scope of law limited—a fact that may itself explain why the British have not found it necessary to codify their constitutional views in a formal constitution. Again, only Britain has a government that can trace its pedigree through centuries of gradual development, even beyond the serious constitutional conflicts of the seventeenth century. Nowhere else, in consequence, have so many aspects of premodern government survived in political offices, procedures and attitudes. But it is not the old alone that is unique in the British political system: only Britain, for example, has a party system consisting of two tightly disciplined parties, and such political parties are very modern phenomena indeed.

The contemporary German party system does approximate the British, both from the standpoint of the number of parties and their tendency to act cohesively as electoral blocs in Parliament (which is essentially what one means by party discipline), but the matter is one of approximation only, and it might be foolhardy to project present political tendencies in Germany into the future.

Most important of all, Great Britain alone of all the countries dealt with here has managed to maintain, over a long period of time, effective democratic government, if by this we mean a great capacity for constructive action on the part of responsible political leaders. British Governments have suffered neither the acute instability nor the near-paralysis that characterized the Weimar Republic and the Third and Fourth Republics in France. Their capacity for action has been great enough to let them carry through a large-scale remodeling of British social and economic structure in this century, chiefly in a brief space of five years after World War II. This remodeling, moreover, was accomplished strictly within the limits of the traditional constitution and by a set of leaders who, far from being Stalins or Bonapartes, were rather mild and colorless even by British standards. It follows that the capacity for action of British Governments is not derived solely from the abilities of British leaders to use the political system effectively: from their charisma or iron control over great party machines. Where a Clement Attlee or a Neville Chamberlain exercises quite as much power as a Winston Churchill or a Lloyd George the power exercised must be an attribute of the political system rather than of the individual wielding power. This inherent capacity for effective action, is the truly distinctive characteristic of British government, one it shares with practically no other important democratic system. In the cases of the Bonn Federal Republic and the French Fifth Republic, for example, one may certainly suspect that the systems' demonstrated capacity for action is due to the personal status or skills of Adenauer and de Gaulle; in any case, neither of these systems has yet demonstrated that it can function equally effectively without charismatic leadership at the top.

To what can this inherent capacity for action be attributed? The question is important not merely as a puzzle in political sociology but also because the tendency to attribute the effectiveness of British government to the wrong causes has done real damage in other countries. It has sometimes been assumed that if one wants a government as stable and active as the British, one need simply imitate the more important characteristics of the British machinery of government. Wherever this was done, unintended consequences at best, disaster at worst, followed. For example, the power of the British executive to dissolve Parliament was written into the organic laws of the French Third Republic only to fall into total disuse for peculiarly French reasons.[1] And while this did not happen in the Weimar Republic it might have been much better if the power of dissolution had atrophied there too, considering the unfortunate uses to which it was sometimes put.

This does not mean, of course, that the machinery of British govern-

---

[1] See below, pp. 287, 289.

ment is irrelevant to the way the system works, but that machinery alone cannot explain its effectiveness. What makes British government so uniquely effective is not only its organization but the peculiar environment (including the political culture) in which the organization of government functions.

The Bases of Effectiveness

British government would not be as effective as it is if it were not for two factors, one cultural, the other structural. The cultural factor is the British conception of authority, which attributes to leadership a far larger scope of legitimate independent action than that of any other democratic country—"independent" action meaning action taken on the leaders' own initiative rather than as an expression of popular or parliamentary will. The structural factor is the disciplined two-party system, which almost always provides a united leadership backed by a marvelously obedient majority of legislators: "solid masses of steady votes."[2] These two factors may be considered the immediate causes of effective parliamentary government in Britain. How do they operate?

The principal advantage enjoyed by British government over most other parliamentary systems is the stability of its cabinets. Since the turn of the century Britain has had one cabinet for every five or six in France, despite the fact that British governments, no less than French, can be deposed by adverse votes of confidence in the legislature or simply by defeats on policy. This stability has a great many desirable results. It enables ministers to learn the ropes of governing (no easy task in this age of highly technical legislation); it prevents excessively abrupt changes in policy; it allows governments to plan their legislative activities far in advance and to introduce long-range projects without fear of interruption in mid-implementation, so to speak. The crucial reason why the British have had such cabinet stability and the French have not (discounting for the present the Fifth Republic, which is, after all, still in its infancy—and may never grow out of it) is of course that the British have had a disciplined two-party system and the French an undisciplined multiparty system. In a multiparty system, cabinets are necessarily based on party coalitions—unless, as has happened in a very few countries, including postwar Germany, a single party can get an absolute parliamentary majority—and coalitions, in the nature of things, are bound to be less stable than one-party governments. A two-party system alone, however, will not inevitably

---

[2] The phrase is that of Walter Bagehot, author of a classic account of British government, *The English Constitution,* published in 1867. Bagehot thought that parliamentary government could not be made to work without such obedient and reliable majorities.

produce stable government, for the parties themselves may be coalitions, united only for certain particular (e.g., electoral) advantages, as they are in the United States. In Britain, however, the two major parties are not mere electoral coalitions parading under a common label. They are "solid masses" because they almost always vote as unified bodies on parliamentary issues in accordance with instructions by the party leaders or caucuses. Occasionally, to be sure—very infrequently—British parties split. Sometimes also there are "free votes" in Parliament (votes on which M.P.s may, with their leaders' permission, vote as their consciences, not their leaders or party caucuses, direct). On such occasions there will be a certain amount of cross-voting in Parliament. But this is very unusual; the reports of "divisions" in the British Parliamentary Reports (*Hansard*) almost always show a steady mass of Labourites in one column and a solid phalanx of Conservatives in the other. The system works with such marvelous consistency that it is not unusual for an M.P. to criticize his party in a parliamentary debate and later to vote with it in the actual "division," although party discipline, rigidly applied, demands not only a member's vote but also his silence, or sometimes, indeed, his public support of policies with which he privately disagrees.

This, by almost any standard, is a remarkable state of affairs and goes a long way toward explaining the unique effectiveness of British govern-ment. But it does not fully explain it. For it is not only cabinet stability and the consistent ability of the British legislature to make constructive decisions that makes the British system effective, but also the great leeway it offers for independent leadership. The plain fact is that in both parties —although perhaps more in the Conservative than in the Labour Party— it is the party leaders rather than the party caucuses who determine how their disciplined supporters are to vote. Nor is this fact grudgingly con-ceded by the supporters simply as one of the hard facts of party life. On the contrary, it is regarded as being somehow natural and right, the way things should be: "legitimate." Voluntary submission to leadership is, even today, in the age of mass democracy, a vital part of British political culture.

The habit of deference to political leaders and in general social be-havior, which Bagehot made the keystone of his analysis of British politics almost a century ago, is generally glossed over in more modern com-mentaries. The tendency in these commentaries is to stress what we have come to regard as modern democratic attitudes, and not without reason. The British do profoundly believe in basic civil and political liberties; they insist that public authority be exercised in conformity with "the rule of law"; they believe in the binding force of the popular mandate. But the first two of these principles, however congenial to modern democrats, originated in much older (especially medieval) notions of constitutional government, and are wholly reconcilable with non-democratic forms of government. Only the principle of the mandate is truly modern and distinctively democratic, and that, significantly, is subscribed to by the British in a very ambivalent and peculiar way.

In most democratic countries the idea of representative government, if not its practice, involves a simple set of principles: ultimate authority lies in popular will, which is expressed in the election of candidates whose chief function is to enact the policies for which they campaigned and to represent the interests of their constituents. In Britain the matter is much more complicated. British ideas of representative government stress not only the derivative character of political authority (i.e., that authority lies *in* popular will) but also its independent character (i.e., that authority is exercised *over*, or *regardless of*, popular will). These two ideas are of course inconsistent, but the British believe in both nevertheless; indeed this very want of logic explains why their conception of authority, democratic though it is, leaves such abnormally great scope for leadership.

It is probably correct to state, as a general rule, that the British expect their rulers to *govern* more than to *represent* them. The people who govern Britain are, of course, representatives in the sense of being popularly elected. But once they get into Parliament they are not expected to act as mere delegates of those who elected them. This means, first, that their constituency is supposed to be the nation as a whole; hence the curious fact (curious, at any rate, to Americans) that members of Parliament are not required to reside in the constituencies they represent. Undoubtedly, British M.P.s perform certain of the representative functions familiar in our own country, such as going to bat for their constituents in the administrative departments, but it would be thought improper for a member of Parliament to make himself a mere middleman between his constituents and Westminster. Even more important, the representatives of the British people are presumed to have a certain legitimate independence even from the public opinion of the nation. The ultrademocratic idea that Parliament is, so to speak, an assembly of the nation in miniature and that it is consequently the will of the nation, not the will of Parliament as such, that makes parliamentary decisions legitimate, never took as deep root in Britain as elsewhere.

This emphasis on government over representation comes out even more clearly in the fact that the British do not even expect Parliament as such to govern them. They not only permit, they even expect, a particular section of Parliament—the Cabinet—to govern, pretty much independently of the private will of the ordinary members of Parliament. In fact they would be very surprised if a large number of ordinary M.P.s ("backbenchers") had independent political wills and insisted on voting their private convictions. The relationships of the Cabinet to Parliament are very much, in gist, like the relationships of Parliament to the nation. The Cabinet is expected to represent the majority in Parliament, in the sense of being chosen from the majority; but once it is chosen it is expected to be more than a mere mouthpiece for the "public opinion" among its supporters.

In a brilliant essay, L. S. Amery has expounded the dual nature of the British conception of authority.[3] This conception he distinguishes from the Continental view of representative government which derives from the French Revolution and which makes political power a delegation from the individual citizen through the legislature to an executive dependent on the legislature. In contrast, the British constitution, today as in the distant past, has two basic elements: an initiating, directing, energizing element —nowadays the Cabinet—and a checking, criticizing element—nowadays the House of Commons and especially the Opposition. Given this notion of authority, it follows that "Parliament is not, and never has been, a legislature, in the sense of a body specially and primarily empowered to make laws." The function of legislation is mainly exercised by Ministers, while the principal task of Parliament is to secure full discussion and ventilation of all matters as a condition of giving its assent to what the Government does. "Our system," he concludes, "is one of democracy, but of democracy by consent and not by delegation, of government of the people, for the people, with, but not by, the people."

The bi-polar structure that Amery traces back to the Middle Ages and makes the central feature of the British constitution does not mean that Britain is not democratic. It means rather that British democracy has grown up within a certain framework of authority to which it has been obliged—perhaps at the sacrifice of some consistency—to accommodate itself. The idea of the mandate expresses the belief that Governments are responsible to the people for their major acts and policies. As the suffrage has been broadened and particularly since the Reform Act of 1867 this idea has been taken more and more seriously. In 1903, for example, Chamberlain raised the tariff question so that at the next general election the public might give a "mandate" on it. In 1923 Baldwin dissolved Parliament, not because of an adverse vote of confidence or a defeat on policy, but solely, he alleged, because he felt he could not undertake tariff reform (then a very important issue) without obtaining an expression of popular will on the matter. The principle of the mandate is certainly a part of British political culture, and, what is more, is frequently acted upon.

---

[3] L. S. Amery, *Thoughts on the Constitution* (Second ed.; London, 1953).

But mandate theory has never fully replaced the idea of independent authority. Even when it is invoked it is frequently little more than normal political cant, a convenient stick with which to beat one's opponents when better arguments are lacking. Some very important policy decisions have been made, even in the heyday of mandate theory, for which no mandate has existed, without in the least outraging anyone's constitutional feelings; thus Baldwin, who felt he could not reform the tariff without a specific mandate, gave women the equal suffrage without the slightest suspicion of one. Much more important, it seems to be generally recognized that the Government ought sometimes to ignore its lack of a mandate, or even to act counter to a mandate, if doing so would be definitely in the national interest—a loose principle which may cover a multitude of independent actions. The case most frequently cited to make this point is the famous "Baldwin Confession" about Britain's failure to rearm against the Nazi threat before 1935. Baldwin argued that until 1935 every government had been given a mandate for disarmament and collective security under the League of Nations, and that the country's mind on the issue had been revealed emphatically at general elections and by-elections; hence he felt rearmament could not legitimately be undertaken until 1935, when some sort of mandate for it was given.[4] The position taken against this argument by Baldwin's opponents was simply that the Government—having, as it claimed, a clear apprehension of the military danger and the futility of the League of Nations—should have acted in the best interests of the nation anyway; that in fact it was its *duty* as the Government of the country and His Majesty's ministers, to do so, regardless of any electoral consequences. We need not determine which of these views has greater merit. It is enough to note the fact that both could seriously be advanced in the first place. It may be true that one or the other conception of the authority of government is invoked only when it is politically convenient to invoke it, but the great point is that both conceptions can be used for political convenience, i.e., to make an impression on the public. Both conceptions, however inconsistent, have solid roots in British political culture.

The British party system and the most basic British conceptions of authority are marvelously complementary in their effects. Both tend to produce strong and stable leadership and a great capacity for positive action. What is more, the practical working of the disciplined two-party system in a sense reconciles the illogical inconsistencies of the ideas of authority, or at least keeps the British unaware that these inconsistencies exist. For what is in fact an independent exercise of power can always be

---

[4] A very vague mandate, it should be noted. The Tories merely inserted an ambiguous reference to rearmament into their election program.

made to appear derivative by the solid masses of steady votes in Parliament. And just as the party system supports the ideas of legitimacy, so these in turn support the party system, for the meek submissiveness to leadership by ordinary M.P.s itself reflects the habit of deference in British society. But while political deference and the two-party system reinforce and support one another they do not cause one another. To find why they exist at all we must probe more deeply.

The Bases of Political Deference

GRADUAL POLITICAL DEVELOPMENT

What accounts for the ready acceptance of independent leadership by the British? The very nature of their ideas of authority suggests the answer. The important thing to note is that these ideas represent the dominant strains in Western ideas of authority since the Middle Ages. The idea of limited government in accordance with a somehow transcendental (superhuman) law is the cornerstone of medieval constitutionalism. The idea of the independent authority of the sovereign is the contribution of the age of absolutism, in England the Tudor and Stuart periods. The idea of the mandate is the basis of modern representative government. Can we not infer that the British permit such great scope to leadership because modern ideas of derivative authority have been merely superadded to older ideas of independent authority? And if that inference is correct, is not the ultimate cause of political deference in Britain to be found in the gradual, almost entirely peaceful, development of British political institutions, a process in which each new age has established its characteristic political attitudes without ever fully replacing those of preceding ages? A glance at British political development will serve to emphasize this point and to make it less abstract—and is particularly necessary in the examination of British government, for in no other country is the past so much alive, in both the visible and invisible layers of political life, as in Britain.

THE MEDIEVAL BALANCE

British political history certainly differs strikingly from the histories of the other countries treated in this book, and this is true even of the remote past, the Middle Ages. Most contemporary texts on British government hardly pay any attention to medieval England, except to mention piously the "signing" of the Magna Carta in 1215 and the early, but rather mysterious, origins of parliamentary representation. Much less mentioned, but undoubtedly the most essential political difference between England and the Continent in the Middle Ages, is the fact that in England the problem of creating strong central authority out of feudal anarchy and chaos seldom seriously arose, while on the Continent it was the dominant theme of medieval political development. In the early eleventh century, effective central authority hardly existed anywhere in Europe. It was weak even in Anglo-Saxon England, though not so weak there as in most of Western Europe, where, in response to the cessation of Mediterranean trade and the exigencies created by the raids of Norsemen and Magyars, political authority had gravitated mainly into the hands of the holders of local lands and fortifications. Authority, as an adjunct of land and as a matter of contractual relationship, had become located not only in a myriad petty principalities but dispersed in a chaos of criss-crossing obligations, too confusing and illogical to be described here.

This chaotic system served a purpose upon coming into being, but lost its *raison d'être* when the conditions that created it ceased to exist. In some areas of Western Europe, however, effective central authority survived in, or early grew out of, feudalism. One of these areas was Normandy—and Normandy, as every schoolboy knows, conquered England in 1066 and effectively superimposed its central political institutions on the local institutions of Saxon England. William dispossessed the Anglo-Saxon earls, replaced them with his own loyal supporters, and kept close control over all the great landholders of the realm and all important appointments, such as those of bishops. He also converted the existing institutions of local government—for example, the office of the sheriff—into obedient instruments of the King rather than creatures of the local areas themselves, and royal justice was greatly extended in the realm, again at the expense of local judicial institutions.

A highly centralized England thus emerged full-blown in the eleventh century, when central government was still largely nominal elsewhere. Struggles about central authority did take place in England, and during the "anarchy of Stephen" (1135-54) the whole machinery of centralized government came close to being permanently wrecked; but after Henry II (1154-89) restored it, the real authority of the monarchy over a unified England was hardly ever questioned. The importance of this fact of early centralization under feudalism can hardly be exaggerated.

In the first place, early centralization spared England from perhaps the most fundamental and divisive of all questions of political culture, that of the very unit of authority with which people are to identify. In some important parts of Continental Europe, this problem, arising originally out of the collapse of universal empire, the feudal fragmentation of authority and the pretensions of great princes, was not solved until the late nineteenth century (e.g., in Germany and Italy); everywhere on the continent it was a persistent problem until well after the Middle Ages.

In England, however, the fact of effective centralization allowed a strong sense of national unity early to emerge; the creation of an awareness of national identity was never one of the tasks of modern statecraft there. Issues concerning the boundaries of the national unit did arise after the Middle Ages—for example, in relation to the monarchy's holdings on the Continent, the Celtic fringe in Wales and Scotland (where weak separatist movements still exist today), the colonial empire, and the Irish question. Some of these issues, in fact, were deeply divisive, as such issues always are; the Irish question, for example, not only involved England in bloody civil war outside the country but almost led to internal war in England itself, as recently as the eve of the first World War. But a central core of national identity—the idea of England—always underlay these peripheral questions. This early consciousness of national identity is perhaps the first instance of two recurrent themes in British political development: one, the fact that consensus on some political issues has nearly always alleviated the intensity of conflict over others; the second, that "fundamental" problems of political culture (the nature of the political unit, the question of proper governmental structure, the questions of the proper scope of government, the particular relations between government and society and between national government and the international system) have not tended to arise in combination, but have come up singly, only after others had ceased to be in serious dispute. After Stephen, there was always some sort of cement to bind the English, even in the worst times of political strife, and always something to make disagreement seem less than absolute.

Secondly, the very existence of effective central authority tended to concentrate the great political struggles of early English history on efforts to contain authority rather than to establish it. Elsewhere the very fact of central government had to be created against a recalcitrant feudalism that had the most obviously unfortunate consequences upon life: lack of elementary personal safety in the face of constant feudal warfare; a chaotic system of tolls, taxes, weights, measures and coins that impeded trade; criss-crossing jurisdictions and a confused variety of laws and customs that prevented legal certainty and opened the door wide to arbitrary power. Where these conditions prevailed, the predominant political need was for the expansion of strong and unified authority. But in England, where such authority already existed, the perfection of its procedures could go hand in hand with limitation of its ambitions.

However contradictory it may seem, English political development in the Middle Ages did consist of two concurrent trends: on one hand, the constant rationalization and improvement of central power, and, on the other, the growth of constraints upon it. Central government became more efficient with the gradual development of routine administration (that is, an embryonic bureaucracy), the separation of the national Treasury from the Royal Household, the growth and consolidation of an obedient machinery of local government carried on by sheriffs, lords lieutenant, and justices of the peace, and the extension of the rules and jurisdiction of royal justice. At the same time, however, rights and privileges against the king were solemnly affirmed in charters and "constitutions," and Parliament gradually developed—first as mere royal council; then as council, rudimentary representative body and control (chiefly through the granting and withholding of monies); and finally as council, representative assembly, control and concurrent law-making power. This development of Parliament took a long time, and one can hardly say exactly when Parliament in any of its roles really first came into being, despite certain landmark dates like 1213 (when knights were first admitted to the Great Council) and 1295 (the date of the "Model Parliament" of Edward I, in which practically all social elements were "represented"— barons, clergy, knights and burgesses). Suffice it to say that it had become recognized as a law-making body by the time of Henry VI (1422-61) when statutes came to be made "by the King's most Excellent Majesty *by and with the advice and consent of the Lords Spiritual and Temporal, and Commons, in this present Parliament assembled, and by the authority of the same"*—a formula still used today at the head of every act of Parliament (except those made under the Parliament Acts of 1911 and 1949). Thus, the effectiveness of royal government was not established in opposition to the autonomy of the King's subjects, or the controls they could exercise over the King, or the methods by which they could participate in royal decisions. All these developed in sometimes uneasy but always close parallel—one could almost say unity. And this also is a persistent theme in British political development. Strong government was rarely equated with autocracy, or responsible government with anarchy; government and representation, government and liberty, did not appear as antithetical principles, but as complementary aspects of a single process. It was very different on the Continent.

A further consequence of this difference between England and the Continent lies in the realm of expressive symbolism. One important aspect of the political symbolism of any society is its gallery of heroes, especially its schoolboy heroes. In the nature of the case, the early heroes of the Continental countries are, almost without exception, the great centralizing kings—creators of central power like Philip Augustus and Saint Louis in France and the great Saxon kings in Germany. In Britain, however, both the creators and the controllers of power are part of early heroic lore; not only William the Conqueror and Henry II, but also the barons at

Runnymede and Simon de Montfort, are in the pantheon of English Greats. A symbolism serving the ends of both strong government and effective control was thus established at the most primitive levels of British political consciousness and helps still today to reconcile values which might elsewhere appear irreconcilable.

Finally, one should note that because of early centralization under feudal institutions the struggle for and against central power never acquired in Britain the aspect of a conflict between feudalism in all its trappings and a thorough-going anti-feudalism. Feudalism, it should be emphasized, was not merely a particular governmental arrangement, but rather something like a way of life. It had a great many faces. It involved certain economic patterns and notions: for example, that land was not "owned" in any outright sense but held, inalienably, in trust and for use. It involved certain notions and practices of social stratification: that society was a complicated and settled hierarchy of statuses and that high status conferred duties as well as privileges and low status rights as well as duties. And it involved certain political beliefs and values as well as political structures: for example, that authority should never be arbitrary, that political relations should be regulated by contract and precedent and law defined as little as possible by human agency, and that authority, while awful and sacred (even in the direct sense of close relation to religion), should be restricted to certain spheres and serve only certain functions. This complicated set of preferments and restraints was never attacked at every front in England, simply because the system as a whole did not seem inimical to the basic functional needs of society. Parts of it changed, in the Middle Ages and subsequently; others remained intact; the modernization of Britain proceeded *from* a feudal base rather than *against* it, so that at no time in British history are feudal notions (if not practices) entirely nonexistent. To be sure, feudalism also left a certain heritage in other European countries. But elsewhere feudal notions became associated with the interests and culture of certain segments of society, while in Britain they survived—modified, to be sure—in the general culture, the "British way of life." And this fact provides perhaps the first example of still another persistent pattern in British politics and social life, that "heaping up of geological strata" in society of which Bagehot makes so much, that grafting of the new upon the old, in which each modifies the other without displacing it entirely.

To put all this in a sentence: Britain emerged from the Middle Ages with a consensus upon the most basic of all elements of political culture, and with a series of social, cultural and political balances—a balance between feudal and non-feudal practices, a balance between symbols of power and restraint, and, above all, a balanced constitution, in which effective central power blended with effective central and local control, a high degree of local autonomy and a high degree of participation in affairs of state. This central idea of balance between disparate elements of structure and culture persists throughout the rest of British political history. The balances change; so do the mechanisms by which they are acted out. But change is never abrupt, never revolutionary in every sense (swift *and* violent), and never so one-sided as to destroy the very idea of a balanced government and society.

Continuity and Change in Modern Times

What the historians please to call "Tudor "absolutism"" provides a case in point. Certainly Tudor absolutism (the rule of Henry VII, Henry VIII, and Elizabeth) was never quite as absolute as Continental absolutism. The Tudors governed vigorously and more personally than previous monarchs. They knew how to get their way. They made institutional innovations which supported their power (such as the Court of Star Chamber and the Court of High Commission) and adapted others, especially the Privy Council, to their own uses. Parliament was largely acquiescent. In all that they fit the mold of European absolutism. But Parliament was still used, at least to give a tinge of national consent to royal decisions; the Tudors either never felt safe, or never wanted to do, without it, however summarily they treated oppositional parliaments and coddled compliant ones. So also that other great institution of medieval constitutionalism, the common law courts, with their administration of a judge-made law of precedent, contined to operate alongside royal courts administering royal law. Will and consent, decree and custom, continued to coexist, even though the balance shifted to the former. What is more, the shift in balance occurred largely because of expediency and techniques of statecraft; it was supported by the memories and fears of baronial anarchy arising out of the Wars of the Roses and achieved by the great skill of the Tudors in making the political balances work in their favor. It was not nearly so much a reflection of change in fundamental political values and beliefs, although the Tudors, by their very success, strengthened the idea of autonomous executive authority and weakened those of custom and consent. Upon the medieval ideas of government under transcendental law and contract, they grafted the idea of the great independent authority of the sovereign, but not so as to eradicate entirely the medieval ideas and institutions.

The great constitutional struggles of the seventeenth century which produced the last revolutionary violence in British history can be interpreted as efforts to maintain this "Elizabethan compromise" against both royalist and anti-royalist ambitions. From the outset these struggles present to us the extraordinary spectacle of revolutionary violence for conservative ends. The initial struggle was against the absolutist pretensions of the Stuarts who succeeded to the throne through James VI of Scotland (James I of England) in 1603. These absolutist pretensions were more serious than those of the Tudors because the Scottish Stuarts had less of a feel for the subtle compromises of English government and because a very one-sided royal absolutism was developing, as a kind of model for England, on the Continent. At the same time, they were less palatable to the English since memories of baronial anarchy had faded and the Stuarts had little skill in political manipulation. Civil war broke out in 1640, after a long series of lesser political storms, but those who resorted to violence were (with certain exceptions of course) hardly political extremists. In essence, they wanted little more than royal adherence to the established balanced constitution, particularly in regard to such fundamental matters as taxation and justice.

But violence always inflames political passions, and the defense of the constitution soon turned into regicide and the establishment of a radical republican "commonwealth" under Cromwell (in 1649). The commonwealth substituted for the ancient constitutional balances a government under a rationally devised (but far from democratic) "instrument of government," the first written constitution in European history. Now, however, the struggle against Stuart ambitions became a struggle against republican extremism, with Parliament the center of resistance as it had been the focal point of opposition to royal power. The republican constitution did not long survive Cromwell's death in 1658, and in 1660 monarchy was restored under Charles II. The restored King governed with a judicious regard for the expected constitutional forms (and a considerable lack of personal drive) but his successor, James II, who had neither his "insight" nor his "indolence," tried to circumvent Parliament, to revive ancient royal prerogatives long since regarded as lapsed and to attack the monopolies of the Church of England. The result was James' expulsion from the realm, largely through the machinations of the parliamentary notables, and the establishment upon the throne of a monarchical pair more willing to comply with parliamentary power, William of Orange, the stadtholder of Holland, and his wife Mary, James' eldest daughter.

What emerged from these struggles was a new constitutional balance, but a balance all the same, between executive power and parliamentary control, aristocratic privilege and popular participation, fundamental law and circumstantial will. Parliament, representation and common law now were in the ascendant, as in Tudor and early Stuart times they had been in relative eclipse, but they were not supreme, any more than royal power had earlier been absolute. The celebrated Bill of Rights of 1689 does read like a one-sided catalogue of Parliamentary powers and individual (especially Protestant) rights: it appears to be a charter of constitutional government under parliamentary supremacy. However, in the crucial non-documentary reaches of political life—that is to say, in political culture and actual political practices—monarchy remained a counterweight to Parliament. The King still chose the members of his Privy Council and appointed ministers and other officers of state; the ministers were still regarded as *his* ministers and their policy as his policy; the principle of ministerial dependence upon a parliamentary majority was not yet established.

Only gradually in the eighteenth century did the idea become entrenched that executive prerogative and powers should be wielded by a cabinet representing a majority in the House of Commons, and even then not as a result of ideological struggle but as a consequence of the weakness, Continental provincialism, indifference and linguistic troubles of the early Hanoverians, and the ill fortunes (later madness) of the more power-minded George III. Cabinet government (like parliamentary representation earlier) established itself almost imperceptibly, and what is more, cabinet government as the British understand it involves the exercise of both royal and parliamentary authority. The rise of the Cabinet involved a relocation of executive power rather than a decline of it. So the essential balance of British political life remained intact, even while the institutions in balance changed—that is to say, even while Crown Powers shifted from King to cabinet and the parliamentary center of gravity from the Lords to the Commons. The idea of parliamentary supremacy was grafted upon that of executive initiative, just as the latter had been grafted upon medieval "constitutionalism," the two being reconciled in the idea of a cabinet exercising Crown powers but representative of and responsible to the parliamentary majority.

The democratization of British politics in the nineteenth and twentieth centuries involved little more than still another restructuring of the balanced forces of the constitution and another grafting of new upon old and ancient principles. Revolutionary violence, aiming at a utopian reconstruction of society, was never required to accomplish it. Like the "absolutism" of the Tudors, and like the ascendancy of Parliament and the growth of the modern cabinet system in the eighteenth century, the expansion of the franchise was achieved more through acquiescence than intense struggles. The conservative forces sometimes yielded gracefully, sometimes indeed pushed the process along on their own initiative; and thereby, perhaps intentionally, they made it appear that democracy did not require any fundamental reconstitution of political life. If such a reconstitution did occur, and it did, it did not occur through anyone's deliberate intention, or indeed prevision, but through the force of the situation created by an expanded franchise and rationalized constituency system.

4b Democratization was accomplished not only peacefully but rather slowly. In Germany, by way of contrast, universal adult male suffrage was granted abruptly at the beginning of the Bismarckian Empire; in Italy, after the enfranchised portion of the population had been less than 15 percent since 1870, something close to universal male adult suffrage was granted suddenly in 1913. In Britain, however, the extension of the franchise and the equally important reform of the constituency system proceeded in easy and gradual stages, despite the absence after 1832 of intense opposition. The celebrated Reform Act of 1832 itself made a rather modest beginning to the process. Under the Act 143 parliamentary seats were redistributed in such a way as to give more representation to grossly under-represented urban and rural areas and less to certain greatly over-represented areas, especially the infamous "rotten boroughs"; but nothing like a system of numerically equal constituencies was introduced. The suffrage was widened, through the redefinition of a complicated set of property qualifications, by about 455,000 voters in the whole United Kingdom (England, Wales, Scotland and Ireland), but nothing remotely like universal suffrage came into being. From the standpoint of enfranchisement, the less famous Reform Act of 1867 (carried by a Tory government) was a good deal more important than that of 1832, since it added about a million new voters to the electorate and, still more important, brought in the bulk of the urban working class. While the Act of 1832 also redistributed some seats, the most important statute in that regard was probably the Representation of the People Act of 1884, which not only admitted another two million voters (approximately) to the franchise but attempted, for the first time in British history, to apportion seats in the country according to some fixed standard, rather than by the old method of taking representation from some constituencies and giving it to others—although even the Act of 1884 did not create really equal constituencies.

Despite these reforms, property qualifications continued to govern the right to vote until 1918, when universal adult male suffrage was granted, while adult female suffrage, also first introduced by the Representation of the People Act of 1918, did not become universal until 1928. The twentieth century reform acts also further rationalized the constituency system, but anomalies dating to very early times, like the special representation of universities and plural voting by possessors of premises in more than one constituency (restricted, but not abolished by the Act of 1918), continued until 1948. In 1944, at last, a permanent Boundaries Commission was set up to keep a continuous watch on the distribution of parliamentary seats and recommend changes to Parliament; but since the Boundary Commission was also instructed to respect old local government areas as much as possible, and to consider factors like geographic extent as well as population, considerable discrepancies in the size of constituencies still exist in Britain today. In that sense, the process of democratization has not been completed even yet.

No one should underestimate the significance of this long series of reform acts, spanning more than a century of British history. If the seventeenth century in England presents the curious spectacle of moderate and conservative violence, the nineteenth and twentieth centuries present the equally curious spectacle of peaceful revolution in British political life. Democratization entailed enormous consequences for British government and politics. It led to a showdown between the House of Lords and the Commons, in the course of which the British Parliament became, from some points of view, virtually unicameral. More significant, it produced the modern system of mass parties. While men spoke of "parties" before, these, until well into the nineteenth century, were merely shifting factions of parliamentary notables, supplemented after 1832 by local registration societies to get out the vote. The great disciplined electoral bodies of today, with their cohesion both in Parliament and outside, their mass memberships, bureaucratic officials, complex finances, internal constitutional processes, research bureaus and publicity departments originated only after the Reform Act of 1867, with the founding of the National Union of Conservative and Constitutional Associations in 1867 and the National Liberal Federation in 1877. The modern party system, in turn, greatly modified the British political system. It put executive power on a new and powerful basis, augmenting the ancient authority of the Crown with the relentlessly disciplined votes of the parliamentary majority. It also provided a new source of policy in the inner councils of the party; indeed it led to a general shift of the decision-making scene from parliamentary deliberation to internal party affairs. Not least, an obvious connection exists between the growth of British democracy and that of the modern social service state (or welfare state)—the gradual enlargement of governmental control over, direction of, and participation in previously "private" economic and social relations. And this development, as we shall see in Chapter 10, further modified many aspects of British government.

Democratization, in short, altered profoundly the character of British political competition (the pattern of politically active interests); it altered, directly and indirectly, the processes of decision-making (the pattern of power); and it altered the pattern of policy produced by the pattern of power—and through policy, still further, the pattern of power itself. Yet there never occurred any wholesale reconstitution of the political system, never any attack on the essential balance of executive power and parliamentary control, or on the idea of lawful, constitutional, even traditional process, or on the ancient symbols of government. Vox *populi* was added to Law and Higher Authority, not put in their stead.

All this provides the necessary factual background to the point with which we started: that the ultimate reason for "political deference" in Britain is to be found in the gradual, predominantly peaceful development of British political institutions. This process permitted old values, beliefs and symbols constantly to modify the new, so that the medieval sanctification of authority and the absolutist realization of autonomous power never really yielded to modern libertarian and populistic ideas. The British constitution grew, in more than a metaphorical sense, by prescription, a heaping up of strata of belief, where those of the French and Germans grew out of a succession of sudden, even violent, upheavals. True, in France and Germany also old political beliefs are still very much alive. But where in these countries the incidence of new upon old beliefs produced profound social fissures, in Britain, as a result of the slow tempo and piecemeal character of constitutional change, the various ideas of authority are combined in a single, generally shared, political culture.

This does not mean, however, that British political ideas have remained rooted in tradition while British society and government have become modernized. It is difficult to conceive of the survival of the ideas of authority without a concomitant survival of institutions to express them, or of deferential attitudes in politics that have no basis in other forms of social behavior. And indeed both the institutions of British government and British social structure contain ancient elements similar to those of British ideas of authority, which provide the ideas with a solid social basis.

CEREMONIAL INSTITUTIONS

In the case of governmental institutions there is of course the vast paraphernalia of titles, offices, rules, apparatus and procedures which have survived from previous eras: the peers, the Lord Chancellor, the common law, the Speaker's Mace, the "calling for candles," and a thousand similar things. No other country has discarded so few of its offices and processes in the course of its political development; seeing a Lord Mayor's parade in London is like seeing a pageant of all British history. Few of the ancient offices and processes, of course, perform any longer the functions they once performed. Like the monarchy, they have become transformed from "efficient" into ceremonial institutions, into mere ritual, the chief purpose of which is just to be formal and dignified and to edify the eyes and heart.

No other democratic system, in consequence, provides such a feast for the sentiments as the British. However, the ceremonial trappings of British government, from the monarchy down to the barristers' wigs, are not to be dismissed as mere theatrical scenery simply because they are now chiefly adornment upon more prosaic but more effective institutions and processes. They too are part of the pattern of effective power in Great Britain because they affect, however indirectly, the way authority is exercised.

Merely by existing, the ceremonial institutions keep the past concretely alive in the present, and thus obscure the radical changes that have certainly occurred in British government, in however piecemeal a fashion, since the Middle Ages. We have discussed how the Reform Acts changed the relations between Parliament and people, and the rise of parties altered the sources and strength of authority. We could add many other important changes which have occurred in British government in the last century: parliamentary procedure was overhauled; the role of the Cabinet and the methods by which it is formed were changed; so were the organization of public administration and a multitude of less important things. But the important point to grasp is that at the end of the century the government did not visibly appear to have changed very much. The Monarch was still there; so were the Lords; so was the Privy Council; so was the Chancellor of the Duchy of Lancaster. However much the structure of government had changed, it had not *manifestly* changed, a fact which has helped to keep intact the old ideas of authority as well.

What is significant about the ceremonial institutions, therefore, is first and foremost that they expressively symbolize the predemocratic conceptions of authority and thus keep them vividly alive in the popular mind. One cannot sit through the most ordinary session of the House of Commons without becoming aware that one is not only in a democratic assembly but also, and more palpably, in the presence of awful and superior majesty. There it is in the great golden mace on the table, the dignified Georgian figure in the Speaker's chair, the obsequious bows in his direction by even the most radical members—indeed, some members of Parliament after bravely going upon the hustings have been rendered speechless by the mere sight of the Speaker's wig. And if the impression of an ordinary session in the Commons is majestic, how much more so is a session in the Lords or an extraordinary session like the Opening of Parliament, when the Commons dutifully trudge to "the other place" on gracious invitation and dutifully listen, while standing, to the gracious Address from the Throne. The same thing applies to the Courts; the wigs are important because they symbolize an attitude, and therefore also, even if in a roundabout way, a practical fact; they are not simply scenery.

Indeed, the predemocratic institutions—the monarchy, the Lords, the

Lord Mayor, etc.—have an almost complete monopoly on the expressive symbolism of British politics. There simply is nothing of democratic vintage to compete against them except dry and abstract slogans. This helps to inject into British political culture a pervasive set of non-democratic attitudes, and it also gives Britain something that few other democracies possess: a set of intelligible symbols of government and authority that fully enlist the fancies and emotions of her people. Bagehot once said that monarchy is the only form of government fully intelligible to ordinary people and the only kind of government in which they will take a sustained personal interest:

> To state the matter shortly, Royalty is a government in which the attentions of the nation are concentrated on one person doing interesting actions. A Republic is a government in which that attention is divided between many, who are all doing uninteresting actions.[5]

Certainly there is a tenable point here. Constitutional government and party government are hard things to be conceived clearly by ordinary minds; they are too legally abstract and too complex in practice to be fully intelligible to anyone but professionals, if indeed they are fully intelligible even to them. Hence, the popular mind affixes loyalty to symbols (the flag, the constitution), and the most effective of all such symbols are real-life persons who can be cheered, speculated upon, gossiped about and idolized. It is not insignificant in this connection that the British royal house, despite the fact that it is composed mainly of very ordinary people, should be as newsworthy in America as it is in Britain.

The ceremonial institutions therefore make for strong government in two ways: by symbolizing and preserving predemocratic attitudes and by endowing public service with a dignity, hence prestige, it possesses in few other democratic societies. "I wrote books," one Englishman is reputed to have said, "for twenty years, and I was nobody; I got into parliament, and before I had taken my seat I had become somebody." "English politicians," says Bagehot, "are the men who fill the thoughts of the English public . . . and it is hard for the ordinary spectators not to believe that the admired actor is greater than themselves."

CLASS STRUCTURE AND CLASS CONSCIOUSNESS

Deference in politics is paralleled, indeed perhaps maintained, by deference in general social behavior. Even in this age of the welfare state the British lower classes are still surprisingly deferential in their attitudes towards the British upper class, a fact which helps to explain both why politics and administration (at least on the higher levels) are still very

---

[5] W. Bagehot, *The English Constitution.*

much in the hands of upper-class people and why they can wield such strong authority. Indeed, the most substantial remains of the past in present British behavior are to be found not in government but in ordinary social life. The social ideologies associated with the rise of democracy, especially egalitarianism, have probably had a less substantial effect on British life than democratic constitutional theory itself, although British class relations have themselves modified the impact of democratic constitutional theory on British government.

From the standpoint of anything that can be stated in bare and lifeless figures, or very easily and directly observed, Britain is certainly one of the most modern of societies. It has all the external trappings of modernity: a large population, declining in its rate of growth; a very low death-rate; a positive balance of migration; a great growth in the number of elderly persons; small families, predominantly of the isolated conjugal type; a steeply falling number of domestic servants; urban concentration of the population and a large industrial working class; the decline of primary services (agriculture, fishing, mining, and quarrying) and the growth of manufacturing, building, transport, communications, commerce and finance at their expense; an increasing number of "professionals" and executives; a vast network of secondary associations, including powerful trade unions, business and farmers' organizations, and professional bodies; universal education; vast numbers of scholarships for higher education; high mobility, vertical and horizontal; a very large and constantly growing middle class; declining differences in incomes and wealth; substantial social services; dynamic technology; crowded highways and parking problems; blighted railways; labor-saving gadgets galore; commercial television, scandal sheets and other carriers of mass culture of every description; nuclear weapons; ubiquitous advertising and public relations; paperbacks; exurbanites. Yet all this, in a sense, is only the surface of society, not its core. Objective modernity is a kind of mask for a pervasive subjective non-modernity, and nowhere is this clearer than in social stratification.

There is a vivid description of the British class system in the first chapter of H. G. Wells's *Tono-Bungay*:

> In that English countryside of my boyhood every human being had a "place." It belonged to you from birth like the colour of your eyes, it was inextricably your destiny. Above you were your betters, below you were your inferiors, and there were even an unstable questionable few cases so disputable that you might for the rough purposes of every day at least, regard them as your equals. Head and centre of our system was Lady Drew, her "leddyship," and . . . Miss Somerville, her cousin and companion. When I was a boy I used to always think of these two poor old creatures as superior beings living, like God, somewhere through the ceiling.

Then there came and went on these floors over our respectful heads, the Company. . . . on the lowest fringe of these real Olympians being the vicarage people, and next to them came those ambiguous beings who are neither quality nor subjects. The doctor in Bladesover ranked below the vicar but above the "vet," artists and summer visitors squeezed in above or below this point according to their appearance and expenditure, and then in a carefully arranged scale came the tenantry, the butler and housekeeper, the village shopkeeper, the head keeper, the cook, the publican, and second keeper, the blacksmith (whose status was complicated by his daughter's keeping the post-office), and so forth. Dominating all these memories is the figure of my mother who knew with inflexible decision her place and the place of everyone in the world.

This is a description of rural society in the late nineteenth century, when the English caste system was particularly rigid. Much has altered since, but nothing has changed so fundamentally as to make Wells entirely inapplicable to the present. Consider what another Englishman wrote at the height of World War II:

The classes that in a crisis trust each other cannot in fact speak to each other. Even if their language is mutually intelligible (as it is not always), they have little or nothing to say to each other. The resident foreigner takes many years to learn the truth that you never come to the end of the English class structure, that new castes and sub-castes are forever being discovered. In despair, the observer may come to the conclusion that the English class structure consists of forty-odd million classes and that the one thing those classes have in common is Englishness, which may be nothing more (or less) than an unconscious acceptance of this odd state of affairs as right and natural for Englishmen. In no Western country is class-consciousness so widely spread, so much taken for granted.[6]

The war itself has undoubtedly made the system less rigid than it used to be; but even the war has not altered things in gist. It may be easier nowadays to engage an English stranger in conversation over a drink than it was once, but the pubs are still divided into public, private and saloon bars, and there are still great distinctions among the types that frequent them, in what they drink, and in how they amuse themselves. The "Bladesover" system, as Wells called it, still exists, even after a half-century of progressive Education Acts, democratization and socialization, and it is probably the key to everything that is distinctively British and perplexing to the foreign inquirer.

Grasp firmly—said Wells—that all England was Bladesover two hundred years ago; that it has had Reform Acts indeed, and such-like changes of formula, but no *essential revolution* since then; that all

---

[6] D. Brogan, *The English People* (1943).

that is modern and different has come in as a thing intruded or as a gloss upon this predominant formula; and you will perceive at once the reasonableness, the necessity, of that snobbishness which is the distinctive quality of British thought.

That this snobbishness is itself a residue from premodern times, and therefore a result of Britain's lack of "essential revolutions," can be seen in the factors which determine one's place on the social stratification scale. These factors express typically aristocratic values. In a nutshell, what one is matters less in determining one's "place" than who one is: as the sociologists say, achievement is less important than ascription. Achievement matters, of course. If it cannot make one really "U" in Nancy Mitford's rather exotic sense it can at least make one near-U, and, indeed, British society has always been characterized by considerable social mobility. But the achievements valued most are themselves reflections of aristocratic values. The right education matters perhaps most of all. Next to that come the things which the right educational institutions—the better "public" schools and Oxford and Cambridge—inculcate (and which can perhaps be learned nowhere else), the right manners and tastes: correctly accented speech, the right vocabulary, wit, certain kinds of dress, the right religion (High Church is upper class, Low Church is not), the right preferences in sport (cricket, rugby football, rowing, not soccer, dog racing or darts), in food and drink and entertainment. Least important perhaps is unmitigated wealth. Affluence helps one up the social ladder, but chiefly by making it relatively easy to acquire the right education and to indulge the right tastes: to become a "gentleman." British class stratification is therefore a matter of social rather than economic stratification and in this sense reflects the hierarchical ideas of aristocratic days.

Deferring to one's betters does not, however, imply being callously exploited or abjectly submissive. The extent to which deference is rendered is highly limited, especially nowadays. An immaculate accent will not buy precedence in a queue, or an extra allowance on the ration book, or an extra vote (a university degree did buy one up to 1948). Moreover, deference can be a matter of mere formality rather than outright submissiveness, and much of the deferential behavior of the British no doubt is ceremony pure and simple; thus, the fact that the British secretary habitually addresses her boss as "sir" does not mean *ipso facto* that she feels differently toward him from the American secretary who habitually calls her boss by his first name. British politics are certainly more democratic than a bald description of British class structure might lead one to expect.

Nevertheless, so deeply ingrained a set of behavior patterns as support the British class system are bound to affect political life. The upper classes are still today, despite democratization and economic leveling, ascendant: in the Cabinet, in Parliament and in the Civil Service; and, what is more important, their ascendance is almost beyond dispute. No doubt the composition of the upper classes has changed since the nineteenth century and no doubt that there are more people of dubious social standing in positions of power today than there used to be, but the intrusion of lower strata into the higher circles of public life is less remarkable than the persistence of upper class domination. Democratization has put their reign upon another footing, party politics and the popular mandate, but the idea of the ruling class has been able to survive the broadening of the franchise simply because it has a solid foundation in public attitudes and behavior.

Bases of the Party System

However great the readiness of the British to accept strong leadership may be, this fact would not be important if the political system did not so constantly provide strong leaders. The reason it does is, of course, the disciplined two-party system; but what accounts for that?

It is very difficult to give a full explanation of the British party system, but one necessary element of it can be stated very simply. This is the extraordinarily pragmatic approach of the British to politics. There could be no two-party system and no party discipline—no meek marching into the division lobbies, no ready sublimation of private political beliefs—if the British were not so remarkably willing to compromise their political convictions. People are not likely to split into merely two camps on any single issue and certainly not on combinations of issues over protracted periods; hence the two-party system—unless indeed it is a multiparty system in disguise—presupposes a persistent willingness to compromise opinions. But under what conditions will people habitually compromise political opinions? Clearly, they are unlikely to do so if they profoundly and passionately believe in them, or if their convictions are derived not from isolated appraisals of isolated cases but from some general, all-inclusive ideology. There is no compromise with dogma. The fundamental secret of party discipline and the two-party system in Britain, therefore, is that British politicians, as a general rule, are not warm partisans, and, as someone has said, are "hard to work up to the dogmatic level." The prevalent political atmosphere is "empirical," "pragmatic," "unideological"—however one should put it. Few politicians seem to have a deep emotional or a profound philosophical stake in their positions and there exists a remarkable willingness to treat issues on their individual merits rather than on the basis of general political theories. Extremism is as hard to find on the Left as on the Right; the British have no deep doctrinal attachments to socialism or free enterprise, or indeed to any other set of dogmas. Closely related to this is the fact that the atmosphere of parliamentary debates is unusually courteous and rational.

But why are the British so calm and pragmatic in their approach to politics? Why are they almost never moved to rioting in the House of Commons and what keeps their disagreements so consistently out of the realm of metaphysics? Here it may be tempting to invoke the mysteries of the Anglo-Saxon soul, i.e., to say that the British are simply tepid and prosaic people. It is difficult to believe this. The crowds that cheer the royal outings are certainly not tepid crowds and the British have produced (but rarely followed in action) their fair share of political "philosophies." Nor is it necessary to be as mysterious about the phenomenon as this. Indeed, one may find a less obscurantist explanation for the sober atmosphere of British parliamentary politics in the very intoxication of the crowds that cheer the queen. This needs to be explained in a somewhat roundabout way.

Once upon a time an M.P., accused by an opponent of making an anomalous statement, replied that he was delighted to hear it because the British are a people who like anomalies; and that moreover they had been able to operate democratic institutions so effectively precisely because they were an "illogical" people. The point was made facetiously but, in a curious way, it is both true and important. The British are "illogical," first, because of their profound emotional attachment to persons and institutions that are, from a superficial practical standpoint, mere glitter and gloss and probably unjustifiable in terms of the Briton's own conscious political values. They are illogical, second, because they leave such a vast range of their political behavior to usage rather than to rationally devised rules and processes. But these, one may argue, are the very things that account for their extraordinary pragmatism in politics and therefore also, indirectly, for the effectiveness of their parliamentary system.

First of all this means that the British, although they probably have as much need for emotional behavior as any other people, can act with sober pragmatism in parliamentary politics because their political passions are channeled toward and satisfied by other aspects of their political system: their ceremonial institutions—above all, of course, the monarchy. Party politics, that is to say, are insulated against excessive emotional behavior simply because the political passions of the British have other outlets in a set of generally accepted and politically innocuous (if not irrelevant) institutions. Where the political emotions do not readily find such outlets they tend to fix themselves on other objects, frequently political ideologies. Such ideologies, more often than not, are held for emotional rather than rational reasons and, above all, have the function of enlisting the passions of people who want at least to appear "reasonable" in their political behavior.

The emotional value of political ideologies, however, is not their only *raison d'être*; they have an even more important function. By providing comprehensive theories of politics (or indeed life in general) they make it unnecessary to deal with individual issues on their individual merits; in short, they make is unnecessary for people to think and to deliberate. Ideologies are like theoretical sausage machines; one feeds in problematic meat at one end and out comes a string of policy sausages at the other, beautifully integrated and consistent. And because they obviate real thought on individual issues they can become terribly necessary under certain conditions, particularly when the political system presents an unusually large number of unresolved issues, or, putting the same point another way, when an unusually large area of behavior is subject to political decision-making. This point can perhaps be clarified best by an analogy with individual behavior. We know that individual men tend to break down—frequently, indeed, as the French sociologist Durkheim found, to commit suicide—when they are confronted with the need of making a vast range of decisions. The human personality seems capable of handling only a limited range of problematic choices and when the range becomes too large, when too much action becomes subject to rational deliberation rather than to authority and conditioning, *anomie* (as Durkheim called it) is likely to result. But suicide, or some other obvious derangement, need not be the inevitable result of *anomie*. Indeed, it may be more normal to respond to the situation by compulsively seeking out and subscribing to some comprehensive ideology that makes thought superfluous. This does not mean that human beings are incapable of making rational decisions on problematic choices; it does mean that the smaller the demands on their reasoning faculties the more likely they are to use reasoning, and not some pseudo-reasoning.

The British, then, are highly immune to ideologies—pragmatic in outlook—not only because their passions are channeled out of ordinary politics but also because the political system confronts them, comparatively speaking, with a narrow range of unresolved issues. And this in turn is due to two factors. First, it is due to the very weight attached to usage in British political ideas. Questions that are highly explosive issues in other societies—for example, the basic question of the proper organization of government and proper procedure—are left in Britain, to a very large extent, to be settled by custom. Second, it is due to a factor mentioned at the very beginning of the chapter: the existence of broad political agreement on questions not settled by habit—broad agreement not only on the constitution but even on policy. This agreement is seen most clearly in three things: the absence of any important extremist groups, Right or Left; the lack of constitutional issues among the major parties; and the reconciliation of the Conservative Party to the welfare state largely instituted by the Labour Government of 1945. It is a very old axiom of political science and of common sense that people are more likely to reconcile their political differences by rational discussion if they have a large range of views in common. But, even more important, a large area of political agreement simply limits the range of problematic choices and thereby enables men to approach the issues in a more sober and open, i.e., rational, frame of mind.

If political pragmatism does not sufficiently explain why the British *do* have a disciplined two-party system, it does at least explain why it is *possible* for them to have such a system. A full and sufficient explanation would no doubt take into account also the habit of deference to political leaders, the fixed idea, derived from the very mechanics of parliamentary government (the constant alternation of Government and Opposition), that government is somehow naturally conducted on a bi-polar basis, the special need for large-scale party organization created by the single-member constituency electoral system[7]—perhaps even the peculiar seating arrangements of the House of Commons.[8] But none of these things could be of the slightest significance if it were not for the spirit of British politics; that is indispensable and fundamental, for without it none of the other forces pushing in the direction of a disciplined two-party system could begin to do their work.

Democracy in Britain

We have dwelt at length upon the extraordinary capacity of the British political system to produce strong leadership—even when the leaders are not commanding personalities—partly because it *is* so very unusual for a democratic system to produce such leadership so consistently. But is Britain really a democracy?

Ultimately this is a semantic issue and no more. But no one will deny that British government and politics have at least some of the more important characteristics generally considered democratic. If mandates are not the only source of authority, a clear mandate, once given, is considered absolutely binding. Ordinary people have considerable opportunities to participate in the political process, not only in elections but through parties, interest organizations and ideological associations. The channels through which they participate are highly regularized and institutionalized. They are regularly presented with choices among com-

---

[7] For a discussion of this point, see below, pp. 175-177.
[8] See p. 124.

petitive sets of rulers and the essential civil liberties which alone make political liberty effective are scrupulously preserved. Thus, if the Cabinet— as some writers have alleged—is practically a dictatorship, it is a dictatorship strongly tempered by democratic processes that are not mere façade.

Even more important, British Governments are powerfully restrained by some of the very factors that account for their great power in the first place. That the British constitution has very ancient foundations, that it has developed by accretion rather than upheaval, means that it contains not only authoritarian elements but also the restraining values of pre-absolutist constitutionalism. The idea of a binding law not subject to human will, the ideas of due process and limited government, the ideas of parliamentary authority over finance and its rights as a committee of grievances—all of which are medieval—have survived in British political culture quite as much as the absolutist notions added later. There is, then, in Britain a powerful "constitutional morality" that does quite as much to tame the leaders' power as democratic processes. The authority of the leaders is accepted as something independent, but it is also *contingent* upon their adherence to rules that tradition and the sense of the nation prescribe and the restriction of public action to areas that, in the constitutional sense of the nation, are subject to public action. No leadership would be considered authoritative if it suspended elections (except in war), imposed censorship upon the press, kept Parliament in dissolution, quarreled openly within itself, or even perhaps merely violated those niceties of parliamentary procedure that the British sense of ceremony insists upon. And by far the most important of the rules on which constitutional morality insists are rules guaranteeing the parliamentary opposition full rights of debate and criticism on measures introduced by the Government, the chance to ask questions about the conduct of administration, and the chance to air grievances in special debates—in short, rules especially useful in imposing discipline upon the rulers themselves. "To discipline Parliament ministers must first discipline themselves" because they operate "within a framework of established expectations"— these phrases by H. J. Laski put the point exactly.

This framework of established expectations is all the more constraining because it is so widely agreed upon and puts such a high value on usage. Consensus on policy and process may set in motion a chain of effects that ultimately produce strong leadership, but consensus in its very nature limits the exercise of such leadership to what is consented to. That the British are so widely agreed upon the essential outlines of the postwar welfare state may give British leaders great power to institute certain social and economic measures, but it puts an equally powerful limit on their ability to institute others. So, even more, does the attachment to usage.

Thus, the Labour Government of 1945 was able to enact a program of social and economic legislation unparalleled in scope among democratic societies; but when it tried to reform certain aspects of the cumbersome, time-wasting, traditional processes for enacting financial legislation in the House of Commons it had to settle, in the face of powerful opposition, for only one small and very insignificant change.

In short, whether Britain is a democracy or not, British government is at least supremely constitutional in character. Indeed, British political culture contains within itself a sort of check-and-balance system, in that it makes simultaneously for active and limited leadership, the twin purposes of any separation of powers. And this is the case because British conceptions of legitimacy are a unique combination of democratic and predemocratic notions, expressed in a set of governmental processes that daily revive and re-enact the past, in a society where ideas of equality and hierarchy coexist in easy inconsistency.

[5]

The Pattern of Power:
The Cabinet

Cabinet and Parliament

The central structure in the pattern of power of the British political system is the cabinet. It does not, of course, act in a vacuum. Its freedom of choice is hemmed in by the influence of many other centers of power—in the parties, in the civil service, in groups among the electorate. We can conceive of a political situation in which such a body would be in effect powerless in the face of such influences, obliged merely to record the decisions already made elsewhere. The electoral college in the United States is in this position, in fact able only to register the results of the presidential contest in the various states. So also is the Supreme Soviet in relation to the higher organs of the Communist Party of the U.S.S.R. While not by any means without limits, the wide freedom of choice normally enjoyed by the Cabinet makes it the natural place to begin a study of the distribution of power in the British system.

Bagehot, in a classic and still useful formula, said that the Cabinet is "a combining committee—a hyphen which joins, a buckle which fastens, the legislative part of the state to the executive part of the state." It is not, however, merely a glorified liaison committee mediating between the legislature and the executive; nor will it do to describe it, as it has often been described, as the executive committee of the majority party in the House of Commons. This formula suggests too much dependence on Parliament, too much "democracy." To be sure, Cabinets are almost invariably composed of the leaders of the majority party in Parliament and

Parliament can unmake them as well as make them, so that, in a sense, the Cabinet exercises only those powers that Parliament suffers it to exercise. But when one penetrates behind appearances the Cabinet turns out to be a very curious legislative committee indeed. In the first place, it may include men who are not members of Parliament at all. Much more seriously, it possesses certain powers that make it not the creature but the master of Parliament. For example, as Parliament can unmake the Cabinet, so the Cabinet can unmake Parliament, by dissolving it and calling new elections. Again, Parliament is not entitled to be informed of Cabinet proceedings, and many things done in Cabinet are in fact withheld from it. In addition, the Cabinet possesses a kind of veto over certain kinds of measures—specifically those involving expenditures of money (i.e., most important bills)—even if they are wanted by an overwhelming majority of Parliament, because constitutional usage provides that such measures must be initiated by a Minister of the Crown. Not long ago, for example, the House of Commons, in a lopsided vote, came out for an increase in M.P.'s salaries; but so unsupreme is Parliament in matters having a financial aspect that the Cabinet's refusal to introduce legislation killed the project more effectively than any presidential veto in the United States.

Undoubtedly, the Cabinet can dictate to Parliament chiefly because of the brute political facts that make for party discipline in Great Britain, but that is not the only source of its authority. It also derives power, both directly and indirectly, from the fact that it has taken over the powers historically lodged in the Crown, powers that are not directly dependent either on parliamentary grant or sufferance. "Powers of the Crown" of course means powers considered to inhere in the sovereign: the Queen's "prerogatives." In the distant past these were quite considerable but in the course of centuries more and more inroads into them were made. Some were signed away by "contracts" between king and "people" (e.g., *Magna Carta*); some were taken away by prohibitive legislation (e.g., the prohibition of the early royal privileges of pre-emption and purveyance); many simply disappeared through long disuse. But the residue is not negligible. It is a prerogative of the Crown to make peers and create other titles of honor, to appoint a large number of public officials, to pardon criminals, to perform all acts of an "international character" (declaring war, making treaties, carrying on diplomatic relations) and to summon, prorogue and dissolve Parliament. It is not, of course, the Queen herself who does these things. The sovereign, as the classic formula goes, has only "the right to be consulted, the right to encourage and the right to warn": in short, to influence her ministers. It is the ministers who in fact exercise the "prerogatives." Nevertheless, this does not mean that the powers of the

Crown are, indirectly, "parliamentary" powers after all. It means simply that the Cabinet is the repository, at one and the same time, of powers flowing from Parliament and from the monarchy, of derivative and independent powers. The Cabinet has, therefore, a dual character. On one hand it is the leadership of Parliament; on the other, it is also the institution that it was the historic function of Parliament to limit and control the Crown; and as the latter it is something more than the former, something more powerful, more mysterious, and more august.

Is it any wonder that there has been a great deal of talk in recent decades about "cabinet dictatorship" in Britain? Certainly even the barest outlines of its functions make it appear suspiciously omnipotent. The Cabinet defines the lines of national policy; it controls and co-ordinates administration; it arranges parliamentary business and introduces the vast majority of bills; it is responsible for all expenditures and taxes; it controls appointments to great offices of state. This does not mean, of course, that the Cabinet is a "dictatorship" in any serious sense. But certainly when the British refer to the Cabinet as *the* Government they do not do so as a mere matter of form. How then is the Cabinet constituted and how does it discharge its tremendous responsibilities?

How a Cabinet Is Constituted

SELECTION OF THE PRIME MINISTER

The first step in the constitution of a Cabinet is the appointment of a Prime Minister, who in turn appoints the other Cabinet members and non-Cabinet ministers (or rather "advises" the Queen that they be appointed although her action is mere formality). The appointment of the Prime Minister is one of the few remaining functions of the sovereign that are of any importance, although this power too is so limited by convention as to be almost an empty formality. The general rule is that the Queen must appoint whatever leader is capable of commanding the support of a majority in Parliament.

In the vast majority of instances the need to select a new Prime Minister arises under conditions that pose no problems at all and leave the monarch no free choice among various candidates. Nowadays elections generally culminate in an outright majority in the House of Commons for one of the two major parties and each party almost invariably has a recognized leader. The Queen's function after a national election therefore is simply to ask the known leader of the successful party to form a Government. When a Government suffers a parliamentary defeat—a rare occurrence in this day of tight party discipline—it has two courses open to it. It may dissolve Parliament and appeal to the electorate by means of a new election, or it may resign—in which case the Queen will call on the recognized leader of the opposition party (and he is always known because he draws a government salary) to form a new Government. If a Prime Minister dies or resigns there usually is a recognized second-in-command to take his place. Difficulties arise only when the majority party has no recognized leader or no recognized second-in-command, when there is no clear majority, or when the majority party is torn by dissension.

In 1931, Ramsay MacDonald, then Prime Minister of a Labour Government, felt obliged to offer his resignation because of serious dissension in his Cabinet. In opposition at the time were not only the Conservatives, but also a substantial group of Liberals. If MacDonald had simply resigned without tendering advice, the king might have had some freedom of choice of a successor. As was his right, however, MacDonald advised that the king confer with Conservative and Liberal leaders, both of whom recommended that the king ask MacDonald to continue as Prime Minister, but at the head of a coalition Government. While this undoubtedly was the King's personal preference also, it gave him no opportunity to act independently and on his own. Similarly, the resignation of Neville Chamberlain in 1940, although taking place in an unusual parliamentary situation, did not result in any significant exercise of power by the king. Chamberlain, the head of what was essentially a Conservative Government, lost the support of a large block of his normal supporters in the House, although he did not suffer an outright defeat. He concluded that since Britain was at war, it would be necessary to form a coalition Government including all parties. Finding that Labour would not serve under him, he consulted with two leading Conservatives, Winston Churchill and Lord Halifax, on the question of whom he should advise the King to summon. Halifax having bowed out, it was clear that the duty would fall on Churchill, who proceeded to form his famous wartime Government.

When Harold Macmillan became Prime Minister after Sir Anthony Eden resigned early in 1957, it looked to many observers as if the Queen had passed over the obvious and proper choice. This was R. A. Butler, former Chancellor of the Exchequer, who was generally regarded as the second-in-command to Eden and who had presided over the Cabinet during Eden's long absence from the country before his resignation. We do not yet know the inside story of this surprise. We do know that the Queen acted on the advice of certain elder statesmen of the Conservative Party. It has also been said that behind this advice lay the fact that during the Suez crisis Butler had aroused the strong hostility of certain sections of the party. In consequence, as soundings in the party showed, the supporters of Butler would serve under Macmillan, but those who preferred Macmillan would refuse office under Butler. Again, however, as in the other cases mentioned above, the sovereign in fact had no real freedom of choice.

Before the middle of the nineteenth century the monarch often had a real choice among rival candidates for the Prime Ministership, but in recent generations the mechanics of the two-party system have generally ground out the man for the job, without difficulty.

SELECTION OF THE CABINET AND MINISTRY

The first task of the Prime Minister is to appoint his Cabinet and Ministry. While all Cabinet members are Ministers, not all Ministers are Cabinet members. Nowadays, a Prime Minister has nearly one hundred political appointments to make upon taking office and the vast majority of these appointments are to officers having ministerial status. There are, first of all, about two dozen administrative departments (such as the Treasury, the Admiralty, the Ministry of Health, the Home Office, the Colonial Office) to which Ministers—"Departmental Ministers"—must be appointed. Then there are a small handful of ministerial positions which involve no departmental duties and to which the Prime Minister generally names important politicians whom he wants to serve him as general advisers; e.g., the Lord President of the Council, the Lord Privy Seal, the Chancellor of the Duchy of Lancaster, the Paymaster General, and whatever "Ministers without Portfolio" the Prime Minister wishes to create— usually none, since the ceremonial ministries enumerated provide ample scope for the appointment of general advisers. Then, since 1941, a number of ministers called "Ministers of State" have been in existence; their purpose has been to assist the Departmental Ministers of important and overworked departments while having a higher status than the parliamentary Secretaries of the Ministries. The latter are also Ministers, but a lowlier variety. Technically they are not "Ministers of the Crown," since they are not appointed by the Queen; their main purpose is to assist the Ministers, especially in their parliamentary duties, and most of them are young men who are being trained for bigger and better things. Finally, there are still a few other persons who have ministerial status, most notably the Government Whips, whose chief function is to help the Prime Minister ride herd on his supporters in the House of Commons and who are generally made Lords of the Treasury or given appointments in the Royal Household, all ceremonial positions we need not worry about.

Not even the British, with all their gift for committee work, could operate a Cabinet composed of all these people, or even of the Departmental Ministers alone. Hence, it is up to the Prime Minister to determine which of them shall sit in the Cabinet, and the Cabinets of the present century have in fact had memberships varying from an even half dozen to close to two dozen, the size lately having been between sixteen and eighteen. The great and old Departments of State—the Treasury, the Foreign Ministry, the Home Office, etc.—almost invariably rate Cabinet seats; the less important Ministries sometimes manage to get representation, e.g., when they are headed by a Minister who has a relatively high status in his party or when they deal with a subject that for the moment looms large in the public eye. Thus, when Aneurin Bevan was Minister of Health during the years when the National Health Service was brought into operation, the Ministry of Health rated a Cabinet seat. But when the important Mr. Bevan was replaced by the relatively less important Mr. Marquand the Ministry was dropped from the Cabinet. One cannot therefore be absolutely sure, from one Ministry to the next, what Ministers will have Cabinet status.[1]

Constitutional convention gives the Prime Minister complete authority to decide who will be members of his Cabinet. His actual power, however, is greatly circumscribed by political realities. Every Prime Minister has certain eminent and powerful colleagues whose appointment to the Cabinet is a foregone conclusion. Every party, in the nature of the two-party system, has wings of opinion whose leaders must, in the interest of harmony, be included. Hence, a certain number of Ministers *known* to have been objectionable to their chiefs (e.g., Joseph Chamberlain, Sir William Harcourt, probably also Aneurin Bevan) have found their way into the Cabinet. Again, every Ministry (and indeed every Cabinet, in-

---

[1] Compare, for example, the Labour Government of 1949 and the Conservative Government of 1955. Ministers included in both were the following:

(1) Prime Minister and First Lord of the Treasury (it has long been customary for the Prime Minister to assume the title "First Lord of the Treasury")

(2) Lord President of the Council (Leader of the House of Commons under Labour)

(3) Lord Privy Seal (Leader of the House of Commons under the Conservatives)

(4) Secretary of State for Foreign Affairs

(5) Chancellor of the Exchequer

(6) Lord Chancellor

(7) Secretary of State for the Home Department

(8) Minister of Defence

(9) Chancellor of the Duchy of Lancaster (also Minister of Materials in the Conservative Government)

(10) Secretary of State for the Colonies

(11) Secretary of State for Commonwealth Relations

(12) Secretary of State for Scotland

(13) Minister of Labour and National Service

(14) President of the Board of Trade

(15) Minister of Education

(16) Minister of Agriculture and Fisheries (also Minister of Food under the Conservatives)

The Minister of Health was included in 1949 but not in 1955, the Minister of Pensions and National Insurance was included in 1955 but the two Ministers responsible for these things in 1949 (before the Ministries were combined) were left out. Thirteen Departmental Ministers were left out in 1949, eight in 1955.

cluding the Socialist Cabinets) contains some peers to represent the
Government in the House of Lords.[2] There is a certain amount of geographical selection—a Scot and a Welshman are almost invariably
included. Certain men come in because a powerful and therefore indispensable man espouses their cause; in fact "combinations"—by which one
man refuses to enter the Government unless certain others are also chosen
—are known. A good many men are selected almost on the basis of
seniority, for having served long parliamentary apprenticeships as faithful
party wheel-horses; a few have the influence—e.g., family connections—to
force their way into prominent positions; and Junior Ministers are usually
selected on the recommendations of their seniors. Indeed, even the division of Cabinet offices is not freely up to the Prime Minister. Powerful
and eminent politicians are frequently in a position to pick their places.
And it should not be forgotten that when a party is out of power it forms
a "shadow Cabinet," certain of its leaders being charged with leading the
opposition in specific areas of policy. These men consequently have a
powerful claim to the Ministries of their special areas.

None of this means, however, that the Prime Minister merely recognizes
a series of *faits accomplis* on taking office. Much is still left to his discretion and the days when he sees his colleagues to discuss appointments are
days of great suspense outside No. 10 Downing Street and, one gathers,
no little excitement inside. "It is like the Zoo at feeding time," said Lord
Salisbury. Ramsay MacDonald, in 1929, remarked to Hugh Dalton, then
a promising young man being offered an undersecretaryship: "It's been
terrible: I have had people in here weeping and fainting." The Prime
Minister can keep, and has kept, out the most eminent of politicians and,
as he can appoint a man, so also he can dismiss him. While dismissals of
Ministers have been few and far between they have occurred, and so have
forcible transfers of Ministers from one job to another. The Cabinet is
the Prime Minister's Cabinet and the Ministry is the Prime Minister's
Ministry, just as much as it is a party Cabinet and Ministry.[3]

How the Cabinet Works

COLLECTIVE RESPONSIBILITY: SECRECY

Much of the Cabinet's procedure is shaped by two of the most basic
constitutional conventions applying to its operation, the rule of collective
responsibility and the rule of secrecy in regard to Cabinet business. One

---

[2] The appointment of a certain number of peers to ministerial positions is required
by law.
[3] But it is worth noting that dismissals of Ministers were far more common in the
nineteenth than in the twentieth century, because, no doubt, of differences in the
importance of party.

former Prime Minister stated the rule of collective responsibility thus: "For all that passes in the Cabinet each member of it who does not resign is absolutely and irretrievably responsible, and has no right afterwards to say that he agreed in one case to a compromise, while in another he was persuaded by his colleague." "This means," explained Lord Morley, "that the Chancellor of the Exchequer may be driven from office by a bad dispatch from the Foreign Office, and an excellent Home Secretary may suffer for the blunders of a stupid Minister of War." The British Cabinet, in short, is a truly collective leadership; the acts of each member are the acts of all, and all stand or fall together. This does not mean that all Cabinet decisions must be taken unanimously; majority decisions are enough. What the rule does require is that if a Minister (Cabinet or non-Cabinet) wants to take his dissensions into the public light he must resign his office, as Aneurin Bevan did in 1951 after it was decided to put charges on National Health Service dentures and spectacles, or as Anthony Eden did in 1938 because he disagreed with Neville Chamberlain's appeasement of Hitler. If he does not want to resign, he must refrain from opposing the Cabinet's decision in public and indeed must support it in Parliament, before the party and before the public, not only by obediently voting for the Cabinet's decision but even by speaking for it. Lord Melbourne once said after a Cabinet meeting in the early nineteenth century: "By the bye . . . what are we to say? Is it to make our corn dearer, or cheaper, or to make the price steady? I don't care *which*: but we had better all be in the same story."

Collective responsibility no doubt imposes strains on the Cabinet as a whole and on individual Ministers. Even on the most unimportant level of Cabinet mechanics it creates certain difficulties, which a looser, more American, conception of the Cabinet's operation might obviate. For example, there is a great reluctance to take votes in the Cabinet, and consequently a tendency to spin out discussion, since the Cabinet tries to conceal its divisions even from itself. When votes are taken, all sorts of subterfuges are used to prevent the exact divisions from becoming known; and, as we shall see below, the doctrine of collective responsibility used to make for a very inadequate system of Cabinet records. How then did the doctrine originate and what purpose does it serve in the current operation of British government? Why is it one of the fundamental rules of the constitution?

The notion of collective responsibility first developed in the eighteenth century—when Ministers were still the King's Ministers in a real sense—as a protective device used by the Cabinet against the king. As long as Ministers stood or fell individually it was relatively easy for the sovereign to dominate them, since someone could always be found to replace an individual Minister. But to replace a whole Ministry was another matter. Subsequently, the rule proved as useful a protective device against Parliament and party as against the sovereign. The opposition is deprived of the opportunity to set Ministers against one another and embarrass the Government. Likewise, factions within the majority party itself are prevented from promoting the political fortunes of this or that minister at the expense of his rivals in the Government. The notion of collective responsibility, therefore, has a curiously paradoxical historical significance. In its infancy it played a role in the development of parliamentary government; subsequently, as the dominance of Parliament over Crown and of the majority party in Parliament was established, it served as a disciplinary device over the parliamentary hordes and thus helped to preserve that degree of executive independence that is the hallmark of the British parliamentary system. In either case the rule served to increase the power of the Cabinet.

There are exceptions to the rule of collective responsibility, and there need to be, since it is manifestly impossible to take all administrative and policy decisions, even the most important, in Cabinet. In fact, the Cabinet as a group transacts only a small proportion of ministerial business. The vast majority of decisions are taken by individual Ministers, the rule being, in gist, that nothing is to be brought before the Cabinet unless it is the subject of serious political controversy or unless serious disagreements between different departments exist—and woe to the Minister who imposes on his frantically busy colleagues by repeatedly bringing unnecessary business before them. Hence, the notion of collective responsibility is not so overdone as to become a manifest fiction: there is such a thing as individual responsibility as well. If, for example, a particular Minister is seriously unpopular, the Government may improve its public relations by dismissing him (forcing him to "resign") or by reshuffling offices. It is even possible for the Government to force an individual Minister to take responsibility for what was really a Cabinet decision in order to save its own skin, although this, admittedly, is very exceptional. The case usually cited is that of Sir Samuel Hoare's resignation over the so-called Hoare-Laval Plan in 1935. With the Cabinet's knowledge and approval, Hoare, the Foreign Secretary, had made an agreement with Laval, then French Prime Minister, approving a partition of Ethiopia as a means of appeasing Mussolini. When word of the agreement was "leaked," a storm of wrathful protest swept Britain. The Cabinet bowed, repudiated the agreement and dropped Hoare from office.

On the other hand, it is not quite so unusual for the Cabinet to leave questions "open," so that Ministers may publicly say what they please about them. One Government, the National Government of 1931, composed of Conservatives, Liberals, and a few Labourites, took the unprecedented step of engaging in a public "agreement to differ" over extremely important points of policy, for the sake of preserving if not true unity then at least a semblance of it in the face of the great depression.

Just as there are exceptions to the rule of collective responsibility, so are there chinks in the Cabinet secrecy it helps to preserve. When responsibility is publicly fixed on some individual Minister, Cabinet secrets tend to tumble out. Even more, when individual Ministers feel constrained to shed the chains of collective responsibility by resigning, revelations usually are made, the rule being that any resigning Minister may explain his reasons to the House and, if given permission to do so by the Crown (and permission is usually given), may then reveal Cabinet transactions.

The rule of secrecy is enforced by an oath taken by all Cabinet members as Privy Councillors and by the Official Secrets Acts, which forbid the publication of Cabinet documents. But it is not really law that makes British Cabinet members so very secretive; as usual, the law takes second place to practical considerations. Cabinet secrecy, like collective responsibility, is a defensive device against outsiders; indeed the two concepts developed together, the latter presupposing the former and both being directed against the same "enemies." Even more important, perhaps, secrecy makes for free expression by Cabinet Ministers and for speed in the transaction of business. If Ministers were aware that their remarks in Cabinet would be made public, their Cabinet behavior would certainly be different from what it is. They would probably suppress a good many facts and their statements would lose that frankness and brevity that make plural decision-making possible under modern conditions.

ORGANIZATION AND PROCESS

But however useful the rule of secrecy may be from a practical standpoint, there was a time when it drastically interfered with the efficiency of the Cabinet. Before the first World War the rule was taken so seriously that no Cabinet records were kept and no Minister was even allowed to take notes on Cabinet discussions. The only exception was the Prime Minister, who was permitted to take cursory notes of decisions to enable him to report accurately to the sovereign. The results, as government became a constantly more pressing affair after the leisurely days of Peel, can be imagined. They are vividly suggested in a famous note from Lord Hartington's private secretary to Gladstone's secretary in 1882: "Harcourt and Chamberlain have both been here this morning, and *at* my Chief about yesterday's Cabinet proceedings. They cannot agree about what occurred. There must have been some decision, as Bright's resignation shows. My Chief has told me to ask you what the devil *was* decided, for he be damned if he knows." Nevertheless, it was not until 1916 that someone

(Lloyd George) did something about the situation, and then of course it
was the stress of war that helped to break down the old convention, both
by showing the need for displacing it and by creating an atmosphere of
urgency in which the change could be made.

Since then, a set of records (the Cabinet "Conclusions" or, as they are
more generally known, "minutes") has been kept and the Cabinet has
been provided with a Secretariat to keep them and in other ways to
facilitate Cabinet business. Something of the old rule, however, lives on
in the brevity and anonymity of the records kept by the Secretariat.
Nothing like a stenographic record is taken. A Cabinet "minute" usually
summarizes the documents on which the Cabinet has had to make a
decision, sets out the gist of any pertinent statement of *fact* made in discussion and of the general arguments urged by a member, and then gives
a full statement of the decision taken. The notes on which the "minute"
is based are taken by a member of the Secretariat. The Cabinet tries to
preserve its privacy at all costs and tolerates only as few outsiders as
absolutely necessary, even from its own staff. This also is a convention
with a purpose. Herbert Morrison, an important member of the postwar
Labour Government, has pointed out that when "strangers" are present
in the Cabinet a certain constraint is likely to fall upon discussions, and
certain things that would certainly be talked out in a conference of party
colleagues, particularly items of political strategy and tactics, are likely to
be suppressed.[4]

The Cabinet Secretariat itself was taken over lock, stock, and barrel
during World War I from the Committee of Imperial Defence[5] and today
consists of a Permanent Secretary, two Deputy Secretaries, an Under-
Secretary, a Senior Assistant Secretary and five Assistant Secretaries, a
rather intimate group of extremely high-powered and privileged officials.
The original purpose of the Secretariat was to keep records of Cabinet
decisions, but by the end of the war it was clear that it could facilitate
Cabinet business in a great many other ways as well and its duties have
therefore gradually increased, as has its staff. Guided by the Prime Minister, it prepares the Cabinet agenda; it sees to it that all items of Cabinet

---

[4] Meetings on "political" subjects are in fact held without the presence of a member
of the Secretariat and, of course, no records of such meetings are kept.
[5] The Committee of Imperial Defence was created shortly after the turn of the
century, for the purpose of co-ordinating defense measures and basing military policy,
both in peace and war, on consistent plans. It had only one permanent member, the
Prime Minister, but the persons usually attending, besides the Prime Minister, included
the political heads of the military departments and the Commander in Chief, with the
heads of the military Intelligence Departments as joint Secretaries and a clerk from
the Foreign Office to keep minutes. As the Committee's work grew, and as it proliferated, as Committees will, into a large number of subcommittees, it gradually acquired
a sizable Secretariat to prepare the agenda, keep minutes and perform liaison work
with other departments (notably the Foreign Office) interested in defense policy.

business are properly supported by memoranda and that the memoranda are properly circulated to the proper people at the proper time; it makes sure that non-Cabinet Ministers involved in an item of Cabinet business are present at the relevant discussions. At times the Secretariat has also included special advisory and fact-finding bodies; for example, during World War II and for some time after it included an Economic Section and a Central Statistical Office, which, in fact, did most of the fact-finding and thinking on which central economic planning was based.

No doubt the work of the Secretariat has made modern Cabinets somewhat more efficient than their Victorian counterparts, but even so it may be difficult to see how the Cabinet can be an efficient instrument of government. First, there is its size. It is notoriously difficult for large groups to transact business jointly and the Cabinet, nowadays, is certainly a large group. In the nineteenth century, Cabinets rarely had more than a dozen members and after the first World War a special committee—the Machinery of Government Committee of the Ministry of Reconstruction —decided that this was just about the ideal size. Between the wars, however, Cabinets grew to as many as twenty-two members, and the usual size nowadays is sixteen to eighteen. But even this figure includes only Ministers of *regular* Cabinet status and does not give an accurate idea of the number of persons who participate in Cabinet discussions, since non-Cabinet Ministers interested in items of policy before the Cabinet are almost invariably called in for its conferences. The *real* size of the Cabinet makes it verge upon a public meeting.

Since there is general agreement on the desirability of smaller Cabinets —and since in times of urgency, especially war, Cabinets have been greatly reduced in size[6]—it seems clear that forces beyond the control of Prime Ministers are pushing the Cabinet's size in an undesirable direction. One of these forces is obvious: the growth in scope and complexity of the pattern of policy. This expansion of government business has led to a proliferation of administrative departments and every administrative department, by custom, has at least a claim to Cabinet representation. But this is not the whole story. The custom of excluding the less important administrative departments has long been established and from an administrative standpoint it is surely enough to allow the Ministers of the excluded departments to sit in on Cabinet meetings dealing with matters falling within their jurisdiction. Hence, it seems reasonable to assume that certain other factors are of greater importance than the proliferation of Departments. One perhaps is sheer habit: the custom of including departments in the Cabinet if at all possible, a legacy of the

---

[6] Lloyd George's War Cabinet had five members; Sir Winston Churchill's Inner Cabinets during the second World War consisted first of eight, then seven, members.

more intimate administrative days of the nineteenth century. Another is a matter of politics: Cabinet membership is the greatest political prize short of the Prime Ministership. The more powerful party men are rewarded with it the less gnashing of teeth and intriguing there is likely to be in the Prime Minister's party; and the larger the number of Cabinet members the less onerous the burden of selection upon the Prime Minister. The rules of political calculation in this instance simply outweigh the rules of administrative calculation, as indeed they usually do in a democracy.

Closely related to the size of the Cabinet as a factor making difficult its efficient operation is the great pressure of business it must discharge nowadays. The good old days when a Prime Minister could keep a personal check on all the administrative departments, acquaint himself with all problems of policy and express informed opinions on them, ended with Peel.[7] Gladstone tried to emulate his great predecessor for some time but as he grew in age and wisdom he gave up the attempt—and government in Gladstone's day was ridiculously simple compared to what it is today. A Cabinet that tried to keep its fingers on all the hundreds of pulses of modern public life could hardly manage with a mere twenty-four hours in the day. Yet the Cabinet scarcely meets more often today than in the days of Peel himself; it usually has two meetings a week lasting about two hours each. Nor could it be otherwise. Cabinet members have far too many non-Cabinet duties to spend a very large proportion of their time in No. 10 Downing Street. They are parliamentarians and must spend a good deal of time in the house; they are the high command of a political party with electoral purposes to achieve; they are ceremonial figures who must often preside at public functions; they are the heads of administrative departments, which they are supposed to supervise. How then does the Cabinet economize its business so as to make ministerial life bearable? How can it perform its plethora of functions in a mere four hours a week?

The first labor-saving device it uses, as we already know, is to leave as much as possible to the decision of individual Ministers. Another is full interdepartmental discussion of business involving more than one administrative jurisdiction. But undoubtedly the most important of all the devices that help the Cabinet do its work are the Cabinet committees, usually composed of a small number of Cabinet members but sometimes also of non-Cabinet Ministers and distinguished non-parliamentary experts. These committees perform what amount to Cabinet functions in certain specific areas of policy. Like individual Ministers they may refer

---

[7] Sir Robert Peel was Prime Minister from 1834 to 1835 and from 1841 to 1846.

questions to the Cabinet for decision or decide them themselves (any Minister being allowed to appeal a committee decision to the Cabinet). But since their function is to relieve the Cabinet of work most questions are nowadays decided in committee rather than in full Cabinet session.

The use of Cabinet committees can be traced back to the nineteenth century, but they began playing a prominent part in the machinery of government only in the twentieth, as the pressure of Cabinet business continually grew. A vivid conception of the quantitative changes that have occurred in the process of government in the last few decades can be gathered from a brief glance at the development of the Cabinet Committee system during the last generation. In 1929, apart from the Committee of Imperial Defence and a small number of *ad hoc* committees formed from time to time for special purposes, only one Standing (i.e., permanent) Committee was in operation—the Home Affairs Committee. This, moreover, performed a technical rather than deliberative function, its duties being confined to the examination of Bills about to be presented to Parliament. Most business was transacted by the full Cabinet. In contrast, the post-World War II Labour Government used no fewer than seventeen Standing Committees. The most important were: (1) the Defence Committee, presided over by the Prime Minister, and including among its members the Foreign Secretary, the Minister of Defence (as Deputy Chairman), the three military Service Ministers (the First Lord of the Admiralty and the Secretaries of State for War and Air), the Minister of Labour and the Minister of Supply—with the Chiefs of Staff usually present at meetings; (2) the Lord President's Committee, a kind of general purposes Committee on domestic policy; (3) the Economic Policy Committee, again presided over by the Prime Minister himself, and responsible for high economic policy and the supervision of economic planning; and (4) the Legislation Committee, which consisted of the Lord Chancellor (the presiding officer of the House of Lords and the head of the whole judicial system, but appointed by the Prime Minister), the Law Officers (Attorney General and Solicitor General) and the Chief Whip, the function of this Committee being to examine the drafts of Parliamentary Bills, important delegated legislation, and to keep an eye on the general progress of the Government's legislative program. Alongside these Standing Committees there also existed a great many *ad hoc* Committees (e.g., the Committee on the National Health Service, the Committee on the Distribution and Marketing of Meat, Fruit and Vegetables) while the Standing Committees themselves frequently proliferated into large numbers of subcommittees. Finally, there were undoubtedly also certain informal groups of the sort that generally develop in a large Cabinet but are not dignified by the term "Committee," the most important being the small clique of trusted cronies and high-powered politicians that generally clusters around the Prime Minister, consituting a sort of inner Cabinet, where, in all likelihood, most great decisions are made.

THE PRIME MINISTER

One writer on the British Constitution has put the position of the Prime Minister in a nutshell: "The Government is the master of the country; and he is the master of the Government." It follows, in the curious logic of British government, that the Prime Minister's status should be as "conventional," i.e., non-legal, as that of the Cabinet he heads, and the law knows him only as a man who draws down £10,000 a year[8] through the Ministers of the Crown Act 1937. Yet the British constitution vests him with wide authority and his actual political power is surely as great as that of any of the Presidents or Prime Ministers of other democratic countries. The Prime Minister is the "first" of the Ministers, in the sense that he has powers they do not possess, that he is frequently in a position to get his way over powerful opposition, and that even the weakest of Prime Ministers have been, in one sense or another, dominating figures. As Hopkins once wrote to Roosevelt during World War II: "Churchill is *the government* in every sense of the word." But, there is also another side to the matter. The Prime Minister, even during a war and even if he is an overwhelming figure like Churchill, functions within certain boundaries that, in view of their historical origins, it is not far-fetched to call a framework of ministerial equality. If one were asked to compare him with the American President one might do it thus: the Prime Minister, because of the concentration of responsibility in the Cabinet and the discipline of British parties, has, as a general rule, far greater powers than the President, whose freedom of action is severely limited by the separation of powers, but the President can usually exercise his powers far more independently as an individual than can the Prime Minister. The British executive is a plural executive, in spite of the predominance of the Prime Minister.

The Prime Minister's indubitable "firstness" over his colleagues is the result of a large number of causes, some constitutional, some party-political, some psychological. Constitutionally, he acquires special eminence from the fact that all ministerial offices derive from him and depend on him, that it is he who make and unmakes Ministers. Legally, ministerial offices are conferred by the sovereign and are a private matter between her and the Minister concerned. Constitutionally, however, all offices are at the Prime Minister's disposal. Apart from his powers of appointment, he

---

[8] Reduced by the Churchill Government to £7,000.

may dismiss a Minister simply by notifying him and the sovereign that he desires to replace him with someone else; and he may cause the utter dissolution of his Government simply by resigning, something, certainly, that no mere Minister is able to do. A second constitutional factor that gives him an especially august position is that he alone, of all the Ministers, may make great decisions without the approval of the full Cabinet. It is generally accepted as constitutional for the Prime Minister to act in the name of the Cabinet, if the matter at issue urgently requires decision and it is not feasible to decide it in Cabinet in proper time. In actual fact, the Prime Minister frequently acts on his own initiative even when the urgency of a situation does not require it, but in these cases he can assert himself not so much for constitutional as for party-political reasons. He is the "Leader" of his party and this, particularly if he is a Conservative, gives him great powers over party policy, both in form and practice. The relevant forms vary between the two major parties,[9] but in practice the powers of Conservative and Labour Prime Ministers are not greatly dissimilar. In both cases, the ultimate sanction behind the Prime Minister's powers to assert himself, to make independent policy statements and to commit his party to them, is the omnipresent fear of a split in the party if his statements are publicly repudiated. To split a party in Britain is to deliver the Government into the hands of the enemy; hence, even when certain members of a party are deeply out of sympathy with its leader they treat him in very gingerly fashion. They may resign from office and criticize, but they rarely launch a direct attack on the leader and in public they usually swallow their disagreements altogether. There are in consequence few resignations over policy disagreements.

Closely related is another party-political factor that contributes to the Prime Minister's power: the fact that general elections in Great Britain are fought, to a large extent, between two rival candidates for the Prime Ministership. These two are more in the limelight than any other candidates. They lead what Gladstone called the "popular agitation" in the nation, while others stick to their constituencies. It is usually their voices that issue from the B.B.C. and their faces that smile down from the hoardings. And a great many elections, since Gladstone and Disraeli set the fashion, have been, to all intents and purposes, popularity contests between rival party leaders.

Here we come to the third group of factors that set the Prime Minister apart from his colleagues, the psychological factors. The Cabinet is always thought of as *his* Cabinet; the Government as *his* Government; he is, in popular imagery, something apart from the minor stars in the Cabi-

---

[9] See Chapter 8.

net galaxy. This popular conception is reinforced by the fact that of all
the important "efficient" officers of government he comes closest to having
also an important ceremonial function. He frequently represents the nation
on ceremonial occasions; he is second only to royalty itself as a national
symbol. And if he has a colorful personality, a caricaturable face, and is
the master of certain kinds of stage business (like Churchill's V sign and
Baldwin's amazingly convincing impersonation of an ordinary country
squire) he may even rival the monarch as a symbol.

What factors then circumscribe his powers vis-à-vis his colleagues? For
his position *is* severely circumscribed, even in the cases of the most colorful Prime Ministers under the most auspicious circumstances. A most
striking example occurred during World War II, when Prime Minister
Churchill and President Roosevelt met on H.M.S. *Prince of Wales* to
work out the Atlantic Charter. Harry Hopkins, who had earlier reported
that Churchill was *the government*, was struck by the fact that while
Roosevelt seemed to be completely on his own, willing and able to commit
the American people to anything that might be agreed upon on his personal authority, Churchill seemed unable to take a step without getting
in touch with his War Cabinet in London and especially his second-in-
command, Clement Attlee. In three days, more than thirty communications passed between the *Prince of Wales* and Whitehall. Churchill
obviously operated within a restraining framework of "collective leadership"
to which the American President, under similar circumstances, was not
subject.

The factors guaranteeing this collectivity of leadership are, primarily,
two. One is that the idea of ministerial equality is deeply ingrained in
British constitutional morality and that the idea of the committee rather
than the individual boss as a decision-making agency is deeply ingrained
in every Englishman's experience. The British use committees for managing practically everything, from lawn-tennis and social clubs to the Cabinet
itself, from the kindergarten to the geriatric home. Discussions, consultations, negotiations, are a matter of almost everyone's daily experience, and
this accounts both for the fact that the British so often make collective
decision-making work and for the fact that they insist upon it even under
the most difficult circumstances. But there is also a practical consideration
that enforces collective decision-making in the Cabinet: the fact that
British Ministers are, as a general rule, men of some political standing,
whose views it is never quite politic to ignore, and also, as a general rule,
men of more than ordinary capacities, whose views it is never quite wise
to ignore. In the first respect, if not the second, they differ markedly from
American Cabinet members, many of whom frequently have no political
experience, let alone important political standing. But even in the second

respect they probably outstrip other species, if only because British ministers must usually spend long apprenticeships and pass a series of difficult tests before they can qualify for high office. Certainly a man who is a bad parliamentarian—who cannot convincingly marshal a set of facts and arguments, hold his own in the cut and thrust of debate, turn a phrase and think coherently on his feet—has no chance of achieving high office, and people who *can* do these things well are not likely to be mere yes men for any Prime Minister.

Social Origins of Cabinet Members

Since much was made in the previous chapter of political deference in Great Britain, and of its corollary, the existence of a relatively cohesive political elite drawn from the upper social strata, a look at the social origins of cabinet members is required to round out this description. Just what sort of people tend to attain cabinet status? Have the social origins and positions of cabinet members changed in such a way that one can speak of a significant decline of upper class predominance in the highest elite positions of British government? And are there any great differences, in terms of social status, between Labour and Conservative governments? Do they represent "counter-elites," in any significant sense of the term?

If we date the beginning of modern democratic government in Britain to the Representation of the People Act of 1884 (as sensible a date as any) and take 1924 as the turning point between Conservative-Liberal and Conservative-Labour party conflict (also a sensible date, since in the election of 1924 the Liberal vote fell from 30 to 18 percent and the Labour vote rose from 30 to 33 percent) we get two fairly distinct periods of nearly equal duration to compare with one another. Comparing cabinet members in these two periods, we notice first perhaps a sharp decline in the number of those who have aristocratic origins and a considerable increase in those who were born into the working class. From 1886 to 1924, 69 of 160 cabinet members came from aristocratic families (the peerage and baronets, excluding those whose titles were themselves rewards for political services), but from 1924 to 1957, only 63 of 238 came from such families, a drop from 43 percent to 26 percent (Table 1). At the same time, cabinet members of working class origin rose from 1.5 percent to 20 percent, while those of middle class origin stayed approximately even at around 55 percent. Note, however, that while the great majority of the British population is working class and the aristocracy only a tiny fraction of the total, the latter was still more heavily represented in cabinets than the former. To have one cabinet member out of four is a striking performance indeed for a hereditary aristocracy in a period of popular democracy, including three periods of socialist government and two of coalition. And one should bear in mind as well that to be working class in origin does not necessarily, in a highly mobile society like Great Britain, make one working class oneself. At any event, to speak of aristocratic domination of the Cabinet in modern "democratic" Britain is not so very far-fetched.

Take education as another measure of the social status of cabinet members. In the period 1886-1924, 79 cabinet members (50 percent) had attended public schools, no less than 64 of them (two out of every five) Eton and Harrow; 125 (three out of four) had gone to a university and 112 of these to Oxford and Cambridge. What was the position in the period 1924-57? In this period, 174 cabinet members were educated in public schools—72 percent, compared to 50 percent in the earlier period! Of these, 127 (53 percent) had attended the so-called Clarendon Schools (the nine great public schools singled out for inquiry by the Clarendon Commission of 1861-64: Eton, Winchester, Westminster, Charterhouse, St. Paul's, Merchant Taylors', Harrow, Rugby and Shrewsbury) and 84 (more than one in three) Eton and Harrow alone. In others words, the great public schools had altogether maintained their grip, with a slightly less dominant, but still dominant, role played by the two most exclusive ones; if anything, they were more influential even than before.

At the same time, 72 percent of all the cabinet members had gone to a university—about the same proportion as in the earlier period—with 55 percent going to Oxford and Cambridge alone. Here again, there is little change, beyond a slight decline in the predominance of "Oxbridge." Add to this that the occupations represented in the cabinet hardly changed at all from one period to the other, with landowners, men of independent means, lawyers (mainly barristers) and business executives leading all the rest by far, and the picture that emerges is unmistakably one of a ruling elite hardly changed by radical democratization and "proletarian" politics. Furthermore, even the rise in politics of many sons of the working class has not seriously affected the all-important educational background of cabinet members. By and large, the working class sons who have got on in politics in recent times have made their way through the agencies which "socialize" mobile people into the upper strata, universities and public schools.

These are overall figures, of course, and for periods when the Tories were in power much more often than the Liberals and Labour. How then does the social composition of Labour cabinets compare to the overall figures? Have Labour cabinets been genuine counterpoints to the persistent theme of elite domination? To some extent—but not quite as much as one might think. At any rate, one would have difficulty making the Labour leadership out to be a full-fledged "counter-elite," presenting not only an alternative set of rulers to the voters but also representing social strata not represented among the Tory leaders.

The two Attlee governments of 1945-51 included two aristocrats out of a total of 32 cabinet members (compared to 8 out of 43 in the Eden and Macmillan governments of 1955-57) (Table 2), but even two aristocrats is "over-representation" when one considers the proportion of aristocrats in the total British population. Fourteen other cabinet members had middle class origins and sixteen working class origins—so that the aristocracy and middle class combined were represented equally in the cabinet with the far more numerous working class. In this connection, however, we should note that the Eden and Macmillan governments included no one at all of working class origin (and also that 10 out of 35 members whose origins were middle class had married into the hereditary aristocracy, so that about 40 percent of the most recent Tory cabinet members had aristocratic connections). A fairly distinct difference between party leaders thus emerges when one considers their family backgrounds. But in both parties there is an equally distinct social difference between leaders and supporters, with the leaders including a considerably larger number of men with high status origins, aristocrats in the Conservative Party and middle class men in the Labour Party, and a large middle class overlap between the parties.

When we consider the education of cabinet members this difference becomes somewhat less distinct. Twelve of the Labour cabinet members, or nearly 40 percent, had attended public schools, with 8 of them (25 percent) going to one or another of the Clarendon Schools. In both cases, this proportion was much higher than among Labour M.P.s—40 against 23 percent in the first case, 25 against 2 percent (!) in the second. And among Labour M.P.s the proportion of public school boys was much higher to begin with than in the country as a whole, and still higher than among Labour supporters. Sixteen of the 32 Labour cabinet members had attended university in a country where less than two percent of the population does so, and nine of the sixteen were Oxbridge men. The Eden and Macmillan cabinets did include a rather larger proportion of public school boys (32 out of 43) and Oxbridge men (27), so that there is some educational difference between the party leaderships—but again, a difference only in the degree of "over-representation" of the highest status groups.

One could almost say, without oversimplifying beyond a reasonable extent, that elite members with high status upon birth tend to dominate the Conservative Party, while elite members who acquire elite status themselves, mainly through education, tend to furnish the upper leadership of the Labour Party. In both cases, however, there is a close connection between social elite and political elite. And one should not forget that it has in fact been the Tories, with all their aristocratic origins and connections, their domination by Eton, Harrow and Oxbridge men, and the vast "over-representation" of men of independent means among their leaders, who have been in power most often in the age of the mandate and the welfare state.

TABLE 1 **Social Status of British Cabinet Ministers, 1924-1957**
(in percent)

CLASS ORIGIN		EDUCATION		OCCUPATION	
Aristocratic	26	Public Schools	72	Independent	28
Middle Class	54	Clarendon Schools	53	Law	20
Working Class	20	Eton-Harrow	35	Businessmen	12
		University	71	Trade Union Leaders	12
		Oxbridge	54	Lecturers	5
				Military	3

TABLE 2 **Comparison of British Conservative and Labour Ministers, 1945-1957**
(in percent)

CLASS ORIGIN	CON- SERV- ATIVE	LABOUR	EDUCA- TION	CON- SERV- ATIVE	LABOUR	OCCUPA- TION	CON- SERV- ATIVE	LABOUR
Aristocratic	25	6.5	Public			Independent	42	—
Middle Class	75	44	Schools	97	40	Law	20	13
Working			Clarendon			Businessmen	27	3
Class	—	50	Schools	70	25	Trade Union		
			University	90	50	Leaders	—	39
			Oxbridge	80	30	Lecturers	—	30

[6]

The Pattern of Power:
Parliament

The Symbolism of the House of Commons

The British monarchy and Cabinet pose a striking paradox: one is dignified by the most solemnly formal constitution ritual, but has only the most peripheral relevance to the actual conduct of British government. The other is dignified by neither legal forms nor constitutional ritual, but is of the most crucial significance from a practical standpoint. If we elevate this curious circumstance into a general law—the more "dignified" a British political institution the less its practical significance—Parliament immediately confronts us with a serious ambivalence. It is a curious mixture of ceremony and improvisation, of ancient usage and modern invention, and this perhaps is explanation enough for the many learned disputes about its role in British government. In any case, the mixture of old and new, formal and informal, is the most palpable thing about the House of Commons the moment one enters it. It is the essence of its atmosphere, and the atmosphere of the House is a matter of practical no less than aesthetic significance. To understand fully what Parliament is and does one must experience it, even if only vicariously.

Let us imagine that the reader is sitting in the visitors' gallery of the House for the first time. No doubt his first impression will be of the physical appearance of the House. This, even if he does not find it attractive, he will almost certainly find surprising. In particular, if the visitor has seen other legislative chambers, he will be surprised by the unique size and seating arrangements. From the standpoint of size it is little more than a glorified Town Hall. It seats fewer than two thirds of its members, despite the fact that it makes no space-consuming concessions to members' comforts (such as desks and individual chairs) but seats them all on long benches, with the august representative lap the only support for papers. The chamber measures roughly three thousand square feet, while the American House of Representatives, despite a much smaller membership, commands more than four times that much space. The prevailing atmosphere of the House of Commons can, therefore, only be described as intimate—except on great occasions (e.g., before an important "division") when, with over six hundred odd members crowding into a space designed for 346, the chief impression is one of excitement and expectancy.

The feeling of excitement at such times is further increased by the seating arrangements. In most of the world's legislative chambers members sit in semicircular or straight rows, all facing a rostrum from which members address the chamber and from which its presiding officer conducts the proceedings. The impression is of an auditorium facing a stage on which individual legislators play the star turn. In the House of Commons, however, members sit on two sets of long benches, graded upward and facing each other, one at the left, the other at the right of the Speaker, who sits at the head of and between the rows of benches. To the right of the Speaker sit the Government and its supporters, Ministers on the front bench (or Treasury Bench, as it is sometimes called), ordinary members ("backbenchers") grouped behind them like obedient and anonymous soldiery. On the other side sit the Opposition, the "Shadow Cabinet" on the front bench and its own soldiery arrayed on the benches behind. The two groups face each other like football teams in a scrimmage, and when members make their verbal cuts and thrusts, they inevitably appear as the members of a team, not as individuals temporarily elevated, in splendid individuality, to the national tribune.

Since the present House of Commons is only a few years old (the old House having been destroyed by German incendiary bombs in 1941) neither its layout nor its small size are accidental. Despite certain obvious discomforts, it was decided to make the new House of Commons almost exactly like the old, not alone because of attachment to the past but because it was widely felt that the physical character of the House somehow affected the character of its proceedings. For example, Mr. Churchill, the most insistent spokesman for the small Chamber, felt that the whole style of debate in the House would be changed for the worse if the House were enlarged; that the effects of meeting in a large and half-empty hall (and the House is rarely full even now) would be depressing; that the old sense of crowding urgency on great occasions would go; and even that the clean-cut two-party system would be endangered if the seating arrangements were altered.

The next thing the visitor to the House will notice is the general tone of its proceedings. It is here that he will be impressed most by the curious mixture of formality and informality. In some ways the House of Commons is the most formal of all legislative chambers. Its deliberations are governed by procedures most of which are hoary with age and many of which are pure ceremony of the quaintest sort, procedures that either no longer serve a useful function or have long since been adapted to new uses while maintaining their old form. The visitor may, for example, be in the House when it is getting dark. Suddenly the cry goes up: "Mr. Speaker, I call for candles." True, candles have not been used to illuminate the House for decades but if a member were to say, "Mr. Speaker, how about putting the electric lights on," he might, with the same effectiveness, make his request in Swahili. The rules of parliamentary procedure include a multitude of precedents set by rulings of the Speakers over the centuries. Until the late nineteenth century, in fact, almost all the business of the House was covered by usage, there being only a small handful of Standing Orders, as the rules deliberately adopted by the House to regulate its proceedings are called. Since then the S.O.s have grown by leaps and bounds, but by far the greater part are still a matter of custom.

For such a solemn and ceremonious set of rules a solemn and ceremonious presiding officer is appropriate, and the House of Commons does not fail to provide him. If any physical evidence of the continuity of British parliamentary institutions were needed, Mr. Speaker would furnish it. There he sits in his chair (his "throne" one should perhaps say), looking like nothing so much as the frontispiece from a biography of Handel, with his flowing wig, his black satin knee breeches, his buckled shoes and long black gown; a figure straight out of the age of squirearchy. He is an arresting figure, and not only does he look much prettier than his French counterpart, who sits in the bourgeois drabness of modern evening dress, but he is far more authoritative. To cite a simple example: if the French National Assembly gets out of hand the President of the Assembly rings a bell, an act which often merely augments the prevailing din. But if the House of Commons becomes disorderly (as it rarely does) the Speaker almost always manages to restore order without recourse to mechanical devices merely by rising from his chair, the rule being that when Mr. Speaker is on his feet all members must be off theirs. And only at times of riotous turmoil does he resort to the ultimate, almost unfailing, method of getting order: putting on his hat. His powers over debate, the putting of motions and questions, and over members' conduct, are vast and to some extent arbitrary.

But even more important than his formal powers is the readiness with which his rulings are obeyed. No doubt his effectiveness as a presiding officer is, in large measure, due to the same factor to which the monarchy largely owes its popularity, the fact that his political impartiality is completely established and unquestioned. He is the very embodiment of the rules of procedure and, like the rules, neutral. This neutrality is guaranteed in numerous ways. The Speaker is elected for the life of a whole Parliament, not as in France, for a single session, and will be re-elected, by a convention dating back to the early eighteenth century, as long as he wishes. Speakers, like monarchs, thus are generally in office for long periods and acquire the usual venerability of age and experience. Although elections to the Speakership may be contested by the parties, only men who have not been violent partisans are put up and the aim is always to secure a unanimous election. Finally, once a man has become Speaker, he is divested of his political personality, so to speak, in a number of ways. Although he continues to be a member of Parliament his constituency chores are taken care of by another member. He may vote only if there is a draw in a decision and then only to preserve the status quo; he never takes part in a debate (absolutely never); and his seat is never contested by the other party ("never," in this case, in the Gilbertian sense; there have been four contests for the Speaker's seat since 1714).

But whatever the sources of the Speaker's power, he has it—and does not greatly need it. The normal tone of the House is orderly and polite; it is a chamber with an aristocratic past and with palpably aristocratic habits. True, the prevalent politeness is to some extent backed by rules. For example, in referring to another member a member speaking in the House must never use his name but refer to him by a ceremonious title: "the Honorable member for ———" (if he is an ordinary M.P.), "the Right Honorable member" (if he is a Privy Councillor), "the honorable and learned member" (if he is a lawyer), "the honorable and gallant member" (if he is a former officer in one of the armed services) or "the noble Lord" (if he is an Irish or Scottish peer not entitled to sit in the House of Lords, or the son of a great nobleman, in possession of a courtesy title). These ceremonious titles are not conducive to belligerence, however much venom certain members manage to inject into them. Again, the Speaker is empowered to see to it that members use only decorous language and may have obstreperous members removed by the Sergeant-at-Arms and, indeed, suspended from the House altogether. A brief but representative list of expressions ruled unparliamentary in the late nineteenth century includes: "cowardly," "a poltroon," "of remarkably fragile honour," "a bigoted, malevolent young puppy," "the reverse of the truth," "bloodthirsty," "mendacious."

But it would be mistaken to suppose that the *politesse* of the House is merely a matter of rules. The rules and precedents are often overlooked, particularly when they are picayune, and Messrs. Churchill and Bevan, among others, have unburdened themselves of expressions that would have astounded the fastidious Speaker Denison in the nineteenth century. The courtesy and good humor of the House are rather a part of its spirit. They come out most clearly and under least compulsion when a member has made a "maiden speech," his first essay in the House of Commons. No matter how miserable the speech, the next speaker, whether friend or foe, will congratulate him on an eloquent and informative performance, express the pleasure of the House in hearing it and the hope that the member will be heard from frequently on other occasions.

This courtesy toward the maiden speaker is also a rule, even if it exists merely in the intangible spirit of the House. It is part of the ritual by which the House never lets one forget that it is both an ancient and a solemn institution. The House, no less than the monarchy, appeals to the form-worshipper, the pomp-worshipper, that dwells in most of us. Yet, for all its formality, it is, as the visitor will immediately sense, basically an intimate and informal place. Here, of course, is where its size plays an important part. It is, for example, not unusual for the great table which supports the golden Mace to support also the gangling legs of some elongated front-bencher. Members present in the House of Commons sit in almost every conceivable posture: some, like Balfour, on their shoulder blades; others reclining on their sides. And there is an almost constant coming and going, bowing in and bowing out, and conferring behind the Speaker's Chair. But the prevalent informality is most notable in the speeches. British parliamentarians need suffer neither the academic pompousness of German legislators nor the incessant Fourth-of-July oratory of the Americans. The tone of the House of Commons is conversational rather than declamatory, witty rather than learned, and it could hardly be otherwise. In so small a chamber, lectures and orations invariably sound ludicrous—except on the greatest of occasions or when delivered by semi-legendary figures like Sir Winston Churchill. Moreover, it cramps the orator's style to be compelled to speak in his place, in the midst of a multitude, rather than from a special tribune. It equally cramps his style to have no desk to put things upon, nor even a rail on which to lean. It cramps his style not to be allowed to use a prepared speech or even special notes.[1] And, not least, since all remarks in the House are to be addressed not to other members but to Mr. Speaker, a man can sound ridiculous haranguing a crowd of one. Speeches, therefore, tend to be calm. They

---

[1] The House permits only Ministers making important announcements of policy, where every word counts, to read their speeches.

also tend to be concise, partly because that is the tradition of the House, partly because the Speaker may immediately suppress all irrelevant remarks and tedious repetitions, but partly also no doubt because the crush of modern business demands dispatch.[2]

But informality is not all. The House can be a mercilessly discourteous audience, particularly if a member departs from its mores, and it is always a tough audience. A. P. Herbert, never one to tremble before a crowd, called it the "Torture Chamber," and with good reason. In almost any circumstances, members, unless they are completely bored, will keep up a running fire of interjections. But if the speeches offend the House, a merciless cacophony may break loose. The would-be orator, for example, will almost certainly be engulfed in a tumultuous rustling of papers, stamping of feet, coughing and sneezing, or, as has happened once or twice, such a continuous chorus of "hear, hear" that he cannot be heard. The House is (generally) courteous and calm; but it is never easy on speakers in the sense that it will tolerate nonsense or lack of decorum or blatant unconventionality.

Class Composition of the House

The right word for the atmosphere of the House of Commons is, if not aristocratic, at least gentlemanly, and no doubt it is so gentlemanly because it is predominantly filled with "Gentlemen." True, the House is not as homogeneously composed of Gentlemen as it was in the eighteenth century, when it was controlled by the aristocracy (younger sons) and gentry, the true and original Gentlemen. Nor is it even as uniformly "gentlemanly" as it was in the nineteenth, after the influx of the new upper and upper-middle classes. Universal suffrage and the rise of the Labour Party have inevitably injected into the House a previously alien strain, so that one cannot today draw up an occupational chart of the members without using such categories as "Railway Clerks," "Commerce: clerical," "Skilled Workers," even "Unskilled Workers." As classes and groups, previously excluded from politics, have risen in political power in the country, their representatives have made their way into the House of Commons. From this some observers have concluded that the character of the House has profoundly changed. But has it?

There can be no doubt that the House of Commons, as a *whole*, is still predominantly upper-class and middle-class in composition. About one

---

[2] In more leisurely days, conciseness was not one of the virtues of the House of Commons. In 1797, for example, Lord Colchester made the following note in his diary: "In the House Mr. Grey moved a vote of censure on Mr. Pitt for his conduct. . . . Only Mr. Grey, Mr. Pitt, and Mr. Fox spoke. The debate began at half-past six, and lasted till one in the morning.

half of all the members in recent Parliaments had attended universities, nearly a third of them Oxford and Cambridge, and, as for secondary schooling, about one out of every six had been to Eton. In the Parliament of 1951-55 there sat 95 lawyers (most of them barristers, the higher echelon of the British legal profession) and 74 professional writers; and, on the Conservative side alone, about 100 company directors, 30 "farmers"[3] and 24 bankers and business executives. But one scarcely needs statistical documentation for this. The visitor to the House can immediately experience its dominantly higher-class character simply by listening to the members' voices, examining their dress, observing their table manners in the House of Commons restaurant, and so on.

It must be admitted of course that the Labour benches are less solidly "respectable" than the Tory benches. "They look like a bunch of damned constituents," as a Tory M.P. was heard to mutter when the new Labour hordes flocked into the House after the landslide of 1945. But it would be difficult today to tell a Labourite from a Tory as easily as all that. One reason is that the House of Commons, by virtue of its well-defined character and style, tends to make people over in its own image, and its style is pronouncedly upper class. If new members are not yet domesticated to the upper strata when they enter it the House will almost invariably carry their training a long way. Aneurin Bevan, a devotee of class conflict, has realized this as well as anyone else, and chafed under the fact:

> The atmosphere of Parliament, its physical arrangements, its procedure, its semi-ecclesiastical ritual, are . . . all profoundly intimidating for the products of a board school system who are the bearers of a fiery message from the great industrial constituencies. . . . To preserve the keen edge of [their] critical judgment [they] will find that [they] must adopt an attitude of scepticism amounting almost to cynicism, for Parliamentary procedure neglects nothing which might soften the acerbities of [their] class feelings. In one sense the House is the most unrepresentative of representative assemblies. . . . It is a social shock absorber placed between privilege and the pressure of popular discontent.

But there is another reason for the pronounced degree of surface homogeneity in the House and a much weightier one, namely that Labour members are themselves surprisingly higher class and do not, as a general rule, need to be House-broken. Here two points are particularly worth noting. First, as Labour representation in the House of Commons has increased in the course of the twentieth century, the number *and proportion* of upper-class Labour members has also risen. To cite only one example: in 1936 the formal education of 49 per cent of Labour members had

---

[3] Mainly owners of estates.

been limited to elementary school and only 17 per cent had been to a university; in 1951 the figures were 24 per cent and 33 per cent respectively. In a decade and a half, the proportion of lower-class membership was halved and that of higher-class membership doubled. It is almost as if the ruling classes had begun seriously to infiltrate the new party once it showed signs of becoming politically important.

Secondly, it seems fairly clear that, just as the Liberal Party was the chief means of entrance into politics of the new upper classes of the nineteenth century, so the Labour Party has become the chief means of entry of the latest additions to the upper strata. The social composition of the House has undoubtedly changed in the last century, but so has the content of the social stratification scale. The expansion of higher education, particularly the scholarship system, has channeled into the higher strata people effectively excluded before, and one sizable chunk of society in particular has become "respectable": the members of certain professions. Only a half century ago—certainly not more than a century ago—doctors, solicitors (the lower echelon of the legal profession), journalists and schoolteachers were still frowned upon as artisans rather than gentlemanly professional men.[4] Today they are almost, if not quite, as respectable as gentlemen "farmers," military officers, and those who live off private means. Once this is realized the figures on the social composition of the House of Commons become very suggestive. In 1958 more than half the Labour members belonged to what we generally consider the professions, and among these the largest chunk consisted of schoolteachers, the second largest of journalists, and another sizable chunk of solicitors. There were 30 journalists on the Labour side and 19 on the Conservative; fourteen Labourites were solicitors against eleven Conservatives; and—most striking of all—59 Labourites were schoolteachers as against a mere two Conservatives. The actual number of "professionals" on the two sides was about even, but the Conservatives drew the vast majority of theirs from the old professions, the first to become "respectable": barristers (66 to 21 for Labour) and military officers (47 to 2!).

The Work of the House of Commons

What precisely is it that all these proper people do in their solemn habitat? What is the role of the House of Commons in the actual conduct of British government? What is its power in the whole scheme of decision-making? What are the specific functions through which this power is exercised?

---

[4] Note, for example, Dickens' treatment of them in *Bleak House, Nicholas Nickleby* and the *Pickwick Papers*.

TABLE 3   **Education of British M.P.s, 1950-1951***
          (*in percent*)

EDUCATION	TOTAL	CONSERVATIVES	LABOUR
Public School	52	85	22
Eton-Harrow	17	35	2
Secondary School	20	12.5	27
Elementary School	27	2.5	51
University	49	59	42
Oxbridge	34	50	18

* This period was chosen because of the almost perfectly even split in the House between Labour and Conservative. The present House, being Conservative-dominated, is still more elitist in composition.

TABLE 4   **Principal Occupations of British M.P.s, 1950-1951**

OCCUPATION	TOTAL	CONSERVATIVES	LABOUR
Barristers	84	50	29
Military Officers	51	49	2
Journalists and Authors	46	18	27
Teachers and Lecturers	43	4	39
Miners	38	—	38
Clerks and Secretaries	33	6	27
Landowners	25	23	—
Solicitors	24	10	13
Manufacturers	23	16	7
Civil Servants	18	13	5

These are crucial questions about British government and, needless to say, they are not easy to answer. There are, however, two extreme positions that we can dismiss. One is that the power of Parliament is "transcendent and absolute," in fact as well as theory. The simple truth is that the House of Commons is dominated by the Cabinet, primarily by means of the stern weapons of party discipline. But from this it does not follow that the other extreme view is correct: that Parliament is merely, as Ramsay MacDonald once said, an electoral college, a body that dutifully registers the people's will in electing an executive and then deserts the field to the men of its choice. Unlike the American electoral college, it remains in session after performing its electoral functions, and it is certain that what it does in session is of some consequence, though of less consequence than the transcendental absolutists make out. To determine how much less we need to examine its work in some detail.

LEGISLATION

"The chief function of Parliament," said the famous lawyer Maitland, "is to make statutes." On the surface, of course, he is right. The House of Commons spends more time discussing bills than doing anything else.

It is the principal house of the British legislature, and no statute can have the force of law unless enacted by it. Neither, however, would any statute have the force of law without the royal assent, yet no one thinks of the Queen as having any real legislative function. The problem to solve is to what extent the time Parliament spends discussing bills is of practical consequence.

Any legislative process may be dissected, for analytical purposes, into three stages. Registering Yeas and Nays is only the last of these stages. The first is the initiation of bills, including not only the conception and drafting of legislative projects but also the business of introducing them in the legislature and deciding which projects the legislature is to discuss. Under modern conditions no legislature can allow all of its members indiscriminately to introduce legislation and then thoroughly discuss all the projects. Some method is required to decide what the legislature is to consider, when, and at what length. And whoever is empowered to decide this has great powers over legislation—something like a veto in fact. The second stage of the legislative process is, of course, "deliberation," i.e., debate to determine the pros and cons of a legislative project by means of discussion among open-minded men. Such deliberation the classic philosophers of popular government (e.g., Bentham) considered to be the very heart and soul of "legislating." The purpose of the legislative process, they felt, is to give expression to popular will; this is done by debate among the people's representatives, from which emerges a decision registered in a vote.

Who then determines what legislative business is to come before the House? To what extent do its discussions conform to the classical model? And when the members troop into the Division Lobbies[5] do they really decide whether the Bill before them is to become law or has that already been decided?

So far as initiation is concerned, Parliament as such clearly does not legislate, since the business of introducing legislation is almost completely monopolized by the Government. The legislative projects of "private members" (i.e. backbenchers, ordinary M.P.s) hardly ever obtain even a hearing. As the table below shows, bills are conceived and promoted by all sorts of different agencies, in and out of the Government. But very, very few can ever be more than a gleam in someone's eye unless the Cabinet agrees to act as parliamentary midwife. Ministers must "introduce" them, however they "originate."

There are both constitutional and practical reasons for this. One consti-

---

[5] Translation: vote. The method of voting is for members to walk through two special rooms, one *for* the Bill (or motion), one *against*, where a count is made and the names are registered. It is a time-consuming method of voting but, as Herbert Morrison has pointed out, a socially pleasant one.

tutional reason is the rule that all legislation involving financial expenditure must have the consent of the Crown; and, much, if not most, important legislation involves the expenditure of money. But more important than this definite rule is a sort of general constitutional prejudice, not shared by other democratic societies, that introducing legislation is somehow rightfully the business first and foremost of the Government. There is, as usual, a democratic rationalization for this attitude. Parties

TABLE 5   Sources of British Legislative Projects
     (Session 1936-1937)

Cabinet	9
Administrative Departments	27
Voluntary Associations (i.e., pressure groups)	9
Government Policy, under known outside pressure	3
Administrative Departments, after consultation with "voluntary associations"	7
Local Government Associations	2
Private Members (on own initiative)	2

contest elections on platforms and once a party has won a majority, it is argued, democratic principles demand that its program should have priority in the legislature. This, however, is probably little more than a rationalization. Few parties assume office with mandates for such a vast amount of legislation as did the Labour Party in 1945 and in an average session legislation for which a mandate has been given occupies only a tiny fraction of the time spent on bills. In the session dealt with in Table 5, for example, only one project (out of seventy) was derived from the election program and the vast majority of the rest had only the loosest connection, if any, with a mandate. British Ministers enjoy their legislative privileges because of the widespread belief that it is the business of the Government to govern and because party discipline puts them in a position to monopolize the parliamentary timetable. This conclusion is reinforced by the fact that the practical considerations making for ministerial monopoly of the legislative agenda—e.g., the pressure of important business—also exist in other countries, without producing similarly cavalier attitudes toward the legislative rights of private members.

If a private member wants to introduce legislation he can do so only on certain days predetermined by parliamentary usage, and the generosity of the Government in power.[6] By long usage, Wednesdays and Fridays are private members' days, Fridays for Bills and Wednesdays for motions.[7]

---

[6] And under the Ten Minutes Rule. This is so complicated and insignificant that it is better ignored.

[7] "Motions" here refers to non-legislative motions. It is necessary in the House of Commons to hinge every debate on a specific motion. Hence, if a member simply wants to criticize some particular ministerial act or aspects of a policy, he must put down a motion. This may or may not be debated, depending on whether it is allowed to go on the actual agenda.

Since the beginning of the war, however, few Wednesdays and fewer than the traditional number of Fridays have been available to private members, so that the old tradition seems in process of being superseded by a new one even less kindly to the backbencher. During the war, of course, the Government had abundantly good reason for taking away all private members' time, and after the war the Labour Government, with a vast mandate to fulfill, had an equally good reason for monopolizing the timetable. Thus, for almost a decade no "private members' Bills" were dealt with in the House of Commons.

The Government, then, practically monopolizes the initiation function. But what of the other two stages of the legislative process? Is the decision to enact or reject a bill the result of "deliberation" among the members of Parliament or not?

This question may seem foolish since the House of Commons undoubtedly debates legislative projects at great length and with great seriousness. In fact, it debates prospective statutes more frequently, if not more thoroughly, than almost any other legislature. Before a bill can become an Act it must pass through five (sometimes six) stages. The first stage, after drafting, is called the First Reading, and is largely perfunctory. The Minister in charge of the Bill to be introduced, being called upon by the Speaker, rises and bows to the Chair; the Clerk of the House of Commons reads out the title of the bill from a "dummy" which has been laid upon the Table (so seriously does the House take its ritual make-believe); and the Minister then names the date on which the next stage in the passage of the bill, Second Reading, is to take place. The bill is now printed and distributed to members and, on the appointed day, the Second Reading takes place. This involves a debate, sometimes very long, in which the main principles of the bill are discussed, but the main principles only. This means, among other things, that amendments to the bill may not be moved. If the bill is approved after the debate it goes to Committee—usually one of the Standing Committees,[8] sometimes a Committee of the whole House. Here only the details of the bill are discussed, the fundamental principles having been accepted on Second Reading. This is the stage, consequently, at which amendments to the bill may be moved, provided only that they do not conflict with the previously adopted general principles of the bill. When the Committee has finished its deliberations it reports the bill back to the House (Report Stage), whereupon another debate on the details generally takes place. Then comes the final stage of the process, Third Reading, when there may be still another debate on general principles; and while by this

---

[8] See below, p. 239.

time the House usually has little left to say, on some occasions Third Reading debates have been as tense and thorough as debates on Second Reading.

Thus there are plenty of opportunities to debate both the principles and details of bills. But it is doubtful whether the House really deliberates when it debates, if by "deliberation" we mean the formation of opinion through discussion or if we imply that the debates have significant effects on the contents of Bills. A. P. Herbert liked to refer to the House of Commons as the "Gas Chamber" and, so far as the effects of its debates on the contents and success of legislative projects are concerned, that, to all intents and purposes, is all it is. Normally it is certain that any Bill introduced by the Government will pass, substantially in the form in which first submitted, whatever splendid oratory, indisputable facts, and tight logic may be advanced against it in the Chamber. The reason, of course, is party discipline. As long as discipline holds, the Government need not really convince anyone of the soundness of its proposals. It need only send out a three-line Whip to its supporters, a letter "urgently requesting" each member's presence in the House at such and such a time when a division is expected to take place, and the troops will obediently march in and do their job, regardless of what is said in the debate.

The House, then, is not a deliberative body, and, this being the case, we need not consider its role in the third stage of the legislative process at any length. Except for an occasional "free vote" private members vote not upon conscience or conviction but upon compulsion. The real deliberative agency in Britain, then, seems to be the Cabinet, and not only because it can make its supporters troop into the Division Lobbies. It can also—together with the leaders of the Opposition—dominate the parliamentary debates themselves by arranging with the Speaker who is to be allowed to speak.[9] And it possesses one other great advantage, compared to the Governments of other countries: it can always see to it that the House votes on a Government bill in the form submitted, by preventing distortion through important amendments, since amendment is not permitted until the principles of a bill have been approved.

However, as the table on the sources of legislative projects will suggest, the Cabinet does not fully monopolize the deliberative function. It is, in essence, merely the decisive apex of a very complex structure of decision-making, involving all sorts of forces (the party in and outside Parlia-

---

[9] Formally, the Speaker decides who is to participate in a debate. If members wish to speak they must rise in their places upon the conclusion of the previous speech, and the first one to "catch the Speaker's eye" will be named to speak. In practice, however, the leaders of the Government and Opposition pretty much arrange the order of speaking to suit themselves. Lists of the principal speakers are submitted to the Chair and the Speaker generally calls out the prearranged order.

ment, the civil service, pressure groups) that press upon the Cabinet and, by constant intervention, help shape the principles and details of legislation. It is this constellation of forces, rather than any single body, that "deliberates" on legislation, in the sense we have used the term. But in this constellation of forces Parliament itself undoubtedly plays a role. Like the parties, the press, the bureaucracy, and the pressure groups, it can exert influence on the Cabinet's decisions, sometimes important influence. Its debates frequently reveal flaws in bills and lead to the acceptance by the Government of technical changes. More important, on at least a few occasions Parliament has caused the Government either to withdraw unpopular legislation or to introduce popular measures it had not intended to introduce. The Education Act of 1936, for example, was withdrawn after heavy criticism in the House. A few years ago the House persuaded the Government to raise old-age pensions against its previous will. And it was the Labour rank and file that persuaded the Government to nationalize Civil Aviation and to reduce compulsory military service from eighteen to twelve months. The list of such cases is impressively short; but it covers only the *publicly* known cases, not the considerable influence exerted by members of Parliament behind the scenes, through the Parties, the committees of the Parliamentary Parties,[10] and informal consultation, both before and after the formal introduction of bills. The fact is that British Governments, for all their great powers, go to very great lengths to ascertain and accommodate the views of the parliamentary rank and file. The power of the House of Commons to kick out a Government may not be a very real threat in this day and age, but it is always there as a silent reserve, a sword of Damocles hanging over the Government. Nor can a Government afford for very long to be consistently criticized by its own supporters, even if they obediently vote for it in the divisions.

CONTROL OVER ADMINISTRATION

This deflationary appraisal of the legislative function of Parliament will not surprise anyone acquainted with its history. The primal function of Parliament was neither to legislate nor to govern but to advise and control those who did govern. Even in the heyday of Whig parliamentarism this notion of the function of Parliament persisted. Burke, for example, explicitly says that Parliament is primarily a "controul" over the Government on behalf of the people. And just as it is fashionable today to argue that Parliament does not really make the laws, so also it is fashionable to maintain that its real function—the work it does really well—

---

[10] See below, pp. 188-189.

is to control the administration of the laws. To determine whether this is so or not we need to examine first the means by which Parliament exerts such control: the Question Period, debates on motions to adjourn and motions of censure, and the machinery for supervising delegated legislation.

The first hour of every sitting day (except Fridays) is set aside for questions to Ministers about matters for which they are responsible. Any member of Parliament may ask up to three "starred questions" a day (i.e., questions for which an oral answer is to be given by the Minister in the House)[11] and these questions may and do cover the whole range of governmental activity and the nation's life. By prearrangement, different Ministers appear on different days and answer questions put to them as they appear on the Order Paper. Members may add oral supplementary questions if a reply given by the Minister seems unsatisfactory. And the usual impression given by Question Time is of rapid-fire give and take that puts the Minister to a severe test. Nothing the House of Commons does is more surely calculated to expose weaknesses in a Minister; nothing the Minister does is more likely to impress or disenchant the House. No doubt most of the Minister's prepared answers are fed him by his civil servants, but no permanent official can fully protect the Minister against the supplementary questions that members may ask after an answer has been given to the original question. Ministers and bureaucrats dread the Question Period, religiously prepare their answers, and anxiously try to anticipate Supplementaries.

By usage, Ministers are always required to make some answer to questions, while a member may ask about anything he likes, provided he observes certain specific rules. If these are transgressed, the Clerks of the House may change his question or throw it out altogether. Questions must be short and framed so as to elicit facts and not opinions. The subject matter must be one for which the Government and the specific Minister questioned are responsible (e.g., questions about the private lives and transactions of citizens are clearly out of order). A question already answered cannot be put again in the same session. Questions must not repeat rumors or gossip. Their language must not be ironical or hypothetical or argumentative, and must in general be such as would be admissible at other times in debate. (Thus, "Whether the Foreign Secretary agrees that it would not be obvious to anyone but a complete ass that the rearmament of Germany, which he proposes, will prevent the reunification of that country," is out on almost every conceivable ground; while

---

[11] Unstarred questions are answered in writing, but since most questions are meant not only to elicit information but also to publicize a subject, to put a Minister on the spot. or to provoke a debate, starred questions predominate.

the question, "Whether the Home Secretary is not a well-meaning but in-
flated solicitor" would be admitted only after removal of the adjectives.)
These rules are designed to prevent loose and abusive questions. But they
do little to take the bite out of Question Time.

If an answer given by a Minister is considered unsatisfactory, even after
Supplementaries, members have several methods available to prevent the
matter from being buried. If, for example, the matter urgently requires
debate, it may, under Standing Order 9 of the rules of procedure, be brought
to debate on the very same day. The member who wants such a debate
must rise and say, "Mr. Speaker, I beg leave to move the adjournment of
the House on a definite matter of urgent public importance, namely
that . . ." The Speaker must then decide whether the matter is really
definite,[12] urgent[13] and public;[14] and if he finds that it satisfies all three
criteria (and forty members of the House agree to the debate) then
all prearranged business comes to an end at seven o'clock that day and a
debate on the adjournment motion begins. Again, a motion to adjourn is
usually made at the end of each daily sitting, and debate on this motion
can also be used to go into a subject raised during Question Time. The
House automatically adjourns at 10:30, but at ten the regular business of
the day is almost always interrupted. A motion to adjourn is then made
and this motion leads to debate until 10:30 on a subject raised by a member, usually to air an individual or local grievance, sometimes to air a
subject of the most general importance. Similar debates, obviously useful to expose acts of administration, take place on the eves of periodical
holidays, e.g., Christmas, Easter, Whitsuntide and the Summer Recess.

Debates on motions of censure may be used in extreme cases to air
matters a government wants to hush up. Such motions, like motions of
confidence, involve a solemn and direct challenge to the Government by
the leaders of the Opposition. But unlike motions of confidence, which
are concerned with general policy, they are concerned with specific ministerial actions and are thus used especially to attack administrative behavior.

Finally, there is the machinery for the control of delegated legislation.
This is important, if only because so much legislative power is now delegated by Parliament to Ministers and the Cabinet. Parliament simply lacks
the time and technical knowledge for certain kinds of legislation, while
others require a flexibility in rule-making that would be impossible to
achieve if Parliament laid down specific provisions. Delegated legislation

---

[12] The motion must not deal with more than one subject; it must deal with a particular case rather than being couched in general terms; it must not be hypothetical;
official information must be available.

[13] The matter must have happened recently and require immediate attention.

[14] The matter must raise a "larger issue" and not merely involve an individual or
local grievance.

—to be precise, rules with the force of law made by the executive under a broad authorization of Parliament—now accounts for around a thousand "statutory instruments" (the technical legal term) a year, some of very great length and complexity. It far overshadows regular Parliamentary legislation, at least in quantity, and it has multiplied five-fold in half a century. Needless to say, this is a matter that worries a great many people, and much has been written about what Chief Justice Lord Hewart called "the new despotism"—the despotism of the bureaucrats who in fact not only administer but also make most of the rules under which people in Great Britain live.

The obvious means for controlling the rule-making powers of the bureaucrats is to require parliamentary approval of the rules they make. The requirement may take two forms: "affirmative resolution" (i.e., a specific vote of approval without which the statutory instrument cannot acquire legal force) or "nullifying prayer" (a negative vote that prevents an instrument from going into force). In examining statutory instruments laid before it for approval or disapproval the House gets help from a special committee of its own members, the Select Committee on Statutory Instruments, created in 1944 to examine all pieces of subordinate legislation and to call to the attention of Parliament any which seem to require special examination. The Committee is assisted by Speaker's Counsel, an expert lawyer and parliamentarian. It is not permitted to register opinions but only to call the attention of Parliament to certain instruments.

How effective is all this machinery? Does the House really "control" the executive in any more meaningful sense of the term than it "legislates"? That it has a great many opportunities to go into matters of administration there can be no doubt. It has perhaps more such opportunities than Congress, and certainly enjoys one incalculable advantage over it: the fact that Ministers are actually present in the House, where they may be challenged, interrogated and embarrassed. The formal doctrine is that, as a general rule, for every administrative action some Minister is liable to answer in the House of Commons, and not only to answer but even to resign, if a grave error of judgment, a serious transgression of law, or abuse of power is involved. British Ministers enjoy none of the comfortable protections of the separation of powers. But is this stern doctrine more than theory? When the House discusses matters of administration is it doing anything more than going through the motions?

Unfortunately, again, there is probably more to be said on the negative than the affirmative side. For example, despite the doctrine of ministerial responsibility for acts of administration, a vast range of public activities nowadays is practically exempt from parliamentary control, i.e., the activities of independent authorities, like the public corporations that administer the industries nationalized by the Labour Government, and those of certain semi-independent authorities created for the specific purpose of exemption from normal political supervision. The number of these agencies is large and they deal with a vast area of activities. Indeed, next to the growth of delegated legislation, their development is probably the most significant constitutional development of the last three decades.[15] But the difficulty is not only that much administration is exempted from parliamentary control. Much more serious is the fact that the means for supervising the activities subject to parliamentary supervision are not as effective as they are sometimes made out to be.

Consider, for example, the case of delegated legislation. Parliament is so spendthrift with its legislative powers because it does not have the time or knowledge for certain kinds of legislation, and if these factors keep it from legislating in the first place they also prevent the effective supervision of administrative lawmaking. Nor is the Select Committee on Statutory Instruments of great help. It is better than nothing. But it is, after all, composed of ordinary M.P.s, it has an enormous amount of work to do, and, in fact, it has called to the attention of Parliament an average of only a dozen statutory instruments a year (out of a thousand) since its inception. In addition, much delegated legislation is not even made subject to parliamentary approval or disapproval, but need only be laid before the House for a certain period or, indeed, sometimes not even that. Most important of all, of what use are resolutions and prayers against statutory instruments if the Government calls out its majority to back them? And this point applies equally to all the other means of controlling administration.

In gist, the House of Commons is no more a controlling body than it is a legislative body—and no less. The same considerations apply to both activities. Party discipline not only gives ministers an effective monopoly over legislation but also immunity from parliamentary control, if they choose to press it to its ultimate extremes. But they rarely choose to do so. Annoying adjournment debates are rarely, if ever, forestalled, even if they could be. Questions are generally answered scrupulously. Occasionally a master of evasion appears (like Gladstone, who used to wrap his answers to Questions in such a cloud of abstract metaphysics and cumbersome technicalities as to leave his listeners numb). But most Ministers make an effort to give an honest accounting to the House; and the fact is that the departments do take immense pains over Questions.[16] Similarly,

---

[15] They already existed in the nineteenth century, but in nothing like the present quantity.
[16] Indeed, it has been frequently alleged that this is not an altogether unmixed blessing. As Hugh Gaitskell has said: "Anybody who has ever worked in a Civil Service

while nothing absolutely needs to be done about uncovered grievances, something usually is done about them. The House of Commons, then, does at least affect the course of administration, and it affects it for much the same reasons it can affect legislation. But, also as in the case of legislation, the controls the House of Commons exercises over administration are exerted jointly with other bodies. The House of Commons is simply one part in a complex framework of control. The airing of a grievance or exposure of an administrative error in the press may be as effective as a debate in Parliament; so also may direct representations to the Minister and discussions in the House of Lords.

PUBLICITY

In essence, then, the position in the case of both legislation and control is that the Government is vastly more independent of Parliament than the transcendental absolutists suggest, and yet far more willing to listen to Parliament—to take its advice, redress its grievances, cater to its preferences—than would a true Cabinet dictatorship, indiscriminately wielding the Whip over its disciplined supporters. In part, this self-effacement of the Government is certainly a matter of "constitutional discipline." But there are important practical sanctions as well; above all, the fear that certain kinds of ministerial behavior may lead to dissension in the majority party, and fear of the repercussions actions in Parliament may have in the electorate. The first of these practical considerations is easy enough to grasp. Insofar as the Government's position rests on party discipline it would be suicidal to alienate a sizable chunk of its supporters. Party dissension is now the main factor that compels an occasional Government to resign. Precisely for this reason, however, the fear of dissension is perhaps less of a limitation on the Government than might appear. If a party split occurs, everyone in the party suffers, leaders and led alike. The Opposition comes in and they are usually "worse" than the leaders of one's own party; the party goes into the wilderness and the streams of normal political advancement may dry up for a protracted period. In short, the specter of dissension keeps the rank and file in line no less than it restrains the leaders. The Government's fear of repercussions in the electorate at large is therefore, in all likelihood, a more powerful constraining factor than fear of intraparty disagreements.

Apart from democratic morals, the chief reason for the Government's scruples about opinion in the electorate is, of course, that it is compelled periodically to put its fortunes to the electoral test. While exercising

Department would agree with me that if there is one major thing which leads civil servants to be extremely cautious, timid and careful and to keep records which outside the Civil Service would be considered unnecessary, it is the fear of the Parliamentary question."

power it is always preparing for the next general election. But even this would not be a sufficient explanation for its generally scrupulous sensitivity to pressure and criticism were it not for another fact: that Parliament —much more than the American Congress, for example—is in the public limelight to a really extraordinary extent. For example, the sales of the daily *Hansard*—which, like the Congressional Record, records verbatim the parliamentary proceedings—have been as high as 12,000 copies and those of the *Weekly Hansard* as high as 16,000 copies. Ordinarily, a publisher who sells that many copies of a light novel considers himself fortunate, and *Hansard* is not light, however much fiction goes into it. In addition, the British press gives remarkably extensive coverage to Parliament. *The Times* and *The Guardian* carry nearly verbatim reports of the debates; even the yellow journals have their special Parliamentary Correspondents; the British Broadcasting Corporation gives a nightly fifteen-minute report on Parliament (usually delivered by an M.P.). Even the humor magazine *Punch* has a sizable and usually serious section on Parliament in every issue, while, in contrast, the *New Yorker* restricts itself to an occasional brief report of a ridiculous extract from a Congressman's speech. Parliament, by the standards of many other countries, gets a great deal of publicity, and one may suspect that this publicity makes a particular impact on that small proportion of the population—the floating vote—that actually determines the outcome of elections.

In a sense, therefore, the proceedings of Parliament are of consequence because a sufficiently large number of people *believe* they are of consequence, although it is not only misconceptions of Parliament's proper role that cause people to take an interest in the parliamentary proceedings. Most important, perhaps, the House of Commons provides a thrilling arena for political conflict, an arena of a sort no legislature in a separation-of-powers systems can match. The floor of the House of Commons is the place where all the leaders of the great parties constantly confront each other in face-to-face conflict—questioning, prodding, debating. The reader need only imagine a political forum in which, almost daily, President Kennedy, Mr. Stevenson, Mr. Nixon, Vice-President Johnson, and Senator Goldwater have at each other. Such a forum would be bound to be more in the public eye than Congress, even if it exerted less practical weight. But we have nothing to rival the House where Gladstone and Disraeli faced each other, year in and out, in constant, direct conflict.

All this may explain why Parliament spends so much time debating Bills and exposing acts of administration, even if the results of its proceedings are so frequently a foregone conclusion. Parliament, in short, has still a third function, additional to legislation and control of the executive. It is, as John Stuart Mill said, the nation's Congress of Opinion no less than its Legislature and Committee of Grievances. It has what Bagehot called a "lyrical" as well as a legislative and controlling function. How well does it perform *this* function?

On this question, at least this much must be said in favor of Parliament: its debates are generally conducted on a surprisingly high intellectual level, and it provides an unusually large number of opportunities for general policy debates and wastes little time on technical and provincial matters, which are not likely to be of great import to anyone except experts and a few interested parties. This is due, in the first place, to the very fact that the substantive powers of members over legislation and administration are so severely limited. If parliamentary debates are unlikely to lead to many changes in a Bill—if no concessions are to be won for Little Wopping or the Brotherhood of Turf Accountants on the floor of the House—there is simply no point in meddling with detail and all the reason in the world for general analysis. Hence, parliamentary debates tend to be rather more interesting and informative than the proceedings of other legislatures. Then too, there are special debates, held every year, designed specifically to be general policy debates, i.e., to inform more than to decide. Every session of Parliament, for example, begins with about a week of such debate, the Debate on the Queen's Speech. The tradition is that when Parliament begins a session the sovereign addresses it in the House of Lords, outlining—in a speech written, of course, by the Cabinet —the main business to be transacted that year. Then a debate takes place that covers the whole range of the speech itself. An equally important vehicle for general policy debates is afforded by the Debates in Committee of Supply (which are discussed in Chapter 10) and by debates on motions phrased in very general terms.

All this is to the good; but even here entries must be made on the negative side of the ledger. The chief one is the severe lack of time for adequate parliamentary discussion. Parliament nowadays has so much business to transact that everything must run according to a strict timetable and debates are almost always severely limited by Governments that have the necessary support to limit them. Three devices may be used for this purpose: closure, "guillotine" and "kangaroo." Closure may be moved by any member after debate has gone on for some time. The Speaker must then decide whether the Opposition has had a fair day in court on the subject under discussion and, if he decides that this is the case, the question is immediately put to the vote. If carried with the support of at least 100 members the debate is finished. Needless to say, Governments have little trouble stopping debate when they want to by this means. The "guillotine" (or closure by compartments) is an even more drastic weapon: it can be used to limit debate before it has ever begun. In essence, a guillotine motion is a Government motion that sets out at what precise time the various stages of a parliamentary proceeding are to end, e.g., so much time for Second Reading, so much in Committee, so much time for the Report Stage, and so on. When the appointed time comes the ax falls on the debate and the next item of business follows, whatever important people are still to speak, however many aspects of the question have not yet been discussed. Finally, as a further limiitation on discussion, the Speaker, in putting amendments to debate, has the power to skip over any he does not consider important or representative of significant sections of opinion. This power is called the "kangaroo."

In limiting debate (and, as we shall see below, in devising the parliamentary timetable) the most scrupulous regard is given to the wishes of the Opposition, which, in fact, directly controls a great deal of Parliament's time. This point is of very great importance, for insofar as publicity is one of the chief functions of Parliament it is correct to say that the Opposition is more important than the Government in the House of Commons. After all, it is chiefly the Opposition that prods, probes, criticizes and exposes those in power.

It should not be supposed, however, that in publicity we have finally found *the* function of Parliament—its particular and peculiar task in the British scheme of government. Again, it is a function that it shares with many other agencies: the press, radio and television, the soapbox orator in Hyde Park, party meetings and conventions, party publications, ethical societies, and so forth. But the dignity and solemnity of the House, the excitement that pervades its debates, and the decisiveness the public attributes to its proceedings undoubtedly make it the most powerful among all the various agencies of political expression.

The House of Lords

So far we have practically equated Parliament with the House of Commons. Needless to say, this is misleading. Parliament includes also the House of Lords. Indeed, from a strictly formal-legal standpoint it includes the Queen as well, for in legal theory Parliament is the absolute and final lawmaking authority in Britain and no law can be enacted without the Royal Assent and the solemn ceremonies attendant upon its grant in the House of Lords. Formally speaking, laws in Britain are made by "the Queen *in* Parliament," not the Queen *and* Parliament. Common sense, however, rebels against including the monarch in the concept of Parliament, if only because the power of the Royal Assent is today a mere formality, never withheld from parliamentary enactments. And one may be tempted to relegate the House of Lords to the same category of antiquated ceremony, and discount completely its role in parliamentary affairs.

For several reasons, however, this is not permissible. One is that the House of Lords exemplifies much that is significant in British political life, even in its ceremonial capacity. The ceremonies themselves are not without consequence, as we have seen, and in no case can one see more vividly the manner in which the British have adapted old institutions to new purposes throughout their history, or the tenacity with which they cling to the forms of their government, than in the evolution of the Lords. Secondly, the House of Lords is even today not without certain formal powers. It definitely plays second fiddle to the House of Commons, but it participates in the actual process of British government much more than the monarchy. And in the third place, if one does not consider the formal-legal powers of the House of Commons but its actual functions and powers, as we have done here, then the House of Lords acquires a much greater practical significance, for it plays its own part in the complicated structure of actual legislative deliberation, control over administration and political publicity sketched above. This makes it necessary to consider in some detail the history of the House, its composition, and its present power and functions.

EVOLUTION

The origin of the House of Lords is usually traced to the Great Councils of the Norman Kings. These Councils, generally summoned three times a year, consisted of "the great men of England" (there was as yet no concept of a peerage), archbishops, bishops, abbots, earls, thegns and knights, and performed simultaneously judicial, advisory and deliberative functions. By 1258 the Council had become known as "parliament," although no one knows the exact beginnings of the term. At that time, separate assemblies for nobles and commoners did not yet exist, nor was the right of permanent attendance on anyone's part recognized. Although the greatest in the realm were nearly always called to attend it, the Great Council consisted of those men, high or low in station, whom it pleased the King to summon. In the fourteenth century, however, the greater and lesser members of the Council took to meeting separately and by the fifteenth century a clear distinction between Lords and Commons was made. By that time also the notion of the hereditary right of peers to attend Parliament had become recognized (although, in typically English manner, it was not formally ratified until 1625, when the King tried to keep the Earl of Bristol from attending the House of Lords and the House itself decided that the practice was "illegal," i.e., unprecedented). In the fifteenth century also, as mentioned earlier, a true sharing of authority between monarch and Parliament developed.

In the earliest stages of parliamentary development, a distinction was made between the powers of the Lords and Commons which definitely favored the Lords. According to the old formula, statutes were made in England "by the *advice* of the Lords and *request* of the Commons"; but already in the fifteenth century the concurrent authority of the two Houses seemed to be generally recognized. The Lords were always referred to first in legal formulas and they retained sole possession of Parliament's judicial function—a very important power in an age when legislation in the modern sense was uncommon. On the other hand, financial powers gradually gravitated to the Commons, which, after all, represented the classes most heavily hit by royal requests for monies—and the power to grant and withhold monies was then, as now, the most efficacious means of controlling executive power. It would be only a slight simplification to say that by the seventeenth century, the Lords had become the judicial and deliberative, and the Commons the controlling, element of Parliament.

In the civil wars of the seventeenth century the power of the House of Lords was for the first time seriously attacked by the Commons. With some exceptions, the Lords were loyal to the monarchist cause, so that, in 1649, the Commons declared that the House was "useless and dangerous and ought to be abolished." Thereafter the Lords ceased to meet, but were restored as a separate chamber when the Commonwealth collapsed in 1660. A long period of struggle between the two Houses followed, centering chiefly on the financial privileges of the Commons. In this struggle the House of Commons was uniformly triumphant. What had long been tacitly recognized now was explicitly affirmed: that money bills should always originate in the Commons and could not be amended by the Lords—that finance was, in fact, a prerogative of the "lower" house. At the same time, the principle became established that Governments should be responsible in Parliament only to the Commons, that is, that they could not be voted out by the Lords. In 1712, the practice of creating new peers wholesale so as to give an existing Ministry adequate support in an unfriendly House of Lords was first used, and has been recognized as legitimate ever since. It is, of course, the ultimate weapon a Government supported by the Commons can use to coerce the Lords into giving it its way, and has been successfully threatened on some vital occasions in more recent history, though never again actually employed.

In the eighteenth century, consequently, it was hardly any longer appropriate to speak of the Lords as the upper house and the Commons as the lower. The power position of the two Houses had become reversed; conservative England had achieved by peaceful and gradual process what revolutionary England had sought vainly to accomplish by abrupt and violent means. Yet the power of the Lords even in this period should not be slighted. Peers generally held the greatest offices of state and, what is far more important, were able to control, through local influence and the anti-quated system of constituencies, elections to the House of Commons, sufficiently to "operate the system" there. We thus get in the eighteenth century a curious accommodation between formal authority in the Commons and actual power in the peerage, and one may even suspect that the Commons were able to gain the upper hand over the Lords largely because the aristocracy could pursue its interests through the former as easily as through the latter.

The Reform Act of 1832, however, began a gradual erosion of aristocratic influence over elections to the Commons. The process was a slow one. As Trollope's parliamentary and Barsetshire novels show so vividly, the "Dukes of Omnium" still could practically appoint members to many rural seats. But the decline of aristocratic influence was continuous all the same, and by the end of the century, party had almost completely displaced peerage as an electoral force.

During this period of electoral reform, the Lords were on the whole still acquiescent in the rule of the Commons; it took some time to realize that the old "system" was being undermined. By the 1880's, however, with the franchise greatly extended, the constituency system reformed, and new radical forces in the House of Commons, the Lords became increasingly a center of Tory resistance against Liberal policy. The great preponderance of peers was, needless to say, Conservative; in 1905, for example, on the eve of a Liberal victory which still ranks as the most one-sided in British history, only 45 of 600 peers were Liberals. The Liberals in power created many new peers, but the majority of these had a disconcerting habit of turning Tory once they were actually in the Lords. Liberal measures were rejected in the Lords in the period 1881-1883 and the Second Irish Home Rule Bill was defeated during Gladstone's last government. The only thing that kept matters from coming to a boil was that the period from 1886 to 1906 was in fact a period of almost unbroken Tory ascendancy—and the old constitutional arrangements still worked well while the Tories were in power.

The great Liberal landslide of 1906 at last brought about a showdown between the two Houses. The Liberals were intent upon achieving important reforms, some of which, like the abolition of plural voting and a new system of assessing land values for purposes of taxation, ran counter to the most obvious Tory interests. The Conservatives, however, relentlessly used their power in the Lords to block almost all but minor reforms. Not for half a century had the Lords insisted so comprehensively on their prerogatives as the upper house. For three years, nothing was done in the face of this virtual constitutional revolution except to talk ominously of reform. Then, in 1909, the Liberals at last made their challenge to the

House of Lords, and made it on the best ground possible, the Budget, long recognized as a Commons' prerogative. The Government's Finance Bill of that year threatened to introduce vital social reforms by financial means, above all heavier taxes on wealth, the taxation of unearned income, and, least palatable to the aristocratic Tories, a reassessment of land values. The Lords rejected the Bill, not indeed illegally, but contrary to long practice; and no doubt that was just what the Liberals intended. They now called an election (in January, 1910), in the course of which parliamentary reform was practically the sole issue, and received another clear-cut, though reduced, majority. Thereupon a broad measure to curb the powers of the Lords was introduced and accepted by the upper house when the King let it be known, upon Prime Minister Asquith's request, that he was prepared to swamp the House with Liberal peers if it proved recalcitrant.

The Parliament Act of 1911 put drastic limitations on the Lords. In essence, it provided, first, that money bills passed by the Commons must be passed by the Lords without amendment within one month after being sent up, or else would be considered an act of Parliament anyway upon receiving the Royal Assent—it being up to the Speaker of the House of Commons to determine whether a bill qualifies as a money bill; and secondly, that any other public bill passed by the Commons in three successive sessions could be enacted with the Royal Assent if rejected each time by the Lords, provided only that two years had elapsed between the first discussion and third passage of the bill in the Commons. In short, the power to veto or delay money bills of all descriptions was completely taken from the Lords and their power over other legislation was reduced to a suspensive veto of two years.

This drastic measure did not end the agitation for reform of the Lords. The incidents from 1906 to 1911 left the House in bad odor altogether on the Left and attacks upon it continued. Some people considered its very nature anachronistic and obnoxious, and pressed either for outright abolition or a completely different basis of membership (the Act of 1911 had ominously announced that a completely different second chamber was the Government's ultimate intention). Apart from the fact that a hereditary upper house was ideologically repellent to the radicals, the possibility was recognized that the Lords could still seriously obstruct a reform program by delaying measures for two years—by interfering, for example, with the planning of parliamentary time or preventing a majority from carrying out certain of its policies before the next election. Curiously enough, the Tories themselves chimed in with this chorus for more reform, not, indeed, further to weaken the House but to strengthen it by altering its membership in one way or another. Conservatives became more and more interested, for example, in schemes making possible life (that is, non-hereditary) peerages—particularly when it became constitutional practice to exclude peers from the Prime Ministership and, ordinarily, other offices of the first rank, a practice not designed to please the heirs of newly created peers. They also became interested in excluding from the House the many "black sheep" or "backwoodsmen" who never attended it, or attended only to frustrate parliamentary reform and attempts to decrease judicial violence—such as flogging—and thereby subjected the whole membership to ridicule. They also became champions of methods designed to increase attendance in the Lords, above all by payment of expenses or salaries in guise of expense allowances.

Indeed, the concern with parliamentary reform gradually shifted altogether after 1911 from the Left to the Right. On the whole the Left seemed increasingly satisfied with the status quo. The Labour Government of 1945-50 did enact, in the Parliament Act of 1949, a further curtailment of the Lords' powers, by reducing its suspensive veto to one year, largely out of fear that the Lords would kill the nationalization of iron and steel by delay. But Labour's basic attitude since the war has been indifferent acceptance of the Lords or else the confident expectation that the House will simply atrophy from disuse. The Conservatives, however, have carried through in recent years some potentially very important changes. They introduced first a kind of voluntary disqualification for politically indifferent peers by permitting them to apply voluntarily for "leaves of absence" from the House if they did not intend to attend "as often as they could." No one was compulsorily excluded but, surprisingly, more than a quarter of those eligible did actually decide to opt out. They then introduced a payment of three guineas (nine dollars) per attendance, ostensibly for expenses, although travel expenses were already granted in 1946. Finally, the present Government enacted a bill providing for the grant of life peerages and for the first time admitting women (but not the wives of peers) into the House.

All this was done with the unenthusiastic support of Labour, for the object of the Conservatives was obviously to improve the quality of the House and assure it a steadier attendance—in short, to strengthen it without changing its essential character. The judicious use of the reforms—for example, the appointment to life peerages of a number of Labour supporters, male and female—seems, however, to have nipped in the bud any nascent resistance to the new dispensation. The idea of the life peerage, after being discussed uneasily for almost a century, seems indeed to be already recognized as the normal way to raise men to the Lords, so much so that the recent grant of a hereditary peerage to the former Archbishop of Canterbury caused a considerable public stir. A few jokes were made about the "baron ladies" who entered the House two years ago, and a few sarcasms expressed about the three guineas per attendance. On the whole, however, the latest reforms of the House have already become established as normal "constitutional" structure—that is to say, they are hardly noticed any more.

A number of general points about British politics are illustrated by this narrative. It shows how British government has changed as a result of democratization and the rise of radical Liberalism and Labour. It also shows how old institutions persist in Britain by being converted from "efficient" into "ceremonial" institutions. It shows further how the ground for such changes is often prepared by previous arrangements, in this case the close identity of interests, prior to democratization, between Lords and Commons which induced the former voluntarily to efface themselves while it was possible to work the House of Commons system. And finally we can see in it some of the mechanisms which make the process of constitutional accretion possible: the appeal to past balances of power in order to legitimate new versions of these balances; the great pliability and practicality of the British Conservatives, indeed their willingness to lead the process of constitutional reform when it cannot be averted and might be turned to their own purposes; and the equally great pragmatism of the radicals, as illustrated, for example, by their willingness to settle for the Parliament Acts of 1911 and 1949 after it became clear that abolition was not necessary for practical purposes.

COMPOSITION

Before considering what the Lords do, let us sketch briefly who they are. Prior to the reforms of 1958 the House had approximately 860 members, which made it the largest legislative chamber in the world. About 800 of these members were hereditary peers of England, Great Britain or the United Kingdom (i.e., possessors of peerages created prior to the Treaty of Union between England and Scotland, or between that Treaty and the creation of the Irish Free State in 1922, or thereafter). Of the other members, 26 were bishops of the Church of England (the "Lords spiritual"); nine were Lords of Appeal (lawyers appointed to the House for life under an act of 1876 to improve the ability of the House to discharge its judicial functions as the highest British court of appeal); sixteen were elected representatives of the peers of Scotland, who do not individually possess the right to sit in the Lords (unless also possessing peerages of England, Great Britain or the United Kingdom—as many do); and the rest were the few surviving representatives of the old Irish peerage which, prior to 1922, elected 28 representatives to the House for life. Thus the House has always included a small number of non-hereditary members, to which have recently been added a number of the new life peers and half a dozen baronesses.

There is still another reason for not exaggerating the aristocratic character of the House, or drawing too stark and simple a contrast between its members and those of the Commons. About half of the present House can date their peerages back no further than the present century, about a fifth are peers only of the second generation, and another fifth are newly ennobled peers—a good many of them self-made men. In the Lords, one can hear about as many accents as in the Commons and find about as large a variety of occupations; the day when the great landowning peerage monopolized the House is long since past. The House of Commons is in fact today the largest recruiting ground for the House of Lords. At any rate, there is not much essential difference between the members of the Lords and the Conservative members of the Commons, and that between Lords and Labour is diminishing. This is due partly to the growing gentlemanliness of Labour M.P.s and partly to the fact that many former Labour Party leaders and functionaries, as well as trade unionists, cooperators and radical intellectuals, have recently been raised to the peerage, along with the men of commerce and industry and retired military commanders who have always furnished the bulk of the new peerage. Of the 116 men created peers in the period 1945-1954, 35 could be considered only middle class and 23 only working class, according to a Fabian Society pamphlet—a rather considerable proportion.

One should also note, in this connection, that there is a considerable difference between the membership of the House and those who actually attend its sessions and participate actively in its deliberations. The membership is the largest of any legislative chamber in the world, but attendance and active participation are by far the smallest. It has been estimated that only about sixty peers are "regular attenders," that is, as likely to be found in the House or its vicinity during sessions as not; that perhaps another twenty are "frequent" attenders; and that another twenty or so "casuals" attend the average session. The average number of peers who vote in divisions is only about eighty, and very few issues seem capable of drawing a much larger number. The abolition of capital punishment, which brought 333 peers into the House in 1956, leads the rest by a wide margin, while other issues which have drawn a large House in the past include liquor control, the establishment of commercial television and changes in the Anglican Prayer Book. Among more strictly political issues—that is, matters of high policy—only constitutional reforms affecting the House itself and an occasional question concerning empire, commonwealth and spheres of influence (the plans for Indian constitutional reform in 1934 and 1935, for example, or the Suez intervention) seem able to arouse the "backwoodsmen." When we come to actual participation in debates, the figures are just as dreary, although they have steadily increased in the present century. The majority of contributors to House of Lords debates hardly ever speak at all, and speak only very briefly when they do; and the number who speak often, say ten times a year, is no larger today than the number of regular attenders, and used to be a great deal smaller.

These figures are important not only in themselves, but also because the proportion of Labourite peers is particularly large among the regular attenders and frequent participants (about a third in both cases). Moreover, peers of first creation tend to be rather more active proportionally than those who inherit their titles; from 1951 to 1954, for example, 65 of 128 very or moderately active peers (defined as peers who spoke at least ten times during the period) were first holders. And among these active peers, a very large proportion have been members, often important members, of the Commons, a good many before inheriting their titles.[17] Thus, when one looks at the actual attenders and participants in the business of the House of Lords the differences between it and the Commons tends to dissolve, or anyway to become less sharp. The Lords remain predominantly conservative and are somewhat more aristocratic (in the social, not legal, sense) than the Commons, and they include a small active coterie of men representing long established, traditionally political, aristocratic Tory families, who in fact play a very large part in its affairs. But forgetting the paraphernalia of the two Houses, observation of the Lords' debates after those of the Commons is very likely to induce a feeling that one has seen it all before, the men as well as the manners, especially in these times of Tory government.

FUNCTIONS AND POWERS

Upon first glance, the powers of the House of Lords would seem to be so negligible as to be hardly worth discussing. No doubt it is one of the chief repositories of solemn ceremony in British political life, gorgeous to look upon and entrancing to watch. Nowhere in British life is the past so vividly and instantly alive in the present. But what do the Lords actually do? What would be missed if they were not there? Their constitutional powers over the shaping of legislation has been reduced, as we have seen, to the puny right to delay bills for one year, and even that right, which does not legally apply to money bills, is seldom exercised—perhaps just because it is so inconsequential. Control over the executive is impugned by the fact that Governments are responsible only to the Commons. And

---

[17] For more details, as well as the most comprehensive modern treatment of the House of Lords, see P. A. Bromhead, *The House of Lords and Contemporary Politics: 1911-1957* (London, 1958).

from this it follows that really great occasions of state, those solemn challenges to a Government which, in Bagehot's words, rivet the public's attention, are also confined to the House of Commons. As in the case of membership, however, so in the case of functions it will not do to draw too sharp a contrast between the Commons and the Lords. We already know that the powers of the Commons are a shadow in practice of what they are in theory. We need only add that those of the Lords are a great deal more consequential in actuality than they appear in form —that the Lords are a factor in the total British decision-making pattern, no doubt less significant than the Commons, but nonetheless a factor to include in an overall description.

In regard to legislation, the Lords possess four formal means of making themselves felt: by rejecting bills passed by the Commons, amending them, acting as the House in which Government bills are first introduced, or through the introduction of bills by private members. The first of these means can in fact be almost ignored; the Lords today do not consider it proper to reject bills passed in the Commons, particularly Government bills. As the Parliament Act of 1949 shows, the Labour Government of 1945-1951 was afraid of the possible effects on its overall program of delaying tactics in the Conservative-dominated House of Lords, but not a single significant Government measure carried in the Commons during this period was rejected in the Lords (unless one counts the Parliament Act of 1949 itself), not even the Iron and Steel Nationalization Bill for the expedition of which the act of 1949 was carried. The House of Lords did balk at the vesting date prescribed by the bill and gained an indirect concession of delay from the government; but it went along, reluctantly, with the bill itself. It also defeated a clause in the Criminal Justice Bill of 1947-1948 abolishing (subsequently restricting) the death penalty, but this clause had not been in the original bill, and was inserted as a result of a private member's amendment and carried on a "free vote" in the Commons.

Insofar as it affects legislation carried in the Commons, the House of Lords does so almost entirely through the process of amendment. An enormous number of Lord's amendments are put, and while most are withdrawn upon discussion, a number ultimately find their way into the statutes. Those that do, however, are mainly minor technical amendments and, as often as not, inspired by the Government itself. The legislative process of the Lords affords the Government a chance to tidy up or improve proposed legislation; that indeed is its chief practical utility. Quite often the Lords—not least the technical experts among them—find legal or other flaws in bills which escaped the scrutiny of both the executive and Commons; quite often they have good ideas which recommend themselves to Ministers (who generally take great pains to talk things out privately with peers who get legislative notions); even more often changes in legislation first suggested in the Commons are actually inserted in the Lords, after the Minister has had time to "take them into consideration" (i.e., discuss them with his civil servants and affected interest groups). Then too, the House of Lords offers the Commons a chance to save a certain amount of precious time by considering Government bills before they go to the lower house. About a quarter of all bills, and sometimes more, in fact originate in the Lords, though never, legally, money bills or, by custom, measures of important policy. The majority of bills introduced in the Lords are minor bills of various descriptions, particularly those which the membership of the Lords is particularly competent to consider, like complex legal questions and bills dealing with agriculture and forestry—the House, after all, includes many of the great lawyers of the realm and an unusually large number of "farmers." One should not, however, exaggerate the benefits to the Commons of introducing bills first in the Lords, since the real object of doing so is not to save the Commons' time but to keep the House of Lords occupied at the beginning of each parliamentary session and prevent a congestion of business at the end. But some saving of time no doubt does accrue to the Commons from the procedure.

Finally, the House of Lords may also be used to introduce private members' legislation; it is in fact far more readily available for this purpose than the Commons. No formal restrictions are put on private members' time in the Lords (though time is always made available to the Government when it wants and needs it) and all that is necessary to introduce a private member's bill is just to introduce it. Time to discuss it, once it is introduced, is always found, and, for technical procedural reasons we need not dwell upon here, bills are hard to keep from actually coming to a vote once they come up for debate. But there is a very important catch in all this. Private members' bills carried in the Lords must also be carried in the Commons before they can become law, and in the Commons the stern impediments to private members' legislation discussed above apply. For this reason, private members' bills are introduced about as rarely in the Lords as in the Commons, and generally only to bring them to public attention, to appeal for the Government's support, or to take a sounding of parliamentary and public opinion on a subject.

If all this gives the impression that the legislative powers of the two Houses are about equal, in consequence and inconsequence, that is just what is intended. The chief difference between the two Houses in regard to legislative debate is that the House of Commons includes practically all the great political leaders, both in and out of power, and is therefore much more the scene of long drawn-out, intense debates, aimed ultimately at the electorate and, through the electorate, at future policy. Debates on legislation in the Lords tend to be much shorter and less exciting than in the Commons, sometimes being little more than mere formalities. And this means also that the publicity function of the Commons, and its function as a control upon administration, must be correspondingly greater, for ultimately both depend on the extent to which debates have a public impact.

The House of Lords, however, does have advantages over the Commons which to some extent compensate it for the absence of great men and the lack of great occasions—in addition to the fact that some great men (including a handful of cabinet ministers) do sit in the Lords and that Lords debates are also widely reported in the quality press which influences the British elite. One of the advantages of the House is that its time is much less stringently controlled than that of the Commons. Because little time is normally required for legislation, a good deal remains for general debates on issues of broad policy, which inform the public, or administrative detail, which put pressure on the executive. Indeed, the characteristic activity of the House is debate upon private members' motions of every degree of import, while in the Commons only ten Wednesdays per session are available for this purpose. Moreover, while very few questions are ever asked in the Lords, those that are asked can often turn into exchanges resembling full debate, due to a lack of control comparable to that in the Commons over "supplementaries" and lack of an explicit time-limit on question-time. The House in fact is governed by very few formal rules. It is the least governed legislative chamber in the world because it exercises the greatest amount of self-control. Its presiding officer, the Lord Chancellor, has far less authority than the Speaker of the House of Commons—partly because there are so few rules to enforce and partly because, by one of those typically British twists of illogical logic, his seat is technically outside the boundaries of the House and he himself consequently not a member of it while presiding.

Another point often made in this connection is that party discipline is much less strict in the Lords than in the Commons, and that individual opinion and independent judgment are therefore much less stultified. This point, however, must be severely qualified. Although no dissolution can threaten the House of Lords, no central electoral funds can be withdrawn by party organizations and no member of the Lords need fear for his seat, the fact is, however strange it may seem, that party discipline in the Lords nowadays is just about as strict as in the Commons—a fact which alone should make one suspicious of any simple structural explanation of the phenomenon of party discipline. Cross-voting between adherents of the two main parties is in fact extremely rare and the instances of it have been steadily diminishing. And discipline extends beyond voting. Conservative peers tend to voice Conservative views in debates, and Labour peers the views of the Labour leaders, all without special whipping and threatening. The chief difference between the two Houses in regard to discipline is simply that debates in the Lords have less the appearance of a contest between two dedicated teams; there happen to be more independents in the Lords. To that extent, but that extent only, the conception of a House of individual judgments holds.

And many of the independents—as well as of the party peers—are men of notable achievement and great special skills. Even more is made of that by apologists for the House of Lords than of its supposed independence from party. In expertise, it has been said, the Lords considerably outstrip the Commons, and no doubt this is true as far as membership is concerned. On economic questions, it is doubtful that the Commons have anyone to match Lord Robbins, or on social questions Baroness Wootton. And who in the Commons, in the period when Keynesian economics became the source of official economic policy, could match the expertise of Lord Keynes himself? But with this argument also one must be very careful. The fact is that the potential of the House of Lords is rather greater in regard to expert judgment than the actuality. Few of the great experts take much part in the Lords' debates; they are often too busy outside and often too old when they enter the House, and they are much more diffident about speaking than the politicians, even when they have greater reason to speak. The debates of the House are in fact carried on mainly by politicians "promoted" from the Commons, or by the would-be politicians among the hereditary peers. Taken all in all, they are no more and no less intelligent than the debates of the Commons. But this is not to say that the occasional interventions of a Keynes or Robbins, Montgomery or Alexander, Hankey or Vansittart, Dawson or Webb Johnson, Cherwell or Beveridge, are not matters of great use or moment.

In essence, then, the House of Lords does contribute something to legislation, control and political education. However much ceremonialized, it is still a term in the "efficient" pattern of British politics and government —i.e., in the pattern of power. And one can even imagine, in the dim future, a House of Lords outstripping the Commons in certain respects as a result of recent changes in its composition. It is a fact that the House of Commons no longer attracts quite as much talent as in the past, when a seat in Parliament was part of the aspiration of every sort of notability. How could it do so in these days of the automaton M.P.? The quality of the Lords, however, is very much on the upgrade, and, with the gradual elimination (by death or choice) of the "backwoodsmen" and a great increase of life peers, one can envisage the House becoming an assembly of great notables from every walk of life, with correspondingly great popular and political influence. But that is merely guessing. For the present, the Lords are neither a spent force, nor more of a limitation than the Commons on the central fact of British political life—cabinet government.

The Transcendence of the Government

"The government of a nation by a large assembly of its elected representatives," says Walter Bagehot in *The English Constitution*, "is nothing less than a miracle." The government of Great Britain at least does not refute this proposition, for it is certain that Parliament does not govern Britain. Far from being transcendent and absolute, it is at most one force in a great complex of forces that press upon and limit those who do govern. And this conception of the role of Parliament applies not only to the functions discussed so far but even to its role as an "electoral college." Parliament does not exclusively determine who is to govern. The electorate, the parties, and, to a lesser extent, the chosen Prime Minister, do that, although Parliament certainly plays a crucial part in the education, testing and weeding out of prospective Ministers.

But it is the Government that is transcendent, however much it is forced to operate in a framework of pressure and control. And, in all likelihood, that is why the miracle of effective parliamentary government has come to pass in Britain. Parliament leaves ample scope for leadership and *expertise*, assigning to others the functions for which popular assemblies of popular politicians are generally unsuited: the definition of coherent national policy, the elaboration of technical detail in legislation, the superintendence of departmental administration. It provides its leaders with the means necessary to enact their policies: reliable majorities in the House of Commons and guaranteed priorities in the allocation of parliamentary time. But it does all this without becoming a mere rubber stamp imprinting legitimacy on the dictatorial actions of the Government, a mere ceremonial institution like the monarchy.

The true relationship between Government and Parliament can be seen most clearly perhaps in two crucially important activities of Government. One of these—the planning and control of parliamentary time—has already been dealt with to some extent in this chapter. The other, which has not yet been touched upon at all, is financial legislation and control of expenditure. But since both of these subjects are of particular importance in the functioning of the contemporary welfare state, they will be discussed not here but in Chapter 10, where the relationships between the policies and processes of British government are analyzed.

[7]

The Pattern of Power:
Administration

Ministers and Civil Servants

A hundred years ago it would have been perfectly possible to analyze
British government adequately with little more than a passing reference to
the bureaucracy. Today this would be like doing *Hamlet* without the
Prince of Denmark. The Civil Service has grown, in Britain as elsewhere, at
a phenomenal rate: from about 20,000 in 1832 to 100,000 at the turn of
the century to 700,000 in 1950. Needless to say, it has a far greater range of
functions to perform. And its character has changed profoundly because
of professionalization. What was once a field entirely for patronage, a safe
haven for those who had failed elsewhere or wanted an easy life, has
become, since Gladstone, in 1872, acted on the famous Northcote-
Trevelyan Report, a career service for which the Firsts of Oxford and
Cambridge grimly compete. Indeed the intellectual level of the British
civil service is unusually high even by the standards of other contemporary
civil services, because of the way in which its members are recruited. And
not only has the intellectual level risen: the service has acquired an *esprit*,
a style, a corporate consciousness and a tradition as well. All this makes
of it an effective instrument of government, one without which the administration of modern policies could hardly be imagined.

But is it not perhaps too effective: so effective as to undermine the
power of those whose instrument it is supposed to be? Undoubtedly
certain factors tending to decrease the power of private members of Parliament—the pressure and technicality of much modern business—tend also

to erode the power of their leaders and to shift power to the permanent officials in the administrative departments. To some observers it appears that the Cabinet occupies the "central" position in the pattern of power only in the sense that it is a focus for two decisive streams of pressure that tend to coalesce into policy through its mediation: political pressure from the electorate, bureaucratic pressure from the Departments. That, at any rate, is what a noted writer on British government, Sir Ivor Jennings, thinks. "The civil service *governs*; the Ministers *control* the process of government"; and he quotes approvingly Sir William Harcourt's aphorism that Ministers exist to tell the civil servants what the public will not stand.

Whether this is really so or not, and to what extent, is a point difficult to settle, because we have even less inside information about the Civil Service than we have about the Cabinet, and we have perhaps least information of all about the actual relationships between Ministers and their permanent officials. Almost nothing ever leaks out about these relationships from either side. The Minister is a wonderfully effective buffer between the Civil Service and the public: it is always he who gets the praise, and it is always he who takes the blame, even to the point of resigning for the errors of his officials. There is undoubtedly much to be said for this arrangement. Above all, by keeping politics out of the Civil Service, it helps to keep the Civil Service out of politics, and the undesirable evils of the Congressional fishing expedition are spared the British Civil Service. But it also tends to keep the British public as well as political scientists in the dark about one of the most crucial aspects of the governmental process. Nor do the memoirs of Ministers illuminate the subject very much. No Minister likes to admit being a puppet for his permanent officials; all have a stake in preserving the fiction of the constitutional myths on the subject. Hence, as K. B. Smellie[1] has said, in the biographies of statesmen the few references to their official collaborators are as complimentary but also as uninformative as tombstones.

On the civil servants' side the darkness is just as impenetrable, if not more so. They are prohibited, under the Official Secrets Acts, from publicly divulging information, on pain of criminal penalties. They write regrettably few memoirs and when they do write them they are invariably and frustratingly discreet. Lord Beveridge has said that the Civil Service works under a sort of modern version of the Benedictine monastic rule: "poverty, anonymity, and obedience"; and there can certainly be no question about the anonymity aspect of the matter, nor the poverty. Do they keep the vow of obedience as strictly as the other two?

Constitutional theory is unequivocal on the subject. Policy-making, as

---

[1] K. B. Smellie, *A Hundred Years of English Government* (1937).

we usually understand that term, is supposed to be the province of the political chiefs. The permanent official is expected to advise, suggest and warn, but beyond that he is supposed to keep his hands clean by seeing to it that whatever the Minister orders is done. This insistence upon neutrality is reflected in a number of formal rules governing official behavior. For example, civil servants are not themselves permitted to be candidates for Parliament. If they work in Departments that have administrative relationships with local governments, they are not allowed to stand for local office. Similarly, they are not allowed to speak or canvass for political candidates and are not supposed to comment on public affairs in books or articles, even on affairs not handled by their own Departments. In the 1930's, for example, an official in the Ministry of Health was dismissed for writing an article, under a pseudonym, commenting on British policy in the Italo-Ethiopian war.

It is inevitable, however, that the Civil Service should not be as submissive or self-effacing vis-à-vis the political officials as the constitutional myths require. Ministers, after all, are usually amateurs in their fields, while their permanent officials are professionals, with years of *expertise* to draw upon. Ministers tend to be men skilled in the art of swaying opinions, "expressive" minds; civil servants tend to be men skilled in the art of analyzing problems, "analytical" minds; and the two kinds of minds rarely coexist in the same person. Every Department, moreover, is a storehouse of traditions and precedents, of routines that make the whole machinery run smoothly; in every Department, therefore, there is bound to be a certain amount of intractable administrative inertia that even the most dynamic Ministers will not be able to move. Not least, of course, the Minister is heavily dependent on his permanent officials for his own advancement. That impressive mastery of detail, those subtle, well-organized arguments that mark him out as a man to watch, presuppose conscientious briefings and coaching by the anonymous eminences in his Department. Indeed, it is perhaps the most ambitious Ministers, those most eager to make a splash in Parliament, that tend most easily to become puppets in the hands of officials.

Undoubtedly, enough is known to make it certain that civil servants sometimes dominate their Ministers, even if the Minister is "strong" and the subject a matter of great importance. Ernest Bevin, for example, was anything but a weakling, but, in contravention of his party's publicly expressed policy, he entirely swallowed the Foreign Office line on Palestine, imposing on Palestine a fiercely repressive pro-Arab policy of the sort the Foreign Office had promoted ever since the Balfour Declaration of 1916. Yet, there are things to be said on the Ministers' side too. Compared, for example, with French Ministers, British Ministers have a very long life.

expectancy in office and, in consequence, far greater opportunity for acquiring *expertise*; and those who attain office are, on the whole, men of very considerable ability. Secondly, it is certain that when a party has a clear mandate, the Civil Service is generally powerless to impose its own will, at any rate without revealing that it is doing so. It would indeed be difficult to find any instances of a clear mandate that the bureaucracy has sabotaged. Similarly, if a Minister is a man with settled convictions and some force of character, he will generally have no trouble getting his way in his department, as did Arthur Henderson at the Foreign Office, Sir Kingsley Wood at the Post Office, or Lloyd George at the Ministry of Munitions in the first World War.

But more important than either the clarity of a party's mandate or the forcefulness of a Minister's personality is the simple fact that civil servants are also to a really remarkable extent constitutionally disciplined and will not sabotage policies politically decided upon or otherwise go beyond the boundaries of official propriety. Cases of administrative corruption are amazingly few in Great Britain, particularly in view of the low salaries paid and the very great opportunities for augmenting them. From this standpoint, the Civil Service has indeed a kind of monastic quality. But whatever the forces that make for its incorruptibility, they also make for its political reliability, for a certain deference to Ministers in no sense warranted by objective considerations. Sir Robert Morant, for example, did his "very best and utmost" to make the Education Bill of 1906 a workable measure, even though it reversed a great deal of the Education Bill of 1902, which he had fathered. And there was the famous case of the official in the Colonial Office who, when informed that his Minister intended to bring up the question of salaries in West Africa, replied that, as soon as he had learned whether the Minister wanted to raise them or to lower them, he would prepare, "in either event, a perfect case."

It was widely felt, however—not least by the British socialists themselves in the early days of the Labour Party—that the political neutrality of the service would break down if a socialist Government ever came to power. But many of the Ministers in the Labour Government of the 1920's have paid tribute to the co-operative attitude of their officials, and not a single one has complained. This, however, was not considered decisive evidence of the political reliability of the Service by some commentators, since MacDonald's Labour Governments were never in a sufficiently strong parliamentary position to undertake major social reforms. The real sabotage was to come when and if Labour ever won a really workable majority. It did win such a majority in 1945, it promptly embarked upon the most sweeping program of social reform in British history—and it carried the program through without a jot of visible sabotage or obstruction by the bureaucracy.

But why had the loyalty of civil servants toward a socialist Government been doubted in the first place? What interests could conceivably impel them to use their power to thwart the policies of their ministerial chiefs? To understand the reason, it is necessary above all to understand that the internal structure of the Service faithfully reflects the class structure, and, to a lesser but still important extent, the economic inequalities, in British society. This is due mainly to the fact that the recruitment system is closely geared to the educational system, which, as pointed out previously, is the chief determinant of British class differentiations. Except for certain "industrial" employees (e.g., men performing certain mechanical tasks in the Post Office), certain purely departmental officers (e.g., inspectors of various kinds), and certain professional men (doctors, lawyers, engineers), the Civil Service is divided into five "classes" (the so-called Treasury Classes), for each of which a different examining and recruiting method is used.

At the top of the pyramid is the *Administrative Class*, numbering altogether about 4,000 men and women. About 100 new members, between the ages of 20 to 24, are recruited to this class annually, chiefly by means of stiff written examinations, which test general intelligence and academic competence,[2] and the preponderant majority are graduates of the better public schools and the ancient universities, i.e., higher-class people. Those who are not higher class become higher class soon enough upon entering the Administrative Class. The members of this Class monopolize the higher grades of the Civil Service and recruits to it assume important duties not long after their brief probationary period. They are the elite of the Service. Just below them is the *Executive Class*, numbering about 60,000 members and engaged mainly in responsible but routine jobs for which "policy" is established by political officers and members of the Administrative Class. Members of the Executive Class are recruited at various levels, but most between 17½ and 18½ years, i.e., among those just completing secondary school and not going on to universities. Next comes

---

[2] Two methods of examination are, in fact, used. Method I involves two written examinations, one in subjects testing general intelligence, "culture," and information; another on academic subjects varying from Arabic to zoology, among which the candidates have free choice; in addition there is an interview by a Board selected by the Civil Service Commissioners designed to test the candidate's "personal" as distinguished from his more academic qualities. The aim is not to discover special skills so much as general ability. Method II, instituted experimentally after the War, involves an adaptation of procedures developed during the War for the selection of Army officers. It also includes written examinations, but more stress is put on the close observation of candidates over a two- or three-day period under a variety of conditions. At one time candidates were assembled for weekends at a country estate for the purpose but at present the Civil Service Selection Board conducts its observations in London.

the *Clerical Class*, composed of people who do most of the actual routine work of the Departments (correspondence, record-keeping, etc.), and recruited mainly between the ages of 16½ and 17½. Finally, there are two very low classes, specially reserved, in characteristic British disdain for the weaker sex, to women: *Clerical Assistance*, recruited between the ages of 15 and 16 and requiring only an elementary education, and the *Typist Class*, which speaks for itself.

It should be noted that each of these classes is practically a self-contained unit, in the sense that there is little mobility between the classes. There is more mobility today than there was twenty years ago; but in the normal case, once one is, say, in the Clerical Class one is in the Clerical Class for life, with little chance for crashing through to the Executive Class and certainly none whatever of getting into the Administrative Class.

With few exceptions, therefore, the higher rungs in the Civil Service are the private preserve of the able sons of the upper classes, although a gradual increase in members of lower-class origin has been taking place. A recently published study of members of the administrative class above the rank of assistant secretary showed that in 1929 only 7 per cent were children of manual workers or domestic servants; while in 1939 and 1950 the percentages were 10 and 17—an increase, but not a sizable one when it is considered that these categories account for the large majority of the whole population. Only 5 per cent in Britain live off private means or belong to the main professions or are owners and managers of important businesses, but 32 per cent of the higher Civil Service are sons of such people. Twenty-eight per cent of adult males are in unskilled or partly skilled occupations; but only 3 per cent of the higher Civil Service come from such backgrounds. And these 3 per cent are not "lower-class." By their achievements in the Service, and no doubt also by their educational backgrounds, they are absorbed into the upper classes.

It was widely believed that people so linked with the upper classes would not take kindly to a powerful socialist Government. In fact, whether they did or not, they carried out the tremendously ambitious reforms of the Labour Government of 1945 without a murmur. This may not be absolutely conclusive, but it certainly suggests that Sir Warren Fisher's classic formulation of the role of the Civil Service is substantially correct:

Determination of policy is the function of ministers, and once a policy is determined it is the unquestioned and unquestionable business of the civil servant to strive to carry out that policy with precisely the same good will whether he agrees with it or not. That is axiomatic and will never be in dispute. At the same time it is the traditional duty of civil servants, while decisions are being formulated, to make available to their chiefs all the information and experience at their disposal and to do this without fear or favor, irrespective of whether the advice thus tendered may accord or not with the Minister's initial view.[3]

In the final analysis, British Ministers and officials have something vitally important in common that may account for the easy surmountability of the differences between them better than anything else: a shared agreement on the forms and procedures of government—a constitutional consensus that seems to be quite independent of class position and political interest. Indeed, nothing perhaps illustrates more clearly the significance of British constitutional morality than the wide difference between the latent powers and actual role of the Civil Service under *any* Government.

TABLE 6   Social Composition of the British Higher Civil Service* 1950
(*in percent*)

FATHER'S OCCUPATION		EDUCATION	
Professionals, Owner-Managers	70	Public Schools	48
Clerks and Workers	27	Clarendon Schools	11
No Gainful Occupation	3	Secondary Schools	43
(independent means)		University	63
		Oxbridge	47

* Assistant Secretaries and above.

The Departments

Ministers and civil servants come face to face in the administrative Departments. It is here that the foreigner would find himself most at home, since the British administrative Departments are not greatly different from those of other countries, a fact which happily makes it unnecessary to embark on lengthy and tedious recitals of technical administrative detail here. But even the Departments have a few peculiarly British characteristics.

One feaure which sharply distinguishes the British from American Departments, for example, is the extent to which the higher administrative positions in the former are filled by career officials—civil servants. Except for the Ministers themselves and two or three Junior Ministers in each Department, no political appointments to executive positions are made. Even the Junior Ministers are in a rather different position from, say, the politically appointed American Under–Secretary. They cannot, for example, overrule, on their own initiative, decisions or suggestions made by the career officials in the Department; only the Minister himself can do that. They are there merely to help the Minister and to learn the departmental ropes, but they are in a sense outside the real departmental hierarchy. This runs from the Minister directly to the Permanent Secre-

[3] Evidence before the *Royal Commission on the Civil Service, 1929-1931.*

tary (who is the highest of the career officials, the general manager of the Department and the chief adviser to the Minister on both matters of policy and administration) and from the Permanent Secretary to one or two deputy secretaries, a small number of assistant secretaries, and, below these, the principals and assistant principals of the Department, the lowliest members of the Administrative Class.

The fact that career officials have all the higher departmental positions makes the smooth change to a powerful socialist Government all the more remarkable, of course. When there is a change of administration in the United States problems of administrative loyalty simply do not arise, at any rate on the higher levels, since the new administration is in a position to replace the higher officials with its own politically reliable appointees. It is still assumed in America that not only the heads of the Departments but also their higher assistants ought to be in political tune with the President. Not so in Great Britain. A change in Government involves changing only about a hundred officials, some seventy of whom are little more than water boys for the Ministers.

Another aspect of the departmental system an American would find rather curious is the very large number of Departments—about thirty altogether. Perhaps nothing conveys more vividly how very much the functions and powers of Government (if not the constitutional myths and processes) have changed in the last two centuries. In the middle of the eighteenth century, the departmental structure was very simple and concerned with little but "basic" governmental activities. There was a Treasury (the most ancient of all the Departments, because the first to be separated from the Royal Household), concerned, of course, with financial administration; a Secretary of State, dealing with domestic and overseas matters in general; an Admiralty; and the offices of the Lord Chancellor, the Lord President, the Lord Privy Seal and the Chancellor of the Duchy of Lancaster, then rather less purely ceremonial in function than they are today. The whole structure was concerned with collecting and expending revenues, keeping the domestic peace, carrying on war and diplomacy, and little else. Almost the whole of the complex modern departmental structure has grown, by a series of convulsive cellular splits, from this exceedingly primitive structure. The Secretary of State, for example, has become a very large number of Secretaries of State, all in charge of their own Departments, but all considered constitutionally a single entity, since they all derive from a single entity. In 1782, foreign and domestic affairs were separated for the first time, by the creation of special Secretaries of State (the Foreign Secretary and Home Secretary); in 1794 they were joined by a Secretary of State for War; in 1854, by a Secretary of State for the Colonies. And there matters rested until the twentieth century, when a rash of new Secretaries of State broke out: one for Commonwealth Relations, another for Scotland, and, in the last Churchill Government, one for the Co-ordination of Transport, Fuel and Power.

A similarly large number of Departments has grown out of the Privy Council: the Board of Trade, the Ministry of Education (via the Board of Education), and the Ministry of Agriculture and Fisheries (via the Veterinary Department under the Privy Council). These offspring of the Council have, in turn, sired further Departments: for example, the Ministries of Labour, Transport, Food, and Fuel and Power, all of which issued from the loins of the Board of Trade in the present century. Still other Departments grew out of the authorities supervising the poor relief, sanitation and health activities of local authorities in the nineteenth century, e.g., the Ministries of Health and Housing. Significantly, only a few of the most modern Departments were directly created by legislation.[4] The rest can, in characteristic British fashion, trace their ancestry back to the days of the Plantagenets.

The multiplication of Departments has caused a great deal of anxiety, since it has brought a host of administrative problems into being, particularly problems of co-ordinating the necessarily related activities of the various Departments, so as to prevent duplication and inconsistency. The famous Machinery of Government Committee (the Haldane Committee), which sat after the first World War, recommended, for example, a sweeping reorganization of Departments into a small number of divisions —for finance, national defense, foreign affairs, research and information, production, employment, supplies, education, health, and justice—rather on the American model. This has not been done, and the chief reason is to be found in another aspect of British departmental administration that is far more peculiarly British than those mentioned so far: the tendency of British administrators to set up co-ordinating committees, large and small, formal and informal, solemn and frivolous. It has been said that when two or three Englishmen get together they form a club; it might also be said that when two or three English officials get together, they form a committee. "We are," said Sir Winston Churchill, "overrun by them, like the Australians were by rabbits." But the mania for committees at least saves the British from the need to create formally streamlined, rigidly co-ordinated administrative machinery. Even if such machinery were created it is doubtful that it would replace the present wealth of committees, since service on committees is part of the everyday experience and training of almost every Englishman, and thus built into his social and political reflexes, so to speak.

---

[4] E.g., the Ministries of Pensions, Defence, Supply, Works, and Civil Aviation.

More will be said about the methods used to co-ordinate administrative activities in Chapter 10 but we should mention here a Department that itself bears much of the responsibility for co-ordination, and, in addition, is by far the most important of all the administrative Departments. This is the Treasury. Its unquestioned pre-eminence among the administrative Departments is due to a number of factors. There is, in the first instance, its position as the most ancient of the Departments, a rather intangible factor that, in a country like Great Britain, has very tangible effects. Like Parliament itself, the Treasury is in possession of ancient ceremonies and ritual, solemn forms that no upstart Department can match. Equally significant, the Treasury is invested with importance by public attitudes, i.e., by the fact that it is *believed* to be the greatest of the Departments. It gets prestige from the fact that its head, the Chancellor of the Exchequer, is a prominent politician and, often, the next in line to the Prime Minister; that he holds forth in Number 11, Downing Street, next to the Prime Minister's residence; and that the Prime Minister himself dignifies the Treasury by taking the title of First Lord of the Treasury. But by far the most important reason for its pre-eminence is that it discharges a number of functions that affect the work of all the other Departments and thus exercises a great amount of control over them and the power to co-ordinate their activities.

Treasury control, like Cabinet government itself, is one of the vital facts of the British Constitution. It involves, above all, the following activities: financial control, economic planning, supervision of the Civil Service, and supervision of the internal organization and methods of the Departments. Financial control is exercised in three ways: by control over the departmental Estimates (i.e., requests for annual appropriations); by the power of *virement*, i.e., the power to authorize Departments to shift funds from one expenditure subhead in the appropriation to another; and by the power of prior approval, based on the rule that all departmental innovations involving finance must be cleared with the Treasury before being undertaken, or discussed with it before being taken higher up to the Cabinet level. More will be said about these means of control when we discuss the administrative problems raised by the modern welfare state in Chapter 10, which is also the appropriate place for discussing the Treasury's planning activities. But it should be evident, even from this bare enumeration of financial functions, that the Departments can take almost no actions having financial implications, save routine actions, without the intervention of the Treasury.

The Treasury's control over the Civil Service gives it equally pervasive powers. Actually, there is no law giving it power to control the civil servants in other Departments; but for a number of reasons it has acquired the power, and it exercises it today almost without question. Because it is desired to have a unified national Civil Service rather than a number of different departmental services, central supervision of the Service has to be vested in a single body and this power has irresistibly gravitated into Treasury hands: partly because of the Treasury's power of the purse, party because it is the Prime Minister's own Department, partly because its special co-ordinating and controlling functions have long been recognized. One of the two Permanent Secretaries of the Treasury is therefore known as the Head of the Home Civil Service, and its Establishment Division trains the assistant principals on entry into the Service, and, in general, supervises the other Departments' personnel administration by the distribution of circulars on the subject. Strictly speaking, these circulars do not require compliance; theoretically each Department may run its own personnel affairs and has an Establishment Division for the purpose. But this freedom is much more formal than real, because of usage and, perhaps more important, the Treasury's power to punish financially any failure to comply. Finally, in view of these pervasive powers over finance and personnel, it was althogether natural that, when it was decided to create a special agency to keep an eye on the Departments' internal organization, and their methods of administration—in short, to create a sort of board of efficiency experts for the Departments in general—it was decided to lodge this function in the Treasury too. It is now performed by its Organization and Methods Division.

Thus, the Treasury supplements the broad co-ordinating functions of the Cabinet itself. There can be no doubt that, next to the Cabinet, it is the principal center of power in British government, so important in fact that it has been argued that the Treasury is no less than a "balance" against the ministerial structure as a whole, almost a kind of permanent Third Chamber, rather than a mere cog in the administrative machine. However this may be, the Treasury is clearly so important that the efficiency of the general administrative structure, and especially, the degree of its suitability to modern purposes of administration, depend, above all, on the Treasury's own organization and methods.

[8]

The Pattern of Interests:
Parties and Pressure Groups

The British governmental process presupposes a tightly disciplined two-party system.[1] In Chapter 4 several reasons, centering on certain features of British political culture, were invoked as explanations of this system. This is not by any means the only line of analysis taken by writers on the subject. In contrast some writers have stressed the homogeneity of the British people and—a related point—the absence of pressure groups from British political life. Others have given much weight to legal structure, especially the electoral system and the power of dissolution. The tight internal organization of the parties themselves has also been considered as a reason for their discipline and strong leadership. None of these approaches gets at the underlying factors, but all touch on such important matters that they are worth discussing at some length.

---

[1] The Labour and Conservative Parties are not the only parties, of course. The Liberal Party is still a live force in the country, however much a spent force in Parliament. In both 1945 and 1950 it polled about 9 per cent of the vote although it ran candidates in only some of the constituencies (304 candidates in 1945, 475 in 1950, and only 109 in 1951 when its popular vote shrank to 2.6 per cent). The Communists, while never amounting to much, have elected M.P.'s (one in 1922, 1924 and 1935 and two in 1945) and other parties successful in parliamentary elections have been the Independent Labour Party (which broke with the Labour Party itself in 1932 and has most of its support in Scotland), the Commonwealth Party and the Scottish Nationalists. Independents have also sat in Parliament from time to time. But the size of the vote polled by minority parties and independents has been so small—save for a transitional period when the place of the Liberal Party was being taken by Labour—and their representation in Parliament so very inconsiderable, that we may properly call the British party system a two-party system. It comes as close to it, in form and actual party behavior, as any party system ever has. It remains to be seen whether the present (1962) Liberal revival necessitates an alteration of this judgment.

Pressure Groups

That the British party system is a reflection of the homogeneity of the British people is not true simply because the British people are not particularly homogeneous. Anyone who asserts they are does not know them. Ethnically they are no more alike than the people of most countries, and a good deal less than many. From the standpoint of speech, manners, and consumption patterns, they are far less alike than the people of the United States; just compare the voices of the Cockney and the inhabitant of Mayfair, a short bus ride away. Religion?—there are very great differences indeed. If there is any homogeneity in Britain it is to be found in the dominance of urban life, and this has little more than statistical significance. The truth, one suspects, lies somewhere between Disraeli, who thought Britain was two nations, and Dennis Brogan, who thinks the number is closer to 44,000,000. The kindest view to take perhaps is that writers who emphasize British homogeneity confuse homogeneity with agreement, or suppose that any coherent culture is necessarily "homogeneous." France, with a far more chaotic party system, is not manifestly less homogeneous, and neither is the United States. We can dismiss this argument out of hand.

A related and more serious point concerns the role of interest groups in British politics. It is sometimes suggested that the pattern of interests in British society is far more simple than that of the United States or Continental countries and that accordingly pressure groups—organizations advocating these interests in the political arena—are of negligible importance. Where pressure groups do thrive—as in the United States—they prevent the tight integration of opinion and leadership in large political parties. On rare occasions, such as presidential elections, the various groups in each party pull together, but this unity is ephemeral and effective for very limited purposes. Britain in contrast—the argument concludes—can have two large integrated parties because interest groups are relatively few and pressure groups do not divide political opinion into a myriad of jostling factions.

Undoubtedly the pattern of power among political parties is conditioned by the pattern of interests in the society. But in Britain, as in any modern industrial society, the pattern of interests is complex and diverse and in the British political system pressure groups are correspondingly numerous and active. True, political science has discovered the existence of British pressure politics only recently, but this has not been due to their insignificance. In the words of one of the discoverers, they are at once "numerous, massive, well-organized and highly effective"—indeed perhaps more massive, organized and effective than the pressure groups of the United States.

That it took so long to stumble upon them may be blamed on the adhesiveness of old political theories and also on the fact that British pressure groups work through channels far more inconspicuous and difficult to detect than those used by American pressure groups. The distinctive traits of interest group politics in Britain may be examined in terms of the patterns of power, policy and political culture. More specifically we need to look at certain aspects of governmental structure, of government activities and programs, and of political attitudes in the British system to understand how British pressure groups operate and why they operate differently from those in other countries, especially the United States.

It is a general rule that where there is power, pressure will be applied. The distribution of power in the American system practically compels interest groups to concentrate a very great deal of their activity on Congress, which, for many reasons—the separation of powers, lack of party discipline, the role of its committees, its powers over the budget, etc.—is a highly useful instrument for interest-group purposes. Power in Britain is concentrated in the parliamentary leaders. It follows that pressure groups, to promote their interests, must influence the leaders, and this they can do effectively only by putting pressure on them directly or by acting through agencies that can, above all the parties and civil servants. Parliament, of course, also has some influence with its leaders, hence it is not entirely useless for British pressure groups to try to influence M.P.s. But compared to the pressures exerted through parties and civil servants their parliamentary activities are secondary.

The need to focus pressure on the bureaucrats is reinforced by the activities of British government. First, the vast scope and technical character of decision-making required by welfare-state policies has led to the devolution of more and more decision-making authority to the bureaucracy, so that there is in Britain a vast amount of executive legislation. Equally important, the decision-making powers delegated to the Departments are likely to be of special concern to interest groups. General policy, of course, is still predominantly made by the Government, but technical details, especially the sort needing fairly frequent revisions (e.g., how much money is to be paid to doctors in the British Health Service; what prices to guarantee to the farmers; on what basis to grant or withhold licenses to build, import, issue securities or acquire raw materials), are taken care of by the Departments—and such details are likely to be of as great concern to interest groups as policy in its broad sense.

Finally, the tendency to focus pressure on administration is reinforced by British attitudes toward politics. In this connection we must first realize that the British, compared to Americans at any rate, tend to be rather unsuspicious of group politics. Their political tradition is far less individualistic than the American and the intervention of "corporations" between the individual will and public policy is considered nothing reprehensible. Indeed the medieval corporatistic conception of society may still be said to have a stronger hold on British attitudes than more modern individualistic notions, however much British philosophers may have developed individualistic political theories influential in other countries. The importance of these attitudes is that they encourage institutionalized contacts between "lobbyists" and decision-makers and tend to remove inhibitions on the part of civil servants against regular relations with interest-group representatives. Hence there is very close and continuous collaboration between pressure groups and civil servants: so close that in some instances groups affected by departmental activities have been almost directly assimilated into the Departments without anyone seeming to think this remarkable. And the tendency of pressure groups to focus their activities on the Departments is reinforced by a second factor: the consensus on broad policies in Britain today. Parliament is mainly concerned with such broad policies. The filling out of framework legislation, however, is the work almost exclusively of the executive. This means that disagreements and conflicts of interest are often more acute in the sphere of executive decisions than in that of parliamentary decisions. Again the effect is to shift the focus of politics from Westminster to Whitehall.

It is therefore on the departmental level, where everything is less "visible," less exposed to public scrutiny, than on the parliamentary level, that the bulk of British pressure-group politics takes place. Interest groups do not make nearly so much use of Parliament as they did in the eighteenth and nineteenth centuries when it was a much more important place. But Parliament, as we have seen, is not yet totally in eclipse and the fact that interest groups still find it worthwhile to exert some pressure on it is itself evidence of this. Many British associations, for example, make use of Parliamentary Agents: law firms specializing in parliamentary business and hired by interest groups to scrutinize bills and Regulations, to draft bills and amendments for submission to Ministers and private members, and, in general, to keep an eye out for the group in the House. The National Farmers Union, the National Federation of Property Owners, and the Institute of British Launderers, among many others, are known to have such Agents under permanent retainer. They are, it should be noted, perhaps the closest thing to our professional lobbyists the British have.

Again, Parliament is full of people who are themselves members of interest groups and act as their spokesmen in Parliament: "interested M.P.s," as they are generally called. There are large numbers of honorary officers or former officers of interest organizations on both sides of the

House and they may represent their associations as much as their constituencies. Indeed, it has been argued that there are more "lobbyists" in America than in Britain simply because pressure groups are far less comprehensively represented right in Congress than in Parliament, and statistically speaking this seems sensible enough, the majority of Senators and Congressmen being lawyers, i.e., representative of only a single interest group. Finally, and most curiously from an American standpoint, many members of Parliament are paid a regular salary and/or their election expenses to represent the views of certain groups in Parliament. It is difficult to say just how many of these "retained M.P.s" there are, but over a hundred receive payments from trade unions alone and we know that many other organizations (e.g., the National Union of Teachers and the National Association of Local Government Officers) hire parliamentary spokesmen.

There is absolutely no secrecy or subterfuge about all this. It is all widely known and nowhere deplored, simply because the British are not afflicted with our extreme individualist biases. Indeed, only two formal rules restrict the interest-group representative in Parliament. Any M.P. having a personal financial interest in any subject before Parliament is expected to declare his interest before taking part in the debate, although this does not apply to an M.P. who is "merely" retained by an interest group; he must have a direct personal pecuniary interest, e.g., be an importer arguing in favor of the lifting of import controls and not merely in the pay of an importers organization. Secondly, no threats may be used, no bribes offered (retainers are not bribes), no money payments or "social privileges" (e.g., membership in a club) withheld or withdrawn to induce a member to take a specific stand on a specific issue. That is a "breach of privilege" and punishable by the House sitting as a High Court. The M.P. after all is a member of Parliament before he is a representative of anything, constituency or interest group.

But what precisely can all these people do to make it worthwhile to hire them in the first place? They can of course raise questions. They can put down motions for debate and see to it that their associations' views are stated when Parliament performs its lyrical function. They can move amendments or try to influence ministerial decisions by personal interviews or by representations before the special committees of the parliamentary parties. These are not altogether useless powers. But the fact remains that as parliamentary powers have been shifted more and more to the parties and departments of state, so also, logically enough, have the activities of the interest groups.

The Labour Party is in large degree an association of pressure groups. While the structure of the Conservative Party is not formally corporate in character, it is nevertheless true that most business organizations—from small trade associations to large organizations like the Federation of British Industries, the National Union of Manufacturers, the Economic League and Aims of Industry—are aligned, although not openly affiliated, with the party. There is, for example, a great deal of overlapping of membership between the committees of the Conservative and Unionists Associations and the committees of trade associations. And we know that on a number of occasions Conservative policy has been made by negotiations between the Tory political leaders on one hand and employers' organizations on the other. The exertion of group pressure through the parties, however, has important drawbacks that keep the parties from totally absorbing and transmitting such pressures. Since parties exist chiefly to win elections, only groups having large numbers of members or great economic power are likely to be consistently influential in party councils. For the same reason, no party can afford to become too narrowly identified with any limited set of interests. After all elections are won by winning over the floating voters. It is also unwise for interest groups to become too openly affiliated with any one party, if only because that party is not likely to be constantly in power and therefore in a position to promote the group's interests. And not least, parties rarely make more than very general policies, i.e., the sort of policies on which there is substantial agreement in all sections of society. From every standpoint, then, we are driven toward administration as the chief area of interest-group activity.

Contacts between administrative officials and interest-group representatives are almost too numerous and variable to describe, but for the sake of simplicity they may be divided into four categories. First, there are formal interest-group deputations and negotiating committees either sent out by the pressure groups themselves or invited to enter into consultation by the government Departments. For example, when the National Health Service was being drafted between 1945 and 1946 constant meetings took place between the Minister of Health, his officials, and a formally constituted British Medical Association Negotiating Committee. Again, annual agricultural production plans and prices are worked out by negotiations between the Minister and representatives of the National Farmers Union. Secondly, there is a great deal of informal contact between the officers of private associations and their opposite numbers in the bureaucracy —contact by telephone, via social gatherings, luncheon, teas, in the pub and at Lords (the Yankee Stadium of cricket), perhaps even in the tube on the way to the suburbs. One cannot describe the whole variety of such contacts, but no doubt almost all minor and routine problems are handled in such informal ways. Third, private associations are directly represented on government committees. The Federation of British Industries, for example, has representatives on some seventy government committees, the Trades Union Council on sixty. The National Union of Manufacturers in 1950 was represented on, among *many* other committees, the Dollar Exports Council, the Dollar Exports Advisory Executive, the Anglo-Canadian Trade Committee, the Consultative Committee for Industry, the Trade Negotiations Committee, and the Customs and Excise Committee. Finally, pressure groups are used directly in the administrative process, not only to help the Departments formulate policy but even to help them carry it out when it has been made. Thus, the Ministry of Food (which was in existence during the war and much of the postwar period, but is now defunct) operated almost entirely through various Food Distributors' Associations, to the point that the Ministry's policies were actually carried out by the trade associations to which they applied. Similarly, the Ministry of Supply for a long time controlled the iron and steel industry through the Iron and Steel Federation, a private trade association.

That private pressure groups should not only have ready access to the bureaucracy but even help it administer and formulate government policy in a formal way would be objectionable in a society in which more individualistic ideas prevailed, but the British not only take this sort of thing for granted; they positively encourage it. Indeed, the very fact that the British consider "corporatistic" politics so normal may account for the fact that their political scientists for so long ignored British pressure groups. There just was nothing unusual to take note of. However this may be it is clear that we cannot explain the British party system in a simple way by merely conveniently denying the existence of British interest groups.

The Electoral System

That Britain has a two-party system is frequently attributed to the British electoral system, specifically the fact that the British have a simple-plurality, single-vote, single-member, constituency system. This means: (a) that Britain is divided into a number of constituencies of roughly equal size; (b) that each constituency elects a single member of Parliament; (c) that the candidate polling the highest vote in any constituency is elected for that constituency regardless of the size of his vote; (d) that voters may vote for only one candidate, and are denied what is technically known as the "alternative vote."[2] Such a system, so the argument goes, inhibits the development of small parties because if a party is not large enough to

---

[2] I.e., a vote for a second, third, etc., choice. In some electoral systems, if all candidates fail to get an absolute majority, second choices are added to the original totals, and so on until some candidate does poll an absolute majority. The aim is to prevent the election of representatives who are strongly opposed by most of their constituents.

win pluralities in a sizable number of constituencies it cannot gain a large parliamentary representation. Hence, since it would be wasting its time trying to work through Parliament, it is more likely to attempt influencing the public by other means, including working through one of the major parties. What discourages the activists in minor political groups also discourages their passive supporters. To vote for a minor party is generally tantamount to "wasting one's vote"; hence minor political groups can rarely count on receiving electoral support equal to the amount of sympathy they command in the country. Finally, small political groups in Britain take a financial risk in contesting elections: the Representation of the People Act (1918) provides that every candidate must deposit £150 at the time of nomination, the deposit being forfeited to the Treasury if he fails to obtain one-eighth of the total vote.

It is true, of course, that these considerations do not prevent the British party system from changing: note the decline of the Liberal Party and the rise of Labour in this century. But the decline of the Liberals in a sense confirms more than refutes the argument, since it indicates that the electoral system tends to preserve the two-party system in form even while its "content" is changing. It does this in two ways. First, the Labour Party managed to establish itself, even as a minor force, only by its affiliation and co-operation with the Liberal Party in its early years. "Lib-Lab" collaboration early in the twentieth century meant co-operation by Labour and Liberal ministers not only in Parliament but also in the elections, i.e., undertakings by one or the other party not to contest certain seats in order to prevent three-cornered contests from splitting the vote in favor of the Conservatives. Thus, in the early years of the century, Britain had what amounted to a two-party system, despite the existence of three parties, the moral being that only groups that can adjust themselves to the two-party system can hope to establish themselves as important political forces. And once Labour, having established itself, cut the umbilical cord to the Liberal Party, the parliamentary decline of the latter was swift and comprehensive, as the table below indicates. It is usually argued that this swift disintegration of a party that in 1906 had won one of the greatest majorities in British history is incomprehensible if one does not take into account the intolerances of the electoral system for more than two important parties. Once Labour had become a significant electoral force it was increasingly difficult for the Liberals to win pluralities, hence parliamentary representation in any fair proportion to their popular support. And once this had happened, the electorate increasingly shifted away from the Liberals, even in cases where Liberal sympathies had not been lost.

Yet electoral systems like the British have not always produced party systems like the British; indeed, in some cases (for example, pre-fascist

TABLE 7   Results of British General Elections

	CONSERVATIVES		LABOUR		LIBERALS	
YEAR	SEATS	PER CENT OF VOTE	SEATS	PER CENT OF VOTE	SEATS	PER CENT OF VOTE
1922	346	38	142	29.5	115	29
1923	258	38	191	30.5	159	30
1924	419	48	151	33	40	18
1929	260	38	288	37	59	23
1935	431	54	154	31	21	7
1945	212	40	394	48	12	9
1950	298	43.5	315	46	9	9
1951	321	48	295	49	6	3
1955	345	50	277	46	6	3
1959	365	49.4	258	44	6	6

Italy) such systems have produced almost diametrically opposite results: very complex multi-party systems. This surely means, at least, that the single-member constituency system alone is not sufficient explanation for the British two-party system. Nor is it reasonable to expect that it should be sufficient. After all, if it is advantageous under the single-member constituency system to form large parties capable of insuring pluralities in large numbers of constituencies, it is similarly desirable to form large parties under other electoral systems for other purposes, above all the ultimate purpose of winning power. The larger, more inclusive and cohesive a party is, the greater its chance of success in *any* context and under any electoral system. Hence, it seems reasonable to infer that if a country has a very large number of small parties, its party system must be the result of considerations which override mere electoral calculations. But electoral systems clearly can influence party structure and behavior only via electoral calculations. In Great Britain such calculations are exceedingly important, but that is because of the broad range of political agreement in British society and the moderate, pragmatic attitudes of British politicians. It is this that makes it possible for voters to shift from one party to another just for the sake of casting a useful ballot, and for politicians to compromise with one another for the mere purpose of jointly achieving power. Thus, the British electoral system tends to compress British parties into the two-party mold because it functions under the specific conditions outlined in the first chapter. Explaining the British two-party system by means of the electoral system does not, therefore, refute the argument in Chapter 4; it presupposes it.

The Power of Dissolution

The fact that British Governments enjoy an unlimited power to dissolve Parliament is frequently invoked to account for the extreme docility of M.P.s vis-à-vis their leaders. Here again it is easy to see the sense in the argument. When the supporters of a Government desert their leaders they may face a dissolution and new elections in which the recalcitrant M.P.s may lose their seats. Or, even if this does not happen, the other side may win a majority in Parliament. And in any case, elections cost money and consume time, in short, are nuisances better avoided. Hence, if there is a disagreement between leaders and supporters on one hand and, on the other, a three-line whip demanding compliance with the leaders,[3] British M.P.s usually swallow their convictions and comply.

But this argument too is refuted by brute fact. The power of dissolving Parliament has existed in many countries—France, Germany, Italy—without leading to any pronounced docility on the part of M.P.s, and it is not difficult to find reasons why, under certain conditions, dissolution provisions should be useless as disciplinary devices. First, the power to dissolve Parliament can be used by leaders to exact compliance only if in fact they are willing to use it; but what guarantee is there of that? In the French Third Republic they were not willing to use it, because of the widespread association, after 1877, of the power of dissolution with authoritarianism.[4] An even more instructive case is postwar Italy. Here an unlimited power of dissolution exists, there are no popular prejudices to inhibit using it, and on several occasions since 1950 Governments have fallen that might legitimately have appealed their case to the electorate. But not a single dissolution has occurred, chiefly because of justified fears that elections might lead to gains for the extremist parties—Communists, Monarchists and neo-Fascists—and the belief that surrendering power to a new set of moderate leaders was preferable to taking a chance on that.

Conversely, the power of dissolution can have a disciplinary effect only if members of Parliament are in fact generally unwilling to incur the risks and discomforts of new elections. But again, they may not be. Where politicians tend to be very dogmatic it may simply be impossible for them to compromise their *Weltanschauungen* for electoral convenience. Where they represent constituents whose predominant interests run counter to the proposals of the leaders (and where the relationship between representative and constituents is very close) it may be far more risky for the representative to defy his constituents than to defy his party leaders. In

---

[3] Individual M.P.s are notified weekly, in writing, about impending parliamentary business by the party Whips. Under each day's business it is standard operating procedure to state: "Your attendance is [particularly] requested." When this is underlined once, it means, "Come if you like but don't put yourself out by any means"; underlined twice it means, "Stay away if necessary but it really would be much better if you were present"; underlined thrice, it means, "You had better have a first-rate excuse for being absent, or else it is highly likely that we will do something terrible to your political career." What this "something terrible" is will be clearer below.
[4] See below, p. 287.

Britain, Governments are ready to dissolve Parliament when they are defeated and M.P.s highly reluctant to have dissolutions occur; but to understand why this is so—why, in short, the power of dissolution in Britain *does* produce party discipline—we must know more than that the power exists.

Apart from the fact that the power of dissolution is recognized as a legitimate prerogative of leadership, the willingness to use it on the part of British Governments is due to the fact that they are not excessively reluctant to risk having their opponents come to power. And this attitude, in turn, reflects the fact that their own outlook is highly pragmatic and that of their opponents sufficiently like their own. Again, we are driven back to consensus and moderation in politics as the decisive factors. As for the general unwillingness of M.P.s to risk elections, a slightly more complicated explanation is required. The decisive fact probably is that ties between representatives and constituents are extraordinarily loose in Britain. Very few, if any, M.P.s owe their position primarily to their close relationships with their constituents and the M.P.'s function, in popular attitudes, is not so much to represent a district as to help constitute a majority. This implies that his relationships to his party are more important than his relations with the constituency, and party organizations are massive and national, not provincial, in character. For these reasons, among others, the British vote for the party label rather than individual candidates, so that to be deprived of the party label (i.e., to refuse to stand as a regular Labourite or Conservative, or to be refused permission to do so) usually means to be doomed, politically speaking.

The postwar Labour Government offers two instructive examples. In 1948, 37 Labour M.P.s, including a gentleman named Platts-Mills, sent a telegram of good wishes to the Italian pro-Communist Socialist Nenni. When called upon by the Labour leadership to withdraw the telegram all but Platts-Mills complied; whereupon Platts-Mills was deprived of the right to stand as a regular Labour candidate at the next General Election and dropped by his local Constituency Party (Shoreditch and Finsbury, a very leftist district). At the next election he polled only 18 per cent of the vote as against the official Labour candidate's 53 per cent. Not long after, another Labour M.P., Konni Zilliacus, was deprived of the party label by the leaders. Unlike Platts-Mills, however, Zilliacus was retained as a candidate by his local Labour Party; but despite this, when the national party sent in a national candidate to contest the election, Zilliacus polled only 15 per cent of the vote, against an official Labour vote of 45 per cent.

The power of dissolution, therefore, works as it does in Great Britain because of the overwhelming importance of the official party label to the voters. But why is the label so important? It is not enough to say: "Because in parliamentary systems one is really choosing a Government when choosing a representative," for the simple reason that the party label is not nearly so important in other parliamentary systems. It is important in Britain, first, because ideologies are not, and second, because of the very existence of a highly disciplined two-party system, which makes voting for independents tantamount to wasting one's vote. But that leaves us enmeshed in a hopelessly circular argument and takes us back again to the point from which we started.

One possibility remains: that party discipline, if not the two-party system, is the result of certain aspects of British party organization itself. This argument we cannot dismiss quite so briefly as the others. We must first examine in detail the organization of the major parties and the distribution of power within them.

Party Organization

The organization of the political parties represents the truly new in British government, superimposed upon the old because of the constant extension and reform of the franchise since the Reform Act of 1832. Mass democracy (or should one simply say mass suffrage?) has produced mass parties profoundly different from the intimate, informal factions of pre-reform days. One can discern four phases in their development. The first comes after the Reform Act of 1832 itself. At this stage British electoral organization was still extremely primitive by modern standards, largely because the Reform Act itself was not a very revolutionary innovation. Before 1832 almost no party organization existed outside Parliament, local electoral affairs being managed by local "notables" while national parties were in fact merely ephemeral factions of individual and independent M.P.s. The Reform Act changed this in two respects. To make sure that voters entered their names on the electoral registers local registration associations were formed, still chiefly under the control of local notables—and never for the purpose of nominating candidates. At the same time, embryonic national political organization emerged in two political clubs (the Carlton Club, founded by the Conservatives, and the Reform Club, founded by the Liberals, both in the 1830's), both composed of M.P.s, candidates for seats, and provincial notables, and acting as primitive co-ordinating bodies for the local associations and liaison committees between local and parliamentary politicians. The second stage in party development consists of the union of the local registration societies in formal national organizations, the Liberal Registration Association (founded in 1861) and the National Union of Conservative and Constitutional Associations (1867); this, of course, was the crucial step in the transition from informal local to formal national electoral organization.

Stage three then elaborated what stage two merely foreshadowed. The local associations became fully open to membership and "representative" in form; the national associations acquired stable organization (national councils and executive committees, with formally determined membership, meetings and functions); and a party bureaucracy (professional election officials) made its appearance. But even at this stage, following the Reform Act of 1867, the party system as we know it was not yet fully developed, chiefly because the parties in Parliament still vastly overshadowed the party machinery outside. In fact, both the National Liberal Federation (founded in 1877) and the Conservative National Union were used chiefly as vehicles for arousing popular enthusiasm and endorsing the policies of the parliamentary leaders. Thus, at this stage of their development the national electoral associations had a democratic structure but not yet a democratic policy-making process. Stage four then consists of the gradual emergence of a more democratic kind of decision-making in the national party organizations, a gradual shift of some power from the notables in Parliament to the representative and bureaucratic party organizations outside of Parliament.

But it is vastly important to note that this process has not gone so far as to make the parliamentary politicians mere puppets of the party organizations. The parliamentary leaders still tend to dominate the party machines, however much the development of the organized mass parties has cut into their former independence. And they dominate the machine not because they are "bosses" in the American sense but just because they *are* parliamentary notables. This indicates that even the present party system, however much the product of democratization, has its roots firmly in the pre-democratic past. And this is true not only of the Conservative Party, which has a very long history, but even of the Labour Party, which came into being just at the turn of the century. Appropriately enough, the dominance of the parliamentarians over party conventions and officials is greater in the former than the latter, but the similarities between them are perhaps even more important than the differences.

MEMBERSHIP ORGANIZATION

All the members of the Conservative Party belong to the party as individuals rather than as members of other organizations. The Labour Party also has individual members, but most of its membership—over five out of six million—consists of members affiliated with the party as groups, making the Labour Party very largely a federation of politically minded but primarily non-political organizations. Most important among these affiliated groups are the trades unions, since they supply almost the whole of the affiliated membership—although only about 60 per cent of all trade unionists belong to the Labour Party.[5] Affiliation is by individual unions rather than by the national organization of the British trade union movement, the Trades Union Council (T.U.C.), and under the Trades Disputes Act of 1946 members of affiliated unions may "contract out" of Labour Party membership by signing forms to that effect. This, however, does not mean that 60 per cent of the trade union movement consists of active supporters of the Labour Party; it means only that 60 per cent have not signed the contracting-out forms. One can get a more accurate idea of the number of "active" Labour supporters in the trades unions by considering pre-1946 figures. Before that year members of affiliated unions had to sign a form stating their positive willingness to contribute before they could be charged a political levy, and while this was the rule no more than 30 to 45 per cent of trades union members were affiliated with the Labour Party. Hence, it seems proper to infer that nearly half of the presently affiliated trades union members are in the party out of inertia or forgetfulness rather than positive conviction.

Among other affiliated organizations are a co-operative society[6] and certain socialist and professional societies: the very important Fabian Society, the Haldane Society (a society of socialist lawyers), and the Socialist Medical Association, none having more than a few thousand members.[7] Almost all the non-union members, therefore, are individual members, as are the more activist union members themselves.

In both the Labour and Conservative parties, individual members are organized in local associations that correspond to the parliamentary constituencies and are therefore generally called "constituency parties." These associations are, in the case of both parties, organized in a "representative" manner[8] and have three principal functions. First and foremost, their task is to electioneer and recruit members to the parties. In this they have the assistance of professional election agents: men with special skills in electoral propaganda and special knowledge of election laws and local political conditions, usually trained in the national headquarters of the

---

[5] This figure is for 1953, when total trades union membership was 8,088,450, of whom 5,071,935 were dues-paying members of the Labour Party.

[6] The Royal Arsenal Co-operative Society.

[7] In 1955, trades unions accounted for 5.5 million members, co-operative societies for 28,000, individual members for nearly a million and socialist societies for a mere 9,000, about 6,000 of whom were members of the Fabian Society.

[8] For example, in the Labour Party individual members are grouped in wards and all may attend ward meetings. The constituency parties themselves are governed by General Management Committees, consisting of delegates from the ward committees, special women's sections, and organizations affiliated with the local party (e.g., trades union branches). Constituency organization in the Conservative Party is not significantly different.

parties and always subject to the approval of the national organization. (The Labour Party, it might be noted, has fewer such agents and pays them less than the Conservative Party, for the simple reason that the Tories have more money.) Secondly, the constituency parties choose candidates for the parliamentary seats, and third, they send representatives to the national conventions of the parties.

THE SELECTION OF CANDIDATES

Choosing a parliamentary candidate is not, however, a purely local affair (as it tends to be in the United States). In both parties the local choice is inoperative until centrally approved and often the real choice is made by the national leaders. The need for central approval is quite explicit in the case of the Labour Party. Its constitution provides that selection of a candidate "shall not be regarded as completed until the name of the person has been placed before a meeting of the National Executive Committee,[9] and his or her selection has been duly endorsed," endorsement being conditional on acceptance and conformity to "the Constitution, Programme, Principles and Policy of the Party" and an undertaking by the candidate to "act in harmony with the Standing Orders of the Parliamentary Labour Party." The penalties for non-compliance are severe: the party label will be withdrawn and so will financial support from the national organization, the Leader of the party will refuse to send to the voters the usual formal letter of endorsement of the candidate during the election campaign and no parliamentary bigwigs will be sent into the constituency on his behalf. The result is almost certain defeat. While exercising a veto over local nominations the national party leadership may also recommend to the local party consideration of a particular candidate, usually a bright young man or a worthy member of the party bureaucracy, who will often be adopted by the local party.[10]

It has been said that control over the selection of candidates is much stricter in the Labour Party than in the Conservative Party, but while no doubt it is more explicit, the actual processes by which Conservative candidates are selected are, in practice, very similar. Again, the local party does the choosing. But a special national committee (the Standing Advisory Committee on Parliamentary Candidates) and a Vice-Chairman of the Party Organization frequently suggest candidates from a specially prepared file and keep an eye on candidates adopted. Approval from the center is necessary before selection of a candidate and the adoption of a

---

[9] For a description of this committee, see below, p. 185.
[10] But not always. After the split in the Party of 1931, for example, the constituency parties commonly passed over the names of ex-ministers recommended for adoption by the national leaders.

persona non grata will have the same consequences as in the Labour Party, with very much the same ultimate effect.

NATIONAL PARTY ORGANIZATION

The national organization of the Labour Party is simply the national instrument of the local and affiliated organizations. That of the Conservative Party is more complex because it is composed simultaneously of bodies representing the constituency associations and bodies that act as agencies for the parliamentary notables, especially the Leader. This structural difference is, as we shall see, symptomatic of certain more important differences between the two parties.

The official national organ of the Labour Party membership is the annual party Conference, attended by representatives of local parties or affiliated organizations, plus representatives of regional party organizations and certain members sitting ex officio (e.g., members of Parliament, prospective Labour candidates, and delegates of the Labour League of Youth). The total number of members qualified to attend was 2,604 in 1950. The Conference spends its time debating reports from the party leaders in and out of Parliament, important statements of policy (e.g., the party program), and resolutions submitted by affiliated organizations. For purposes of voting each affiliated organization is permitted as many votes as it has members, so that about five million votes are cast by trades unions, one million by the constituency parties, and only 60,000 by the socialist societies and the Royal Arsenal Co-operative combined, all usually in "blocks."[11]

The Conservative Party has not one but two large conventions every year: the meeting of its Central Council and that of the party Conference. These two bodies do not seem very different. True, one meets in the spring, the other in the autumn; one (the Conference) has a truly gargantuan membership of 5,000,[12] the other numbers a more modest 3,600; but both are composed of the same people: chiefly representatives of the constituency organizations,[13] Conservative M.P.s and peers, prospective candidates and important party bureaucrats. Nevertheless, the two bodies are not in theory duplicates of one another. The Council is the governing body of the National Union of Conservative and Unionist Associations, i.e., of the members. The Conference is the annual meeting of the party— and party and party members are *not* considered identical by the Con-

---

[11] The figures are for 1950. The Labour Party constitution does not require block voting, but it is customary and delegations rarely split.
[12] The actual attendance, as in the Labour Party, is usually not much more than half this total.
[13] Four in the case of the Council, seven in the case of the Conference.

servatives. The *party*, to be sure, includes the party members and their associations, but it also includes something more: the parliamentary notables and their Leader. It goes without saying, of course, that these notables are themselves members of the party, but—and this is the crucial point —their role as party members is something separate from their role as the party's parliamentary notables; so that it is proper to say that the Conference is composed of party members and parliamentary notables in their role as notables, while the General Council is composed of party members, including the parliamentary notables. The same people, by and large, are involved. Nevertheless, the distinction is not mere hairsplitting, because it represents an attitude within the Conservative Party—i.e., the independence of parliamentary notables from party—that is of great constitutional significance and has important practical consequences.

Both parties have special bodies to manage their affairs while the annual meetings are not in session. That of the Labour Party is called the National Executive Committee and has 28 members: 20 elected by affiliated organizations (12 by the trades unions, 7 by the constituency parties, and 1 by the rest), 6 elected by the Conference as a whole (5 women and the Party Treasurer, who is a person of importance precisely because he is the only male chosen by the whole Conference), and 2—the Leader of the parliamentary party and his deputy—sitting ex officio. The NEC meets monthly and is, according to the party constitution, "subject to the control and directions of the Party Conference, the Administrative Authority of the Party." Its powers over party organization are, however, impressive and it has, besides, a special voice in policy-making. It is the NEC that controls the party bureaucracy, which in turn takes care of routine administration; and, above all, it is the NEC that has the power to enforce party discipline by expelling individual members or disaffiliating organizations. Its disciplinary actions, to be sure, are subject to review by the Conference, but the Conference almost always overwhelmingly endorses the NEC's decisions. In regard to policy, the NEC, together with the parliamentary leaders, makes up the party's election manifesto, its reports and resolutions set off many of the most important Conference debates, and its members are accorded certain special privileges in these debates.

The Conservative Party also has an Executive Committee, a mammoth organization, having approximately 150 members.[14] But the Conservative Executive Committee is not quite in the same position as that of the

---

[14] Hence it does most of its work through a General Purposes Sub-Committee; but even that is twice as large as the NEC of the Labour Party. The membership of the Executive Committee consists of area representatives of the constituency parties and principal officers of the Party, both in Parliament and the party bureaucracy. It is assisted by a very large number of Advisory Committees.

Labour Party. Like the Central Council, the Executive Committee is merely an organ of the constituency associations and is chiefly concerned with routine organizational matters and the preparation of the meetings of the Central Council. And unlike Labour's Executive Committee it shares control over national party work with a very complicated series of other bodies that are not representative of the constituency organizations and most of which have far more important work to do.

One of the most important of these other organizations is the Central Office, the permanent party headquarters where the party bureaucrats do their work under the guidance of the party Chairman. There is a remote equivalent of the Central Office in the Labour Party, the Head Office in Transport House. But the Labour bureaucracy is directly under the National Executive Committee, and the party Secretary (who heads the Head Office) is its creature and that of the National Conference—thus making the Labour bureaucracy a tool if not an offshoot of the membership organization. Over the Conservative Central Office, on the other hand, the members of the party have virtually no control. Its Chairman and two Vice-Chairmen are appointed by the party Leader in his capacity as leader and its function, to put it succinctly, is not to help the constituency associations, but to act on behalf of the parliamentary notables.

Alongside the Central Office is another party organ chiefly composed of party functionaries, the Research Department. This is, in a sense, the Tories' answer to the Fabian Society: a body of expert research-workers who advise the party leaders on policy and who brief Conservative M.P.s on issues before Parliament and help them, if necessary, to work up their speeches. The importance attached to the Department may be inferred from the fact that its chairman, a direct appointee of the party Leader, in the postwar period was R. A. Butler. Finally, there exist on the national level a number of important National Advisory Committees, which, while including some representatives of the National Union, are certainly less the instruments of the Union than of the notables. By far the most important is the Advisory Committee on Policy; its chairman and deputy chairman are both appointed by the party Leader, while Parliament and the Executive Committee of the National Union contribute seven members each. There are also two Advisory Committees on party finance, both having representation from Parliament, the National Union and the party bureaucracy, but both also effectually under control of the Leader. Finally, there is the Standing Advisory Committee on Parliamentary Candidates previously mentioned; 5 of its 8 members coming from the membership organization and 2 from the Central Office. In practice, however, the main responsibility for party candidates is vested in the Vice-Chairman of the Party Organization—an appointee of the Leader, and not even a member of the Advisory Committee.

It will be seen that while in the Labour Party there is a straight flow of authority from the grass-roots organizations to the Conference, from the Conference to the National Executive Committee, and from the NEC to the party Secretary and bureaucracy, in the Conservative Party authority flows in two channels: from constituency associations to Central Council to Executive Committee, and from the Leader to the Central Office and the Research Department; whereupon the two streams of authority become amalgamated in a series of bodies deriving authority from both: the party Conference and the advisory Committees. But all the important bodies—those dealing with policy, finance, parliamentary candidates, research and party administration—are either under the direct jurisdiction of the Leader or headed by officials he appoints.

From what source, then, does the Leader of the Conservative Party derive his immense authority? The official selecting committee, until 1937, consisted simply of the Conservative members of the two Houses of Parliament and the party's prospective candidates—in short, the actual and potential parliamentary notables. In 1937, however, a sop was thrown to the rank and file (and the democratic principle) by the addition of the Executive Committee of the National Union to the group. But since this only involved adding some 100 votes to the 1,000 votes already qualified, it did not produce any significant shift in power from parliamentarians to the rank and file. The one-thousand-odd Conservative members of the House of Commons and the House of Lords still far outweigh the nearly three million dues-paying members of the party in selecting the man to lead them in Parliament, to govern the country when the party is in power, and to control the party's most important extra-parliamentary organizations. Moreover, it would be wrong to suppose that even these one thousand really determine who the Leader is to be in every case. Often they merely ratify a decision already made, usually by very few people. This is especially likely to happen when a Conservative Prime Minister dies or resigns and is succeeded by another Conservative leader. In that case, the sovereign, advised by whom she selects to advise her, names the succeeding Prime Minister, who is then elected Leader of the party. Thus, upon Churchill's resignation in 1955, Eden was named Prime Minister and subsequently Leader of the party.

Nothing suggests more unequivocally that British parties too have roots in the past than the Conservative Leader's authority and the method by which he is elected. It is not only that parliamentarians play such an important role in choosing him but that even they refrain from wielding their formal powers when a Conservative has already been named First Minister of the Crown. And it is not only that the Leader can control the party bureaucracy; he has a host of other independent powers as well that give him a position of power unrivaled in other democratic parties. It is he who appoints the party's Chief Whip; it is he who appoints the party's Shadow Cabinet when it is in opposition; most striking of all, he alone can authoritatively commit the party to policy or present an election program. In 1945, for example, the Conservative Party had no party program at all; there was merely "Mr. Churchill's Declaration of Policy to the Electors."

The Labour Party Leader enjoys nothing like the same explicit authority. Indeed, in terms of the party constitution, no Labour Party Leader exists at all. The Parliamentary Labour Party (i.e., the Labour M.P.s) does, to be sure, elect a leader, but the words of the party constitution make him only the Leader of the parliamentary party, not the Leader of the Labour Party. While this distinction is of little practical importance the fact remains that the post lacks many of the formal powers explicitly given the Conservative Leader. Not the Leader but the parliamentary party appoints the Chief Whip; nor does he appoint the members of the Shadow Cabinet—again, the parliamentary party does—or the head of the party bureaucracy. He does not autocratically pronounce policy; on the contrary, final authority over the formulation of policy, as over all other party concerns, is vested by the party constitution in the party Conference, its "sovereign" authority. Not least, when the Labour Party is out of power its Leader is elected annually, unlike the Conservative Leader who holds his position as long as he likes, until he dies or resigns, presumably as a symbol of his "independence" from the party machine.

In the Labour Party, therefore, the formal powers of the Conservative Leaders are assigned partly to the organization of the party outside Parliament and partly to the Parliamentary Labour Party. The latter differs rather strikingly from its Conservative counterpart precisely by the fact that it is assigned powers that the Conservatives commit to their Leader. Strictly speaking, indeed, the Conservative Party has no parliamentary party in the Labour sense at all. It does have a series of committees composed of Conservative backbenchers that advise the Leader on policy (if he wants their advice) and help him to gauge rank-and-file feelings. There are about twenty "functional" committees, the principal officers of which form a Business Committee that has ready access to the Leader, and in addition there is the more amorphous "1922 Committee," composed of all the backbench Conservative members, the function of which is simply to elicit rank-and-file views to be communicated to the Leader, the Chief Whip, and other "notables." But it is not even pretended that these backbench organizations can make decisions binding on the leaders.

In the Labour Party, on the other hand, the parliamentary party has much greater formal power—at least when the party is in opposition. It is the governing organ of the party in Parliament. Its policy decisions are binding on all Labour members and, as we already know, its "Parliamentary Committee" (elected by the Labour members of the House of Commons) is the Labour Shadow Cabinet. The Whips are its own instruments, not the Leader's, and the Leader himself is its annually elected creature. When the party is in office, however, all this abruptly changes. Although its Leader is invariably named Prime Minister, the parliamentary party does not choose the Cabinet, that being the Prime Minister's prerogative. At the same time it ceases to make decisions binding on all the members of the party, including the leaders. It becomes in fact rather like what the Conservative parliamentary party is all the time: a series of "Study Groups," headed by a "Liaison Committee" that, like the Conservative Business Committee and the officers of the "1922 Committee," keeps the leaders in touch with sentiment on the benches behind. This dual character of the Parliamentary Labour Party is, as we shall see in the next section, indicative of something very important.

Power Relationships in the Parties

So far we have discussed only formal organization; but this is mere skin and bones. What are the vital organs of the two parties? Where does power to make binding decisions really reside? We know where it is formally lodged: in the Labour Party the Conference is sovereign, in the Conservative Party it is the Leader. But one must never accept such formal provisions at face value. When one inquires further into the matter, even as sketchily as we shall here, the two parties turn out to be not so very different from one another after all, one being far less democratic, the other far more, than they pretend to be. Let us consider the Labour Party first, that being the more complicated case.

It has often been asserted that the Labour Party is not in fact a democratic organization because it is dominated by the leaders of the more powerful trades unions. Statistically the point is well taken. Not only are five out of every six votes at the Conference cast by the trades unions but of the eighty unions affiliated with the party six account for more than half the membership.[15] Financially the point is well taken too; most of Labour's money comes from political dues collected by the unions. And the fact is that the Party and the unions have only rarely been seriously at odds. But none of this means necessarily that the Labour party is "undemocratic," even if we concede that the trades unions themselves are not in every case models of democracy and have been, on the whole, like-

---

[15] The Transport and General Workers Union (830,000 members), the National Union of Mineworkers (651,000), the Amalgamated Engineering Union (595,000), the General and Municipal Workers (400,000), the National Union of Railwaymen (366,000) and the Union of Shop Distributive and Allied Workers (317,000).

minded on important questions of policy.[16] For money and voting strength
at the Conference are not the only determinants of power in the Labour
Party.

A considerable amount of money certainly is needed by the party, but
money alone will not make it successful. To achieve its purpose—i.e., to
win elections—the party also needs "activists": people to run the constituency parties, to canvass for members, to get out the vote and to whip
up enthusiasm, and this the agents cannot do alone. But the party activists
are to be found almost entirely in the constituency parties; even the
activist trades unionists generally join constituency parties and act through
these rather than the unions. For this reason alone the unions cannot
consistently bully the Conference against the opposition of the individual
members. After all, what good would it do to sweep Conference after
Conference only to find that the constituency parties will not energetically
work for the program during a campaign? The socialist societies and the
Parliamentary Party have special weapons too with which to assert themselves. The Fabian Society is still the brains of the movement: the party
research organization and its chief source of ideas—not nearly so much as
it was in the heyday of the Webbs and Shaw and H. G. Wells but still
enough to give it influence. And the Parliamentary Party gains power
from the very fact that it is the party's arm in Parliament. It is required
to enact into law the party program; it has the special prestige that all
British parliamentarians possess; and its leaders are the party members
most in the public eye, not least during election campaigns.

The Labour Party, then, consists of a series of countervailing powers—
trades unions, constituency party activists, socialist intellectuals, and members of Parliament—each of which is useful if not indispensable to the
others. Intraparty decision-making involves the interplay of all these forces,
and this explains why Labour policy has been consistently neither as left-
wing as that of its "left-wing enthusiasts" nor as right-wing as that of the
"dull-witted and conservative trades union officials." (The epithets are
Beatrice Webb's.)

The quantitative power of the trades unions, moreover, is greater in
the Conference than on the National Executive Committee and greater

---

[16] "Like-minded on important questions of policy" does not mean unanimous on all
questions of policy. There are, in fact, important political splits among the six largest
unions. Three (the Transport and General Workers Union, the Mineworkers, and the
General and Municipal) have been consistently conservative in the past, while the
Railwaymen, Engineers and the Distributive and Allied Workers have been consistently
left-wing. These divisions are not of course fixed. Under their present leader, Frank
Cousins, the Transport and General Workers have been veering left while, after the
death of James Figgins, the Railwaymen were practically bound to veer right. On
the whole, however, the bulk of the trades unions have been considerably to the right
of the constituency parties.

on the NEC than in the Parliamentary Party. And it is not as great among the parliamentary leaders as among the parliamentary rank and file. But the NEC undoubtedly has greater power than the Conference as a whole; the party in Parliament frequently dominates the party outside, and the parliamentary leaders (especially the Leader) can usually control the parliamentary party. This is important both to appraise correctly the power of the unions and to understand the party's actual decision-making processes.

The annual Conference neither is nor could be, in practice, what it is supposed to be in theory: the party's sovereign decision-making body. Two thousand people, meeting for four and a half days in some crowded seaside resort to consider some three to four hundred resolutions, to debate the voluminous reports of their leaders and to hear their addresses, cannot make policy as a truly deliberative assembly. They can and do raise an occasional row, and sometimes—very infrequently—they win out in a conflict with the leaders. They played a decisive role in 1918, again in 1935, and still a third time in 1954. But each time, it should be noted, the "leaders" were divided among themselves.[17] They sometimes, by the tone of the discussions, stiffen the attitudes of the leaders[18] or soften them. But for the Conference to carry a point against a united NEC or, even more unlikely, an NEC united with all the parliamentary luminaries, is exceptional indeed, and when it does it is usually ignored. No doubt this means that the NEC is adroit at adjusting itself to any strong sentiment among the rank and file. But it means much more clearly that the NEC simply tends to dominate the Conference—that the Conference is a rally, a chance for the activists to become acquainted, a chance for the leaders and would-be leaders to show their paces, a chance for the people at the top to feel out sentiment at the bottom, but little more.

Again, the parliamentary party holds a specially privileged position vis-à-vis the party outside, especially when the party is in power. It holds such a position, above all, because British constitutional practice does not tolerate government by party caucuses. The Government is supposed to be carried on by Her Majesty's Ministers, not by a party's bigwigs. Her

---

[17] In 1918, the Parliamentary Party wanted to remain in the Lloyd George Coalition but a special party Conference demanded withdrawal; the NEC, however, was in favor of withdrawal as against the parliamentary leaders. In 1935 the Conference in effect dictated to a divided parliamentary party on the sanctions issue. And in 1954 the Conference decided the party's attitude on German rearmament, again because of deep divisions among the parliamentary leaders and on the NEC.

[18] As in 1936, on the issue of the party's attitude toward the Spanish Civil War, and in 1944 when the Conference wrote into the party program a clear commitment to public ownership of land, heavy industry, banking, etc., against an NEC resolution recommending more ambiguously the transfer to the state of "power to direct the policy" of various sectors of the economy.

Majesty's Ministers have access to information not available to ordinary people. Their duty is (according to Mr. Churchill) first to the country, then to their constituents, and only then to their party. They alone understand the problems and are in control of the parliamentary timetable.[19] Hence, how could ordinary people presume to dictate to them?

That this is no empty constitutional theory may be illustrated by an incident that occurred in 1945 while the wartime Coalition Government was still in office. Mr. Attlee, a member of the Coalition, was to accompany Mr. Churchill to the projected Potsdam Conference. The then chairman of the Party, Professor Harold Laski, declared shortly before the meeting of the Conference that the party could not be committed to any decisions that had not been debated by the NEC or the Parliamentary Labour Party. Churchill seized on this with enthusiastic indignation. Would a Labour Government really be a dictatorship of the National Executive—a body "unknown to the British Constitution"? Would government secrets communicated to Labour Ministers as His Majesty's Privy Councillors be communicated to members of the Executive who were not subject to the Privy Councillor's oath of secrecy? Mr. Attlee answered with a statement that may be taken as definitive. The Parliamentary Labour Party consults with the NEC before the opening of every parliamentary session and at any other time it wants to consult with it, but "at no times and in no circumstances has the National Executive Committee ever sought to give instructions to the Parliamentary Labour Party arising out of the consultation. Indeed . . . it has no power to do so."

There can be little doubt that Parliamentary Party here means first and foremost the parliamentary leaders, although their powers are undoubtedly much greater when Labour is in office than when it is not. Consider the following comment by R. T. McKenzie on the fate of the party's "Study Groups" under the Government of 1945:

> Those Members of Parliament who expected that the Groups would give them a chance to take part actively in policy-making have had their hopes rudely dashed. From the start the Ministers made it clear that they did not look on the Groups in this light. The Ministers' reasons for taking this position were twofold: They felt that constitutionally they could not reveal proposed legislation to a few Members before presenting it to the whole House; and they believed that as a practical matter it would be risky to discuss legislative proposals with Backbenchers because the latter might speak for only a narrow minority of the Party, or they might "leak" to the press, or they might try to obstruct or alter Cabinet proposals. Some Backbenchers have come to feel that the group meetings are a waste of time, or, even

---

[19] See below, pp. 235-240.

worse, that they are a means of keeping the rank-and-file occupied with trivial tasks so that their influence would be minimized.[20]

And it has been argued that Clement Attlee emerged as a strong figure after becoming Leader not only because he was much more than he appeared to be on the surface—"a sheep in sheep's clothing," Winston Churchill once called him—but because his position carried with it certain inherent powers and prestige, with which it invests even the meekest occupant. Very few Prime Ministers indeed have failed to make use of these powers. The plain fact is, as a writer on British government recently said, that "in spite of . . . Labour's tradition of back-bench participation in policy-making, the parliamentary leaders have maintained a sphere of independent action probably as wide as that of the Conservatives' leadership *when in power.*" But we have reason to think that the privileges bestowed upon the leaders in power also enhance their influence in opposition.

The row between the Labour Party Conference and parliamentary leaders in 1960-61 over defense policy illustrates this account of their power relations. In 1960, the Conference passed, by very small majorities, two resolutions calling for unilateral nuclear disarmament and, for all intents and purposes, a more qualified commitment to NATO. The parliamentary leadership predominantly, but nothing like unanimously, opposed both resolutions. This illustrates that Conference does sometimes take an independent position—when the leadership itself is not very cohesive. (Since the Conference majorities were due to some important last-minute swings by certain trades unions, it also indicates that the unions do not by any means always act as a coherent body of opinion in the party, or as a unified counterforce to radical left-wing opinion.) Far from suggesting, however, that the Labour Party is not dominated by its leaders, the aftermath of the incident shows how powerful they are even in the face of clear and unmistakable Conference decisions. Most of the leaders in Parliament refused to accept the decisions as binding, and all efforts to make them adhere to the Conference decisions failed. Moreover, in the year following the Conference the parliamentary leadership gradually closed ranks around a position still very different from that of the 1960 Conference. Immediately certain bodies of opinion, mainly unions, rallied to the leaders, contrary to their earlier position. At the Conference of 1961, the parliamentary leaders won out, and by a considerable margin.

We should realize, however, that the Labour leaders' sphere of independent action rivals that of the Conservative leaders not only because the Labour leaders have more power than formal party theory suggests but

---

[20] R. T. McKenzie, *British Political Parties* (1955).

also because the Conservative leaders have less. Certainly, the Leader of the Conservative Party does not wield in practice the comprehensive powers assigned to him by theory, at least not single-handedly and arbitrarily. Backbenchers, the "ardent partisans" (as Churchill put it) outside Parliament, the research members of the party—all wield influence as in the Labour Party, and for similar reasons. These reasons are that winning elections is the overriding purpose of the party—among the Conservatives even more than the Labourites—and that the Leader cannot win elections by himself. That point was made unmistakable by the General Election of 1945. The Conservatives then had a Leader as popular personally as any democratic Leader is likely to be. They waged a campaign which did little but exploit Churchill's popularity. They let him arbitrarily declare policy and manage the electioneering. And they were crushingly defeated by the Labour Party.

That this experience had important effects can be seen in the way party policy has been evolved since 1945. Before that the normal practice had been for the party to put forward men and for the men to propound measures, more or less as they went along. After 1945 a clamor arose, particularly among the younger members of the party, for concrete statements of *party* policy with which to counter Labour actions and propaganda. By 1950 two very lengthy documents setting forth such policy, the *Industrial Charter* (1947) and *The Right Road for Britain* (1950) had been published. To be sure, the parliamentary leaders played the dominant role in the preparation of these documents. *The Right Road*, for example, was worked out under the supervision of a committee of the Shadow Cabinet and clearly made subject to the Leader's veto. Material for the deliberations was prepared by members of the Research Department, a draft was prepared by the special Committee, which was submitted to the Leader and other prominent Conservatives for approval, published, and then approved almost unanimously at the Conference. But the fact that the parliamentary notables took the lead in the preparation of the document is not as important as the very fact that such a statement of policy was prepared at all. For although it was not formally accorded the status of an election program—that would have been much too abrupt a break with usage—and although Churchill truculently announced to the Conference that he still intended to make "personal" policy, a declaration of policy so overwhelmingly supported by the party and so widely distributed in the country could not fail to affect Conservative policy in Parliament.

The Right Road was made at the top and acclaimed at the bottom, but this is not different from what happens in the Labour Party. And as in the case of the Labour Party, the rank and file, usually docile, more anxious to cheer than to carp, has on occasion forced its point of view on the leaders. The best recent example is the housing debate at the 1950 Conference. The Conference was debating a routine motion condemning Labour's housing policies. In the course of the debate a speaker mentioned that 300,000 houses should be built annually. The figure caught on like "a prairie fire"; speaker after speaker repeated it amidst the constantly growing enthusiasm of the delegates. There can be no doubt that the leaders would have preferred a nicely ambivalent resolution, leaving them a free hand to build as many houses as they felt proper in the course of developments, but the delegates were not to be denied. At last, Lord Woolton, the Chairman of the party, arose and accepted the figure on behalf of the leadership, "to bloodcurdling yells of triumph from the floor," according to the *Observer*. Nor was the incident ignored. The Conservative Government of 1951 did proceed to build 300,000 houses, and the Minister in charge of the housing program, Mr. Macmillan, promptly became a celebrated figure in the party. The prairie fire of 1950 was certainly exceptional, but none the less significant for that. It suggests that in the Conservative Party, as in the Labour Party, the leaders are not unconditionally independent of the pressures arising from the rank and file in and out of Parliament.

Thus, one of the most striking characteristics of the two major British parties is that despite having utterly different formal structures their actual decision-making powers are strikingly similar. Labour has avoided "caucus government," the Tories autocracy; both are in fact oligarchies tempered by a sense of dependence on mass support. Is it not reasonable to infer that this is so because both parties function under conditions that forcefully push them in the same direction?

The first of these conditions is the prevalence of certain political conventions and attitudes throughout British society, especially those that have their roots in predemocratic times. These explain better than anything else the dominance of the Leader in each party. There is, first of all, the long tradition of personal leadership by parliamentary notables, dating to the time when parliamentary parties were really personal factions and when the concept of the mandate was practically unknown. Inevitably this tradition of commitment to a leader plays a greater role in the Conservative than in the Labour party, but it has probably affected the latter too by being a parliamentary tradition—part of the style of the House. More important, Parliament has always been regarded as something other than a convention of delegates, either of parties or of constituencies; its legitimate function, in short, is "to govern the country," not (in the first instance at any rate) to legitimize local or party interests. This applies most forcibly of all, of course, to the members of the Government. To be one of Her Majesty's Ministers, a member of the Cabinet and of the Privy Council, is to be set aside from mere party, not only in the sense of being given a special responsibility for the *national* welfare but in the sense of being given a special right to make policy toward this end. The actual (not formal) distribution of power in British parties, therefore, even in the case of the Labour Party, is deeply affected by the more ancient and non-democratic aspects of the Constitution. This emerges most strikingly from the fact that when Labour is in power its Parliamentary Party acquires a structure very similar to that of the Conservative Party while its leaders formally cut themselves off from the party organization in Parliament and cease to be bound by its decisions.

But just as the structure of action in the Labour Party is affected by the non-democratic aspects of British political life so that of the Conservative Party is affected by its democratic aspects. Whatever Conservative Party theory may say on the subject, it is a violation of British political sensibilities, including Conservative sensibilities, to ride roughshod over popular sentiment. To ignore such sentiment is barely legitimate, but to defy it is clearly not. Outside of their Constitution the Conservatives do pretend that they are a democratic group. Equally important is the much more tangible fact that the Conservatives no less than Labour must seek to win power by means of universal suffrage, and that mass democracy imposes certain inescapable institutional conditions on a mass party; that was the great lesson of 1945. Mass democracy in its very nature requires ardent enthusiasts, party bureaucrats, party research offices and mass finances, as well as popular leaders. Hence, just as it gives to the socialist intellectuals and local Labour Party activists powers to balance off against the trades unions, so it gives to the enthusiasts of the National Union and the intellectuals and bureaucrats of the Conservative Central Office and Research Department countervailing powers against the parliamentary notables. Party democracy may be accepted only truculently by the Tory Leader, but it is, in some degree at least, a necessary consequence of electoral democracy, however much modified, in both parties, by more ancient traditions.

Party Organization and Party Discipline

To what aspects of party organization, then, can party discipline be attributed? One obvious possibility is the screening of parliamentary candidates by the national headquarters of both parties. Such screening no doubt helps to eliminate some blatant heretics, but whether it does more than that is doubtful. There is, in strict point of fact, little cautious screening of potential M.P.s by the party oligarchs, chiefly because blatant heresy is itself unusual among British politicians. And attributing party discipline to central screening begs the question of why the local party organizations so meekly submit (as a general rule) to central control, and why there is a kind of party discipline outside Parliament that helps to make possible party discipline inside Parliament. After all, effective central screening of local parliamentary candidates is not simply a technical device that can be used in any country as people please. It may itself be a consequence of the same factors that make for party discipline in Parliament; in any case, it presupposes conditions that are far from universal.

The most important of these conditions in Britain is the importance of the party label to successful political candidacy. But is the party label successful qua party label, as we supposed in a previous part of the chapter, or because of the concrete penalties that follow its withdrawal? The chief penalty it entails is of course withdrawal of central financial support, but that, while certainly annoying, is not so severe a handicap to the constituency parties as might appear. In the Conservative Party the constituency associations are very well able to fend for themselves financially. In fact, the chief financial function of the Central Office seems to be merely to redistribute funds from the more to the less well-to-do constituencies.[21] This is not of course the case in the Labour Party, at least not to the same extent. But British elections are in any case relatively inexpensive and financial considerations in consequence not so pressing as might be thought. Few candidates spend more than £1,000 in a campaign and most considerably less, since there is much less general hullabaloo in a British election and time on radio and television are furnished free by the B.B.C. This sum is hardly out of reach of most constituency parties, particularly since the trades unions often directly support the campaigns of Labour candidates.[22] Thus, financial support from the center, while always welcome, is not so vitally necessary in either party as to account for their extraordinary obedience to central advice on candidacies.

There are two other important objections against theories attributing party discipline in Parliament to the power of the party organizations outside. One is that the party organizations of both parties are themselves much more under the control of members of Parliament than M.P.s are under the control of the party organizations and that the high cohesion of external party machinery, like discipline in Parliament, is due to the dominance of the parliamentary leaders. Hence, while their domination over external party machinery reinforces the dominance of the leaders over

---

[21] Two-fifths of the Conservative associations are helped by the national party organization with money collected from other local associations.

[22] 140 in 1950 and 138 in 1951. Trades unions may contribute up to £300 annually to any constituency party and pay up to 80 per cent of any candidate's election expenses.

the parliamentary parties, it is more plausible to attribute both to the same basic causes than to make one the determinant of the other. Finally, if the power of external party organization (including financial power) were the decisive determinant of party discipline in Parliament we should expect to find more solid discipline on the Labour than on the Conservative benches; yet, if anything, the opposite is the case.

This fact itself suggests that the explanation of the British party system developed in Chapter 4—that it is a result, essentially, of the British political "spirit"—is correct. Although the outlook of the Labour Party, like that of the Conservative Party, is predominantly pragmatic, attachment to "principles," dogma, even ideology is considerably more common among Labourites (especially the extreme left wing) than Tories, though still uncommon enough. Hence it is the Labour Party—and before Labour it was, for similar reasons, the Liberal Party—that always seems in danger of suffering party splits as the result of irreconcilable opinions, and it seems always to be the extreme left wing whose opinions are intractable. The Conservatives, even when divided (as over Suez in 1956-57), never seem in great danger of splitting. The decisive factor inducing the disciplined two-party system then is the British "genius for political compromise," and this is not so much the result of the political disadvantages always entailed in severe internal party disagreements—these disadvantages after all exist also where parties are not disciplined—as of the peculiarly British conditions earlier discussed.

[9]

Party Goals and the
Pattern of Policy

Elusiveness of British Party Goals

Parties are organizations that pursue goals (or "interests") by means of electoral competition. In the previous chapter, we discussed the organizations and something of the character of the electoral competition, but nothing has yet been said about the goals. Undoubtedly it is necessary to go into this subject if one is to have a rounded picture of British politics. It is, however, an extremely difficult and elusive subject to discuss.

How precisely does one find out what party goals are in a country like Great Britain? The most obvious way, it would seem, is by looking at actual party programs: the parties' official statements of policy. But such programs are constantly changing in the light of circumstances and, not least, the particular exigencies of electoral competition; they express the pressure of environmental conditions and the sheer will to power as well as the more basic normative values of party leaders and members. In other words, they raise the problem, familiar enough to Americans, of how seriously one should take what such programs say. A look at the Labour Party program of 1945 would tend to a certain extent to mislead us about party goals today, and a look at the program of today could mislead us similarly about those of tomorrow. Even more is this true of actual policy when a party is in power. The policy of a Government, as we saw throughout the discussion of the British structure of decision-making, reflects party goals only alongside many other forces, not the least of which, besides hard and fast conditions, are the influence of the bureaucracy, the pressure of the social groups with which the government has to deal, and the difficult problems of managing parliamentary time, adequately preparing and drafting legislation, and coordinating different aspects of policy that bear upon one another. Taking Labour's financial policies in 1947 and 1948 at face value, for example, we would have to conclude that Labour favored both a policy of easy money and devil-may-care spending and one of hard money and tight budgetary control, whereas in fact both policies represented adjustments to economic conditions and the views of Treasury officials at least as much as Labour values. All one can really infer from these policies is that Labour favors the adjustment of economic policy to economic circumstances and expert opinion, which is something, but not much. Both electoral programs and governmental policies can be taken only as indicators of party goals, not as the goals themselves.

Even more serious difficulties than these arise when one tries to pin down British party goals. One is the very pragmatism of the British parties. In other countries one can often represent party goals by coherent, well articulated political "philosophies"; party ideology tends to provide a certain continuity of outlook and a certain insensitivity to shifts in circumstances and opinions. In Britain, however, one can speak at most of certain vague dispositions, never raised to the dignity and pretentiousness of philosophy, as characterizing the parties—or only of their tendency to favor more the vested interests of some social groups than others, or to respond more intensely to certain symbols than to others. A further difficulty arises from the fact that Britain is a highly consensual country; this has as its corollary the fact that party policies do not tend at any time to be starkly opposed but rather to converge upon one another, often appearing more similar than different. And most important of all, British parties are aggregative parties *par excellence*. They do not represent any particular social interest or opinion but a great many, quite a few of which are hardly very compatible. Because they consist of many wings of opinion and cater to many social groups, differences within the parties are often as marked as differences between the parties as a whole (if indeed one can speak of them as wholes)—and sometimes more so. Today, for example, the moderates in the Labour and Conservative Parties probably have rather more in common than the Labour moderates and the extreme left, or the Tory moderates and the extreme right; and this is not unusual in British party politics.

Our approach to party goals in Britain must therefore be rather complicated and indirect, and the result rather impressionistic. A differentiation of party goals which makes clear contrasts between Labourite and Tory and disentangles policy altogether from environmental conditions and the national consensus might be intellectually tidy but would seriously mislead. The procedure we shall use, consequently, will not be to draw a set of well-ordered and comprehensive normative profiles of the parties. Rather we shall look at the whole interplay of programs, policies, dispositions, conditions and consensus, concentrating on that most cardinal fact in postwar British domestic policy, the highly developed social service (or welfare) state. We shall first discuss its origins, to illustrate how objective conditions, general political consensus and particular forces of opinion coalesced in the policy of a particular party, the Labour Party, which governed Britain from 1945 to 1951—and thus incidentally also set the stage for the discussion of the effects of policy on the pattern of power in Chapter 10. Then we shall look at what the Conservatives have done with the welfare state since coming to power in 1951, and at how Labour has responded while in opposition. Some sense of party differences should emerge from this, and will be augmented by a more general discussion of essential differences in party attitudes at the end. The total effect may be somewhat ambiguous, but so it must be.

Origins of the British Welfare State

Since the end of World War II Great Britain has acquired a very highly developed welfare state. This means simply that the state has assumed a high degree of responsibility for the condition of the British economy and for the economic welfare of every member of British society. It tries, by public direction, to assure an economy that is highly productive, financially stable, and capable of selling the exports that Britain must sell to survive. At the same time it tries, by public policy, to assure full employment and guarantees to all members of society, even those who cannot be employed, a certain minimum standard of subsistence. The principal means employed to achieve these ends have been three: nationalization measures (i.e., measures transferring certain privately owned business concerns to public authority), economic planning and control measures, and redistribution-of-wealth measures (i.e., measures designed to transfer wealth from the well-off to the not-so-well-off).

The welfare state, however, is certainly not an exclusive development of the postwar period. Long before the Labour landslide of 1945 Great Britain had a certain amount of public enterprise (most of it, incidentally, the creation of Conservative Governments), at least a little public economic planning, and a good deal of public economic control and social security legislation. The development of the welfare state is a long and continuing story and to find its origins one must go back at least to the middle of the nineteenth century, when the first public health measures were enacted. But this unfolding of the welfare state has been tremen-

dously accelerated in the postwar period, and in this period occurred also
the culmination of the more important trends in socio-economic legislation that can be traced to earlier times. What forces, then, induced the
British to create a highly developed welfare state in this period?

No doubt much of the explanation may be found, as usual, in attitudes
—in subjectively conceived social values and objectives. The postwar
British welfare state crowned with success half a century of political agitation by trades union Labourites and Fabian socialists. But it is mistaken
to think of the British welfare state purely in these terms. To a considerable extent, its development was a matter of need no less than choice.
Certain objective forces ("objective" in the sense that they were given in
the environment of policy and not subject to anyone's choice) did as much
to impel Britain in the socio-economic direction she has taken since the
war as any political agitation, a fact reflected in the startlingly close agreement among the parties on social and economic issues. To some extent
this consensus on policy may be due to the remarkable ability of the
Tories to trim their program to any prevailing wind of doctrine, but the
kindlier and perhaps more accurate construction to put on the matter is
that choice among policies in postwar Britain has been severely limited by
given conditions that party politics cannot wish away.

The most serious and intractable of these conditions is the British international economic position. Everyone knows that international trade is
a matter of life or death for Great Britain; that she is heavily dependent
on imports of foodstuffs and raw materials to support her population and
keep her factories running; and that, as a corollary, she must have large
and reliable export markets for her manufactured goods in areas that can
supply her needs for primary materials.[1] Unfortunately, the international
economic outlook for Britain has been bleak and growing steadily bleaker
for a very long time, and World War II came very close to delivering the
economic *coup de grâce* after a long history of deterioration.

Although British war losses, in cold statistical terms, were not as serious
as those sustained by Germany and Russia, or, for that matter, France, in
a relative sense, particularly in view of her desperate dependence on international trade, they were perhaps the most devastating, because the
least easily replaceable, of all. A few statistics will vividly tell the tale.

---

[1] Francis Williams, in *Socialist Britain* (1948), points out that before the war,
"nearly three-quarters of all the food [Great Britain] ate came from abroad, 55 per
cent of her meat, 75 per cent of her wheat, 85 per cent of her butter, all her tea,
cocoa, and coffee, three-quarters of her sugar. . . . Moreover, with the single exception of coal, the raw materials upon which her major industries depended were largely
or wholly imported; all the cotton, all the rubber, five-sixths of the wool, practically
all the petroleum, two-thirds of the iron ore, most of the timber." About a quarter of
the national income went in payment for imports of various sorts.

Between 1939 and 1945, more than one billion pounds of Britain's overseas investments (chiefly "dollar" investments) had to be liquidated in order to raise foreign currencies with which to buy war equipment and supplies. In the same period, Britain's external debt rose from £760,000,000 to £3,355,000,000, leading to vastly increased pressure on her foreign currency resources in both principal and interest payments. And, again during the same period, "reserves" (meaning actual holdings of gold and United States dollars) dwindled from £864,000,000 to £453,000,000, while shipping, a reliable earner of "invisibles" before the war, dwindled from 22,100,000 to 15,900,000 tons. In short, on V-J Day victorious Britain was bankrupt, with no long-run relief in sight; and this situation was confounded still further by certain postwar events, particularly the loss of Eastern European markets as a result of the cold war, and the loss of India, Ceylon and Burma, which had previously been more or less exclusive British trading areas.

The American loan and Economic Cooperation Administration aid provided short-run relief but could hardly be a permanent solution of Britain's economic problems. What was needed first and foremost was a vastly expanded volume of exports and an import bill kept down to the minimum. Exports were needed to fill the hiatus left by the vanished invisible earnings from British overseas investments and the supply of services (e.g., shipping).[2] But how was the necessary surplus of exports to be achieved? Clearly, postwar Britain had to export much more than prewar Britain. But, objectively, postwar Britain was hardly in a position to produce as much as prewar Britain, because the war had done a serious amount of property damage, not least to productive facilities. Hence, the required volume of exports could be achieved only by the severe curtailment of domestic consumption. But this also was no easy task. The war had created a large unrequited demand for consumer goods in Great Britain just as it did elsewhere. Personal possessions had deteriorated no less than capital equipment. Nearly half a million houses had been destroyed or damaged beyond repair. Another three and a half million needed repairs, major and minor. No hospitals had been built since 1938, nor any schools, or other public buildings.

The danger therefore was that Britain would consume herself into destruction rather than export her way to recovery, particularly since manufacturers could make fortunes almost without effort in the starved home market or in other easy markets in soft currency areas, instead of going into the highly competitive and sales-resistant hard-currency markets, especially the North American markets. Under those conditions no post-

---

[2] Before the war, invisibles paid for one-fifth of all British imports; after the war for only one-fiftieth.

war Government could have taken a chance on an undirected economy. The Labourite socialists therefore had a high degree of public planning and control thrust upon them, however much they might have been predisposed to central economic controls in the first place.

The need for a great deal of public intervention in economic affairs was further accentuated by the internal condition of the British economy. It goes without saying that the seriousness of the international economic problems was inversely proportional to the internal efficiency of British industry, which, quite apart from the results of war damage, was (and is) quite low. A single figure will suffice to illustrate the point: a study done in identical years in 32 manufacturing trades showed that the ratio of productivity between the United States and Britain has been at a level of 216 to 100 in favor of the United States, and countless visiting productivity teams on both sides have confirmed the impression conveyed by this ratio. To some extent, the internal difficulties of the British economy may be the result of the very factor one might expect would have given it the greatest advantage over those of other countries: Britain's head start in the industrial revolution. There is perhaps such a thing as an overdeveloped economy no less than an underdeveloped economy, and Britain is the chief case in point. For example, the older capital equipment is, the more it consumes in maintenance and repair. From this standpoint it is extremely suggestive to note that Britain has, since the war, devoted on the average 20 per cent of her national income to capital formation rather than consumption expenditure—a strikingly large proportion—and yet has managed to increase her total capital resources only very slightly. To some extent this no doubt is due to the capital investment devoured by war damage and war neglect, but it also reflects the relatively great age of much of Britain's industrial plant. Again, once a country has acquired a highly developed industrial apparatus—once it has committed a large proportion of its capital resources—it is extremely difficult, for psychological as well as physical reasons, to scrap and totally renew sizable portions of it, thus keeping up with the technical level of more recently industrialized societies.

To make a long and very complicated story short, there has existed in the postwar period a sort of permanent economic crisis in Britain, partly as a result of changes in her position wrought by the war, partly as the result of the continuation of long-range international economic tendencies in her disfavor, and partly as the result of a long series of provisional circumstances so strung together as to constitute almost a permanent emergency. Invisible earnings have not been recovered to prewar level; the terms of trade, despite some bright periods (e.g., during the Korean War), have been steadily worsening; tariff walls impede exports; and German and Japanese competition has revived to a dangerous degree. The cold war has demanded the diversion of goods desperately needed for export or home consumption to defense, and colonial crises have put a similar drain on equipment and manpower. Not least, there has been considerable inflationary pressure on the domestic market.

Given all these handicaps, the economic recovery made by the British in the postwar period has been astonishing: a large postwar deficit in invisible payments and receipts had been turned into a small surplus by June 1948. The current accounts balance of payments was changed from a deficit of £630,000,000 in 1947 to a surplus of £30,000,000 a year later (though it soon went into the red again). And exports were enormously increased, especially to the Western Hemisphere, in the midst of severe domestic shortages (in 1948 they were 60 per cent greater than in 1938). But these achievements have not been sufficient to remove the pressures pushing Britain in the direction of the welfare state, at least in its economic planning and control aspects. The volume and severity of controls have been relaxed by both Labour and Conservative Governments in the course of the postwar period, but Britain has not been able to achieve a position in which she can take a real chance on the risky and wasteful luxuries of free enterprise.

But it would be a gross distortion to suggest that the British were dragged kicking and screaming into the postwar social policy by blind and irresistible economic forces. Most of the postwar social policy certainly was the product of a startlingly broad "ideological" consensus in British society. To understand the origins of the British welfare state we need consequently to grasp the reasons for this general agreement on its desirability in British society. Why the overwhelming Labour Party victory in 1945 and, even more important, why so little disagreement among the parties, of the sort that raged in America, on how to proceed in the postwar world? After all, objective economic conditions cannot explain the broad agreement on comprehensive social insurance and state responsibility for a national minimum. On the contrary, strict economic calculation would have tended to justify much less generous public policies toward individuals in favor of social welfare as such.

In this connection it is vitally important to note that Britain has little, if any, doctrinal *laissez-faire* tradition of the sort to be found both on the Continent and in the United States, so that it was relatively easy for the idea of the social service state to entrench itself in all sections of opinion. The official British social philosophy of most of the nineteenth century— if any social philosophy may be so described—was Benthamite utilitarianism, and this is sometimes thought of as liberal and in the classic *laissez-faire* tradition. But erroneously so. The utilitarians were never committed to—indeed, they explicitly attacked—the grandiose social metaphysics, the providential apparatus of natural law, by which classical *laissez-faire* liberalism was justified. They were in favor of *laissez-faire* only because the loosening of legal restraints on economic activity seemed to them conducive to their sole categorical imperative, "the greatest good of the greatest number." Hence, their *laissez-faire* opinions were always pragmatic and conditional and, above all, coupled with a very considerable tendency toward public manipulation, both to reform rationally the existing exercise of public authority and—more important—to exert public authority in areas where it had not been exercised before. Benthamite utilitarianism tended toward the negative state or the positive state, without any consistency of doctrine, depending solely upon whether public authority or private liberty seemed most conducive to public welfare. It was, in short, a typically British sort of creed. Before the middle of the nineteenth century it was still predominantly *laissez-faire* in its preferences; after that it was gradually transformed, particularly by John Stuart Mill, into a near-socialist creed.

Apart from utilitarianism, the most influential intellectual movements in the last century or so (politically speaking) have been Oxford Idealism and Fabian Socialism, both of which preached doctrines anything but *laissez-faire* in character. Fabianism may be regarded, for all practical purposes, as manipulative utilitarianism taken to its logical conclusion, leavened with a tender-minded humanitarianism and ornamented with a few ill-digested concepts and theories from the Continental socialist ideologies. Idealism, a philosophy elaborated chiefly from German antecedents by an impressive succession of influential Oxford professors—T. H. Green, F. H. Bradley, Bernard Bosanquet—also justified the social-service state, although on far less pragmatic grounds than either post-Benthamite utilitarianism or Fabianism.

All these movements were, of course, largely "intellectual" movements rather than popular ideologies, however much more influence they wielded than the usual American intellectual movement. But they reflected an altogether different movement which had perhaps greater influence on modern British society than any other: the Evangelical movement. The importance of Evangelicalism in molding both private and political morality in Great Britain can hardly be exaggerated. One famous historian has attributed the fact that England escaped without lower-class revolution in the nineteenth century largely to its influence, and if this means that Evangelicalism induced attitudes among the upper classes that helped to take the curse off the Industrial Revolution and the callousness from bourgeois liberalism the theory is substantially correct. Out of it grew a number of complementary political and economic strands. In the working class it induced both a certain resignation to the condition of being a

worker and a commitment to an essentially ethical, fundamentalist socialism; at any rate, the non-conformist chapel, for a long time, was the chief
center of British trade unionism and socialism. Among the upper classes
it induced chiefly a crusading private humanitarianism, an almost incredible amount of philanthropy, of which the names of Edwin Chadwick
and Lord Shaftesbury have become symbolic. The movement was not
restricted to non-conformists but gradually won adherents also among the
Anglicans, if only as a defense against the rapid strides of the non-conformist sects. As a result, Britain was well on the way toward acquiring a
welfare state by private philanthropy long before she acquired one by
government legislation, and when the postwar welfare state came into
being much of it simply involved taking over facilities previously provided
by voluntary (mainly charitable) associations: hospitals, ambulances, certain insurance services, and so on. But the important point to note here
is that the Evangelical influence, as much as and more than the British
tradition of pragmatism, blocked the way for the entrenchment of the
harsher *laissez-faire* doctrines as well as the harsher reactions to those
doctrines.

Inevitably, these currents of thought were reflected in party politics. It
is almost useless to search British party history for a free-enterprise party.[3]
It may be easy enough to find parties looking out for business interests
but this is not the same thing as ideological commitment—pronounced
mental predisposition—to a free-enterprise system. The Conservatives, for
example, engaged in a downright indecent wooing of the lower classes in
the nineteenth century, trying, like Bismarck in Germany, to steal the
thunder of the social reformers and thus to preserve the submissive loyalty
of the lower classes to the aristocracy. Thus, Disraeli's Tory Democracy
envisaged an alliance between "the cottage and the throne"—the lower
classes and the aristocracy—by which the latter undertook to enact broad
social and economic reforms in return for the political support of the
former—and it should not be forgotten that the most crucial extension of
the franchise in the nineteenth century, the Reform Act of 1867, was
made by Disraeli's Conservative Government. When Harold Macmillan
wrote his book *Reconstruction* in 1934 he showed that the tradition of
Tory democracy was then still very much alive in Tory ranks. His book
was a staunch defense of capitalism, but a capitalism conceived as a sort
of super-New Deal, involving a high degree of public planning, cartel-like
controlling councils over various sectors of industry jointly operated by
management and trade-union leaders, guaranteed annual wages to employees, and an extensive range of public social services, among other
things in kind. This Conservative tendency toward economic radicalism

---

[3] Only certain wings of the nineteenth-century Liberal Party qualify.

is no doubt the result, in part at least, of political opportunism, but it also reflects the aristocratic foundations of the Conservative party, particularly the aristocratic tradition of paternalism and social service, which powerfully reinforced the Christian motivations of great nineteenth-century reformers like Lord Shaftesbury.

The Labour Party's welfare state was less a radical innovation than an extension of and compromise between all these currents of ideas, powerfully reinforced by "circumstances": the constantly more serious and more perceptible deterioration of Britain's economy from neglect and old age, the traumatic impact of the Great Depression, and, most important of all, the impact of the second World War. The war pushed Britain into the present welfare state not only by its effect on the British economy, but even more by its impact on social thought. The worst problems of prewar society vanished in the war. Unemployment disappeared and a major effort was made to share the resources of the country fairly among all by rationing, price controls and subsidies, the net result being, strangely enough, a greatly increased standard of living for most of the British population. The chief condition of this desirable state of affairs seemed to be collective effort and a deep community consciousness in the whole nation—a feeling of neighborliness and fraternity unprecedented in British history. The War therefore strongly consolidated opinion behind the idea of dealing with the problems of peace as with those of war; by public planning, collective controls, and social guarantees to every individual of a "fair share" of the national wealth. It is no exaggeration to say that Göring's Blitz was the force that coalesced all the converging strands of Christian humanitarianism, utilitarian pragmatism, Idealistic statism, Fabian socialism, and aristocratic paternalism into the social program pursued since the War. In outline, at any rate, the whole program was sketched in the two Beveridge Reports that appeared in the course of war—one on Social Insurance, the other on means to ensure full employment by public policy—and that all parties were pledged to implement as soon as circumstances would permit.

In view of all this it is not surprising that most of the social policies resorted to by the postwar Labour Governments actually originated outside the party and the Fabian Society; that they were subscribed to by almost all sections of political opinion; and that they seem now to be accepted, in essence, almost as a natural feature in the social landscape.

The Welfare State in Operation, 1945-1951

NATIONALIZATION

When Labour set about nationalizing a number of important industries the step was widely represented in America as revolutionary in character, and, except perhaps for the socialized medical services (which also involved nationalization of a sort), the nationalized industries have received more publicity abroad than any other aspect of the welfare state. It is not difficult to understand this foreign emphasis on socialization measures, but it is nevertheless misplaced. There certainly was no wholesale expropriation of private property of any revolutionary sort; all that happened was the transfer, at generous (perhaps overgenerous) rates, of the stock of a few enterprises from private to public hands. Most of the British economy is still privately owned and, indeed, Labour seems committed even today to nationalizing no more than about one-fifth of the economy. The only industries and businesses nationalized were the Bank of England, coal, electricity and gas, inland transport (railways, canals, road haulage), iron and steel, air transport and cable and wireless—strategically important sectors of the economy all, but still only a fraction of the sum total of the economic establishment. It follows that nationalization was approached as a means rather than an end in itself and that greater weight was attached to other aspects of the welfare state.

Moreover, the ground for the postwar nationalization measures had been prepared by the Liberals and Conservatives at least as much as by Labour. It was the Liberal Party that began the whole trend toward public enterprise by the creation of the Port of London Authority (which owns and operates docks and harbor facilities on the lower Thames) in 1908, and the Conservatives powerfully pushed the trend along by the creation of the Central Electricity Board in 1926, the chartering of the British Broadcasting Corporation as a public corporation in 1927, and the creation of the London Passenger Transport Board in 1933 (by a Conservative-dominated National Government). Equally important, almost all the postwar nationalization measures (iron and steel being the sole exception) were undertaken as the result of the findings and recommendations of Conservative-dominated investigating committees: the Bank of England measure, for example, as a result of the Macmillan Report, coal because of the Reid Report, gas because of the Heyworth Report, and electricity because of the McGowan Report. And not least, nationalization, as carried out by Labour, had much less effect on the structure of the industries nationalized than might be supposed. There was no revolutionary upheaval in management, or in the organization of the industries, or in labor relations, or even in commercial practices. The change from private to national enterprise, as the more radical Labourites learned to their displeasure, involved changes in form much more than in substance. Nevertheless, one should not deflate the nationalization program too much. It is noteworthy because it provides an excellent insight into the attitudes that gave rise to the British welfare state and because it has raised, despite its modesty, serious institutional problems.

A great deal can be learned about the character of modern British socialism by an examination of the reasons that induced the nationalization measures. Nationalization may be the result of two very different kinds of reasons, one essentially "ethical" (or doctrinaire, ideological, philosophical, theoretical—whichever term is preferred), the other essentially "pragmatic-economic." The older socialist arguments for nationalization were overwhelmingly of the ethical variety, even in the case of the Fabians. For all their managerialism, the Fabians' distaste for "unearned increment," their distrust of large private power concentrations, and their ethical preferences for industrial democracy were as decisive in shaping their views as their criticisms of the wastefulness of private enterprise. But throughout the twentieth century the case for public enterprise was shifted more and more onto pragmatic-economic grounds. Thus, in *Let Us Face the Future*, the Labour Party's election manifesto of 1945, it was stated that only industries "ripe or overripe" for public ownership should be nationalized. And a pamphlet issued in 1948 to clarify this rather ambiguous formula (*Public Ownership, The Next Step*) pointed out that this meant industries having one or preferably more than one of the following characteristics: that the industry be (1) *a basic supplier of raw materials*; (2) *monopolized by a large trust*; (3) *inefficient*, because unable to find finance for capital investment, or split into units too small for economical operation, or burdened with a very low standard of management; (4) an investor of capital on a very large scale; (5) suffering from very *bad industrial relations*. Except for the neglect of the fourth consideration, the postwar program of nationalization faithfully followed these highly pragmatic criteria.

The Bank of England,[4] for example, was nationalized for the following reasons. First, because the Bank already had such close relations with the Treasury that nationalization was essentially only a formality. As Chancellor of the Exchequer Dalton put it, "the Old Man of the Treasury and the Old Lady of Threadneedle Street should be legally married to avoid any further danger of their living in sin." But these close relations rested mainly on an informal basis and, it was feared, depended on a community

---

[4] Since American readers can hardly be expected to be familiar with so strange a foreign phenomenon as the Bank of England, a brief description is probably in order. The Bank is a sort of cross between an ordinary bank, a Federal Reserve Bank and the Treasury itself. It was a private bank until 1945 but handled all government funds, all foreign transactions, made loans, set interest rates, etc. It acted in close alliance with the Treasury, but its directors could and sometimes did act independently. It was owned by private investors but actually run by a Court of Directors that was not elected but was a sort of self-perpetuating oligarchy.

of outlook and interests between the Bank's directors and the people in the Treasury that would. cease to exist once a socialist Government achieved full power. This fear was the result particularly of beliefs that financial policy between the wars had been made less by the Treasury than by Mr. Montagu Norman (later Lord Norman), the Governor of the Bank from 1920 to 1944, and that, on a number of occasions, the Bank had actually used its position to sabotage government policies. Hence, the second reason for nationalization: to make the Bank a reliable and obedient tool for economic planning, and particularly an instrument with which to control the activities of the private banking system for public ends. At one time, indeed, Labour Party theoreticians had argued the necessity of wholesale nationalization of the banking system for purposes of financial planning to maintain full employment, but this more am- bitious proposal was dropped in favor of nationalizing the Bank of Eng- land only and giving it general powers of direction over the private banking sector.

The case for nationalizing the coal industry was even more strikingly pragmatic. Coal is the only raw material found in anything like abund- ance domestically. But this industry, on which the whole of Britain's industrial life depended, was in desperately bad condition in 1945 and had been for some decades before. It had given no evidence of being able to straighten out its difficulties and absolutely none of being able to com- mand the capital investment necessary to expand and improve to the level required by the planned postwar expansion of production. Hence, what, other than transferring the industry to public ownership, could be done? Almost everything that could have been wrong with the industry was wrong with it. It suffered from all sorts of geological disadvantages. It was technologically hide-bound and backward, and organized in a wasteful way. It was afflicted with bad working conditions: rates of accidents and occupational sickness were shockingly high and getting worse almost yearly.

Needless to say, labor relations in the industry were not cordial. The miners hated management with an implacable hatred and quit the in- dustry at every opportunity, sometimes at the greatest hardships, even during the Great Depression, thus slowly robbing it of precious manpower, the more precious because of its inadequate technological condition. Man- agement, in turn, behaved according to the worst stereotypes of the capitalist. For all the faults of the industry it never missed returning a profit, not only because the owners skimped on wages, but also because they economized on maintenance, reserves and replacements, taking out everything possible in dividends and fixing prices by cartel-like arrange- ments that allowed even the most marginal of mines to return a profit at the worst of times. A number of investigating commissions had found these facts out between the wars and a number of schemes to correct the situation had been tried, none with any significantly good effects. The last straw came when, during the war, a government controller had to take charge of the industry. No government could possibly have avoided nationalizing the industry after the war.

The reasons underlying Labour's other nationalization measures (electricity, gas, railways, road transport, civil aviation, and iron and steel) confirm the point suggested by the cases we have examined. Labour did not nationalize because it was doctrinally convinced of the superiority of public over private enterprise (although some Labourites undoubtedly were so convinced) but either to rescue vital industries from decay or bring under public control sectors of industry vitally important to effective planning. This conservative character of postwar nationalization can also be seen in the fact that nationalization was not used to achieve any real copartnership between labor and management in the direction of the industries, much less to achieve industrial democracy in the old and usual sense of the term. And this is particularly worth noting since industrial democracy, in one sense or another, was, once upon a time, the whole *raison d'être* of nationalization. In 1919, for example, the Annual Conference of the Labour Party instructed its Executive Committee to work out a scheme for the actual control of industry by workers in which the only problematic point seems to have been whether workers in general or only workers employed in the specific industries concerned should control nationalized enterprises. By the end of World War II, the last spark of syndicalism had apparently gone out of the Labour movement. In the nationalized industries, either no arrangements for workers' participation in management were made, or they were made only for the very lowest management levels (e.g., at pit level in the coal industry), or given such nominal advisory functions, shared with so many other interests (as in the case of the Transport Consultative Committees) as to make them almost valueless. In short, as if to emphasize the non-doctrinaire, almost involuntary, character of its nationalization program, the Labour Government saw to it that, except for the rationalization of industrial organization and similar purely utilitarian considerations, things after nationalization would be very much as they had been before. In view of this, it is not surprising that nationalization appears to have had no exhilarating effects on the workers in the nationalized industries and to have increasingly disillusioned the trades unions.

CENTRAL ECONOMIC PLANNING AND CONTROL

The idea that it is the responsibility of government to direct the economy into socially desirable channels and that the market cannot be relied upon to produce spontaneously an optimum of social welfare is now deeply entrenched in Britain, and central planning is accepted as normal rather than extraordinary procedure. But even in their approach to economic planning and control the British are essentially pragmatic. This is most evident in their preference for certain kinds of planning over others, particularly in their preference for certain "loose" kinds of planning requiring a minimum of direct interference in private decision-making. British postwar planning has been "open-ended" and predominantly Keynesian in character—"open-ended," in the sense that it has not aimed at specific distant goals in the manner of the Russian Five-Year Plans but relied mainly upon short-term adjustments to changing economic conditions in light of certain broad criteria (to increase production, reduce the import-export gap, prevent unemployment, and so on); Keynesian, in the sense that British planners have tended to rely far more on indirect, financial methods of steering the economy (budget policy, control of the interest rate, etc.) rather than on direct physical controls to achieve their objectives. That is not to say that direct physical controls—like price controls, rationing, allocation of scarce materials, special licensing requirements—have not been used; in the nature of Britain's postwar situation they had to be used to a very large extent. But the tendency has been to use a minimum of such controls and, to whatever degree possible, to scrap them in favor of more indirect methods.

A brief word on Keynesianism is in order here, since, together with Fabianism, it provides the chief theoretical foundation of the British welfare state and has probably replaced classical Fabianism as the orthodoxy of the Labour Party. This of course is not the place for even a sketchy exposition of Keynesian theory, but at least the basic attitude of the Keynesians should be understood. Like the *laissez-faire* theorists, the Keynesians believe that the economic system operates in accordance with determinate laws—in predictable patterns—and that it is not chaotic. Unlike *laissez-faire* theorists, however, they do not believe that spontaneous market activity (free enterprise) necessarily and mechanically leads to the most desirable social results. But unlike the socialists, Keynesians do not believe that to solve the economic problems created by free capitalism, capitalist society must be remade in an entirely new image. On the contrary, they want to save capitalism by using the mechanics of the market —after these mechanics are properly understood—to guide the system into desirable directions, avoiding cyclical economic movements, unemployment, inflation, etc. And this they feel can be done with a minimum of bureaucracy and little limitation of entrepreneurial freedom, by purely fiscal methods (e.g., by public spending, taxation policies, or control of interest rates)—methods that would sacrifice few of the virtues of economic individualism while preventing its more unfortunate effects.

These ideas—and Keynesian methods as well—have been the very essence of British postwar planning. The first objective of such planning has been the maintenance of a high and stable level of employment; never again was there to be unemployment of the sort that had existed in the nineteen-thirties. The chief means used to ensure full employment have been two: (1) the maintenance by the government of a level of expenditure considered adequate to provide full employment (i.e., the main proposal of the Beveridge Report on Full Employment) and (2) control of the location of industry. The latter was considered necessary to maintain full employment for the simple reason that adequate total "outlay" alone could not assure jobs for everyone if demand for labor were "misdirected," i.e., if it arose in communities having a scarcity of labor rather than in communities having a surplus. And demand for labor, in the absence of proper policy, is always likely to be to some extent "misdirected" if labor is less mobile than inanimate resources, which it is everywhere, but especially perhaps in Britain. To solve unemployment problems due to low mobility of labor it was decided to bring work to the workers by persuading or compelling new industries to build in specially designated areas. This was done partly by the Distribution of Industry Act 1945, which compels any manufacturer intending to build establishments above a certain size to notify the Board of Trade, which might then presumably plead with him not to go (like everyone else) to London, but to a so-called "Development Area." Even more was accomplished by the requirement that licenses for new construction had to be obtained from the Ministry of Works, which could of course issue such licenses only on condition of construction taking place in the Development Areas.

The economic situation prevailing after the war made it crystal clear that full employment, however important, could be neither the sole nor even perhaps the overriding purpose of planning. Even more important— because, in the long run, the availability of sufficient employment itself depended on it—was the need to maintain a decent balance of payments, particularly with the dollar area. The chief means used to achieve this objective fell into two categories: means used to control and reduce imports, and means used to assure an adequate level of exports. For the first purpose, the most obvious device—import licensing—was employed. For the second, both direct and indirect methods were used. Certain manufacturers were "induced" to sell a certain proportion of their production abroad by certain government sanctions, and necessarily so since extremely easy profits were available in home markets compared to very uncertain ones in areas to which Britain had to export. And, in addition, especially high "purchase taxes" were put on certain items, to discourage excessive domestic demand for them no less than to achieve a certain leveling of incomes.

Closely related to this second objective of British planning are two others, which are both, in a sense, ends in themselves and subsidiary to other purposes of planning: the need to maintain "adequate balance" in production and the need to guard the economy against inflation. "Adequate balance" in production simply means that scarce capital goods and materials are not squandered frivolously, but used in the most economical way, in accordance with national priorities, where most needed. This objective, of course, required a vast machinery for deciding the allocation of materials, channeling investments, and issuing licenses, which, in a sense, constituted the very heart of the planning process. Inflation was feared, as it was everywhere, for its effects on the domestic economy, particularly on certain income groups whose money incomes are not highly adjustable, but equally for its possible effects on the export program, since rises in domestic prices would, of course, lead to increases in export prices or to currency devaluation, which has its own disadvantages. The chief means used to prevent it were what one would expect: a high level of income taxation to siphon off purchasing power, appeals for wage restraints and dividend limitation, profit taxes, and, in some cases, direct government subsidies to producers and distributors to limit the prices of certain specific good.

To achieve all these objectives and to exert general control, direct or indirect, over the economy the government acquired control in one way or another over the following things: foreign exchange, domestic credit, capital issues (securities), prices, incomes, the allocation of materials, and the distribution of labor. In addition to these specific powers, the general condition of the economy could be influenced by direct government expenditures (which grew from about 6 per cent of national income in 1907-08 to about 40 per cent in 1949-50); by direct government investments (which, in 1949, accounted for about one-third of all investments, while another third was made by industries and services in which the government plays a large role); by direct public employment of a vast labor force (one-third of all the employed); and by informal influence exerted over both trade unions and employers, especially, of course, trade unions under the Labour Government.

But we have not yet discussed what was and is perhaps the most crucial objective of all postwar British economic policy—most crucial because all other objectives involve it in one way or another. This was to stimulate productivity, not only in absolute terms, but, even more important, relative to other countries. That is to say, what was needed was not merely a statistical rise in productivity—that was something easy to achieve in most industries as a result merely of technical advances. What was needed, even more, was a rise in productivity, if not to the American level then at least to that of the more efficient competitive European countries, since, in the final analysis, Britain's economic welfare depended upon her ability to keep step with or outstrip the economies of her competitors. But here too, despite the urgency of the matter, the Labour Government was surprisingly circumspect about maintaining the system of private enterprise. Essentially, its approach was the following: first, it established a number of Working Parties, composed of employers' representatives, trade union representatives and independent specialists,[5] to study conditions in the more important industries and to report on means to improve their productivity, based on maintaining the system of private enterprise. Then, it established a series of Development Councils, constituted after the tripartite pattern of the Working Parties, the chief task of which is to do joint research for the industries concerned (by means of funds compulsorily levied on the industry) and to make recommendations, which various parts of the industry may or may not choose to accept; the whole matter being put on a purely voluntary basis, except for the use of certain special financial inducements to "persuade" certain industries to use their Development Councils. Given British industrial conditions, nothing more solicitous of the privacy of private enterprise could be imagined.

In central economic planning, then, the approach of both parties has been to rely on fiscal policy as much as possible; in stimulating productivity, the emphasis has been on "industrial self-government," a friendly synonym for what, in other countries, would be called monopoly. Only in respect to one sector of the economy, agriculture, was a sterner approach adopted, and this more on the statute books than in practice.

Agriculture was already a major problem area in the British economy long before the war, but it became an even more serious problem during and after the war. Because of Britain's international economic position, it was clearly necessary for her farmers to produce as much as possible of her requirements in foodstuffs, although obviously self-sufficiency was out of the question. Increases in agricultural production were particularly required since one of the basic axioms of the "fair shares" policy was to raise average nutritional standards, which, prior to the war, were, for one of the more highly developed and civilized countries, appallingly low. But British agriculture was poorly equipped to meet the task required of it. In the words of an American observer:

---

[5] Seventeen such Working Parties were established, for the following industries: cotton, boots and shoes, carpets, china clay, heavy clothing, light clothing, waterproof clothing, cutlery, furniture, glassware, hosiery, jewelry, lace, linoleum, pottery, wool, jute. Their reports are gold mines of information on British industrial conditions.

On the eve of the Second World War *virtually everything* was wrong with British agriculture. Farming methods were badly out of date, the land was deteriorating, and all classes of the farming population . . . were becoming impoverished.[6]

In the 1930's, the reaction of the predominantly Conservative Government of the period was characteristically Tory: to establish a number of agricultural cartels (Marketing Boards, to use the technical term) controlled by the major domestic producers, to give these cartels legal power to regulate the sale of commodities at any stage between producer and consumer, and to supplement their authority with periodical grants of special aids and subsidies to the Boards. Seventeen such semi-official monopolies were created, and British agriculture, which previously had been ruggedly, though almost disastrously, individualistic, was to a very large extent brought up to the industrial level of corporatization.

On the whole, postwar policy has been not to undo the policies of the nineteen-thirties but to supplement them with new legislation, the Agriculture Act of 1947. This was essentially a bargain between government and farmers by which the government obligated itself to find assured markets at guaranteed prices for most of the British farmer's produce, in return for an undertaking on the part of the farmer to manage his land efficiently, in accordance with certain rules of good estate management and husbandry. Under the Act, the Minister, through negotiations with representatives of the farmers (the National Farmers' Union), works out annual agreements on the commodities to be produced and the prices to be paid for them, the N.F.U., representing as it does some 80 per cent of all the British farmers, undertaking to see to it that production is oriented toward certain annual, mutually agreed targets. In return, the farmers are obligated, under the Act, to cultivate their lands efficiently, on penalty of being dispossessed by the Minister of Agriculture.

These are the harsher measures referred to above. The Agriculture Act of 1947, in fact, came very close to being a nationalization measure, in the sense that all farms privately held are now held only conditionally, the conditions being set by the government. But, as might have been expected, the bark of the legislation has been much worse than its bite. There has been no wholesale confiscation of farm land, nor is there likely to be, even in cases permitting a legal case for dispossession to be made. Farmers who do not live up to the required standards are given every opportunity to remedy their ways before the ax falls and to see to it that the ax does not fall without sound reason. In addition, supervision of the practices of farmers is exercised through County Agricultural Committees, composed

---

[6] R. A. Brady, *Crisis in Britain* (1950).

of local farmers, who tend, not incomprehensibly, to be rather soft on the farming practices of their neighbors. And perhaps most important of all, there seems to be genuine reluctance on the part of the authorities to use the harsher provisions of the Act. In fact, almost no confiscations at all have taken place, even in glaringly bad cases.

REDISTRIBUTION OF WEALTH

The purpose of both nationalization and economic planning has been to increase the efficiency of the British economy. The purpose of redistribution-of-wealth measures is to distribute its benefits more equally by means of public services financed by heavily discriminatory taxation. These measures fall into four categories.

First, the state provides a large range of compulsory social insurance services, based on the recommendations of the Beveridge Report on Social Insurance and Allied Services of 1942. The Beveridge Report's proposal that the state should assume responsibility for providing all Britons with security "from cradle to grave" by means of compulsory public insurance was approved almost unanimously in Britain, both parties being pledged to implement it in the postwar period—a fact which indicates the impact of the war on British opinion. As a result the British now have a remarkable series of social-security measures providing for income during sickness, disability, unemployment, maternity, widowhood, and old age, while special grants are provided for maternity and burial expenses. In short, almost every conceivable exigency of life is covered. These measures are, of course, insurance measures, but they also involve some redistribution of wealth since they are financed only partly from the contributions of the insured, their employers being forced to make sizable contributions to the insurance funds.

Secondly, there are certain "public assistance" measures, financed entirely out of taxation. The purpose of the public insurance measures was, of course, to make "relief" to the poor unnecessary: to replace public charity with enforced voluntary thrift. But it was impossible, even with the greatest foresight, to provide for all conceivable contingencies by means of insurance. Moreover, it was decided, for reasons stated in the Beveridge Report, to base the insurance services on flat-rate contributions and flat-rate benefits, i.e., to have everyone covered by the system pay the same contribution into the national insurance fund and receive the same benefits for various contingencies. But the same contingencies can create different degrees of need under different circumstances: hence, provision was made for special "assistance" in special cases.

Third, certain public services and payments, paid for out of taxation, are provided directly to the public. All British families receive a weekly "family allowance" of eight to ten shillings for every child (after the first). For a long time after the war the local authorities also provided certain foods: e.g., orange juice, cod liver oil and bananas, to families with children, partly for hygienic reasons and partly to see to it that very scarce foods were devoted to the most urgent uses. But most important under this category—indeed perhaps the most ambitious project undertaken by the Labour Government—is the National Health Service. Since 1948, all people in Great Britain have been entitled to receive either free of charge or for payment of very small charges all medical services (including general practitioner, specialist and hospital services) and a large number of auxiliary services: dentistry, ophthalmic care, drugs, health visiting, after-care, convalescent care and home nursing. One can get some idea of the importance of the project from the fact that it consumes annually some £400 million, which is the largest item of civil expenditure in the budget and some 4 per cent of the total national income. The Health Service also involves employment of over 300,000 persons, which makes it one of the largest consumers of man power and physical resources as well. And not least, it is the only aspect of Labour policy that reflects the basic value of classical socialism (to each according to his needs) and that displaced a pre-welfare state system of services with an almost completely new one.[7]

Fourth, certain measures used by the Labour Government were intended to make available to the public goods considered basic necessities of life, at prices everyone could afford to pay. In certain cases, for example, direct subsidies were paid to producers in order to keep their prices down; in others the government itself bought goods in bulk (e.g., meat) and sold them to distributors at a loss. These devices were coupled with retail price fixing and, in cases where special shortages existed, rationing. The items chiefly affected were clothing, food and housing—although not all clothing, food and housing. In the case of clothing, for example, the Government subsidized and fixed the prices of certain kinds of cloth and ready-made garments ("utility" clothing) to make them easily purchasable, while putting special purchase taxes on other, especially high quality, expensive cloth, the idea being to make available to everyone adequate clothing at low prices, at least partly by penalizing those who insisted on being fashionable. A similar system was used in the case of foods. Not all foods were subsidized, but only "basic" foods not naturally available in such abundance that market mechanics could be relied upon to keep their

---

[7] "Almost" completely new because some remnants of the old system of medical services still exist. Some hospitals—for example, "private" hospitals (i.e., those run for profit), some denominational hospitals and trade-union hostels—were not taken over by the Ministry of Health. There is also still some private medical practice, since neither doctors nor patients were compelled to go into the Health Service. But over 95 per cent of both are in it.

prices down. Even in the days of the most rigid austerity one could live a gourmet's life in Britain, but only at a considerable cost, since the prices of non-subsidized and non-rationed foods were raised by the very fact that others were both subsidized and rationed.

All this necessarily involved a considerable leveling of economic differences in society. It is impossible to say just how much in absolutely precise terms, but a few figures will convey at least a general idea of the shift in income distribution. During the postwar period about 40 per cent of total national income in Britain was disposed of by public authorities (compared to approximately 20 per cent in the United States). Not all this 40 per cent, of course, was redistributed income. About half of it went into "running the government," some of it was "redistributed" to the upper and middle classes themselves, and some of it came from taxes paid by the lower classes. Making these allowances, it is generally estimated that some 10 per cent of national income was actually given to people as "free income" in the form of gifts, via the state, from the well-to-do. This is reflected in the fact that real income in the working class (even before "free income") was up 16 per cent over 1938 while the real incomes of salary earners were down 19 per cent and those of dividend earners down 4 per cent. Again, while in 1938, 7,000 people had reported incomes of over £6,000 (then worth $30,000), in 1948 only 70 people had such incomes (then worth $17,000); but at the same time the number of people living in comfortable circumstances, i.e., earning a good but not spectacular living, increased immensely.

But even in the case of economic leveling by means of "fair shares" policies, one can find more than a trace of characteristic British caution. The leveling process was not carried as far as it might have been; certainly postwar Britain was not made into an egalitarian society. The social distances between rich and poor were reduced but the rich were not abolished. But how could one become rich, or even merely stay rich, under Labour policies? The answer is: by living off wealth amassed before the war, or by making large "capital gains" (these, incongruously, were never taxed by Labour), but chiefly by "diddling" the tax collector. It is safe to say that a good many of the larger British incomes are the result mainly of unreported earnings, rigged expense accounts and similar devices. This does not mean that postwar Britain is a plutocrat's paradise, but only that the welfare state has left at least some room for acquisitive activity, conspicuous consumption, and for savings and investment.

One can also see the cautiousness of Labour's approach toward leveling in the fact that it made no innovations whatever in the field of education— and education, as we have seen, is an important source of social differences in Britain, certainly more important than unadorned wealth. It is true that a comprehensive Education Act was enacted by the coalition in 1944 and that its provisions made it easier for gifted lower-class children to make their way into the better secondary schools and universities. But the Education Act of 1944, while opening the educational system more than in the past, did not alter the system in any significant sense. The fact that the sweeping program of the Labour Government of 1945 made no provision for education can therefore only mean one of two things: either that Labourites were unaware of the role of education in determining British social stratification, or, much more likely, that they were not prepared to carry the Cautious Revolution to the deepest roots of the British social system.[8]

The Welfare State Question Since 1951

Throughout the discussion so far the consensual elements which went into the development of the British welfare state have been emphasized. The Conservative Party did of course do its job as the official Opposition while Labour was in power. It carped and criticized and moved amendments; but only on iron and steel nationalization among the major measures did any flare-up of drastic conflict occur, and that measure happened to be the one about which Labour itself felt least confident. The iron and steel industry undoubtedly fits one of Labour's criteria for nationalization: it was a vital industry for purposes of economic planning. Unlike coal and the public utilities, however, it was not a derelict industry, incapable of doing the job required of it, but, on the whole, vigorous, profitable, and progressive. Moreover, iron and steel production was already closely supervised by the Government and a central organization of the industry itself, making obstruction of the Government's economic program unlikely. It was not accidental, therefore, that the industry came far down on Labour's schedule of priorities for nationalization, and that the Government was so willing to accommodate the House of Lords in the matter of delaying the actual transfer of ownership. In view of this, the import of the conflict over iron and steel nationalization should not be magnified.

On other important measures, Conservative opposition was either constructive, or perfunctory, or concerned with marginal details, or incensed with the manner in which legislation had been drafted, or concerned with airy generalities in favor of free enterprise and self-reliance rather than with concrete alternatives. How, after all, could the Tories have done

---

[8] One important aspect of the postwar welfare state, at once a nationalization, planning, and social welfare measure, has not been discussed here. This is Town and Country Planning, designed to achieve general control over land use in Britain. This legislation is so intricate, however, that even a superficial account would consume more space than a general work such as this permits.

more? Objective circumstances press upon Tories as well as Socialists. Also, public opinion overwhelmingly favored the social service state and the Conservatives have ever had a lively interest in getting into office. Furthermore, their own program in 1945 was not so very different from Labour's, nor in any deep sense repugnant to their own ethos. Churchill's declaration of policy to the voters did put great emphasis on personal leadership and went in for a good many resounding flourishes which sound impressively unsocialistic—"this is the time for freeing energies not stifling them," "Britain's character has been built on character and daring, not on docility," "we stand for the fullest opportunity for go and push," and the like; but wherever the declaration got down to brass tacks it sounded more than a little like Labour's program: full employment through Keynesian economic policy, public housing, price controls, subsidies, the planning of land use, compulsory insurance, socialized medicine, and so on. In its essence, then, the Labour program went into effect with the formal opposition but, in most respects, public acquiescence (and perhaps private blessing) of most of the Conservatives.

For this reason, it is hardly surprising that some of our discussion of the welfare state under Labour was conducted in the present tense. No wholesale dismantling of Labour policies occurred when the Conservatives returned to power in 1951. Yet the past tense did enter the discussion—the Tories have in fact modified a good many parts of Labour's program. At first, they went about the business of modification very circumspectly; but their slowness to introduce changes was attributed by many Labourites solely to their narrow electoral victory in 1951, when Labour still polled a larger popular vote but lost due to the distortions of the electoral system. After that, however, the Conservatives went from strength to strength to the point that they hardly are in any danger of losing office in the foreseeable future. Did they use their power, unprecedented in British history, to make very radical changes in domestic policy? How serious are the modifications of Labour's program they have carried out, especially since their second postwar victory in 1955, and what has been Labour's response?

In regard to nationalization of industry, the Conservatives—with two exceptions—have merely held the line between the private and public sectors of industry created by Labour. No additional industries have been nationalized, while two, iron and steel and long-distance road haulage, were returned to private hands, both shortly after the Tories' return to power. Moreover, the nationalized industries today still look very much the same as under Labour. The Conservatives have undertaken no structural changes, except only for minor ones introduced for purposes of managerial efficiency. They may have appointed a somewhat larger number of directors of private firms to the industries' boards and higher managerial positions than Labour would have done, but no wholesale changes in controlling personnel occurred, not least because the managers and directors of the industries already had a decidedly capitalistic flavor under Labour.

It is doubtful that the picture in regard to nationalization would have been very different if Labour rather than the Conservatives had been in power during the last ten years. Through most of this period, the Labour party as a whole has drifted away markedly from nationalization even as a means for achieving its goals (let alone as an end worth pursuing in itself); only the extreme left wing seems still to attach much importance to the idea. A pamphlet of 1949, *Labour Believes in Britain*, did list for probable nationalization certain industries not scheduled earlier: sugar, cement, chemicals, industrial insurance, cold storage and meat slaughtering. Basically, however, the plan was to investigate these industries to see whether they were "ripe" for nationalization rather than to nationalize them without further ado; and when Labour was returned in 1950 it did not in fact propose any new nationalization measures, ostensibly because of its very small majority, but really also, one may suspect, because of uncertainties about the idea of nationalization. The Party's electoral manifesto of 1955 marked a shift at least in degree from its programs in 1950 and 1951: it merely envisaged the return to public ownership of the denationalized industries and added sections of the chemical and tool industries for further nationalization.

In 1957, an important change in the very nature of Labour's approach to power and control in industry was added. In the pamphlet *Industry and Society*, the party proposed in the future to acquire a voice for the government in industry, not by outright nationalization but by purchasing shares in private firms on the open market with funds largely derived from contributions to national social insurance schemes. Industries that "fail the nation" were still to be nationalized, but no particular ones were mentioned and it was assumed that government participation in the private sector would ensure a more responsible management as well as provide a healthy influx of new capital where needed. The importance of this program of course lies in the fact that it committed the party directly to preserving the whole structure of private industry by making government merely a participant in its arrangements; the public corporations set up earlier to run the industries were already a large step in this direction,[9] but not nearly so obvious a step as the proposals of *Industry and Society*.

These proposals were incorporated into Labour's electoral manifesto for 1959, which also reiterated Labour's intention to renationalize road

---

[9] See below, pp. 208-212.

haulage and iron and steel and then, upon repeating the vague "fail-the-nation" formula, said "we have no other plans for further nationalization." By the election of 1959, in short, nationalization was little more than a memory among Labour goals and vague verbal threat against defective managements. Indeed, after the election a movement was launched to delete clause 4, committing the party to the ideal of public ownership of production facilities, from the party constitution. But the attempt rallied in opposition the party traditionalists as well as leftists, became confused with stocktaking on Mr. Gaitskell's leadership, and in any event seemed rather pointless from a practical standpoint—so that, in the end, nothing came of it. Since then, no important changes in Labour thinking have occurred, although a recent proposal by the leadership (not yet official party policy) does incorporate one new and possibly far-reaching idea: the nationalization of building land in order to speed slum clearance, improve town and country planning, and end speculation in land values. This proposal also mentions, still very vaguely however, that nationalization might be used against great concentrations of industrial power (reminiscent of the "ethical" position on public ownership of earlier years) as well as wasteful industries and those already dependent on the state for their very existence, like the aircraft and pharmaceutical industries.

Undoubtedly there are many reasons for this gradual erosion of the ideal of public enterprise. As the squabbles over the issue with the extreme left indicate, it marks the triumph of Keynesian manipulators in the party over the more old-fashioned socialists. It also reflects pragmatic adjustments to popular attitudes, which are undoubtedly running overwhelmingly against nationalization. The performance of the nationalized industries has ranged from dismal to uninspiring, as indeed it had to in view of the nature of the industries taken over—most of them antiquated, long starved for capital, long mismanaged, and engaged in a losing battle against strong competitive industries. In a sophisticated sense one could in fact argue that nationalization has greatly improved some industries and at least kept others from deteriorating much further: none of the industries is now subsidized out of public funds, organization has been rationalized and productivity increased, and prices have gone up less than in the private sector. But what people note is not difficult comparative statistics but the occasional power cut, the dirty and less frequent trains, and the very fact that prices increase. They were led to expect too much of the nationalized industries by Labour itself and so have been widely disillusioned by their performance.

No doubt a massive public relations campaign against nationalization by business has contributed to the shift of attitudes; in the electoral campaign of 1959, business spent four times as much on advertising as the Conservatives, and fourteen times as much as Labour. But we should note that the disillusion has been perhaps most marked in the trades unions, and that in the unions it has been due most probably to the infinitesimal changes which nationalization made in the actual power structures of the industries. The management of the industries changed very little after the transfer of ownership; many of the old executives and directors were kept on, and for this reason, among others, hierarchical relations in the industries, labor-management consultation, and negotiations over conditions of work have improved little from the unions' point of view. The form of ownership was changed, indeed, but not the actuality of power, hierarchy and control. To cite but one set of relevant figures: in 1956, there were 272 full-time and part-time board members in the principal nationalized industries, and of these, 106 were also company directors in private businesses (many holding ten or more directorships and chairmanships). These men inevitably brought to the boards the attitudes, as well as the skills, of the business world. Another 71 board members were "technicians and professional managers," many of them men who had held important positions in the industries before nationalization. Only 47 represented the Labour Party, trades unions, or the cooperative movement. The unions' response to this situation has been largely indifference to the whole idea of nationalization—unlike that of some leftwing intellectuals (and, to be accurate, a very few union leaders), who have argued rather for nationalization measures better designed to realize the old socialist values than for the desertion of the idea itself.

From all this it should be apparent that the difference on nationalization between the parties is much more one of degree than kind. Certainly one can say nothing so simple as that one party is for nationalization and the other against it. That formula might fit the extreme left and far right in the two parties, but both parties are still predominantly moderate. Nor do the parties differ very much in their predominant conceptions of the purpose of nationalization or of the proper structure for public enterprises. One can easily envisage a Conservative government nationalizing industries which "fail the nation" (after all, they practically started the whole business), or Labour not nationalizing anything further unless very drastic failures in the private sector occur.

The parties' approaches to economic planning and control similarly differ in degree rather than kind. The Conservatives did dismantle most of the direct economic controls in existence in 1951, but the process of shifting from direct controls to indirect measures had already begun and been carried quite far while Labour was still in power. By 1951, indeed, one could hardly any longer speak of "planning" by the Labour government in any meaningful sense; rather economic control had taken the form increasingly of forecasting economic eventualities and trying to adjust to them in good time in order to prevent any crisis in employment, prices, investment, or the balance of payments; and the means used toward these ends had gradually shifted from materials allocation, price controls, rationing and licensing to financial and budgetary measures. Economic planning and control in that sense are quite as congenial to the Tories as to Labour; indeed the overall differences between the parties on this subject are diminished by the fact that there is no notable extremist planning faction in the Labour Party to match the minority group of American-style free-enterprisers among the Tories. The relative simplicities of public ownership and financial levelling arrest the attention of the emotional socialist far more than the intricate technical problems of economic planning.

If there are notable differences between the parties in regard to economic planning and control, they are the following three. The Tories are rather less dedicated to planning in principle than Labour; they will readily use economic planning and control devices when circumstances seem to require it, but more pressing circumstances are required to make them act than would be the case under Labour. They are also less ready than Labour to use direct controls. And in regard to indirect controls, their policies tend to be predominantly stop-and-go adjustments to short-range trends and they seem to be much more addicted than Labour to the manipulation of indirect taxes (sales and excise taxes) and of interest rates, devices which affect consumers in the middle and lower income ranges and small businessmen much more than either large concerns or people who are really well-off.

This point has a bearing also upon the parties' attitudes toward the distribution of wealth in society. On this subject, if on any, the parties' attitudes are significantly different, although even in this case one cannot really speak of stark and total opposition. The Tories are certainly committed to the social service state. However, the idea means to them something strikingly different from what it means to most of the Labour Party. To Labour the idea connotes a state which uses its powers to lessen considerably economic stratification, provides on constantly more equal terms the facilities needed for self-realization and improvement, and makes widely available the basic amenities as well as necessities of life. Not that anything like this was achieved under the postwar Labour government, or that certain Labour policies, or lack of Labour policies, did not have contrary effects. But this is the dominant image of the social service state in Labour minds. To the Tories, however, the social service state means Beveridge, and nothing more: full employment and a decent, but not too decent, minimum guarantee to all, balanced by the need for incentives to individual enterprise, self-reliance and the operation of a substantially free market. Hence the parties draw the boundary between state and individual responsibility at different points; put different amounts of emphasis on payments for state services, direct or by insurance; differ in their attitude toward means tests for public benefits; and differ also in the extent to which they encourage private welfare schemes in place of governmental services.

The Conservatives have in fact altered a good many of Labour's redistribution of wealth schemes since 1951. To be sure, some of these modifications were also anticipated by the Labour Government. For example, it was a Labour Government which first began withdrawing subsidies, price controls and rationing schemes when certain necessities became more abundant after the war; in ending such measures for distributive purposes altogether, the Tories, at most, carried out more quickly what Labour would have done in any case. It was also a Labour Government which first instituted charges on certain services supplied by the National Health Service. The Conservatives merely continued and, quite recently, extended the Labour charges, and have certainly not made them prohibitive in nature. In this case, however, important differences of attitude governed the parties' actions. The Labour Government applied its charges during the economic emergency created by the need to rearm during the Korean War. We have no reason to doubt its announced intention to remove the charges when the economic situation improved. A substantial body of opinion which loathed the charges always existed in the party—indeed, it was the dispute about the charges, even more than about rearmament as such, which caused Aneurin Bevan's famous resignation from the Cabinet in 1951. No such body of opinion exists on the Conservative side. The Conservatives kept the charges in effect, and increased them, despite the lack of any discernible economic compulsion. They did so, they said, because most people could in fact afford to pay them, and those that could not could recover their money by appealing to the National Assistance (i.e., relief) authorities. That motive for Health Service charges, it will be easily seen, is very different from Labour's, and represents another conception altogether of the welfare state.

It has been alleged that there was even more to the Conservative extension of the Health Service charges than they said: that the charges were extended to enable the government to give tax concessions to the upper income brackets. It is difficult to determine whether this is so or not, but it is a fact that tax concessions to the better off were in fact made shortly after the extension of the charges—and were themselves followed in quick succession by increases, under pressure of an economic crisis, in indirect taxes bearing most heavily on the lower income groups. None of these measures, however, involved any enormous sums; they do not imply that the Tories are unqualifiedly tough on poverty and tender toward wealth, but only portray certain differences in the dispositions of the parties.

In addition to the imposition and extension of charges, the withdrawal of subsidies and price controls (including, recently, most rent controls), and the greater use of indirect taxes, the Conservatives have modified Labour's levelling measures in three other ways. One of these is to finance a somewhat greater proportion of the public welfare services out of insurance contributions rather than general tax funds—in other words, to have the recipients of benefits pay for them indirectly. In the four years between 1957 and 1961, for example, the insurance contribution to the National Health Service was approximately trebled, although it should be noted that even under Labour a small fraction of the cost of the Health Service was taken out of insurance contributions and that, despite the recent increases in insurance payments, the Service is still financed mainly out of taxation—that it is still an important channel for the redistributing of wealth. Secondly, the Conservatives have made a wider use of "public assistance" (relief) based on means tests than Labour: we saw an example of this above in the case of Health Service charges. And third, a good deal of encouragement has been given to private welfare schemes (such as private pension plans), by means of tax advantages and the refusal to extend welfare legislation to areas not sufficiently covered by the existing schemes.

Some Labourites even argue that, very indirectly and covertly, the concessions made to such private schemes tend to neutralize to a large extent the redistributive effects of the government's welfare measures. They claim that enormous sums are lost to the government through the tax reliefs and exemptions involved, and that private pension schemes in fact spread earnings over longer periods and free them from taxation. They also claim that large sums are lost to the Exchequer through the wide use of other fringe benefits for employees, especially those in the executive brackets: health services; child allowances; death benefits; personal expenses for travel, entertainment, dress and equipment; meal vouchers; motor cars; season tickets; housing; holiday expenses; children's school fees; and many others. Britain, according to their account is still two nations—not so much of poverty and wealth, but of those whose wages constitute their total personal income and those for whom the taxable salary is merely a kind of base pay; and this difference is particularly marked in old age, when one part of the country becomes dependent on very meager public old age benefits (about seven dollars a week, until recently regardless of previous income) while the other often retires with large lump sums in separation pay, sizable free life insurance policies and a pension going well into four figures per annum and designed to sustain the standard of life a person had before retirement.

While Labour was in power, it made no direct attack on such inequalities—partly, of course, because they were not then quite so marked as now. Recently, however, the party has concentrated an increasing amount of its fire on getting rid of the expenses and fringe benefit "swindle," putting a tax on capital gains and devising a public pension plan geared closely to previous earnings and guaranteeing a sizable income in old age. In the election campaign of 1959, the pension issue was in fact one of the really serious bones of contention, with Labour arguing for a completely revamped scheme of retirement benefits and the Conservatives taking the wind out of their sails by increasing pensions by ten shillings in 1958 and then propounding a plan making very slight modifications in the old system of flat-rate payments and contributions.

A fair-sized gap has thus developed between the parties in regard to social welfare measures. A similar gap seems now at last to be developing between them on education. The Conservatives want to improve the present school system by building more schools, training better teachers, providing to able students more opportunities to rise on the educational ladder—to attend universities and "grammar schools" (public university preparatory schools)—and improving schools which do not prepare for higher education so as to make them less disturbing to parents. But they want to keep the present system; Labour wants to change it. In the election manifesto of 1959, the Labour Party proposed comprehensive high schools on the American model in place of the present division of secondary schools into three kinds (one kind preparing students for higher education, another essentially for white-collar and technical jobs, and a third for manual trades). At the same time the party proposed to end the present system of examination which channels children at age eleven into one stream or another, with little hope of subsequent change. More recently still, the party has even made a first mild attack on the public schools. It has not come out for abolition; but it does want the public school system "integrated" with the state schools, in the sense of some reasonable division of functions between them and more state control over the public schools' activities. The party's plans in this connection are still, however, extremely vague; one can say little more about them than that changes stopping a long way short of ending the public schools system are being discussed. Even this, however, places the party far beyond its position on education when it was in power, and helps to make party differences in regard to social policy perhaps more striking than they have been at any time since 1945.

Party Goals: A Summary

From the data in the previous section a number of broad inferences regarding party goals emerge. One—and it should be specially emphasized, since we have talked so much about party differences—is that a solid basis of consensus undoubtedly exists between the parties. Labour does not want to nationalize all industry and the Conservatives do not want to have a purely private economy; both parties believe in close governmental direction of economic life; and the Conservatives want at least a guaranteed minimum for all—comprehensive freedom from all kinds of misery. Although the parties differ on many details, on the most fundamental of all substantive political issues, the broad relations between government and society, their positions are remarkable close. And even on details, agreement is perhaps greater, though for obvious reasons less discussed, than disputes. After all, the great creations of the postwar Labour Government, from the National Coal Board to the Health Service still exist, and have in many respects fared better under the Tories than under the socialists.

This does not mean, however, that the parties do not offer the voter a meaningful choice of policies. To say, as an English writer on politics once did, that a British election is merely a kind of census for determining who thinks himself Conservative and who Labour is vastly to exaggerate a small amount of truth. There may be no Great Issues between the parties today. There may not even be anything comparable to the tariff and imperial questions of the nineteenth and early twentieth centuries, both persistent themes of passionate party conflict. But for anyone who cares about details of policy as much as questions of basic political philosophy, the parties offer enough for rational choice. And there is at least a chance that some sort of Grand Debate, comparable to the tariff and imperial questions, may now be developing between them on defense and international policy—the sort of issue which increases conflict within the parties as well as between them. At any rate, from an initial position of full commitment to the cold war and nuclear armaments, the Labour Party has gradually been drifting toward the championing of disengagement in Europe and, if not unilateral nuclear disarmament, the idea of a "non-nuclear club"; Labour seems to have become reconciled to let Britain play a secondary role in international power politics, while the Tories have pursued their own version of *grandeur*. One should not (at present) make too much of this, or of other, more minor, differences between the parties on colonial questions and the problems of European integration; but neither should one play down these differences altogether.

The parties offer the voter a meaningful choice. But one should also say that this choice is not between rival ideologies—between comprehensive social philosophies. Hence, to a Frenchman, or a German accustomed to the rivalry of political *Weltanschauungen*, they might not appear to offer any choice at all. Only from the perspective of a pragmatic approach to politics do the differences in party goals assume significance.

Just for that reason, as we said earlier, it is difficult and perhaps foolhardy to draw any overall normative profiles of the parties which pretend to represent permanent party differences rather than ephemeral emanations of electoral competition. Nevertheless, two general and persistent differences between the positions of the parties probably exist:

(1) Even when party policies closely coincide, the conceptions and propensities underlying them are often different. We saw this in the case of the Tory and Labour approaches to social welfare measures, and it is equally true in other cases. Both parties are sufficiently free from detailed and dogmatic preconceptions to be able to adjust policy readily to pressing environmental needs, whether arising from the growth of a superannuated population, or international economics, or the East-West power struggle, or the struggle for development and independence in non-Western areas. Hence the frequent convergence of their policies. Yet these policies are often thought of as emanations of different value schema and different sets of expressive symbols. There is a difference between granting state welfare services as a kind of aristocratic obligation to the lower orders in a hierarchical society and granting them because of a belief in fundamental human equality. There is a difference between the idea of a great and powerful England and the idea of a British obligation to participate in the common democratic struggle against despotism. There is a difference between wanting to reduce overall social inequalities and wanting to give men chances to improve themselves. But the policies rationalized in these terms may be nearly identical. Just because the underlying conceptions tend to differ, however, the responses to environmental pressures may differ also in some respects; convergence does not mean identity. The symbols and shibboleths of party conflict—God, country, hierarchy, authority, commonwealth, property, opportunity, enterprise, and power, for the Tories; equality, freedom, community, peaceability, restraint and "social justice," for Labour—do not govern conduct as rigidly as dogmatic ideologies, but serve as something more than mere language for clothing opportunistic responses to random pressures.

(2) While the moderates in the two parties are often closely alike in their persuasions, both parties have wings of more extreme opinion—groups of men who are less pragmatic in their approaches to politics, more concerned with the particular vested interests of certain social

groups, more divided in the symbols to which they respond and the shibboleths they preach. If one were to contrast merely these extreme wings—the colonialists, the violence-minded, and the doctrinaire free enterprisers in the Conservative party, and the pacifists, unilateral disarmers, nationalizers and extreme levellers in the Labour party—one might get something akin to party conflict patterns in France and, until recently, in Germany. Sometimes indeed these extreme groups split from the main bodies of the parties (it is always they who split) and offer separate choices in elections, usually without success. Neither wing has, or has had, or is likely to have, any chance of achieving power on its own. Yet within the parties each has a certain effect. Furnishing as they do many of the party militants, and representing as they do bodies of opinion which, though small, can swing plurality elections, the party extremes constantly have a bifurcating effect on party policy. They are a counterforce to the consensus and pragmatism which predominates in British political life and thus help, as it were, to keep the party struggle honest— something more than electioneering by different segments of the same elite. And this makes the extremists very useful, for without them democracy might seem to have little point in so harmonious a society as Great Britain.

[10]

The Impact of Policy on the Pattern of Power

Policy and the pattern of power are interrelated. The pattern of power produces policy and carries it out. Policy, in turn, affects the pattern of power, first of all through affecting the political interests in society and secondly, more directly, through its impact upon the machinery of government. In this chapter we shall discuss certain aspects of this inter-relation, concentrating on the institutional significance, as it were, of the highly developed welfare state. In essence, the welfare state raises two important institutional problems: whether a form of government developed prior to the age of positive government can effectively discharge the tasks which positive government sets, and whether such a form of government can survive a radical change in governmental functions without crucial modifications.

The development of the welfare state has certainly changed the British political system in several important respects. The sum total of government activities has grown immensely. Moreover, the government is now engaged on a large scale in unprecedented *kinds* of activities, especially the direct provision by the state of goods and services to the members of society (medical care and drugs, many sorts of insurance, coal, transportation, electricity, gas, and entertainment, in addition to the more traditional public goods and services, education and postal services), and the direct assumption by the state of certain decision-making functions in areas previously subject solely to private decision-making, e.g., by means of price controls, rationing, or the allocation of capital goods. Contemporary

British government, then, is something novel, both in scope and kind. But the machinery of government that has to perform the new functions developed in times when government was a more leisurely activity and much less directly concerned with the direction of social and economic affairs. Hence the first problem posed by the interrelation of power and policy in the welfare state: To what extent is the structure of government, as developed in the past, appropriate to the efficient performance of the tasks of the welfare state? To what extent has it been possible to make the necessary adaptations and adjustments? And to what extent are these adjustments compatible with the values and structural requirements of democratic, responsible, parliamentary government?

The second problem is to assess the significance of the institutional changes made under the impact of welfare state policies from the standpoint of the overall structure of British government. It is possible that structural innovations made with no more revolutionary intention than to achieve efficient administration may create changes on the most fundamental level of the governmental process: in the distribution of effective power. On the other hand, the extent and nature of structural innovations for welfare-state purposes have themselves been limited by ancient usage and contemporary values, simply because Britain is a country where usage counts for a great deal and where welfare-state values do not have a monopoly on the political sentiments. The impact of the welfare state, on the British machinery of government involves, in fact, an interplay between the exigencies of effective administration on one hand and the injunctions of constitutional values on the other. The question is whether the latter are sufficiently powerful to neutralize the former, or the former the latter, or whether British government today still involves a substantial balance between old values and new requirements.

Parliament in the Welfare State

The eclipse of Parliament—that is, the shift of decision-making powers from the House of Commons to its leaders and to the administrative Departments—is not solely or even primarily a result of the welfare state. The process was already well under way before 1945. Parliament never possessed "sovereignty" in the sense that French Assemblies have possessed it; and what drained away its powers in the twentieth century was the development of a highly disciplined, national two-party system, much more than welfare-state policy. Nevertheless, the welfare state undoubtedly has acted as a catalyst on the process, because of its demands for special technical knowledge in decision-making (which an assembly of politicians, in the nature of things, can hardly be expected to possess) and because of the tremendous volume of business Parliament would have to transact if it tried to preserve the old balance between its own decision-making powers and those of other agencies.

THE PARLIAMENTARY TIMETABLE

The unavoidable impact of the welfare state on British political institutions can certainly be seen most clearly in the effects the sheer quantitative pressure of business has had on parliamentary transactions. In almost every decade in the last century the number of days spent in session has increased: from 111 "sitting-days" in 1865-74, to 127 in 1895-1904, to 149 in 1925-34, to an enormous 172 in 1954; and that, one may suppose, is just about the maximum.[1] But even this brutal extension of the session has not sufficed to arrest certain regrettable tendencies discussed in an earlier chapter: the vast increase in the amount of executive legislation, the severe curtailment of parliamentary debates, and the decline in the powers and status of private members. Even if no tremendous constitutional issues are raised by the pressure of business and its consequences the matter raises such great practical difficulties in the conduct of government that we ought to take a closer look at how parliamentary time is allocated.

The timetable (agenda) governing parliamentary business is announced weekly by the Leader of the House of Commons, whose chief function is to control the allocation of parliamentary time and who is usually a very high-ranking Cabinet officer, on a par with the Chancellor of the Exchequer and the Foreign Secretary in the upper echelons of the Cabinet. The announcement is usually made on a Thursday, in response to a "private notice question"[2] by the leader of the Opposition. It is frequently followed by a row, as private members protest against the omission of pet subjects. But these rows almost never achieve their object against the hordes of automatic supporters of the Government. This does not mean, of course, that the parliamentary agenda is arbitrarily determined by the Government and forced on the Opposition. On the contrary, it is invariably the product of close consultations between Government leaders and Opposition leaders, Government Whips and Opposition Whips, and while it is the Government that decides, it almost invariably does so with scrupulous regard for the reasonable requests of the Opposition. Indeed, as we shall see, the Opposition not only has influence with the Government in regard to the parliamentary timetable but directly controls a very sizable chunk of it.

---

[1] Parliament cannot, of course, spend 365 days a year in session. One must subtract from the total week ends (130 days per year, counting Fridays as half-days) and time for holidays (perhaps another 45 days, including a summer holiday of civilized length).
[2] Such questions are not printed on the Order Paper and are therefore used whenever it is desirable to secure an answer to a question without delay.

While the parliamentary agenda is announced weekly it is in fact planned, in broad outline if not in narrow detail, for a much longer period: a whole session or, indeed, the whole five-year tenure of a Government. Such long-range planning is supremely necessary for a Government with a sizable mandate (like the Labour Government of 1945) since without it the sheer pressure of parliamentary business could prevent enactment of its program. Hence, it is scarcely surprising that the institution of long-range planning of the parliamentary agenda was one of the first innovations brought about by the postwar welfare state. The whole process in fact was begun by the Labour Government of 1945.

When Labour came to power in that year it was confronted by a very nasty problem in regard to parliamentary time. It had an unusually large mandate to fulfill as a result of its victory in the General Election. It had to pass through Parliament certain absolutely urgent bills not a part of its program (for example, the annual Army and Air Force Bills). It was confronted by volumes upon volumes of bills wanted by individual administrative Departments and advocated, at Cabinet level, by various Ministers. And there was the usual clamor for the usual masses of legislation by pressure groups. Clearly, there was no chance whatever of submitting all the legislative projects involved to Parliament. But how was it to decide which projects to introduce and in what order?

The first task was to calculate the amount of time available for legislation. This could be done by taking the total number of sitting-days in the session and subtracting from it time for the following things:

(1) *Private members' time*, i.e., time set aside for backbenchers to put down motions for debate or introduce legislative projects.

(2) *Opposed private Bills*,[3] which are debated evenings after 7 P.M. at the discretion of the Chairman of Ways and Means,[4] time being taken for such business out of Government, not Opposition or private members', time.

(3) *Debates on urgency adjournment motions;* the time required for this also comes out of Government time, at the virtual discretion of the Speaker.

(4) *Debates on motions of censure;* the tradition here is that when-

---

[3] Private bills are not to be confused with private members' bills. The latter are simply "public bills" introduced by private members. Public bills lay down legal provisions pertaining to the whole community or general classes of the community (doctors, drivers, pedestrians, etc.). Private bills deal only with specific local, corporate or individual interests. Such bills must be passed whenever, for example, a local authority wants to introduce some new service (say a bus service) or whenever an organization created by Act of Parliament (e.g., a railroad) wants to do something that its parliamentary charter does not authorize. Parliament transacts a vast amount of such private business, most of it routine, only disputed projects coming before it for debate.
[4] One of the presiding officers of the House.

ever the leaders of the Opposition put down such a motion the Government is required to make available out of its own time at least one whole day for debate.

(5) *Debates on subjects on which very large numbers of members want debates*, especially non-party or foreign policy subjects, for which, provided public demand in Parliament is large and vociferous enough, permission to use the Government's time is hardly ever refused.

(6) *Annual financial business,* to be described below. The time devoted to financial business, much of it under the direct control of the Opposition, accounts for by far the largest chunk of time not under Government control (approximately 45 days every year).

(7) *Other kinds of routine or recurrent debates*, such as the Debate on the Address (6 or 7 days per session), debates on the eves of periodical holidays, and on the reports of the nationalized industries (although these are not yet a firm fixture in parliamentary usage). Here again, much time is actually at the disposal of the Opposition.

(8) *Debates on Statutory Instruments*.

(9) *Government motions,* i.e., motions designed to obtain endorsement of some Government action, or proposed Government action, where no formal parliamentary motion is really required, or motions to obtain an expression of parliamentary opinion for any purpose.

After subtracting time for all of these purposes from the probable total of the session, something in the neighborhood of 70 days was found to remain for the Government's legislative business. This, however, was only the first, and the easiest, of the calculations that had to be made. In addition, a fairly elaborate scheme of priorities for projects had to be devised. Then, it was necessary to calculate how much time each Bill to be submitted would require in the House. Finally, all these calculations had to be converted into a schedule for the five-years' legislative business and the schedule itself adjusted and modified as unforeseen circumstances arose. Herbert Morrison, who was Mr. Attlee's Leader of the House, has described the whole process, accurately enough, as the "slaughter of the innocents," the knife being wielded by a special Cabinet Committee (the Future Legislation Committee, headed by Morrison himself) in close consultation with Ministers, whose chief contribution to the process seems to have been endless and impassioned pleading for their own pet projects.

All this illustrates two important points, apart from the sense in which the welfare state has affected the governmental process. One is the amazingly tight control British Governments have over parliamentary time.[5]

---

[5] Compare the power of British Cabinets over the parliamentary agenda with that of French Cabinets under the Fourth Republic. Nothing illustrates more strikingly the differences between the two systems.

It is this, of course, that made it possible for the Labour Party to enact such a thoroughgoing program of reform. Secondly, the process by which parliamentary time is allocated illustrates that the considerable powers of British Governments are exercised in a disciplined and constitutionally "moral" way, with due respect for parliamentary usage and in close collaboration with the Opposition. But "Opposition" here, it should be noted, means the leaders of the Opposition, not any mere backbencher. When negotiations regarding parliamentary time take place through what the British call "the usual channels," it is the actual and potential leaders of Parliament (or their Whips) who do the negotiating, while private members can exercise influence on the agenda only through their spokesmen. Indeed, the item of traditional parliamentary business that is usually encroached upon by Governments to eke out the meager ration of time is Private Members' Time. The sanctity attaching to Opposition time does not at all attach to backbenchers' time, and that is important.

Because of the negligible role played by private members in the planning of the agenda, the close collaboration between Government and Opposition leaders is all the more important to prevent arbitrary control of parliamentary business by the Cabinet. And because of this perhaps the most regrettable consequence of the constriction of parliamentary time has been to subject the easy collaboration between Government and Opposition on the agenda to severe strains which indeed may ultimately have important constitutional consequences. There is some evidence that, because of acute pressure of business, Governments are becoming rather less tolerant of Opposition demands for time than they used to be; note, for example, the great increase in the number of guillotine motions (almost always opposed by the Opposition). On the other hand, the Opposition seems to be discovering that it can use the pressure of time in the House as a political weapon, as did the Conservatives in 1951 when they tried to break the Labour Government by subjecting it to a long series of all-night sessions debating delegated legislation.[6] Thus pressure of business, however prosaic and merely quantitative a change, has not only produced difficulties in calculation and procedural adaptations (like the increased use of the guillotine or of parliamentary committees), but may even produce changes on the far more fundamental constitutional level, i.e., in the relations between Government and Opposition.

Could anything be done to relieve the pressure of business? Writers on British government have made a great many minor suggestions[7] and one

---

[6] Motions on delegated legislation are not subject to the Hour of Interruption at 10 P.M. and therefore are ideal instruments for obstructing other parliamentary business or breaking overworked Ministers.

[7] E.g., omission of the Financial Resolution Stage in the discussion of Bills, reducing the number of debates on financial legislation, reducing the amount taken for private Bills, omitting certain forms of parliamentary ritual, etc.

major one: a drastic change in the parliamentary committee system. The House of Commons has been frequently criticized for taking too much legislative business in Committee of the Whole House.[8] This, it is argued, is unwise, since the purpose of the Committee Stage in legislation is to save time for the whole House and to get the sort of free, easy, intimate and technically informed debate one is unlikely to have in a large assembly. But the consideration of legislative business in Committee of the Whole House is a deeply ingrained tradition that, despite constant attempts at reform, has tenaciously persisted. Governments have rarely let "great measures" get off the floor of the House of Commons at any phase of their passage and at present it is generally agreed that Bills of "first-class constitutional importance" should be considered by Committee of the Whole House rather than one of the smaller Standing Committees.

More seriously, there has been much criticism of the Standing Committees of the House themselves, chiefly on three grounds. One is that they are not specialized committees—like those in Germany and the United States, which deal with special functional categories of legislation (Agriculture, Finance, Foreign Affairs, etc.)—but general purpose committees which deal with any legislation brought before them, regardless of subject. Secondly, the British committees have been criticized for their enormous size. Each consists of around sixty members (selected so as to duplicate the proportions of Government and Opposition supporters in the House itself). That means they are really miniature Parliaments, each almost as large as the American Senate, and hardly the sort of place where business can be transacted expeditiously. Finally, it has been alleged that the committees are too few—in fact there are only five, called Committees A, B, C, D and Scottish, although other countries seem unable to do with fewer than a dozen or two, not counting subcommittees.

There can be no doubt that a committee system consisting of a large number of small specialized committees would be more powerful than one consisting of a small number of large general-purpose committees. If any confirmation is wanted, it is surely provided by the Fourth Republic. But that does not necessarily mean that the former is preferable to the latter. Committees of the French and American variety tend, more often than not, to produce an alternative leadership, frequently in open conflict with Cabinet ministers, so that although the system might save time, it might also impair the coherence of policy. Again, in small committees— even if they do not develop the compulsive oppositional tendencies of French committees—Governments can scarcely have as much control over their majority as in large ones and are therefore far more likely to be defeated, or embarrassed by undesirable amendments. The defection of

---

[8] A Committee of the Whole House is simply the whole House of Commons with the Speaker not in the chair.

one or two supporters may indeed mean complete loss of control over a legislative project on such committees; hence Governments are likely to be even more reluctant to let important Bills off the floor of the whole House than they already are. Thus the institution of a committee system designed to dispatch parliamentary business might, paradoxically, succeed only in slowing it down.

There is no easy way to adapt Parliament to conditions created by the welfare state without severely altering its role in British government. And if the choice is between an expeditious Parliament and one from which coherent and consistent policies emerge then surely welfare-state values themselves require that expedition be foregone.

FINANCIAL BUSINESS

Because of the emphasis put on financial planning and control in the British welfare state it is particularly necessary for the Government to have control over financial legislation in the House of Commons. Planning by means of fiscal methods can be successfully done only under certain institutional conditions. At a minimum, it presupposes that the planners have some sort of effective control over public spending and taxation, a requirement rarely met in domocratic countries. But in Britain the Government's control over finance is, if anything, even greater than its control over the parliamentary agenda, so great in fact that it may be misleading to attribute to Parliament any practical role in budget-making at all. When Parliament debates financial legislation, for example, it almost never actually debates financial policy—how much money is to be spent, for what purposes, on the basis of what sort of revenues—but uses the debates for purposes of airing grievances against administration or for criticizing policy. Even more striking, British Governments are so absolutely sure that their financial proposals will be adopted by the House that they begin contracting for expenditures even before the annual Appropriation Act is passed; and the House is so sure that it will adopt the Government's financial policies that it gives legal sanction to the tax proposals even before it had a chance to discuss them. Nothing is more puzzling to the foreign observer than the fact that the House debates financial proposals after it has, in effect, adopted them, and nothing should be more instructive. It makes it clear that the House, whatever it may be, is not a deliberative assembly, deciding policy by exchange of views.

British financial policy is made in two overlapping phases, one concerned with appropriations and culminating in the annual Appropriation Act, the other with taxation and culminating in the annual Finance Act. The process of appropriation begins every year sometime in February when the Estimates are introduced in the House. These are departmental requests for money needed in the impending financial year, collated and reviewed by the Treasury and presented to Parliament in the case of the armed services by the appropriate departmental minister and in the case of other services by the Financial Secretary to the Treasury. Ultimately the estimates are embodied in the annual Appropriation Act, which is usually not passed until some time late in July or early in August. Since the financial year starts on April 1, provision needs to be made for departmental expenditure pending passage of the Appropriation Act. This the House does by voting before April 1 part of the total sum for which departments have asked. Before that date also the House will vote various Supplementary Estimates requested to cover departmental expenditure in excess of the amounts appropriated for the current year.

For all this business the House has set aside a total of twenty-six days—the Supply Days—which are fitted into its work at various times from February until the middle of the summer. On most of these days the House, sitting as Committee of Supply, concerns itself with the estimates of a particular Department. These debates, however, are not normally on financial matters, such as how much money should be provided for a Department or for one of its services. They center rather on Department policies and programs. Thus a grant to the Ministry of Housing and Local Government might be the peg on which is hung a debate over whether the Government in its public housing program is making an efficient use of manpower. The estimate for the Post Office has afforded an opportunity for debate on increased telephone charges—in Britain, it will be remembered, the Post Office owns and operates all tele-communications—and the Foreign Office estimate has been used to set in motion a wide-ranging debate on the foreign policy of the Government.

In essence, then, debates on expenditure provide convenient pretexts for airing grievances and propagandizing the electorate; hence, also, it is entirely appropriate that the twenty-six Supply Days should be Opposition time, that is, days on which the leaders of the Opposition may determine what subjects the House is to discuss.

The situation in regard to taxation is little different. As in the case of expenditure, tax policies are decided by the Treasury and the Cabinet long in advance of April 1. They are submitted to Parliament sometime in April on what is called "Budget Night," when the Chancellor of the Exchequer appears before the House of Commons to deliver a long speech explaining not only the Government's proposed tax policies but also its financial policy in general for the year. In recent years, indeed, the Budget Speech has almost invariably been a high-level exercise in applied Keynesian economics, particularly so when Hugh Gaitskell, a former teacher of economics at London University, was Chancellor. Needless to say,

Budget Speeches are not, and have never been, intrinsically enjoyable affairs, except perhaps in the hands of such a great Budget speaker as Gladstone, who "was the only man who could lead his hearers over the arid desert, and yet keep them cheerful and lively and interested without flagging." Nevertheless, Budget Night is a great state occasion, when the House is crammed to capacity, when Extras are published and almost everyone in Britain is in a state of excitement; the reason being, of course, that the Chancellor's announcement of policy is much more than a mere announcement; it *is* policy and therefore affects everyone where he is likely to be interested most. After the Budget Speech, which is likely to last some hours, the House immediately passes all the tax resolutions (except one which does not actually affect the level or limits of taxation), so as to allow the Government to collect all the new taxes immediately. Then, having approved the tax proposals, the House proceeds to debate them (*sic*), basing its debates on the one unapproved resolution. The debates, first on the Chancellor's budget proposals, then on the Finance Bill brought in to give them effect, last in sum about two and a half weeks, and are distributed, like the debates on expenditure, over a period of some months, while the Government acts on the safe assumption that the outcome will be favorable.

From the standpoint of welfare-state values, this is almost an ideal system. At least it means that the British Parliament is no barrier to effective fiscal planning, unlike the more powerful Parliaments of other countries with their chronic propensities to increase proposed expenditures and reduce taxation and to turn out budgets less by means of con- sidered economic planning than by haggling among ministers, committees and private members.

If the system has flaws they are that financial business is profligate with parliamentary time and that the system operates, as in other countries, on an annual basis. Of all the activities of Parliament, financial business is by far the most time-consuming. There is, moreover, a great deal of repetition in the financial debates, one general policy debate seemingly following another, with roughly the same speakers saying roughly similar things time and time again. More seriously, objections can be lodged against the whole idea of annual budgets as inappropriate to the activities of the social- service state. The periods for which funds are given and the intervals at which financial policies are reviewed do affect the efficiency of administra- tion, simply because economic conditions do not conveniently change to coincide with the beginning of new financial years. A certain sum designed to buy so many airplanes or hospital beds may, because of changes in price levels, turn out to be wholly inadequate for the purpose, while a certain fiscal policy may be made obsolete by the outbreak of a war, or an American tariff change, or a shift in the terms of trade.

These problems are not, of course, insoluble within the framework of annual budgets. It is always possible, if a Department's funds run unexpectedly low, to submit Supplementary Estimates for additional appropriations, and it is always possible to introduce new Budgets in face of unexpected circumstances. The real problem, however, is posed by services requiring appropriations for periods longer than a single year, and many of the new state services require precisely that. The clearest case, perhaps, is the hospital part of the National Health Service. The function of the new hospital authorities, the Regional Hospital Boards, is to plan the general character of the hospital system: its organization and distribution, the conversion of facilities for purposes of optimum utility, the expansion of facilities, the building of new facilities, the hiring and firing of higher personnel, etc. None of this can be done without money and little of it within the space of a year; it just takes longer to build new hospitals, or nurses' annexes, or to convert a maternity hospital into a tuberculosis sanatorium. But funds are voted on a yearly basis and experience has shown that plans made on the basis of one year's expenditure may be nullified, even when implementation has already started, by appropriations made in light of the following year's own peculiar exigencies. There has, consequently, been some agitation for breaking the single annual budget into a number of different budgets, running for different periods—a social-service budget perhaps, an armed-forces budget, and a routine departmental budget—or for annual budgets from which certain services, like the hospital service, are exempt. But it is easy to see the flaw in this. Granted that special budgets would be fine for special services, what becomes of the over-all financial planning function of the Government? In the final analysis, the difficulty is that welfare-state policies have not only introduced new institutional demands, but a large set of different and *contradictory* ones, the administrative requirements of different kinds of welfare-state policies not always being conveniently the same.

Administration

THE PROBLEM OF CO-ORDINATION

Inevitably, the most conspicuous adjustments to the welfare state have been made in the administrative system, the most visible change of all being a very considerable growth in the number of public employees and administrative agencies. This in itself is not perhaps very important. But the growth in the number of civil servants and administrative Departments since the advent of the "positive" state has given rise, indirectly, to at least one serious problem: how to co-ordinate their activities. Co-ordination is required both in policy-making and in the administration of policy. In the case of policy the most obvious reason is the desirability of pursuing a consistent line toward a single set of goals. But equally important is the fact that the policies of one Department almost always impinge on others, even when they are not directly related, and even if only in the sense that new policies frequently involve new charges, so that the adoption of one Department's policies almost always means the frustration of another's. The purpose of co-ordination in policy-making, therefore, is not only to achieve consistency but, perhaps above all, to assure that precious commodities (money, materials, parliamentary time, certain types of manpower) are distributed so as to do the most good, by a kind of marginal utility calculation, rather than being allocated by the blind forces of competition between Departments and Ministers. In the case of the execution of policy, co-ordination is necessary simply because the work of Departments can never be entirely self-contained, and it is especially unlikely to be when the number of Departments is very large and specialization very narrow.

The need for administrative co-ordination is not, of course, something peculiar to the welfare state, but the welfare state has accentuated it by making the machinery of government more cumbersome and complex and by extending government activity to areas in which faulty co-ordination is particularly annoying and wasteful. A good example is housing. Under the Labour Government it was necessary for five major Departments to collaborate before any house could be built in Britain. The Town and Country Planning Ministry had to clear the site, the Board of Trade had to provide certain raw materials, the Ministry of Labour manpower, and the Ministry of Works building licenses, while the Ministry of Health was responsible for housing policy as such. Faulty co-ordination among these Departments could have physically ruined the housing program: sites might have been cleared where no houses were ever built, building materials allocated where no sites were made available, labor assigned where no permission to build had been given. And what applies to housing applies, with a vengeance, to over-all economic policy. That frightful muddles rarely occur (they do sometimes occur) attests to the effectiveness of British co-ordinating machinery.

This machinery works on many levels of British government. At its apex is, of course, the Cabinet, concerned almost exclusively with the co-ordination of policy in the broadest sense. The Cabinet is, in theory, responsible for settling all departmental disputes and smoothing out all friction, but its actual role as an instrument of co-ordination must not be exaggerated. In fact, it acts largely as a high court of appeal settling such disputes as are brought to it (and under modern conditions Ministers are always reluctant to bring even serious disputes before it) and as a body making "high policy," which simply cannot be bothered with all the petty details of co-ordination. Much more is done by Cabinet Committees, although these again are concerned chiefly with very general problems or very notable disputes. The bulk of the work, here as always, is done not by Ministers but by officials, and by the Treasury, the traditional co-ordinating Department.

On the official level co-ordination is achieved in a variety of ways. A great deal is accomplished by multiple appointments, i.e., appointing the same person to related jobs in different ministries. The Chief Medical Officer of the Ministry of Health, for example, has for a long time also been Chief Medical Officer in the Ministry of Education, under whose jurisdiction falls the School Medical Service. Another co-ordinating device is the joint Advisory Committee, i.e., a committee advising a particular Department (or the Cabinet) on which representatives of various other Departments are invited to sit. More important than either of these are the ubiquitous interdepartmental committees, referred to in a previous chapter; more than anything else—even party discipline—these committees are the distinctive hallmark of British government. They exist for all sorts of purposes, from the broadest to the narrowest. There is, for example, an interdepartmental committee for housing and, on the other extreme, there was formed, shortly after World War II, a "Committee on the Spontaneous Manifestation of Personal Gratification on the Cessation of Hostilities." There is also a famous story about a Foreign Office official whose job was to do nothing but make the rounds of Committees the Office was represented upon, and who spent all his time riding about in a taxi, looking in on a committee, smoking a pipe, then taking off again for the next committee.

All this may sound ludicrous, but it is effective chiefly because the British Civil Service is imbued with a tradition of co-operation like that of no other country. Indeed the most effective method of administrative co-ordination in Britain is simple informal contact among members of the higher Civil Service, of which the more ephemeral kind of interdepartmental committee is merely the least informal instance. Members of the Administrative Class have, generally speaking, similar backgrounds, tastes and manners. A good many of them know one another very well, indeed are related to one another. All become, upon entering the Class, members of a very close-knit in-group, having a tradition, a common speaking voice, a common education and common manners. This sort of thing helps to "cement" the executive structure.

But this informal network is concerned more with the co-ordination of administration than of "policy." The co-ordination of the latter is accomplished, in the sense of consistency, mainly by ministerial committees, and, in the sense of deciding the marginal utility of projects, chiefly by the Treasury. The latter is a particularly suitable agency for balancing departmental proposals against one another since it has "control" over both finance and establishments (i.e., staff), both of which are likely to be immediately affected by important innovations, and both of which are likely to raise the issue of "balance" (the utility and disutility of various projects relative to one another) in its starkest and most easily comprehensible form. It is moreover a particularly effective agency for balancing departmental proposals since in fact no successful appeal against its decisions is possible in Parliament, once they have appropriate ministerial support. The only way to challenge the Treasury's decisions is to take the issue before the Cabinet itself. But there appeals on anything but the most urgent and notorious matters are likely to be resented, while, in any case, the Chancellor of the Exchequer is almost invariably one of the most powerful members of the Cabinet itself. Disputes between the Treasury and other Departments do arise and are sometimes taken all the way upstairs, but more often than not the Treasury seems to get its way. But how precisely does the Treasury balance departmental projects?

The review of departmental estimates prior to their submission to Parliament is only one of a number of such means, and while it affords an excellent chance to examine departmental outlays as a whole, weighing them against one another, it is perhaps less important than another means of Treasury control: day-to-day or week-to-week control. This involves, in essence, an obligation on Departments to obtain Treasury approval for any changes in departmental activities having a financial aspect, a rule which, typically, has no statutory basis but arises out of long tradition. In practice, this rule makes the Treasury an omnipresent partner in almost all departmental planning. The Treasury therefore "controls" departmental projects not only by its power to make trouble by disapproving but also through the tendency of Departments to bring the Treasury in on their plans at an early stage. Once it has been called in, the Treasury of course brings to bear the Treasury view on the Department's planning, that is, a government-wide view that is, ideally at least, thoroughly informed on general economic policy, general policy priorities, means likely to be available to staff and finance new projects, and the plans of other Departments to draw on these means. Co-ordination by the Treasury, therefore, is not something done once a year when the Budget is prepared, but a continuous process.

Since control of economic planning of the British sort is essentially a matter of co-ordinating economic policies, and since the British prefer financial to other kinds of planning, it is not surprising that the chief responsibility for it is lodged in the Treasury. But the Treasury merely plays the pivotal role in a rather complicated set of planning arrangements, which, due to the importance of economic planning and its unprecedented character among government activities, we will look at in some detail.

THE ORGANIZATION OF ECONOMIC PLANNING

It is perhaps significant that the organization of planning and the process by which it has been carried out have been so very much in the established British administrative tradition. The burden of work has fallen on the inevitable committees, ministerial, official and joint advisory, and what these committees do is, in essence, not so much to pursue rationally predefined quantitative goals as to adjust and reconcile conflicts (achieving "balance") in light of broad criteria. Perhaps this is due to the fact that the British have a genuine preference for a type of planning so loose as to be hardly planning at all, but little more than surveying, forecasting and compromising. Yet the essentials of postwar planning organization came into being in reaction against economic planning machinery considered too loose to be effective. It is therefore plausible to infer that the "traditionalistic" organization and process of planning result from an inability to adjust administrative usage to the new functions of the state.

Until 1947 the Labour Government tried to carry out economic planning solely by means of the time-honored methods of plural authority, shared by a number of Departments, ministerial committees and interdepartmental committees, with the Cabinet the nominal unifying agency. Chief responsibility for economic planning was vested in a special ministerial committee, the Lord President's (Mr. Morrison's) Committee, except for the export drive and fiscal policy, which were managed by the Board of Trade and Treasury respectively. Under those three focal points of responsibility, at the official level, worked a number of interdepartmental committees, headed by a committee of the permanent heads of the main economic Departments, "the central economic team," which did the important work of gathering data, preparing forecasts, framing plans and supervising their execution. This entirely catholic mode of organization, working in the traditional way (by constant adjustment and compromise), was discredited by the severe economic crisis of 1947 and scrapped for the sake of "tighter" machinery; but precisely of what sort? The "logical" step would perhaps have been to institute some rigidly centralized form of planning organization: perhaps a super-Minister of economic affairs, in direct control of all subordinate economic depart- ments; perhaps an economic general staff drawn from the various Departments but in a position, unlike the usual interdepartmental committee, to issue orders from its central vantage point. These, or similar "centralist solutions," seem almost corollaries of the prevalent desire for more positive and more coherent economic planning. But in fact little more was done than to shift the chief responsibility for planning from a Cabinet Committee to the Treasury, a change that did not, and could not, change the essential character of planning organization and process. It did simplify things by placing the co-ordination of economic policy in the same Department as that of fiscal policy, but that is all. That planning organization and process, even after the metamorphosis of 1947, still followed the loosest traditions of British administration will be seen from even the sketchiest description.

The planning machinery that emerged from the crisis of 1947 must be dealt with on two levels, ministerial and official.[9] On the ministerial level the planning function was vested in the Chancellor of the Exchequer as the head of the Treasury and, at Cabinet level, a small Economic Policy Committee, chaired by the Prime Minister and consisting of the Ministers of the chief economic Departments. On the official level, the work was done by the Economic Section of the Cabinet, the Central Economic Planning Staff, and a large number of special interdepartmental committees. The Economic Section, manned by professional economists, was chiefly responsible for gathering comprehensive economic data. These data became the raw material for the work of the Central Economic Planning Staff, which was now, as the committee of permanent heads of economic Departments had been before, the "thinking part" of the whole structure, its function being, in essence, to make decisions to be ratified by Ministers.

Despite this centralization of planning organization, interdepartmental committees of the orthodox kind continued to operate, two of particular importance: the Investment Programmes Committee and the Import Programmes Committee. But in view of this, one may ask what purpose was served by the transfer of planning "responsibilities" from a ministerial committee to a single department? What was the function of the Economic Affairs Division of the Treasury, other than to provide chairmen to the various interdepartmental committees concerned with economic policy? Herbert Morrison has supplied the answer.[10] "It was the duty of the [Central Economic] Planning Staff and the Economic Section *to see that*

---

[9] There is also what one might call a consultative level, consisting of bodies on which business and labor as well as government are represented. These consultative bodies are of great importance since they furnish information of actual field conditions, provide expert advice, and help to "sell" government decisions to the people who must make them work.

[10] *Government and Parliament.*

the consequences of taking action in one field were considered in relation to our problems as a whole." The activities this implies are very much in the tradition of Treasury control and British administration in general. The function of the CEPS was to determine, on the basis of data supplied by the Economic Section, what the common economic problems were and to publish the findings, together with the general policy proposals, in the annual *Economic Survey.* The *Survey* was not to be an operational plan but merely a broad analysis of the situation and a modifiable statement of policy. Planning was to remain open-ended in the sense of not aiming at rigid quantitative goals, but it was to be systematic nevertheless, in the sense of being carried on under conscious, suitable and informative criteria. The *Survey*, in short, was a sort of Platonic ideal, not a working blueprint for planning. Nor could it have been anything else, in view of the methods by which planning decisions were actually made. Two aspects of this method are especially important. One is that the initiative for action in economic as in financial matters was allowed to remain entirely in the hands of the operating Departments. It was they who initiated requests for materials or suggestions for their allocations; it was they who developed capital schemes and proposed import quotas. The Treasury, as in the case of departmental Estimates, simply brought to bear on these departmental proposals the "Government view," as defined by the work of its corps of economic planners, especially in the *Survey*. Moreover, bringing the Government view to bear on proposals did not mean exercising an arbitrary veto or peremptorily altering departmental schemes. The method of bringing it to bear was in almost all cases negotiation and the end of negotiation was to achieve "agreement" on general Government policy. The Treasury, in short, for all the centralization of planning functions after 1947, never made itself more than a specially important party in the interdepartmental economic team. Considering the severity of the economic crisis of 1947, the economic adjustments made were certainly impressively mild. Why? Is not the obvious answer that the tough solutions that might have been adopted are alien to some of the deepest traditions of British politics and administration? The British have a firm tradition of collective responsibility, a system of leadership in which no single Minister can order other Ministers about but in which decisions are made collectively by the heads of Departments. This is "Cabinet democracy." Inevitably, this method of high-level decision-making has affected the character of lower-level decision-making. Since departmental decisions, if important enough, may ultimately come up against the collective give and take of the plural executive, even the lowest-level decisions are often the result of interdepartmental consultations, designed to prevent higher-level squabbles. Hence the absence in British administration of those clean lines of command that are the joy of American and German professors of administration. The Treasury style of co-ordination, in which commands are not given but interdepartmental consultation is highly institutionalized, fits the system perfectly. A supereconomic department, able to give direct orders to other Departments, would have been profoundly out of tune with it.

But this not only explains the mildness of the reforms made in the planning machinery after 1947. It also helps to explain why British planning has been so mild and limited in scope, so consistently wary of explicit direction toward predetermined quantitative goals. Planning by consultation and compromise, in the style of Treasury co-ordination, clearly lends itself only to open-ended planning, and best of all to planning by financial methods. No doubt British liberalism has something to do with the cautiousness of British economic planning, but so also has the intolerance of the British administrative system for an activity unsuited to the traditions of the plural executive.

THE PUBLIC CORPORATION

The welfare state has altered the structure of British administration chiefly by the great multiplication of administrative bodies standing outside the regular departmental system. Of these, the public corporations that operate the nationalized industries are of course the most prominent, although other "autonomous" or near-autonomous agencies have been created to operate the National Assistance Program, to distribute financial grants to the universities, to supervise government-sponsored scientific research, to manage the National Parks, and to administer the Agriculture, the National Health Service, and the Industrial Development Acts.

There are many differences among the various public corporations, but all have at least one thing in common: a high degree of administrative independence, and this in four senses: first, in the sense of political autonomy, i.e., the relative absence of ministerial control over the corporation and of ministerial accountability to Parliament for the corporation's affairs; second, financial autonomy, i.e., freedom from ordinary government budgeting and therefore Treasury Control;[11] third, autonomy in regard to personnel, i.e., exemption from normal civil-service procedures in regard to the recruitment of staff, promotion, pay and pensions; and fourth, freedom from administrative procedures that are standardized among the Departments. It should not be difficult to see why administrative bodies having these characteristics should have been chosen for the

---

[11] Most public corporations in Great Britain are financed, like any private business establishment, by selling goods and services to the public and by borrowing funds from the public or the Treasury.

purpose of supplying goods and services to the public. One need only consider what the operation of the nationalized industries by the ordinary Departments would have meant: questions in the House of Commons on any aspect of their activities, the scrutiny of their work by parliamentary select committees, and Treasury control over their finances and personnel. As a result administrators in charge of the nationalized enterprises would have become reluctant, under the constant threat of parliamentary criticism, to take quick and risky (that is, "businesslike") decisions, and procedure would have become rigidified into the usual civil-service routine. There might have been outright interference for political purposes in the day-to-day affairs of the enterprises as well, quite apart from parliamentary criticism. The public corporations might not have been able to attract adequate personnel, because of the low level of civil-service salaries and the limited opportunities for ambitious young men in a civil-service system. And there would have been excessive centralization of administration, under a Minister responsible to Parliament.

For all of these reasons, public corporations were considered appropriate instruments to use wherever businesslike administration was especially desirable. The prewar public corporations—the British Broadcasting Corporation, the London Passenger Transport Board, the Port of London Authority and the Central Electricity Board—were therefore given a remarkable degree of autonomy, ordinary political control over them amounting to little more than the appointment of board members by the Minister and, in the case of the B.B.C., a periodical review of its charter. Since the war, however, the British have had something of a change of heart about such very independent corporations and, in fact, the public corporations created since 1945 are not nearly so autonomous as their predecessors. Why not?

In the first place, it was widely felt that the old arguments about the incompatibility between politically responsible and businesslike, efficient management were much exaggerated. Some people indeed felt that making the managers of the nationalized enterprises politically responsible would stimulate effort and initiative rather than the opposite. After all, the public corporations were, in effect, public monopolies; and without either competition or political criticism to prod their managers, what, save an inherent "sense of workmanship," was to keep them from becoming lazy and slovenly? In addition, certain ordinary government Departments were in fact already engaged in providing goods and services to the public, some with notable efficiency. The British Post Office, for example, is big enterprise in the most exacting sense. It deals not only with letters and parcels but also telegrams, cables and telephones, certain technical aspects of sound broadcasting, runs the largest savings bank in the country, and pays government pensions and allowances. And there are relatively few complaints about it.

Secondly, many of the postwar public enterprises were nationalized at least partly to facilitate national economic planning; consequently, it would have been absurd to give these enterprises independence from the control of the planning authorities. But whether public enterprises were nationalized for planning purposes or not, there was in any case to be central economic planning, and this made it clearly undesirable to create a series of public monopolies, all in basic industries, that might pull in entirely different economic directions. Prewar Governments were not committed to central economic planning; hence they could afford to give the public corporations much more autonomy than could postwar Governments.

It will be evident from this that the public corporation poses a serious dilemma. On one hand, it seems advisable to prevent the more regrettable consequences that might follow from ordinary departmental administration; on the other it is equally necessary to prevent excessive administrative autonomy; yet any step to prevent the one is always likely to lead to the other. Is there a golden mean?

If there is one it is safe to say that the British have not yet found it, although their solution of the problem may superficially seem very convincing. This solution rests on a distinction between the "general policies" of the nationalized industries and their "day-to-day management," the theory being that the latter is properly the private function of the corporations while the former is the sphere in which political control may be constructively exercised. But however sound this solution may be in principle, it immediately raises some uncomfortable problems in practice: one, the very old problem of how precisely to distinguish between policy-making and administration; another, by what specific arrangements to prevent political control of routine management while assuring political control over policy. Confronted by these problems the British have simply taken refuge in muddle.

The powers of Ministers over the nationalized industries fall into three main categories. First they may appoint and remove members of their governing Boards—a traditional but not therefore a negligible power. Second they possess what are generally called "specific powers," varying a great deal from one case to another, although some of the powers involved are exercised over all the corporations. For example, all the corporations must furnish statistics and other kinds of information on request; in all cases, also, the Minister must approve large-scale capital outlays. Finally Ministers have in all cases been granted power to issue "general directions" to the Boards of the industries. It will be seen at once that these powers are both extensive and, in the last case, vague. One cannot therefore get a clear idea of the scope of Ministers' powers by reading the statutes, since everything depends on how they interpret their functions vis-à-vis the Boards.

Just how they have done this is very difficult to determine, but from the shaky evidence available two points emerge. One is that, *on the whole,* the Ministers appear to have been reluctant to interfere in the affairs of the public corporations. Between 1946 and 1951, for example, not a single "direction" was issued by any Minister to a Board. Secondly, Minister-Board relationships, despite common tendencies, vary a good deal from one case to another, not so much because of differences among the statutes as because of the vagueness of their terms and differences in how they are interpreted. For example, under the Labour Government of 1945, the Minister of Fuel and Power seems to have interfered a good deal in the public corporations under his jurisdiction, the Minister of Transport hardly at all, for no immediately discernible reason other than temperament and, to some extent perhaps, the public notoriety of the industries under their jurisdictions.

Relationships between the Minister and Parliament (specifically, the extent to which Ministers are answerable in the House for the activities of the public corporations) are, if anything, even more muddled. The subject, in fact, is so much in flux that it may be misleading to say anything definite about it at all. Parliamentary questions are both the clearest and most contentious case in point. In principle, once again, the matter is simple: Ministers must answer questions on subjects for which they are responsible and may refuse to answer all others. But this straightforward formula tells us almost nothing at all since we do not know precisely how to determine the extent of a Minister's responsibilities. And, in fact, a host of uncomfortable problems, contradictory procedures and absurd formulations have emerged within the boundaries of the formula. At one time it was held by the Speaker that Ministers were liable to answer only those questions about the postwar public corporations that they were liable to answer about the prewar corporations—a patent absurdity since the role of the postwar corporations was altogether different. A great deal of squabbling has revolved around whether questions resembling questions a Minister has previously refused to answer should simply be thrown out by the Clerks or whether the Minister should in every case decide whether to answer the specific question or not. Still more squabbling has taken place about whether Ministers were answerable to Parliament only for those actions they actually take in regard to the Boards or also for Board activities they *might* arrogate to themselves. Most of all there has been quarreling about what constitutes policy and what administration—

whether the lateness of a train is a matter of policy, whether the late-ness of fifty trains is, whether a power cut that ruins thousands of Sunday dinners is not something more than a matter of administration, and so on.

But this muddle is not accidental, any more than the looseness of British economic planning. It is, indeed, inevitable and suggests an im-portant lesson about the institutional significance of the welfare state, namely that the adjustment of institutions to the requirements of the welfare state has been difficult simply because these requirements are so different and contradictory. In this case, the main contradiction is between the management of public enterprises and the commitment to central economic planning: the one requiring a great deal of administrative autonomy, the other demanding very little. The British have dealt with this contradiction only by evolving seductive generalizations while mud-dling along from power cut to power cut, fare increase to fare increase, in an eclectic, experimental spirit from which a proper solution of the general problem may or may not emerge. It is difficult to see that anything else could have been done.

The Impact on Politics

Apart perhaps from the "conversion" of the Conservative Party to "social-ism," the chief impact of the welfare state on politics has been in the area of interest-group activity. In essence, the welfare state has had three effects on such activity: it has accelerated the tendency of interest groups to concentrate pressure on the Administration, intensified their efforts and made them more powerful. Concentration on the Administration is simply the result of the further shift of decision-making powers to the Administra-tion, especially the growth of executive legislation. And it is not just the large volume of delegated legislation that is relevant here but the fact that administrative Departments rather than Parliament make most of the decisions in which interest groups are particularly interested. The Na-tional Farmers Union is certainly interested in broad agricultural policy, the sort made presumably by "political" processes; but it is safe to say that it is more interested in the production targets and minimum price arrangements that are worked out each year, principally at the administra-tive level, under existing legislation. The British Medical Association is undoubtedly interested in broad medical and sanitary policy, but it is far more intensely and immediately interested in the terms of service under which Health Service doctors work, and that is a matter left almost en-tirely to executive decision-making. The welfare state has made pressure group activity more intense simply because private associations have more to gain or lose from government decisions than in the past. The Commit-tee on Intermediaries, reporting in 1950, found that the public then annually made some 19,000,000 applications for licenses, permits, and similar things to government Departments—and this on the basis of an incomplete survey and without reckoning certain routine and simple applications, like applications for food ration books. To give the reader a more concrete idea of what this involved, the Ministry of Supply had to deal annually with some 1,500 applications for licenses to manufacture, 54,000 to acquire steel, 20,000 to acquire cotton, 400,000 for stockholders' licenses for acquisition of iron and steel products—and a host of other applications for similar purposes. It will be seen at once that for many individuals and firms the success or failure of applications can be a vital matter, the result being a vastly increased use of "intermediaries" (people with influence, special knowledge, legal skills) to push along individual applications and intensified interest-group activity to influence the grounds on which administrative decisions are made.

All this is simple enough. But why should the welfare state have increased the *power* of interest-group activity? This question will be easier to answer if we first understand what factors tend in general to make pressure groups powerful. Three such factors seem particularly relevant: the size of the group, its ability to supply *expertise*, and the extent to which its co-operation with government is required. *Size* is important for obvious electoral reasons, so important in fact that certain large groups in society—particularly if the political loyalties of its members are not fixed, or not known to be fixed—can achieve their objectives even without bringing direct pressure to bear on the government. The case of old-age pensioners in Great Britain is a good example. Their number is constantly growing both in absolute terms and relative to other social groups. Hence, there has developed in recent years a kind of competition for the old-age vote in the form of promised increases in old-age benefits. Before the general election of 1955, for example, both parties committed themselves to raising old-age pensions and the Conservatives opportunely raised the pension shortly before the election actually took place. Very similar things also apply to other relatively uncommitted groups, such as schoolteachers and farmers.

A group's possession of *expertise* can make it politically effective for two reasons. First, because laymen always tend to feel a certain deference toward professionals; and the more a mastery over a subject presupposes *expertise* (rigorous training, like professional training) the more likely this is to be the case. The civil servant or the politician is always likely to feel that farmers know farming, architects building, and doctors medicine, and therefore also the right policies appertaining to farming, building and medicine. Secondly, and more concretely, Departments, in making decisions, may genuinely need skills that only members of the interest group can provide. Finally, the power of a pressure group depends on the *extent to which its co-operation is required*. One simply cannot, for example, carry out an agricultural policy without getting farmers to co-operate, as the Soviets have had opportunity to discover on innumerable occasions. While the need for a group's co-operation does not of course guarantee that it will achieve its political objectives it does limit the extent to which these objectives can be frustrated, even in totalitarian countries, and limiting the extent of undesired policies is merely the obverse of winning legitimation for desired policies.

British interest groups tend to be more effective now than in the past, first, because welfare-state policies have in a curious way increased the size of interest groups. Size here should not be understood in the usual sense but as something one might more appropriately call "politically effective size." In determining the political effectiveness of a group what matters is not only its absolute size (e.g., the number of people who are farmers, or doctors, or veterans) but also how many of the members of the group are actually organized for political action, on the general principle that even in democratic politics the cohesive battalions are more effective than the disorganized ones. In this connection it is noteworthy that as the state has expanded the scope of its activities over British agriculture the number of farmers belonging to the National Farmers' Union has also increased, until today the N.F.U. includes almost all the farmers in Great Britain.[12] And this is not only because organization pays, but also because government policies have deliberately encouraged the formation of comprehensive voluntary associations, particularly by making such associations official negotiating bodies, giving them permanent membership on advisory committees and even assigning them roles in the administration of policy. Thus, under the Agriculture Act negotiations are carried on not with "farmers," but the National Farmers' Union. Under the National Health Service Act it is not, in practice, the "profession" that deals with the Ministry of Health and furnishes members to advisory, disciplinary and administrative committees, but professional organizations, especially the British Medical Association and its local branches.

Perhaps the clearest example of how the other two factors (*expertise* and the need for a group's co-operation) have increased the power of interest-groups in the welfare state, is medicine. First of all, medicine is a field in which the gulf between professional and layman is particularly deep, partly because of the very demanding training required of a doctor, partly because of the deeply rooted popular attitudes toward medicine. The

---

[12] Membership growth of the N.F.U. has been as follows:

| 1919— 88,889 | 1940—132,401 |
| 1929—111,500 | 1948—194,000 |

doctor is always something more than the professor of an arduously acquired skill; he is more a magician, an initiate into a particularly subtle mystery, than a mere graduate of a difficult course of technical training. Secondly, a great many of the decisions that officials in the Ministry of Health must make require professional knowledge or touch intimately upon clinical practice: for example, a decision as to how to distinguish a "medicine" from a "food" for the purpose of setting limits on what general practitioners may or may not prescribe, or decisions on the conversion of hospitals, the purchasing of medical equipment, types of medical report forms, the organization of the maternity services, and so on. Finally, it is obvious that a socialized medical service requires, above all else, a co-operative medical profession—for example, the service must be able to attract and hold the better specialists, especially for purposes of full-time service, since the majority of doctors are always likely to enter a service used by a majority of patients. In view of all this it should surprise no one that the British Medical Association has been a wonderfully effective pressure group from the outset of the Service. It is constantly consulted by the Ministry and it rarely fails to get anything it wants very badly. The B.M.A. badly wanted an Amending Act to the National Health Service Act guaranteeing that the profession could never be paid salaries (the Minister had already given a verbal promise to this effect); it got it. When a large number of Registrars (young doctors training in specialties) were to be dismissed from the hospitals and diverted into general practice the B.M.A. violently objected; only a few were in fact dismissed. No single recommendation of the National Health Service Council (a professional advisory committee on the Health Service) has ever been suppressed or even just turned down by the Ministry of Health. One of the chief reasons for the remarkably general acceptance of the Health Service in the British medical profession—and it is almost universal—may in fact be that, having dreaded bureaucratic enslavement, the profession has now realized that bureaucrats tend to be very reasonable, malleable and accommodating people, at least where doctors are concerned.

The Cabinet Today

From what has been said it follows that the contemporary distribution of effective power in British government is different from what it was in Bagehot's day or even just a generation or two ago. But how different? Parliament certainly debates less thoroughly and controls less comprehensively than it used to; autonomous and semi-autonomous administrative organizations do much more than they used to; an increasing proportion of government decisions are made neither in Parliament, nor the Parties, nor the Cabinet, nor the Departments, but in non-official associations. But has the essential organizational principle of British government been significantly affected by welfare-state pressures, i.e., what Bagehot called the real secret of the British Constitution, the concentration of responsibility ("fusion of powers") in the hands of the Cabinet? The distinctive product of eighteenth- and nineteenth-century politics in Great Britain undoubtedly was Cabinet Government; and Cabinet Government was the proper institutional expression of the constitutional attitudes discussed in Chapter 4. But has the welfare state had any significant impact on the Cabinet and its role in the machinery of government?

One can argue with some force that it is precisely here, where one would perhaps least expect it, that the welfare state has had its most revolutionary impact. We may indeed be in the midst of one of those crucial metamorphoses that are the very essence of British constitutional development and seem to recur with a startling regularity: the conversion of an "efficient" institution (in this case the Cabinet) into a ceremonial institution, by a draining off of its practical functions until little more than empty formalities remain. The transformation is certainly not yet complete and has not, of course, gone nearly as far as the conversion of the Privy Council into a ceremonial body. "It is just possible," a British journal recently said, "that the British Cabinet is still an important body." But it is certainly a very different body from what it was once and we have good reason to think a less important one.

The Cabinet has changed, in the first place, from a small and intimate discussion group into a large and complicated piece of administrative machinery. It has become as large as it is at least partly because of the growth of state activities and the consequent multiplication of administrative Departments, particularly if we take its size to be determined not by the number of Ministers having official Cabinet status but the number who actually participate in Cabinet deliberations. The Cabinet has become a complicated machine, because of its size, and also because of the character of the decisions it has to make and the activities it has to supervise and co-ordinate. The Cabinet, after all, is, like Parliament, composed primarily of professional politicians and is, if anything, even more pressed for time than the legislature. For all of these reasons it cannot possibly be what it was when Bagehot discovered that the fusion of powers in the Cabinet was the secret of the British Constitution.

The position of the Cabinet in the British machinery of government has changed in two ways under the pressure of welfare-state policies and of the modern party system, and both involve a draining off of its powers. On one hand, some of the former functions have become concentrated in fewer hands. The making of high policy, in particular, seems to be increasingly concentrated in the hands of the Prime Minister and a small group around him, sometimes composed of great Ministers, sometimes merely of the Prime Minister's intimates. Some of the greatest decisions of state seem in recent times to have been made by such special juntas and presented to the Cabinet almost as *faits accomplis,* over the known disagreement of certain Cabinet members. This diversion of effective power from a whole body, functioning collectively, to a special segment of it is also what happened to the Cabinet's historic predecessors: the House of Lords, the King's Council, the Privy Council and the Cabinet Council. Concomitantly, other Cabinet functions have become dispersed to an almost unfathomably complex administrative and deliberative machinery. Decisions once made collectively in the Cabinet are now made by Cabinet committees, by individual Ministers, bureaucrats, the Treasury, official committees, party machinery, and even private associations; and, most often, by interaction among all of these bodies. If power is concentrated anywhere in the British machinery of government it is concentrated not in the Cabinet but in this complex framework of decision-making, the Cabinet itself—i.e., the body that meets three or four hours a week in the Cabinet Room of No. 10 Downing Street—being no more than a part of the framework. But what precise role it plays as a collective entity is far from clear. It has been suggested that its real function is to act as a court of appeal when disputes arise within the normal decision-making machinery; but if the analysis here is correct the change in its functions is even greater than that.

Conclusion

We can now answer in a general way the general questions raised at the beginning of the chapter: whether a form of government developed in another era can survive the institution of socialist policies, and whether such policies can be effectively administered within the limits imposed by a constitutional system evolved for different purposes, however much altered for the sake of the policies. The answers are rather complicated but can be stated briefly thus:

Perhaps the most basic institutional requirement that must be satisfied if welfare-state policies are to be successful is strong democratic leadership: a high degree of executive control over the legislature (e.g., the allocation of time, financial policy-making, and probing into the affairs of public enterprise) and the administrative machinery; a high degree of co-ordination in policy-making and administration; and considerable continuity and stability of leadership. This is clearest of all in the case of economic planning, where everything depends on the concentration of decision-making powers in the hands of an agency pursuing consistent objectives by coherent means. Now British Cabinet government, as we saw particularly in the case of the budgetary process, seems to satisfy this requirement nearly to perfection, because of its stability and because its very essence is the integration of decision-making powers. It appears to be, compared to other parliamentary systems, and compared also to presidential systems, a marvelously appropriate instrument for the purposes of the social-service state, despite the fact that it has not been perfectly suitable in detail to all particular welfare-state objectives.

But Cabinet government seems, chiefly under the impact of the social-service state, to be itself undergoing a fundamental transformation, the essence of which is the scattering of decision-making powers and thus the loosening of leadership. Resting as it did on a beautifully simple idea—that the same leaders should initiate policy, supervise its execution, and co-ordinate administration, being accountable for all they did to the people's representatives—it worked effectively in the beautifully simple nineteenth century, but seems to be dissolving into something hideously complex under the complexities of twentieth-century politics and policies. But if this is indeed the case, what becomes of the suitability of the British machinery of government to welfare-state purposes? Is not the answer to our problems an ironic one: that welfare-state socialism would function best under an institutional framework that Britain once provided but that welfare-state socialism itself is transforming into something much less suitable to its own aims?

The effect of the welfare state on British government and politics can best be described as "pluralization." In the case of government we see it in the dispersion of Cabinet powers to numerous other agencies—so numerous a universe of agencies that it is extremely difficult nowadays to affix definite responsibility for any but the very highest and most routine policies (those decided either by the Prime Minister and his coterie and those which are strictly intradepartmental). In the case of politics, we see it in the gravitation of influence from the integrated two-party system to the complex universe of pressure groups of every variety. This pluralization of government and political competition may transform the British political system far more fundamentally than the decline of the Crown and the rise of democracy ever did, even if it does so much less obviously. Above all, the rise of Parliament and the electorate never seriously altered the fundamental balance of British political life between the concentration of authority in a cohesive executive and that of control in a relatively integrated set of representative institutions. But can we really speak of a concentration of authority in Britain today in anything more than form? Or of a concentration of control, when the principal pressures upon executive government come from a myriad semi-private groups rather than the parliamentary representatives? And how could such a government perform the essential task of the social service state: to substitute rational, consistent and coordinated direction by means of public policy for the chaotic adjustments of unintegrated private actors?

The supreme irony of the institutional impact of the welfare state may be that, attempting to overcome the supposed irrationalities of free-market relations, it has made a previously integrated government itself into a kind of free market—a polycentric universe of many actors, official and unofficial, each exerting pushes and pulls upon the others, in such a way that only certain equilibria of forces, not rational and consistent decisions, emerge. At least that is a possibility to be contemplated, if not a palpable accomplished fact.

[11]

Prospects

When one reviews the character of contemporary British government and politics, and, even more, when one reflects upon British political history, one is immediately struck by a number of remarkable things. Britain has long been blessed by a high degree of political integration, of which the broad consensus on the Constitution and on policies is only the most remarkable instance. The British conception of authority highly corresponds to the British pattern of effective power, in the sense that political decisions are in fact made largely as they are ideally supposed to be made. The result of these two things is a minimum of tension in the political system and therefore a very high degree of political stability—stability both in the sense of stable Governments and the even more important sense of a stable constitution. Moreover, stability in the first sense is reinforced by the character of the British party system, while stability in the second sense is supported by the fact that British political processes are effective enough to satisfy a large volume of political demands, so that no important group need be alienated from the system because of its inherent inability to effect the group's political aims. Is such a system likely to undergo any important changes in the foreseeable future?

Even if "Cabinet government" is being transformed into something different from its classic form under the situational pressures of welfare-state policies, this does not imply any vitally important change in the British political system. How important, after all, is the redistribution of certain Cabinet functions compared to the persistence of a disciplined two-party system, or the continued existence of broad political agreement, a "ruling class" and the deferential attitudes it elicits, or indeed even the very tone of British government? True, these things are themselves undergoing changes. But so far only in content, not in form. Thus, what the British are agreed upon today is not what they agreed upon fifty or even twenty years ago, but the existence of broad agreement itself has not changed. Recruitment into the ruling class, its composition, the depth of the sentiment of deference—all these have changed, but deference to leaders and to the social strata expected to supply leaders still exists. And it is these things—party discipline, consensus, deference, and the survival of the past in the symbols and ceremonies of government—that make Britain what it uniquely is: an unusually effective democratic system, resting on a remarkable political culture in which a host of logically irreconcilable attitudes (democratic and non-democratic, autocratic and responsible, liberal and collectivist, hierarchical and egalitarian) are smoothly integrated.

However, we cannot simply assume that these things will not change, if we proceed from the conviction that British politics is not the result of British genes, but of determinate historical forces and, indeed, a certain amount of luck. From what sources might basic changes come?

One possible source is the welfare state—not as much in its impact on governmental institutions as in its impact on political attitudes. There are no violent antagonisms between socialists and anti-socialists, as we have seen, but welfare-state socialism has created psychological tensions in other senses. Curiously, it has produced much unrest among its most ardent supporters, the radical Left. One reason for this unrest is that the Tories have so smoothly adapted themselves to the welfare state that many people in the Labour Party have felt bereft of a program. The result has been much compulsive seeking after policies with which to counter the political appeal of the Conservatives—one sometimes feels almost any policies. It is altogether possible that such policies will ultimately come from that section of the party that has become disillusioned with the achievements of postwar policy and feels it is imperative to go far beyond it. There is certainly much feeling among the more radical Labourites that the objectives of 1945 have not been achieved despite the enactment of the Labour program. Post-welfare-state Britain, after all, is not so vastly different from pre-welfare-state Britain in certain—to the left-wing Labourites, important —respects. What has become of industrial democracy in the nationalized industries? What has happened to economic planning under the Treasury? Granted that economic leveling has been considerable, has there been enough of it, and what has become of social leveling? Does the educational system not still maintain all the old, deplored social distinctions? People who deplore the cautiousness of the cautious revolution are not of course in control of the Labour Party. On the contrary; there has been a right-wing as well as a left-wing reaction against the disappointments of the welfare state in the party, and at present the right-wing is in control. But we cannot be sure that in Labour's frantic groping for new ideas it will retain control.

Among Conservatives there is also some disgruntlement. The Conservative Party has made the best of most of the new order, but not all of its supporters have adapted themselves smoothly to it. It must be remembered that many people have had to make major readjustments to the new condition of things: especially people with fixed incomes, the salariat, and indeed the whole middle class—the class that has been truly leveled down. We must remember also that many avenues of achievement have been narrowed for the ambitious and that it has been made difficult if not impossible for many members of the upper classes to sustain a way of life they had come to regard as natural: taking periodic trips abroad, sending their children to boarding schools, having more than one servant, and so on. Not all have adjusted gracefully and there are certainly pockets of deep resentment in British society. It would be wrong to suggest that all British suburbia is seething with discontent, but undoubtedly more than a lunatic fringe is alienated from postwar policy.

The welfare state, in short, is resented on one extreme as having done too much and on the other as having done too little. That perhaps is only natural and, since only extremes are involved, not very serious. The question is whether there is any chance that the still rather minor disagreements over social and economic policy might deepen into fundamental and intransigent political conflict.

There can be no doubt that the gulf between the parties on socio-economic policy has widened in recent years, and that may be an indicator of things to come. The Conservative Party in power has consolidated and improved some of the social services introduced by Labour (for example, it has embarked on the first sizable postwar hospital building program under the National Health Service) and held the line on others, but in the area of economic leveling its policies have tended to be rather retrogressive. Meanwhile Labour, despite its moderate leadership since 1951, has moved ahead on many fronts—far more than the chronic left-wing dissidents in the party sometimes seem to realize. In the field of public ownership the proposal to embark on a massive copartnership between the state and private investors in business is certainly an important step in the direction of a still more mixed economy—not, of course, a step toward industrial democracy and the total eradication of private business, but then neither was the nationalization program of 1945-1951. Also, of late, the Labour Party's official policy has again begun to mention a few specific industries as likely candidates for outright nationalization, and indeed a few, like the pharmaceutical and aircraft industries, not definitely considered before. While the left wing of the party has battled about constitutional formulas, the leadership thus has almost imperceptibly committed itself to go considerably beyond the status quo of 1951—and what the Tories seem to want. The gulf between the parties has become greatest, however, in the area of economic redistribution. In that area, Labour wants to demolish the presently most powerful bastions of economic privilege: tax loopholes, tax concessions, and the enormous difference in benefits between private and public welfare schemes; while the Tories, both by acts and omissions, have rather widened the economic differentiations of society even without an outright direct attack on the national minimum and comprehensive social security. And not least, a real issue between the parties seems to exist at last in the often neglected but, particularly in Britain, all-important field of educational policy. As a result, the general election of 1959 presented to the voter far more serious issues of policy than any election in the present writer's memory; and since the election policy differences have grown still greater.

Even so, the differences between the parties are still the sort of differences which might arise between men who are substantially like-minded. They have no constitutional overtones. They are not supported on either side by full-fledged ideology. They involve no fixed dogma, unresponsive to reasonable argument or the pressure of environmental conditions. Britain still has consensus and a predominantly pragmatic approach to politics.

What could seriously affect this state of affairs—if anything could—is the present distribution of power between the Conservative and Labour Parties. The marginal victory which the Tories won in 1951 has now grown into a heavy preponderance, in parliamentary seats if not in popular support. (See above, p. 177.) The Conservatives have won three successive general elections since 1950 and increased their margin over Labour in each case, something which has never happened before in British history. Only five percent of the popular vote divided the parties in 1959. But then only three percent did in 1955; and in 1951 the popular vote was practically evenly split, with a slight advantage to Labour, while in 1950 Labour had a three percent and in 1945 an eight percent lead over the Tories. Nothing like that continuous dissipation of electoral support by a major party has ever happened before in British history. More significant than these lifeless figures, perhaps, is the fact that the shift from Labour to Tory voting can be correlated, with an almost eerie closeness, to changes (which are likely to continue) in the occupational structure and population distribution of Great Britain, particularly shifts from manual wage-earning to white-collar, salaried employment and movement from the urban centers to the suburbs and new towns. Not only do the figures themselves tend to coincide (Labour has lost an average of about one half percent of the voters per annum since 1951 and there has been a shift of approximately one half percent per annum from manual to salaried employment) but election figures show that the greatest gains to the Tories tended to accrue in the newer suburbs and among those who recently made the leap, still large in Britain, from the blue to the white collar.

Labour's policies themselves have had not a little to do with the social changes which have benefited the Conservatives so greatly, but that does not alter the fact that the Conservatives have reaped the political rewards. Add to this the fact that in a country like Britain the Tories have, and always have had, a large advantage, accruing from basic social attitudes, over the radical parties—that it is they who symbolize the continuity and ancient origins of British politics, the majesty of monarchy, the authority of the executive, political deference—and one can see why there should be talk today of one-party government in Britain. It has in fact been said that the Tories have actually been in power almost continuously since the origin of the modern party system, with only interludes of radical rule (like those of 1945-1951 and 1906-1914) and coalition government (usually itself dominated by the Conservatives), and no doubt there is something in this. But nothing like the present Conservative ascendancy has ever been known before. And barring the sort of accidents which the optimists in the Labour Party envisage, or a lasting Liberal revival, it is likely to continue, in a society where class conflict, never very acute, is in decline, where upward social mobility is great, and where the delicate internal balances of the Labour Party make any large-scale adjustment to changed electoral conditions difficult and unlikely.

Perhaps hyper-stability is better than acute instability of government. Perhaps it is possible to have democratic one-party rule. Opposition does continue, even if it has no real chance to govern. Bodies of opinion not represented in the Government can exert influence through that alternative channel of representation, pressure group politics. But the dangers in such a situation are also obvious. One is that the governing party, feeling itself out of danger, will launch a more serious attack on the existing order in favor of the interests of its more affluent and militant supporters— in the case of the Tories, the right wing of the party. Another is that the opposition will grow increasingly intransigent and obstructive because of its frustrations, withdrawing, for example, the easy collaboration on parliamentary business which is presupposed by much of British government; and that it will also become more extreme in its policy formulations and irresponsible in its criticisms. Americans had at least a taste of that sort of thing during the twenty years of Democratic hegemony. Moreover, since Labour's poor record since 1951 has been made under moderate leadership, it is not altogether unlikely that the left-wing militants will in the long run gain over other sections of the party. In all of these ways, the tone of British politics and the substantive differences between the parties might change considerably, altering the character of the whole pattern of government we have described.

This is not meant as prophecy, of course. It is speculation. The issue is, in a way, whether British political culture is strong and autonomous enough to persist in the face of a radically changing distribution of party power— strong enough to allow responsible and moderate government and opposition, pragmatic politics, and easy procedural collaboration to continue even under very unfavorable conditions; and we have at least as much reason to think that it is as that it is not. In the past, it always was.

There is, however, another source of potentially great tension in British society today. It is not the result of the British pattern of purposes and interests but of the British situation in the postwar world: specifically, the need for the British to adjust themselves to being a second-rank international force.

In the immediate postwar period the British faced the task of reconstruction and their other immense economic problems with equanimity, even enthusiasm. Sir Stafford Cripps's austerity measures were received with resolution. People endured the queues and the shortages with great good nature. Even the miners occasionally worked on Saturdays. But all this was in the flush of victory, when it was not clear, as it certainly is now, that Britain would never recover her prewar eminence. Had the outlook seemed less hopeful one wonders whether such trials would have been endured so good-humoredly. It is one thing to feel that one is reconstructing one's society and quite another to feel that one is barely keeping it afloat. A magnanimous gifts of sovereignty to a former dependency flatters the ego; forcible dislodgment even from a mere sphere of influence does not. Recent events, of course, have made it clear, even to the most die-hard chauvinists perhaps, that Britain is no longer top dog. But for a number of reasons we cannot yet be sure that the necessary psychological readjustments to the new "situation" will be made as successfully and smoothly as have the economic adjustments.

It is certainly not inconceivable that the international decline of Britain will create disruptions in her internal political culture. Most seriously of all, it may endanger the survival of that broad consensus that has for so long characterized British politics and given Britain such great stability. This agreement was due at least partly to the acceptance by the lower classes of upper class leadership and the satisfaction by the upper classes of demands for important political, social and economic reforms; in short, deference on one hand and moderate reformism on the other. But neither of these is unconditionally a part of British political culture. Submission to leaders, although having a solid basis in British social structure, may have been predicated upon their success in governing, and that success has never, since the eighteenth century, seemed as questionable as it does today. But on what ground other than its inherent fitness to govern, as measured by success, can a political class retain its hold upon the popular imagination? By expressive symbolism perhaps; the sheer theatrical pomp and show and the fairy-tale romance of ceremonial institutions. But between symbolism that exalts and symbolism that seems empty burlesque the dividing line is thin. Even the most ancient and solemn ceremonial needs a basis of belief, and that, in Britain, one suspects, was always supplied by a universal British conviction of the rightness of British institutions—the Anglo-Saxon genius for self-government, as the Anglo-Saxons used to call it. Can it survive national relegation to the second rank?

Conversely, upper-class (especially Conservative) moderation, the second condition of consensus, has also shown signs of cracking. Certainly the Suez affair was not a result of good pragmatic sense. This, of course, should not be taken as conclusive evidence that the British Conservatives have finally lost their genius for sensible adjustment. Upper-class (and indeed also lower-class) jingoism is nothing new in Britain. Nor is immoderation in foreign relations. Indeed, one of the more curious aspects of British political behavior has always been the abrupt metamorphosis Britons seem to undergo when dealing with non-Britons, especially colonials. And, not least, if there have been significant divisions among the British they have been, even in the past, most acute in the case of foreign and imperial, not domestic, affairs. But if international frustrations continue to produce the bitter animosities among the parties generated by Suez it is not unlikely that these animosities will be reflected also in intransigence on domestic issues.

The most somber possibility therefore is that the two sources of tension in British society, domestic and international, may reinforce and deepen each other. That they can do this is clear. After all, did not the Bevanites transfer their domestic socialist frustrations into a championing of international neutralism? What then would happen if the Conservatives, in a mistaken diagnosis of Britain's international problems, unmade the welfare state in a really serious way—or if Labour, in search of issues, made international relations a greater bone of contention than it has? Already the left wing is desperately trying to do so.

That a society has achieved remarkable stability; that its political culture is highly integrated; that its concept of authority closely corresponds to its structure of effective power; that its decision-making processes are effective enough to satisfy a large volume of political demands—all this means that it is relatively safe from instability as a result of its internal dynamics, but not that it is absolutely immune to major change. For, first, no society has absolute control over its situation, and culture and situation obviously are related. And, second, the purposes on which a society is agreed may themselves, in operation, have deeply problematic and divisive consequences.[1]

---

[1] Forecasting, in a social science textbook, is notoriously foolhardy. This chapter illustrates the point. Since it was written, the Liberal Party has scored some remarkable successes in by-elections, drawing votes mainly from economically mobile elements of the population whose class position is, actually and in their own minds, not very firmly fixed. For this reason, speculation on the possibility of a one-party system is now (July, 1962) rather less common than speculation about the effects of a three-party system—or a return to two-party government through the benefits accruing to Labour from the shift of Tory to Liberal votes. However, it seems pointless to elaborate on these possibilities; there have been too many abortive Liberal revivals in by-elections in the past to make the present Liberal upswing, considerable though it is, appear definitive and lasting. Only one thing seems certain. The British party system is at present in flux toward a still unknown destination.

Part Three

THE FRENCH POLITICAL SYSTEM

by Nicholas Wahl

Excerpts from Addresses to the French People by Charles de Gaulle, 1945-1962.

As President of the Provisional Government, to the drafters of the Fourth Republic's constitution, December 31, 1945:

We have begun to reconstruct the Republic. You will continue the job. No matter how you do it, I think I can tell you in good conscience . . . that if you fail to take into account the absolute necessity of authority, dignity, and responsibility for the Government, you will go toward a situation where one day—I predict it—you will bitterly regret the course you will have taken.

As a leader of the opposition under the Fourth Republic, September 7, 1947:

Do you think the nation can go from one crisis to another without being led by a strong, disinterested, and stable Government? Yesterday I warned you. Today I tell you again. We need a regime in which the state has leadership that is leadership and to which the people have given the mandate and the means to impose the national interest, no matter what happens.

As a private citizen, after the first Algiers uprising, May 15, 1958:

The degradation of the state results infallibly in . . . national dislocation. . . . In the past the country, from its depths, placed confidence in me to lead it to salvation. . . . Today, before the trials that are once again surging forward, let it be known that I hold myself ready to assume the powers of the Republic.

As the last Prime Minister of the Fourth Republic, September 4, 1958:

The new constitution has been created so that the country may be efficiently led by those whom it mandates and to whom it gives the confidence which generates legitimacy; so that there should exist above political battles a national arbitrator. . . . This, then, is what inspires the the constitution which on September 28th will be submitted for your approval. . . . If you approve, the result will be to make the Republic strong and effective. . . .

As first President of the Fifth Republic, January 30, 1959:

> The first hurdle to cross was the confusion of powers which paralyzed the state and led to civil war. Today we have crossed it. We have new institutions and our problems are being taken care of. I have named a Government that I judge worthy and capable of accomplishing its difficult mission. . . . If things should go wrong, the arbitrator, with your support, will henceforth have the means to set things right.

As President of the Fifth Republic, after the second Algiers uprising, January 29, 1960:

> If I have put on my uniform to speak to you today on television, it is to indicate that I am doing so as General de Gaulle, as well as the chief of state. . . . Certain people in Algiers, in order to impose their will on the nation, on the state, on myself, have entered into insurrection . . . rising in arms against the authority of France. . . . I speak now to France: Well, my dear and old country, here we are once again together, facing a great trial. . . . By virtue of the mandate the people have given me and of the national legitimacy I have embodied for twenty years . . . I ask everyone to support me, come what may.

As President of the Fifth Republic, after the third Algiers uprising, April 23, 1961:

> An insurgent power has been established in Algeria. . . . See how the state is being flouted, the nation defied, our power shaken. . . . Look where France may go in contrast to what she is becoming. . . . Men and women of France, help me!

As President of the Fifth Republic, after the end of the Algerian war and on the eve of Algerian independence, June 8, 1962:

> What had to be done was done. But, as everyone saw, it is because the new institutions enable the state to act—whereas the old ones only hindered it—that the government can make decisions instead of constantly equivocating, and that it stands fast instead of forever tottering and stumbling. Above all, women and men of France, everyone has seen that the loyal confidence which you have massively bestowed upon me has spurred and sustained me day after day and that this direct agreement between the people and the one who has the responsibility of leading it has become, in modern times, essential to the Republic.

[I 2]

Conflicting Ideals of Authority

The Two Historic Traditions

The uniqueness of French political instiutions lies not in their instability or lack of effectiveness but rather in the length of time they have remained unstable and ineffective. Today, as during the nineteenth century, observers distinguish three basic traits characteristic of French politics. First there is the unstable, antagonistic relationship between the legislative and the executive, one far more unsettling than the usual competition between branches of government in other constitutional systems. Until the coming of the Fifth Republic in 1958, this unstable relationship produced the frequent and apparently capricious changes in the executive for which France was famous. Since then the new constitution has mechanically eliminated Government* or cabinet instability, but it has failed both in altering this basic antagonism and in reducing its dangerous effects upon the efficiency of policy making.

Second, there is the relative ineffectiveness of French political institutions in the face of immediate and long-range problems, both foreign and domestic. Before 1958 short-lived Governments were rarely in power long enough to carry out effective programs; but then, as now, the real trouble came from the absence of a line of confidence and responsibility running from public opinion, through a working majority in parliament, to a coherent Government both willing and able to act. True, in the face of many problems such as the Algerian war, there *did* exist a popular

---

* It should be noted that in European politics the word "Government" frequently refers to the administration alone, and in particular to the political executive or cabinet. To distinguish this usage from the more general meaning, the word is capitalized when reference is being made to the cabinet or the executive branch.

consensus in favor of a solution as well as a potential majority in parliament. But while the Government may have been willing to act in accordance with the popular will it has often been unable to do so, as was the case in Algeria.

The third trait of French politics is the reason for this frequent impotence: the often turbulent and near-surface violence of French political competition reflects the continuing existence of large groups of citizens permanently hostile to the constitution. Unlike similar minorities in England and Germany, they are able to challenge the will of the popular majority as well as that of the Government. Why all this should be true of France and not of the other major democracies is explainable by the peculiar qualities of French political culture, which will be explored below. The point to be made now concerning these three basic traits of French politics is that they have all prevailed for many years—at least since the early eighteenth century when absolute monarchy, that form of government first perfected by French genius, was initially challenged. Long before the Great Revolution, British writers of the eighteenth century were already noting the vagaries of French political life and, of course, attributed this to shortcomings in the flighty French character. Indeed, these three traits were as prevalent under monarchies as under republics, under dictatorship as under parliamentary democracy —and France has tried all of these since 1789.

One could argue, however, that in one respect French politics and government have been quite stable: unlike German, British, and Russian government, which have changed continually, French government retains its outstanding characteristics notwithstanding new constitutions and new political personnel. It is, for this reason, essentially unreformed government, in which changes that have occurred have not replaced pre-existing institutions but rather have simply been grafted onto existing customs and laws. Thus the restored monarchy in 1814 retained much of the revolutionary and Napoleonic regimes; the restored Napoleonic Empire of the mid-nineteenth century retained much of the monarchic experience; the restored Republic of 1870 retained much of both the monarchy and the Empire; and after World War II the new Fourth Republic retained much of the old Third Republic of prewar days. Today the Fifth Republic not only represents an extension of many policies and reforms suggested or initiated by the Fourth Republic, but it has also left unchanged most of the administrative institutions of the previous regime.

As a consequence, there exists a great legacy of the past in French political institutions. For instead of an integration of the past with the present, there has been a piling-up of different and often incompatible political institutions that has made French government a cumbersome patchwork, vulnerable to instability, lacking effectiveness, and generally ill-adapted to modern problems. The situation may be compared, hypothetically, to one that would have prevailed in the United States had the institutions created by the Articles of Confederation been largely preserved after the adoption of the Constitution. But in France the situation was further complicated by the fact that on the plane of political culture the area of agreement over political institutions had been narrowing steadily since early in the eighteenth century. France has long been known as the nation of the Great Revolution, the cradle of democracy and reason, the mother of innovations in style and ideas. But it is often forgotten—and particularly by Americans—that France was also the nation that perfected political absolutism and that has epitomized reverence for the traditional, above all in economic and social customs. In political ideas, therefore, France has developed a split personality that has been perpetuated by the historical experience of the nineteenth-century revolutions and by the peculiar resistance of French society to social and economic change. Thus, for example, partisans of authoritarian government have had, since the Revolution, four chances to create regimes that ultimately paid homage to principles of the *ancien régime*—the last one being as late as 1940-44 in the Vichy Government of Marshal Pétain.

Nor has France undergone the rapid industrialization and soaring urban population growth that constituted the potent material force in favor of democratic government in Great Britain. Unlike the latter, whose society became predominantly urban as a result of industrialization, French society became more complex, with her industrial sector simply added on to an agricultural and commercial sector that hardly gave way to the new economic forces. Politically this meant that parties and interests committed to old France were not obliged to transform themselves in order to represent new France. The increasing social complexity was therefore mirrored in the accretion of political factions, each fighting for its class, interest, or historical "layer." It was then natural for the more conservative among them to look to the administrative and elitist institutions of government to protect them, while the "new" classes looked increasingly to suffrage and parliament as their protectors. The booty of an internal political war since 1789, the French political system was permanently cast into two competing and hostile institutional patterns, rendering its neutrality—and therefore a true constitutional settlement—impossible.

Unlike France, the governmental structures in Britain, Bonn Germany, and the United States have become relatively "neutral": in none of these countries are the basic constitutional or customary rules of political life seriously challenged by social or political forces. A true constitutional settlement exists in each country because competing groups in society agree at least on the proposition that existing political institutions can serve their interests as well as those of their rivals. What is the quality of political institutions and of a system as a whole that produces this "neutrality," this true constitutional settlement? Undoubtedly it is a quality of balance imparted by a successful blending of the competing principles of authority within each institution and hence within the system as a whole. The British cabinet and Prime Minister embody the principle of command, to be sure. Yet England's ancient tradition of popular deference to decisions taken by Her Majesty's Government for a generally recognized common good has nurtured, over the years, the prudent exercise of command by cabinets and Prime Ministers. This, in turn, has been favored by a parliament and a party system that kept the executive in close touch with opinion, and, together with the tradition of deference, it has allowed the principle of command to be automatically tempered by the principle of consent. The German Chancellor, especially Konrad Adenauer, is very much a symbol of command. Yet in the Federal Republic an ultimate sensitivity to what public opinion will allow, bred by a direct connection with a truly national governing party and the vigilance of an effective opposition party, makes for a similar blending of the principles of command and consent.

In other words, the effectiveness of the executive in Britain and Germany is due not only to the simple awareness of the citizen that the executive's orders may be backed up by force, but is also due to the citizen's recognition that these orders are legitimate because, in the British case, Her Majesty's Government is traditionally considered to have a superior wisdom, and, in the German case, the Chancellor's decisions reflect the will of a genuine popular majority. French citizens, while often only too aware of the force that lies behind the commands of the executive, have rarely had a Government that has been able to convince the mass of them that its commands spring from popular consent or that they are in an unbroken tradition of policies for the common good. Since this quality of blending principles of authority is to be found at all levels of British and German government, one can truly call them, with only a slight deformation of Aristotle's concept, systems of "mixed government." Unlike the French political system, such government does have a satisfactory degree of cooperation between the executive and the legislative branches. This in turn allows generally effective policies to be administered, which in turn reduces to impotence groups of citizens who oppose the constitution.

Mixed government has never existed in France because the aristocratic principle of command and the democratic principle of consent, instead of becoming blended within each institution and thus assuring balance and cooperation among them, individually became *fully* embodied in *different* and ultimately antagonistic institutions. The French parliament, unlike its British counterpart, never developed respect for an executive with some independence and from the time of the Kings to the present has always sought to absorb executive functions. This was, of course, largely in reaction to the tradition of an executive armed with a centralized administration that was far too powerful and omnipresent to be truly compatible with any parliament, and hence with the very principle of limited government. The history of French political institutions is the history of two traditions of politics, two approaches to the solution of political problems that have never been successfully merged or brought into compromise. It is, indeed, the history of two sets of political institutions that since the eighteenth century have ruled France consecutively.

From the beginning this dualism in political traditions was reflected in a dualism in French law and jurisprudence. The rights of the state and its administration are dealt with by "public law" while the rights of individuals form "private law." Although since the Revolution the state has been equated with the collectivity or the will of the people, nonetheless the ancient dualism exists and Frenchmen still are tried for crimes against the state under a jurisdiction different from that relating to crimes against their fellow citizens. There has developed, therefore, a coexistence of two primitive patterns of politics, the state-minded administrative pattern and the individual-oriented representative pattern. Unintegrated and unreformed, they remain competitive and mutually hostile because they are supported by hostile groups in society. For it is a sad fact that there still exist in French opinion groups that believe that these primitive models can each produce effective government independent of the other. In brief, the principle of mixed government has not been realized in modern France.

Modern governments such as the British or German have powerful bureaucracies and potent executives as well as alert and effective representative assemblies. What distinguishes them from French government is that a decision has been made and respected as to the proper relations between institutions of administration and execution and those of representation and criticism. In the case of Great Britain the decision was made by a gradual constitutional settlement in which the proper relations between Crown, Cabinet, and Commons were regulated by custom and law. In the case of Bonn Germany a balance was created by the deliberate decision of a constituent Parliamentary Council, to which all parties have since adhered. In the Soviet Union the decision in favor of government by an elite—the Communist Party—was made by a revolutionary act to which subsequent generations have been obliged to adhere.

Although France has often settled the relationship between the legislative and executive branches in theory—that is, in a constitution—in practice, in the last two Republics and in the present Fifth there has never been a true blending of the principles of authority and the two historic traditions of politics embodying them. Under the Third and Fourth Republics a parliament with the essentially "revolutionary" vocation of constantly increasing its prerogative over other branches of government coexisted with an equally anachronistic centralized and omnipresent administration that made even the typically short-leased tenants of the executive branch seem a threat to popular sovereignty. With the representative tradition prevailing, however, political life then was marked by long periods of "immobilism" in which little was done because the executive had been deprived by the legislative of the authority to act. These were interspersed with short periods of frantic activity when a temporarily empowered executive suddenly "liquidated" pending problems while parliament waited in a self-imposed abdication.

Behind the scenes, meanwhile, there was pursued a permanent struggle between the bureaucracy, eager to exploit periods of governmental paralysis in order quietly to impose its expert will, and the leaders of parliament, constantly on guard in order to checkmate moves of the administration that tended to pare down their powers. It would not be an exaggeration to say that for part of the time under the Fourth Republic France was ruled by civil servants whose vocation was ultimately to preserve the status quo, and for another part of the time by the leaders of shifting parliamentary majorities who succeeded more often in undoing the work of the bureaucrats than in effecting new policies. When France did have short periods of effective government, the head of the executive, the Prime Minister, managed to become independent of his majority by a direct appeal to public opinion and both obliged the bureaucracy to do his will and was able to prevent parliament from undoing it. For brief moments, therefore, individual Governments in the administrative tradition of politics did emerge under the last two Republics, though constitutionally the representative tradition with its dominant parliament was the norm.

However, the administrative tradition has become the rule constitutionally since the establishment of the Fifth Republic in 1958. The new institutions reflect the usual reaction against the tradition of politics inspiring the previous regime. Yesterday's parliamentary omnipotence has given way to today's executive omnipotence and the blending of traditions and principles of authority has once again been neglected. Once again France has had the opportunity to create the one kind of regime she has never experienced—mixed government. But once again the Fifth Republic has remained true to the historic pendular movement by establishing a system well within the administrative tradition of politics. The nation's long history of constitutional instability must probably continue.

The ancient coexistence of two hostile political traditions in France clearly has deep-seated causes. It has been suggested that Frenchmen have developed, by virtue of upbringing and culture, an ambivalent attitude toward all authority. On the one hand, a Frenchman dislikes face to face relations with either wielders of authority or with those with whom he shares authority directly. He prefers, rather, to have decisions made centrally by some impersonal and presumably expert but distant authority. Thus one of the reasons advanced for the long maintenance of the centralized bureaucracy created by Napoleon is simply that Frenchmen approve of having many delicate political decisions made for them by experts in order to assure some sort of abstract justice. It explains, too, why there has never been more of a movement in favor of autonomous local government in France. On the other hand, Frenchmen are also very eager indeed to protect their individual liberty of action, to prevent abuses of power by the centralized political authority, and to have a constant veto over its decisions. Hence, it is argued, the growth of institutions like an all-powerful parliament, whose job in the eyes of Frenchmen is to watch over the "ideal" decisions of the executive branch, often taking away its leader, the Prime Minister, in order to check its momentum.

Many other explanations of this dualism in conceptions of authority in French political culture have also been advanced. The most famous one, of course, is the purely ideological theory of the "Red and the Black." According to this much documented view there are the popular forces of progress on the Left, marching under the ensign of the revolutionary motto, *Liberté, Egalité, Fraternité.* On the Right, marshaled against these popular forces, are the aristocratic legions of reaction, committed to the restoration of the past and supported by economic and social elites as well as the Catholic Church. But such an essentially ideological analysis is inadequate, for the conflict between the two Frances during the past century and a half has been far more complex. The alignment of forces at first was not that of the aristocracy versus the people, but rather part of the aristocracy versus the middle class. While the original cleavage may have indeed occurred along ideological lines of traditionalism versus liberalism, by the middle of the nineteenth century economic and social interests became the sources of conflict. By that time, moreover, the middle class had allied itself with the aristocracy to oppose the rising working class. The two Frances were no longer those of the late eighteenth century, yet the basic cleavage remained, and, what is most important for our analysis, so did the opposed political institutions around which the original conflicting ideologies had been formed. And in their exclusive faith in either the administration or the representative assembly, Frenchmen have perpetuated the dualism of conceptions of authority that continues to provide the cultural framework within which political forces carry on their struggles.

These struggles, for which French politics are so famous, are not really between Left or Right, nor between the forces of tradition and those of progress, nor between the working people and the upper classes, as Marxists argue. Rather they have primarily been struggles between two shifting coalitions of social groups, each one attached to certain political institutions embodying a pattern of power and decision making that they believe conforms to their interests. The historic terms of Right and Left, progress and reaction, have long lost much of their analytic value in the context of French politics. For many years the competition for power has been between classes, parties, and pressure groups, which, at a given time, look primarily to either the executive and its bureaucracy or to parliament and its party leaders for redress of grievances or policy making. Nor is it rare that the same class, party, or pressure group will support the administrative pattern of decision making on one issue, only to switch to the representative pattern on another issue, if it feels its interests may best be served by doing so.

The fault lies not in the fickleness of French political forces, however— this is a universal trait. *The real vice lies in the continued availability to Frenchmen of two unreformed myths about how political decisions may best be made and two unreformed sets of political institutions that give pseudo-reality to these myths.* This dualism has been the malady of French politics, chiefly responsible for preventing the emergence of an effective parliamentary government in which the institutions of leadership and those of democratic consent work together. Before examining the institutions themselves, a brief recapitualation of French political and constitutional history may help to illustrate the foregoing discussion and show the causes for France's inability to integrate her two historic traditions of politics and thus produce a system of mixed government adapted to modern needs.

A Century of Constitutional Instability

The reasons for France's failure to develop satisfactory parliamentary government during the Third Republic lie in the period 1789-1870. During this time four developments appeared that have had critical influence on the evolution of her political institutions. First, there occurred the Great Revolution, which precluded the continuity of a natural evolution toward limited, or constitutional, government. Second, under Napoleon there was created a bureaucratized dictatorship whose institutions became permanent. Third, there followed the introduction of a defective parliamentary regime in which a multiparty system and constantly changing Governments were encouraged by monarchs who continued to seek unfettered personal power. Fourth, under Napoleon III there emerged a corrupt economic liberalism that, unlike its British counterpart, refused to nurture true parliamentarism, but opted for authoritarian government.

In his study of the French Revolution, Alexis de Tocqueville shows that rather than the extreme harshness of conditions in eighteenth-century France, it was, in fact, the increasing liberalism of the monarchy that encouraged the taking of the Bastille. There is, indeed, much to indicate that the years just prior to the Revolution were producing at least a *de facto* limited monarchy. Louis XVI had hardly the unlimited authority of Louis XIV and he repeatedly found himself bowing to the wishes of the rising middle class, as expressed in the *Parlements* of Paris—the quasi-legislative law courts. Even after July 14, 1789, there was still the possibility of preserving the continuity of legitimate government, for superficially the king seemed willing to accept constitutionalism. But unlike his British counterpart, the French king lacked the realism to understand the permanence of the middle class's demand for power. While paying lip service to the first revolutionary assembly, he plotted secretly to restore absolutism —and this time, that of the seventeenth century! On the side of the revolutionaries, too, the moderates lost power and in 1792 the First Republic was proclaimed, thereby ending the monarchy and rejecting the British alternative of constitutionalism within the framework of legitimacy. This act proved that a decision as to the form of government could be taken by a handful of mortal men. The king and his administration were replaced by the sovereign assembly and its administration, ostensibly representing the will of the people. Thus was born the revolutionary myth of popular sovereignty and its institutional form—the all-powerful representative assembly. At the same time, of course, the remnants of feudalism were eliminated and a nominally democratic society was decreed.

Naturally the great mass of the French people remained aloof from these changes and judged proceedings in Paris against simple human standards. When wartime conditions as well as imprudent policies created a disorder that went beyond any that existed under the *ancien régime,* the time was ripe for reaction. Napoleon seized the opportunity and restored order and authority—but not the royal order and authority, for this the Revolution had seemingly exiled forever. At this point the legitimacy of hereditary government was joined in limbo by the new legitimacy of popular government, the supporters of the two forms of government often going into at least a spiritual exile. There thus began the process of division in French society that has been one of the sources of political instability. Because no one emerged the clear winner in the Revolution, the battle was fought over and over again during the nineteenth century. Each crisis became a revolution because each side hoped, this time, to win the final victory.

Napoleon both achieved and undid the Revolution. His creation of a military order in society, thanks to highly centralized bureaucratic government, forcibly established the national unity and equality of treatment that the Revolution had sought. But it accomplished these ends by the constraint of absolute monarchy rather than the consent of democracy. He accepted the Revolution's destruction of feudal privileges and the rise of the commercial middle class, but he promptly created a new aristocracy based largely on this middle class and committed henceforth to his person for its status. There was thus established still another political faction, one made up of Frenchmen whose status depended not on the existence of a hereditary king, nor on the creation of a democratic republic, but on the existence of a military dictatorship to which they paid allegiance in return for social peace.

The fall of Napoleon ushered in the Restoration of the Bourbon monarchy (1814-30) and the July Monarchy (1830-48). But the return to legitimate monarchic rule in 1814 did not bring back the *ancien régime*. Louis XVIII introduced a form of parliamentary government, having spent his years of exile in England where he had been impressed by the prevailing governmental system. The peculiar hybrid of parliamentarism that emerged between 1814 and 1848 differed considerably from its British model. Responsible for this was the king himself, who, unlike his British counterpart, sought to retain a maximum of his personal prerogative behind the form of a largely advisory parliament. The king was in fact assured of predominance over parliament by three factors: First, the Governments he named were rarely homogeneous, thus making it difficult to hold any one party accountable. Second, Governments were responsible to the king alone, who could name them and dismiss them at will. Third, unlike the British king during this period, the French monarch made no effort at organizing solid Government majorities in Parliament against which the rest of parliament could organize a similarly solid opposition. As a result, parliament was divided from the start among many small, competing groups. This the king welcomed, for it allowed him to rule unfettered by the responsible criticism of a single and powerful parliamentary opposition.

Moreover, while in England there was a constant effort to increase the suffrage, in France succeeding monarchs made the suffrage more, not less, limited. Parliamentary government therefore was not allowed to develop healthily in France at the time it was being successfully adopted in Great Britain. France's two constitutional monarchies, however, did maintain the principle of elected assemblies and the centralized bureaucracy, the former to retain the loyalty of the rising middle class, the latter to assure more effectively the monarch's ultimate control. Representative institutions were used as means, not ends, and no effort was made to educate the population for a more responsible political role.

As a consequence, when another revolution established the Second Republic in 1848, French society was not much more democratic than it had been in 1789. The new Republic was declared in a predominantly agricultural country that was naturally conservative and monarchist. As the First Republic had been, the Second was the work of Parisians—a coalition of the Parisian "people" and the middle class, chafing under the king's repressive policies. But unlike the earlier experience, 1848 was characterized by the participation of people who called themselves socialists. The threat to private property thus appeared and the revolutionary coalition foundered upon it when the fearful middle class leaders abandoned their pressure for universal suffrage and representative government. Again a Napoleon— the great one's nephew—came to restore order, instituting a plebiscitary dictatorship that exploited the conservative majority in public opinion to give a democratic sanction to his regime.

Now parliament was reduced to even greater impotence than under the Restoration and the July Monarchy. The administrative tradition of government prevailed, civil and political rights were severely curtailed, and the emperor continued his uncle's policy of winning a large degree of consent for his rule—from business to peasantry and even the city workers—by means of a paternalistic economic and social program. The result of this was that the opposition to his tyranny was reduced to its smallest expression in a group of doctrinaire intellectuals. Bonapartism again struck a lethal blow at liberalism and its political form, parliamentarism. Yet under Napoleon III the middle class ultimately came to hold great power and the mass of the people developed a superficial feeling of participation without the aid of representative institutions. Indeed, Napoleon III successfully identified limited suffrage and parliament with the memory of the oppressive constitutional monarchies, hence for a time thoroughly discrediting parliamentarism as a conservative invention in the minds of the urban population. Thus was born the latent bias for Caesarism that time and again was to threaten constitutionalism in France in the years to come.

The Second Empire survived military defeat no better than had the First. The victory of Prussia in 1870 left France in the throes of another revolutionary convulsion, Paris being in the hands of a socialist "Commune" while in Bordeaux a moderate republican government set about making peace with the victor. For the second time in French history—the first had been in 1848—the French people were called to the polls in a free election. Reacting against both the extremist democratic Commune in Paris and the military adventure of the latest Bonaparte, they returned a conservative majority to the National Assembly that was dedicated to constitutional monarchy. The constitution drafted in 1875 reflected this renewed desire to escape the alternation between extremes that had dogged France since the Great Revolution. But this does not mean that the bulk of either the people or the National Assembly were finally united on basic political values. The constitution on which they finally agreed was like an armistice between opposing armies, in which supporters of the two rival traditions of politics agreed to a momentary compromise without surrendering their hopes for a "pure" system to be established in the future. There was thus created a parliamentary government, again patterned on the British, and studiously poised halfway between the "assembly" regime of 1792, which provided for an all-powerful, unicameral legislature, and the one-man rule of the Bonapartes.

The Third Republic: 1870-1940

The constitutional laws of the Third Republic created a system of government that seemed excellent—at least in theory. Their vital innovation was a real separation of powers that appeared to provide a safeguard against the extreme of a demagogic legislature in the hands of a revolutionary elite as well as the danger of a dictatorial chief of state in the Bonapartist tradition. The lower house, the Chamber of Deputies, was invested with broad legislative powers and assured by the constitution of a fixed period every year for its deliberations, as well as various other prerogatives. It shared with an upper house, the Senate, the duty of electing the head of the executive branch of government, the President of the Republic—who also served as chief of state. The latter chose his Ministers, had the right to propose legislation, and could dissolve the Chamber, with the approval of the Senate, and call new elections. Although personally he was invulnerable to the Chamber's hostility, his Ministers were declared collectively responsible to parliament.

On the face of it, the constitution seemed to provide France at long last with true "mixed government." Although separation of powers and ministerial responsibility were provided for, it soon became apparent that the drafters of the constitution had left the executive in a potentially predominant position. In particular, there was no mention in the laws of 1875 of the office of Prime Minister, that is, the truly responsible head of the executive. It was assumed that the President of the Republic would exercise all executive duties, just as the king had been, in effect, head of Government under the constitutional monarchies. Since the President of the Republic was elected for a seven-year term and was not responsible to parliament, abuse of the executive power of dissolving parliament appeared possible. And indeed this is not surprising when it is remembered that the drafters were monarchists who actively hoped for the day when the contending pretenders to the French throne would come to an agreement and the monarchy would again be restored.

But the intention of this royalist majority was never realized and a conservative republic became, in the words of its first President, Adolphe Thiers, "the regime that divides us least." As the years went by without a decision as to which branch of the French royal family would rule, conservative opinion became reconciled to the only available guarantees against the "risks" of universal suffrage: the powerful surrogate for a king, the President of the Republic, and centralized administration, which the Republic retained in its full Bonapartist form.

The crisis came on May 16, 1877, when Marshal MacMahon, the royalist who had been elected second President of the Republic, decided to dissolve the Chamber of Deputies. While this was within his constitutional rights, it was interpreted by growing democratic opinion as a sudden return to the pre-republican administrative tradition of government. For the President's motive was to dismiss a Chamber that refused confidence to a conservative ministry that he had named and desired to retain. When the new elections returned an even larger hostile majority, it became evident that genuine republicanism and the representative tradition of government had become rooted in public opinion. MacMahon bowed to the popular will, named a ministry responsible to the new republican majority, and the true political history of the Third Republic began. During the following years the growth of an industrial working class swelled the ranks of true republicans and as a result further increased the power of the parties committed to making the Republic truly democratic. Thus with the principle of ministerial responsibility to parliament established, the Prime Minister came to assume most of the executive power. But the reaction to MacMahon's "coup" had been so strong that vigor and initiative on the executive's part were henceforth discouraged.

From the constitutional point of view the history of the Third Republic may be divided by World War I. From 1877 to 1914 there was a marked trend toward revising the 1875 constitutional balance between the executive and the legislature in favor of the latter. From the first World War to the fall of the Republic in 1940, the governmental system, lacking an effective executive power, proved unable to meet new problems and there resulted a radical increase in ministerial instability. Again, informal means were found to institute a countertrend in which the executive was strengthened at the expense of the legislative.

The most permanent characteristics of French government, however, were developed during the earlier period. Prior to the first World War France was still far from being a fully industrialized nation, and her largely small-town and rural population had not only a poor opinion of the Paris government, which under dictators and revolutionary mobs had brought grief to the country, but also felt little objective need for government intervention in their everyday lives. After all, France was well endowed with natural resources, and was fairly independent of world trade. It was felt that government was necessary to keep order and protect the frontiers, but beyond that could only serve as a source of oppression and unnecessary expenditure by the nation. Indeed the victory of the middle class republicans after 1877 was accompanied by a victory of the economic principle of *laissez faire* that reached proportions unknown in other major powers, except for the United States. The scope of governmental policy was severely limited and this eliminated pressure for reforming the governmental system—of little importance in French life at the time.

These conditions produced traits that are still very much present in French government today. First there is the importance of ideological issues and verbal partisanship. This is partly due to the relative unimportance, in early Third Republic politics, of economic and social issues such as factory legislation and the income tax question. These questions were raised but were not resolved until after the last threat to the Republic was laid to rest in the Dreyfus Affair. Certainly, too, the verbal effervescence was in part born of a reaction against long years of censorship. For if France became the nation of free speech par excellence, it was only because government control over political opinion and its expression had been so much a tradition during the long period in which the administrative tradition of politics prevailed.

Second, there is the amazing individualism of French politics—the importance of personalities, of local and regional issues, and hence the lack of discipline that pervades all levels of politics. Again reference to France's past provides the cause: personal discipline, intellectual consistency, the sacrifice of personal motives for collective ends, are all required in political systems where the politicians are actually responsible for most political decisions. But in France where no tradition of local government existed, where a powerful administration, with agents in every locality, determined the minutest matter, there was little objective need to be responsible. Things would get done the way "the state" wanted them whether political leaders acted responsibly or not. Most of them, outside of the few who held ministerial posts at any one time, conceived of themselves as members of either the opposition or a potential opposition, and thus no effort was made to moderate criticism or temper ambitions. Overturning a Government became as much a means of opening a general competition for ministerial posts as it was for registering disapproval of Government policies. French experience seemed to suggest the rule that parliamentarism increases in irresponsibility and instability in inverse proportion to the role members of parliament have in the actual determination of policy.

But if the continuing existence of a monarchical bureaucracy appeared to interfere with the full prerogative of the parliament, why did this supposedly sovereign body permit the conservative institution to flourish? Why didn't the victorious republicans decentralize French government, thus reducing the role of the ancient central bureaucracy in policy formulation? The Third Republic was produced in a compromise between conservative friends of the administrative tradition, who wanted as little democracy as possible, and progressives of the representative republican tradition, who wanted wide-sweeping social reforms and political changes. Neither having a clear majority in the early years, a compromise was necessary, the terms of which were neatly put by Thiers when he warned, in 1871: "the Republic will be conservative or it will not be at all."

This compromise provided for the retention of the centralized bureaucracy, which guaranteed order, in return for a representative assembly elected by universal suffrage and, later, limited local self-government. But by 1900 progressive republicans, finally in control of the government, became aware of the advantages of a centralized bureaucracy, with its police and local government organizations. In the aftermath of the Dreyfus Affair they learned that such institutions could be used as effectively against conservatives as the latter had used them against republicans in 1848 and 1871.

Moreover, the progressive republicans had slowly transformed the 1875 regime into something quite different from what it had originally been. After MacMahon's retirement only nonentities were chosen for President of the Republic. The true chief of the executive was the Prime Minister, who with his cabinet became totally responsible to the Chamber of Deputies. Nor did the President of the Republic attempt to reaffirm the independence of the constitutional executive by using the power of dissolution. Almost eighty years had to pass before a French parliament was dissolved before its term was formally reached. At the same time indirect methods were used to decrease the power of conservative forces in society. An attempt was made to ensure the secular state school's monopoly on education. Then the powers of local government authorities were increased in an effort to withdraw at least some power from the conservatively recruited central administration. Finally, and most important, progressive republicans sought continually to decrease the power in France of what they considered the most potent conservative influence—Roman Catholicism, until 1905 recognized and supported as the official French church.

The climax of this struggle between those who had never accepted the Republic as permanent and the growing number of devoted republicans came in the famous Dreyfus Affair. Beginning in 1894, the affair became the last pitched battle between the social groups loyal to the administrative tradition of government and the politicians of the representative tradition. Captain Dreyfus was a victim of a judicial error in which the honor of the French army was at stake. The case was exaggerated out of all proportion because of the excellent opportunity it offered both friends and enemies of the democratic Republic to fight what they thought would be a decisive ideological battle. The army, along with the Church, remained one of the last strongholds of pre-republican and authoritarian sentiment. Everyone in France who opposed further democratization of society—and with the rise of socialism this had come to include many socially conservative republicans—opposed rectification of the error on the grounds of *raison d'état* (reason of state), the higher logic that must prevail over abstract justice and individual rights. Those who favored the trend toward separation of church and state, and the general dominance of the representative tradition, urged revision of the error and a full pardon for Dreyfus even if it meant dishonor for the army—and often many urged this in order to discredit another bastion of conservatism, rather than in order to uphold the rights of an individual.

By the time the Dreyfus decision was reversed in 1906 important political changes had taken place that were partially responsible for the revision. The rise of the Socialist Party had brought a powerful ally to the democratic forces, which helped assure the primacy of the Chamber over the executive and thus seemingly neutralize a conservative civil service. Church and state were separated in 1905, the influence of the army was reduced, and the balance of political power shifted into the hands of the lower middle classes, represented by the Radical Socialist Party. The great battle of political reform had been won.

But at the same time France was slowly and almost unnoticeably losing its world position. In the years before World War I her birth rate fell, her industrial development lagged in relation to the major powers, and her colonial expansion was seriously challenged. The battle for a democratic republic had so absorbed her political energies that the need for social and economic reforms had been overlooked. Nor were the political reformers who had won power in the years before the first World War prepared to embark on these social and economic changes. Except for the socialists, the progressive forces proved vehemently opposed to bestowing upon the executive, necessarily the agent of social and economic change, the new powers required for meeting the problems of an industrial society. Had they not recently won the long fight to weaken its independent role in France?

The war radically altered the conditions of French politics. Its enormous physical and economic costs served further to weaken France's world power. Yet wartime needs had demonstrated the virtues of strong executive leadership and Clemenceau's exercise of this power seemed to reveal by contrast the impotence and irrelevance of the highly verbal parliamentarism of prewar politics. It was not surprising, therefore, that the conservative partisans of the administrative tradition of politics should have won a great victory in the first elections after the armistice. Hope was rekindled for the possible reversal of the prewar victory of democracy after the Dreyfus Affair. And the old ideological battles around the state monopoly of education, around the influence of the Catholic Church, and around the power of the administration vis-à-vis parliament were all revived. But added to these were a new set of pressing political problems resulting from the economic effects of the war and the Soviet revolution in Russia.

The rise of communism in France had two important influences on French politics. It weakened the strength of the democratic Left by attracting socialist voters to an extremist party that kept aloof from the rest of the nation. And by frightening the more conservative members of the democratic parties it inspired the formation of authoritarian political groups on the Right that gained new strength for their old battle against the Republic. Now these groups could claim that the democratic parties were not strong enough to resist communism. These party developments made the formation of moderate Government coalitions more difficult than before the war and made their existence more precarious as well.

The real breakdown of French political institutions under the weight of problems for which they were not adapted did not come until the decade before World War II. Then a combination of domestic and international crises started the country on the road that brought the Third Republic to an end. The government had, after all, been conceived by nineteenth-century liberals, who had assumed that the scope of public policy and governmental power had been too broad under Napoleon III. While intentionally retaining his centralized bureaucracy as an organ of order and control, they allowed executive power to wither away, producing thereby a parliamentarism that had difficulty acting in times of stress. Under the vastly increased responsibilities of government created by economic depression and international troubles, the archaic structure of French government began to show serious signs of breakdown.

From 1932 on ministerial instability became chronic. The average life of a Government during the next eight years was four months, as compared to eight months in 1914-32 and ten months in 1870-1914. The growth of extremist groups on the Right that advocated direct and violent action against the government was a tangible sign of public disaffection from the regime. Indeed, as the Great Depression settled on the major

industrial countries a feeling of revolutionary potential appeared throughout the world, which in France was encouraged by the rapidity and seeming frivolity with which Governments came and went. In February 1934,
extreme Rightists rose in a mass demonstration on the Place de la Con-
corde in Paris to protest the government's incapacity to manage the
country's affairs. They attempted to cross the Seine and invade the Chamber of Deputies, once again producing for posterity a "revolutionary day"
in the spirit of 1789, 1830, 1848, and 1870. Though France was now thoroughly republican and democratic and no real threat to the constitution
emerged, the Popular Front, a coalition of all the left-wing parties, was
formed, ostensibly to protect the Republic against the resurgent Right,
but in fact to seize the opportunity to enact long-needed social reforms.

The Popular Front, however, served largely to weaken French unity in
a world threatened by war because it seemed to integrate the Communist
Party into national political life. France in the 1930's was still very much
an agricultural country, with 48 per cent of the population living off the
land, and only a small minority of the remaining 52 per cent could have
been considered members of a modern economy. In a word, for all the
hue and cry of its intellectual politics, very much in the revolutionary
tradition, France was basically a conservative country in 1936. Yet since
1932 the Communist Party had gained over half a million votes in the
election and over fifty new deputies. And in Germany and Italy another
form of revolutionary movement, Fascism, was claiming that the wave of
the future was behind it. In these circumstances Frenchmen of all opinions
began to realize just how ill adapted to the twentieth century their country
had become. The choice for many seemed to be between Fascism and
Communism, but at any rate the viability of traditional liberal and republican government appeared to them doubtful. It was in this state of
mind that the French were called upon to prepare for World War II.
Amazingly, great efforts were made and when war came in 1939 France
had an impressive war machine readied. But beneath the surface the
divisions and unsettled problems of the preceding two decades created the
potential of collapse. It remained only for the spectacular defeat of the
French army and the *de facto* abdication of the country's leadership to
make this potential a reality. In June 1940 the defeat of the army and the
resignation of the Government of Paul Reynaud constituted indictments
against which the Third Republic had no recourse. In July the authoritarian Vichy regime was created, led by Marshal Pétain, who re-established
the administrative pattern of government in the best pre-republican tradition. The Chamber and Senate were replaced by an appointed advisory
council and the civil service was put in complete charge of policy making
as well as policy execution. As in 1870, a regime that had increasingly lost

the confidence of the people failed to survive a military catastrophe—only this time the regime was the Republic.

The Rise and Fall of the Fourth Republic: 1940-1958

During the critical last years of the Third Republic two groups of reformist critics of French political institutions appeared both in and out of party politics. One group, made up largely of conservatives and anti-Communists, urged that the old-fashioned parliamentary democracy be streamlined in accordance with the model presented by the new dynamic powers of Nazi Germany and Fascist Italy. Another group, drawn from among the younger members of the center and moderate left parties, as well as from civic reform groups outside of politics altogether, urged a rejuvenated and energetic Republic, reformed to meet the challenge of new problems, rather than scrapped in favor of a return to the authoritarian tradition of the monarchy and the Empire.

After the armistice of June 1940, France was divided by the Germans into a zone, occupied and governed directly by them, and a zone, with its capital at Vichy, administered by a French government nominally free of German supervision. This nonoccupied zone was ostensibly ruled by Marshal Philippe Pétain, the aged hero of World War I, who became the figurehead for a government in the hands of the conservative and authoritarian reformers of the Third Republic. At the same time, however, in both zones as well as in the French colonies overseas and among Frenchmen in London, there developed a spirit of resistance to both the Vichy policy of collaboration with Germany and its attempt to transform France into an authoritarian country. It was quite fitting, therefore, that the second group of democratic reformers should become leaders of this resistance. Within metropolitan France underground resistance movements were created and in London General Charles de Gaulle organized Free France, which was ultimately to become co-ordinator of all French efforts to re-enter the war at the side of the Allies.

De Gaulle's efforts, although at first primarily military, became inevitably political. He correctly reasoned that an appeal to continued resistance in the name of the discredited prewar Republic would inspire little enthusiasm. Moreover, he knew that the leaders of active resistance within France were almost exclusively young reformers or marginal politicians for whom defeat had come as a vindication of their long-standing demands for change. De Gaulle saw that to enlist their cooperation Free France would have to promise a Fourth Republic after victory. Thus from 1942 onward the General and the leaders of the internal resistance movements formally planned new economic and political institutions to be created after Liberation. But the secret of de Gaulle's great personal hold on the loyalty of the French, the secret of his power as President of the Fifth Republic, lies not only in his espousal of the cause of reform during the war. For Frenchmen of all opinions the sudden defeat by Germany in 1940 and the increasing collaboration of the Vichy regime with their country's victors created a real crisis of national self-respect. The very existence of a French fighting force within the Allied camp and the ultimate presence of a French officer at the German armistice negotiations in 1945 were the meager conditions for regaining some sense of honor. Charles de Gaulle, as leader of those French who continued to fight and as the one who created a place for France among the victorious Allies, naturally became the symbol of this sense of honor.

Since the Resistance was as much opposed to returning to the Third Republic as it was to the Vichy regime, constitutional and reform projects studiously sought to avoid the pitfalls of both a weak and anarchic parliamentary democracy and a tyrannical dictatorship. As in 1875, constitutional thinking during the war years sought to balance institutions of the administrative and representative traditions of politics. True mixed government was the goal: executive and legislative powers balanced and assured of a responsible yet independent coexistence by the separation of powers. When liberation came in 1944 hope was high, for the past four years had seemed to eliminate all the forces that favored one or the other of the extreme forms of government under which France had long suffered. On the one hand, the blind conservative partisans of government by an administrative and social elite had been thoroughly discredited by their roles in the collaborationist government of Pétain—truly the government of administration *par excellence*. On the other hand, the prewar parties and politicians, who had failed to produce the necessary leadership and had become identified with ineffective government and ministerial instability, had also been discredited by the rapid collapse of the Third Republic in 1940. What seemed to emerge in 1944 was a new political elite, inexperienced, young, yet enthusiastic and in many ways more realistic and adapted to modern times than had been the old cadres. This was reflected in the first Constituent Assembly, elected in October 1945 in order to draft a new constitution: over 90 per cent of the members had no previous national political experience.

And yet very potent seeds of the past were imbedded in the new French politics. After having denounced de Gaulle and the Resistance as agents of British imperialism, the French Communist Party hastily recanted in 1941 when Hitler attacked the Soviet Union. Subsequently the party became one of the most active and popular elements of the Resistance. However, leadership of the Resistance remained firmly in the hands of the moderate non-Communist reformers, who were committed to establishing an efficient parliamentary government in which a strong executive balanced a vigorous legislative. De Gaulle, as leader of the French resistance movements, naturally loomed as head of the first postwar French government. But for the Communists de Gaulle and the principle of a strong executive represented the major obstacles to their assumption of power after the war. Thus even prior to liberation the Communist Party urged a truly "revolutionary" constitution that would assure a predominant representative assembly in which, of course, they expected presently to gain a strong if not a near-majority position. As for de Gaulle, their only formidable competitor for post-liberation popularity and organizational drive, the Communists made an effort to discredit him with the moderate reformers by encouraging a whispering campaign about his alleged plans for dictatorship.

The Communist Party thus made itself heir to the pure revolutionary tradition that during the nineteenth century constantly had urged an "assembly regime" in which the legislature in effect performed executive as well as legislative functions. Naturally their activity tended to inspire a reaction of fear on the part of French conservatives. Many who had at first hoped for a balanced constitution now reacted against Communist extremism by reviving activity on behalf of a predominant executive and bureaucracy. It was natural that General de Gaulle should become their leader as he constituted the only other real focus of public sympathy in the country. As a consequence, by the time debate over the exact terms of the Fourth Republic's constitution began, French politics were once again divided along the classic lines of the representative, democratic ideal of authority versus the administrative, elitist ideal.

Of course neither de Gaulle nor the conservative parties supporting him sought to institute a dictatorial regime on the monarchist or Bonapartist models. Rather they sought simply to assure effective government by remedying the defect of a weak and unstable executive that the experience of the Third Republic had revealed. Yet the opposition of the Communists, who urged reducing the formal powers of the executive even further than they had been reduced by custom before the war, automatically thrust de Gaulle and his supporters into what appeared to be the anti-republican camp. Fearful that the Communists would be successful at the elections by posing as the only truly republican party, the moderate reformers abandoned both de Gaulle and their early intentions of creating a strong executive to balance the traditionally powerful legislature. Although the 1946 constitution did not incorporate the radical "assembly regime" of the Communists, it nonetheless went far toward legally institutionalizing those customs of the Third Republic that had led to the weakening of the executive branch.

True, a token effort had been made to give the Prime Minister increased powers and to make the defeat of a Government more difficult. But in practice none of these new provisions prevented the reappearance of instability, which soon approached the record of the Third Republic during the interwar years. The short period of social and economic reforms—including nationalization of the natural gas, electricity, and coal industries, the major insurance companies, and the commercial banks—did not dispel the growing disillusionment over the fruits of the Liberation. Again, as at the beginning of the Third Republic, the political system was the product not of consensus, but of a compromise between two coalitions of political forces clustered about the two historic traditions. Instead of mixing the two ideals of authority, they juxtaposed them.

Thus the new constitution, drafted by Resistance leaders who supported the representative tradition, established the legislature as the dominant branch of the government. But General de Gaulle and the more conservative political leaders around him managed to retain intact the highly centralized and essentially pre-democratic bureaucracy, the institution essential to the administrative tradition. Nor did de Gaulle's departure from the Government change matters: the threat of a Communist coup made the Resistance leaders realize that a centralized bureaucracy, and especially a strong police organization, was absolutely necessary. Yet in the matter of positive government action to resolve France's many postwar problems, the partisans of the representative tradition continued to insist on the primacy of parliament's role. But parliament, divided among many parties and unable to produce stable Governmental majorities, showed itself incapable of acting swiftly and effectively. Soon after the Liberation period it became clear to many Frenchmen that there was arising a serious disproportion between the range of governmental responsibilities created by the constitution and postwar social reforms, and the authority, stability, and efficiency of the supposedly new governmental system.

In brief, defeat, occupation, resistance, and liberation had not liquidated the burden of the past in the French political system. They had simply created a number of new layers in French political culture that were further to complicate and hinder the already cumbersome operation of French government. To the ancient enmity between partisans of the administrative and representative traditions were added the vexatious issues of the German occupation and collaboration versus resistance; "Gaullist" and "Pétainist" were added to the collection of epithets that envenomed political debate. The new political personnel soon slipped into the classical categories of French politics, given new names but still fighting the ancient battle of the two opposing ideals of authority.

Those interests seeking economic and social changes looked to parliament and encouraged it to remain vigilant against attempts by the civil service to prevent "progress." Those interests opposed to such changes looked to the administration and hoped for a strong executive to protect them against "anarchy" and "revolution." Between parliament and the civil service, the cabinet, properly the source of policy-making, remained simply the changing agent of changing majorities in the legislature. The result of this struggle has been what the French call *immobilisme*—a lack of effective governmental action on pressing public problems because of a lack of agreement on the proper solutions. The prime beneficiaries of such a situation have been the various groups and the extremists of all colors who live on discontent.

The collapse of the Fourth Republic was very much the work of forces hostile to the regime that exploited discontent over government *immobilisme* in the face of the Algerian problem. The Algiers revolt by European settlers and elements of the French army in May 1958 simply created the situation that these forces had long awaited in order to bring about a change in political institutions. But even more important a factor in the Republic's demise were certain trends in French society that sapped the regime of its popular support and thus made both the work of demolition and construction easier for the founders of the Fifth Republic. By a strange coincidence, the French Institute of Public Opinion asked a sample of Frenchmen in January 1958—only four months before the revolt in Algiers —what they would do in case of a coup against the Republic. Only 4 per cent replied that they would oppose the coup actively, while a majority admitted flatly that they would do nothing at all. Why did the Fourth Republic have so few defenders in 1958?

One of the trends that undermined the regime originated during World War II. Frenchmen of all opinions at that time had agreed that after the Liberation there should be no return to the chronic political instability of the Third Republic—the prewar regime in which they had also lost their confidence. Many of them actually attributed the humiliating defeat by the Germans in 1940 to the weakness of their country's governmental system. But while there was almost complete unanimity on the need for a new constitution in 1945, the one adopted the next year for the Fourth Republic, and the subsequent record of that regime, proved a huge disappointment to these hopes. As political instability and ineffective government reappeared in the postwar years, the French again lost faith in their form of parliamentary government.

This gradual decline in faith took a sharp dip around 1954 due to a curious phenomenon. That year there occurred the conjunction of the most outstanding success and the most glaring failure of the Fourth Republic.

The long effort of economic planning and reconstruction inaugurated after
World War II finally blossomed into a vigorous industrial boom and a
sudden and widespread rise in the standard of living. But that same year
the Republic's long and fruitless effort at maintaining her prewar colonial
empire intact ended with the humiliating defeat of the French army at
Dien Bien Phu and the subsequent loss of France's Asiatic domain of
Indochina. At the same time the outbreak of the Moslem rebellion in
Algeria and the stirrings of independence movements in other French holding in Africa threatened to reduce France even further to the simple status
of a continental European power.

As luck had it, the very success of the French economy had served to
magnify the failure of the nation's postwar attempts at regaining her
traditional international prestige. For, as France progressed into the years
of economic prosperity after 1954—a period her neighbors Britain and
Germany had known earlier—the gap widened between the mediocre reality
of France's world power position and the suddenly revived national aspirations for the status of a great power. On the one hand French workers
and businessmen alike had come to feel both a new confidence in the
future of their country as a viable economic unit and a new pride in her
growing contribution to the free world's technological and cultural progress. On the other hand, they were puzzled and disturbed by the continuing ridicule with which French political institutions were regarded, by
the feebleness of the French voice in the decisions of the Western Alliance,
and by the rapidity with which French dependencies throughout the world
sought to divorce themselves from the motherland. Unfairly perhaps (for
the magnitude of the problems facing France in the 1950's would have
challenged the effectiveness of any system of government) the blame was
placed upon the regime. To Frenchmen of all classes, the fault still seemed
to lie with that ancient malady—the instability of French Governments
and the ineffectiveness of their policies.

The situation was ideal for the revival of antiparliamentarism and nationalism, related political movements that have prospered intermittently
since the late nineteenth century whenever Frenchmen felt that the reality
of their country's power was radically out of proportion to her potential
and her most cherished historical traditions. In the years before World
War I, when a sudden industrial boom accompanied the bitter competition
with Germany on the international scene, these movements had found
widespread support. Similarly during the last years of the Fourth Republic
the mounting prosperity and the continuing reverses internationally
widened the gap between national aspirations and France's world prestige.
The result again was that the demand for political reforms grew in a
rather inarticulate yet striking manner. The reactionary Poujadist move-

ment was the first to notice the success of the nationalist appeal to public opinion. Then in the elections of 1956 it was the leftist Mendès-France coalition that unconsciously exploited the same current of opinion with its appearance of energetic leadership and its promise of national revival symbolized by the seven-month reign of its leader in 1954-55. Finally, during the two years preceding the Algerian crisis, the nationalist predisposition of French opinion came to affect all political parties. The Communists began to soft-pedal their appeal for Algerian independence; the Socialists, who in Robert Lacoste had one of the leaders of the French Algeria faction, forgot their 1956 election pledges of a negotiated peace in Algeria; the Radicals turned from Mendès-France who, by remaining true to his policy of colonial disengagement, had lost his nationalist appeal of 1955; the conservatives gave new vigor to their traditional nationalism, fearful of the attraction the many new ultranationalist and authoritarian groups would have for their own followers. The near unanimity of French opinion behind the invasion of Suez in 1956 was final evidence of the new nationalist atmosphere of the country.

But by all odds the most important effect of this new "mood" was upon the professional army leadership. Smarting under repeated humiliations since 1940, France's army leaders developed a new awareness of the political dimension of their responsibilities. Reasoning that their defeat in Indochina was more the result of vacillation by unstable and incoherent Paris Governments than of defective strategy and tactics, they vowed this would not be the cause of their defeat in Algeria. With their vast administrative functions in Algeria, and their proud faith in the social mission they were accomplishing for the Moslem population, the army came to abandon their traditional neutrality. In order to assure both victory and their social mission they placed increased pressure on succeeding cabinets for a steadfast prosecution of the war against the Algerian rebels. This was accompanied by frequent rumors of plots against the regime by a number of particularly irate military leaders. Symbol of national prestige, traditional hero of nationalist movements, the army received encouragement from everyone who sought to reestablish French power and reform French political institutions.

In retrospect it now seems that throughout these developments the Gaullists, whose fortunes were never lower than during these years following the retirement of their leader, were inevitably and often reluctantly looked to for leadership of the revived French nationalism. The Vichy and often fascist background of the extreme nationalists and the Algerian settlers prevented them from trusting the Gaullists, although they were obliged to recognize that they were the best-connected in government and influential private circles. Nor were the Gaullists universally respected by the army command, although their leader was recognized as the only political force that could serve as a cover and justification for their eventual revolt against Republican authority. But the fact that with the leaders of the Republic the Gaullists shared a common Resistance past meant to realistic plotters that the followers of the General would be generally considered the oldest and least dangerous of the nationalist and anticonstitutional opposition and hence the one that would generate the least resistance from authorities. Thus even without the active leadership of de Gaulle, the Gaullists in May 1958 proved to be the thread of Ariadne, guiding all the forces committed to the overthrow of the Fourth Republic. It was this thread that was carefully and consciously twisted into the fuse that ignited the explosion of May 1958 which swept away the old regime.

The Nature of the Fifth Republic: A Return to the Administrative Tradition

What kind of political system has de Gaulle created? Is his regime, originating as it did in a military coup, simply a moderate and sophisticated form of dictatorship? To answer this it is first important to realize that few aspects of the Fifth Republic were improvised in the heat of revolutionary fervor. There was little of this fervor because of the orderly and legal demise of the Fourth Republic, something de Gaulle had firmly insisted upon. The Gaullists, it should be remembered, had been organized as a political movement for over ten years and had long matured their constitutional reform plans. The new regime, therefore, copied very closely the model prescribed by de Gaulle in his 1946 campaign against ratification of the constitution of the Fourth Republic. In its details the constitution of 1958 adheres closely to projects elaborated by the General's chief associates in the intervening years. Indeed, it was one of de Gaulle's chief advisors of that early period, Michel Debré, who was primarily responsible for drafting the new constitution and who, as the first Prime Minister of the new Republic, established the precedents of practice. Indeed, it has been the predominance of de Gaulle's ideas and policies, and the lack of a revolutionary fervor in the new regime, that has led to an extreme nationalist opposition to the Fifth Republic, made up of rightists and fascists, activist elements among the Algerian settlers, important elements of the Army, and others who have felt that de Gaulle used them to return to power and then dropped both them and their ideas.

In many respects the new Republic is also simply an extension of policies and reforms that had been painfully attempted during the last years of the previous regime. The various economic measures, for example, which have managed to make of the French franc a "hard" currency since 1958, had all been tried and had failed to "take" under the Fourth Republic.

Many of the administrative reforms carried out by the new regime had been conceived during the previous one but, for lack of ministerial coherence and stability, could never be applied. Generally, most of de Gaulle's domestic policies are new only in the sense that they have enacted into law proposals made by civil servants and politicians during the Fourth Republic. In the past some of the proposals remained stillborn because no majority could be found for them in parliaments which shied away from reforms threatening powerful interest groups. When proposals were introduced for legislation, few of the Governments remained in power long enough to see them through to final enactment.

The areas in which the new Republic has sought to be truly novel are foreign affairs and political institutions. While enjoying greater international prestige than its predecessor—due less to its institutions and policies than to the person of its President—the Fifth Republic has by and large followed a foreign policy that French national interests and the international power struggle had long ago dictated to the Fourth Republic. As for political institutions, the new regime attempted to resolve the longstanding problem of Government stability and hence to satisfy popular demands for political reform. Ostensibly the new constitution meant to adapt institutions to the needs of a nation entering the stage of advanced industrialization. But in this respect, too, the Fifth Republic has proven unable to break with the past, showing itself less revolutionary in practice than many expected. If technically there have been only two Governments since January 1959, over three years' experience with the new institutions has seen the "instability" of the new Ministers reach a cadence almost as great as before. And if one refers to the three basic traits of French politics, mentioned at the outset, one notes, first, that relations between the executive and the legislative branches have been as antagonistic as ever; second, that stable solutions to the most pressing economic and foreign policy problems are still not assured; and third, that violence in political life and even the threat of a revolutionary change in regime are still realities in the France of mid-1962.

As one commentator on French politics has put it, the Government crises of the past have been replaced by the less frequent, yet potentially more dangerous crises of the regime itself. Under the Fourth Republic a three year period would have recorded the making and unmaking of five or six Governments. During the first three years of the Fifth Republic there has been only one cabinet, but there have been two attempted *coups d'état* in Algiers, at least two stillborn conspiracies, and one officially admitted plot against the life of President de Gaulle. In addition there have been frequent periods of "attenuated *coup d'état*," when systematic rumor and the "intoxication" of public opinion by right wing opponents of de Gaulle's policies aimed at frightening the Government into voluntarily reversing its decision to end the Algerian war by a negotiated peace with the Moslem rebels. With such a record, one can hardly claim that political stability has been achieved by either the institutions or the policies of the new regime.

If in practice, then, the Fifth Republic has not proved to be a complete break with tradition, constitutionally it is unquestionably an innovation, if neither original nor effective. On paper the regime has been endowed with the essential features of traditional parliamentary government, primarily distinguished from past forms of this kind of government by its dominant double executive. Under the Third and Fourth Republics, a powerless President of the Republic and a Prime Minister who rarely could hope to remain in power for much more than half a year were both subordinated to an all-powerful lower chamber of parliament. Now much of the latter's power of policy making has been transferred to the executive authority, shared unequally by an almost omnipotent President of the Republic and a Prime Minister who can henceforth look forward to a long tenure in office.

Such a regime is a radical departure from all past French experience, yet it is not really a dictatorship in the modern sense of the word. For although the powers and the intentions of the first incumbent make the President resemble an absolute monarch, and although the direct relationship between de Gaulle and public opinion is somewhat Bonapartist, the election of the President and the constitutional restraints on the exercise of his powers clearly distinguish the regime from usual examples of one-man rule. Three years of experience have shown the style of the Fifth Republic to be really that of a Roman dictatorship. A moderate, indeed liberal authoritarian rule has been legitimized by frequent appeals for direct approval, either by referendum or by simple acclamation. Whether this system is less democratic than the Fourth Republic is difficult to say—at least for this author. Many Frenchmen have felt that the previous regime, with its all-powerful parliament deciding matters among a small group of party leaders and with little reference to public opinion, was essentially oligarchic and not democratic. De Gaulle, while all-powerful like the parliaments, is at least trusted and popular, which they were not, and his policies have usually met little public resistance. When they have, as in the case of his agricultural policy, de Gaulle has simply conceded to public pressure.

Behind such concessions to pressure groups—"intermediaries" as de Gaulle would call them—lies the basic reason why the Fifth Republic can not be classed as a dictatorship. Neither de Gaulle nor his first Prime

Minister, Michel Debré, were interested in creating a source of energy, or motive power to impose their policy decisions against the resistance of pressure groups. In modern times a true dictator has required a social force, organized throughout the country, to assure ultimate obedience from the citizen no matter how unpopular some of the government's decisions might be. Whether it was a totalitarian party, a national police force, the army, a paramilitary formation, or a combination of them, dictators have maintained their rule and effected their policies through the discipline and pressure that a loyal corps created at every level of public affairs. Not only has de Gaulle refused to allow the transformation of the new Gaullist party into something resembling such a source of discipline and pressure, but he has made little effort to assure the loyalty of the police or army by illegal purges and has not extended the government's intervention into the Frenchman's everyday life. Indeed, the ineffectiveness of many of his policies can be traced to precisely the failure of the near-majority Gaullist party to mobilize public support in the country, and the imperfect execution of his decisions by agents of the Government such as bureaucrats, police officers, and army personnel.

Critics of the Fifth Republic, however, still point to the way in which all public policy is dominated by the decisions of the executive and principally by the will of one man, de Gaulle himself. It is true that with the decline of party activity popular participation in politics has seemed to wither dangerously. But when, save in times of special crises, have the French, so accustomed to centralized policy making, ever participated as directly and genuinely in political life as do the British and Americans? The abundance of party rhetoric and a popular obsession with the game of parliamentary maneuvering were hardly indices of a healthy body politic under the Fourth Republic. No, rather than representing a break with democratic representative government, the Fifth Republic is a break with the French form of parliamentary government, which has proved usually to be neither effectively democratic nor genuinely representative, even when on the surface it appeared to be so. The disaffection of the French from the Fourth Republic, which had been founded as a more "democratic" system than its predecessor, indicates that at least in its declining years it had ceased to be a "thing of the people"—a *respublica*, the origin of the word "republic."

From the point of view of constitutional law, and notwithstanding the extreme separation of executive and legislative powers, the determining fact is that the Prime Minister remains responsible to a majority in the lower chamber, which alone can remove him from office. But this responsibility before parliament does not make the regime even a close cousin of the parliamentary government practiced elsewhere in Europe.

Formally this is because of the severe limitations placed upon parliament's power to endanger executive stability, and the severe curtailment of its legislative powers. But even more important in differentiating it is the role de Gaulle has given the President as chief of state: monopolizing decision making in the major areas of policy, revising constitutional practice at will, and ruling under emergency powers for periods extending beyond the emergency. Unsatisfactory as it might be, probably the only thing that can be said is that the Fifth Republic is a new form of parliamentary government, having a predominant double executive. It is, also, of course, the first form of French parliamentary government that is fully in the administrative tradition of politics.

One of the problems involved in this return to the administrative tradition by a republican regime is that in the past this tradition has been associated with reactionary and anti-republican forces. In France, where historical memories of political grudges are potent influences on opinion, this has meant that many liberal Frenchmen identify the new constitution with the kind of illegitimate dictatorship France has experienced more than once. For them the only kind of government that is legitimate is the kind of parliamentarism France knew under the Third and Fourth Republics. Some conservative Frenchmen consider the Fifth Republic equally illegitimate, not because it is authoritarian, but because it has used its new power to liquidate France's colonial empire and to encourage the modernization of her economy. For the great mass of Frenchmen, however, the legitimacy of the new institutions depends simply on whether they work, whether they succeed in solving the problems of French society and maintaining the good life they have enjoyed for the past few years.

As long as de Gaulle is in power his personal legitimacy will probably cover failures of policy and institutional defects. But the new constitutional order itself has yet to become legitimate as a result of general agreement over its effectiveness. Although the magnitude of political problems such as Algeria has been largely responsible for the continued ineffectiveness of French government, the burden of proof still remains on those who argued under the Fourth Republic that a change in institutions was the key to successful policies. The return of General de Gaulle and the adoption of an entirely new constitution have provided this viewpoint with a good test situation—and students of politics with a good opportunity to note the essential features of French political culture that persist no matter what the constitution.

Usually formal institutions are less important in the study of political systems than are political forces and the informal but concrete processes of policy making. Under the Fifth Republic the Algerian crisis and a changing French society have thrust political forces into a transition period while de Gaulle has made the executive the dominant source of policy making, thus temporarily promoting the influence of formal institutions. Moreover, the newness of the constitutional order and the great pretentions of its creators also require an initial analysis of the constitution and how it has worked since its adoption. This look at the theory and practice of the new institutions is needed at the outset in order to understand the framework within which political forces and policy making are confined and the problems involved in legitimizing the new regime.

[13]

The New Constitutional Order:

Theory and Practice

General Philosophy of the Constitution

On June 1, 1958, General de Gaulle was legally invested as the last Prime Minister of the Fourth Republic. The next day he was empowered to revise the constitution drastically, the condition he had posed for assuming power and had urged continually since the document was first adopted in 1946. Having thus given the General full constituent powers, the last parliament of the Fourth Republic disbanded, never to meet again. By the end of August de Gaulle's cabinet had completed its draft of the new constitution and on September 28, 1958, the document was presented to the French people for their approval in a referendum. Although 80 per cent of the voters favored the new constitution, their endorsement was less for the long and poorly drafted legal text than it was for the temporary dictatorship of a familiar and prestigious national leader, returning to power in a potentially dangerous crisis. Yet the French knew that much more than the formal rules of government would be changed in the months to come. For even though most of the leaders of the Fourth Republic supported de Gaulle's reforms, what the French and the world were to witness in 1958 was the beginning of an attempt to change the basic ideas, methods, and styles for managing political life. It was the tenth of its kind France had known since the Revolution of 1789.

Unlike its predecessor, the constitution of the Fifth Republic was not drafted by a representative assembly but by General de Gaulle's Minister of Justice, the veteran Gaullist, Michel Debré, assisted by the cabinet and a group of experts. It was a fitting origin for a document that promoted the executive to dominance and embodied plans that partisans of the administrative tradition had urged since the Third Republic. For although the constitution closely reflects the thinking of the Gaullists, most of its features are not really innovations but rather long-debated remedies for French political ills. For this reason alone, it has been argued, there can be no permanency in the new regime because, while it has corrected many of the defects of the Fourth Republic, its preoccupation with abuses of the past has blinded it to the needs of the present.

Nor was the philosophy behind the changes very novel. De Gaulle and his followers had long been urging a strengthened and stabilized executive because they felt it was a prerequisite to the restoration of French power in the world. The reasoning of the drafters, therefore, was basically simple: a strong and stable executive is the key to effective government, which in turn is a prime condition of great power status. Frenchmen, the Gaullists assume, are united in their desire for greatness though they continue to be divided bitterly over the means to achieve this end—hence the country's ancient political division and multiparty system. Thus, they reasoned, executive stability and power could not be assured in France in the manner employed by England—that is, by a cabinet's dependence upon the absolute control of a parliamentary majority by one of the two parties monopolizing representation. Accordingly, parliamentary government under the Third and Fourth Republics had been essentially an "assembly regime," with the legislature dominating the executive but itself unable to provide effective leadership because it lacked either a majority party or the ability to produce stable coalition majorities among the factious parties.

They therefore concluded that as long as the dominant Assembly reflected the many divisions of French opinion, this branch of government should not be allowed to control the policy-making function nor should it be allowed to paralyze executive action to resolve problems that, as de Gaulle always puts it, a "dangerous world" can produce at any moment. In the General's mind these partisan divisions are permanent traits of the French national character, produced by innate qualities of the "race" and the peculiar nature of French historical experience. How can it be thought, de Gaulle has said only partly in jest, that the multiparty system is anything but permanent and natural in a country that prides itself on having over two hundred varieties of cheese? This being the case, the Gaullist argument ran, the only way to assure executive stability and power was to make the executive much less dependent on shifting parliamentary majorities and to endow it with a vastly enlarged competence.

The radical separation of powers implied in this analysis did not lead de

Gaulle to embrace the principle of presidential government, however. Not only did the June 2, 1958, grant of constituent power exclude this system by specifying that the new constitution had to provide for ministerial responsibility to parliament, but de Gaulle was himself hostile to the presidential principle at that time. The General has often stated in private that he believes the French to be basically monarchist in their attitude toward government. This implies, above all, the need of a chief of state who is usually above the wear and tear of everyday politics and in a Kingly (and Gaullist!) fashion "belongs to no one yet belongs to everyone." A President who is both chief of state and chief of the executive, and leader of a national party to boot, could hardly fill this prescription. Nor would a presidential system allow either the ritual sacrifice of a Prime Minister to the demands of the specially fickle French opinion, or the wise chastisement of an inevitably irresponsible parliament by dissolution at times of deadlock between the legislative and the executive.

What was clearly needed, then, was a modified form of parliamentary government, with a double executive, one part of which remained technically responsible to the lower house, and a parliament whose control over both the life and composition of the cabinet, as well as the content of policy making, was curtailed. The constitution of the Fifth Republic sought to embody this Gaullist analysis through two major changes in traditional institutions. First, it transformed the formerly powerless chief of state, the President of the Republic, into a unique and potent crisis executive. The fact that the first years of the new regime have been especially crisis-ridden has meant that under de Gaulle's interpretation the President's powers have extended into almost all areas of public policy. Second, the constitution has completely reorganized the relations between the normal executive—the Prime Minister and his cabinet—and the National Assembly, in order to reduce the latter's role in the legislative process and limit its ability to make and unmake Governments. The results of these changes have been to eliminate ministerial instability during the first three years of the regime and to consign policy making almost entirely to the reinforced double executive. The constitutional order described in the following pages refers not only to the provisions of the 1958 document, but also to the organic laws (*lois organiques*) completing the constitution, enacted subsequently by parliament, and to such nonconstitutional texts as the parliamentary rules of procedure that affect seriously the functioning of the formal governmental system.

A Powerful Crisis Executive: The President of the Republic

General de Gaulle's personal experience during and after World War II led him to believe that the two essential duties of the French Presidency should be to assure the regular functioning of the state and to guarantee the nation's independence and territorial integrity. In June 1940, as a junior member of the Third Republic's last ministry, he viewed from the inside the liquidation of all political authority in the face of onrushing military defeat. He notes in his memoirs that during those fateful days he was particularly struck by the fact that "the President of the Republic abstained from raising his voice, even within the Cabinet, to express the supreme interest of the country." Later, as the leading critic of the policies of the Fourth Republic, he was again convinced that it was the constitutional impotence of the President that at least partly explained why ephemeral Governments were allowed, in his eyes, to bargain away much of France's independence in treaties and alliances.

ELECTION

But in order to have the authority "to express the supreme interest of the country" in time of crisis and to watch over its independence, the President could no longer be elected simply by the two houses of parliament as under the Third and Fourth Republics. Since, as we have seen, presidential government was rejected by common consent in 1958, direct election by the people was not considered at the time of drafting. It was argued, moreover, that because the new President was to be chief executive of the French Community as well as French chief of state, he could be elected only by indirect suffrage, given the difficulties in organizing direct elections throughout a varied and far-flung range of overseas dependencies. The solution was a special college of 81,761 official electors that included members of parliament, local government representatives of metropolitan and overseas departments, members of overseas territorial assemblies and those of the assemblies of the member states of the Community, and, finally, by far the largest group (72,500 out of the 81,761), members and delegates of the township and municipal councils of France and her overseas departments.

A body of this size, it was explained, would be less likely to disperse its votes among many candidates than would universal suffrage in a multi-party system. At the same time, however, such an electorate would be more prone to choose an outstanding national leader as President than would parliament, ever jealous of its own influence over policy matters *vis-à-vis* the executive. Clearly, the first election of a President that took place under this system on December 21, 1958, was not a good test of these assumptions. General de Gaulle's candidacy was supported by all the major political parties except the Communists, who presented an official candidate, as did a small non-Communist left group left by Pierre Mendès-France. No electioneering took place and, between de Gaulle's huge popularity and the completely *pro forma* nature of the two other candidacies, it was no surprise that the General won 78.5 per cent of all the votes cast. Whether such an electoral college will always choose an outstanding national figure who can serve as a symbol of national unity, and whose vast authority will always be considered legitimate by a majority of the people, is open to doubt. The College is far from representative of the population: over one half of the presidential electors come from rural and small-town France that represents but one third of the total population. It is by no means certain that in normal circumstances such a majority would elect a personality whose leadership can be respected by the urban worker as well as the rural notable.

FORMAL POWERS

While retaining all the ceremonial prerogatives of the chief of state under the Fourth Republic as well as the old seven-year term of office, the new presidency has additional powers meant to deal with the new responsibilities of the position. Since the Prime Minister and his cabinet are still responsible to the lower house, the National Assembly retains a reduced yet real power to block executive action. In order to provide the Government with a normal means of escaping this danger, the President's power of appointing to high administrative office has been expanded, as has his role in negotiating treaties and international agreements, again in case parliament blocks the action of the Government. If conflict between parliament and the Prime Minister persists, or if for any reason he sees fit, the President now has the discretionary right to dissolve the National Assembly at any time after its first year—and this on his own decision and with no condition required other than consulting the Prime Minister and the presiding officers of parliament. Short of the threat of dissolution, the President can urge cooperation on parliament as well as place directly before it his personal views, by means of written messages that are read for him to both houses. And as an additional executive arm to use against either the obstinacy or "error" of parliament, de Gaulle had included in the constitution the President's right to submit legislation directly to the people in a referendum (Article 11). Thus, usually on the proposal of the Government (but by joint resolution of parliament in the rare case it is the Government that is judged to be in "error"), the President can ask for popular approval or disapproval of a law or international agreement that he judges to have the effect of seriously changing the constitutional order. In less serious cases of infringement on this order, he can ask that a bill be reviewed by the new Constitutional Council, which is empowered to declare it unconstitutional.

Under the Fifth Republic de Gaulle's first exercise of this right to call a referendum had the effect of extending the constitutional powers of the Presidency. On January 8, 1961, he asked the people to vote on a law that formally concerned the reorganization of France's future relations with Algeria. In reality, the purpose of the referendum was to appeal above the heads of the lawmakers and the party leaders for a direct personal vote of confidence on the eve of a new phase in his efforts to end the seven year old Algerian war. It had the effect of showing that the people supported his policy of self-determination for Algeria as well as demonstrating once again his continued personal popularity. The success with which he has more than once used this device—in January 1961 over 75 per cent and in April 1962 over 90 per cent of the voters followed his wishes— as well as his own view of the President as a sort of Republican monarch, suggests that while de Gaulle holds that office more frequent use of the referendum to bolster presidential power might be expected.

Last, but hardly least, among the new powers of the President is the veritable blank check conferred by the famous Article 16 of the constitution. If the threat to French independence or the danger to the regular functioning of the institutions—either from within or without—is so great that all the specified powers are not sufficient, the President can decide completely on his own to become temporarily omnipotent, taking any executive or legislative measures he alone considers necessary. This emergency powers clause places as a limit upon this prerogative only the obligation to consult other governmental authorities and to keep parliament in session. Haunted by the memory of France's collapse in 1940, de Gaulle insisted on this "institutionalization" of the President's will to protect the continuity of the French state in a world increasingly marked by international crises. As Michel Debré also put it, the threat of nuclear war now creates the need for such an emergency power for the man who is to symbolize the unity and continuity of the nation.

No one, however, forecast in 1958 the condition under which Article 16 would for the first time be actually invoked on April 23, 1961. It was in reaction to the attempt by part of the French army to seize power in Algeria, pursue to the bitter end the war against the Moslem nationalists, and probably either upset the government in Paris, or oblige it to accept their will. De Gaulle promptly declared: "I have decided to put in force Article 16 of our constitution. Starting today, I will take, if necessary directly, the measures that will appear to me to be demanded by the circumstances." Contrary to expectations, the measures de Gaulle did take during the five months he kept the emergency powers in force were primarily of a technical nature, including neither structural reforms nor unorthodox repressive acts. The abundant criticism his use of Article 16 provoked, therefore, had less to do with the content of his acts or the original justification for using the clause than with the length of time beyond the immediate emergency that de Gaulle maintained the emergency powers. It was fear of what de Gaulle could do and what precedents he could set rather than what he actually did that motivated the rising protests that finally obliged him to relinquish the powers on October 1, 1961.

SUCCESSION

As for the future use of Article 16, after de Gaulle leaves office it can be said, for example, that, while the provision at least gives a President already having the will to act the required legal power, it certainly cannot endow a man with the will to take extraordinary action if he is not naturally suited for emergency situations. Nor is the electoral college of the Presidency, as originally conceived, likely to guarantee that after de Gaulle such a strong personality will be elected or—what is even more important —that his action under Article 16 will be universally considered legitimate. For judging from both de Gaulle's limited use of these powers and reaction to the measures taken, even a man whose legitimacy seems assured by history and frequent appeals for popular approval has not been spared bitter criticism. It was this growing concern for assuring the legitimacy for his successor's decisions both under emergency and normal circumstances that led de Gaulle in 1961 to suggest a revision of the constitution that would institute the direct popular election of the President.

On the one hand the probability of a succession crisis, dramatized by the attempt on de Gaulle's life in August 1961, has raised doubts about the normal provisions for filling a sudden vacancy. According to the constitution it is the President of the Senate, or upper house, who temporarily takes office while preparations for the election by the college of some 80,000 presidential electors are made (Article 7). Given the doubts about the ability of such a relatively unrepresentative body to choose a man who would be universally respected even under "normal" circumstances, how less likely would this respect emerge in the conditions of internal and international crisis that now appear normal for France? Only direct popular election, it is now reasoned, can give a successor to de Gaulle the authority and legitimacy that was his through the gift of history. Moreover, the progressive granting of complete independence to most of the states of the Community has obviated a major argument in favor of the original provision for indirect elections. The chances, therefore, are good that the next major constitutional change in the Fifth Republic will provide for popular election of the President, a reform that could easily encourage the evolution of the regime toward full presidential government.

A Stabilized Government

LIMITS OF THE NEW STABILITY

The various constitutional limits on the National Assembly's powers to deny the Government legislation and to ultimately force it from office have thus far assured the cabinet a tenure in office that approaches that of Great Britain and West Germany. This does not mean, however, that stability of tenure has been accompanied by stability of cabinet personnel and Government policy. No amount of constitutional engineering can prevent changes in a majority (or, for that matter, changes in the extent to which a single party within the majority supports the cabinet) from affecting the coherence and continuity of policy. Under the new regime the Government is still responsible to a majority made up of a coalition of parties with differing views and with each one often divided internally by factionalism. Under these conditions both the make-up of a cabinet and the continuity of its policies remain subject to a certain amount of instability. Realizing this, President de Gaulle told the first meeting of the Debré Government's Council of Ministers in January 1959: "You represent, gentlemen, the Government of this legislature. There will be no other." He meant, of course, that he would dissolve the Assembly at the first sign of a return to the old patterns of executive impotence and instability.

Yet when Prime Minister Debré resigned in April 1962 only eight of the twenty-one principal ministers still held the same jobs they did the day they heard those words. The first thirty months of the Debré cabinet saw seven new men appointed to principal ministries whose incumbents were either dismissed or switched to other posts. This represents a "renewal" of fully one third of the posts, as compared to an average "renewal" of about 40 per cent affecting the principal ministries of the four cabinets that ruled during the last thirty months of the Fourth Republic before de Gaulle's return. What these figures reveal is that, while cabinet instability has been eliminated by the new constitution, the immutable dynamics of French politics have continued to produce at almost the old rate a less dramatic yet just as familiar form of instability: the instability of individual ministers.

Under the Third and Fourth Republics Prime Ministers were often obliged to dismiss or transfer Ministers whose presence in certain posts became incompatible with a shift in the Government's parliamentary majority. In many cases the "renewals" were caused by a clash of views between the individual minister and the Prime Minister. In many cases these changes resulted in the so-called "dislocation" of the Government's majority, the ultimate resignation of the Prime Minister, and the opening of a ministerial crisis. When the Government was able to hold its majority together after such a ministerial "rearrangement" (*remaniement*), it was commonly said to have passed through a "dry crisis" (*crise sèche*). The early experience of the Debré Government has shown that while the new constitution makes the executive invulnerable to the collective instability of the old ministerial crisis, it can not protect it against the threats to the continuity of policies and ministerial personnel that are inherent in the French multiparty system and in the fragility of coalition government. Today the "dry crises" caused by resignations, dismissals, transfers, and the threats of resignations of individual ministers continue to be the way in which the Prime Minister adapts to sudden shifts in parliamentary majority, the pressures of volatile public opinion, changes in political circumstances, as well as simple disagreement within the cabinet, individual failure to handle a job, and, in some cases, the displeasure of the all-powerful President. But whereas in the past the first three situations might have led to the fall of the Government, and an often serious change in over-all policy, a ministerial "rearrangement" no longer holds this danger. (See Figure 1)

CONFIDENCE VOTE AND CENSURE PROCEDURE

The reason for this, of course, is that the cabinet is now supplied with so many powers not subject to approval by the Assembly that it can count on enacting most of its vital policies for the low price of occasional minor changes in program and the personnel shifts of the "dry crisis." Before examining these new powers it is worthwhile noting that the making of a Government under the Fifth Republic proceeds in much the way it did in the past. The President names the Prime Minister who, along with the Ministers the latter then chooses, may or may not be a member of parliament. As in the past, the "Prime Minister-designate" then seeks a vote of confidence from the National Assembly. Though the Government is explicitly responsible only to the directly elected lower chamber, the new constitution permits the Prime Minister to request approval of a general policy statement from the upper house, renamed the Senate (Article 49). Consonant with de Gaulle's long-standing intention to reestablish true bicameralism in France, this measure allows the Government to apply at least moral pressure upon a hostile Assembly by seeking Senate approval of the new cabinet's program.

Although no formal Assembly investiture, as was the case in the past, is called for by the constitution, Prime Minister Debré created the precedent of interpreting Article 49—which allows the Prime Minister to ask the Assembly for approval of the Government's program by a simple majority vote—to mean that such a vote should be asked for immediately after nomination by the President. This precedent was followed by Georges

Pompidou soon after he formed the second Government of the Fifth Republic on April 15, 1962. The same article also permits the Prime Minister to risk the life of his Government on a piece of high priority legislation by posing the classical "question of confidence" before the Assembly—the source of most cabinet crises under the Third and Fourth Republics. But unlike the past, the constitution eliminates the danger formerly involved in this executive effort to discipline its majority in order to accomplish its program. Article 49, paragraph 3, now specifies that a bill on which the Government has pledged its responsibility is automatically considered adopted, no matter what the actual vote in the Assembly, unless that body has voted a formal motion of censure of the Government.

This drastic measure, obliging the Government to resign immediately, was never employed under the Fourth Republic. Its use under the Fifth, either alone on a general policy matter, or in connection with a bill on which the Government has staked its life, involves conditions that sharply reduce its potential as a threat to the life of the cabinet. A motion of censure must now be signed by at least one tenth of the Assembly's membership and, after a forty-eight hour waiting period, must be voted by an absolute majority of all deputies. If the motion is not adopted the Government remains in office, the bill is considered passed even if more deputies voted against it than for it, and the sponsoring opposition deputies cannot introduce another such motion during the same session, unless it is in connection with another bill on which the Government has engaged its life.

In the new confidence vote procedure all the advantages are now on the side of the executive. The Prime Minister has a full two day period during which he can mobilize the support of his majority. Even if there was a coherent opposition of two hundred members, which has not been the case since 1958, the requirement of sponsorship by one tenth of the 552 members would mean that no more than three such motions could be introduced in each session. Indeed, given the deep divisions in the present Assembly opposition, even one motion of censure per session has not been easy to arrange. During the first three and a half years of the new regime, only seven such motions came to votes, an average of less than one per session. (The mandate of the sixty-eight deputies from Algerian constituencies was cancelled by decree following the independence of Algeria in July 1962. This, together with temporary vacancies, reduced the total number of deputies to 480. Since the opposition lost relatively more Algerian deputies than did the Pompidou Government majority, this reduction of seats has given the present cabinet further protection against a motion of censure.) Aware of this invulnerability to censure provided by the divided opposition and the cohesion of the large Gaullist group in the lower house, Prime Minister Debré actually used the confidence vote twice on high

FIGURE 1   Longevity of Governments, 1900–1962

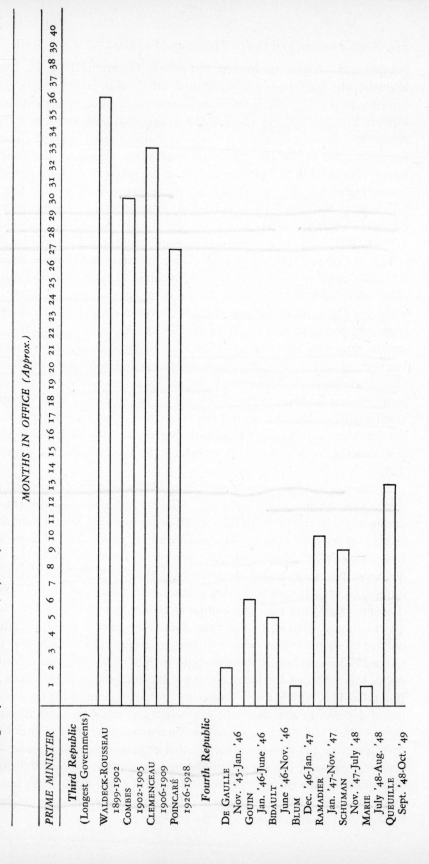

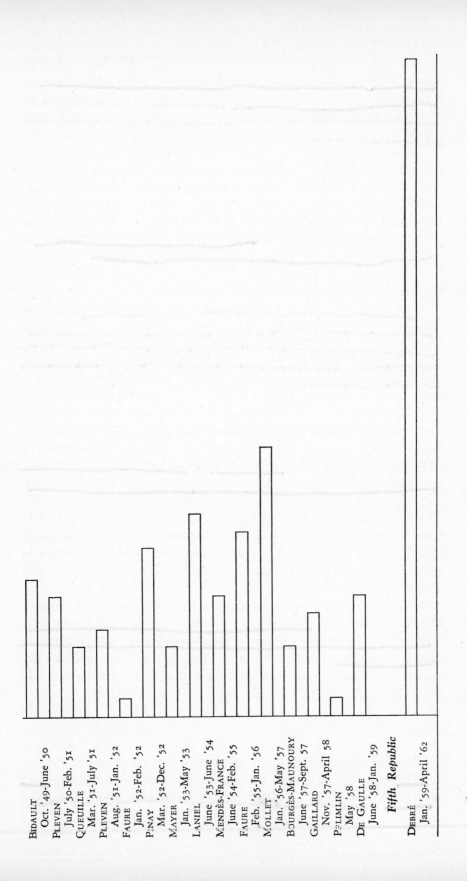

BIDAULT
Oct. '49-June '50

PLEVEN
July '50-Feb. '51

QUEUILLE
Mar. '51-July '51

PLEVEN
Aug. '51-Jan. '52

FAURE
Jan. '52-Feb. '52

PINAY
Mar. '52-Dec. '52

MAYER
Jan. '53-May '53

LANIEL
June '53-June '54

MENDÈS-FRANCE
June '54-Feb. '55

FAURE
Feb. '55-Jan. '56

MOLLET
Jan. '56-May '57

BOURGÈS-MAUNOURY
June '57-Sept. 57

GAILLARD
Nov. '57-April 58

PFLIMLIN
May '58

DE GAULLE
June '58-Jan. '59

Fifth Republic

DEBRÉ
Jan. '59-April '62

priority bills in order to oblige passage of legislation for which he knew there was no parliamentary majority. Since there was no majority for an alternate Government either, the motion of censure failed and Debré's priority legislation was automatically considered passed. But this somewhat cynical use of the constitution to enact legislation without, indeed against, the will of parliament has been cited frequently as the innovation of the new regime that is most thoroughly out of keeping with French legal traditions. Its continued use will signify an increasingly hopeless attitude of the Government toward the principle of ministerial responsibility under present party conditions and a further alienation of parliament from the principle of self-discipline and cooperation *vis-à-vis* the cabinet.

Controls over Parliamentary Criticism

By combining the vote of confidence with the cumbersome censure procedure the new constitution has reduced the danger of executive instability connected with a test of responsibility taken at the Government's initiative. It has also reduced the threat of instability when such tests are provoked at *parliament*'s initiative. Under both the Third and Fourth Republics the lower house had various means of questioning and criticizing both the Government's policies and it execution of the laws. Each of these involved a vote that was regarded by the executive as either a warning of growing parliamentary displeasure or an actual confidence test. By far the most potent of these methods was the "interpellation"—a formal question or critique, put to the Government orally by a deputy, usually with little prior notice, and having immediate priority over anything being debated at the time. The interpellation was followed by a general debate, usually unlimited in time, in the course of which a Minister answered the question, other deputies added their views, and various "motivated" motions to return to the agenda—automatically suspended for the interpellation—were presented for votes.

Because of the provision for general debate, unknown in the British question procedure, interpellation represented an ideal and constantly available opportunity for enemies of the cabinet to harass it and even to force it from office. For by the end of a long interpellation debate, a discussion that usually began on a specific aspect of Government policy had often developed into such a wide ranging critique of the executive that the Prime Minister was prompted to consider the vote on the motion to return to the agenda as tantamount to a vote of confidence. If the motion that passed carried a hostile "motive," the Government knew it had little hope for maintaining its majority and enacting its program.

Today this political arm of parliament against the executive is almost eliminated. In order to interpellate the Government a deputy must now be ready to challenge openly its existence by means of the difficult censure process used in connection with votes of confidence called by the Government. The only methods left to parliament by the new constitution for criticizing the executive, short of censuring it, are oral questions, with or without debate, and the written questions. The latter, traditionally but a means for obtaining free and official legal advice from the administration for a deputy's constituents, have recently become more general in scope in reaction to the difficulties encountered in using even the harmless oral question procedures. Oral questions may now be put only on Friday afternoons, in the Assembly, and Tuesday afternoons, in the Senate, for in the minds of the constitution drafters the British model of a limited but regular process for parliamentary criticism of the executive had to be introduced in France (Article 48). In regard to the oral question without debate, the Minister or his representative replies, and the questioning deputy alone has five minutes to rebut the Government's answer. When a debate follows a question, any deputy can participate but, in order to prevent the oral question with debate from being transformed into an interpellation that escapes the censure procedure, no vote of any kind is permitted at the close of discussion. Thus once again the parliament is deprived of an opportunity to formally and collectively pass judgement on the Government, unless in effect an alternate majority has emerged which allows the censure motion to pass.

The practice of the Fifth Republic has proved the effectiveness of these new limitations on parliamentary power over the executive. During the last eight months of the Fourth Republic, 86 interpellations were tabled and 203 oral questions without debate were submitted, the former obviating the need for oral questions with debate. For a similar period in 1960 no interpellations were tabled, only 15 oral questions with debate were asked in the place of interpellations, and only 53 oral questions without debate were put to the Government. Furthermore, a close look at this practice reveals that, rather than the formal constitution, it is informal French political custom that has made the regular question period as an arm of parliament against the Government so difficult to import from Britain.

The first problem has been the massive absenteeism of deputies on question days, coming as these do at the end or beginning of the parliamentary week when members are often en route to their constituencies. To be sure, this could have been avoided, but, even had they been placed earlier in the week, the fact that no vote of a resolution or "prayer" (*voeux*) expressing parliament's collective view is permitted after debate reduces interest in attending question sittings for the average deputy. This in turn means that the oral questions that are asked on those days are usually of a technical and specific nature, further reducing interest in attendance.

Even when important political questions are submitted, they are usually posed in the order they are tabled and hence there is little assurance that the important ones will be debated on a given Friday. And when, by chance, such a question does come up and the Government judges it "inopportune," it can easily persuade the steering committees of each house to postpone the offending question or, *in extremis*, simply refuse to send a Minister to reply, which automatically postpones the question. Finally much of the tension generated in Britain's daily question hour is absent on question day in France because Ministers usually read long, boring replies or worse, send their assistants to read them. There is thus little of the sharp atmosphere of dialogue between Government and parliament that is promoted by the short, incisive, often witty, improvised reply of the British Minister.

The heart of the matter is, of course, the absence of a real tradition of constructive dialogue between Government and parliament in France. The formal channels of parliamentary criticism of the executive were used by deputies in the past as long as they involved the possibility of unmaking a Government whose policies they feared or of initiating the process of making a new one in which they or their party might be represented. Question procedures in France have never been part of the process of compromise, correction, and, indeed, collaboration, between the two branches of government that they were in Britain. This is because the French party system makes both Government majorities and opposition minorities so unstable that all parties are more often potential opposition parties than they are actual Government parties. Under these conditions question periods are functional to the French political system only if they directly promote ministerial instability. By trying to impose the British practice of regular but limited opportunities for criticism, the new constitution has failed to appreciate the way in which the French multiparty system in this, as in so many ways, makes such borrowings impossible. Nor, it should be added, have the precedents of the Debré Government, steeped as it was in the administrative tradition of French politics, encouraged the effectiveness of question day. Surely neither its elimination of embarrassing questions nor the haughty and state-minded habit of its Ministers, often former civil servants, of reading long, involved replies to general policy questions, demonstrated a real interest in creating a constructive dialogue with parliament. As of this writing, it is too early to judge whether the Pompidou Government will allow such a dialogue to develop.

If the question procedures offer little chance to endanger the life of a Government by direct parliamentary initiative, there remains, nonetheless, a slim alternative available to parliament through provoking a Government into asking for a confidence vote on a statement of general policy. During the early months of the Debré Government, when its majority was absolutely loyal, it often opened such wide-ranging debates in order to demonstrate its hold over its majority as well as to allow the opposition to vent its frustrations at being unable to muster a motion of censure. It is conceivable that, unable to touch the Government directly by such a motion, a small opposition could create enough public and parliamentary outcry and stall the legislative process enough to oblige the Prime Minister to ask for a vote of confidence on a declaration of policy. In this case the motion of censure procedure is avoided and a simple hostile plurality in the vote after the debate obliges the Government to resign. But unlike the old interpellation, it is the Government that initiates this test of strength. As its majority gradually lost its early solidarty, the Debré Government showed an awareness of the danger involved in allowing a simple plurality test on a policy declaration and refrained from submitting them for confidence votes. Since the question period has failed to acquire any potency, this trend further decreased parliament's opportunity to criticize the Government.

A series of secondary innovations, established by the constitution, organic laws, or parliamentary rules, also tend to reinforce executive stability. Ordinary sessions of parliament can not last for more than five and a half months per year, as against at least seven (and often much more) during the last regime. This reduces in time the Assembly's opportunity to challenge the Government. The number of deputies has been cut down from over 600 to about 550 and the minimum size of the Assembly's party groups has been set at 30 members. From about a dozen groups in the last years of the Fourth Republic, there are now but six official groups in the Assembly, roughly equivalent to the six major party groupings in the country. Since group leaders were among the most important potential ministers—or *ministrables,* as the French call them—this reform has reduced by half those deputies with the strongest vested interest in the cabinet crisis. (The cancellation of the Algerian deputies' mandate reduced the Assembly to 480 members in July 1962 and resulted in the disappearance of the Assembly group to which most of them belonged, bringing to five the number of party groups in the lower house.) Moreover, this ancient ambition for ministerial office and the naturally related interest in executive instability were the targets of the controversial constitutional provision obliging a newly appointed minister to resign his seat as a deputy or senator (Article 23). Whether or not this has in fact curbed parliament members' unwholesome appetite for Government instability is impossible to document. As will be seen in connection with policy making, however, it did probably account in good part for the poor relations between the Debré Government and its majority. Having lost their official positions as leaders of the legislative branch, the few parliamentarians in the cabinet lost at the same time much of their influence among their former colleagues.

The constitution has also struck a blow at the group leaders' power by weakening their former control over the votes cast by their troops (Article 27). The informal traditions of public life in France, such as multiple office holding, long weekends in the constituency, and busy Paris legal and commercial jobs, have long been responsible for a high rate of parliamentary absenteeism. This had made voting by proxy the rule rather than the exception (as in other parliaments) under the Third and Fourth Republics. Usually, moreover, the group leader or his representative voted the whole group by what was in effect a blanket proxy. This considerable power has been eliminated by requiring that most voting be "personal," long the rule in other legislatures, whereby members "divide" on most votes by walking through lobbies, as in England, or personally casting "Yes" or "No" ballots inscribed with their names. In theory members can now receive only one colleague's proxy, which must be personally given, and duly registered with officers of the chamber before the sitting, and which can last only for a specified time, in no case more than eight days.

According to the rules of procedure in the Assembly, proxies were to be allowed only in a limited number of situations such as illness, or temporary missions abroad. In practice, however, the heavy hand of tradition has once again struck down the intentions of the founders of the Fifth Republic. The deputies who, as secretaries of the Assembly, issue proxy permissions, have proved extremely sympathetic to their colleagues' excuses and have approved many marginal cases of absence. Then, too, thanks to the introduction of electrical vote registration in 1959, an illegal form of proxy voting has developed. Deputies planning to be absent for totally inexcusable reasons, and eager to avoid the stringent new sanctions for unexcused absences, now often leave their personal keys to the voting switch on their desks with a friend or with the group leader, who, with a pocket full of voting keys, regains the powers of the old blanket proxy. And just to assure absolute immunity to sanctions for absenteeism, both houses by tacit consent have simply cut down the number of occasions when a "personal vote" is required. During the last two and a half years of the Fourth Republic one thousand such votes were taken; for the first two and a half years of the Fifth only 138 were recorded. Thus the personal habits of French parliamentary life—so contrary to parliamentarism practiced elsewhere—have been accommodated by either illegal proxy voting or by confining most votes to a show of hands involving no identification of the members. The intention of the new Republic's founders to give France "true" parliamentary government has again been confounded by the power of custom.

The Threat of Dissolution

The final reinforcement of Government stability that must be noted belongs fully to the classical tradition of parliamentary government. The new constitution gives the President of the Republic the uninhibited right to dissolve the Assembly after its first year. Theoretically this power should "discipline" a Government's majority by making its members less prone to allow a cabinet crisis for fear of being sent before their electors by the President. It is a return to the constitutional theory—if not the practice—of the Third Republic, and a thorough break with that of the Fourth, during which dissolution was available to the Prime Minister, not the President, under conditions most difficult to realize. There has been no real test of the effectiveness of this executive power over the legislative branch during the first years of the Fifth Republic. The stability of the Debré Government depended not, on the threat of dissolution, but rather on the unexpected cohesion of the near-majority Government party, the Gaullist "Union for the New Republic," on the constitutional obstacles to the passage of a motion of censure by the small and divided opposition, and on the popular pressure maintained in favor of the Government by repeated personal appeals of General de Gaulle.

Dissolution by the executive usually serves to discipline and preserve a majority only when the existing party system provides a clear choice of opposition to the electorate, and when most deputies depend more on a national party organization than on local machines and local reputations. Although France has moved closer to such a party system in recent years, it still lacks the kind of politics in which executive dissolution can be a fully effective deterrent to the Assembly's tendency to frustrate the Government's actions and to the volatility of coalition majorities. In this respect, as in the others noted above, the early experience of the Fifth Republic has demonstrated the irrelevant nature of certain of the formal provisions of the new constitution. In the case of those that, indeed, successfully did guarantee the stability of the Debré Government—such as the confidence vote procedure—the record also revealed their artificiality. Behind the engineered stability of the Government there remains a traditional party system unable to produce either a true governing majority party or a stable governing coalition. As the Debré Government completed its third year in office, the early cohesion of its majority showed signs of decay under the continuing stress of the Algerian problem and the redoubled attacks of economic and social pressure groups. During the Fourth Republic this growing fragility of the majority would have led to immobilism of Government policy at least, if not to the fall of the Government itself after a sudden shift in the majority. But under the Fifth Republic even immobilism of policy can be avoided by a Government thanks to the radical subordination of parliament's role in the process of policy making by another set of constitutional innovations.

A Parliament Subordinated to the Executive

Nothing reveals more clearly the drafters' prejudice in favor of the administrative tradition of politics than those provisions of the constitution limiting the role of parliament in the policy-making process. This has been accomplished by a substantive change restricting parliamentary competence to a limited number of policy matters and three procedural changes providing the executive with new means of intervening in the legislative process in order to achieve its ends. It is worth noting at the outset, however, that as important as these changes are they are mostly extensions of reforms undertaken during the two previous Republics in order to reduce parliament's preponderance in policy-making. For long before the Fifth Republic, the problems created by policy *immobilisme* and the need for effective executive action in crisis led parliaments to make sudden and often total grants of legislative authority to the executive. Indeed, two such grants made *in extremis* were responsible for ending the lives of the last two regimes in the representative tradition of politics. Since the new Senate was expected to check the National Assembly's power, the election of its members is dealt with in this section. The election of members of the lower house of parliament is described in Chapter 14.

THE SHRUNKEN DOMAIN OF THE LAW

The first and most important change has been instituted by Article 34 of the new constitution which, in effect, inverts the previously existing relationship between parliamentary law-making and executive rule-making. Under the last Republics the policy matters subject to law-making were unlimited while executive rule-making was confined to the application of laws or to matters that parliament expressly empowered the Government to deal with. This was in accordance with the classical theory of democratic parliamentarism, which formally still applies to the English case. But in the latter, the disciplined two-party system and the power this gives the cabinet have, in effect, resulted in the Government's quasi-monopoly of policy-making through the device of delegated legislation. In France the multiparty system and the absence of stable coalitions have meant that parliamentary omnipotence in law-making usually made the legislative process, hence policy-making, long, cumbersome, and often productive of policies that were but formal compromises of basically irreconcilable attitudes. The inability of a divided parliament to take action on important problems during the crises of both the Third and Fourth Republics led it to extend voluntarily the Government's rule-making power in areas that had originally been reserved for legislation. This was accomplished by those French forms of delegated legislation known as "decree-laws" (*décrêts-lois*) under the Third Republic and "framework laws" (*lois cadres*) under the Fourth. Today these former emergency practices have been normalized: the Government makes most policy by issuing decrees and ordinances while parliament's role in the process as lawmaker is limited to a specific number of subjects mainly determined by the constitution. The Government's rule-making power, therefore, normally covers all policy matters not specifically reserved to parliament.

Furthermore, "for the execution of its program" according to Article 38, the executive may ask parliament to grant it power temporarily to take measures by ordinance that constitutionally are among the subjects reserved to legislative competence. Parliament does not have the reciprocal right, however, to exceed this "domain of the law," unless a special organic law, passed under conditions far more stringent than ordinary legislation, has been enacted to enlarge the list of its reserved policy subjects. Actually, this "domain" does include the bulk of policy matters traditionally dealt with by parliament: civil rights, the penal and civil codes, taxation, the budget, electoral laws, nationalization, education, social security, national defense, and social and economic plans and programs. Moreover, the practice of the Debré Government had the effect of somewhat extending this list by allowing deputies to add amendments of a clearly regulatory nature to Government-sponsored economic bills, thus enabling them to acquit their "duties" to constituents and pressure groups. Yet the over-all effect of limiting the subjects of parliamentary competence has been to discourage the gross legislative activity of parliament. In 1957, under the Fourth Republic, there were 990 bills tabled in the two houses while in 1959, under the new regime, this figure reached only 340. This reduction of parliamentary participation in policy-making has in turn released the Government from its former heavy, and often worried, preoccupation with what the legislature was doing on a policy matter it too was trying to resolve. Similarly, it has also released the Government from having to wait upon a slow legislative process in those many instances which it can now deal with directly by rules. This is especially true of the budget bill, which in the past was especially subject to parliamentary dismantling. Delays in its enactment often extended into the fiscal year for which it was drafted and the general financial management of France suffered as a consequence. Now Article 47 permits the cabinet to enact the budget by ordinance if parliament has not passed it within seventy days of its presentation.

The Speedier Legislative Process

A second set of constitutional changes has authorized the executive to intervene directly in parliament's lawmaking process in order to expedite passage of laws it considers important. By inscribing many of the rules of this process into the constitution itself, the primacy of parliament in the already limited area left to it has thus also been restricted. The most important new provision is in Article 48, which gives the Government the right to have its own bills, or private members' bills it has approved, placed first on the agenda of the two houses every day, save the one reserved weekly for questions. This means that the Government has an almost absolute control over the bills parliament discusses and enacts for, by picking and choosing among those tabled, it can eliminate bills it does not want to have either enacted or even discussed. The practice of the Fifth Republic has demonstrated the efficacy of this provision, which, in effect, places the legislative process in the hands of the executive. At the start of a legislative session the Prime Minister announces the policy matters he will submit for legislation. Every two weeks thereafter the Government sends each house a list of Government bills, or Government-approved private members' bills, slated for priority debate in the order set forth on the list. The steering committees of the two houses have the right to suggest changes in this order, but the Government can insist on maintaining its priorities. Indeed, the Government can by-pass these committees altogether if it chooses.

Thus by the simple expedient of so loading the agenda with Government bills that no time was left for anything else, the Debré Government was able to exclude private members' bills it opposed, dilatory debates on irrelevant motions and demagogic resolutions, and even members' questions of personal privilege and discussions of matters of parliamentary housekeeping. Indeed, it was said that the Government on occasion actually "packed" the agenda in order to head off certain embarrassing debates and refused to give priority to certain important questions for fear of being rebuffed by parliament in their ultimate disposition.

The sheer number of laws passed every year under the Fourth Republic, as well as their variety and detail, was also an index of parliament's once massive involvement in policy-making. Since Governments' coalition majorities rarely coincided with majorities on the parliamentary steering committees (and even when they did Prime Ministers' control over them was weak), each house remained completely master of its agenda. They employed this advantage usually in order to provide priority hearing to those legislative matters that were important to the most powerful interest groups and political parties. The absence of executive control over the parliament's agenda in France, therefore, resulted in the passage by the Assembly of an average of 286 laws per year between 1946 and 1951. For the same period the British House of Commons passed an average of only 56 laws. Even as late as 1957, after the Assembly had agreed to limit its legislative production, 198 laws were still voted. Most of these laws, it is true, were of Government origin but, unlike the British ones, a large number of them had been introduced at first as private members' bills or were Government bills that incorporated private members' amendments as the price for passage. Almost invariably this meant new expenditures not called for by the budget, and hence they wrought havoc with the executive's financial and economic programs.

Today the constitution has dealt with this problem by adopting the British practice of prohibiting the introduction of private members' bills that imply an increase of Government expenditure or a reduction in tax revenues (Article 40). It has also armed the Government with means to assure passage of its priority legislation, in the form originally presented and with sufficient speed to deal with the problem for which it was intended. In Britain this modern requirement of speedy and effective policy-making in a wide field of complex matters has long been met by executive control of the legislative process and executive rule-making as the normal form of policy decisions. The small number of laws passed annually, almost all of Government origin, implies that each of them must delegate wide quasi-legislative power to the cabinet, which makes policy by decree—"statutory instruments," in British parlance. This curbing of parliament's theoretically unlimited law-making power in Britain is made possible by firm executive control of the majority, which in turn is due to the party system.

Similar limitation of parliament has been finally achieved in France by new constitutional arrangements and the statistics testify to their efficacy: in 1959 only fifty-two bills were passed by parliament and among them only one originated with a private member. Indeed, of the five hundred-odd private members' bills introduced during the first three years of the Fifth Republic, only twenty-one were allowed as far as the agenda by the Government. But whereas in England it has been a delegation of authority by parliament and majority party control that resulted in a self-limitation of legislative production, in France this has been created by the artificial fiat of a written constitution. By assigning the Government the right to monopolize parliament's own agenda, the constitution has imposed bonds on parliament that now produce results similar to those achieved in Britain by more "natural" methods. As shall be seen in the chapter on policy-making, this artificial mechanism has added to French politics a new cause for friction between the executive and the legislative.

Long after a bill is on the agenda the constitution continues to maintain the Government's influence over its fate. In the past, unlike its British counterpart, the French parliament rarely opened debate by considering the Government's original bill. Rather it first discussed its own committee's report and then proceeded to debate and vote upon either a much revised version of the Government bill or even one of a number of totally different "counter-bills" (*contre projets*) proposed by private members. This allowed deputies representing interests affected by the legislation to have the maximum opportunity to "protect" their supporters. First, they could disfigure the bill in the preliminary discussions of the permanent specialized committee, where most deputies representing groups interested in the committee's subject had seats. Then later they could amend it or even totally alter it in the public debate on the committee's report. Today this is no longer possible for, as in Britain, consideration of all Government bills begins with a statement by a Minister, explaining the motives and expected results of the legislation proposed, thereby preventing the terms of discussion from being set by the parliamentary opposition or by deputies committed to particular interests (Article 42).

Often this Government statement now comes even before the parliamentary committee has begun discussion, thus offering the executive a chance to influence the earliest stage of the legislative process. By providing for the Government's opening of debate, the drafters of the constitution had hoped primarily to encourage a general, and not a specialized or "interested," judgment at the important committee stage. They tried to assure this by giving both the Government and parliament the right to call for creation of *ad hoc* committees for most bills (Article 43). It was assumed that such a procedure would avoid the special pleading inherent in the old permanent specialized committees dominated by "interested" deputies. But unwilling to make a complete break with French practice, the drafters also provided for the traditional committees, reducing them from the nineteen existing at the end of the Fourth Republic to six (Article 43). It was felt that, for the few bills sent to the permanent specialized committees, passage would be expedited by eliminating the time-consuming and inefficient cross reference required by the detailed breakdown by subject represented in the old system of many committees. Undoubtedly, too, it was expected that by being limited to six, the new specialized committees would have an average of 100 members each, thus becoming unwieldy little subparliaments, ill prepared to engage in the painstaking and usually interest-inspired dissection of Government bills parliamentary committees had been famous for in the past.

Once again the traditions of French political life have frustrated the hopes of the constitution makers. The system of specialized committees was adopted by the French parliament at the turn of the century precisely in order to assure important economic and social groups that their defenders in parliament would always have a chance to influence legislation affecting them. Since farmers, for example, continue to exert as much pressure on their representatives as before, parliament under the Fifth Republic has adopted practices and drafted rules of procedure that have successfully offset the aims of the constitution. Thus, neither house has created many *ad hoc* committees for bills but rather has sent them immediately to one of the specialized committees. Nor has the Government insisted on the *ad hoc* treatment because the new parliamentary rules have made their creation a long and complicated process, thereby defeating the expedition and ease that had originally been cited in their favor. As for the six specialized committees, the two dealing with economic and social matters—membership in which is most attractive to the parliamentary representatives of pressure groups—have each been assigned no less than 120 members. (The old specialized committees had 44 members and the *ad hoc* committee now has but 33). Since a deputy can belong to only one specialized committee, the size of the two most sensitive ones allows the maximum number of "interested" deputies to belong and thus to meet what they consider their responsibilities to their constituents. Moreover, the awkward size of these new committees has led to the formation of unofficial subcommittees, which do the real work of examining bills. According to reports, these have become just as specialized in focus and as particular in judgment as were those of the old regime. Finally, debate in the plenary sessions of these huge committees has tended to become a dress rehearsal for the highly political discussions of the public debates. As a result, the committee stage is often stretched out for many weeks, delaying passage of a Government bill, save in those cases when the executive requests the "urgency" procedure.

But once a bill is finally reported out of committee for a second reading before parliament, the Government again disposes of new constitutional means to prevent delaying tactics and serious alteration of its text in the full-scale debate. Under Article 44, the Government can now reject amendments from the floor that threaten the essence of its legislative proposals, as well as move its own amendments to restore items dropped by the committees. It should be said that in practice the Debré Government refrained from exercising these powers, partly to avoid further friction with a parliament already too aware of its new impotence, partly because it had a more effective method to ensure passage of the original version of its bill. This is the right, still under Article 44, to call for a "single vote" at any time during the debate—on the part of a bill being challenged, on only those amendments it has proposed or accepted, or on the whole bill—if the course of debate reveals that general opposition is growing. A request for such a "single vote" (*vote unique* or *vote global*) automatically suspends the usually disfiguring article-by-article consideration in public debate and, on short notice, obliges deputies either to accept totally the Government's version of the bill or be responsible for its final defeat. Of all the constitutional changes in procedure, it has been this one that has caused deputies the greatest chagrin for, unlike the Senators, they have ultimate responsibility for the form in which a bill is passed. Yet when the Government calls for a "single vote," they are unable to satisfy their constituents' interest in changes even to the extent of getting a simple hearing for their amendments in open debate.

The possibility of asking for a "single vote" in order to save the heart of a Government bill or to stave off crippling amendments existed under the Fourth Republic but only if the question of confidence was posed. This was a slow mechanism, requiring approval of the Council of Ministers and a twenty-four-hour waiting period that led to further delays in the legislative process. Today, without rejecting deputies' amendments outright or invoking the always risky question of confidence, Fifth Republic Governments are able to preserve both the letter and the spirit of their legislative proposals. The price the Debré Government paid for employing this effective arm against parliament was the firm determination of many deputies to change this provision in the constitution as soon as a majority for reform could be mustered. In order to avoid this reaction the Debré Government could have used the "single vote" more sparingly, even allowing some modification of its legislative proposals in public debate. An alternative would have been to allow parliament to vote resolutions criticizing Government policies on question day, thereby releasing its frustrations and showing its constituents some tangible proof of concern for their special interests. The traditional pressures of French politics must be allowed such orderly channels of expression or else they will ultimately break the constitutional straitjacket imposed upon them by the Fifth Republic.

The possibility of dilatory and obstructionist tactics by deputies during debate has been curbed by the Assembly's new rules of procedure, thereby also aiding the Government in expediting legislation. Such famous delaying procedures as the "prejudicial motion" and the "adjournment motion" have been prohibited during legislative debates, while moving the previous question and sending a bill back to committee have been limited. The possibility of wide-ranging critical debates on the pretext of a vote approving the minutes of the previous day's sittings or moving the closure of the day's discussions have been eliminated. The President of the Assembly now enjoys a series of new disciplinary powers also tending to expedite debate and limit parliamentary prerogative. During unlimited debate he can decide when the Assembly has been "sufficiently informed" by a deputy; he can refuse to allow a deputy to read a long speech, insisting on extempore delivery; he can close general discussion after two deputies of opposite views have been heard. More important still, the President under the new rules can impose sanctions on a member who disturbs the good order of debate, without asking for a vote from his peers as he formerly was obliged to do.

When the two houses have passed differing versions of a Government bill and speedy passage is threatened by a prolonged "shuttle" (*navette*) between them, the Prime Minister may now convoke a joint conference committee (*commission mixte paritaire*) to iron out the remaining differences (Article 45). If it comes to no agreement or if the two houses fail to pass the conference committee's compromise—to which only Government-approved amendments may be added—the Prime Minister can then ask the Assembly to rule definitively on either its original version or on the one proposed by the committee. The experience of the Debré Government has actually been to use the joint conference committee stage as still another means to impose its will on parliament. For by proposing and accepting amendments in the committee, which reestablish provisions originally rejected by majorities in one or both houses, an additional chance to bully through its own version of legislation has thus been created.

THE SENATE AS ALLY OF THE EXECUTIVE

The third source of executive strength in policy making—at least in the minds of the constitution drafters was the newly reinforced power of the upper house, which today has reverted to its prewar name of Senate. Historically upper chambers in France belong to the administrative tradition of politics. The great revolutionary assemblies were unicameral and it was not until Thermidor and the Empire that an upper house was created, precisely in order to limit the action of the popularly elected lower house. Indeed, Napoleon I frankly called his upper house the "Conservative Senate," and the authoritarian regimes of the nineteenth century all used a Senate as a counterweight to a more broadly based lower house. The constitution of the Third Republic did not alter this tradition but in fact continued the imperial practice of providing for lifetime Senators. Although this provision was soon abandoned and the Senate developed into a thoroughly republican body, it did retain its more conservative character thanks to the mode of election of its members. Senators were then elected for nine-year terms—over twice as long as that of a deputy—and not by direct popular election, but by an electoral college made up of the deputies, members of departmental councils, and delegates chosen by municipal and township councils. The latter dominated the group and as a consequence the Senate became very much the "grand council of the townships of France," as Gambetta put it. But this was its purpose, for part of the price republicans had to pay for the 1875 constitution was to assure the royalist and conservative majority in the founding assembly that the popularly elected Chamber of Deputies would be checked by an upper house in which more conservative provincial France would have a permanent majority. Indirect election by a college in which the more numerous rural townships had a natural majority seemed to guarantee this. The result was a Senate that throughout the life of the Third Republic was more traditionalist in economic and social matters than the Chamber of Deputies.

In the revolutionary atmosphere of 1944-46 the first reflex of the drafters of the new constitution of the Fourth Republic was to omit an upper house all together and return to the unicameralism of the true "assembly regime." But the prospective power of the Communist party in a single, all-powerful legislative body led the drafters to agree that a counterforce of some sort would be necessary, if only to delay passage of legislation. A drastically weakened version of the prewar Senate was therefore created and named the Council of the Republic in a further attempt to indicate its special status. Until 1954 the Council was a purely advisory body without the right to initiate legislation and in theory unable to delay the Assembly's version of a text for more than two months. The constitution specified clearly that the Government was responsible only to the Assembly, which alone invested a cabinet, and it allowed the lower house to reject any of the Council's amendments by simply adopting its own version of a law by the same majority the Council had used. At the same time the mode of election, being substantially the same as that of the old Senate, had made the Council the preserve of elder statesmen and the representatives of provincial, agricultural, and small-town interests. Given the undeniable importance of these sectors of French society and the growing strength of parties sympathetic to them, the advice of the Council became increasingly respected, and in 1954 the constitution was amended to return to the upper house much of the power of the old Senate.

The new Senate of the Fifth Republic is made up of 306 members whose seats are distributed among the départements (France's principal administrative units) according to population. (After Algeria was declared independent in July 1962, the mandate of the thirty-four senators from Algerian constituencies was cancelled by decree, reducing the new Senate membership to 272.) As in the past, they are not elected directly by the people but rather by electoral colleges in each department, composed of the department's deputies, its locally elected departmental councilors, and delegates chosen by the department's township and municipal councils. This amounts to a total Senatorial electorate of some 100,000, slightly more than the total under the Third and Fourth Republics, due to an increase in the number of delegates from the larger cities and towns. However, urban electors are still very much in the minority and this underrepresentation makes the new Senate retain its traditional role as spokesman for rural France. To be eligible for election candidates must be thirty-five years of age, twelve years older than for the Assembly. The traditional Senatorial term of nine years has been reestablished, with renewal by thirds every three years. Members for the populous departments are elected by a system of party lists and proportional representation, while in the less populated departments a two-ballot, majority system is employed. Because the electorate is small there is little official campaigning, the influence of local reputation, party regularity, and personal connections being the decisive factors. Successful candidates, therefore, are usually local "notables," well known to the politicians of the department and strongly supported by one or more of the important interest groups of the region.

Unlike the Council of the Republic, the new Senate has formally the same legislative prerogatives as the Assembly, save, of course, in the cases of the budget and other financial bills, which must originate in the lower house. Otherwise, the Senate can bury a bill by simply refusing to consider the version sent up from the Assembly. However, since the executive controls the agenda of both houses, this power to block the will of the Assembly can only be exercised if the Government finds it useful to keep an Assembly bill out of the Senate, perhaps in a rare instance of private member legislation. As described above, the Government can always dissolve the resistance of the Senate to a Government bill already passed in the Assembly by calling for a joint conference committee and ultimately falling back on the Assembly for passage in case of further Senatorial intransigence.

On the other hand, its greater role in lawmaking has made the Senate a potential lever of the executive against Assembly resistance to the Government's legislative program. Thus the cabinet can instruct friendly Senators to restore in their reading of a bill items originally rejected by the lower house. This can be especially effective on the reading of a conference committee text when only Government-sponsored amendments may be moved. In the contrary case of legislation dear to the deputies and opposed by the Government, however, the latter can refuse to call a conference committee and thus condemn the bill to an endless shuttle between the houses unless the Senate accepts the Assembly bill.

In addition to the services it can perform for the executive in the legislative process, the Senate can also be used to reinforce Government stability, thanks to a number of minor constitutional innovations. For, although the cabinet is still responsible only to an Assembly majority, it can ask for Senate approval of a general policy statement and thereby impose pressure on the lower house. Even more important, the Government can ask the Senate to act on the budget if the Assembly fails to rule within forty days of its presentation, thus again allowing for pressure on the lower house. Then, too, by generally increasing the dignity of the Senate, the constitution has by this fact devalued the formerly dominant prestige of the Assembly and limited the legitimacy of its pretentions *vis à vis* the executive. To this effect it is the President of the Senate who now becomes acting President of the Republic in case of a sudden vacancy, and not the President of the Assembly as before. Moreover, not only does the Senate's presiding officer now share equally with the Assembly President a number of important nominative and procedural powers, but he now also comes directly after the President of the Republic and the Prime Minister in the official protocol of precedence.

The new constitution, therefore, makes the upper house potentially both a passive and an active ally of the executive against the Assembly. When the Government refrains from using its powers to expedite the legislative process, the enhanced prestige and reestablished law-making role of the Senate brakes the Assembly's policy-making momentum. When the Government so chooses, by calling for a conference committee, asking the Senate for approval of a policy statement, or presenting a budget to the Senate, it can enlist the upper house in its struggle to impose the executive will on the Assembly. This assumes, of course, that there exists a majority in the Senate more favorable to the Government than the one in the Assembly. In the minds of the constitution drafters this condition would be favored by the Senators' relative seniority in age, their lengthened term of office, and, especially, their indirect election by a college of notables, which released them from the direct pressure of public opinion to which deputies were subject.

As a matter of fact, these conditions have not favored a Government majority in the Senate during the first years of the Fifth Republic and as a consequence Prime Minister Debré's use of the upper house against the Assembly was much curtailed. Constitutional engineering fell once more under the weight of politics when in the Senatorial elections of 1959 many Fourth Republic politicians, who had lost their Assembly seats the year before in the Gaullist sweep, became Senators. Indirect suffrage by local officeholders had meant that the traditional politician rather than the "new man" had the clear advantage. And to make matters worse for the Government, the Senatorial elections took place months after the original Gaullist victory at a time when resistance had already built up to a number of unpopular economic policies. While Debré's party, the Gaullist UNR, held 40 per cent of the Assembly seats, it had less than 10 per cent of them in the Senate, and its contribution to the solidity of the Prime Minister's majority in the upper house was proportionally less effective. Consequently, the Debré Government was often unable to muster Senate majorities for bringing into play expediting devices like the "single vote" and pressure devices like Senatorial approval of policy statements. On the contrary, the large percentage of opposition Senators and many Fourth Republic holdovers has made the Senate both a passive and active ally of the divided and impotent Assembly opposition. In the face of frequent Senate defeats, the Debré Government was often obliged to interrupt the legislative shuttle between the houses and force final passage of a bill in the Assembly where its majority was stable. It has been the growing fear that the Senate could become a permanent critical forum for both powerful interest groups and anti-Gaullist politicians that has led de Gaulle to consider a constitutional revision, reducing once again the Senate's legislative role. Moreover, to dilute the strength of party representation, de Gaulle's old idea of electing to the upper house delegates from economic, social, and professional organizations has also been revived.

Actually, this desire to offset the parliamentary influence of party leaders and pressure groups—whom de Gaulle irritably refers to as "intermediaries"—has been partly satisfied by the somewhat greater use being made of a consultative organ of government, the Economic and Social Council. The members of this body are either delegated by trade unions, professional groups, and voluntary organizations interested in social policy, or appointed as experts by Government decree. While still having only advisory powers as under the Fourth Republic, the Council is now meant to serve principally as an advisor to the executive and not to the National Assembly as before. The Government is obliged to submit its economic and social legislative proposals, as well as its general economic plans for the nation, to the Council for advice. But since it now can name one third of the membership rather than less than 8 per cent as under the last regime, the Government usually can expect that the reports on these matters will favor its views and hence strengthen its case *vis à vis* parliament. The Council also continues to have the function of recommending legislation to the Government and receiving the views of interested groups on bills and general economic and social problems, somewhat in the manner of the Congressional investigating and legislative committees in the United States. If it so desires, the Government can obviously urge its nominees on the Council to encourage policy recommendations it favors, thereby short-circuiting the influence of the "intermediaries" at work on the deputies. The Government can also suggest to pressure groups that their interests may best be served by appearing before an organ like the Council, which directly advises the powerful executive, rather than by appealing to the deputies or the political parties of a weakened and divided parliament.

AN ULTIMATE CHECK ON PARLIAMENT:
THE CONSTITUTIONAL COUNCIL

The fourth and last source of executive dominance lies in the new procedure for testing the constitutionality of laws after they have been enacted by parliament. Their minds ever focused on the experience of the Third and Fourth Republics, the drafters of the new constitution saw in the entirely new Constitutional Council a final barrier to parliamentary initiatives that interfered or were incompatible with effective executive action. In traditional theory and practice, the law of parliament had been supreme and the machinery for judicial review was rudimentary, with its development considered contrary to the sovereignty of the people as expressed by parliament. The Fourth Republic made a feeble step toward creating an organ of judicial review in its Constitutional Committee. But not only were a majority of its members chosen by a partisan vote in the Assembly, thus affecting their independence and objectivity, but also its powers were extremely limited and, in fact, it was hardly ever used.

Title VII of the new constitution breaks with this tradition by making the Constitutional Council almost an independent organ of government. It is composed of all former Presidents of the Republic and nine other members, three chosen by each of the Presidents of the two chambers plus the incumbent President of the Republic, who also names one of the members chairman. The Council has a number of special powers of surveillance that are potentially very important. Besides assuring the regularity of the election of the President and members of parliament, and the procedures followed in referenda, it must approve the rules of procedure adopted by the two houses of parliament. By this provision the drafters hoped to prevent any indirect effort by parliament to escape the new constitutional bonds placed upon its powers *vis à vis* the executive. It is also the Council that alone decides when the sudden incapacity of the President requires his temporary replacement by the President of the Senate, or whether new elections should be called for his permanent replacement. The Council must be consulted by the President of the Republic on the use of the emergency powers under Article 16, as well as on every measure taken under those powers.

As a more frequently used tool against parliament, however, the Council may be asked by the cabinet to strike down proposed private members' bills or deputies' amendments to Government bills which it considers deal with matters outside the specified domain of law-making and hence within its own rule-making prerogative. It may also use the Council to extend its rule-making powers by asking it to decide whether a matter that was a subject of legislation before the Fifth Republic now comes within the purview of executive rule-making. All organic laws that supplement the constitution are automatically reviewed by the Council to test their constitutionality, thus providing another check on any indirect effort to change the intentions of the drafters. Finally, the Government and the President of the Republic (as well as the Presidents of the two chambers) can ask the Council to nullify a law or treaty that is considered incompatible with the constitution. It should be added that the right of appeal to the Council in order to limit the Government's rule-making power is available to parliament, although, as shall be seen below, present conditions make this unlikely.

Thus, not only has the new constitution surrounded parliament with strict curbs on its political power to unmake Governments and on its legislative power in policy-making, but it has also created an organ to act as watchdog, seeing that parliament remains within its status of inferiority. The activity of the Council during its first years has demonstrated its efficiency in this respect. On the Government's request in 1959 it prevented a senatorial attempt to reintroduce a pale form of interpellation, that once potent arm against the cabinet, by striking from its new rules of procedure provisions allowing a vote of a resolution after an oral question with debate. Since then the Government has had little recourse to the Council in order to disallow parliamentary initiatives, simply because the Presidents of the two houses, convinced the Council would continue to rule in favor of the executive, have applied a rigid internal discipline over the tabling of laws and amendments in order to prevent further embarrassment to their assemblies. This has, of course, affected the reputation of the Council as a supposedly independent organ of Government and, indeed, the present solid Gaullist majority on the Council confirms this doubt. Five of the nine originally appointed members, named by de Gaulle and the Gaullist President of the Assembly, had been active in Gaullist political movements and were presumed to be personally devoted to de Gaulle and his constitutional ideas. Since then this Gaullist majority has been preserved, suggesting that if de Gaulle were to leave the scene suddenly, this majority might well become the main legal obstacle to a reconversion of the Fifth Republic toward a more traditional form of parliamentarism. Were this majority of political circumstances to change, however, a looser interpretation of the present constitution might prevail, thus allowing a gradual and orderly transformation of the document by Council decisions, much as the United States Supreme Court has affected constitutional law and practice.

Contractual Cooperation with Former Dependencies

In no field of policy has the ineffectiveness of French political institutions been so apparent as in relations with overseas dependencies. In a world swept by national independence movements, the immobilism of French policy led to the worst results. Neither an all-out effort to maintain control over Indochina and North Africa nor genuine promises of autonomy and gradual independence on the British model were made. The ensuing defeats in the Far East, the sudden concessions on Tunisia and Morocco, and finally the outbreak of the Algerian rebellion in territory long considered "part" of France were the principal causes of the crisis of public confidence in which the Fourth Republic fell. In 1958 de Gaulle and the drafters of the new constitution sought to reconcile their desire to maintain direct control over France's last African colonies with the mounting pressure for independence on that continent. The solution they chose was a relatively liberal one: a flexible structure called the "Community," which preserved French dominance over most important decisions of the African states' domestic and foreign policy, yet explicitly provided for both their evolution toward complete autonomy and even total independence. Two years later the course of events had led to such independence for all of France's African dependencies as well as to a radical change in both the theory and practice of France's relations with them. Once again the formal text of the new constitution had failed to contain the ebullience of politics, this time external to France.

The Original "Community" of 1958

The constitution of the Fourth Republic established a fairly complicated structure for governing France's overseas dependencies, called the French Union. Those dependencies not officially considered "overseas departments" of France were nonetheless represented in the French parliament as "overseas territories." Those that had theoretically acceded to complete internal autonomy were called "associated states" and were represented in the advisory body known as the Assembly of the French Union. In 1958 the latter organ was abolished and representatives of the overseas territories that chose to remain associated with France in the referendum of September 1958 no longer sat in the Paris parliament. Eliminated, thereby, were most of the African deputies who had little interest in much of the French parliament's proceedings but who bargained their votes indiscriminately among the parties in return for political and personal favors. The Community, as the new structure was called, consisted of France and almost all of her sub-Saharan African territories, dignified with the name of "member states." (At the referendum only the former territory of

Guinea voted to become completely independent and hence remain outside the Community.) The link between France and these dependencies was extremely flexible and indeed represented primarily a procedure for constant consultation and accommodation rather than a fixed division of powers. However, by the terms of Article 78 of the new constitution, a certain number of specified matters such as foreign policy, defense, economic and financial policy, and decisions regarding strategic raw materials were prohibited to the governments of the African member states and placed under the competence of the common organs of the Community.

These organs were solidly dominated by France's President of the Republic who was also President of the Community and in whose election, it should be recalled, overseas dependencies participated. He presided over the principal organ of the Community, the Executive Council, made up of the French Prime Minister and the Prime Ministers of the member states, as well as their cabinet colleagues involved in matters common to the Community. There was also a Senate of the Community, made up of delegates from the various legislative assemblies, in which metropolitan French delegates had a clear majority. However, since the powers of the Senate were advisory and since it did not meet for more than two months per year, it seemed unlikely that the Senate would play an important role in the new structure. There was also a Court of Arbitration of the Community, which ruled on conflicts among the member states and whose members were appointed by the President.

While the full grant of local autonomy and the clear recognition of the members' right to independence, as provided by Article 86, placed the Community a far cry from France's old colonial policy of centralism, the Paris government still retained very strong control over the policies of the members. In keeping with de Gaulle's view of the new Presidency as the defender of France's national power, this control was vested principally in the new chief of state and was therefore not subject to the vagaries of the French parliament, which the drafters of the constitution considered responsible for France's loss of Indochina, Tunisia, and Morocco. Thus the administration of the Community, including control over the areas of "common" interest, was directly under the President. It was he who convoked the Executive Council, presided over its meetings, made the decisions on the common matters between its quarterly sessions, and in substance ultimately handled all major policy problems for the African governments.

However, unlike the previous structure of the French Union, the Community allowed for an infinite number of opportunities for negotiations between the President and the representatives of the African states, not to mention the psychologically vital safety valve represented by the formally stated right to independence. Lastly, although organic laws and constitutional changes affecting the Community were largely within the competence of the Paris government, the President had enough power to make important concessions of further autonomy to a member state if the pressure for complete independence grew too strong.

THE NEW SYSTEM OF "COOPERATION"

It was this power that de Gaulle employed in 1959 and 1960 to completely transform the Community into what is now a loose confederation of sovereign states. By granting what he called "international sovereignty" to those states remaining in the Community and by maintaining close ties to those who chose independence outside of the Community, de Gaulle changed both the letter and spirit of the original structure. Today the member states' relations with France are governed, not by the French constitution, but by a series of bilateral treaties. The essence of these relations is now cooperation between formally sovereign states, not the association of partially autonomous states with a predominant power. As for those African countries that for varying reasons chose to remain formally outside the community, their relations with France are for practical purposes the same as for members. In the words of Maurice Duverger, a leading French political scientist, the "constitutional Community" of 1958 has given way to a new "contractual Community."

Strictly speaking de Gaulle's personal grant of independence to all the original members of the Community was in contradiction with the constitution. For not only did he avoid the complicated procedure of Article 86, by which independence was to be accorded, but he also proclaimed that independence did not mean *ipso facto* withdrawal from the Community, as the same article clearly stated. In the circumstances de Gaulle had little choice but to act quickly and on his personal responsibility since the rapid movement of all of Africa toward freedom and the consequent growth of internal pressures for full sovereignty in the member states made it obvious that continued French presence in Africa depended on immediate action. In June 1960 the situation was regularized by the passage of a constitutional law eliminating the incompatibility between independence and membership in the Community.

The original institutions of the Community, such as the Executive Council and the Senate, which dealt with decisions within the "competence of the Community" as defined by the constitution, no longer exist. There are now occasional meetings of a new body called the Conference of Chiefs of State, but it, as well as a projected Interparliamentary Senate and a series of intergovernmental committees, is purely consultative, if not indeed ceremonial. Political and security matters of common concern are now treated bilaterally through the foreign ministries and, like all France's foreign relations, are discussed in the cabinet. More likely, however, the important matters are decided in frequent meetings between de Gaulle and his Prime Minister and their African counterparts or representatives. Formally, the President of the Republic is still President of the Community, but since the member states no longer participate in his election and since constitutionally he no longer dominates decisions taken within the "competence of the Community," the President's role is—theoretically —ceremonial, like that of the Queen's in the British Commonwealth.

In practice, however, the prestige of de Gaulle, the presence in the African states of many vital French technical advisors and teachers, and the huge financial contribution of France to their budgets makes the French government extremely influential in the policy making of the new nations. And, although a new version of the original Court of Arbitration is planned, conflicts among states and even power struggles within them are being regularly arbitrated on an informal, *ad hoc* basis by the French President and his Prime Minister. To aid him in these primarily informal functions, de Gaulle has a staff headed by a trusted personal assistant with the title of Secretary General of the Presidency for Community and African and Malgasy Affairs. Since the bulk of these bilateral relations concern the vast variety of French economic and technical assistance that requires the participation of many French ministries, a coordinating body on the cabinet level, named the Council for African and Malgasy Affairs (Madagascar being technically outside of Africa) has been created. Presided over by the President, the Council includes the Prime Minister, the Minister of Foreign Affairs, the Secretary General of the Presidency for Community Affairs, the Secretary of the Government (who heads the Council's staff), and the Minister of Cooperation.

It is the totally new Ministry of Cooperation that plans and administers the aid programs to the new states. With the approval of the Prime Minister and the cabinet, the Minister of Cooperation deals with French ministries closely involved in the programs, such as Finance and Education, as well as with the representatives of the governments receiving aid. The Minister makes no distinction between states still formally within the Community and those now outside, for all France's former African colonies and trust territories have bilateral and even multilateral economic and technical assistance treaties with her. This indicates that in practice there is really little difference between the kinds of relations France now has with her former dependencies. Bilateralism is the rule and the Presidency and the Ministry of Cooperation are the principal points of contact the former colonies have with France.

Of course, the amount of French assistance and the extent of political coordination in international and security affairs varies among the African states. The exact degree is somewhat reflected in the formal status of each former dependency *vis à vis* what remains of the original "constitutional Community." The following list shows roughly, and in descending order, the closeness of the ties binding the new nations to France. All of them, it should be remembered, are now fully independent.

1. Six members of the revised Community: The Central African Republic, The Republic of Chad, The Republic of the Congo (Brazzaville), The Gabon Republic, The Malgasy Republic, The Republic of Senegal.
2. States having bilateral agreements similar to those of the above but formally outside the Community: The Republic of Dahomey, The Republic of the Ivory Coast, The Republic of the Niger, The Republic of the Upper Volta (these four states are loosely federated in the Council of the Entente), The Islamic Republic of Mauritania.
3. Former United Nations Trusteeship territories with close ties to France but formally outside the Community: The Republic of Cameroun, The Republic of Togo.
4. Former French colonies, generally hostile to France, maintaining no political or security coordination, and receiving only the slightest economic and technical assistance: The Republic of Mali, The Republic of Guinea.

Conclusion: The Victory of Practice over Theory

French constitutions have forever been the victims of French politics. Louis XVIII's constitution tried to impose the British form of limited monarchy and two revolutions later France was a Republic. The restored monarchy in turn gave way to a constitutional order establishing a second Bonaparte's one-man rule that by 1870 had almost turned into parliamentary government. The constitutional laws of the Third Republic were meant to enshrine the executive but could not prevent the legislative from becoming dominant. And the Fourth Republic enshrined the legislative, only to find it necessary to repeatedly violate its constitution in order to provide effective executive action. The first years of the Fifth Republic have demonstrated that France still lacks a constitution compatible with her politics.

It seems clear after three years' experience that the drafters of the new constitution were overly concerned with the defects of the Fourth Republic's formal institutions and not enough concerned with both the traditional habits and the new trends and circumstances of French political life. Thus, it has been the Algerian war and the political passions it has unleashed that have led de Gaulle to totally dominate decision making and reinterpret the President's role. It has been more the Gaullist electoral victory of 1958 than the constitution that assured the Debré Government its longevity. It was the unexpected cohesion of his party more than the constitution that guaranteed victory for the Prime Minister's legislative program. It has been the permanence of parliamentary and other informal customs that has caused the proxy vote and other banned practices to elude the constitutional prohibition. It has been the unexpected election to the Senate of veteran anti-Gaullists that has made of that body a hindrance rather than a help to the cabinet. All of these unforeseen factors have been produced by either the resistance of old or the rise of new political forces—in short, the traditional problem of conflicting ideals of political authority. Driven by different historical circumstances, French constitutions have always foundered on the same reefs.

The Variety of Political Forces

The Withering of Traditional Politics

The coming of the Fifth Republic cast a pall of silence and paralysis upon the normally turbulent life of French political parties. After three years the hush over party politics remained, though the increased activity of pressure groups and the threat of violence from elements of the army and their extremist civilian allies created another kind of turbulence and instability. Both the new constitution and the Algerian crisis have contributed to a transformation of political life that the French term "depolitization." Public attention has shifted from the essentially political arena of parliament to the actions of a single man. And the competition for power has shifted from among the highly political parties of the past to a struggle between that man, Charles de Gaulle, and a new set of "intermediaries" between state and nation.

In terms of the future of French democracy the decline of the traditional parties during the first years of the new regime is of special interest. Parliament's reduced role in policy making and its inability to threaten seriously the tenure of the Government have meant that its debates are no longer as interesting for the public as they used to be. Consequently, French parliamentarians, like politicians everywhere, were less moved to make speeches when no one was bothering to listen. As for party activity, a vicious circle of causes reduced its intensity to a point that inspired fear for representative government on the part of many observers. This growing "depolitization" was evidenced by trends affecting all parties as well as the behavior of Frenchmen at the polls. Formal party membership, vital for the supply of the "militants" who produce party activity, continued to decline steadily. Attendance at party meetings of all sorts was poor and the striking record of eligible voters' failure to vote in by-elections, local elections, and in the much publicized referendum of January 1961 also confirmed this trend away from traditional politics.

TWO THEORIES OF PARTY DECLINE

Two sets of explanations are offered for this phenomenon. There is a "devil theory" that sees de Gaulle as the principal cause for the disaffection from politics. Many who in varying degree are hostile to the General and his new institutions argue that by reducing the power of parliament and assuming personal responsibility for major policy decisions, de Gaulle has eliminated the *raison d'être* of political parties. This, in turn, has sapped the morale of politically active Frenchmen, hence the decline in party activity, which, in turn, is responsible for the public's lack of interest in elections and other forms of political participation. Such an attitude, to complete the circular analysis, further demoralized the party organizations and their leaders, convinced as they were that their words had come to have little echo in the country. Since de Gaulle's ancient dislike for parties as they have developed in France is well known, the argument was finally embellished with the claim that "depolitization" was the ultimate purpose of the General in his constitutional reform of 1958. An opinion unstructured by parties, freed of "intermediaries" between itself and the state, was just what an authoritarian de Gaulle wanted from the start, his critics have insisted.

A more subtle explanation, taking into account both changes in French society and trends in French political behavior, attributed the "depolitization" to a complicated and longer process. Indeed, rather than being its cause, de Gaulle and the Fifth Republic were seen as the results of a growing reaction against the old parties and the parliamentary system they literally "occupied." It is true that the decline in party membership and the slow-down in party activity were both well under way during the last years of the Fourth Republic. Public opinion polls and analyses then agreed that traditional party programs and activities were increasingly considered irrelevant to France's problems by large sectors of the public. In general, the parties' rather abstract diagnoses of French ills, based as they were on past ideological issues, were being viewed as out-of-date by a society more and more bent on concrete problems of individual well-being and less and less convinced of the wisdom or feasibility of radical social change.

By 1958 Communism had lost its dynamic and had become the theology of an apparently irreducible, if stabilized, segment of alienated opinion. Democratic socialism had lost its reformist image to a reality that made of the French Socialist party first the spokesman for France's large body of government employees and only second the representative of the liberal lower middle class. With the slow disappearance of the popular mystique of a united Europe, the Christian Democratic party, the M.R.P., lost the principal distinction that separated it from other conservative parties— parties that had never been considered anything else than political "fronts" for various business and agricultural interests. As for the attraction of the Radical party, that misnamed amalgam of conservative economic ideas with mildly liberal political attitudes so important in prewar France, it never really took hold in opinion after 1945 and its popular identity with traditional parliamentarism served to speed it toward oblivion after the collapse of the Fourth Republic.

Associated with these long-range trends were the political circumstances created by the Algerian war. Various combinations of traditional parties had attempted to find a solution and all had failed. A socialist Premier whose party had campaigned for a negotiated solution tried a policy of intensified military repression; more conservative Premiers, formally committed to maintaining France in Algeria, hinted broadly at some sort of a negotiated peace. By 1958, therefore, opinion had become convinced of what many political leaders had been saying in private for some time: none of the traditional parties had a solution, and, even if they did, none of the traditional political leaders could make it stick against the will of the army and the Europeans in Algeria. Undoubtedly one of the unrecognized causes for the eclipse of the once popular Pierre Mendès-France was the fact that, like all other party leaders, he had no solution to offer either. But in terms of politics the crisis of 1958, more than a crisis of creative ideas and solutions, was a crisis of public confidence in the usual cadres of French political life. It had long been reflected in the disaffection from the parties and their leaders, and even before the Algerian war it had been reflected in the growth of activist nationalism and sudden electoral shifts to passing phenomena like Pierre Poujade, the antitax demagogue, and Mendès-France, both men who rightly or wrongly were for varying periods considered outside the "system" by large numbers of Frenchmen.

Thus when the Algiers coup of May 1958 brought de Gaulle back to power after over twelve years in retirement, "depolitization"—a popular turning from traditional party leadership—had long since been in progress. It is true that once in office again de Gaulle did nothing to encourage the revitalization of the party system. Indeed, he did nothing to encourage the development of even the Gaullist party, the Union for the New Republic, whose very reason for existing was loyalty to the General and his policies. But setting aside de Gaulle's prejudices about French parties, it can be legitimately asked whether the creation of a dynamic party system is the responsibility of a crisis leader. The very appeal to a Solon or Lycurgus signifies the abdication of responsibility on the part of traditional party leadership. If French politics are to be reborn, it must be the work of the politically active in France and not another act of a miracle man. It must also be added that the continuing Algerian crisis remained a major obstacle in the way of such a rebirth. The French are a realistic people who realized that de Gaulle represented the only political force that could impose a solution in Algeria. Disappointing though this might be for doctrinaires of democratic theory, Frenchmen in general have been glad that de Gaulle has taken from their shoulders the responsibility for Algeria and other difficult political problems—problems that their own political divisions made impossible to resolve in the past. In brief, then, France during the early Fifth Republic was still not ripe for a revival of politics in either its historic French form or, more hopefully, in a form better adapted to the need of its emerging modern society.

This has not been a healthy situation, to be sure, and there were many who wondered whether or not it signified a decline in the democratic reflexes of France. They claimed that whatever the faults of the old political system, the existence of vigorous parliamentary debate and an active party life at least offered a forum for public discussion of political issues and a means for challenging executive authority—both vital for the health of French democracy. Others have been inspired by the present crisis to ask themselves whether genuine democratic politics have ever really existed in France, or, at least, what aspects of French democracy led opinion to its disaffection from the party system. Some of these skeptics have wondered whether the absence of a direct link between opinion and the executive, provided for in Britain's cabinet government and in America's presidential system, is responsible for the disaffection. Another group of "neo-democrats," as they may be described, has insisted that the absence of responsible local government and other institutions of popular participation on the lower reaches of the political process has made the growth of French democracy so fragile. Finally, there are those who argued that the low level of party activity was natural in a country that was still reacting against a system in which such activity often appeared to be considered more important by its participants than was effective government.

Trends Revealed by the 1958 Elections

Yet whatever the causes for the decline of French politics, it cannot be denied that modest and potentially important trends in the alignment and comparative strength of political parties and other political forces have appeared since the coming of the Fifth Republic. Political circumstances, recent institutional changes, as well as the evolution of French society, have combined to alter somewhat the expression of traditional French political opinion. Although there has been no sharp reduction in the number of political parties, a certain simplification of the party system has resulted from three developments: the apparently permanent decline of the Radical party and its elimination as a parliamentary force; the decline of the extreme right as an electoral power, marked by both the eclipse of Poujadism and the failure of the "French Algeria" nationalists to attract voters in recent elections; and the emergence of a near-majority party in the National Assembly, the Gaullist Union for the New Republic. It is true, of course, that Radicals might still become Ministers, deputies, or Senators; that extreme Rightists still have influence over the Government through the action of pressure groups and the army; and that the U.N.R. might never become a genuine majority party or, for that matter, even remain a force in French politics. But continuing trends in French society seem to be dooming the Radicals and the extreme rightists as popular movements, and favoring instead parties like the U.N.R., if not the U.N.R. itself. The urbanization and thorough industrialization of French life, the decline of traditional rural and small town elites, the disappearance of small-scale commercial enterprises, and the growth of white-collar and managerial classes associated with modern industry have been some of these long-run trends. (See Table 8)

TABLE 8   **Major Party Strengths in French Legislative Elections 1928-1958 (Percentage of Vote Cast for Deputies)**

	THIRD REPUBLIC			PROVISIONAL GOVERNMENT		FOURTH REPUBLIC			FIFTH REPUBLIC 1958 (1ST
	1928	1932	1936	1945	JUNE 1946	NOV. 1946	1951	1956	BALLOT)
Conservatives	47	46	42	14	13	13	12	15	20
MRP				25	28	26	12	11	12
Gaullists						2	22	4	18
Radicals	23	25	22	11	11	12	10	13	8
Socialists	18	21	20	24	21	18	14	15	15
Communists	11	8	16	26	26	29	26	25	19

It has also been these trends that, in large part, are responsible for the weakening of the Communist party's hold upon the working class. While it cannot be said that the decline in the party's popular support is permanent, nor that its electoral decline since 1958 has been strikingly important in absolute terms, it is nonetheless probable that the Communists will not be able to mobilize an average 25 per cent of the voters at future elections as they once could. The growth of modern industry, originally a source of strength for the most "revolutionary" party of the Left, has slowly altered the structure and outlook of the working class. New industrial processes have increased the proportion of skilled workers, many of whom are paid monthly wages, which makes them consider themselves closer to the white-collar class than to workers still on an hourly rate. Prosperity has turned French workers into mass consumers and has brought their way of life closer to that enjoyed by all "nonproletarian" groups in society. This new stake in economic prosperity has, in turn, made them more reluctant to engage in purely political protests of the kind the Communist party staged in the early postwar years. The very fact that their relative prosperity can in no evident way be traced to the agitation of the party, long isolated from power and influence, has itself tended to weaken the Communist grip on its once loyal and monolithic social base.

At the same time the continuing exodus from the poorest agricultural regions has reduced the bastions of Communist rural power, while the decline of small, marginal business enterprises has eliminated many sources of bitter labor-management struggles, which in the past helped to maintain party loyalty. By 1958 it remained only for the potency of de Gaulle's personal appeal and the general disaffection from the Fourth Republic, which Communists shared with all Frenchmen, to reduce the party's percentage of the electorate to less than 20 per cent.

THE RECENT EVOLUTION OF POLITICAL FORCES

Since the general elections of 1958 there have been no tests of political opinion that have provided further insights into the evolution of these new trends in French politics. The various by-elections, the local elections in 1959 and 1961, and the referendums of January 1961 and April 1962 have, however, confirmed the conclusions suggested by the 1958 results. The disaffection from traditional forms of political participation continued, as evidenced in a rate of nonvoting that exceeded even the unusually high rate for by-elections and local elections under the Fourth Republic. Indeed, the all-time record for nonvoting in France was made in June 1961 at a well-publicized Parisian by-election when, on the second ballot, 62.5 per cent of the eligible voters failed to appear at the polls. During the same month at local elections for cantonal representatives on the councils of the *départements*, France's major administrative units, a thirty year record was broken, with 43.5 per cent abstaining from the ballot. Even at the referendum of January 8, 1961, at which de Gaulle asked the country to approve his Algerian policy and staked his personal prestige on the issue, 23.5 per cent refused to go to the polls, a full 8.45 per cent over the rate of nonvoting in the historic referendum of September 1958. No amount of official propaganda was able to maintain participation at the 1958 rate, though it must be said that for many who abstained from voting this attitude was itself a form of participation. Thus on the basis of the most recent electoral statistics there is no evidence to indicate a forthcoming revival of politics in terms of participation at elections.

As for relative party strength, little can be added to what has already been said about the new trends. The four by-elections of 1959 showed, as did the municipal elections that year, a temporary revival of Communist electoral power, if only by 8 per cent over the party's 1958 percentage of the total vote. This revival was no longer apparent in the Communist showing at the cantonal elections of June 1961 when they simply maintained the level achieved at the previous cantonal balloting of 1955. It must be added, however, that all local elections have limited relevancy to national political opinions, including those that show a Communist revival. The only interesting results of these various local elections concerns the modest success with which both the Gaullist U.N.R. and the Christian Democratic M.R.P. have put down roots in provincial France. At the June 1961 cantonal elections the traditional representatives of rural France, the conservative Independents and the musty Radicals, both lost a good number of seats to these two parties. Although it is difficult to give a trustworthy national interpretation of the results of elections in which local issues predominate, it might be considered that this move away from the traditional representatives of the countryside is further evidence, however scant, of a desire for new political styles on the part of an electorate undergoing serious social change.

The results of the referendum early in 1961 are difficult to interpret in terms of party strengths, but some general conclusions can be drawn. As in 1958 the Communist party directed its faithful to vote "No" to de Gaulle's request for "Yes." However, an analysis of the heaviest "No" voting areas shows that they do not cover traditionally Communist sections of the country. Indeed, even less than in 1958 did Communist voters obey the directions of their party. The increase of the "No" vote from 1958 to 1961 was attributable mainly to a large vote of the extreme right against de Gaulle's Algerian policy, judged to be too liberal by partisans of "French Algeria." Yet, the fact that most of the 18.37 per cent of the eligible voters who cast "No" ballots were undoubtedly Communists demonstrated at least how feeble was the strength in electoral terms of the extremist right wing. This was again proved by the complete rout of all "French Algeria" candidates at the local elections of 1961 as well as at the Paris by-election of that year. Perhaps the least that one can say about the referendum of 1961 is that it showed that de Gaulle's personal prestige was still very high and that his self-determination policy for Algeria was widely approved by public opinion. The results laid to rest once and for all the argument that Frenchmen basically were against any concessions in negotiations with the Moslem rebels. But while the referendum showed the weakness of the parties and the strength of de Gaulle's raw prestige, it might be wise to note that the affirmative vote was as much a sign of popular eagerness to end the war as it was a mark of support for the General. As a consequence, it is not surprising that, with the cease-fire in Algeria finally signed in March 1962, the referendum of April 8th approving the agreement with the Moslem rebels and, in effect, agreeing to the independence of Algeria, saw over 90 per cent of the voters answer de Gaulle's appeal for an affirmative vote.

In the fall of 1961 rumors of an approaching general election brought a modicum of hope to the leaders of France's parties. Discontent among the farmers and general public criticism of the Government's domestic policies gave special promise of fruitful campaign issues. All parties, moreover, saw in National Assembly elections an opportunity to capture public attention, tighten party organization, and rekindle militant loyalties. Yet a certain uneasiness reigned over party life, for the years of relative eclipse have been accompanied by a corresponding rise of three other political forces, which have competed for influence over opinion and decision making. During the past few years the trade union movement has, to a limited extent annexed some of the functions of the parties of the left, and conservative pressure groups have done the same for the parties of the right. In the west of France two deputies elected in 1958 were sponsored primarily by the catholic trade union and farmers' movements. Similarly, the passing of parliament from the front of the political stage has prompted trade unions to be more active in representing all the interests of their members *vis à vis* the government. In accordance with this trend the Catholic and Socialist trade union movements have debated the possibility of breaking with the formal traditions of French labor that eschew direct participation in electoral activity. Even a wing of the Communist-dominated labor union, the C.G.T., has indicated an interest in finding means for increasing the influence of the working class within the existing society rather than waiting for the "great night" of revolution. While the day that sees the emergence of a "French Labor Party" is still far off, the first prerequisites for such a new political force are, perhaps, being slowly forged in these highly tentative efforts of French trade unions to participate directly in political competition.

Less hopeful a trend for the future of democratic processes was the increasing influence of the army over both political life and the government. De Gaulle's refusal to maintain by force French sovereignty over Algeria and his policy of negotiation with the Moslem rebels led to the creation of an alliance between activist army elements and extremist politicians. This new "military party" came to exert a power in France often as important as that of the traditional parties. Indeed, the army might well be in power in France today were it not for the countervailing personal influence over public opinion enjoyed by Charles de Gaulle. No realistic analysis of political forces operating in 1962 is complete unless an attempt is made to evaluate the power that is de Gaulle's by historical accident and that is as important as that of parties and ideologies deeply rooted in the evolution of French society. It should be noted once again, however, that neither the permanence of de Gaulle's personal influence, nor the rise of a politically minded trade union movement, nor the appearance of a military veto power would have been possible had not France's traditional multiparty politics declined in its hold upon opinion. This is, perhaps, the central fact of political life under the Fifth Republic.

Old Intermediaries: Parties and Pressure Groups

THE ORIGINS OF THE MULTIPARTY SYSTEM

Historical and Ideological Sources. The variety of political opinions in France is as long-standing as her governmental instability. But although this variety antedates the coming of parliamentarism, its responsibility for increasing instability was greatly heightened when the establishment of universal suffrage and the subsequent organization of mass parties brought public opinion directly into politics. In general, therefore, while French parties in their present form are of relatively recent origin, their ideas and their social bases developed during the nineteenth century. On the whole this is equally true of England, yet there only two major parties emerged, while multipartism developed in France. It is true that the British tend to approach political problems in a more pragmatic and empirical manner than do the French. This is not so much because the British shun all doctrine and ideology as because basic national purpose rests with them on such deep consensus that problems of policy can be approached pragmatically. France's lack of consensus, and hence her more sectarian and doctrinaire approach to politics, is, like Britain's consensus and pragmatism, the product of, first, a series of historical and political accidents, and second, certain social, cultural, and economic factors.

Long before the nineteenth century, English kings had sought, or had been forced to seek, the opinion of others in the making of governmental decisions. At first it had been only baronial councils, but by the late eighteenth century it had long been accepted that the king made his decisions "in parliament." While the British crown progressed continually toward greater self-limitation, the French monarchy in the early nineteenth century progressed just as steadily toward greater centralization of all political decisions in itself. Because policy was made by the king and his administration, it was unnecessary for opinion to be organized effectively by parties in order to alter the administration's views—which in all cases would prevail. Because of these situational factors political opinion became unrelated to policy making, and, in its irresponsibility, tended to disperse along lines having more to do with general ideas, social interests, and personality cliques than with the pros and cons of concrete policy. Even with the limited introduction of parliamentary government and the limited extension of the suffrage during the nineteenth century, French kings were reluctant to share their sovereignty. The French Prime Minister remained a personal agent of the royal will, unlike his British counterpart, who gradually became a true party leader, mustering the support of a majority in parliament to which he ultimately became responsible. In France the king viewed parliament as an institution of the political opposition and he saw in its growing divisions into groups a guarantee of his own supremacy. Thus a vicious circle was created: the office of Prime Minister in France had little independent power and therefore attracted few men of talent and leadership; because few such men became Prime Minister the office was not expanded and an executive power responsible to parliament, yet effective and stable, failed to develop.

As for the variety and abstractness of French political ideas, especially those of the Left, it must not be forgotten that they originated in a long and bloody revolution that attempted to destroy not merely a Government, or even a political regime, but a whole society. When it succeeded, many revolutionaries sincerely believed that they had wiped the slate clean and could begin constructing French society anew. Consequently, they set about devising plans and ideologies that dealt not simply with the immediate problems of the day, but with grandiose plans for remaking the intellectual, economic, and political life of the country along radically libertarian lines. Naturally those who opposed the revolution opposed it totally and adopted the mode of thought of the revolutionaries to do so. Thus royalists and conservatives in general rejected the fact of the revolution and urged a return to a divine-right monarchy even more illiberal than that which preceded the Revolution. They too sought in politics a means of totally revising society rather than simply meeting problems of the day. To complicate matters further, the Napoleonic experience introduced a new theory that combined authority with consent and a limited social equality. This was meant to be as total a substitute for revolutionary theory as revolutionary theory had sought to be for the monarchical tradition—indeed all the more so since it claimed to be a synthesis of the two!

Finally it must be noted that the revolutions of the nineteenth century and the uncertain future of the Third Republic during its early years all tended to nurture the hopes of partisans of the many political opinions that rejected the democratic republic. They were discouraged from compromise by the constant rise and fall of constitutions, and political crises such as the Dreyfus Affair. Thus France's chronic constitutional and political instability was a leading factor in the development of her many different political forces as well as being itself an effect of their multiplicity. The structure of political power in France, being multiple and varied, encouraged a sectarian and ideological style of politics. This in turn prevented an easy integration of political forces even when circumstances were favorable for unity among partisans of rival ideals of authority.

Social and Cultural Sources. It has been stated earlier that the most striking characteristic of French political institutions is that they are "unreformed," i.e., that they have not been adapted to changing conditions. In large part this is the consequence, as we have seen, of French society itself being unreformed. Of all the great powers France presents the largest number of outcroppings of past economic and social ages. By the end of the nineteenth century Britain and Germany were thoroughly industrialized while Russia was still very largely agricultural. But France, although largely agricultural, was already important industrially, and yet retained a large commercial and artisanal sector of its economy, representing a transitional stage of development. Moreover, the bulk of her agriculture was not of the extensive, mechanized type arising in Britain and the United States, but rather was based on a large number of small holdings, exploited by individual peasant families who used methods developed during the seventeenth and eighteenth centuries. Yet some of French agriculture was modern, extensive, and oriented toward success in the competitive world markets. Clearly the interests of this commercial agriculture would not always be the same as those of peasant agriculture.

Similarly France developed a few large, modern industries that operated alongside a majority of small family-owned plants that refused to modernize and amalgamate. Thus, again there occurred a subdivision of interests within a sector of the French economy: alongside a small group of progressive business men, whose productivity was high enough to allow them to make concessions to labor, was a large number of small businessmen whose high unit-cost of production prohibited a progressive wage policy if profit margins were to be maintained.

Finally, the slow progress of industrialization and a low birth rate preserved a distribution of goods and services based on a huge network of small shopkeepers and artisans. Without the pressure of a growing population there was no energy behind a reform of the distribution system. The shopkeepers and artisans shared no interests with either agriculture or industry; they felt that they were increasingly being deprived of their share in the national income by impersonal economic forces such as "big business" and "big labor."

In terms of political opinions, such a kaleidoscopic economic and social pattern produced a number of irreconcilable forces that, unable and unwilling to compromise, continued to prevent movement toward fewer and larger political groupings. First, there was a backward peasantry, tied to ancient production methods and having no more in common with any other group representing the producer's and property-owner's outlook in politics than a very general conservatism. Second, there was a large group of marginal nineteenth-century family businesses whose owners would not and could not form the core of a "reasonable" conservative party prepared to compromise with labor in order to increase productivity and profits. Nor were their interests rightly represented by the minority of dynamic modern businessmen whose high productivity allowed them to be more supple in dealing with labor. Third, there was a huge number of shopkeepers and artisans who, sensing that an evolving economy could bring them only disaster, readily supported antiparliamentary movements that seemed to give momentary promise of delaying if not upsetting the forces of progress. Fourth, there was a large industrial laboring class, totally alienated from a society in which forces such as those mentioned above had retained power and still set the style of values and customs. Unlike the working class in Britain, the French proletariat was a revolutionary class with a long history of conflict with "capitalism." While in England the workers' interests were generally represented by the middle-class Liberal party until the twentieth century, in France the workers and the middle class broke irrevocably in 1848. From then on they became the most violent enemies; consequently all hope was lost for associating the French worker with a "reasonable" reformist movement led by the liberal bourgeoisie.

Thus social and economic factors produced at least three types of conservatism—that of the peasant, the successful businessman, and the marginal businessman; and at least two kinds of progressives—the revolutionary worker and the middle-class reformer. It should be noted that the demands of each of these groups were conditioned more by their role in France's political culture than by an objective economic or social grievance. French and British small shopkeepers may both suffer from the growth of large chain stores. But it is only in France, with her Jacobin tradition of sympathy for the little man against the big and powerful organization, that the shopkeeper can become such a powerful political force. Although Pierre Poujade organized France's shopkeepers into an essentially reactionary movement, much of his success was due to an appeal to this ancient, leftist, Jacobin hatred for *les gros* (the fat ones).

In addition to these basic socioeconomic factors making for distinct, class-based parties, two other cultural factors further increased the number of possible party groups. For, beside divisions along social and economic lines, a serious division along philosophical lines was caused by the continued existence of the Catholic Church question. To this day it remains difficult for two shopkeepers to belong to the same party if one is a practicing Catholic and the other a Freemason and an anticlerical. The reason is that, although church and state were separated in 1905, the Catholic Church is still a partisan, political force for conservatism in the eyes of many Frenchmen. In 1789, of course, this was a fact, as it was during much of the following century when the Church openly supported anti-democratic and later anti-Republican parties and opinions. The Church is no longer solidly conservative, and indeed many individual Catholic leaders are among the most active reformers. Yet it cannot be denied that in the provinces, wherever the influence of the parish priest is strong, the resistance to progress is also strong. The fact that this is commonly due to the economic backwardness of the region and the inadequacy of secular state educational facilities is often not remembered, and the old image of an inherently conservative Church is preserved in the minds of many Frenchmen. Thus on all levels, from workers to businessmen, class and occupational interest is further subdivided by attitudes toward Catholicism.

Clearly, then, many French political parties are associated with a limited historical experience and with often obsolete social groups. Even when they no longer fulfill a real representational need for these groups, however, they often live on because their leaders want to retain them as personal vehicles, exploiting a purely emotional attachment in order to keep the parties alive. The vanity and self-importance of French political leaders has itself been an important influence in perpetuating the multi-party system. With two parties, only two men can be supreme party leaders and potential prime ministers; in a multiparty system, requiring coalition cabinets, the opportunities for top leadership are more numerous. This has been an important factor in preventing the success of most attempts to form permanent larger groups of the relatively small French parties.

THE FUNCTION OF FRENCH ELECTIONS

Beside voting on occasional referenda, Frenchmen go to the polls to elect directly their representatives in local assemblies and in the lower house of parliament, the National Assembly. Members of the upper house, it has been seen, are "indirectly" elected by a special college made up largely of the local assemblies and their delegates. These electors are usually party regulars or local notables, in both cases closely tied to economic or regional interests and, given the underrepresentation of urban areas, have generally a rural and conservative outlook. Consequently, Senatorial elections are rarely tests of the relative strength of political parties in the country at large. On the other hand, elections to the municipal councils and to the assemblies of the larger administrative unit, called the *département* (*conseils municipaux* and *conseils généraux*), are influenced mainly by relatively nonpolitical or at least strictly local issues. This, as well as the lack of any real autonomy on the part of these assemblies, makes public interest in local government elections very slight. Nonvoting is, therefore, traditionally widespread, thus further reducing their value as political barometers.

Electoral Traditions of the Past.   It is in elections to the National Assembly that the great formal tests between political parties take place. But in France these elections have never meant a direct popular choice between alternative Governments as they do in Britain. Nor do they create a direct circuit of responsibility between the Government and a majority in public opinion as do elections in Britain, the United States, and even Germany. An obvious reason for this is that no single French party has been able to amass a majority of the popular vote and hence take complete charge of the executive. It has not even been possible, in normal times, to create two national party coalitions because of the vastly differing relations between the parties from one constituency to another. Historically, moreover, French legislative elections have never had the function of producing a governing majority and thus directly naming a popularly responsible Government, as they do in the British parliamentary system. Rather, legislative elections still retain the purpose assigned to them during the Great Revolution: to select an assemblage of delegates that would check executive power or itself wield that power. The representative tradition of politics, rejecting the principle of an independent executive as undemocratic, viewed the only legitimate relationship between the two branches of government as one of legislative dominance. Although the 1958 constitution has eliminated this relationship in theory and practice, the nature of the party system, the style of electioneering, and the usual behavior of deputies have shown that the traditional function of legislative elections has not changed under the Fifth Republic. Moreover, although the Assembly today is no longer the central institution of the new political system, the Government is still responsible to a majority in the lower house, the composition of which obviously has an affect on the cabinet's make-up and on the fate of its legislative program.

Nor was there any place for elections producing governing majorities in the administrative tradition of politics. After the Revolution elections under the monarchies and empires of the nineteenth century were still not meant to evolve responsible Governments. Kings and Bonapartes excluded elected deputies from participating in the choice of the political executive. When the chief of state did not name all the Ministers personally, he chose a personally loyal Prime Minister who did and who was usually not responsible to any majority in parliament. Coupled with limited suffrage, this exclusion of parliament from a share in choosing the Government reduced the function of representation to insignificance, encouraged demagogic irresponsibility on the part of deputies who saw themselves purely as delegates of local interests, and convinced them, moreover, that henceforth they must seek to wield power directly.

Thus in neither the representative nor administrative ideal of authority was there room for the concept of an executive both responsible and independent. Hence the practice of elections that produced such executives did not develop. For partisans of the administrative tradition of politics, governing was the business of the king and his friends, and not a matter to be determined by a majority; for supporters of the representative tradition the executive was naturally an agent of tyranny, unnecessary once a sovereign assembly was elected to represent the public will. Elections came to be seen as simply the means of producing either a condensed substitute for popular sovereignty, or a delegation of notables, representing the various economic and social elite groups of the nation, whose docile presence in the capital served to attenuate the authoritarian appearance of royal or imperial rule.

The result of this electoral history was that when France suddenly received universal suffrage and representative government under the Third Republic, there existed no natural and tested system of elections that could link the popular will with the executive by means of a parliamentary majority. Instead there were a number of electoral systems that had been chosen by various rulers solely on the basis of their utility in producing a cooperative parliament, one having no real majority, thus no will of its own. One of these systems, perfected under Napoleon III's dictatorship, provided for single-member districts, with the seat going to the candidate who won a majority of the votes on a first balloting, or, failing that, to the candidate having simply the largest number of votes on a second balloting held one week later. The traditional multiplicity of parties excluded the use of the plurality vote criterion on the first ballot, as was possible in two-party systems like those of Britain and the United States. Moreover, Napoleon III found that the two ballotings afforded the Government an excellent opportunity for observing a free test of opinion in the first balloting, and then proceeding to the nomination of "official" candidates and an elimination of strong opposition candidates prior to the second balloting. It was this system essentially that the Third Republic employed for most of its elections from 1875 to 1940, although, to be sure, almost always without the intimidation and official candidacies between the ballotings.

The two-ballot majority system of the Third Republic did not facilitate the emergence of effective majorities. In most districts the first balloting simply served to set the odds on the various party combinations that could confront each other in the decisive second voting. Party diversity was thus encouraged, since various economic and social groups used the first balloting as a preliminary test run to measure the weight of each group organized as a party. Moreover, the system gave an advantage to the parties that were less encumbered with a formal doctrine and a national organization, since they were better able to take advantage of the bargaining that took place in the small local districts between the two ballotings. In consequence the system produced parliaments made up of deputies who had been elected by local party coalitions having little or no relevance to national issues. Nor were these deputies, once inside the Chamber, inclined to organize themselves in groups that reflected their electoral coalitions. From these arrangements it was the loose, largely programless center parties that profited most, for they alone could adopt any position dictated by local or parliamentary circumstances without risking accusations of doctrinal inconsistency.

During the Third Republic, therefore, the former manipulations of the emperor during the week between the ballotings were simply replaced by the manipulations of the local party bosses. The electoral system continued to encourage the party diversity and political irresponsibility that had existed under both traditions of French politics since the Revolution. And parliament, although elevated to the rank of the dominant branch of government, was unable to produce stable majorities. The founders of the Fourth Republic—Socialists (SFIO), Christian Democrats (MRP), and Communists—represented parties that had long opposed the traditional two-ballot electoral scheme. Not only did they consider it immoral, but they also knew that a system favoring center parties, organized locally and endowed with well-known personalities and professional cadres, would hardly help their new party machines, which were organized nationally and depended primarily on a national program and ideology rather than famous names. As a consequence a system of proportional representation (PR) was adopted in 1946 that favored large, nationally organized political parties such as the SFIO, the Communist party, and the MRP. It was claimed, of course, that such a system was also the fairest and the most honest, for it assured some representation to all shades of opinion, which a majority system definitely would not, and it furthermore eliminated the "deals" and obscure party bargaining which the two-ballot system had encouraged at the expense of purity of program. The new system, it was claimed, would thus never frustrate a true manifestation of the popular will.

By the end of the first legislature the Communists had passed into the opposition, and on the Right there appeared the powerful Gaullist opposition. Together these two dynamic movements threatened to attract such a large vote that no moderate majority would be possible. Therefore, on the eve of the new elections in 1951, the then center parties—SFIO, MRP, Independents, and Radicals—decided to alter the election law so as to make sure that the huge Communist-Gaullist popular vote would not be translated into a "negative" majority in the National Assembly. This was accomplished by permitting parties to make electoral alliances (*apparentements*) and giving these alliances all the seats of any constituency in which they won an absolute majority of the votes cast. Within such a winning alliance seats were allocated to individual party lists according to the 1946 version of PR. This new electoral system gave the center parties the opportunity to face the Gaullists and Communists as though the centrists were one unified party and to reduce the representation of these minority groups, as is done normally in plurality voting systems in the United States and Britain. The system worked as intended: the Communists won 71 fewer seats than they would have under the 1946 law, the Gaullists 26 fewer—enough in both cases to assure the center parties a slim but workable majority in the Assembly.

After the Liberation, the Resistance leaders had hoped that PR, party lists, and larger constituencies would help to stabilize and purify French politics by obliging the voter to choose party and program rather than personality and special promises. By creating an electoral system that favored large, nationally organized parties, moreover, it was hoped that the total number of French parties would be ultimately reduced. The experience of a decade showed these hopes to have been in vain. The number of parties was not reduced over the prewar figure and Government stability was not increased. Moreover, the alliances of 1951 reintroduced much of the bargaining and behind-the-scenes deals that PR was supposed to abolish. Yet cleavages between the parties became, if anything, more unbridgeable as a result of the extra power the list system gave to the doctrinaire national party organizations and their leaders. Finally, local issues still had a very potent influence notwithstanding the larger constituencies of the list system, for parties were careful to construct a "balanced ticket" that included representatives of all the regions of the department.

The Electoral System of the Fifth Republic. In September 1958 the approval of the new constitution automatically gave General de Gaulle the power to enact a new electoral law by decree. Long hostile to proportional representation, the General and his followers had always favored a majority system of voting, which they felt would be most likely to bring their movement to power, produce a coherent majority in parliament, and promote a more stable executive. But, as a predominantly urban political party, the Gaullists had strongly opposed the old prewar system of majority voting with its minuscule constituencies in which parochial local issues and local favorite sons had an advantage. Paradoxically, it was a modified version of precisely this system that de Gaulle personally decided upon, clearly against the wishes of his closest associates. The elections of November 1958, therefore, were run in single member constituencies, with the seat going to the candidate who won an absolute majority on the first ballot or, when no such candidate emerged, to the one having a simple plurality on the second ballot run a week later. (This system is called: *scrutin d'arrondissement, uninominal, majoritaire, à deux tours.*)

The new electoral procedure differed from that of the Third Republic, however, in at least two important ways. First, the new constituencies were larger, somewhat less favorable to rural interests, and not quite as gerrymandered as they had been in the past. Second, according to Article 25 of the constitution, candidates had to print under their own names on the ballot the name of a "substitute" (*remplaçant*), a person who would automatically take their seat if, after election, they were named Minister, died, or were appointed to other high public office incompatible with a legislative mandate. If a deputy resigned, and in all other cases of vacancy, by-elections remained necessary. The voting age was left at 21, the age for eligibility as a candidate stayed at 23, and deputies still held office for a maximum of five years. To discourage frivolous candidacies a deposit of 1000 New Francs ($200) was required, to be returned, however, to those who polled at least 5 per cent of the votes cast. The latter were also reimbursed by the government for a limited amount of printing expenses, but the bulk of campaign funds had to be raised individually or by the parties. The use of the state-owned radio and television network for campaign speeches was carefully regulated by law: only parties presenting at least 75 candidates could use its facilities. Many of the smaller parties, consequently, endorsed candidates simply in order to reach the requisite number allowing one of their national leaders to address the nation for five minutes at a time on a number of occasions.

De Gaulle's motives for choosing a single-member, majority system were very significant, for on the face of it this voting procedure seemed to favor traditional, anti-Gaullist parties having ancient local roots, and certainly not the relatively unknown candidates of the Gaullist party, the Union for the New Republic. All indications in the fall of 1958 pointed to a huge electoral victory for those parties that seemed to the electorate as most loyal to the General. The only clearly opposition parties were the Communists and small splinter parties that had left the Radicals and the Socialists, who, in majority, also proclaimed their loyalty to de Gaulle. The Gaullist Union for the New Republic (UNR) seemed destined to be the big winner, especially, as experts thought, if it could make coalition lists with the conservatives. This, of course, was central to the system favored by the Gaullists but rejected by the General. Since such a result appeared to condemn the center parties and the non-Communist Left to a severe election defeat, de Gaulle chose the system that was most likely, according to the experts, to save as many of the Socialist, Radical, and MRP candidates as possible. For, desirous of maintaining his role as a non-partisan arbitrator, the General did not want to be the captive of those parties which had been most vociferous in supporting him or even of the party that had done the most to bring about his return to power. He wished to remain a balancer of forces, free to disavow parties and policies when and if a change in circumstances placed these parties and policies in opposition to the national interest as he saw it.

As it turned out, de Gaulle's attempt to create a more balanced Assembly failed, for so great was his prestige that the Gaullist UNR candidates, identified with his name, swept the field and unseated most of the veteran leaders of the traditional parties. Thus of the 537 incumbent deputies who contested seats in 1958, only 131 were returned by the voters; 265 were beaten, creating thereby a turnover of political leadership exceeded in France only by the elections of 1945. The thirst for new blood, moreover, reduced the average age of the new Assembly from 52 to 49 and vastly increased the number of businessmen and white-collar employees among the deputies. The voting proved that if a national current of opinion was strong enough even an electoral system that favored local issues and candidates could not stem the tide. (See Figure 2)

The 1958 elections, therefore, came close to creating a governing majority and even something resembling a governing party, both of which the representative tradition of politics feared, because they threatened to legitimize a strong executive, and the administrative tradition also feared, because they threatened to limit the executive's liberty of action. For precisely this reason, as shall be seen below, de Gaulle—faithful to the administrative tradition—has resisted the UNR's pretentions to the status of a governing party. The election, furthermore, revealed that the social trends favoring a simplification of the French multiparty system could someday result in the emergence of a genuine majority party or at least a stable majority

FIGURE 2.   Approximate Party Strengths in the National Assembly
(Deputies for metropolitan France)

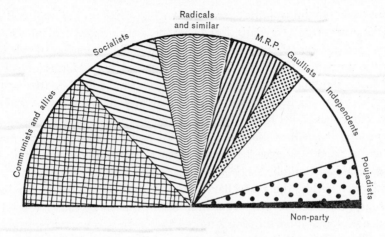

The last Assembly of the Fourth Republic, elected January 2, 1956

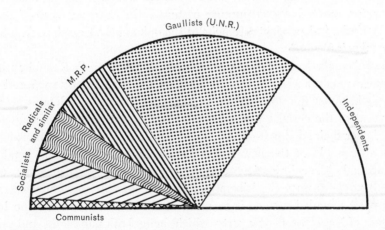

The first Assembly of the Fifth Republic, elected November 23 & 30, 1958

coalition. When this does occur French elections will at last have the
same function elections have in all effective democratic political systems:
the direct designation of a Government by the voters and the creation,
thereby, of a circuit of responsibility between the two of them. Until that
time, however, French elections must remain a process for designating the
delegates of France's varying political divisions, periodically demonstrating the relative strengths of parties, which, of course, are only one category
of political forces.

Major Parties

The Independents and Peasants Party (Centre National des Indépendants et Paysans). Known generally as "the Independents," this is the party representing traditional conservatism. It is essentially a national electoral machine grouping the Paris leadership of conservative movements and supported by rural France and the old-fashioned elements of the business community. The party is strongly opposed to all forms of government intervention in economic affairs except for subsidies to marginal industries and high tariffs for agricultural and manufactured products. The party has consistently fought attempts to reform the tax system by making it produce more revenue from personal income taxes, and it naturally opposes increases in governmental expenditures, except in the cases of aid to Catholic schools and the military establishment. Although a minority within the party has professed a liberal attitude in colonial matters and sees in European unification the modern-day version of France's international "mission," most Independents have continued to oppose every effort at "decolonization," especially in Algeria. But this much-touted nationalism has rarely been reflected in a willingness to pay the price for restored world prestige in any other currency than rhetoric. In brief, the Independents are heirs to the opinion the French usually term the "classic Right."

This is the only party closely associated with the Fourth Republic whose popularity substantially increased between the elections of 1956 and the first held under the new regime. In 1958 Independent candidates won 20 per cent of the popular vote on the first ballot—an increase of fully one-third over their 1956 poll—and 117 of them joined the party group during the early weeks of the new Assembly. The success of the Independents was actually the culmination of a slow but steady rise in favor of conservative candidates since the Liberation. Their victory in 1958, however, was the more remarkable since it occurred at the same time as did the huge victory of the UNR, a new party, which, being both nationalist and popularly identified as closest to de Gaulle, could have been expected to cut into the regular conservative vote. It seems that the increase of Independent votes was made at the expense of center parties such as the Radicals and the MRP, which, by and large, appeared to resist the general desire for constitutional reform. Still strongly supported by the kind of rural conservative notables who dominate the electoral college of the Senate, it is not surprising that the Independents should have maintained their rank as the largest party in the upper house. At the indirect elections of 1959 over ninety Senators with Independent endorsement were elected, a slight improvement over their position in the last years of the Fourth Republic.

The former Secretary General of the Independents, Roger Duchet, has been responsible for this more militant and doctrinaire orientation, in both domestic and Algerian affairs. It was he who swung the party behind de Gaulle in 1958 when he sensed that the Fourth Republic's days were numbered, and it was he who swung the majority into unofficial alliance with the ultranationalists and army officers who during the early years of the Fifth Republic opposed de Gaulle's policy of self-determination for Algeria. Ranged against him was a more liberal minority, generally representing modern business with international ties and thus especially fearful of the American reaction to a Government of the extreme right in France. While it was this minority faction that was represented by three ministers in the Debré Government, much of its influence among the party rank and file has declined, and its veteran leader, the prewar Prime Minister Paul Reynaud, resigned from the party's executive committee in protest against Duchet's attacks on de Gaulle and his Algerian policy. Antoine Pinay, the party's most popular leader in the last years of the previous regime, is today in temporary retirement after having been forced to resign from the Debré Government in 1960 because of his opposition to de Gaulle's foreign and economic policies. Although formerly considered a moderate conservative, Pinay has carefully avoided close identification with either faction of his party in recent months and is thought by all conservatives, including the ultraconservatives, as the most likely successor to de Gaulle as President.

The strategy of the Independents has been to combine an attack on de Gaulle's liberal Algerian policy as insufficiently "national", with sharp criticism of his rule as a "technocratic dictatorship." In this way they hoped to maintain their lines to the ultranationalists among the army and its allies, who as the most dynamic enemies of the regime might bring about its sudden collapse, and also to the center parties and the old Republic's politicians, who might easily be the ultimate receivers of an army-supported succession regime that inevitably went bankrupt. It is this sort of accident that now offers the Independents their only hope for a brief return to power, for the rapid growth of modern business, the decline of rural voting strength, and the competition from the Gaullist UNR promise to eclipse this old conservative party. The slow recognition of this trend against them has driven a once moderate and thoroughly parliamentary movement into ever more direct cooperation with anti-constitutional and extreme nationalist forces.

The Christian Democratic Party or MRP (Mouvement Républicain Populaire). Unlike the Independents, the MRP is highly organized and has a well-defined doctrine, at least on paper. It is heir to the vigorous political tradition of liberal Catholicism and in particular the movement known throughout Europe as Christian Democracy. While practicing Catholics who vote for the Independents are likely to be farmers or conservative businessmen, those who vote for the MRP are usually professional people, white-collar workers, and civic-minded business executives. Although their official doctrine is critical of free enterprise, the MRP under the Fourth Republic usually supported the same conservative policies as did the Independents. Yet historical memories of the long prewar struggle against the antidemocratic, traditional French conservatism, and the desire of its members to differentiate themselves from the backward-looking Independents, have prevented the MRP from being happy in alliance with the "classic Right." The party, as well as the leadership, was formed in a schism from the old Catholic conservatism and during the occupation they were openly hostile to the Vichy regime, whose last defenders are among the present-day Independents. Moreover, Christian Democracy's interest in the social message of the Church is sincere and clashes with what they consider the coldly antisocial outlook of most French conservatives.

It has been the revival of nationalism that has led them to make a modest move back to the liberalism of their origins. Still committed to European unity, eager for a negotiated peace in Algeria, anxious over the influence of the army in the new regime, and increasingly influenced by young and dynamic liberal Catholics from the Christian trade unions and the farmer movements, the MRP has become under the Fifth Republic the most conservative of the liberal parties rather than the most liberal of the conservatives, as it was under the preceding regime. This shifting position has allowed them to maintain, indeed actually improve very slightly, their popular vote—about 12 per cent on the first ballot in 1958, with 56 deputies joining their group in the Assembly, which had stood at 70 in 1956. The sharp decline in representation is due partly, of course, to the smaller size of the Fifth Republic's lower chamber. But partly it is the work of the new electoral law that assured the MRP seats in only those areas where it had strong local candidates who were also recognized by the voters as "new men," untarnished by Fourth Republic reputations and well-liked for local leadership qualities. With losses to the Independents and the UNR in nationalist Alsace and Western France, the party maintained its position only by its new support in areas where Catholic Action organizations had worked in its favor. In the Senate, however—and for the same reasons it lost seats in the Assembly—the MRP actually improved the percentage of its membership. The 34 Senators it elected in the indirect elections of 1959 represent 11 per cent of the total, while during the last years of the Fourth Republic the MRP share of the upper house attained only 8 per cent.

Under the Fifth Republic the MRP was a reluctant, though generally loyal participant in the Debré Government's majority, with three of its members as Ministers. But like the Independents the party's militants and leadership have increasingly criticized both the policies and the autocratic mode of governing of de Gaulle and his Prime Minister. Unlike the traditional conservatives, however, their complaints have centered on the slowness with which de Gaulle was proceeding to a negotiated peace in Algeria. They also wanted the Government to engage itself more thoroughly in the cause dearest to their hearts as Christian Democrats—the economic, and ultimately political, unity of Europe. Consequently, when a cease-fire in Algeria was finally signed, the MRP indicated its approval by increasing to five its Ministerial participation in the Pompidou Government that succeeded the Debré Government in April 1962. But the next month it proved its continued attachment to European integration by ordering the five MRP Ministers to leave the Government following a press conference at which de Gaulle vigorously criticized the party's mystique of a European "supranationality." No longer represented in the cabinet, the MRP continues to be within the Pompidou Government's parliamentary majority, expecting thus to appeal to both pro and anti Government sentiment in public opinion.

The titular head of the party is its President the deputy André Colin, but its principal spokesman and real leader is the Alsatian deputy, Pierre Pflimlin. It was he who, as Prime Minister in May 1958, first resisted the army and settlers' coup that championed de Gaulle's return to power, and then recommended that de Gaulle be legally invested as his successor by the National Assembly. Situated closest to the opposition, although within the Government's majority, the MRP has room for maneuver should new elections bring a more left-oriented majority to power. While it has not engaged in official talks with its former Socialist and Radical allies, the party's thoroughly centrist position, and the good personal relations its leaders have with this opposition, assure it a role in any future coalition not dominated by either of the extremes.

The Radical Socialist Party (Parti Républicain Radical et Radical Socialiste). The Radical party has always been a party of personalities with strong local attachments, loosely organized and barely committed to a program or doctrine. The only constant in its policies has been anticlericalism, and even that gave signs of disappearing under the Fourth Republic when the party was often allied with the Independents on economic and social issues. In these matters the Radicals have been generally conservative, except for the brief period late in the Fourth Republic when their former leader, Pierre Mendès-France, urged them to support government intervention to foster reconversion of backward sectors of the French economy. But because of its emotional loyalty to the ideals of the Great

Revolution, and its rock-bound opposition to the Catholic church, the party has never been comfortable in coalition with the MRP, or, especially, with the Independents. The Radicals remain the lineal descendents of the "radical" wing of the nineteenth century liberalism which championed political democracy, civil liberties, separation of church and state, and basic social reforms—all achieved before World War I. The decline in influence of the small town middle class and the farm population in general, the social bases of this political tradition, has also seen the decline in the strength of the Radical party. Yet between 1906 and 1940 the party was one of the most powerful in France, being the "hinge" group in most coalitions, the element without which a Government could not be formed. This reputation as the principal Government party of the discredited Third Republic also did much to weaken its hold on the electorate in the postwar period.

The coming of the Fifth Republic has almost completed the job of eclipsing the Radical party. Along with the victory of the Gaullist UNR and the sharp decline of the Communist party, this is the most important revelation of the 1958 elections. From roughly 13 per cent of the vote in 1956, the Radicals and the small groups associated with them fell to 8 per cent on the first ballot and to less than 5 per cent on the second ballot in November 1958. Almost a million former Radical voters turned to other parties or abstained from voting. Even more significant was the wholesale elimination of Radicals from the new Assembly: from fifty-odd deputies in 1956, only thirteen true Radicals were elected in 1958. Adding to this figure the representatives of the splinter groups of former Radicals, the total number who could in any way qualify as Radicals came to no more than forty, about half the total of all Radicals two years before. Like the MRP, however, their well-established local positions helped them to maintain, and indeed slightly improve, their percentage of members in the upper house. Favoring parties entrenched in rural and small-town France, the indirect elections to the Senate in 1959 raised Radical membership to over 16 per cent of that body, far in excess of its percentage in the popularly elected lower house.

Paradoxically the virtual eclipse of Radicalism as a political force occurred under precisely the electoral system which that party had long campaigned for under the Fourth Republic, when proportional representation had been the rule. The Radicals were convinced that, as under the Third Republic, their well-known local leaders and their central position between parties of the left and right would promote Radical victories in a two-ballot majority system in small constituencies. What they did not recognize before the 1958 elections was that the sudden rise of nationalism and the popular desire for institutional reform would work toward canceling out such historical calculations and indeed make them appear as the politicians most identified with the old system of politics and hence the great loser. Even Mendès-France, who had tried to change the public "image" of Radicalism by vainly attempting to revitalize the party and give it a new reformist program, suffered an amazing electoral defeat in a rural constituency he had held continuously since 1932. The reason, obviously, was his opposition to de Gaulle. In the same elections there occurred the total elimination of Radical deputies from the Paris region and in the East, areas long closed to the party but that had voted Radical when Mendès-France gave the party an ephemeral reputation of dynamism.

Many of the Radical party's outstanding leaders have deserted to small splinter groups in the wake of the internal crises that rocked the party in the last years of the Fourth Republic. The more conservative among them left in reaction to Mendès-France's attempt to pull the party to the left, while Mendès-France himself left in reaction to both the party's reluctance to follow him and its support for de Gaulle in the first year of the new regime. As a consequence, the party is now in the hands of a young and centrist leadership, quite different from the aging veterans who led the party in the past. The president is currently Maurice Faure, a youthful deputy whose passion for European unity can be expected to urge the party into closer alliance with both the MRP and the Socialists. Other influential party leaders include two young former Prime Ministers, the deputy Felix Gaillard and the Senator Edgar Faure. The president of the party took the Debré Government to task for a foreign policy that he considered insufficiently European and for the slowness with which the Algerian problem was being resolved. At its 1961 congress the Radical party emphasized its role as protector of farm interests in order to maintain if not regain its power over the still important farm vote. Since 1960, when the party lost its official representative in the Debré Government, the Radicals have been formally in the opposition while making it quite clear, in good Radical style, that this opposition was far from immutable. They have, however, increased their criticism of both the regime and its policies in order to remain abreast of the protests of the agricultural interests, which have always represented an important segment of their electorate. Given the slow decline of these interests in a rapidly industrializing France, the Radicals can hold little hope for the future, notwithstanding their new and young leaders. In truth, the only novelty about them as Radicals is simply their youthfulness.

The Socialist Party or SFIO (Parti Socialiste—Section Française de l'Internationale Ouvrière). Formally, the French Socialist party is still in favor of the collectivization of all means of production according to Marxist principles. In fact, however, the party has for many years sought simply to reform French capitalism so that a more equal distribution of the national income may be achieved. It is strongest in the industrial North, where workers in the smaller factories still vote socialist, and in urban areas among the personnel of the nationalized industries, among teachers in all parts of the country, and among white-collar workers. The party organization is powerful and highly bureaucratized, although its membership has remained fairly limited ever since the Communists challenged it for leadership of the working class. From the postwar record of 335,000 regular members in 1945, the number dropped to 120,000 ten years later, to 83,000 in 1959, and to but 79,000 in 1960.

Unlike the Radicals, the Socialists maintained their popular vote in November 1958 at 15 per cent on the first ballot, but like them they also suffered heavy losses among their most famous parliamentary leaders and their representation in general. Only forty-seven deputies joined the Socialist group in the new Assembly, about half the number that were members under the last legislature of the Fourth Republic. Like the Radicals, the Socialists were victims of the new electoral law that encouraged normal socialist voters to vote for the most popular non-Communist candidate on the second ballot—in most cases the Gaullist. In the Senatorial elections of 1959 the Socialists' generally strong local organization allowed them to maintain their position at roughly 16 per cent of the membership.

Actually, the Socialist party, like the MRP, did not suffer as much as could have been expected, given the strong tide against parties identified with the old regime. This is primarily due to the shrewd leadership of its veteran Secretary-General, Guy Mollet. Sensing the new current of nationalism as early as 1956, Mollet refused to follow Mendès-France into an intransigent loyalty to their electoral promises of that year. Indeed, rather than resisting the nationalist current as a good socialist, he actually encouraged it. It was, moreover, under Mollet's Government of 1956-57 that the policy of military "pacification" in Algeria was fully developed and the decision originally taken to reject a negotiated peace. Then in May 1958 when he saw that the Pflimlin cabinet could not master the Army revolt, he supported both the Government and the constitution of General de Gaulle—a man whom he had fought bitterly since the Liberation but who he now realized was both the popular choice and the only alternative to a military dictatorship.

Indeed, it might well be said that Mollet and the Socialist party were the keys to de Gaulle's return to power. For had Mollet not persuaded a majority of his colleagues to vote for the General's investiture, the latter could not have been elected Premier legally—the condition he had set for saving the country from a military dictatorship. This, of course, in no way prevented Mollet from reversing himself in the fall of 1958 and leading his party into a highly subtle opposition after the elections: support for de Gaulle as President of the Republic and for the Debré Government on foreign and Algerian policy, but loyal opposition to the Debré Government on domestic matters. Mollet's opportunism has resulted in the loss of a few of the more left-wing and anti-Gaullist leaders of the party, as well as a few local party federations, to a new splinter organization called the United Socialist Party. But at present the party has maintained remarkably well its hold over a small body of militants and a fairly large number of local office holders, especially in the agricultural south. Indeed, at the local elections of June 1961 the party improved its over-all representation in the departmental councils, in part reflecting the popularity of the new total-opposition line adopted by Guy Mollet the year before.

For as popular opposition to the Debré Government grew over its economic and agricultural policies, its hesitations over making peace in Algeria, and its generally authoritarian style, the Socialist leader Guy Mollet sensed that it was time to lead his party once again into a more intransigent phase. Declaring his opposition to both de Gaulle and the Debré Government's policies, Mollet covered his flanks by appeasing the remaining left-wing of his party. Then as disaffection from the regime arose in 1961 and talk of new elections was heard, Mollet prepared for the usual swing of the pendulum of political opinion by engaging in strategy talks with other opposition parties of the non-Communist left and calling for a vague union of "democratic" forces. There is nothing to indicate that the Socialists will be the victors in forthcoming elections, or even the organizers of an opposition electoral alliance, though for the moment they are the most important party of the parliamentary opposition to de Gaulle and Debré. Yet the future of the non-Communist Left probably remains in the hands of the SFIO whose organization and electorate is still intact, if not flourishing. They have the great asset of a realistic, if uninspiring and opportunistic leader, who has shown remarkable ability in keeping his party in line with changes in French public opinion.

The Communist Party (Parti Communiste Français). The Communist party represents the revolutionary Left in France. This, of course, is an ancient and respected French political tradition, dating from the Revolution of 1789 and from the brutally suppressed workers' uprisings of 1848 and 1871. The revolutionary Left existed in France long before the Soviet revolution of 1917 and the founding of the French Communist party in 1920. As a consequence, many of the Frenchmen who vote Communist are really expressing attachment to an old, home-grown political tradition that today happens to be, in their estimation, best represented by the Communist party. The typical Communist voter is a factory worker, probably in a fairly large, heavy industry and living in or around a city. Somewhat less frequently a Communist vote is cast by a poor farmer or peasant in the backward and mountainous center of the country, an area that has always voted far Left in protest against its low standard of living. The party itself is a highly centralized machine that operates under central direction resembling an army's general staff. Maurice Thorez, although ailing, is still supreme boss, and Jacques Duclos, the party's parliamentary leader, is his chief lieutenant.

Most vigorous in its opposition to de Gaulle and the nationalist current that brought him back to power, the French Communist party registered a loss of 30 per cent of its voters at the 1958 elections. Less than 19 per cent of the electorate cast Communist votes on the first ballot, a proportion smaller than at any election since 1936, and far below the high-water mark of French Communism in November 1946 when the party received almost 29 per cent of the vote. As for its representation in the Assembly, the effect of the new electoral system and the tactics of the non-Communist parties combined with the nationalist tide to all but eliminate Communist deputies from the lower chamber. From 144 deputies in 1956, or roughly one quarter of the total number, the party has fallen to the almost ridiculously small number of 10—about 2 per cent of the present number of deputies. Under the two-ballot system a Communist could get elected only if he had an absolute majority on the first ballot or was able to attract enough normally non-Communist voters or abstainers in order to give him a plurality on the second ballot. As it was, only one Communist won by the first method and only nine were successful in breaking through the anti-Communist barrier created by the other parties, which invariably urged their first-ballot voters to cast their vote for the non-Communist candidate who was best placed to win a plurality on the second ballot—and this irrespective of that candidate's party or program. Thanks to its strong position in a few municipalities, the Party maintained its small percentage of membership in the Senate, which allowed some of its leadership to remain in parliament.

An analysis of the Communist vote shows that its decline was as general throughout France as was its sudden rise after the Liberation. The size of its losses was roughly the same in the industrial North as in the agricultural South and, amazingly enough, at least 800,000 of its former voters turned in 1958 to the Gaullist party—long the bitterest enemy of the Communist party. The remainder of the party's decline from its 1956 total must be accounted for by the massive nonvoting of normally Communist voters. For many Communists who could not bring themselves to vote for de Gaulle's party found that they could not bring themselves to vote against the prestigious Liberator and wartime hero.

The primary cause of this huge defeat in November 1958 is clearly the fact that for the average Communist voter—who, it should be remembered, is not a member of the party—de Gaulle's prestige and the promise he represented of a break with the men and policies of the Fourth Republic proved to be more influential than the party's propaganda. Of importance also was the isolation of the Communists as a result of their attitude at the time of the Hungarian uprising of 1956. Many non-Communist leftists who disliked voting for a nationalist candidate found it less difficult to do so than to cast their second ballot for a defender of Soviet repression even when the Communist was the leftist who had the most votes and hence could win the seat on the second ballot. Finally, the rise in many French workers' standard of living since 1954 had undoubtedly reduced the extent of protest voting for the party. This had already been indicated by a slow decline in the membership of the party's main pressure group, France's largest trade union, the General Confederation of Labor.

In the face of these changes neither the organization nor the leadership nor the doctrine of the party has altered—which has undoubtedly contributed to the decline of the movement's popularity. The most important internal changes have been involuntary ones, brought about by the evolution in the outlook and the structure of the working class. Thus, besides a drop in the party members, there has been a continued aging of the membership, with a decline in both the recruitment of young Frenchmen below thirty and the renewal of membership cards of those who do join briefly. It would seem that the general nationalist current, always strong among French youth, has taken its toll on the Communist troops, as has general French prosperity. Before another general election has taken place it will be difficult to tell whether or not these trends will continue to harm the party. The fact that the party regained its traditional quarter of the electorate in the municipal elections of March 1959 is both a tribute to the usually excellent local Communist administration and a protest against the then recently announced reduction of welfare benefits and food subsidies—rather than proof that the 1958 trends had been reversed. From all appearances the evolution of French society is working against the fortunes of Communism.

The trends of 1958 were confirmed by the voting in the referendum of January 1961 when again de Gaulle's personal prestige drew a good number of normally Communist voters away from the party's opposition attitude toward both the man and his Algerian policy. Later in the year Waldeck-Rochet, the new heir apparent to Thorez, the ailing party boss, announced that party membership was down to 407,000 from 425,000 in 1959 and 430,000 in 1956. Unofficial and more objective estimates place the number of regular members at somewhat more than 150,000, of which at least a fifth are paid party functionaries. This steady decline in membership is principally due to the disappearance of many factory cells in the rapidly expanding modern industries, thus supporting the argument that a changing society is dooming the party in the long run. At the same time the party continues to undergo a long internal crisis resulting from an attempt by a number of minor leaders and Communist intellectuals to steer Thorez and the top leadership away from its traditional Stalinist rigidity and its unwillingness to recognize the relevancy of changes in both the structure of French capitalism and the working class.

Why then does the Communist party remain the largest organized bloc of French political opinion, especially now that prosperity has affected all levels of the population? Undoubtedly the reason for the party's organizational success, and hence its still imposing electoral power, is the fact that it is ever-present in all the activities of French society that impinge on the working class. It is thus able to give a constant and concrete demonstration of interest in the worker's everyday concerns by practical accomplishment as well as ideological argument. Thus when other parties talk of lowering consumer prices the Communist party has actually gone out and organized cooperatives for selling goods cheaply to their members. It has provided legal aid against landlords who seek to evict workers, organized sports and youth programs for underprivileged families, and has often been the first to protest against lockouts and reductions in force by employers. In short, the party does many of the things that the old fashioned, big-city machines used to do in American politics to "buy" the votes of the poor by tangible, not verbal, activity. Indeed, the analogy is especially apt, for one could argue that, had France ever experienced a real reform period in her recent history, the essentially demagogic machine control of the Communist party over the lower classes in France would today be as weak as the control by the big-city machines in the United States.

Few students of French politics today will insist that the future of the Communist party is secure. The best it can hope for now is a military coup against de Gaulle or the coming to power of a reactionary Government after de Gaulle's departure from power, both of which would generate a widespread left reaction within which the party might regain some of its declining influence. For the moment, with the prospect of forthcoming elections the party is trying to leave the isolation that cost it so dearly in the last elections. Under the two-ballot majority system now in effect, local electoral alliances are vital among generally like-minded parties in order to get the maximum benefit from the popular vote. But the party's past record assures it of only the most limited success in negotiations with the non-Communist Left, unless the threat of a right-wing coup re-creates the historical reflex of "republican defense."

The Gaullist Party: Union for the New Republic or UNR (Union pour la Nouvelle République). The nationalist tradition in France has always been a broad one, including left-wing movements like the Radical party of the early Third Republic, as well as partisans of authoritarian reaction like the royalist and antiparliamentary leagues of the interwar period and the more recent party of Pierre Poujade. Although it has usually been conservative groups that have been the most vociferously nationalist since the establishment of the Third Republic, often this was meant mainly to provide a more popular and appealing cover to their essentially conservative or even reactionary ends—as was indeed the case with Poujade. Nationalist parties first flourished in France on the prevailing feelings of inferiority and national decay that followed the German victory in 1870. At the turn of the century and in the period between the world wars there were similar periods when Frenchmen became conscious of their country's relative loss of prestige. Then, as in recent years, nationalist groups chose France's inffective parliamentary government as the main scapegoat. They have, therefore, shared with conservatives a common reverence for the strong executive, the organ of state power that all nationalists believe to be the key to the restoration of national prestige, and that all conservatives believe is vital for the preservation of order and the social status quo.

Unlike conservatives and reactionaries, French nationalists are often quite willing to have the strong executive used to improve the living standards of the lower classes and thereby cement national unity. Present-day cleavages within the Gaullist UNR and between the latter and the conservative Independents stem from precisely this ancient source of irritation. Similarly, suspicion of the reformist aims of the Gaullists as well as hostility to those of their constitutional ideas that maintain the essentials of representative government have forced many extreme rightists like Poujade into the opposition to de Gaulle, thereby reducing their influence completely. Paradoxically, therefore, the return to popularity of the general nationalist current may lead to the decline of antiparliamentary opinion, its place being taken by more moderate groups. The new Gaullist party, the Union for the New Republic, hopes to fill just this position of a moderate nationalist movement, situated roughly in the center of the political spectrum, and committed to an essentially governing vocation. Whether or not it will succeed in these aspirations is far from certain.

Founded by the followers of General de Gaulle, the UNR was the great victor in the 1958 elections and the first French party to approach a majority position in the lower chamber since the late nineteenth century. It is a lineal descendant of the small Gaullist party of the Fourth Republic's last years, the Social Republicans (*Centre National des Républicains Sociaux*), as well as of the large Gaullist movement of earlier years, the Rally of the French People or RPF (*Rassemblement du Peuple Français*). Indeed, most of its leaders, candidates, and militants were members of both these parent groups. Organized Gaullism was launched by de Gaulle in 1947 as a constitutional reform movement, but while very successful at the 1951 elections it was not powerful enough to unseat the center parties from their control of the Fourth Republic. After de Gaulle retired from politics, his followers formed a small party that continued to press for constitutional and social reforms, notably within the Mendès-France government of 1954-55. But they also stressed their nationalism and their intransigence in retaining France's overseas holdings and keeping Algeria French. When the nationalist current swept France after 1956, the Gaullists became its vigorous champions while at the same time calling for a return to power of de Gaulle. It was understandable, therefore, that in 1958 it should be the Gaullists who would profit most from both the massive popular confidence in the General as well as the continued popular desire for national revival and political reform.

However, no one, including the Gaullists, foresaw the magnitude of their 1958 electoral victory—a veritable extension of de Gaulle's personal victory in the referendum of September. With only the scantiest organization in the provinces, the UNR polled an amazing figure for a new party. The share was 18 per cent of the electorate on the first ballot, expanded to 28 per cent on the second ballot, thanks to the massive transfer of votes from the traditional center parties. This was a far cry from the 4 per cent the Gaullists had been able to win in the 1956 elections. Like the losses of the Communist party, the huge gains of the Gaullists were general all over France. Over one third of France's ninety departments gave the party at least 30 per cent of the vote—and this in every region of the country. Unlike its predecessors, the new Gaullist party was as popular in the rural South as in the urban North, due largely to gains from the Poujadist and Radical losses. About one quarter of the UNR vote came from formerly Communist voters while a large amount came from Frenchmen who in their disgust for the politics of the Fourth Republic had never bothered to vote before. As the party most clearly identified with the new tide of nationalism and the desire for a general political house-cleaning, the UNR fell heir to the two million floating votes that had made the successes of previous champions of national revival such as the RPF, Poujade, and Mendès-France.

The 206 deputies who formed the first UNR group in the Assembly were ten times as numerous as the Gaullists in the last Assembly of the Fourth Republic. By 1960 the group had actually grown by a dozen or so new members, either victors in by-elections or refugees from the group of members for Algerian constituencies whose support of de Gaulle's policy in Algeria made their position untenable among the extremists of that group. Thus there now exists a French political party with both a governing vocation and a near-majority representation in the lower house, a development that could ultimately be almost as significant as the adoption of the new constitution. For if the UNR remains united, and if it improves its original popular vote, it could be the initiator of a polarization of political forces in France that would reduce the ancient multiplicity of parties and produce a simplified party system such as that of Germany and Italy, if not a two party system along British lines.

Three years of organizing experience and service as the leading party in the Debré Government's majority, however, have produced only modest evidence that the UNR has initiated this process or even assured its permanence as a center party with a governing vocation in the tradition of the prewar Radicals. While contrary to all predictions the UNR parliamentary groups have in fact maintained their unity, the party has been less successful in putting down roots in the provinces or in producing outstanding new leaders. Its small group of 44 members in the Senate—less than either the MRP or Radical groups—reflects this poverty of organizational strength in rural and small-town France, since the electors of the upper house are precisely the kind of local politicians the UNR has failed to win to its colors. True, in the local elections of June 1961 the number of departmental councilors elected on UNR tickets gave some hope that at last the UNR was beginning to be accepted by the provinces. By-election victories of totally unknown UNR candidates against familiar political figures also have testified to the drawing power of the party label, although this is probably due more to public recognition that the party is the most loyal supporter of General de Gaulle than to the attractiveness of the party's program or leadership. Yet for a party that polled close to four million votes, a membership of perhaps fifty thousand is not very impressive. And the fact that its most active sections are still merely rejuvenated remnants of the old RPF organization, loyal to the Gaullist mystique, indicates how superficial is their hold on the electorate that supported them in 1958.

Sociologically, Gaullist candidates and deputies were similar to the party's militants and to many of their voters. They were largely without previous experience in political office, having been drawn from among businessmen, engineers, shopkeepers, the liberal professions, and the middle range of white-collar workers. Their average age was 46, lower than that of the average deputy, and most of them were urban in both origins and present employment. Neither the working class nor the peasantry was really represented among them, but five of the eight career army officers who became deputies in 1958 were elected on the UNR ticket. A high percentage of them had been active in the wartime Resistance movement and most of them had been members of the RPF. In a word, the UNR represented precisely those social and economic groups that in recent years had become most sensitive to the gap between France's potential and her mediocre status among the world powers.

Since de Gaulle refused to have any direct role in the founding or organizing of the party, the leadership remained collective for the first year or so. It was shared by a moderate faction, led by a young financier named Albin Chalandon and the Gaullist President of the Assembly, Jacques Chaban-Delmas; and a more intransigently nationalist wing led by Jacques Soustelle and Léon Delbecque, the chief architects of the Algerian coup of 1958. The rivalry of the two factions centered about how fully the party should support de Gaulle's policy of self-determination for Algeria and to what extent it should try and become a vast popular movement that could rival the Communists in organizational power and surpass them in control of public opinion. Soustelle wanted the party to persuade de Gaulle to commit France to the "integration" of Algeria and a military victory over the Moslem rebels as well as to proceed to a "conditioning" of French public opinion for the sacrifices this policy would entail. By 1960 the leaders of this "ultra" wing of the UNR had been excluded from membership, with the party becoming more homogeneously Gaullist in Algerian policy and more firmly in the hands of the moderate leadership.

Formally, the party's program is largely reduced to the loyal support of General de Gaulle and the policies of his Prime Minister. This is especially true in respect to Algerian, foreign, and defense policies, matters in which de Gaulle has reserved full decision-making priority. In domestic economic and social matters, however, the party officially took a more reformist liberal line than the one followed by the Debré Government and its conservative Finance Ministers. Thus it continued the old RPF demand for government-instituted profit-sharing and called for more economic planning and a greater amount of public investment for purposes of expanding and modernizing the French economy. With the rise of electoral fever and the prospect of confronting voters who are probably less Gaullist than they were in 1958, the UNR has redoubled its efforts at appearing to be a moderately reformist party of the center, independent in many respects from the Government in power. To this end it increasingly demanded in 1961 that Prime Minister Debré not take its support for granted, but rather negotiate with its parliamentary leaders and make concessions on Government bills that would win the party votes in a forthcoming election. There was even some talk of transforming the party into a "Gaullist Union" that would include genuinely left-wing forces from both other parties and the small left-Gaullist party, the Democratic Union of Labor. Thus even the UNR is thinking of means to exploit what they consider an inevitable swing of public opinion to the present opposition parties in any forthcoming elections. For the moment, however, the UNR remains simply the party-extension of de Gaulle's own personal prestige. Yet the General still refuses to give it either leadership, doctrine, or organization, clearly unwilling for it to become a true Government party, for reasons that will be discussed in Chapter 15. Consequently, the UNR continues to be torn between the desire to have a mind of its own on policy matters, thus creating its own following in public opinion and assuring its longevity after de Gaulle, and the need to remain loyal to the man whose prestige is responsible for its existence.

MINOR PARTIES

Most minor parties have no relevance to a study of the French political system because they are completely outside the circuit of power and, indeed, often serve social rather than political functions for their members. Monarchist, anarchist, and reform groups of many kinds exist as intellectual coteries for small numbers of Frenchmen with eccentric or thoroughly out-of-date political and social ideas. Some minor parties represent the doctrinaire and unassimilable remnants of once powerful national movements such as the prewar Fascist leagues and Pierre Poujade's reactionary tax-protest movement of the 1950's. A very few of these small parties, however, have potential political importance because their leaders personally have national prestige or direct influence with the leaders of major parties or other important political figures who could conceivably bring them to power.

Some of these potentially important parties were formed to provide a semblance of national organization for well-known members and former members of parliament who deserted a major party over policy or personal matters. This is the case of the conservative Republican Center (*Centre Républicain*) led by former right-wing Radicals like Senator Bernard Lafay and the former deputy André Morice. The organization serves as a captive forum for speeches and thus assures the party's leaders of the newspaper coverage an isolated political leader would lack. Other potentially important small parties represent genuine, although tiny, currents of political opinion situated on the margins of the major political movements. They have no parliamentary representation but are led by men with national reputations who either left major parties along with a sizable bloc of militants or who were not asked to join a transformed major party because of their minority attitudes. The foremost example of this category is the United Socialist Party (PSU—*Parti Socialiste Unifié*), a left-wing opposition group led by the former Radical Prime Minister, Pierre Mendès-France, and the former left-wing SFIO Socialist deputy, Edouard Depreux. Until the regular Socialists and Radicals joined the opposition to de Gaulle, the PSU was the only non-Communist Left party in this position. Today it is a rather heterogeneous amalgam united only in a determined opposition to the governing style of the Gaullist regime.

The party has a good sized corps of party workers drawn mostly from the big cities and ranging in outlook from former Communists and present fellow travelers to liberal-minded moderates and technocrats. Although he has no official office in the party, Mendès-France is its most influential figure because of his remaining personal prestige. Most of his views, however, are not typical of the rank and file who, by and large, are doctrinaire Marxist socialists, nostalgically longing for unity of action with the Communist party. An important element of this majority is made up of former deputies and party workers who once formed the extreme left-wing of the regular Socialist party, which they left over its support of de Gaulle and the new constitution in 1958. A minority of the PSU leadership are liberal reformers of middle class background whose personal attachment to Mendès-France and long-standing opposition to the Algerian policies of both the Fourth and Fifth Republics drew them to the party. PSU candidates have had no real success at either parliamentary by-elections or local and municipal balloting. University students of voting age, left-wing intellectuals, liberal bureaucrats, doctrinaire socialist school teachers, and white-collar workers are simply not numerous enough to elect candidates in majority elections, even if their numbers suffice to staff a party. While it is conceivable that Mendès-France might individually be asked to join a left-oriented Government, it is not very likely that the more representative leaders of this party, whose following is so narrowly based, will approach power in the near future.

If the PSU is situated on the margin between the "legitimate" opposition of the Socialists and Radicals and the "revolutionary" opposition of the Communists, the Democratic Union of Labor (UDT—*Union Démocratique du Travail*) represents the marginal current of left-wing Gaullism, between the pro-government Gaullist UNR and the opposition. The UDT has few militants and even less of a following in the country than the PSU, but it has the huge advantage of a leadership that is in close contact with General de Gaulle. Rather than being a left-wing dissidence from the UNR, this organization provides a sounding board for politicians who remain personally loyal to de Gaulle but whose opposition to Michel Debré and the generally conservative leadership of the UNR made membership in the main Gaullist movement impossible and, in fact, not offered. Along with many former liberal leaders of the old RPF, the UDT has among its ranks ex-admirers of Mendès-France, who refused to follow their hero's complete evolution, and middle-class reformers who still dream of the Resistance idea of a left-of-center "French Labour Party" modeled on the British example. In theory, they look forward to a more liberal phase of the Fifth Republic, after new elections, in which they hope de Gaulle will personally endorse, and even lead, a left-oriented coalition of parties and trade unions and in which their marginal position and Gaullist loyalty will give them a share of the leadership. In practice, however, the function of the UDT is to keep politically "alive" for de Gaulle a number of well-known liberal Gaullists such as the former RPF deputies Louis Vallon and Réne Capitant. Their program involves unconditional support of those sectors of Government policy decided by de Gaulle himself and a vigorous critique of domestic economic and social policies that they impute to the conservative Gaullism of the UNR. Their only hope for immediate power has been the possibility that de Gaulle would instruct a successor to Prime Minister Debré to include a left-wing Gaullist in his cabinet in order to reward the party's loyalty and to increase the Government's liberal coloration. This hope was fulfilled in May 1962 when Georges Pompidou, Debré's successor, named a UDT leader as Minister of Labor.

PRESSURE GROUPS

French pressure groups, whether trade unions or business associations, have traditionally avoided direct participation in politics. The former were for years committed to syndicalist socialism, which rejected working through parties in favor of direct and often violent pressures on employers and, especially, upon the state. Unlike unions in Britain and the United States, French worker organizations sought reforms more by trying to enlist the government in support of their grievances and less by direct negotiations with management. Similarly, business interests pursued their political ends directly by behind-the-scenes pressure upon the politicians in the executive and the civil servants. Since the war two developments have altered this pattern and changed the political significance of pressure groups. First, the vast increase in the amount of economic and social planning, in welfare programs, and the complexity of legislation in these fields, has obliged the state to bring representatives of interest groups into regular and official participation in the policy-making process. Besides membership in the Economic and Social Council there are over two thousand separate consultative bodies available in which these representatives can formally present their views on public policy. Not only does this procedure provide information on the proper application of the law, but by associating pressure groups with the formal policy process it has also tended to make their activities more responsible and less demagogic.

A second trend has been the extension of pressure group attention to matters formerly in the domain of parties, such as civil rights and political institutions. This has been due to the growing popular disaffection from the traditional parties and the striking diversification of trade union and even business association membership. Before World War II most union members were manual salaried workers, and business associations spoke primarily for big business. Today the rapid development of the French economy has transformed former manual laborers into white-collar employees, and business associations have been swollen by new members from the growing service industries and from dynamic modern business. Inevitably, the purely economic interests represented by pressure groups have become infinitely varied and, in their search for issues that represent a common denominator, the groups have been drawn to general political questions and national economic policies. Like the increased participation in consultative bodies, this interest in general policy has brought pressure groups into further contact with the organs of government and with political leaders. Some French commentators see in this continual dialogue between the state and voluntary associations, representing professional and social groups, the first sign of a new kind of politics and, perhaps, a new kind of state in which the old parties and their primarily ideological programs will give way to formal corporate representation and more pragmatic and concrete political competition. For the moment, however, one can say that the French government usually pays as much, and occasionally far more, attention to what pressure groups are saying than they do to the pronouncements of the major parties.

The most important pressure groups of French business are the National Confederation of French Employers (CNPF—*Confédération Nationale du Patronat Français*) and the General Confederation of Small and Medium Business (CGPME—*Confédération Générale des Petites et Moyennes Entreprises*). The first has existed since 1936 and represents the kind of big business that in the United States belongs to the National Association of Manufacturers. The second was organized after World War II in protest against the alleged neglect of small business interests by the CNPF and is made up of about three thousand trade associations and regional business groups roughly equivalent in function to the American Chambers of Commerce. In the early years of the Fourth Republic, when the Communist danger was at its height, new left-wing social and economic policies were being enacted, and the French economy was relatively stagnant, CNPF activity mainly involved contributing to anti-communist parties and candidates, propagandizing against the nationalizations, and

CNPF
CGPME

opposing policies that opened the French market to foreign competition. Today, while it is still a rock-ribbed conservative organization, the CNPF is primarily engaged in guaranteeing the best terms for French participation in the European Common Market and helping its members to adapt to the new conditions of both the French and the burgeoning European economies.

The small business organization, representing service and distribution industries and many marginal businesses, is less friendly to the Common Market, more protectionist, more hostile to public investment that might imply tax increases, and more critical of cooperatives and schemes for "modernizing" the economy. Since this kind of business is still very numerous in France, the CGPME is powerful in electoral terms and has many friendly parliamentarians working for its interests, especially among the Independents.

Unlike the British and American trade union movement, French organized labor is divided among three competing union federations and represents as a whole only a small percentage of the total working class. The largest of the three is the General Confederation of Labor (CGT—*Confédération Générale du Travail*), the only important Communist pressure group. But this means that only a large part of the leadership of the CGT is Communist, for most of the rank and file is either non- political or votes for other parties. Often French workers, if they wish to be effectively unionized, are obliged to join the CGT because it is the only union in a plant or the only active one in bargaining with management. Since the CGT is the oldest organization and fell heir to traditional union machinery, its represents at least nominally the majority of organized labor in France. The official and undoubtedly exaggerated membership figure for 1961 is somewhat above 1,700,000 out of the roughly 3,000,000 union members.

Recently the Communist leadership of the CGT has been challenged by a reformist, non-communist minority, which has urged unification of the trade union movement and a rejection of both political alliance with the Communists and the old syndicalist dogma of direct worker action. It has argued in favor of increased union participation in democratic planning, thus indirectly contradicting Marx's prediction of violent revolution and his belief that capitalism could not reform itself. The strengthening of this reformist attitude within the CGT is probable in light of the diversification of working class interests and the success of "reformism" in the membership drives of the other union organizations. The most important of these is the French Confederation of Catholic Workers (CFTC—*Confédération Française des Travailleurs Chrétiens*), which has provided since 1919 a haven for those workers whose religious sentiments prevented them from belonging to the militantly anticlerical and Marxist French trade union movement. The third major national organization is the General Confederation of Labor—Workers' Force (CGT-FO—*Confédération Générale du Travail—Force Ouvrière*), created in 1947 under Socialist party inspiration by dissident leaders of the Communist CGT. The CFTC claims a steadily rising membership that reached 750,000 in 1961 while the less dynamic CGT-FO remained at about 400,000. Unlike the Communist CGT these organizations usually attract workers in the lighter industries, civil servants, and white-collar employees. But the CFTC in particular has made serious inroads into CGT strongholds, thanks to a combative and shrewd leadership. Moreover, its policy of a more active role in everyday politics seems to be gaining approval among the younger generation of French workers.

Yet the relative weakness of the French trade union movement generally—there are about three million members in a total labor force of about fourteen million—and the continued isolation of the working class by Communist control via party and CGT, means that trade unions are without the strength to be as potent a political force as they are in Britain, Germany, or America. Divisions among the three groups over strategy, the lack of economic expertise to match that of management, the insignificant funds for supporting propaganda and strike activities, all contribute to this relative impotence. As a consequence, the leaders of the two "reformist" movements have listened with interest to proposals from various political parties for the creation of a "French Labor Party," which would strengthen the voice of French labor and achieve the trend toward greater union participation in general political action.

The largest farmers' pressure group is the National Federation of Agricultural Unions (FNSEA—*Fédération Nationale des Syndicats d'Exploitants Agricoles*), which groups local farm organizations of all sizes and in all parts of the country. It is dominated by the large producers who maintain their leadership because they fight the battles of the marginal farmer, thus satisfying the mass of backward French agriculture and assuring themselves and other efficient farmers a handsome profit. Recently the FNSEA has resorted to direct action such as calling mass meetings, barricading national highways, and participating in other demonstrations meant to focus the attention of the government and the public on the truly difficult plight of French agriculture. Equally prone to direct action in defense of what they consider their interests are the many veterans' organizations, which, unlike their British counterpart, are sharply divided along political lines. The most nationalist among them were important allies of the activist elements of the army in opposing de Gaulle's policy of a negotiated peace in Algeria. Far less political and more likely to pursue their goals through consultation with the Government or pressure on members of parliament are the numerous movements defending the rights and interests of the family. They have had a special importance in France, thanks to the sponsorship of the Catholic Church and the postwar Government programs to encourage the French birth rate by aiding large families.

Students and teachers belong to pressure groups of somewhat less importance in general political and economic terms, but of considerable influence in large areas of liberal public opinion. The majority of primary and secondary school teachers are organized by the School Teachers Union (*Syndicat des Instituteurs*) and the National Education Federation (*Fédération de l'Education Nationale*). While important in representing the professional interests of their members, these organizations are often more active in defending the civil rights of other Frenchmen and opposing any state aid to the large Catholic school system. In this they are vigorously supported by the generally left-oriented National Union of French Students (UNEF—*Union Nationale des Etudiants de France*), grouping the politically active in France's universities and responsible for managing various state-subsidized services for students.

Ranged against these organizations on the matter of aid to Catholic schools is the powerful Parents' Association of the Independent School System (APEL—*Association des Parents d'Elèves de l'Enseignement Libre*), which in 1958 succeeded in obtaining passage of a new subsidy for the church schools. Finally there are also many *ad hoc* pressure groups constantly being formed by intellectuals and opinion leaders in the context of temporary problems and events. The traditional importance of intellectuals in French political life has meant that the impact of these ephemeral organizations can often be very great. Since the beginning of the Algerian war the organized protest of intellectuals' pressure groups directed public attention to the abuses of civil rights by the army and other agents of the state. Although their public meetings and their manifestos bearing many prestigious signatures had usually little direct effect on Government policy, they often did serve to reveal to political parties what new issues were liable to attract attention and thus to prove politically profitable.

A New Veto Power: The Military Party

In the days before universal suffrage and the rise of mass organizations to contest elections, the word "party" had a meaning that is all but forgotten today. It had nothing to do with divisions in public opinion but rather refered to factions of influential people, in and around the government, who sought by legal and illegal means to mold policy to their interests or at least exercise over its determination a veto power. Historians have thus written of a "courtiers' party," the "Church's party," and even the party of "Monsieur the brother of the King." With little or no mass support in the country, these factions gained their influence from the positions they occupied within the King's household or the government apparatus, as well as from the singleness of purpose with which they pursued a common goal. It is very much in this sense that one could say that a "military party" has constituted one of the most important political forces under the early Fifth Republic and often exercised a veto power over Government decisions.

Its principal active elements were a sizable body of career army officers, a few purely professional French army units like the Foreign Legion and certain paratroop regiments, and a variety of civilians including important individual politicians and generally minor extreme nationalist organizations. They have been united in a fanatical conviction that French greatness, the preserving of Africa from communist domination, and their own personal fortunes all depended on preventing Algeria from becoming an independent Moslem state. This military party included neither the other two armed services, nor the mass of French soldiers, nor even the higher echelon career officers, and it had no single mass organization recruiting Frenchmen or influencing opinion. Yet it was powerful because the circumstances of the Algerian conflict gave its members both psychological and administrative leverage upon public opinion and policy making.

The "party" represented itself as the most patriotic force in France, alone committed to the highest national interest of maintaining territorial integrity. It claimed to be most sensitive to the terrible "drama of conscience" the Algerian problem represented for the army: the choice between blind obedience and a sense of honor. To insist on traditional obedience to the legal government, the military party argued, meant being guilty of dividing the army and obliging officers to act against their beliefs, a telling argument for Frenchmen. But besides these appeals to sympathy and justice, the military party also showed itself to be the political force in France most willing to employ physical violence to support its deeply felt convictions. Finally, when all these levers failed to sway policy in its favor, the party still had the resource of calling upon many officers and civil servants who, by virtue of their functions, prevented the offending policy from being fully executed.

During the last years of the Fourth Republic one could have called the military party a pressure group because of its exclusive committment to the single issue of French Algeria. But during the early years of the Fifth Republic the growing disillusionment with de Gaulle, for whose return to power they felt responsible, made their attitude toward politics both more revolutionary and less circumscribed by Algeria alone. If the Republic—that is, representative government—even under de Gaulle could not give them satisfaction, perhaps de Gaulle and the Republic along with him must be sacrificed. Perhaps, too, the military party should be called upon to give up its only partially effective veto power over Government policy and transform itself into the government and the sole author of policy. Therefore, because of its influence in the early Fifth Republic and its potential as a revolutionary power, the army and its allies must be viewed as having represented a political force at least as potent as the regular party system.

ARMY ACTIVISTS

The rationale for the military party's opposition and the army's frequent insubordination was their belief that de Gaulle and the legal Government were betraying the national interest. The activist elements of the army felt they had a duty above simple obedience to resist this betrayal. Although such reasoning was almost unknown among French military before World War II, it by no means originated in the tensions of the Algerian war. Those officers who cried "treason" at de Gaulle's negotiations with the Moslem rebels often pointed to the General's own historic disobedience of 1940 as their model. Was it not de Gaulle, they asked, who first urged disloyalty on the French army in the face of the then legal Government's decision to lay down arms? And was not his justification at the time a similar appeal to a higher national interest and a sacred duty of continuing the fight to preserve France's territorial integrity? It was, indeed, in this wartime crisis of conscience that many officers who commanded in Algeria were first obliged to "think for themselves" in choosing between conflicting views of honor and obedience. Thus began the intellectual transformation of the French army from an "unconscious machine" to a "party" in the nation.

World War II was also the source of the army's psychologically comforting belief that its defeats in the field were due to the bad judgment of politicians, the failure of political institutions, and the treason of certain parties. After the war many officers felt that they should continue to judge for themselves the political context of their mission, perhaps even influence the Government decisions when the need arose. Dubious when applied to World War II, this thesis of civilian responsibility for military defeat became more plausible in the Indochina war beginning in 1946. The long drawn-out guerrilla struggle with the Communist-led nationalists of Viet Nam ended in defeat in 1954 largely because of the vacillation and politics-as-usual attitude of Paris. Quickly after their withdrawal from the Far East came the retreats from Tunisia, Morocco (which career officers had long considered their special fief), and finally from Suez, where in 1956 the French army believed a technical victory had been erased by the manueuvers of politicians and international pressures. By 1957, when Algeria alone offered the chance to end twenty years of defeat and reverse France's colonial fortunes, a real consensus had developed among career officers that henceforth only success should be the criterion of their action. Moreover, whether it meant open disobedience or not, they felt it must be their judgment of the conditions for this success that should prevail.

Discontent with civilian authority and political "activism" was most widespread among the lower ranks of commissioned officers. Not only had they undergone an intellectual transformation since the war, but also they were affected by social trends that completed their alienation from French society. Unlike the traditional career officer of the past, these captains, majors, and colonels spent most of the postwar years overseas. The average captain in 1958 had spent 88 out of the preceding 144 months away from France and his family. His standard of living and status in a changing society was declining and when he did come home for leave the housing shortage often obliged him to spend his nights in a hotel. But what above all reinforced the sense of alienation of officers was the inbreeding of officer recruitment: by 1958 almost 50 per cent of the military school graduates were sons of officers. The attractions of prosperous civilian professions and the relative decline of army pay had left only the most personally motivated, and hence most inflexible, available for military careers.

Self-righteousness reinforced the sense of betrayal and alienation when many officers came to see their struggle to maintain France in her overseas territories as a fight for the bastions of the West and a new crusade for Christian civilization. Aside from the traditional conservative and religious bias of the military, this view was based on the strategic insight that the "Third World War" had already begun, with the underdeveloped countries as the first theater of operations. The Indochina experience left them with two assumptions that came to underly their politics. First, there was the belief that all native nationalist rebellions were utimately serving Moscow's purposes; and second, that the success of these rebellions was due to their adoption of Chinese Communist techniques of subversive warfare which alone offered the key to a successful Western riposte. Many young French officers learned the first principle of these techniques in the Viet Minh prison camps: the army must operate among the people as a fish lives in water. When they came to Algeria they quickly saw the Moslem rebellion as a similar "war in the crowd" and identified the main objective as the allegiance of the masses and not the capture of terrain. It became clear that their methods would have to be political and psychological, their function governmental as well as military.

During the last years of the Fourth Republic the subversive warfare school among officers won over both civilian and military leadership and Algeria was transformed administratively into a vast "military province." Since the Moslem nationalist rebels (the National Liberation Front or FLN—*Front de Libération Nationale*) sought to dislocate existing social and political structures, to intimidate those who would remain loyal to France, to demoralize opinion supporting the status quo, and to eliminate individuals entirely committed to the French presence, the army believed it would have to interpose itself between the rebels and the Moslem population. This required taking over a variety of governmental functions ranging from education and public health to building roads and creating new villages outside rebel zones. By the end of 1958 1,000 soldier-teachers cared for 59,000 Moslem children who had never seen a French school. Close to 700 new civil administration units had been set up by the army to bring law and reforms to areas that had never known a French administrator. But to cap it all, the army had to discover a powerful myth with which to counter the rebels' call for Algerian independence and this they found in the idea of bringing Algeria up to full parity with metropolitan France.

Such slogans as "integration," "French Algeria," and "one nation from Dunkerque to Tamanrasset" were launched and found useful *vis à vis* the desperate European settlers as well as the hesitant Moslem population. The subversive warfare experts reasoned that the idea of "integration" would reassure the settlers of their future in Algeria and maintain their vigorous pressure against both the Moslem rebels and any attempt by a Paris Government to negotiate with them. Although hardly sharing the selfish motives of the settlers, the army supported them in these pressures and assured the success of the Algiers rising of 1958 that led to de Gaulle's return to power. The General was the candidate of neither the settlers nor the activist junior officers but was accepted as a compromise and an improvement over the party politicians. Very soon after taking office, however, de Gaulle confirmed the fears and suspicions of the "French Algeria" forces.

Sharing neither their conviction that Algeria was the last bastion against international communism, nor their arguments for integration, nor their obsession with the magical properties of subversive warfare, de Gaulle immediately attempted to bring the army to a realistic view of the problem. He transfered many of the activist officers to France, reduced the army's administrative functions in Algeria, formally dismantled the subversive warfare branch, and tried to divert officers' attention from

Algeria by urging vast military reforms to equip the army for the nuclear age. When he officially announced self-determination as the goal of Algerian policy in September 1959, and later even spoke of the emergence of an Algerian Republic, the army knew that de Gaulle was well along the road to a negotiated peace with the Moslem rebels. In October 1959 some of the most fanatical activists planned a coup, only to be discovered by the Government. In January 1960 the unsuccessful rising of the settlers in Algiers offered them another opportunity to force a change in policy. Finally in April 1961 a junta of generals who had retired from active service in protest against de Gaulle's policy took things into their own hands and tried to take over all of Algeria. The coup failed because the mass of the army and French opinion responded to de Gaulle's radio appeals by remaining loyal. But three of the leaders of the "putsch," led by General Raoul Salan, refused to surrender and formed in early 1961 a clandestine resistance movement commanded by other cashiered officers and drawing support from the European settlers. This "Secret Army Organization" (OAS—*Organisation Armée Secrète*) sought to eliminate de Gaulle and bring to power a regime that was fully committed to the maintenance of French Algeria. To succeed they thought they needed the "cover" of well-known politicians and the support of metropolitan political organizations provided by their civilian allies.

Civilian "Ultras"

The transformation of a part of the French army into a nationalist pressure group inevitably brought officers into contact with right-wing nationalists and their political movements. Under the Fourth Republic the more moderate nationalists who were working for de Gaulle's return to power early identified the army's restlessness as a force they could use for their limited goal of a reformed republican regime. However, genuine antidemocratic parties and extreme conservatives also sought to become allies of the army, and it is they who led the rightist opposition to de Gaulle in both parliament and opinion during the last year of the Algerian war. Many officers found this a very congenial alliance because their struggle against a negotiated peace in Algeria—what they called "the sellout"—was inspired by a conviction that any democratic Government, whether led by de Gaulle or politicians, must inevitably lead to French decline. In their view a decadent and soft metropolitan France was unable to understand that Algeria represented the same source of national dynamism and power that the Western frontier once represented for the United States. As long as the majority ruled, they believed, Frenchmen would choose comfort over challenge. The future of France, therefore, required that majority rule and its institutions either be "conditioned" to accept French Algeria or be ignored by the warriors turned philosopher kings.

This outlook found passive and active encouragement from four groups of civilians. First there were the remnants of France's various fascist and authoritarian minor parties that not only approved anything the army did as a matter of doctrine, but also never lost hope that circumstances would kill French democracy and bring them to power. These organizations provided a certain doctrinal basis for the military party as well as a corps of experienced terrorists who were used for direct action ranging from intimidation by bombings to assasination.

A second series of allies were the important nationalist pressure groups, the many right wing veterans' associations. Not only did they share the mystique of subversive warfare with the activists in the army, but also they remained in close liaison with them for purposes of action. These movements provided the organized mass of civilians located throughout France whose unquestioning loyalty to the army and blind courage made them ideal for street demonstrations and ultimately revolutionary action.

The third and by far most important and effective ally of the army was the vast majority of European settlers in Algeria, unwilling to face the prospect of leaving what they considered their homeland and ready to do anything to avoid becoming a minority in an independent Moslem republic. A rough and ready amalgam of Spaniards, Italians, Maltese, and Frenchmen, they share few of France's political and ethical values and have long preferred authoritarian leaders and antidemocratic parties. Fervently royalist or Pétainist in the past, these *pieds noirs* ("black feet," as they were known locally) have always hated de Gaulle and looked to the army as their saviour. The most violent elements of this generally volatile population joined the terrorist teams of the Secret Army Organization which set off the plastic bombs, murdered Moslems at random, and destroyed public buildings in Algeria in the spring of 1962 in the vain effort at forestalling the creation of an independent Moslem Algerian Republic.

Finally, the best known civilian allies of the army were a varied selection of parliamentarians and politicians, most of whom were young and opportunist, totally unknown before 1958, but who achieved notoriety or public office by supporting the "French Algeria" cause. Until he voluntarily exiled himself after the April 1961 coup, the unofficial leader of this disparate clan was Jacques Soustelle, former Governor of Algeria and once the intimate associate of General de Gaulle. After his dismissal from the Debré Government for opposing its policy of self-determination, Soustelle organized various pressure groups in favor of "French Algeria" which served these politicans as forums. Their purpose at the time was to prepare a civilian "front" for an army-sponsored Government to succeed de Gaulle and reverse his policy of negotiation with the Moslem rebels. Soustelle was joined in this activity by a few well known politicians like the Socialist Robert Lacoste, also a former Governor of Algeria, and the former Radicals and ex-Defense Ministers, André Morice and Maurice Bourgès-Maunoury, who became defenders of a "French Algeria" while serving the Fourth Republic. Their positions were dictated as much by personal ambition as by the desire for consistency.

Other veteran politicians like the former MRP Georges Bidault, whose career had long been in decline, saw in the rise of the army the means for his own return to prominence and his revenge against those responsible for his eclipse. Increasingly embittered by de Gaulle's devious policy of bringing peace to Algeria, Bidault finally went into exile and joined the Secret Army Organization. After the cease-fire was signed and an independent Algeria was in view, he declared his intention to continue the struggle for a "French Algeria" and to overthrow the "treasonous" Gaullist regime. When Raoul Salan, the head of the OAS, was captured in Algiers in April 1962, Bidault became his successor and he announced from exile the formation of a "National Council of the Resistance" which was to lead the clandestine fight against de Gaulle and the Fifth Republic. Less than twenty years before it had been the same Bidault who, as chairman of an earlier National Council of the Resistance, had, under de Gaulle's direction, led the last phases of the resistance to the German occupation and the Vichy regime. It had been he who had helped to pave the way for de Gaulle's first rise to power as head of the provisional government of the Fourth Republic.

With the end of the Algerian war and an independent Moslem Algeria now a reality, the attention of the extremists in the military party appears to have shifted to metropolitan France. Ever since the failure of the 1961 army coup in Algiers, the Secret Army Organization has realized that its major stumbling block is de Gaulle and his support in French opinion. While there was still hope of preventing a negotiated peace with the Moslem nationalists, the OAS attempted to undermine this support by a campaign of terror aimed at demonstrating the Government's ineffectiveness and the power of the OAS opposition to an independent Algeria. To this end, the OAS applied the methods of subversive warfare used by the army in Indochina against its own compatriots in order to subvert the legal authority.

But when the OAS failed to prevent the signing of a cease-fire in March 1962, when its principal military leaders, the ex-generals Raoul Salan and Edmond Jouhaud, were arrested, and when it was unable to prevent the organization of the July 1, 1962 referendum in Algeria that affirmed independence, the organization lost its hold on the European settlers of Algeria. The "water" in which the OAS "fish," according to the principles of subversive warfare, must be nurtured thus dried up. With the settlers' leadership choosing to suspend anti-Moslem terrorism in the hope of winning a place for Europeans in the new Arab Algeria, the remaining hard-core of the OAS was reduced to a few army deserters and cashiered officers, most of whom had been implicated in past coups and conspiracies. At this writing it is these fanatical bitter-enders who represent the military party's greatest threat to the Fifth Republic. Abandoned by their civilian allies among the settlers, the military remnants of the OAS were reported to be returning to France in order to seek "revenge" for the loss of Algeria, presumably by continuing their attempts at assassinating de Gaulle. But apart from the possible success of such an isolated act of terrorism—the consequences of which can not be foreseen—the only hope of the military party in gaining power lies, paradoxically, in the future of France's relations with the new Moslem Algeria. If the latter's government allows savage reprisals against the remaining European settlers and forces them to flee to France, the OAS may yet succeed in organizing the most desperate among the returnees into an extreme right-wing political force capable of endangering the Fifth Republic. If de Gaulle's policy of "association" between the new Moslem state and France succeeds, however, and the settlers realize that they have a viable future in Algeria, the OAS will inevitably be reduced to a handful of outlaws whose future is limited to arrest or permanent exile.

De Gaulle and Gaullism

Charles de Gaulle does not recognize the existence of a distinct political opinion called "Gaullism." He has said that all Frenchmen at one time or another have been Gaullists—whenever they placed the national interest above any other interest. Yet in France reference is frequently made to the "Gaullist regime," "Gaullist policies," a "Gaullist majority" in parliament, the activities of a "Gaullist party" or of individuals called "Gaullists," and the rise or fall of "Gaullism" in public opinion. Actually, the influence of de Gaulle in French political life can be identified on three levels. At the time of this writing he is personally the most important factor in the formal decision-making process of government, a level to be treated in the following chapter. He is also the symbolic leader, indeed the *raison d'être* of a major political party, the UNR, the fourth in a series of "Gaullist" parties that has been dealt with earlier in this chapter. But unlike an average party leader who holds high public office, de Gaulle also exerts great influence over the opinions and behavior of the large majority of Frenchmen whose formal loyalties range from communism to extreme conservatism. This dimension of "Gaullism" is the gift of history, the history of the unique relationship that grew up between de Gaulle and the French people during World War II.

The strength of this influence has been statistically measured in six referenda since 1945 and frequently demonstrated by the acclamation of crowds whenever de Gaulle has toured the country as a private citizen or as chief of state. In October 1945 de Gaulle asked the people to approve his quasi-dictatorial powers as head of the provisional government of the Fourth Republic and over two thirds of them did so. In May 1946 his tacit disapproval of the first draft of the postwar constitution contributed to its rejection by the voters. In November 1946 his outspoken condemnation of the second draft resulted in a third of the voters rejecting that draft and almost a third refusing to vote at all, thus making its adoption by barely more than a third seem doubtfully legitimate although legally secure. After his return to power in 1958 his new constitution was approved by nearly 80 per cent and his plans for Algeria in January 1961 were ratified by 75 per cent. Finally, in April 1962 over 90 per cent of the voters approved his cease-fire agreement with the Moslem rebels and explicitly granted him power to bring Algeria to independence. During the first three years as President of the Fifth Republic his many provincial tours were always successful tests of his own popularity even when his Government was being widely criticized for its policies. And when his personal authority and safety were challenged by the rebellions of settlers and army officers in Algiers, de Gaulle's direct appeals for support were answered by such a massive rallying of opinion that the subversion quickly collapsed.

This amazing hold on the loyalties of individual Frenchmen is above all the product of historical accident and is profoundly psychological in nature. It is, however, also the result of de Gaulle's conscious efforts ever since he first appeared on the political scene. The first source of his influence comes from his having been adopted by the French as the symbol of the only self-respect and sense of honor they can muster in their memories of France's role in World War II. But the more consciously fashioned source of his power derives from his behavior and rhetoric during the war, as chief of the Liberation Government, and as a private citizen prior to 1958.

As the wartime leader of the Free French, de Gaulle realized that he would have to become a symbol of national unity and thus he methodically set about to combine nationalist, conservative, liberal, and even revolutionary themes in his radio appeals to occupied France from London. His unparalleled success meant that the Communist worker recognized that de Gaulle led the opposition to the reactionary Vichy regime; the conservative bourgeois felt that de Gaulle was the only leader who could serve as a bulwark against a Communist France after the war; the liberal intellectual was excited by de Gaulle's promises of a vast program of social reform; and the provincial nationalist saw de Gaulle as incarnating a stubborn resolve to eradicate the humiliation of France's defeat and restore her international power. To all of them de Gaulle in London meant the existence of a slim but real argument that France had not lost her honor and prestige in the debacle of 1940.

When de Gaulle returned triumphantly to France in 1944 he made good on the explicit and implicit promises to all of these people. He enacted by decree a vast program of social and economic reform and punished those who had collaborated with the Germans or persecuted the resistance movements. Yet he also prevented the reforms from leading to a social revolution and he limited the power of the communists and the revolutionary Resistance. He brought France back into the war against the Axis and restored her colonial empire. Then he demonstrated his respect for democracy by leaving power when his views clashed with the left-wing majority of the first National Assembly, though he soon after posted his contempt for the ineffectiveness of the Fourth Republic by founding an opposition political movement. Yet when this party failed to win power legally and became increasingly involved in the deals and compromises of the political system, he dissociated himself from it and again preserved—barely—his reputation as being above factions, or, as he put it, "belonging to all, yet belonging to none."

During his years of complete retirement France forgot the few partisan images of de Gaulle and remembered only that he was, after all, the most illustrious of its citizens. The appearance of his brilliantly written memoirs marked a new rise in his popularity, which grew in direct proportion to the immobilism and failures of the Fourth Republic. In May 1958 most Frenchmen agreed with the Communist militant who explained why he refused to follow his party's order to demonstrate against de Gaulle's return by saying: "After all, he *is* a great guy. There at least is a fellow who has not been out for himself all these years."

It is because de Gaulle's legendary wartime role did in fact make him a public hero without peers and because his own efforts made Frenchmen of all opinions feel he was above the factionalism and self-interested politics of the Fourth Republic that he has continued to exert such an influence over his compatriots. Aware of the vital importance to his rule of this hold on their loyalty, de Gaulle, as President of the Fifth Republic, has resumed his practice of direct personal contact with the French people. His frequent speaking trips in various parts of the country are designed to test his popularity and renew his influence in areas where it has been eroded by discontent. De Gaulle believes that the special "national legitimacy" he has "incarnated" since 1940 had its origins in just such direct contacts, either in person or by his wartime radio speeches, and these trips, therefore, are as much a means of revitalizing his own personal confidence and vigor as they are a source of personal power over the people. Whether the Fifth Republic's difficulties and failures will affect this power adversely is something that can still not be evaluated. Since the final resolution of the Algerian problem has provided the major test for de Gaulle as a political force standing above parties and institutions, it is not easy to see what other national crisis could possibly shake the loyalty of Frenchmen in Charles de Gaulle.

[15]

Policy Making
Under Republican Monarchy

The Primacy and Problems of the Policy Process

The purpose of political systems is to produce solutions for the problems of their societies. A country's constitutional structure provides the formal rules and institutional framework that supposedly govern the competition of political forces for the final determination of these solutions. In no political system does either the constitution or the alignment of political forces alone determine the workings and products of the policy process. Formal constitutional procedures are often partially abandoned in policy making. Political forces such as parties and pressure groups have often little direct influence over the final outcome. It is sometimes informal political customs, indirect political pressures, and the influence of supposedly neutral civil servants that are the most weighty factors in producing a given policy. For this reason the policy-making process has a "life of its own" independent of the other aspects of a political system, yet affected by them and constantly undergoing subtle changes as a result of the shifting weight of the factors involved.

Today this process is the most important but also the most obscure part of the French political system. The most that can be said about it in summary is that, for the first three years of the Fifth Republic, President de Gaulle made the most important policy decisions; the Government of Prime Minister Michel Debré was responsible for those lesser decisions which de Gaulle did not make; and parties, special interests, and powerful groups and individuals were successful in using parliament and the bureaucracy to modify both these original decisions and their ultimate impact on French society. The situation, of course, was very different during the Fourth Republic when the preeminence of parliament and executive instability made centrally important the process of making and unmaking the Government by the National Assembly. Policy-making then was simply a function of this process, suffering both discontinuity from the changing cabinets and incoherence from the bargaining required to construct the unstable party coalitions. The severity and persistence of monetary inflation in postwar France, for example, was at least partly due to the uncertainty about economic and financial policies fostered by changing cabinets, and to the ineffectiveness of the policies themselves, born as they were in compromises between incompatible party positions. Conversely one can say that the stabilization of the French franc, the great policy accomplishment of the Fifth Republic, was partly due to the expectation of longevity for the Government and to the consistency of its policies.

The new constitution is responsible for both this longevity and consistency by having ensured the stability of the executive and given it the major role in policy making. Both de Gaulle and his advisor on constitutional matters, Michel Debré, had long made known the first principle of the Gaullist constitution: policy making is the province of the executive, under the control of parliamentary criticism, until the time when the legislative formally withdraws its confidence. Thus the President of the Republic and the Prime Minister and his cabinet became the major sources of policy decisions through the constitutional limitation of parliament's law-making prerogative and the extension of the executive's rule-making power. The artificially engineered Government stability was expected to provide the continuity of policy, and the predominant role of the double executive, independent of parliament and its special interests, was expected to assure coherence of policy.

The first three years of the new regime, however, have shown that the stability of the executive and its quasi-monopoly of decision-making are not enough to produce a thoroughly effective policy process. The policies of de Gaulle and his Prime Minister have succeeded in bringing France's former African colonies to independence, in maintaining over-all economic prosperity and financial stability, and in modernizing the country's judicial and administrative structure. But their failure in matters such as the agricultural crisis and the decline of purchasing power of scattered sectors of society, as well as the long dead-lock over Algeria, have cast some doubt on the effectiveness of the new institutions. Repeated threats to public order and the resistance of important groups have encouraged de Gaulle to extend his constitutional powers and rule France almost single-handed. At the same time reawakening social and economic protest and concern over the advisability of de Gaulle's ambitious foreign policy have led to the progressive disaffection of large parts of opinion and a growing opposition to a technically all-powerful Government unable to resolve domestic problems while seeking great power status in the world. This, in turn, has generated further resistance to policies and has thus revived a vicious circle well known under the Fourth Republic.

Of course, the atmosphere of crisis generated by the Algerian problem seriously affected the debut of the new institutions. Undoubtedly the violence of the military party's reaction to Government policy in Algeria injected a new turbulence into French politics. It was this threat that often led de Gaulle to exceed the letter of his constitutional powers. Perhaps Algeria was also responsible for de Gaulle's domination of policy-making to the total exclusion of parliament and often the Government itself. Perhaps the emergencies of the new Republic's first years have prevented the Government from resolving many domestic problems for fear of provoking additional opposition.

Yet one wonders whether this thesis of Algerian responsibility should not be inverted. Perhaps policy-making in all matters, save the Algerian war, would have been more effective if de Gaulle had allowed greater, not less, participation by parliament and Government in major decisions, hence obliging them to share responsibility and to organize general public support more efficiently. Perhaps even a solution in Algeria would have come earlier if there had existed a powerful link between the executive and opinion in the form of a true party of Government, or at least a stable governing coalition of parties, directly involved in policy making. In other words, it can be legitimately asked whether the ineffectiveness of policies was not at least partly due to the unstructured relationship between opinion and Government, the lack of a transmission belt that continually persuaded and educated citizens concerning policy and informed the Government of the limits on what would be accepted. Executive stability and relative autonomy in decision making must be supplemented by a process of legitimizing policy, which only some system of effective popular representation can provide. De Gaulle's application of the new constitution neglected this process, convinced as he was that his personal legitimacy would adhere to his policies. Experience has proved him wrong and policy making has suffered as a consequence.

If the ineffectiveness of the Fifth Republic's policy process was due to its isolation from opinion, the opposite had been true of the policy process under the Fourth Republic. The latter overcame various resistances to policy by involving the representatives of France's vastly divided opinion in the determination of policy to a huge degree. The compromises required to make or preserve the unstable coalitions and the dominance of the legislative process made policy diffuse, exposed to fickle shifts of opinion or, more frequently, the even more fickle shifts of parliamentary mood. In both Republics the ineffectiveness of policy-making could have been prevented by a system of mixed government that avoided the extremes of isolation from opinion inherent in the administrative tradition of politics and the diffuseness of responsibility and accountability inherent in the representative tradition.

Under the Fourth Republic, however, policy making did at least offer a great advantage to students of French politics. Since it was largely determined by the legislative process of parliament, policy making in the past was widely open to view and indeed too well publicized by deputies and parties eager to justify and broadcast their influence. During the early Fifth Republic the legislative process not only was constitutionally restricted to a limited number of policy subjects, but also was easily dominated by the will of the executive, and hence was usually but a rubber stamp for executive decisions. Both the theory and practice of the Fifth Republic's policy process made its study difficult, for decision-making in the administrative tradition is naturally steeped in secrecy, always characteristic of the executive and its bureaucracy. When, in addition, most important policy was determined by one man, it was natural that an even smaller and more hidden circle of intimate advisers was of central importance, yet by its very nature had to remain obscure.

The problem was still further compounded by the short time observers had to watch the workings of the new regime. The Algerian crisis, too, made any close observation relatively useless, for it brought about sudden changes in policy procedures and responsibilities. Often the process was totally "revolutionized" by de Gaulle's frequent interventions into areas formerly in the domain of the Prime Minister, the bureaucracy, and even parliament. Thus even the description of a fairly stable distribution of responsibilities among parts of the executive branch was impossible. Instead of any systematic analysis, one must be contented with an evaluation of the relative importance of the roles in policy-making held by the major wielders of power in the new political system. These three unequal sources of influence over policy are President de Gaulle, the Prime Minister and his cabinet, and those other minor powers who by trying to interpose themselves between the will of the executive and the people have earned from de Gaulle the title of "intermediaries."

The Role of President de Gaulle: A "Reserved" Sector of Policy for Supreme Arbitration

DE GAULLE'S CONCEPTION OF THE PRESIDENCY

Today the most powerful influence in policy-making is the will of a man who views himself as a "republican monarch." The atmosphere of crisis that has existed ever since he took office and, it must be said, the very logic of his own theory of the presidency, have brought de Gaulle to almost total domination of governmental decisions. This move toward absolute power, however, is not in accord with the letter of the constitution. Article 20 clearly states that "the Government [i.e., the Prime Minister and his cabinet] determines and conducts the policy of the nation." But other constitutional provisions, as well as personal and circumstantial factors, explain why it has been de Gaulle who has "determined" and often "conducted" the policy making of the Fifth Republic.

The office of the President was conceived as a crisis executive and endowed with specified normal powers that largely subjected the Government and its policies to presidential influence. The chief of state was also endowed with unlimited emergency powers, under Article 16, to ensure the safety of the state against internal or external crisis. De Gaulle chose as his first Prime Minister a loyal associate, who made of the Government the executing agency of the President and who thereby allowed the latter's specified normal powers to dominate even day-to-day decisions. Furthermore, two attempts to overthrow the regime and a continuing threat from political forces opposed to de Gaulle's Algerian policy justified use of the emergency powers as well, thus enlarging the constitutional powers of the President to their ultimate limits.

Aside from these formal powers, de Gaulle as President benefits from the personal influence he enjoys over the loyalty and esteem of the French people. His return to office in 1958 was approved by a vast majority of Frenchmen because he was felt to be the only one who could settle the Algerian war, prevent civil strife, and restore France to the status of a great power. This popular image of uniqueness and indispensability comes from de Gaulle's legendary place in history as France's World War II leader. As indicated in the preceding chapter, this power over opinion derives from the peculiarly synthetic quality of de Gaulle's authority, allowing him to be respected by almost every group in French society. De Gaulle has sensed that the special nature of his hold on the French and the authority he exercised thereby was more that of an arbitrator and balancer of forces than that of a leader of a party or a doctrinaire. This personal view of his special leadership qualities was applied by him during the war, during his short tenure as President of the provisional government of the Fourth Republic, and now as President of the Fifth.

The idea of the leader as a supreme arbitrator, above parties and interests, was congenial to both de Gaulle's personality and to his private political philosophy. Like many career military officers of his background and generation, his early political opinion was monarchist. But he was always a thoroughly practical thinker who soon realized that the republican form of government was permanently and legitimately established in France. Indeed, as leader of the Resistance to forces that had replaced the Third Republic with the Vichy dictatorship, he could not be anything but a republican. However, his diagnosis of France's political ills as a republic continued to be tainted by his early monarchism. It was inevitable that his experience in the defeat of 1940 and his early ideas should combine with his role of Resistance leader to inspire a concept of the executive that can best be described as that of a "republican monarch" —a term which aptly describes the President of the Fifth Republic.*

De Gaulle freely admits his belief that the French people, while committed to the forms and processes of a democratic republic, are, like himself, essentially monarchist. He deduces this from a personal interpretation of French history, from his conviction that French political divisions and instability are permanent traits of the national character, and from a certainty that above their divisions over means and day-to-day ends, there is a basic, semiarticulated unity over France's ultimate goal of greatness. De Gaulle believes that only a form of monarchical rule can satisfy these essential conditions of the French body politic. There must be, first of all, a chief of state representing this basic unity and symbolizing the ultimate goal of greatness, who decides matters of the highest policy affecting the nation as a whole and who assures the absolute continuity of state power come what may. His method of policy-making must be typically monarchical, arbitrating among the inevitably multiple political forces, preserving his independence from any one of them in order better to serve as the supreme judge of the nation's general interest.

Under the chief of state is a chief of Government who represents the changing majorities of a volatile political opinion, executes policy decisions of the chief of state, and makes decisions in the remaining policy sector of domestic matters. In this latter realm there can obviously be no single national interest and hence decisions on day-to-day policy will require taking sides, generating partisan passions, and occasionally requiring changes in their authors—the Prime Minister and his cabinet— when the balance of political forces shifts or when mistakes have been made. Clearly, too, a Prime Minister who deals with the most disputatious matters and whose tenure in office is not fixed can serve to attract the partisan attacks, which, if directed at the chief of state, could impair his function as supreme arbitrator.

While something can be said in favor of this theory of isolated policy-making by a monarchical executive, the practice of the Fifth Republic

---

* The term was first coined by Michel Debré during the Resistance. C.f. Jacquier-Bruère (Michel Debré, et al.), *Refaire la France* (Paris, 1945), p. 122.

has not proved its entire suitability for today's France, as will be seen below.

De Gaulle's Objectives as President

The policy objectives pursued by de Gaulle have been simple, traditional, and indeed monarchical. It was almost by reflex that in 1945, as President of the postwar Government, de Gaulle's first move in foreign affairs was to insist, seriously if unsuccessfully, on detaching the Rhineland from Germany, thus approaching that ancient objective of the kings of France—natural frontiers on the East. Today he no longer insists on natural frontiers, for, unlike old-fashioned French nationalists—and de Gaulle considers himself above all a nationalist—the General has always understood his mission in severely pragmatic and realistic terms. "Things being what they are" is a phrase he often uses in announcing a decision he has taken or in an evaluation he has been obliged to make. De Gaulle's whole record shows that his pursuit of French greatness is usually within the context of France's basic capabilities and the world "as it is." He knows that France today can not rival the super powers in influence, but by following a course of friendship with Germany and a progressive unification of Europe he hopes to make France the diplomatic leader of a third major world power. He knows that Soviet power in Europe requires a cooperative western counterforce such as NATO, yet he has insisted on maintaining much independence for France's national army and on building a French nuclear capability in order to ensure her influence within the alliance. He knows that the drive for independence of the former colonial peoples cannot be stopped, yet he has sought to create permanent cooperative links with France's former colonies, in order to assure French cultural and, indeed, political influence in the underdeveloped world, a source of international prestige for his country.

Above all, de Gaulle's policies are all "future directed," aimed at providing France with the resources, physical and psychological, for returning to the front rank of nations when circumstances provide the chance. For de Gaulle is convinced that, like France in the past, great nations will decline in power and their roles will have to be taken by nations that today are waiting in the wings. He is certain that the nation will remain the permanent unit of world affairs and that, while alliances and even confederal arrangements are inevitable results of the interdependence created by industrialism, the nation will always be the ultimate object of human loyalty. To the extent that de Gaulle's decisions affect domestic affairs, he has tried to assure France's financial stability, to encourage the modernization of French industry, to provide means for lessening strife between labor and management, and to foster a revival of France's scientific talents. As in foreign affairs, de Gaulle's policies in these areas mean to guarantee France's future by providing impressive goals for French enterprise that will divert attention from the ancient political quarrels that have dissipated her potential in the past.

It can legitimately be asked whether de Gaulle has accomplished many of these goals and how much of France's prestige and self-confidence he has restored since he returned to office. As in the case of his concept of the Presidency, de Gaulle's image of tomorrow's France and his choice of policies that image indicates are only partially shared by his compatriots. Frenchmen, in fact, do like a monarchical leader and monarchical policies, but they have also come to like values that make it difficult for such leadership and policies to prevail. A great believer in symbols, de Gaulle has restored to the office of the President some of the pomp, formality, and pride once cultivated by the kings. The insistence on little details like the restoration of the chapel in the presidential Elysée Palace, the obligation to serve only native French drinks at presidential receptions, the order for all servants and guards to wear full-dress uniforms most of the time illustrate the traditionalism of a regime dedicated to restoring the grandeur of "eternal France," not merely that of a Republic. Yet France has come a long way since 1789 and even since 1945. Now a heavily industrialized nation, bent on the individual enjoyment of material prosperity and closely sharing these private concerns with the people of neighboring countries, France may not be very sensitive to de Gaulle's symbols. This probable "rationalization" of French values—that is, a decreasing popular sensitivity to certain once potent and emotionally charged symbols of past glory—may yet prove to be the greatest obstacle to de Gaulle's achievement of his personal objectives, many of which are inspired by purely traditional standards of French national greatness.

DE GAULLE'S METHODS AS PRESIDENT

Normal Powers. The method de Gaulle has employed in making policy is appropriate to his conception of the Presidency as guardian of the national interest. Soon after taking power he established a presidential sector of policy that included those questions he saw affecting the nation as a whole and for which he, as "republican monarch," had to assume sole responsibility. These matters included foreign affairs, national defense, relations with the French Community and other former dependencies and to deal with them he created a special policy-making process centered in his office. For each of the subjects de Gaulle had a special assistant on his personal staff who prepared background papers for his personal use and served as liaison with the ministerial department concerned. Each of the "presidential policy areas" had also a form of co-ordinating and consultative "task force," called a "restricted committee" (*comité restreint*), in order to distinguish it from the regular cabinet committees chaired by the Prime Minister. Unlike the latter, the restricted committees are chaired by de Gaulle and composed of members of the executive most concerned with the subject, whether they be Ministers or not. Since the Ministers for all these areas of policy were consciously chosen among senior bureaucrats, de Gaulle knows that he is surrounded by loyal and experienced servants of the state who have little or no committment to parties and special interests as would a Minister who had been a party leader. In this company de Gaulle feels somewhat reassured that the discussion will be as "objective" in terms of the national interest as possible and that his decisions will ultimately be executed by men whose whole lives have presumably been spent in doing just that. Consequently de Gaulle has taken their advice seriously and, if anywhere, it has been in these restricted committees that the strategy and tactics of his decisions have been allowed to be criticized.

Parallel to his meetings with the restricted committees, de Gaulle conducted a series of conversations with individuals whose opinions—either for their wisdom or their representative quality—were of interest. First of all he consulted his loyal Prime Minister, Michel Debré, who, while usually attending the restricted committee meetings, realized that de Gaulle's preeminence in the presidential sector of policy meant that it was really de Gaulle who was Prime Minister in these areas and therefore had to have his own direct relations with members of what was still formally called the Debré cabinet. De Gaulle spent most of his office time receiving many other visitors, a procedure that around the General had long been monarchically called "giving audiences." He listened to other Ministers, to private and governmental experts, to deputies and Senators, representatives of pressure groups, and to anyone who could bring him information or an indication of how important sectors of French opinion might react to policies under consideration. De Gaulle often "gave audience" to as many as twenty visitors a day and, when he was unsatisfied with the information he had gleaned, he appointed members of his personal staff to make on-the-spot inquiries or interview powerful personalities whose visit to the Elysée Palace could prove embarrassing or would reveal de Gaulle's policy intentions.

To gather this information, to prepare the decisions, and to keep watch over the execution of presidential policy, the staff of the Elysée has been vastly expanded over what it was under the Fourth Republic when, in theory and practice, the Presidency was relatively unimportant. In fact, the influence of the presidential staff has risen considerably since de Gaulle's assumption of the office in January 1959. There have been signs that discussions among the staff and *ad hoc* consultations with the Prime Minister and a few loyal associates of long-standing have progressively replaced the formal meetings of the restricted committees, originally the basic instruments of presidential policy making. This trend, of course, has further reduced the participation of the Ministers in the most important policy decisions, many of which they are nonetheless required to execute. Among those personal aides upon whom de Gaulle counted the most was Geoffroy de Courcel, who in June 1940 flew to London with de Gaulle as an *aide de camp* and who until recently managed the Presidency staff as its Secretary General. There was also Jacques Foccart, whose background in intelligence work, trading with the African colonies, and organizing de Gaulle's political party under the Fourth Republic equipped him for the informal jobs of overseeing police and intelligence operations, political liaison, and the formal job of managing presidential relations with former dependent areas. Since Georges Pompidou, the banker and ex-civil servant who succeeded Debré as Prime Minister in April 1962, had formerly been an important personal aide of de Gaulle, it is very likely that the influence of the immediate presidential staff will continue to be extremely important.

After a decision was made its execution became the job of the Government and its Ministers. Unlike the practice under past regimes, the process of execution began where once policy decisions were debated— in the meetings of the Council of Ministers. To be sure, de Gaulle called for discussion of policy decisions, but every Minister knew that on most matters de Gaulle had already made up his mind and that the weekly meetings of the Council, chaired by the President, were merely for purposes of ratification. Discussion, therefore, was usually perfunctory and limited to procedural matters such as the allocation of executing responsibility among the Ministers. Those involved in the presidential sector arc the Ministers of Foreign Affairs, of the Armies (Defense), of Algerian Affairs, of the Sahara and overseas *départements* and territories, and, finally, the Minister of Cooperation, who administers the aid programs to the former African colonies. André Malraux, the renowned writer and personal friend of de Gaulle who served as Minister of Cultural Affairs, also was involved indirectly with the work of this sector.

When the decision was within the rule-making power of the executive, the Minister concerned drafted an ordinance or decree, which, after discussion and approval by the Council of Ministers, took effect immediately. If the decision was within the special authority granted to the executive by a parliamentary delegation of legislative power, a similar procedure was followed. But if the decision was on a matter that was subject to parliamentary legislation, the Minister had to draft a Government bill embodying the decision and then, with the aid of the Prime Minister, the parliamentary leaders of the Government majority had to shepherd the bill through the two houses and into law.

In all these cases the possibilities were numerous for "watering down" the original policy decision taken by de Gaulle. As one observer put it, the Government of good intentions, words, and decisions might well be on the right bank of the Seine (where the Elysée Palace is located) but the "Ministry" of action and execution was on the left bank (where both parliament and most of the executive departments are situated). A Minister in charge of drafting an ordinance might be personally loyal to de Gaulle's intentions but, under the influence of his expert advisers, the pressure of interested groups, and the threat of a reaction from those who will be affected, he might present an ordinance that falls short of the original decision. This was most often true in the past of the Ministers of Defense, loyal civil servants, but heavily subjected to the daily pressures of the military party. Many officers assigned to the Ministry of Defense were or quickly became committed to an intransigent opposition to negotiating with the Moslem rebels. They used their official functions to prevent or to attenuate the execution of Government policies that promoted the chances of a negotiated peace. For example, de Gaulle's decisions to liberate a large number of Moslems from the "administrative internment" they were suffering because of suspected cooperation with the rebels was greeted by the threat of massive demonstrations by European settlers in Algeria. This and later "concessions" to Moslem opinion were made to facilitate future negotiations for peace in Algeria. But the ordinances were not carried out, and, while de Gaulle inquired about their execution at meetings of the Council of Ministers, he rarely made any personal effort to assure their application. With the growing violence of settler opposition to de Gaulle's policy in 1961, it was rumored that very few Paris policies were actually being executed by governmental authorities in Algeria. Yet de Gaulle continued to keep relatively aloof from the process of execution, feeling that becoming involved would not only sap his energies and divert his attention, but would also make him less effective as a supreme arbitrator. After all, if political forces were strong enough to prevent execution of a decision, de Gaulle reasoned, perhaps their strength and their point of view had been neglected in the decision-making. To become embroiled in execution, moreover, is the reflex of the doctrinaire who insists on his policy being enacted. De Gaulle not only sought to keep himself above doctrinaire factions, but was a pragmatic fatalist who believed that the chaos inherent in human behavior could be occasionally controlled but never fully ordered.

Besides being a fatalist de Gaulle believed in always acting at the "right" time, in waiting patiently if the circumstances did not favor the achievement of a given end. He believed that contrary forces had to be "managed" rather than challenged full front, and that his role as emergency leader, as well as supreme arbitrator, depended on keeping free of petty controversies, using his power sparingly and keeping it in reserve until national interest required action. What has made it so difficult to study the Fifth Republic's policy process is that one never knew when de Gaulle would seize upon a major or minor problem of policy or policy execution, judge it to be a matter of national interest, and intervene in its resolution. Not only has he often decided domestic matters that were under consideration by the Government, but he has even extended his authority to the level of constitutional interpretation. In March 1960 a majority of deputies in the Assembly, under pressure from farm organizations, asked for a special parliamentary session to deal with the agricultural crisis. Although Articles 29 and 30 of the constitution clearly leave no alternative to the President but to decree such a session when demanded by a majority, de Gaulle refused to do so. Suggesting that the Assembly was acting on "outside orders," in violation of Article 27, and that a special session would serve only to upset the Government's efforts to resolve the crisis, de Gaulle declared that the request was "compatible with neither the spirit nor the regular functioning of the institutions which I must uphold and assure, by virtue of the popular will and the terms of the constitution." By thus adding to his already imposing array of normal powers this implicit authority to interpret the constitution, de Gaulle created a dubious precedent of constitutional theory. Yet this new power is so closely related to his personal prestige and to his position as the true "father" of the new constitution that there is little likelihood it will ever be successfully used by a successor.

Emergency Powers. De Gaulle's philosophy of leadership is very much in the classical tradition, which sees the monarch achieving his personal goal by neutralizing one force with another and, above all, keeping aloof from the compromises, errors, and negotiations involved in execution, whenever possible. In practice it has meant that the decision-maker concerned with France's most vital problems is voluntarily isolated from policy execution most of the time and does not always worry when his decisions are not carried out. For this de Gaulle has been much criticized and the question has been raised as to whether this monarchical style is suited for problems that are more critical than ever before, and for a society whose complexity and political awareness is far greater than that of the *Ancien Régime*. On the other hand, there is an area of policy making in which de Gaulle's aloofness and isolation is both constitutionally proper and practically necessary. Decisions taken by de Gaulle under the presidential emergency powers clause of Article 16 need only be submitted to the Constitutional Council for advice and require no ratification or even consultation in the Council of Ministers. De Gaulle invoked these powers for the first time in April 1961 after the Algier army coup and he maintained them for over five months.

It was this long maintenance of the unlimited powers after the four day insurrection that attracted criticism, and not de Gaulle's right or wisdom in invoking Article 16 or even the measures he took under its authority. In fact, most Frenchmen agreed that the coup was a threat to "the institutions of the Republic" and hence required extraordinary administrative, judicial, and police measures that could only be taken if existing laws were suspended. Most of the decisions taken by de Gaulle did just that, the only "structural" reforms undertaken being the creation of a special military tribunal for trying the leaders of the army coup and a new set of rules making it easier for the Government to suspend disloyal military officers and civil servants. While the trials were public, many of the sanctions taken against individuals under the new rules were not made public, nor was it clear whether these rules would become permanent. In light of this typical administrative secrecy, the fact that parliament was constitutionally in permanent session was not considered an adequate guarantee of individual civil rights against abuses of state power.

Beyond his use of Article 16, de Gaulle often directly makes policy under the pressure of emergencies without reference to the Government or even the constitution. In these cases he invokes only his personal authority as "General de Gaulle," whose special legitimacy, he has declared, dates from June 1940 and not from his election as President in December 1958. Thus in 1960, when the pressure for complete independence by member states of the Community reached dangerous proportions, de Gaulle ruled that they could accede to that status immediately and still remain members of a "new" Community, long before the constitution was amended to create this "new" legal situation. During the abortive negotiations with the Moslem rebel F.L.N. in 1960 and 1961, de Gaulle gave orders directly to the French delegates without even the usual token consultation of the Council of Ministers. Indeed, it was even rumored that a direct telephone wire had been installed between the Elysée and the chief French negotiator. On many other occasions de Gaulle has announced a policy decision without prior consultation with the Government, in a public speech, in conversations with diplomats or heads of state, and even at Elysée receptions. There was, of course, no open protest from de Gaulle's loyal Prime Minister, nor even much public criticism of the practice, given de Gaulle's continuing status as the indispensable man in a time of crisis and his unique position—indeed, legitimacy—*vis à vis* the French people. Even when these decisions are in the area of domestic affairs, informally reserved to the Government, there is little protest, since the interdependence of policy in times of stress is recognized.

Yet, three years of crises during which he has seen many of his decisions and those of his Prime Minister deformed at various stages of the policy process have eroded de Gaulle's concept of his office and of his personal mission as "republican monarch." On the one hand he has steadily extended his personal involvement in both the taking and executing of policy decisions in both the presidential and domestic sectors. This has meant that he has depended on his personal staff and closest advisers rather than the Ministers and the regular bureaucracy for counsel and has been increasingly drawn into negotiations with the groups and interests involved in the decisions. This direct experience with the intractable flesh of France's body politic has only confirmed his innate fatalism about the possibility of altering human events. Even the greatest men, de Gaulle has come to believe, can only effect historical changes when circumstances are ripe for change. Between these brief moments, such as May 1958, the "republican monarch" must bide his time, serving to remind the French of the little they do have in common, doing what he can to prevent vital national interests from being sacrificed, and waiting for the next moment when action can be taken to press France along her destined road.

The Role of the Prime Minister and His Government: An "Open" Sector of Policy for Administrative Fiat

THE SPECIAL POSITION OF DE GAULLE'S PRIME MINISTER

If an analysis of the President's role in policy-making is really a study of how Charles de Gaulle makes decisions, so, then, an analysis of the Government's role must be a study of how the Fifth Republic's first Prime Minister, Michel Debré, and his Ministers have affected policy. This is necessarily the case at this writing for there has been only one Government to observe at length since the birth of the Fifth Republic, the Pompidou cabinet being in office only since April 1962. But it is also true because the special relationship between Debré and de Gaulle was more influential in determining the Government's role than either the constitution or traditional political custom. Had Michel Debré not been alive when de Gaulle assumed the Presidency in January 1959, someone very much like him would have had to be discovered. For both the theory and practice of de Gaulle's rule depended closely on Debre's personal qualities and on his personal interpretation of the Prime Minister's position.

In order completely to control decisions on most important policy matters de Gaulle needed a Prime Minister so loyal to him directly that he would readily abandon his own convictions, political debts, and personal ambitions. In order to be supreme arbitrator above parties and interests, de Gaulle needed a Prime Minister who would unfailingly take responsibility for many of the most unpopular policy decisions and often accept the blame for the failure of policy made by the President. Yet since parliamentary majorities for legislation were needed and a Government coalition had to be maintained, de Gaulle also needed a Prime Minister who could preserve the cohesion and support of the most important party in the National Assembly, while also willing to compromise his political future by employing the effective, if brutal, constitutional means to force through the presidential program against parliamentary opposition. Above all, de Gaulle needed a Prime Minister who shared his personal view of an objective national interest to be served at any cost, personal or political. Michel Debré, a former high civil servant and a veteran Gaullist parliamentarian whose passionate attachment to de Gaulle dated from World War II, was in the circumstances of 1958-59 the only man who met all of these requirements. Georges Pompidou, De Gaulle's second Prime Minister, is if anything, even more an instrument of the presidential will. Indeed, his only political experience has been on de Gaulle's personal staff and in the civil service, thus leaving him without the knowledge of parliamentary life that occasionally served the ex-senator Debré in his dealings with the legislative branch.

Composition and Function of the Cabinet

The make-up of the Debré and Pompidou cabinets reflects a similar accord with the principles, goals, and methods of de Gaulle's Presidency. Under the Fourth Republic the Prime Minister personally chose his Ministers with primarily political considerations in mind. They had to represent the parties in the Government coalition and the matching of ministerial post to parliamentary leader was made more on the basis of the latter's influence over a bloc of votes than for his technical competence or even his personal relations with the Prime Minister. Although under the Fifth Republic the choice of Ministers still belongs to the Prime Minister constitutionally, the members of the Debré and Pompidou cabinets were chosen in cooperation with de Gaulle. In order that the influence of party loyalty or personal political ambition over policy in the presidential sector could be held to the minimum, the Ministers dealing with this area were chosen among former high civil servants. But given the prejudice of de Gaulle against party leaders and the fact that it was so difficult for parliament to endanger the life of the Government, the number of parliamentary leaders in the cabinet was kept to a bare minimum. Of the twenty-one

T A B L E 9   French Cabinets 1945-1962

PRIME MINISTER	DATE GOVERNMENT INVESTED	RESIGNED	PARTY COMPOSITION AT INVESTITURE (MINISTERS)
PROVISIONAL GOVERNMENT Elections Oct. 21, '45			
Charles de Gaulle	Nov. 21, '45	Jan. 22, '46	5 MRP, 5 CP, 5 SFIO, 3 UDSR, 1 RS, 1 Con.
Félix Gouin (SFIO)	Jan. 26, '46	June 11, '46	7 SFIO, 6 MRP, 6 CP
Elections June 2, '46			
Georges Bidault (MRP)	June 23, '46	Nov. 28, '46	8 MRP, 7 CP, 6 SFIO, 1 UDSR
FOURTH REPUBLIC Elections Nov. 10, '46			
Léon Blum (SFIO)	Dec. 16, '46	Jan. 16, '47	17 SFIO
Paul Ramadier (SFIO)	Jan. 22, '47	Nov. 19, '47	8 SFIO, 5 MRP, 5 CP, 3 RS, 2 UDSR, 2 Con.
Robert Schuman (MRP)	Nov. 24, '47	July 19, '48	6 MRP, 5 SFIO, 2 RS, 1 UDSR, 1 Con.
André Marie (RS)	July 26, '48	Aug. 28, '48	6 SFIO, 6 MRP, 5 RS, 2 Con.
Robert Schuman (MRP)	Sept. 5, '48	Sept. 7, '48	6 MRP, 4 SFIO, 4 RS, 1 Con.
Henri Queuille (RS)	Sept. 9, '48	Oct. 6, '49	5 MRP, 5 SFIO, 3 RS, 1 UDSR, 1 Con.
Georges Bidault (MRP)	Oct. 29, '49	June 24, '50	6 MRP, 5 SFIO, 5 RS, 2 Con.
René Pleven (UDSR)	July 12, '50	Feb. 28, '51	6 MRP, 5 SFIO, 5 RS, 3 UDSR, 3 Con.
Henri Queuille (RS)	Mar. 10, '51	July 10, '51	7 MRP, 5 SFIO, 4 RS, 3 UDSR, 3 Con.
Elections June 17, '51			
René Pleven (UDSR)	Aug. 10, '51	Jan. 7, '52	7 MRP, 7 RS, 7 Con., 2 UDSR
Edgar Faure (RS)	Jan. 20, '52	Feb. 29, '52	8 MRP, 8 Con., 7 RS, 3 UDSR
Antoine Pinay (Con.)	Mar. 8, '52	Dec. 23, '52	6 Con., 5 RS, 4 MRP, 2 UDSR
René Mayer (RS)	Jan. 8, '53	May 21, '53	8 Con., 7 RS, 6 MRP, 2 UDSR
Joseph Laniel (Con.)	June 27, '53	June 12, '54	8 Con., 5 MRP, 4 RS, 3 Gaul., 2 UDSR
Pierre Mendès-France (RS)	June 18, '54	Feb. 6, '55	5 RS, 4 Gaul., 3 Con., 2 UDSR, 1 MRP
Edgar Faure (RS)	Feb. 25, '55	Jan. 24, '56	5 RS, 5 Con., 4 Gaul., 4 MRP, 1 UDSR
Elections Jan. 2, '56			
Guy Mollet (SFIO)	Jan. 31, '56	May 21, '57	6 SFIO, 4 RS, 3 Gaul., 2 UDSR
Maurice Bourgès-Maunoury (RS)	June 12, '57	Sept. 30, '57	6 RS, 5 SFIO, 2 UDSR
Félix Gaillard (RS)	Nov. 5, '57	April 15, '58	4 SFIO, 4 Con., 3 RS, 3 MRP, 2 UDSR, 1 Gaul.
Pierre Pflimlin (MRP)	May 14, '58	May 28, '58	5 MRP, 5 RS, 5 Con., 3 UDSR
Charles de Gaulle	June 1, '58	Jan. 8, '59	4 CS, 2 SFIO, 2 MRP, 2 Con., 2 RS, 1 NP
FIFTH REPUBLIC Elections Nov. 23 and 30, 1958			
Michel Debré (Gaul.)	Jan. 8, '59	April 14, '62	7 Gaul., 7 CS, 5 Con., 4 MRP, 1 UDSR, 1 RS, 1 NP
Georges Pompidou (Gaul.)	April 15, '62		8 Gaul., 5 MRP, 5 CS, 2 Con, 1 RS, 1 NP

ABBREVIATIONS: CP—Communist Party · Con.—Conservatives (usually Independents) · Gaul.—Gaullist (Social Republicans or U.N.R.) · MRP—*Mouvement Républicain Populaire* (Christian Democrats) · RS—Radical Socialists (and similar) · SFIO—Socialist Party · UDSR—*Union Démocratique et Socialiste de la Résistance* (small center party of personalities) · CS—Civil Servant · NP—Nonparty personality most important Ministers in early 1962, ten had spent almost all their public lives in the bureaucracy. Besides the posts dealing with the presidential sector, Justice, Education, Industry and Commerce, and Housing were in the hands of such "technicians." As for the pure political appointees, all of whom, of course, were obliged by the constitution to resign their parliamentary seats on entering the cabinet, they were either loyal Gaullists, personal friends of de Gaulle and Debré from other parties, or relatively unambitious men who represented the wing of their party most loyal to de Gaulle. The situation in the Pompidou Government is only slightly changed, with seven of the principal posts in the hands of veteran civil servants in June 1962. (See Tables 9 and 10.)

Since policy making under the Fourth Republic was subordinated to the problem of assembling and preserving a Government majority, the Prime Minister and his colleagues spent much of their time in constant

TABLE **10** **The Ministers and Their Departments**
(As of June 1962)

Prime Minister
Georges Pompidou (Appointed April 15, 1962), Banker, former civil servant.

Ministers of State

Cultural Affairs	:	André Malraux (Writer)
Overseas Departments and Territories	:	Louis Jacquinot (Former Independent deputy)
Algerian Affairs	:	Louis Joxe (Civil servant)
Scientific Research, Atomic Energy, and Space	:	Gaston Palewski (Former Gaullist deputy)

Ministers

Justice	:	Jean Foyer (Civil servant)
Foreign Affairs	:	Maurice Couve de Murville (Civil servant)
Interior	:	Roger Frey (Gaullist party leader)
Armed Forces	:	Pierre Messmer (Civil servant)
Finance and Economic Affairs	:	Valéry Giscard d'Estaing (Former Independent deputy)
Education	:	Pierre Sudreau (Civil servant)
Public Works and Transportation	:	Roger Dusseaulx (Former Gaullist deputy)
Industry	:	Michel Maurice-Bokanowski (Former Gaullist deputy)
Agriculture	:	Edgard Pisani (Former Radical Senator)
Labor	:	Gilbert Grandval (Civil servant)
Public Health and Population	:	Raymond Marcellin (Former Independent deputy)
Housing	:	Jacques Maziol (Former Gaullist Deputy)
Veterans Affairs	:	Raymond Triboulet (Former Gaullist deputy)
Post and Telecommunications	:	Jacques Marette (Former Gaullist Senator)
Cooperation (aid to former overseas dependencies)	:	Georges Gorse (Civil servant)

Secretaries of State
(Attached to Prime Minister's Office)

Information	:	Alain Peyrefitte (Former Gaullist deputy)
Civil Service Administration	:	Jean de Broglie (Former Independent deputy)
Repatriation Affairs	:	Robert Boulin (Former Gaullist deputy)
Internal Commerce	:	François Missoffe (Former Gaullist deputy)
Parliamentary Liaison	:	Pierre Dumas (Former Gaullist deputy)

negotiations over policy with the leadership of the National Assembly—
the officers of the two houses and presidents of party groups and of the
legislative committees. For this reason alone men having little or no
parliamentary influence could rarely be Ministers. The Government's program often lacked coherence because of the need to compromise basically
irreconcilable views in the momentary majority. And the Ministers' control
over the civil service was imperfect, due to both their short tenure of office
and their lack of technical competence, being usually purely political
choices. While the Fifth Republic sought to change all this, and has,
indeed, gone far toward doing so, what has remained striking is the extent
to which guaranteed cabinet stability, the high percentage of technician-
Ministers, and their ability to keep close watch upon the civil service did
not produce a radically more coherent and effective policy program for
the Debré Government.

The reasons for this derived from the difficult political circumstances
created by the Algerian war and the failure of the institutional changes
of 1958 to alter seriously the constitutionally untouchable habits of
parliamentarians, pressure groups, and civil servants. The Government's
role in the policy process was twofold: it supposedly restricted itself to
simply executing the decisions made by de Gaulle in his presidential
sector of policy while it both made and executed policy in its own "open"
sector of largely domestic questions. Most policy on domestic matters—
an area de Gaulle referred to metaphorically as "decisions concerning the
price of milk"—did, in fact, originate in the Prime Minister's office, in the
ministerial departments, or in meetings of the cabinet and its subcommittees. As in the past the great majority of decrees, ordinances, and
Government-sponsored legislative proposals were still drafted by civil
servants or the personal staffs of the Ministers. But once this had been
done, the cabinet's role in the policy process bore little resemblance to the
practices of the Third or Fourth Republics, even when one had taken
into account the huge reduction in scope produced by the creation of a
"reserved" presidential sector of policy.

Prior to the present regime, policy proposals, after approval by a Minister, usually had to be debated and decided in full cabinet meetings,
chaired by the Prime Minister. Given the problem of unstable Government
coalitions, these deliberations necessarily were those of a general parliamentary strategy board that discussed, in the main, the conditions of preserving
the majority—hence staying in office—and weighed the possible effects of
the policy decision on these conditions. Cabinet meetings in the past had
to subordinate the substantive merits of a policy to an evaluation of its
impact on the cohesion of the parliamentary majority. The participation
of the Ministers in these discussions, therefore, was vital, less for their

judgments on the policy itself, than for their reports on the probable reactions of their party colleagues and their personal pledges to marshal
their party's support in favor of the policy compromises finally hammered
out. Once the cabinet made its decision and assured itself of a parliamentary majority for a policy, the final approval by the Council of Ministers,
chaired then as now by the President, was largely a matter of form, since
the latter's role in the past was largely consultative.

Under the Fifth Republic the constitutionally reinforced stability of
the Government has made the political and parliamentary strategy deliberations of the cabinet unnecessary. Full cabinet meetings, therefore, have
become very infrequent, the full complement of Ministers assembling only
at the long, weekly meetings with de Gaulle at the Council of Ministers.
Between these sessions Ministers have spent most of their time in their
departments, overseeing the execution of policy and consulting with civil
servants on policy proposals. Their participation in purely cabinet decision
making, before the rather formal debate at the Council of Ministers, was
limited to the meetings of various interdepartmental committees (*comités
interministériels*) created by Debré for the substantive discussion of policy
matters proposed by the departments. These groups were the most important stage in the policy process for matters within the Government's
"open" sector of domestic questions. However, the personal influence of
Prime Minister Debré on the composition and function of these committees severely curtailed their use by power-minded Ministers for influencing Government decisions. Conscientious to the point of obsession,
Debré presided over most interdepartmental committees and dominated
their deliberations. As a former civil servant, he preferred the counsel of
the professional expert and often named a high bureaucrat rather than a
Minister to a committee discussing a particularly sensitive matter. Many
of these committees were not formally on the cabinet level, and even those
that were may have had civil servants as members. When he wanted to
avoid a Minister's participation altogether, the committee meetings were
simply formal affairs, while the real decisions were made in informal contacts between Debré, his staff, and the civil servants concerned.

THE PRIME MINISTER'S OFFICE

Obviously this system has reinforced the influence of the Prime Minister
over Government decisions, since he not only could dominate small expert
groups more easily than full cabinet meetings of his peers, but also could,
by simply refraining from creating such committees, chose areas of policy
to deal with personally. To assist him in this task Prime Minister Debré
followed President de Gaulle's lead and appointed a large personal staff
to provide him with background material and oversee policy execution

and policy coordination. There is also a regular governmental department known as the "Services of the Prime Minister," a division of which is called the General Secretariat of the Government. This performs the actual administrative task of policy coordination: collecting the proposals of the Ministers, servicing the interdepartmental committees, drafting final versions of decrees, ordinances, and Government bills, and finally submitting them to the Council of State (*Conseil d'Etat*), a body of high civil servants who act as the Government's permanent legal advisers, empowered to redraft bills if they seem improper or unconstitutional. Other offices grouped under the Prime Minister's direct control deal with substantive and administrative matters of a general or necessarily interdepartmental nature. These include vastly important departments such as the Atomic Energy Commission, the Civil Service Administration, and the Information services, which have been headed by Ministers or lesser cabinet members known as Secretaries of State. Finally, there are lesser services such as the government publications office, the department charged with encouraging scientific research, and the mysterious S.D.E.C.E. (*Service de Documentation Extérieure et de Contre-Espionnage*), roughly France's equivalent of the American C.I.A.

Wherever a policy decision originated, Michel Debré established the practice of consulting a small circle of advisers before taking it to the Council of Ministers for final approval. Among them were members of his staff who informed him of soundings they had made in the groups and interests likely to be affected by the policy. There were members of de Gaulle's personal staff who advised him on their chief's probable reaction. And there were a very few cabinet members whose advice Debré respected, as well as the Gaullist President of the National Assembly, Jacques Chaban-Delmas, who often predicted parliamentary reaction. In reaction to increasing parliamentary opposition to parts of his domestic program during 1961, Debré made an effort to discuss policy decisions with members of parliament before their announcement as executive rules or their presentation to parliament for lawmaking. Much of the criticism of the Fifth Republic has centered on the treatment of parliament as a rubber stamp, by both Debré and de Gaulle, forcing it to pass a bill in the form presented by the Government by using the various constitutional levers on the legislative process. The principal Government party, the Gaullist UNR, has continually asked for the privilege of prior consultation in return for its loyal support of Government bills. They as well as other parties have argued that some concessions to parliament, or at least its consultation, during the early stages of policy consideration would assure speedier passage of a Government bill later, since the predictable objections of pressure groups could be met before public debate began and open concessions became more embarrassing. To meet these requests Debré "delegated" a senior Minister with considerable parliamentary experience to the job of liaison with parliament during the whole policy process, and he increased his own personal contacts with parliamentarians to discuss current policy matters. Prime Minister Pompidou, whose nomination was itself a source of parliamentary irritation, has continued this practice.

THE COUNCIL OF MINISTERS AND DELEGATED LEGISLATION

The final stage of policy making by the Government is discussion and decision in the weekly meetings of the Council of Ministers. While much of the time is taken up with the formal approval of all high administrative appointments below the cabinet level, the Council also must ratify ordinances and decrees before they can be promulgated and approve Government bills before they can be submitted to parliament. The discussion leading up to this approval is often the only chance for most of the Ministers to discuss policy decisions. And because full cabinet meetings are rare, it is also in the Council of Ministers that collective responsibility for policy *vis à vis* parliament and public opinion is taken. Yet, since he presides, the President, who is not responsible to parliament, directs this process and thereby, along with his chairing the only regular full meetings of the cabinet, reinforces his dominance over policy-making. From the little that is known of these meetings it can be said that de Gaulle's rein on the Ministers has been very short. He usually announced his decisions concerning policy in the presidential sector and asked for the "observations" of the Ministers. Few of them were reported to hazard a view, realizing the uselessness of the effort and fearing the irony, if not the wrath, of de Gaulle. But on domestic matters de Gaulle has allowed somewhat more discussion, since it was the Ministers who presented the decisions and since de Gaulle knew that the views of the political Ministers especially reflected the positions of interests and parties that had to be accommodated.

When a policy decision threatened to arouse a storm of public protest or even to endanger the Government's parliamentary majority, the kind of general political strategy discussion that once dominated cabinet meetings occasionally took place, undoubtedly in the Council of Ministers. Similarly the kind of arbitration of conflicts among Ministers over budgetary questions and matters of administrative responsibility that were once decided by the Prime Minister in cabinet meetings was usually handled by de Gaulle in the Council, even though the Ministers were not formally responsible to him. These various assumptions of cabinet functions by the Council, as well as the Prime Minister's preference for policy discussion in interdepartmental committees and his general loyalty to de Gaulle, have all had the net effect of strengthening the President's control over policy.

The Council of Ministers under the Fifth Republic has also grown more important in policy making because it formally issued the ordinances by which the Government implemented the increased delegations of legislative power given to it by parliament. Already under the Fourth Republic the Government repeatedly asked parliament for enabling acts empowering it to "legislate" by decree on matters normally reserved for lawmaking. Especially after the outbreak of the Algerian war in 1954, succeeding Governments asked the legislative branch to declare a "state of emergency" or to accord them "special powers," which meant, in effect, that it would be the Council of Ministers that made law within the fairly circumscribed area defined by the enabling act. The specific decrees had great significance, empowering officials in Algeria to suspend civil liberties, to set up internment camps, and to launch basic economic, social, and administrative reforms. The enabling acts, moreover, allowed the Council of Ministers to make existing legislation consistent with the new decrees, and this without limit of time in the case of the March 1956 "special powers" law.

Under the Fifth Republic the executive's access to and exercise of delegated legislative powers had been further facilitated. Article 38 of the constitution formally institutionalizes the practice of the last years of the Fourth Republic by permitting the Government to ask for parliamentary consent for taking measures normally dealt with by law, on the simple grounds that they were required for the "execution of its program." These grants of legislative authority were supposedly limited by both time and subject, and the Government was expected to table regular bills embodying the ordinances it had issued. In February 1960, after the first unsuccessful army coup in Algiers, the Debré Government invoked Article 38 and, under pressure of events and the Government's normally great control of the legislative process, an enabling act was quickly passed authorizing it to take measures "necessary for assuring order, the safety of the state and the constitution, the pacification and administration of Algeria." Although this delegation of authority was limited to a year, its scope, as this quotation illustrates, went far beyond that accorded by previous enabling acts. The law made no reference to the specific Government program whose "execution" had to be assured, nor did it further define the policy limits within which the Government could act. The delegation of legislative power made no distinction between Algeria and metropolitan France and it allowed the Government to transform its ordinances into permanent legislation within the year.

This 1960 enabling act has been cited as another example of the tendency to expand executive power at the expense of parliament under the Fifth Republic. In particular, the law once again reinforced de Gaulle's personal control over policy for, unlike previous delegations of legislative power, it specified that the ordinances issued must appear "under the signature of General de Gaulle, President of the Republic." The Government undoubtedly felt that the measures likely to be taken required de Gaulle's personal prestige attached to them for popular consent and parliamentary reassurance. Indeed, the first thirty ordinances issued under the 1960 law gave the French Government repressive powers that no other western democracy had available. And as expected, the Algerian crisis and the continued confidence in de Gaulle justified for both the public and parliament the vast increase in the executive's police powers. Less justifiable in those terms, and generally unnoticed, were a number of ordinances Prime Minister Debré asked the Council of Ministers to issue under the same law, but which dealt with subjects totally unrelated to "assuring order" or "the safety of the state." In July 1960, for example, the Government issued an ordinance regulating the home distillation of alcohol, a problem France's government has been grappling with for a century and one certainly not requiring emergency action that automatically excluded parliamentary consideration. In fact, only a month after the February 1960 law was passed, Debré had an ordinance issued on the touchy question of relocating former French settlers in Indochina, in order to forestall further parliamentary discussion of a private member's bill dealing with the matter and passed by one of the houses weeks before the circumstances arose that motivated the enabling act under which the Government acted.

These abuses of delegated legislation are in part the fault of parliament, which in times of crisis has always abandoned any procedures for controlling the Government's use of these grants of authority while they are in effect. Even under the Third and Fourth Republics parliament rarely showed interest in keeping a close watch in order to debate the abuses of delegated legislation that came to light. But under the Fifth Republic these abuses were principally due to the fact that the men most influential in policy making—De Gaulle, Debré, and most of his Ministers—were all partisans of the administrative tradition of politics. Their belief in the existence of an objective national interest has made them see the nation and its problems as submitted to a vast administrative process in which choosing the rationally correct solution is more vital than choosing the one for which there is public or parliamentary consent. None of them were really antidemocratic but they did believe, with de Gaulle, that generating consensus or even consent for a specific policy was usually hopeless in France. When, therefore, the pressure for policy decisions became great, as in times of crisis, their first reflex was to issue an ordinance or decree, and be done with it. If this resulted in the infringement of parliament's lawmaking power or in abusing a grant of delegated legislative authority, there was reference to the "safety of the state" or to *raison d'état*, the ultimate justification of those in the administrative tradition of politics.

For all these reasons the debate in the Council of Ministers over ordinances and decrees not subject to immediate parliamentary approval has been potentially a limited check on executive power. However, since the departure of the conservative political leader Antoine Pinay from the Ministry of Finance, none of the remaining political Ministers had the self-confidence or national following to challenge Debré, let alone de Gaulle. The former civil servants who were the technician Ministers had neither the personal authority nor the inclination to do so, and thus much of the most important policies moved from conception to execution with only the barest exposure to regular and formal criticism.

Negotiations with Interest Groups

To be fair one must mention that Debré often did take policy matters directly to the interested parties for their criticism and advice, thus mitigating the closed circuit of decision-making in the administrative tradition. This was actually thrust upon him by the fact that the decline of parliamentary and party influence had driven representatives of economic and social interests to bring their complaints directly to the Government, often with the hope of negotiating a solution by ordinance or decree, thus eliminating parliament altogether. In at least one case the Prime Minister tried to solve an economic problem by such informal negotiation and compromise rather than by asking parliament or even the Government for action. In March 1961 Debré met with the president of the National Confederation of French Employers in order to obtain from big business the promise not to raise wages over four per cent, which would have favored inflation.

In the case of most domestic policy, as has been mentioned above, the Ministers did meet with the representatives of interested pressure groups, as well as with members of parliament, or had their staff aides do so. But until recently these meetings rarely resulted in a negotiated compromise at the cabinet level between the Government's view and that of the interest or party concerned. This was because of de Gaulle's personal antipathy for what he calls the "intermediaries" that stand between the state and the people and that, according to him, thrive on the promotion of the particular interest over the national interest. One of the results of this view has been that many of the concessions to the "intermediaries" are made below the cabinet level in the bureaucracy, thus transforming civil servants into "intermediaries" along with parliament, parties, and pressure groups. De Gaulle, moreover, saw the Ministers as essentially heads of "bureaux," as a commanding general views the members of his general staff whose prime function is to execute decisions and watch over their officers. Consequently, he often criticized the Ministers for their prior consultation over policy with interested factions, not only because it seemed to him a return to past practices of incoherent policies but also because it enlarged the influence of "intermediaries" over policy making and made the state seem weak.

De Gaulle continually opposed Debré's discussions with trade union and business leaders, and not until the rise of real conflict between the Government and parliament over agricultural policies in 1961 did he allow a member of the cabinet to have the formal job of parliamentary liaison. Yet, oddly enough, de Gaulle himself, as supreme arbitrator, spent much of his day in discussions with the "intermediaries" and had a member of his staff assigned to the task of collecting information on the mood of parliament, the parties, and pressure groups. Indeed, it was often as a result of just such direct contacts that de Gaulle decided to intervene in the Government's realm of policy making. He entered this "open" sector in order to disallow a decision he felt would cause too great a public outcry, such as a Government bill to control the press or a decision to arrest a particularly violent political opponent of the Government. Then too he entered the process in order to assure passage of a bill or the execution of an ordinance that the Government seemed unlikely to achieve alone. But de Gaulle justified these contacts with "intermediaries" in a typically monarchical manner: they were all his "subjects" and as supreme arbitrator he personally had to hear their complaints, for his arbitration might ultimately have to be between the Government and one of the "intermediaries." Until such an occasion appeared, however, it remained useful for de Gaulle to have a Government that, by being relatively intransigent and isolated from parliament and opinion, allowed the "republican monarch" to enjoy a reputation for greater flexibility, thus making it possible for him to exercise his arbitration more fully when he chose to do so. It is precisely these requirements of "republican monarchy" that made the Government's relations with parliament and even the civil service so difficult. If France no longer had a parliamentary form of government this would not be a problem, but it should be remembered that, besides depending upon a parliamentary majority for its life, French Governments must still go to the legislative branch for laws and must rely on the bureaucracy for the execution of policy.

The Role of the "Intermediaries": Modifying
the Executive Will

With important policy made by de Gaulle, with most other decisions made by the Prime Minister and the Government, and with the vast grants of delegated legislation and almost limitless emergency powers available to the executive, why then, should the French political system have continued to appear powerless before many outstanding problems? The Algerian war for three years, the subversion of the military party, the crises of a backward agriculture, the disparity of living standards in other sectors of the economy, were all the object of Government policies, yet they all remained sources of political unrest. General de Gaulle placed the blame for this unrest on what he picturesquely called "the bands of grumblers, churls, and the ill-tempered." On the rare occasions when he admitted that his policies had not been successful, he attributed failure to certain "intermediaries" who interposed themselves between the state and the nation, in order to prevent reasonable policies from being executed. As has been mentioned, these intermediaries were, in de Gaulle's mind, parliament as a whole, the political parties, pressure groups, individual politicians, and even the bureaucracy and other agents of execution like army officers and the police.

Of course, France, like other societies, has many unresolved problems because the policies chosen and executed by the political system have not been adequate to the task. It is true, however, that inaction by the Government, or the adoption of inadequate policies, has often been due to the resistance of important groups having access to all levels of the policy process. Some problems were unresolved because the executive had been obliged to make incoherent or watered-down policies that reflected the disagreement of parties and opinion, very much in the style of the Fourth Republic's ephemeral Governments. Still other problems were not resolved because the interpretation or execution of Government policies by different levels of public servants denatured their impact on society. In all these latter cases the cause for policy failure was at least in part the intervention of "intermediaries" between the executive will and the people. Yet this is both inevitable and universal, having existed under all French regimes, as well as under the effective mixed governmental systems of Britain and the United States, and even under the totalitarian system of the Soviet Union.

In Britain and the United States, however, the harmful effects of the "intermediaries" are limited by allowing them formal and regular participation in the policy process. Parliament ceases to be only a negative "intermediary" when it has a responsible role in policy making. A political party ceases to be simply an "intermediary" when it is in a stable Government or opposition coalition or is itself the majority or opposition party.

Pressure groups are at least less "intermediaries" when they have either the party system or an effective process of consultation by the Government to look to for the redress of grievances. Finally, public servants are no longer "intermediaries" when their neutrality is protected by the existence of alternate channels for the influencing of policy by special interests. The virtue of mixed government is that it transforms all these "intermediaries" into functioning and necessary links between the Government and the people, obliging them thereby to bear some responsibility for the general interest.

Totalitarian systems must also deal with "intermediaries," and it would be wrong to think that force and terror are its only methods for doing so. The single totalitarian party has the function of criticizing the civil servants in their execution of the Government's policies. The party also serves to inform the Government of popular reactions to its policies and the limits of what will be obeyed by consent alone. Naturally, the mechanisms of the police state are the ultimate means of executing the Government's will when consent must be ignored and the interference of "intermediaries" crushed. But both the Soviet government and British government have attenuated the problem of resistance to public policy and its execution by developing a permanent transmission belt between opinion and policy making, whether it be of a democratic or authoritarian nature. Both systems have at least discovered institutions assuring effective policy making within the context of their political culture and values.

France under the Fifth Republic has not succeeded in this for the same reason its predecessors have failed: the refusal to adopt political institutions that can lessen the ancient conflict between ideals of authority. The present regime is in the administrative tradition of politics, and the shortcomings of its policy process are due to the vices of that tradition. The existence of powerful "intermediaries" that hamper policy execution has always been typical of such regimes, from the eighteenth century when the word itself first came into common usage, to the limited monarchies and the empires of the nineteenth century, to the Vichy regime of Marshal Pétain in World War II. Indeed, one might almost say that regimes that formally make policy decisions an executive monopoly are themselves responsible for informally transforming special interests, political parties, and their own civil servants into the very "intermediaries" whose influence they had hoped to escape.

De Gaulle's analysis of the weaknesses of his policy process, therefore, is quite apt, notwithstanding its old-fashioned terminology. The "intermediaries" are responsible for modifying the will of the executive, and together they play the third major role in the Fifth Republic's policy making. Although he has rejected mixed government, de Gaulle is neither a tyrant nor a totalitarian and therefore admits that parties, pressure groups, parliament, and partisan civil servants must be tolerated. Unwilling to suppress his "intermediaries" de Gaulle has been obliged to allow them considerable freedom, although he continued to bar them from the positive responsibility in policy-making that alone would reduce their negative influence.

Parliament: Concessions to Parties, Politicians and Interests

In the first edition of this book the analysis of parliament's role in policy-making under the Fourth Republic began with this flat statement: "While most policy is initiated by the executive . . . it is parliament that is the most influential in determining the ultimate content of Government policies." The present edition dealing with the Fifth Republic shows in two ways how inapplicable this statement has become. Parliament's role is relegated to that of an "intermediary," exerting largely a braking or negative power over policy. And the details of the legislative process, by which parliament once dominated policy, is described, not in this chapter but rather in the chapter on the formal constitutional order. This is to suggest that the legislative process is to a great extent now irrelevant to policy-making and that it is significant today rather as an illustration of how the new constitution subordinates the legislative branch to the executive.

The constitution, however, still requires parliament to participate formally in policy-making, even if its influence is no longer dominant. Article 34 setting up the "domain of the law" requires the Government to go to parliament for legislative approval of the most important policies. When speedy action is required the Government invokes Article 38 and asks parliament for a delegation of legislative authority in the form of an enabling act. After it has issued ordinances under that act the Government must go to parliament to have these ordinances ratified. But, as we have already seen, parliament's role in all these cases does not really add up to a serious influence over policy-making, at least not under the present crisis and monarchical phase of the Fifth Republic.

Sources of Parliamentary Weakness. FORMAL RESTRICTIONS ON PARLIAMENT: The new constitution has had much to do with reducing the impact of parliament on the final policy product. Article 49 has deprived the National Assembly of the power to implicitly jeopardize the life of the Government on every bill submitted by linking the question of confidence to the cumbersome mechanism of the censure motion. The Government now knows that its bill will automatically become law if it asks for a vote of confidence, because the opposition is too divided and today still too small to muster the absolute majority of the members for the motion of censure. The constitution is also responsible for placing almost every stage of the legislative process under the close control of the Government. Article 48 gives the executive the right to monopolize parliament's agenda; Article 44 gives it the right to reject offensive amendments by the technique of the "single vote"; Article 45 allows the Government to call for a joint conference committee for hastening along final passage. Even in the management of its own public debates, a potential forum for criticizing the Government, parliament has been barred from using such mild and traditional levers against the executive as the "indicative vote" (*vote indicatif*), which has no affect on final passage, or even the vote after an oral question, which at least could reveal the "mood" of the house.

Members have usually been careful to avoid tabling their own bills or amendments to Government bills that could be interpreted as dealing with matters outside of the restricted "domain of the law," established by Article 34. Whether right or wrong, they now assume that the Government's protest would always be upheld by the Constitutional Council, given its ruling on the senatorial rules of procedure in 1959. To avoid further such embarrassment, members now "clear" their amendments with the Government before tabling them, thus voluntarily giving up a measure of parliament's independent control over policy.

Private members' legislation has almost disappeared, not only because of the Government control of the agenda, but also because Article 40 prohibits members from tabling bills that involve either a public expense or a reduction in revenue; this thereby obliges private members' bills to be only symbolic.

But the very nature and form of the laws parliament now makes also tend to reduce its role in policy-making. Government bills have become extremely general in their wording, regularly implying a large grant of quasi-legislative power to the executive through the use of its rule-making power to fill in the "details." Under the Fourth Republic parliaments occasionally resolved a complicated and politically delicate policy matter by passing a "framework law" (*loi cadre*), which set the general principles and left the details to executive decision. On most Government bills, however, they fully exercised their jealously guarded right to decide on the minutest detail, if not rewrite the bill altogether, thus making laws longer and more complicated than comparable legislation in Britain. There these results have been achieved due to the cabinet's firm grip on a stable and disciplined majority, allowing it to oblige parliament to pass general laws that give the executive large grants of legislative authority to be exercised by "statutory instruments," the British equivalent of decrees.

The cabinet in the Fifth Republic has often submitted its policy proposals in the form of "program laws" (*lois de programme*) or "orienting laws" (*lois d'orientation*), which set forth the major provisions of a policy or the direction the Government intended to take on a matter but left the details and the methods of execution to executive discretion. Whereas in the past, unlike England, France made relatively little use of delegated legislation, under the Fifth Republic most laws involve various degrees of such grants, and all thanks to the Government's control of the legislative process. The disturbing aspect of this development is that much of the content of French laws is not even indirectly sanctioned, let alone reviewed, by parliament. While de Gaulle remained President one could argue that a majority in the country, if not always in parliament, sanctioned the delegation of lawmaking authority exercised in his name, thereby approximating the approval of the majority party in the British parliament. But given France's multiparty system and the scant likelihood of stable coalitions or a majority party in the near future, it is difficult to see how the growth of delegated legislation could be justified democratically after de Gaulle left office.

INFORMAL RESTRICTIONS ON PARLIAMENT: Aside from the constitution and the perpetual atmosphere of crisis that in France, as in all countries, results in broad grants of legislative power to the executive, there were a number of lesser factors that also prevented parliament from playing a major role in the policy process. The individual deputy or senator continued to remain poorly equipped to criticize the Government's legislative proposals. The French parliament has no equivalent of the American legislative reference service to provide background documentation on legislative proposals, and neither members nor parliamentary committees have adequate secretarial or staff assistance for developing a detailed critique of Government bills. The Assembly's small library is for browsing, not research, and the overworked civil servant attached to a committee has only his home ministry as a source of information. In the past this vacuum of information was partly filled by masses of carefully and attractively prepared documentation originating in the offices of pressure groups. But under the new regime the latter tend to go directly to the Government, the real center of power, and hence spend less time "educating" parliament.

Neither house has made adequate use of question day (Article 48) as a means of criticizing Government policy for reasons that have been described in Chapter 13, as well as for a lack of information and staff. Even public debate has not been fully exploited as a means of focusing critical attention, in part because of the notable absence of experienced and effective parliamentary orators. The defeat of so many veteran party leaders at the 1958 elections brought to the Assembly many inexperienced politicians who have rarely proved a threat to even the modest oratorical

talents available to the Debré and Pompidou Governments. Like every impotent representative body in history, the French parliament has often surrendered to the easy alternative of broad ideological attack on Government
bills rather than pertinent, constructive criticism, even when the policy required no great expertise for being understood. This falling-back on the tired
oratorical styles of the past has hardly endeared parliament to an opinion
already convinced of the inevitable irresponsibility of French parliaments.
Nor does this knowledge of public hostility help to encourage members of
parliament to make maximum use of their right to criticize the executive,
so important a function of parliament in Britain.

THE GAULLIST UNR: A "MOBILE RESERVE":   In truth, however, it must be
noted that, even if deputies chose to use prolonged public debate as a
means of prying concessions from the Government, they would find it
difficult to do so. The President of the Assembly is a loyal follower of
General de Gaulle, a friend of the Prime Minister, and a member of the
UNR, the major pro-Government party. He has generally employed the
increased powers of the office to keep debate to a minimum as well as to
keep other prerogatives of his colleagues strictly within their tight constitutional bonds. The Assembly President's election, moreover, reflects a
party alignment in the lower house that also tends to reduce the influence
of parliament. In the Assembly the Gaullist UNR deputies have proved to
be a stable bloc of about two hundred votes, constantly at the disposition
of the Government. This has provided Prime Minister Debré with what
French commentators refer to by the military term of a "mobile reserve"
(*masse de manœuvre*)—a center voting bloc that, according to the bill
being considered, he could order to the left or right in order for them to
join the bare two dozen additional deputies from the other parties of his
majority needed for an absolute majority of the house. On most votes a
plurality of those present and voting is enough, making it even easier
to muster a favorable vote for Government bills, given the permanent
loyalty of the UNR. As shall be seen below, the party alignment in the
Senate was radically different and represented a minor source of leverage
against the executive. But in the Assembly, with two hundred UNR
votes in his control, Debré could turn to the MRP for the margin of
winning votes on an Algerian issue, when many Independents would be in
the opposition, and later he could turn to the latter for the same margin
on a financial issue when the MRP could no longer be depended upon.
Even when the Senate delayed approval of a Government bill, the Prime
Minister could call for a joint conference committee, secure in the knowledge that the mode of selection of its Assembly delegates would favor the

UNR as the largest party and hence produce a pro-Government majority that would "unfreeze" the bill.

The end of the Algerian war has emboldened parliamentary criticism of the Government and the prospect of Assembly elections in 1962-63 has somewhat reawakened party activity in mid-1962. Moreover, de Gaulle's replacement of Prime Minister Debré with Georges Pompidou, a banker and former civil servant who had never been a professional politician, served parliament as a good excuse to redouble their protests against the executive's monopoly of decision-making. The opposition parties—Communists, Socialists, Radicals, and the scattered representatives of the military party—have increasingly used procedural "points of order" in public debate in order to engage in impromptu criticism of the Government. The parties of the majority—the MRP, disaffected by much of de Gaulle's foreign policy, the moderate wing of the Independents, and even the loyal UNR—have all succumbed to "electionitis" which in France as elsewhere makes parties more sensitive to voters' complaints and more critical of the men in power. But no threat to the life of the Pompidou Government is really involved in this restiveness. Most UNR deputies know that their reelection will depend on their loyalty to de Gaulle and hence they will continue to assure the cohesion of their Assembly group. This, in turn, makes passage of a motion of censure almost impossible given the present party composition of the lower house.

Sources of Parliamentary Influence. During the third year of the Fifth Republic the appearance of violent social unrest among farmers and government workers, the growing public lassitude over de Gaulle's inability to end the Algerian war, and the talk of approaching elections all resulted in a slight loosening of the Government's grip on policy-making. Like the French kings, whose people suddenly shouted their discontent in the streets, or Napoleon III, whose policies proved ineffective, the Fifth Republic has followed the administrative tradition's precedent of making direct concessions to powerful interests and allowing parliament to participate in policy-making—ever so slightly and by the back door. The observation of this trend itself directed attention to the various means that have always been at parliament's disposal to affect policy-making.

It has been certain informal parliamentary customs, if not simply habits, untouched by circumstances or constitutional change, that were responsible for whatever influence parliament still had. These relatively obscure customs were invaluable tools against the executive under the Third and Fourth Republics and have become rooted in French political culture. Under the Fifth Republic they allowed parliament to force minor concessions on policy from the Government; tomorrow, in new political circumstances without de Gaulle, and even without constitutional change, these parliamentary customs may open the way for at least a partial restoration of parliament's once important influence over policy.

PARLIAMENT AS SPOKESMAN FOR PRESSURE GROUPS: Although, as noted above, pressure groups now tend to go directly to the executive, parliament still serves as a link between them and the executive, especially for the more traditional and old-fashioned special interests such as agriculture and small business. In Chapter 13 it was stated that the drafters of the constitution reduced the number of permanent specialized legislative committees and assumed that most bills would be assigned to small *ad hoc* committees for initial examination in the hope that special interests and pressure groups would have less influence over legislation. But, as was also mentioned, the enduring power of these groups over parliamentary behavior has led to the avoidance of the *ad hoc* committees, to the assignment of deputies to the permanent committees dealing with those policy subjects of personal electoral importance to them, and, finally, to the clearly unconstitutional organization of these huge groups into informal subcommittees, each dealing with the policy of a ministerial department, exactly as did the legislative committee of the Fourth Republic. The effect of this unsanctioned return to past practice is that Government bills are first examined by those members of parliament most politically sensitive to the proposals, and hence best prepared to criticize them. A deputy from an important wheat-growing region today is certain to have a seat on the 120-member Committee for Production and Trade, and undoubtedly will also attend the meetings of the informal subcommittee for agriculture. But even more important, this development allows members with close links to pressure groups to mobilize the extra parliamentary leaders of these organizations for direct action on the Government level at the very start of the legislative process.

In the past the organic connection between members representing an economic or social interest and the professional defense organization was a series of "study groups" (*groupes d'étude*) made up of members coming from districts in which a particular interest was powerful. Whether he was a socialist or a conservative, a member from a region where wine production was important could ill afford to remain aloof from the wine growers' "study group." Similarly, the textile industries or road transport "study groups," representing economic interests scattered all over the country, attracted members from every region, regardless of party. Although formally prohibited by the Assembly's rules under the Fourth Republic, these groups flourished then as they do today, notwithstanding the maintenance of the formal prohibition and the vow of the current Assembly

President to banish them. They are usually founded by a member who has a close personal connection with an industry or professional organization, which, in turn, occasionally provided the group members with much needed research and secretarial assistance. Though illegal, they met in rooms of the two houses to hear representatives of their sponsoring interest address them and generally "brief" them on what amendments should be attached to Government bills in order to defend their common interests.

A looser form of connection between parliamentarian and pressure group is provided by such tolerated, though informal, parliamentary institutions as the "intergroup" and the "parliamentary club" (*amicale parlementaire*), organized by such general interest groups as the Catholic school subsidy lobby, the "French Algeria" lobby, and the farm lobby. In the case of both these large formations and the smaller study groups, the link with a particular political party may often be very close and obviously useful. It is no surprise that the Independents are the most avid defenders of small business in parliament after one notes that the president of the "Parliamentary Club for Small Business" is none other than a recent secretary general of the Independent party.

AMENDMENT OF GOVERNMENT BILLS: This informal reestablishment of specialized legislative committees and the activities of various parliamentary interest groupings have both served to provide the constitutionally diminished parliament with powerful backing from social groups in the country. This sponsorship is used by individual members principally to extract detailed concessions from the Government on its legislative proposals. The quasi-elimination of private members' bills and the executive's control of the legislative process leaves only this type of formal influence over legislation in parliament's hands. De Gaulle and Debré shared the administrative tradition's doctrine that policy is essentially the executive's prerogative, and hence they resisted parliamentary attempts at wholesale overhaul of major legislation. But if, as Prime Minister Debré stated, "Government power does not retreat," it often "allowed" its proposals to be slightly dismantled. When, therefore, the pressure of an interest group was judged to be irresistible, the Government usually negotiated with them in secret in order to learn which aspects of the bill were considered most offensive. Then it "allowed" the concessions by authorizing the parliamentary representatives of the interests to amend the bill, eliminating thereby the provisions on which agreement was reached in the negotiations. Members could add these amendments at the committee stage or they could get specific approval for them when the Government called for a "single vote" in public debate or during the deliberations of the joint conference committee when only Government-approved amendments were in order.

By using the amending process to make concessions to special interests, de Gaulle's executive strove to maintain its public image of invulnerability to pressure politics, in contrast to the Fourth Republic, while still permitting the compromises that all political systems had to allow. The process also provided parliament with much of what influence it still maintained over policy, although it must be said that the principles of neither an "objective" national interest nor democratic accountability were served in the bargain. For in the past the very essence of parliamentary dominance over policy making required ultimate decisions to emerge from the highly publicized dialogues between the Government and parliament. While these often ended in a cabinet crisis, they usually made it clear to the public what parties and interests participated in either producing the final compromise or in defeating the Government bill. During the early Fifth Republic executive dominance over policy making not only involved the secrecy of all administrative decision-making but also meant that parliament's role in begging concessions was exercised through rather hidden negotiations with Ministers or their aides. This actually suited both the Government, eager to avoid publicity for its concessions, and most members of parliament, anxious to conceal an open break with an executive headed by a man for whom public opinion still had great respect.

On the whole executive control of the legislative process has reduced the influence of outside interest groups on lawmaking. But the fact that what influence they have retained is now exercised secretly offsets this advantage to a large degree. Nor has this practice improved the reputation of parliament as a forum for constructive debate of national problems. It had long ceased to have this reputation under the Fourth Republic, and its return to old traditions of blatant interest representation as a source of leverage against the executive under the Fifth promises little improvement in the future.

PARLIAMENT AS THE PRESERVE OF OLD PARTY POLITICS: The basic stability of French political culture and style—that is, the motives and expressions of both general political and parliamentary behavior—also has provided the legislative branch with a measure of influence over policy making. The traditional atmosphere of parliament as a "closed arena," with its special unwritten rules of the game and its organic hostility to the executive, has not changed. Even though the Government is effectively represented at every stage of the legislative process and has a large and loyal bloc of votes at its command in the Assembly, the prevailing mood of parliament remains one of grudging cooperation, if not sullen opposition. Since parliament remains a forum for public debate during five and a half months of the year, the Government obviously must make efforts at preventing a current of criticism originating there from spreading to the nation at large. This would have been easier if the senatorial elections of April 1959 had returned a majority similar to the one elected in the Assembly. But the traditionalism of rural and small-town France, much overrepresented in the Senate's electoral college of delegates mainly from the township and municipal councils, served to make the upper house a bastion of the pattern of power that existed during the last years of the Fourth Republic. Hence, the center parties, and, in particular, opposition parties such as the Socialists, Radicals and Communists, maintained their strength in the Senate. As was seen in Chapter 13, this fact reduced the Senate's usefulness to the Government as a lever against the Assembly. More important, however, by returning so many veteran parliamentarians and producing a much larger opposition than in the Assembly, the Senate's elections created a Fourth Republic atmosphere in the upper house which has fostered vigorous criticism, if not much actual obstruction, of the Government's program.

Enjoying the security of election by local notables committed to voting a party line, of long terms in office unthreatened by dissolution, and of freedom from the responsibility for the life or death of the Government, Senators have become the principal spokesmen for all opposition currents of opinion. The constitution, it is true, gives the Assembly the last word on legislation, and the Government, with its control over that body, has never been permanently blocked by Senate opposition. Yet Senators can extract concessions from the Government in the joint conference committees, where their equal representation with the Assembly and their generally superior legislative and parliamentary experience have allowed them to occasionally influence the committee majority and hence the outcome of this crucial stage in the legislative process. For to avoid having to use the confidence procedure to assure final passage in the Assembly, the Government could either accept the joint committee draft or make its concessions to the Senate by allowing amendments in public debate.

At the end of 1961, with the Assembly fearful of taking strong stands for or against the Government due to the critical status of the Algerian problem and the rumors of coming elections, the Senate became especially active as a sounding board for minority views. Neither Prime Minister Debré nor his Ministers were well equipped personally to offset the rhetorical powers of the Senate, or even the Assembly, for that matter. The Ministers who were former civil servants had no experience in parliamentary debate and their haughty attitude when reciting their statements to both houses only decreased the persuasive impact of their speeches. Debré's long career as an intransigent opposition Senator under the Fourth Republic had not trained him to "handle" parliamentary majorities nor did his scrupulously honest, impolitic, and often self-righteous personality help to make his relations easier with a parliament of ironic Frenchmen. By maintaining, therefore, the old rhetorical styles of the past, parliament placed the Government under a handicap when it occasionally tried to effect passage of a bill by persuasion instead of by its potent control over the legislative process.

By providing a forum for abstract ideological argument, in which a Government of "technicians" was uneasy, both houses also provided material for the opposition press. The advent of a regime in the administrative tradition of politics severely limited newspapers' ability to report on how the most important political decisions were made. When they reported and often magnified the general critiques of parliamentary debate, journalists contributed to the "blackmail of the weak" by which parliament forced concessions from the executive. Although the large party press of the Third and early Fourth Republics has declined, most French newspapers still tend to treat political news in a partisan fashion. Members of parliament have always sought to "extend" their personal prestige, as well as the influence of the legislative branch, by writing articles for the press, having their remarks in debate reprinted and commented upon, and by "inspiring" rumors about dissension and weakness in the Government. Their hope has been to encourage or create a current in opinion that would support them in their struggle with the executive. Although the traditional well-placed rumor or scathing front-page article could no longer bring down the cabinet as it could in the heyday of legislative dominance, it still served as a means of threatening the Government. Mindful of the influence over opinion available to parliament through its press connections, both de Gaulle and Debré took pains to explain personally the Government's position to editors. The Debré Government went even further by unofficially sponsoring the creation of a pro-Government popular weekly paper, as well as a Gaullist competitor for the *Journal du Parlement*, a privately circulated paper that specializes in rumor-mongering and printing deputies' articles, both of a conservative, oppositional nature.

THE GAULLIST UNR: ELECTORAL ASPIRATIONS AND MAJORITY PRETENSIONS: Paradoxically, one of parliament's sources of influence over policy was the major Government party, that bloc of two hundred votes in the Assembly that, as seen above, also served to bend parliament to the Government's will. This would, of course, hardly be paradoxical in a parliamentary system such as the British, where *the* Government party serves both these functions, being itself the majority from which the executive emerges as well as a reflection of the sovereign popular will. But the Gaullist UNR was only the *largest* party in a majority coalition and it operated within a parliamentary tradition that has never had a place for a true governing party linking the executive to majority opinion.

The conflict of French ideals of authority has assigned parliament the traditional role of institutional hero for the representative tradition of politics. As such, its formal and informal organization and customs have all aimed to limit or oppose executive power, while its members have viewed themselves as delegates of the sovereign people, posted to Paris to defend their constituents' interests against the bureaucracy and ambitious politicians. The drafters of the 1958 constitution coped with this ancient oppositional posture of parliament by changing its formal organization and procedures so as to weaken its control over policy making. Many UNR deputies originally entered the Assembly with the hope of behaving like members of a true Government party, unaffected by the pressures of special interests or the attractions of demagoguery. But in choosing "artificial" constitutional means for "taming" parliament, de Gaulle and Debré automatically rejected the alternative of a "natural" control over parliament by a governing majority party as in Britain, and thereby dashed the hopes of the UNR deputies. With the reappearance of informal parliamentary customs described above, it has been difficult for the UNR to develop the strange, new reflexes of a governing party, faced as they were with competition from deputies who felt no compunction in behaving as the delegates of special interests and expressing opposition views even when their parties were officially within the Government majority. Had the constitution established mixed government, in which parliament had a larger direct role in policy making, the basic condition for a true governing party as well as for the "natural" control of parliament by the executive would have been achieved.

As it is, UNR deputies have urged the Government to make concessions to important electoral interests for fear that their blind loyalty would result in an advantage for their competitors. No matter how clearly Debré explained to them that their election in 1958 and their steady successes in by-elections since then were due to their loyalty to de Gaulle, they remained vulnerable to the oppositional and often demagogic atmosphere of parliament. The parties' use of the press as a magnifier of public grievances, the "services" that deputies still hasten to provide their electors, the traditional quest for local elected office (facilitated by the informal reestablishment of proxy voting), and the unchanging oratorical style of ideological criticism, have all made the UNR sensitive to the electoral advantages of adopting some of these traditional parliamentary habits and even giving a certain oppositional cast to their behavior.

For domestic affairs at least, this behavior was partly sanctioned by the regime's creation of the two "sectors" of policy making, the "open" one being excluded from the pledge of loyalty to the supreme arbitrator. It has also been encouraged by the political situation in 1961, which has seen the Government's majority undermined by the defection of the most conservative Independents over the Algerian issue. Moreover, talk of new elections inspired the MRP as well as the UNR to criticize the relatively unpopular economic policies of the Debré Government and to press for more popular domestic legislation. The parliamentary leaders of the UNR, therefore, were torn between their duties as commanders of a silent "mobile reserve" at the disposition of the Government and their responsibilities in getting their followers reelected in the face of growing dissatisfaction with the Government's domestic program.

To escape this dilemma the UNR increasingly insisted on the prerogatives of a true governing party, as opposed to a passive bloc of votes. In so doing, it technically increased parliamentary influence over policy making, for the party asked for and received a larger number of ministerial posts. UNR leaders have also succeeded in obtaining permanent liaison between the Government and the parliamentary party groups, although they have failed to persuade the Government to make the UNR the real inspirer of policy and its spokesman in both parliament and nation. Nor is there much evidence that the UNR has extracted more than minor policy concessions from the Government, for, while its program continues to be generally liberal in economic and social matters, the cabinet's policies continue to reflect the more conservative views of the Minister of Finance and the civil service. On the other hand, the MRP Ministers' sudden departure from the Pompidou Government in May 1962 led to a further increase in the number of UNR Ministers. Fully half of the cabinet is now drawn from the main pro-Government party and the latter's former secretary general is prominent among them. Given Pompidou's lack of political experience and his increasingly difficult parliamentary position, it is possible that the influence of the UNR over Government policy will grow.

The UNR, then, served only slightly to increase parliamentary influence during the early years of the Fifth Republic because it was not a true governing party. While Debré would undoubtedly have liked it to develop in that direction, there were indications that General de Gaulle was opposed to the trend. During the first three years of the Fifth Republic his view of himself as supreme arbitrator closely resembled the monarchical model, which assured executive domination by keeping parliament divided and irresponsible. Not only did his theory of a France permanently without consensus exclude the concept of a governing majority, but the very independence and supremacy of the "republican monarch" depended on the absence of a powerful majority party representing a national opinion only the monarch should represent. The result has been that the Government's policies were often at the mercy of a coalition of "intermediaries," undisciplined by a majority party as in Britain. The Pompidou Government's inability to impose many of its policies, however, might well persuade de Gaulle ultimately to sponsor a completely official Government party or coalition, which could provide the "motor" required for effective policy. Talk of his personally leading a broad "Gaullist Union" in the next elections has given currency to this analysis, for de Gaulle's pragmatism has often led him in the past to act against his convictions when circumstances so required.

But meanwhile the executive-enshrining constitution and the preference of both de Gaulle and his Prime Minister for policy-making in the administrative tradition rendered the future of true party government in France problematic at best. For the moment policy is made by the double executive, slightly altered by the "intermediaries" of parliament and its parties, and interpreted by the civil service, an "intermediary" located at both the origin and the execution of policy, and hence of prime importance.

BUREAUCRACY: THE INFLUENCE OF EXPERTS, ADMINISTRATORS, AND INTERESTS

The policy makers discussed thus far, whether de Gaulle, the Government, or parliament, share in common various degrees of political responsibility to the people. As a regime in the administrative tradition, the Fifth Republic has gone far toward isolating the executive from parliament, the parties, and opinion. Yet, ultimately, de Gaulle's executive is accountable for its decisions as the frequent concessions to special interests and opinion demonstrate. The decisions of the executive in such a regime, however, are apt to be especially influenced by the central institution of the administrative tradition: the bureaucracy. In all political systems the function of civil servants and other agents of policy execution, such as the armed forces, requires them to be politically irresponsible, committed solely to the execution of orders coming from the responsible political executive.

Under the Fourth Republic the bureaucracy gained some power over policy-making, due, first, to ministerial instability, which prevented a constant hand on the policy tiller, and, second, to incoherent policies, reflecting incompatible party coalitions, which required considerable interpretation by the civil service before they could be applicable. On the other hand, a powerful and ever-watchful parliament kept bureaucratic interpretation and policy making within the limits of managing current affairs. The highly detailed and copious legislative production of parliament tended to restrict the discretion of the bureaucracy as did the vigilance of the personal staffs of the Ministers.

With the coming of executive stability and potentially coherent policy programs under the new Republic, it was expected that the bureaucracy's independent policy initiatives would be few, even if its influence within the executive branch would grow now that purely political considerations no longer required the expert view to be modified for reasons of parliamentary strategy. Few commentators, however, foresaw the extent to which the bureaucracy and the rest of the politically irresponsible executive establishment would increase their hold on all levels of the policy process. In today's "republican monarchy" career civil servants have been named as principal Ministers; they have had access to the conception of policy by dominating the personal staffs of the major decision makers, de Gaulle and the Prime Minister; they have influenced policy by drawing up the ordinances, decrees, and Government bills. It was the career civil servant, too, who advised parliament in the exercise of its meager role, and due to the decline of that role it was the civil service that bore much of the brunt of informal pressure group interference. Finally it was the career bureaucracy that, in a highly centralized country like France, executed policy directly at all levels, and in its execution had the last word as to the effect of that policy on the citizen.

This direct contact with the conception, drafting, final formulation, and execution of policy was shared by the career civil servants with a very small, yet powerful group of political appointees among the Ministers' staffs and executing agents, such as the army and various police organizations. But the personal preferences of de Gaulle and Debré, as well as the effect of the new constitutional order, have made the career civil servant the most important of the politically irresponsible influences. Rather than being a break with tradition, it was simply the extension of a historical trend that previous regimes in the representative tradition of politics were neither willing nor able to reverse. The reasons for this are circumstantial in part, but are also deeply rooted in French political culture.

l'Etat: The Tradition of Centralized Administration. France's national civil service has potentially the power to affect the lives of its compatriots more profoundly than that of any other democratic country. Aside from its role in the national policy process, it has responsibility for a wide variety of activities such as local government, all social welfare service, some mining and manufacturing, administering the court system, some banking and insurance, most education, all police powers, all public works, and many other matters that in Britain, Germany, and the United States are handled by independent local or regional authorities, if not by private enterprise. This broad responsibility of the central bureaucracy is not only a reflection of the increase in social services and government economic regulation since World War II. It is, rather, primarily a testimony to the survival of an unreformed administrative pattern of policy making for large sectors of French life inherited from the country's authoritarian past.

ORIGINS: It matters not whether they are conservative or liberal, most Frenchmen seem to have long ago agreed that public services are best administered centrally and that some sectors of social life need considerable government supervision. A centralized, permanent, and powerful bureaucracy is the oldest and most characteristic institution of French public life—far antedating democratic institutions. Born in the absolutist days of the seventeenth century, the bureaucracy was from the start associated with that originally French contribution to political thought: the idea of sovereignty. This held that in every political community there had to be one ultimate source of decision making in public affairs. Prior to the Revolution this source was, of course, the king, the creator of all laws, who exercised these powers through his personal bureaucracy or administration. The Revolution was fought to substitute the people for the king as the ultimate source of law. Logically, then, it should have followed that the unitary state and the centralized bureaucracy, which aided the king in making and executing decisions, would also be swept away by the Revolution. Indeed, the more moderate and perhaps far-sighted of the revolutionary leaders saw that the wise corollary of popular sovereignty was local self-government and rigorous administrative decentralization. But the Jacobins, who soon came to power, felt that it was important to retain a central bureaucracy for practical as well as doctrinal reasons.

On the practical level a strong central bureaucracy was needed to prosecute the war revolutionary France was obliged to wage against most of the dynastic powers of Europe. The Jacobins also needed a centralized governmental mechanism in order to impose the victory of the Revolution, largely a Paris affair, on a conservative and generally hostile provincial France. To permit regionalism and administrative decentralization would also have meant allowing many of the last vestiges of the old hierarchical and even feudal society to survive. Most of the hatred of the revolutionaries and indeed much popular discontent even in the provinces had been directed against social inequalities under the old regime. Only a powerful Paris-directed administration, with its regulations and enforcement procedures, could ensure equality before the law in a country used to inequality and privilege.

On the doctrinal side the revolutionaries and their republican successors were never able to rid themselves of a general French cultural compulsion to have a single source of authority in public affairs. According to their interpretation of the ideas of Jean Jacques Rousseau, apostle of the Revolution, the king's single sovereign will was to be replaced by the people's single sovereign will, and the king himself replaced by a representative assembly. Since this assembly could neither be in continuous contact with the people's will nor alone both make and execute the law, there developed the theory that it would act in favor of an abstract collective good and its laws reflecting that good would be executed by a permanent administration.

Such a theory presumed a pure "assembly regime," in which policy would be made by the all-powerful sovereign assembly and executed by a neutral bureaucracy. But as we saw in Chapter 12, events of the nineteenth century did not allow such a regime to develop. Napoleon made the bureaucracy more than ever the center of the policy-making process, although he did retain the revolutionary idea of the collective good in the place of the clearly obsolete ideas of divine right and feudal order. Furthermore, by organizing a regular bureaucratic career, rendering the administration omnipotent, and encouraging an *esprit de corps* for servants of the state, he strongly reinforced the principles of centralization and permanence, and produced a new and much respected occupational category in France.

L'ETAT AND THE REPUBLIC: Down to the Third Republic, then, the administration remained an adjunct of the all-powerful executive, both in making and executing policy. Naturally, it also became the sworn enemy of the more extreme supporters of the revolutionary idea of a dominant assembly. But when the republicans finally came to power after 1877, they again failed to destroy the essentially undemocratic centralized administration. The early leaders of the Third Republic were not the revolutionary hotheads of 1794, but were representatives of the rising industrial middle class that had chafed under the economic and foreign policies of Napoleon III and had suffered under the new system of privileges created by the Emperor. They feared a "strong man" and the return to power of the old aristocratic elites, but they feared equally the radicals in their own party who talked threateningly of a "social and democratic republic." In the realm of economic and social policies, they disliked a strong, interventionist, or positive state, based on a centralized and permanent bureaucracy. But for purposes of defense against a return of the aristocratic elites or a revolutionary threat to private property, they allowed the bureaucracy to remain as the heart of a "policeman's state," which could protect the status quo. However, to guard against the possibility that the bureaucracy, under the leadership of the cabinet, would develop an independent will, they created a dominant role for parliament in policy-making and even introduced limited local self-government.

Unfortunately, they neglected to change the personnel, duties, and methods of the old imperial bureaucracy, whose values consequently remained, during the Third Republic, much what they had been under the kings and emperors. The stability of French bureaucratic personnel in the nineteenth century is indeed amazing: between 1847 and 1852, from the July Monarchy to the Second Republic to the Second Empire, there were hardly any more changes in personnel than in a normal five-year period under one regime. This was again the case for the years 1869 to 1875, when a dictatorial empire became a liberal empire, turning into a royalist provisional republic and becoming finally a true and permanent republic. Most high civil servants, therefore, remained loyal to the traditional administrative concept of a single collective good, which they as servants of the state could alone determine and promote—an idea developed under Napoleon I. France under the Third Republic was, in this sense, as "statist" as she had ever been under the Empire.

But the growing power of the deputies and the calls for reforms from labor and other interest groups—which were soon transformed into electoral pressures and victories—all left the high bureaucrats more convinced than ever that they alone were right. Since they were almost exclusively recruited from the upper middle class and the aristocracy, they tended to resist reforms that were demanded by the rising lower middle and working classes, represented by the Radical Socialist and Socialist parties. Aware of this, these parties attempted to weaken the bureaucracy by fighting for parliament's complete control over the executive. But, as has been noted, the effect of destroying an independent political executive was only to produce ministerial instability, which, if anything, increased the power of the permanent bureaucracy, committed to the social and economic status quo. By striking at the political executive the leftist parties actually were missing their mark, for they weakened the institutions—the Premier and his cabinet—that could control the conservatively oriented bureaucracy. The latter was, moreover, protected from overhaul and reform by the parties and interest groups that agreed with the bureaucracy's conservative outlook and that saw in its power a means of offsetting the threats to private property inherent in universal suffrage during the rise of an industrial working class. These business and agricultural interests were thus the new supporters of the administrative tradition of politics. Taking the place of the aristocratic elites of the monarchies and empires, they formed new social elites that profited from the existence of a centralized bureaucracy, imbued with the traditional bureaucratic pride of office and a self-confidence in its superior policy-making wisdom.

L'ETAT SINCE WORLD WAR II: The partisans of the representative tradition who founded the Fourth Republic in 1944-46 were once again faced with the problem of the bureaucracy, the stability and continuity of which through the nineteenth century, the Third Republic and even the Vichy regime had, as one commentator has put it, "led to the survival within administrative life of principles belonging to vanished political systems." Strong pressures from the Left, led by the Communist party, urged the complete purge of the bureaucratic personnel and its replacement by the revolutionary cadres of the Resistance. A small reformist minority urged some renewal of personnel, but primarily argued for the institution of more democratic and representative methods of recruitment plus a rigorous decentralization of administrative functions, so that the central bureaucracy would no longer have such sweeping powers over all sectors of public life. This, they felt, would eliminate the congenital fear of a strong political executive, which, with a less centralized and omnipotent bureaucracy, would be allowed more stability and thus be able to do a better job of policy-making within the proposed narrower scope of national government action.

Although methods of recruitment were democratized in 1945, neither the wide scope of bureaucratic action nor the upper-class monopoly on the high civil service posts was, in the end, seriously modified. For again the threat of a revolutionary Left, this time the Communists, militated against disorganizing the "policeman's state" at a time when everyone was talking of a possible Communist coup. Even more justifiably, it was argued that the new structural reforms voted, plus the broad and necessary governmental powers for directing the economy during the period of reconstruction, both required the retention of a centralized and experienced bureaucracy. Necessity, therefore, also militated against decentralizing administrative functions, and even against a serious purge of prewar bureaucrats, for fear of a shortage of much-needed expertise. Notwithstanding the desire of the Resistance leaders to eliminate the threat to representative government and democratic policy-making constituted by a bureaucracy that still believed in its independent right to determine Government policies, such a bureaucracy existed throughout the Fourth Republic. As a result it remained the focus for the hopes of partisans of the administrative tradition of politics, and after the Fourth's demise in 1958 it became the backbone of the new regime.

Beyond the effect of culture and historical accident, it must be said that French national character has also been responsible for the growth of bureaucratic control over public life. Frenchmen have always disliked face-to-face negotiations with their fellow citizens over conflicts of personal, economic, and political interests. Whether it is due to a philosophical preference of a Platonic sort or to more deep-seated psychological factors, they have usually preferred to have these conflicts resolved by a supposedly neutral, expert, and all-powerful authority external to the parties in conflict. Hence a court system in which local judges are strangers appointed by Paris rather than named or elected from among neighbors; a local government in which the most important decisions are made by a high official named by, and referring constantly for orders to, Paris. In such a context one can understand how a supreme arbitrator such as de Gaulle finds much instinctive popular approval for his monarchical rule.

Yet in many little ways this phobia for face-to-face negotiations and compromise—the very heart of self-government—seems to be disappearing in today's France. The very complexity of social life has made centralized administration less efficient than it once was, and under both the Fourth and Fifth Republics considerable administrative decentralization has been accomplished, though without weakening the role of the bureaucracy in decision-making. This will occur only when France adopts a system of mixed government in which the civil servants have no choice but to be entirely neutral, having neither the long vacations of the political executive of the past or the policy monopoly of today's dominant executive as avenues to independent and irresponsible influence.

High Civil Servants: Their Outlook and Milieu. THE GRAND CORPS: The most influential members of the bureaucracy are those career civil servants who are "detached" from their regular departments to serve on the personal staffs of Ministers and those who serve in the major divisions of the departments that deal with important policy matters. The latter are the major ministries such as Foreign Affairs, Finance, Defense, Interior, or new departments such as the social services or the nationalized banks, which, while independent of the cabinet, are in close contact with economic and social policy. High civil servants in departments such as Education, Justice, and Industry and Commerce are important, but since their duties are largely either technical or purely administrative they are less influential in the conception of policy and rarely recruited for the Ministers' personal staffs. The most influential bureaucrats, wherever they serve, are principally chosen from among five elite groups of civil servants generally refered to as the "Grand Corps of the State" (*Grands Corps de l'Etat*). These are the Inspectors of Finance, the diplomatic corps, the Court of Accounts, the Council of State and the Prefects. In theory Inspectors of Finance are the top career officials of the Ministry of Finance, as members of the diplomatic corps are in the Ministry of Foreign Affairs and Prefects in the Ministry of the Interior. Similarly members of the Court of Accounts are usually occupied with verification of government expenses, while the Council of State serves as the Government's principal source of legal advice in drafting legislation, as well as an administrative court and supervisor of the civil service. However, many members of these corps of high civil servants are officially "detached" from their ministry or service in order to serve as directors of important offices located in other ministries or in the newer departments. In addition, members of these corps are chosen by Ministers for their personal staffs and brain trusts, while others serve as staff directors for the major legislative committees. Thus wherever Government policy is drafted, turned into law, and finally cast into administrative regulations, there members of the Grand Corps are to be found.

For this reason it is important to inquire into the background, training, and values of these "mandarins" who direct France's potent and active state apparatus. They are recruited, in the main, by a very rigorous written and oral competitive examination, which requires, above all, intellectual ability, plus a liberal education, presence of mind, very articulate written and oral expression, and an undefinable polish or self-confidence born of intelligent, yet persistent cultivation of the ego. These were the requisite qualities of the Grand Corps before the war, when recruitment was almost exclusively from the upper classes, for then as now these qualities were usually products of an education and cultural breeding available only to the well-to-do. Attempts were made in 1946 to democratize the high civil service by allowing subaltern functionaries from modest backgrounds to take examinations, and by creating a National School of Administration to provide a uniform training for all new candidates. However, the oral examination boards were from the start necessarily in the hands of veterans of the prewar Grand Corps who, unconsciously and also for reasons of *esprit de corps*, set standards that closely approximated those that had obtained in the past. As a consequence 65 per cent of the young Frenchmen who passed the supposedly "new" examination in 1945-51 were from business, professional, managerial, and high civil servant families. Only 3 per cent were recruited from agricultural and industrial working class families, while the bulk of the remainder came from fairly well-off artisanal and independent farmer families. There is evidence, moreover, that considerable inbreeding exists since 40 per cent of the candidates are children of fairly well-placed civil servants.

In a country where the standard of living for wage earners is still relatively low, few families of the lower classes can afford to do without the earning power of a son. Hence only an average of 5 per cent of secondary school students and 4 per cent of university students were from the industrial and agricultural working class in recent years. Since higher education is absolutely vital to success in the competitive examination, educational experience and its financial implications provide a sort of prior selection for the high civil service.

RELATIONS WITH BUSINESS: Ever since the beginning of the century the incomes of even the highest civil servants have failed to keep up with the rise in the cost of living. As a consequence the government service throughout the 1920's and 1930's continued to lose prestige and saw many of its most talented members leave for lucrative jobs in private industry. This was understandable, for, after all, high civil servants were drawn largely from the same class as management and the training and expertise derived from government jobs served them well in managerial positions. After World War II this trend continued and, in 1951, 60 per cent of the candidates for the competitive examination admitted that government service for them was but a stepping stone to business and financial careers. Many of the most important private banks and manufacturing companies are directed by former high civil servants. Indeed the heads of the fifteen top private and public banks are former Inspectors of Finance. This brings up the question of whether the community of background between "Big Business" and "Big Bureaucracy" does not represent a threat to democratic processes of policy-making.

There is unquestionably a similarity in outlook and values between the top bureaucrat in an important economic service of the administration and the top officer of a large business. Both are managers and highly competent technicians; both are interested in an efficient and productive French economy; both are slightly contemptuous of unstable and ineffective parliamentarism; finally both have a great faith in technical, empirical, "realistic" solutions to problems. Unlike his nineteenth-century predecessor, today's high civil servant has come to appreciate the need for considerable economic and social policy-making by the central government. Naturally, he has especially come to appreciate the increase in power this trend has given experts in government. More than ever, therefore, the top echelons of the bureaucracy are sensitive to their duties as servants of the "positive state," the administrative tradition that for centuries has served the national interest, as it saw this interest. Today the influential bureaucrats see this interest as modernization of French society and a rise in French economic production. Hence it is alleged that they are relatively accessible to pressure from representatives of the modern and efficient sectors of the economy, such as the big manufacturing companies. Certainly by background and experience a community of viewpoint does exist between these groups. Furthermore, thanks to the many advisory committees of businessmen attached to government departments and to the close personal relations between bureaucrats and their former colleagues in private business, there has long been ample opportunity for many important industries to exert pressure upon the source of the rules and regulations that give law concrete meaning. Under the Fifth Republic this opportunity has remained great, though business is by no means alone in its exploitation.

The "Where" and "How" of Bureaucratic Power. THE PERSONAL STAFFS: Unlike the American public service few political appointments to the bureaucracy are ever made in France. The sole major exceptions are occasional ambassadorial posts and, above all, the personal staffs of the President, the Prime Minister, the Ministers, and other heads of departments. In the past these "Minister's offices" (*cabinets ministériels*) served as the link between the Minister and both his department and the political circles of parliament, the parties, and pressure groups. Accordingly they included career civil servants, "detached" usually from one of the Grand Corps, whose job it was to "speak the language" of the bureaucrats in the department. They also included an assortment of bright young men from the universities and business, journalists, faithful party workers, personal friends, and even members of the Minister's family. It was these purely political appointees who made the contacts, wrote the speeches, and served as the eyes and ears of the Minister. During the Fourth Republic they advised him of parliament's reaction to his policy proposals, of the views influential interests were taking of Government policies he had already authored, of his general reputation among political personalities, and—above all—they kept him informed of which parliamentary leaders or which of his cabinet colleagues were "out to get him."

Since the coming of the Fifth Republic the composition of these staffs has remained roughly the same, but the influence of the "detached" career civil servant has constantly risen at the expense of the party workers and others brought in from the outside. In the first months of the new regime when the meager "revolutionary" atmosphere of May 1958 still persisted, the political Ministers especially appointed men to their staffs who had been personally faithful in party activity, or who had been active in preparing the return of General de Gaulle, or whose presence near them served to reassure the military party, the principal veto power in French politics during the first years of the Fifth Republic. With the Government's stability assured by the new constitution, these purely political appointees were less active as liaison with parliament than as the "delegates" of interests not openly represented in the cabinet, such as the army, extreme wings of the Gaullist party, and left-wing intellectual movements. A Gaullist Minister of Justice, for example, reassured liberal opinion by appointing two left-wing journalists to his staff, while the Prime Minister reassured the military party by naming activist officers and civilian "ultras" to his staff. Although undoubtedly involved in the conception of policy proposals, these political bureaucrats—called "little barons" (*petits barons*) by the opposition press—influenced policy mainly by attempting to short-circuit the wire between decision and execution.

This influence still persists, but de Gaulle's rejection of the military party's solution for Algeria and the coups of 1960 and 1961, in which some of the "little barons" were implicated, resulted in the purging of many personal staffs. The political appointees who remained were relegated to the traditional tasks of speech writing and political intelligence gathering. Their influence over policy conception became slight in comparison to that of career bureaucrats on the personal staffs. Following the example set by de Gaulle, the Ministers relied mainly on these "technocrats" for the choice of the policy programs and Government bills, suggested by their departments, that would be presented for final approval. Proposals for important reforms or personal policy ideas were usually worked up by the Minister and the career men on his staff, who could often use their close relations with their chief to promote a policy they had long cherished. When a policy became law or was cast into ordinance or decree, it was again these career men who aided the Minister in approving or rejecting the many detailed departmental regulations and executing orders that were brought up for signature by the permanent departmental personnel. Finally, these career bureaucrats were also involved in the Minister's political life by their contacts with pressure groups and their drafting of answers to the oral and written questions on his department's activities, posed on behalf of their constituents by members of parliament.

DEPARTMENTAL PERSONNEL AND THE COUNCIL OF STATE: Below the Ministers and their personal staffs are the directors of the department's permanent divisions and offices whose job it is to bring policy problems to the attention of the Minister, suggest their solutions, and adapt policies already made for execution throughout the country. The great mass of relatively minor day-to-day policy originates at this level, as it does in all modern political systems. To the extent that high civil servants dominate the personal staffs, the independent influence of the departmental personnel over policy conception is much limited. But in writing the draft legislation, ordinances, and decrees, these bureaucrats can exercise power over the effect of policy decisions. Indeed, their control over details has given them under the Fifth Republic a certain measure of political control over both their Ministers and the Government's image in opinion.

As was seen in Chapter 13, executive instability has today given way to the "dry crises," marked by the departure of individual Ministers, which permits the Government's adaptation to changes in opinion or parliamentary majority or failures of policy. In the case of a recent Minister of Agriculture, there was evidence that his policies—and hence those of the Government—were bitterly, if quietly, opposed by his departmental personnel. Perhaps under the pressure of farm organizations or perhaps because of their "expert" opposition to his methods for dealing with the problem of declining farm prices, the civil servants effectively negated the successfully passed Government legislation by simply delaying the issuance of the executing regulations. As pleas for government action mounted, the Minister fell under public attack by parliament and the farm organizations for his inaction. This in a regime with an all-powerful executive is potentially more dangerous than if he had acted without success. While it is probable that the Minister in question was at fault for failing to foster effective relations with his departmental personnel, it seems certain that both his dismissal and the Government's reputation for inaction on the farm problem can be largely attributed to bureaucratic power.

The agricultural legislation refered to above was in the form of a long "orienting law" (*loi d'orientation*) that defined the goals of Government action and left the methods and other important details to executive discretion. It was a form of delegated legislation that obviously placed semi-legislative powers in the hands of those who wrote the regulations, specifying the methods and details. One can understand, therefore, why pressure groups, in their efforts to have Government policies modified to suit their interests, have concentrated on the high civil servants. Such a course has also become inevitable as the Fifth Republic increasingly chooses to solve troublesome economic and social problems by direct negotiation with the groups concerned, ratifying these agreements by delegated legislative power or normal decree power rather than asking for laws that would perhaps involve unsettling parliamentary debates. This development has brought bureaucracy into continual contact with interest groups for purposes of actually deciding policy and not just for receiving advice as was the case in the traditional consultative committees of the past. True, these contacts may result in the "education" of pressure groups and their acceptance of policies in the general interest as put to them by the bureaucracy. But whether the increased policy-making power of the civil servants results in more or less pressure politics, it is clear that it does reduce democratic control over policy and raises the problem of technocratic rule.

High civil servants have influenced policy through their special activities in the legislative branch as well as through their normal functions in the executive. Their expert advice was constantly sought by the two houses of parliament in the consideration of legislative proposals. On the staffs of the legislative committees bureaucrats may have important influence in aiding members to amend Government bills. More directly, some of them actually participated in parliament's lawmaking by becoming elected as deputies and Senators and by using their expertise and talent in both committees and public debate. Unlike British civil servants French bureaucrats may run for office without being obliged to resign and while still retaining their rank in the service. The trend, moreover, is toward an ever-increasing number of them in parliament, perhaps because popular reaction against professional politicians and old ideological issues has made career civil servants, along with engineers and businessmen, seem to represent the well-trained "new" political man who talks politics in more modern concrete terms. At any rate, from a low of six high civil servants in the very ideologically minded National Assembly of 1945, the number of those temporarily "detached" from their departments to hold seats rose to twenty-seven in 1951 and thirty-seven in 1958, when the flood tide against the old political personnel was running especially high.

After a policy decision had been cast into the form of a Government bill, ordinance, or decree, it was submitted to the traditional legal counselor of French Governments, the Council of State. This is a group of high civil servants who exercise a small but unique influence over policy. Recruited from among the most impressive candidates for the bureaucratic career, the Councilors correct the drafting errors and advise as to the compatibility of the document with previous legislation and executive rules, and its probable effect in achieving the policy goal. The Council also serves as France's highest administrative tribunal to which individuals can appeal if they believe bureaucrats or agents of the state have executed a law or decree in a way contrary to its purpose, thereby doing them damage. This function of judicial review of the Government's administrative acts often has important after-effects on executive policy-making and, in particular, the Council has been in the past France's major defender of individual civil rights. Under the Fourth Republic it quashed regulations barring Communist students from the National School of Administration on the ground that this was a misuse of administrative powers, tending to infringe upon parliament's legislative prerogative. This sort of decision was easier to take at a time when a powerful parliament existed to support the Council's case against the weak and unstable executive. Under the Fifth Republic the Council's lack of real independence from the executive, the emergencies of the Algerian war, and the prevailing *raison d'état* atmosphere of the Debré Government combined to limit its effectiveness as an *ex post facto* check on policy making and as the protector of civil rights. This again has significance for the problem of protecting individual liberties in a political system so dominated by the executive and its agents.

Policy Execution at the Grass Roots. Once a policy decision is taken, translated into a Government bill, approved by the Council of State, voted by parliament or issued by the Council of Ministers, and interpreted for execution by detailed regulations and orders, a variety of public servants in direct contact with the people see to it that the policy becomes social fact. It is true that by the time they receive the regulations and orders the original decision may well have undergone modifications. But it is also true that both the letter and spirit of what remains may undergo still further change at the hands of those who apply the laws, decrees, and regulations to everyday life.

This final stage of the policy process has always had special importance in France, above all at times like the present when the executive is very powerful. The fact that France has long had a unitary form of government with a highly centralized bureaucracy has meant that Paris dealt with the whole range of public policy and services and enforced its decisions by local public servants under their direct control. Everything—from the cost of a hunting license in the Ardennes and an extra day of vacation for the grammar school students of La Roche-sur-Foron (pop.: 4,548), to the price of wheat and the nation's electoral system—is decided in Paris by law or executive rule and enforced by the employees of the Paris departments responsible for initiating the policy. French citizens, therefore, having such a wide variety of contacts with policy made in Paris, naturally have more occasion to pass judgment on the national Government than do citizens of Britain, Germany, or the United States, where either federal systems or some local government prevail. Frenchmen are also used to judging the effectiveness of policy on the basis of the actions (or nonaction) of the executing agent, no matter what the stated intentions of Paris might be. Finally, since a dominant and stable executive was the Fifth Republic's solution to the ineffective policies of the previous regime, it was expected that the decisions of the new executive would be promptly made and efficiently executed by its local agents. In other words, the citizen's attitudes toward the men in power and the policies they pursue, and indeed the regime itself, have been much affected by the behavior of those who execute the policy of the Paris Government at the citizen's level.

PREFECTS: In theory, whatever is decided in Paris today by law or executive rule is executed tomorrow or the day after in every part of the country. The principal arm of the Government at the grass roots of the policy process is the Prefect (*Préfet*), a high civil servant, employed by the Ministry of the Interior, who resides in the main town of each *département*. It is he who is ultimately responsible for all aspects of local government and the execution of national policies locally. Although elected departmental councils (*conseils généraux*) and township or municipal councils (*conseils municipaux*) do exist, the serious decisions of local government policy are made by the Prefect in consultation with his ministry or another Paris authority. If the locally elected councils resist these decisions, the Prefect can report this to his Minister who is able, upon cabinet approval, to dissolve the recalcitrant elected bodies. Individuals with grievances or a request for special treatment in a local matter can go to their elected local official or even to their deputy or Senator, but chances are they will go to see the Prefect first. Their objective will be to get a special dispensation from this official, such as the suspension of a law or rule in their own particular case. Only if this fails will they appeal to their parliamentary representatives to intercede with the Paris department or the Minister concerned.

Since the Prefect is responsible for the execution of all kinds of policy, he has a miniature "Government" in his *département*, made up of civil servants who are all employed by Paris offices but who live and work in the provinces. There are tax officials who depend on the Ministry of Finance; inspectors and administrators of various kinds who depend on the Ministries of Public Works, Agriculture, Labor, Public Health, Housing, Industry and Commerce, or Veteran Affairs. Traditionally these officials have been honest, loyally and impartially executing the orders of their Paris superiors. But their closeness to the "consumers" of policy, the very fact that they have to live among them, makes for occasional "interpretation" of policy in favor of a local interest. The most striking recent case of local pressure was the frequent inability of Paris to have its orders executed by the Prefects in Algeria, men who were surrounded by a population hostile to the Government and whose lives often depended on not executing the orders they received.

THE POLICE: Assisting the Prefect are a variety of police organizations that, beside enforcing law and order, keep him informed of the local activities of political parties, economic and social developments such as strikes and demonstrations by interest groups, and, indeed, the general "mood" of the population. The latter is important for the Prime Minister, or the Minister of the Interior may often ask Prefects to send them reports on the likely attitude of their citizens toward a policy under consideration in Paris. This bureaucratic approach to public opinion, as well as the sheer plethora of police organizations, has existed in France ever since the kings and emperors, and under liberal as well as conservative Governments. It is further testimony to the persistence of the administrative tradition in French political life and has always been considered indispensable, given the wide range of governmental responsibilities and the highly centralized execution of policy. But this attitude toward opinion and the cooperation of the citizen is also a source of great weakness, for if the Prefect is ever abandoned by his "eyes, ears, and arms," the Paris Government may suddenly feel it has lost its hold on the country. Into the vacuum of self-confidence thus created, revolutionary forces have penetrated in the past and may do so once again.

These vital police organizations are mostly grouped under the central control of the Minister of the Interior who has at his disposal the French equivalent of the American F.B.I., the *Sûreté Nationale,* and a highly mobile national riot police (the C.R.S., or *Compagnies Républicaines de Sécurité*). However, under the Ministry of Defense there are the *Gendarmes (Gendarmerie Nationale)*, an essentially rural police responsible for order where no municipal police force exists, for enforcing military conscription, and for executing the orders of the military courts, which in France have jurisdiction over civilians as well as the military. Given the importance of Paris in French public life the Paris police department has in practice, and at times by law, assumed enforcement and investigatory functions throughout the country. There has been, for example, a corps of "economic police" based in Paris whose job it was to enforce economic and currency regulations.

These various police and the interchange of functions among them have developed gradually, without rational planning. French political culture made it seem logical that, with a unitary government and a centralized bureaucracy, each time a social problem became a matter of public policy, a police organization should be assigned or newly created to enforce Paris decisions. Similarly, when political circumstances changed and a traditional police organization no longer seemed capable of fulfilling its functions, these were quickly transferred to another parallel organization. While efficiency and justice were the expected results, often the proliferation of police has produced a ridiculous competition among them and ineffective enforcement. More serious is the problem of the police under the Fifth Republic. During the Algerian war police officers were the main targets for Moslem rebel terrorists. Before then the police were widely employed to prevent or suppress disturbances by the Communist party. These experiences, as well as the natural affinities of temperament and their permanent grievance against the Government for low salaries, have made large elements of the police partisans of the military party and therefore doubtfully loyal to de Gaulle and the present regime. Commentators have cited this as the reason for the relatively ineffective pursuit of right-wing "French Algeria" terrorists by the police in 1961-62 and the over-zealous suppression of the slightest left-wing demonstration. Yet the Government's stated policy of prosecuting the O.A.S. terrorists of the military party really became accepted as a policy only when the police successfully executed it. And even if the Government had formally decided against ordering the police to break up a left-wing demonstration in favor of a negotiated peace in Algeria, which the Government also sought, suppressing the leftists automatically became policy when the police followed their instincts and "roughed up" the demonstrators.

COURTS: In the case of infractions of the laws or executive rules, the Prefect, his staff, or the police inform the local agent of the Minister of Justice, the public prosecutor. This bureaucrat then proceeds to draw up a case, which is tried in a court system that is also administered by the Minister. According to Article 65 of the constitution, nominations to the bench are controlled by the High Council of the Magistrature (Conseil Supérieur de la Magistrature), appointed and presided over by the President of the Republic and hence formally independent of the Government, as are technically its nominees. There is no jury save in the most serious criminal cases, the defendant being tried before one or more judges who, hardly his peers, are rather civil servants who have the task of finding out whether in fact there was or was not a breach of the rule or law. In its handling of most cases the French court system reflects the administrative tradition of politics. The omnipresence of the government and its bureaucracy in French life makes an individual's trial less a litigation over whether in fact he broke a specified law or regulation and more the public occasion at which he tries to reject the heavy presumption of his guilt in which the proceedings are clothed.

Although most judges are difficult to remove from office, their recruitment, training, and promotional system has encouraged a cautious bureaucratic mentality. Not only have French judges been mediocre in the past, but the organization of the court system made the process of justice often slow and painful for the accused. One of the most successful and important early reforms of the Debré Government in 1959 was a modernization of the judicial system, which promises to improve both the quality of justice and its speed. Yet for the moment local judges remain as subject to popular pressures as are other local agents of the Paris government while, at the same time, their civil servants' mentality makes them overly responsive to the prejudices of superiors upon whom their advancement depends. The policy of the Debré Government, therefore, might well have been to treat Moslem Algerians working in France on an equal footing with native Frenchmen, if only to assure the good will of the great mass of Moslems in Algeria. Yet when a local court habitually applied more stringent punishment to Moslem demonstrators than to French counter-demonstrators, or when it threw out an airtight case against a right-wing

Frenchman accused of murdering a Moslem, the court system was participating in the policy process, if only negatively. Had there been a thoroughly independent judiciary in France this would not have been the case, but such a change depends on a reform of the whole administrative system and indeed a new outlook on the part of Frenchmen themselves on the problem of centralization.

THE ARMED FORCES: France's constant participation in some kind of military action between 1945 and 1962 has meant that an important sector of public policy had to be executed by the armed forces. The evolution of the army's attitude toward both policy and the Fifth Republic has been treated above in the discussion of the military party, but a few words about its influence over the execution of policy during the first years of the Fifth Republic is in order at this point. Fighting a subversive war with an enemy that used guerrilla tactics and terrorism, the French army in both Algeria and metropolitan France was obliged to adopt methods used by the police of all countries in combating crime and subversion. Networks of informants, preventive detention, the torture of captives for information, and even summary execution of terrorists caught in the act were frequent during the Algerian war because the army felt they were technically necessary for suppressing the Moslem rebels. Succeeding Governments under the Fourth Republic as well as the Debré Government tried to limit these practices for it was official policy that constitutional civil rights were to be respected. Under the pressure of both the military party and responsible army leaders, however, the executive's emergency powers and its use of delegated legislation were employed to legalize or at least "cover" many of these army methods.

Ever since the Algiers uprising of 1960 de Gaulle slowly succeeded in cutting back some of the army's judicial and police authority in Algeria. Yet while the Algerian war continued the atmosphere of crisis and the justification of "patriotic" necessity allowed the army to make policy in many areas touching the conduct of the war. Both the Ministry of Defense and the old system of military courts with jurisdiction over civilians also gave the armed forces influence over Government policy and its image before the public. As a country with a famous military tradition and many historic debts to her army, France has long had laws and regulations protecting the army's "rear" among the civilian population. Any citizen's act, therefore, which could be interpreted as having a hurtful effect on the morale or organization of the armed forces was considered an infraction that had to be tried in military courts. In the same vein, the Minister of Defense (or more likely one of the "little barons" on his personal staff) occasionally ordered the seizure of a whole edition of a newspaper that printed an article he or his personnel considered harmful to army morale or that seemed to them as tending to encourage disobedience in its ranks. Thus although General de Gaulle may well have considered publicity about the hopelessness of an army victory in Algeria as necessary and the punishment of an officer who refused to obey Government directions as vital, ministerial orders and the partiality of military courts could rob these policies of effect. It was because of the favoritism of regular military justice that de Gaulle used his presidential emergency powers after the April 1961 army coup to set up a special court for trying the rebellious officers.

With the Algerian war ended, the size of the French army will undoubtedly be reduced and its influence over policy can be expected to decline. Yet, under the terms of the March 1962 cease-fire agreement with the Moslem nationalists, large units of the army will continue to be garrisoned in Algeria, primarily to protect the remaining Europeans and guarantee the terms of the agreement. In light of the past hostility of many officers toward de Gaulle and the idea of an independent Algeria, the complete reliability of the army in this task is at least debatable. As for the bulk of the army which must now be quartered in France, doubts may also arise about its loyalty as a potential executor of policy under present political circumstances. In all countries the Government employs the garrisoned armed forces as a reserve police power in the case of civil disturbances that the normal forces of order can not or refuse to suppress. But if the regular police were to prove ineffective in putting down a strike for power by the extremists of the military party—say the OAS supported by European returnees from Algeria—there is no certainty at this writing that the army will do better than the police. The return of the army to its traditional role as a neutral executor of Government policy, therefore, depends not just on peace in Algeria, but on the "total" solution of the Algerian problem in all its complexity. For the French army to once again be available as a loyal reserve police power and as the instrument of official French national policy alone, it must pass through a readjustment stage during which it has no police duties at all to accomplish nor revolutionary causes to defend.

[16]

Problems and Prospects

As the Fifth Republic enters its fourth year, it is easier to write about the problems of the regime than about its prospects. For notwithstanding the important constitutional changes of 1958, the French political system has retained its most ancient quality: a lack of legitimacy and an aura of impermanence that make it difficult to predict the system's future course. It is as if Frenchmen continued to withhold entire confidence in their political institutions in order to maintain open as many options for change as possible. But as for the problems of the regime, they are many and can readily be described on three different and yet related levels.

First there are the continuing problems of French political life that have sources in the historic dialogue between conflicting ideals of authority —the administrative and representative traditions of politics. Many of these problems have been discussed throughout the preceding chapters, in connection with the "dated" aspects of the new constitution, the persistence of anachronistic political forces, and the survival of a centralized bureaucratic tradition. Second, there are a specific set of problems inherent in the political circumstances and the constitution of the Fifth Republic, as well as in the style of government created by General de Gaulle. The contrast between theory and practice in the new constitution, the dangers of new political forces, and the "reinterpretation" of the constitution according to momentary needs are among some of these problems already treated. Finally, there are general problems of modern democratic government that the current French experience shares with other highly industrialized western societies. What, for example, are the proper relations between interest groups and the government, and how is the growth of bureaucratic influence over policy making to be made politically responsible?

A Self-Defeating Policy Process

All the problems of the French political system are embodied in the policy-making process of the Fifth Republic and bear responsibility for its continuing ineffectiveness. The inadequacy of the Fourth Republic's policy-making was due to Government instability, which produced the incoherence and discontinuity of policies. By eliminating Government instability the Fifth Republic had hoped to make its policy product coherent and continuous, and some progress in economic and financial matters has indeed been made. But much policy remains ineffective because the relatively open compromises of parties and politicians, once responsible for incoherent policies, and the evident discontinuity of cabinets have both been replaced by hidden compromises between the executive and interest groups, now responsible for incoherent policies, and the new discontinuity of influences within an executive branch clothed in traditional secrecy.

Since policy-making is the ultimate purpose of a political system, all political institutions are involved in it in one manner or another. The policy process synthesizes the individual functions of different institutions and, if they are complementary and compatible, the policy product is effective. Under the Fifth Republic this process continues, as it did under past regimes, to express contradictory and incompatible tensions. It remains, consequently, a circular and self-defeating process. Typical of a regime in the administrative tradition of politics, the process begins with de Gaulle's twin assumptions that there does exist an abstract, objective general interest, though concrete political consensus remains impossible in a permanently divided France. In order that the national or general interest will prevail, parliament, inevitably the expression of the divided public opinion, must be largely excluded from policy-making. This means that most government decisions must be initiated in the executive branch, under the primary influence of the supreme arbitrator, the Ministers, and the "technocrats," the high civil servants whom de Gaulle trusts somewhat more than politicians to serve the national interest.

But because de Gaulle believes in the permanence of French social, economic, and ideological cleavages, and yet rejects the methods of dictatorship, he is obliged to make concessions to the multiple interests of the body politic. Since the philosophy of the new regime formally condemns the influence of "intermediaries," such as parties and other groups that stand between *le pouvoir*, the policy-making guardian of the general interest, and *le peuple*, with its many particular interests, the concessions to the latter must be made directly by the agents of *le pouvoir*. Hence the fact that from de Gaulle to the Prime Minister and his cabinet to the bureaucracy in general, there are continual contacts and negotiations with the representatives of particular interests. Like any other nondictatorial regime operating in a pluralistic society, the Fifth Republic has been obliged to discover a method for adapting policy to at least some of the objections of powerful affected minorities, thereby assuring the legitimacy of its rule. But by refusing parliament, the regular representative of particular interests, an effective role in policy making, the Fifth Republic has obliged the bureaucracy, supposedly the agent of the general interest, to become an "intermediary" between the decisions of *le pouvoir* and the wishes of *le peuple*.

The Perils of Ineffective Policy

Thus even in a regime in the administrative tradition of politics provision must be made for the representation of individual interests. When it is the bureaucrat who must "represent" them, it is understandable that he will fulfill this function within his professional context—that is, by short-circuiting a decision that he considers harmful to the interest he is "representing." The high civil servant on a Minister's staff who deforms the intention of his chief in the draft bill or decree he was asked to write may not even be in basic disagreement with Government policy. It may simply be that in doing so he has in mind what he considers a reasonable objection by, say, a trade union leader he recently talked to. Indeed, his motive for altering the Minister's policy may primarily be the desire to avoid later embarrassment for him when the policy comes under public scrutiny. Such "intermediary" action by the high civil servant would be unnecessary if the regime provided for a regular open dialogue between the Minister and the trade union movement through a continuous system of consultation or an effective parliamentary debate.

But at least the civil servant's action is situated at the start of the policy process, removed from an effect on public opinion. Far more dangerous for continued confidence in the regime is an agent of policy execution who refuses to apply new regulations to, say, local shopkeepers on the grounds that the viewpoint of the "independent businessman" has not been given adequate hearing by the Government. And even more fatal in this respect is the refusal of a police officer to arrest, for example, a terrorist of the military party's Secret Army Organization on the grounds that he is, after all, a true "patriot." How much less likely both these "intermediary" actions would be if the executing agent and the policeman had certain proof that the policy they were being asked to uphold carried the public approval of a coherent governing majority of deputies and Senators, that is a majority coalition of parties, which in turn means the support of public opinion—in other words, their own neighbors.

If a political system such as the Fifth Republic in which the executive dominates policy making and commands an omnipresent bureaucracy is still unable to make its decisions "stick," public opinion will ultimately be no more loyal to it than it had been in the case of previous regimes whose policies were ineffective because of executive instability and parliamentary dominance. During the first years of the Fifth Republic the personal prestige of Charles de Gaulle alone has prevented the familiar phenomenon of popular disaffection from reaching the proportions known in the last years of the Fourth Republic. For surely it cannot be said that the new constitution has eliminated the influence of pressure groups, the demagoguery of parliament, the deformation of policy by civil servants, the lethargy of agents of policy execution, the hesitations and disobedience of police and army officers, or the actions of any other "intermediary" whom de Gaulle usually blames for the regime's shortcomings.

This variety of interferences between policy conception and policy execution exists in all political systems. The influence of the civil servant is enormous in British policy making. The growth of a quasi-corporatist procedure for the direct representation of interests within the executive is as great in the United States and Britain, and even greater in Germany, than it has become in France. Yet only in the latter have civil servants become "intermediaries," assuming the political responsibility of negating or deforming policy in the name of economic, social, or ideological interests. This is because the opportunity for assuming such political responsibility does not exist in the same measure in political systems of mixed government. Nor are the regular "intermediaries" of parliament, parties, and pressure groups likely to act in so purely negative a fashion as they do in France when a formal role for them is created in the policy-making process. In its desire to make the general interest prevail and thus maintain public support for the new regime, the Fifth Republic has promoted the executive to dominance over policy decisions. Yet, unwilling either to impose the executive will by force or to allow the normal representatives of a divided opinion to participate in policy making, the regime has given the executive the job of representing interests within itself. The result has been a political system publicly committed to the national interest, yet often serving particular interests and often unable to make its policies effective. The price has inevitably been a growing decline in public confidence, the very thing the Fifth Republic was created to prevent.

The Alternative of Mixed Government

The future of the Fifth Republic will be determined by how many of these problems in policy-making are resolved. Four alternatives can be envisaged of which the most hopeful, if not the most probable, is the continued evolution of the regime toward a system of mixed government.

This could be achieved by establishing a better balance between the executive and legislative branches in the determination of public policy. It is not a mechanical "balance of powers" that is required, but rather an assurance that political parties and parliament will henceforth have a genuine role in the formulation of government decisions affecting society and its constituent interests. Organizing a dialogue between the executive, with its expertise, its over-all view, and the legislature, with its ability to represent special interests and to legitimize government decisions, can result in effective policy. For policy decisions emerging from such a dialogue will be regularly "instructed" about local objections while at the same time bearing the explicit approval of the traditional representatives of popular sovereignty.

But if mixed government requires giving "intermediaries" a positive role in the policy process, it also requires giving the Government the power to execute policy notwithstanding further resistance by the "intermediaries." In the modern democratic context this means linking the executive's authority directly to a majority in public opinion, which only direct popular election of the chief of the executive can accomplish. This is a far more effective way of liberating a Prime Minister, or a President, or even a "supreme arbitrator" from the pressures of parliament than by having him elected, for example, by a special college of local notables and reducing parliament's functionally necessary role in the policy-making process.

Whether France goes all the way toward a presidential system on the American model or maintains a hybrid form of parliamentary government in which it is the Prime Minister who is popularly elected while the President becomes a largely ceremonial figure, the direct election of the effective chief of the executive will encourage party coalitions and ultimately, perhaps, the emergence of a single majority party. Successful mixed government depends, in the last analysis, on coherent governing majorities, for only they can assure true political responsibility, which alone can provide a political system with permanence and legitimacy in the eyes of the people. True governing majorities alone can provide the democratically legitimate motive force that makes policies obeyed and that disciplines the action of the "intermediaries." Only a real governing majority, moreover, can allow both parliament to represent interests and the bureaucracy to exercise ever-increasing functions imposed by modern industrial society, without the first dominating policy making, thus rendering it ineffective as under the Fourth Republic, or the second becoming an "intermediary," and thus usurping political responsibility as under the Fifth Republic.

Other Options for Change

Much more probable than a full turn toward mixed government is the development of a hybrid, transitional political system after de Gaulle's departure from power. There are commentators who insist that the unique features of the Fifth Republic are due more to de Gaulle's personal rule than to the innovations of the new constitution. With de Gaulle gone, they argue, the constitution could be applied in a very different way, retaining features such as the guarantees of executive stability while giving parliament a greater role in policy-making by simply not employing the Government's constitutional powers to control the legislative process and not infringing on its normal lawmaking prerogative. Unless de Gaulle had amended the constitution in order to provide for popular election of the President before his departure, it is unlikely that his successors would be able to do so, and hence the evolution toward mixed government and its coherent governing majorities would not be forthcoming. Yet developments in the party system at the present time indicate that even without the effects of majority election on the national level, a simplification of the party system is in the offing. Perhaps this alternative of a hybrid regime in the administrative tradition will evolve toward a situation not unlike that of the German Federal Republic where a two-party system in effect is operating within a political system in which executive stability has been constitutionally "engineered."

Less likely, though by no means excluded, is a full return to a regime in the representative tradition of politics. More than once in the past the reaction to the failure or downfall of a regime in the administrative tradition has been a pendular swing to what the French call an "assembly regime" (régime d'assemblée), one in which parliament totally dominates the executive and in which policy-making is subordinated to the process of making and preserving party coalitions. Although the formal institutions of the Fifth Republic no longer reflect the representative tradition, it has been shown above that many informal institutions such as parliamentary custom and party behavior still reflect this ancient political reflex. But although many of the older politicians would probably favor a return to the ways of the Third and Fourth Republics, it is doubtful whether public opinion would permit, under relatively normal conditions, such a return to a thoroughly discredited past.

Yet such an extreme alternative cannot be dismissed as a possibility, especially if the fourth option for change is chosen by France. Were a violent political upheaval to take place, such as a coup d'état by the military party, a period of dictatorship could well be followed by another violent swing to the Left. Since the "assembly regime" has been the institutional hero of the revolutionary forces in French history, it is likely that the leaders of the reaction to a regime in the most extreme form of the administrative tradition, unprotected by the personal prestige of de Gaulle, would follow the French practice of choosing the most extreme form of the representative tradition. The Communist party has long been the leading advocate of a radical "assembly regime" and, in view of the fact that its troops would certainly be very active in a revolution against an extreme rightist dictatorship, it would have much to say about the new political institutions.

The problem with this fourth alternative is that one cannot say how probable its realization will be at this writing. The very fact that dictatorship and, indeed, anarchy remain both logical and possible alternatives in the France of 1962 means that the political system today has still not achieved either legitimacy or effectiveness. In terms of the analysis presented in this study, however, it can be suggested that in the measure that institutions of mixed government are adopted by France, the legitimacy and effectiveness of her political system will grow, the conflict between ancient ideals of authority will disappear, the options of the administrative and representative traditions of politics will no longer be present, and the probability of violent political change will decline.

Part Four

THE GERMAN
POLITICAL
SYSTEM

by Herbert J. Spiro

Excerpt from the inaugural address of the President of the Bundestag, Dr. Gerstenmaier, upon his reelection, in Berlin, October 15, 1957.

He who wishes to serve Germany today would do well above all to renounce all illusions and all vain demands, and to grasp the world that embraces us in all its ideological conflict.

What this means for the revision of conventional concepts, such as national sovereignty or the previous form of positive international law—and therefore for national as well as international politics—was recently asked of (*ans Herz gelegt*) the young Federal Defense Force by Federal Constitutional Judge Gerhard Leibholz in a treatise as pregnant as it was brilliant. The ideological, that is, the ethically essential and the existentially decisive for the human being and the world, takes precedence over "demands coming from the national state." So said Leibholz. And I think he is right. What are the needs of national prestige politics in the face of the necessities of our time: to save the human being with his eternal destiny from surrender to unheard-of forces?

Politics is no cocktail consisting of tactics, propaganda, group interests, and prestige needs, mixed for the satisfaction of national or personal thirst for power! True enough, this has happened in the past and is happening still today. . . . If we wish to survive, we cannot deny ourselves the forces of a transformed and refined national consciousness, and we will not save Germany from the fate of becoming a province, a dependent insignificant province in world events, unless we place next to our *economic and organizational achievement an equal spiritual and cultural achievement.* [Applause.]

. . . . Amidst a world full of danger, but also full of previously unknown great possibilities, we begin this parliamentary period. "Where there is danger, that which rescues groweth also." This word of Hölderlin is no vague consolation, but the insight into the secret of the world that rests in God's hands. Here in Germany's capital city, we resume our work once again. It is no political prophecy, but a wish; yes, it is a prayer: may God grant that we complete this work here in a united and pacified fatherland! [*Lively general applause.*]

*Excerpt from a debate on the film industry and censorship in the
Bundestag, April 2, 1954.*

DEPUTY PAUL   (Social Democratic Party):

It is another matter that movie people are interesting for the press—
just as interesting as for instance politicians, including the Federal Ministers. In this connection it must, however, be remarked that the former
are usually more rewarding for the press than the latter, because they are as
a rule—I underline as a rule—more beautiful in figure and face. [*Hilarity
in the center.* DEPUTY PELSTER: Can't always say that!] In the film industry, too, business is sometimes made with dirty things. [*Calls of "Aha"
from the center.*]

But, my most esteemed ladies and gentlemen, we Social Democrats
have not invented this order of society [Very good! *from the SPD. Laughter and calls from the center*] in which one coins gold out of dirt. [*Sustained hilarity.*] After all, it is your view that everything in the world and
in the economy should be subjected to Liberalism. [*Laughter in the center and right.* DEPUTY PELSTER: Socialism is after all the legitimate child
of Liberalism.] But Federal Minister Dr. Wuermeling is not just concerned with the movies, he is only looking for arguments for his ambitions, and these ambitions are of a shady, very shady sort. [*Laughter
and calls from the center:* Oh! Oh!] Herr Federal Minister Wuermeling,
in seeking to castrate the movies [*the President's bell*], is leading an attack
on liberty of the spirit and of artistic creation. [*Applause from the SPD.
Contradictions from the center.*]

When problems of marriage and family life may no longer be treated,
then a part of their intellectual substance is being withdrawn from the
movies. Artists of all times and nations have represented not only the
average fate. They were stimulated to create the unusual, the tragic, and
the problematic. Thus it was from Sophocles to Shakespeare and Goethe
[*Hilarity and calls from the center—the President's bell.*], thus it was
from Schiller's *Luise Millerin* through Ibsen, Strindberg, on into our time.
. . . .

DEPUTY MENDE   (Free Democratic Party):

When the movie *Trip to Marakesh* was shown in Neumarkt-St. Veit,
Father Stehlböck had the penitential bells rung and prayed for the poor
sinner Frau Mayerhofer, owner of the movie theater and wife of Bundestag Deputy Mayerhofer of the Party of the Bavarians. [*Great hilarity.*]
In his Sunday sermon, there occurred the words: "Let us pray against

the delusion of this woman," and "By their fruits ye shall know them." [*Renewed great hilarity.*]

In Bardenberg, on the occasion of the performance of the film *Grosse Freiheit No. 7*, a picket line was formed around the movie theater in order to prevent the public from entering the theater. This was done under the leadership of the local clergyman, who had equipped himself for this purpose with a poster, and by members of the Catholic Film Commission.

Benjamin Constant has proclaimed that democracy, when carried to its extreme, can degenerate into the most terrible stepping stone to despotism. Let us therefore if possible avoid this association of people's sentiments, people's censorship, and people's democracy. A politician and a responsible person in public life must do more than merely listen to the *vox populi*. He has the responsibility, before his conscience and God, to let his actions be determined in the sense of the categorical imperative of Immanuel Kant. [*Vigorous applause from the FDP and the SPD.*]

It seems to me that it would be best to stay with Blaise Pascal, whose *Pensées* the Herr Federal Minister knows as well as I do too. To the question, whether man is good or evil, whether Jean Jacques Rousseau is right with his "*retournons à la nature*," Blaise Pascal replies: Man is neither good nor evil; only misfortune wills that he often becomes a devil when one wants to force him to become an angel. [*Very good! from the SPD.*]

[17]

Continuity and Discontinuity
in German Politics

The Constitution of the Federal Republic of Germany was proclaimed only in May 1949. The government based on this Constitution controls only about two-thirds of the territory and three-fourths of the population of Germany. The rest of the country is a satellite that has been subjected to a forced process of Sovietization. It calls itself the "German Democratic Republic."

Until 1955, the Government of the West German Federal Republic did not even exercise sovereignty over its own territory, but was under strict control by the Allied High Commission. This body consisted of representatives of the United States, Great Britain, and France. Even after sovereignty was granted to the Germans, troops of these three powers remained on the soil of the Federal Republic. Its Constitution was actually written to meet specifications and a deadline, set for 1949 by the Military Governors. The deadline had been preceded by four years of military occupation and military government following the most colossal military defeat and the greatest human migration in history—it brought ten million refugees and expellees into Germany. Before these catastrophes, their "cause": twelve years of totalitarian dictatorship, National Socialism under Adolf Hitler. In 1933, he had destroyed the Weimar Republic, Germany's first experiment with constitutional democracy. The Weimar Republic, in turn, had been born out of the country's first great modern defeat, at the end of World War I, in 1918, and lived—often on the brink of death or suicide—for only fourteen years. Before that, there were the

forty-seven years of the Second Empire, an absolute monarchy with some
vestiges of constitutionalism. And before 1871, Germany had been little
more than what Metternich called it, "a mere geographical expression."

Can there be any basis for comparing German with British or French
government? Offhand, we might well deny it. The differences in historical raw material are simply too vast. Compared with Britain, France
appears unstable. But at least France had already had forty-seven years of
her *Third* Republic, when the German national state was only forty-seven
years old and the Germans were trying to build their *first* Republic at
Weimar. At that time, one could have said: Constitutional politics in
Britain has tradition; constitutional politics in France is supported at least
by the revolutionary tradition; but constitutional politics in Germany does
not even have that. Thus, the Weimar Republic had to start virtually
from scratch. After World War II, in France, one spoke of an easy return
from the Fourth Republic to the Third. In Germany, a return from the
Bonn Republic to that of Weimar, short-lived as it was, would be much
less likely. French society was deeply divided, but at least there seemed to
be general acceptance of the procedures that produced *immobilisme*. German society, upon recovering self-government, faced so many problems that
it should have been rent by even more cleavages. Moreover, it lacked experience with political procedures by means of which these gaps could be
bridged and differences compromised. The Germans had not only to reconstruct government, but also to create the procedures by which disagreements about the goals of reconstruction could be either resolved or de-
ferred. And this at the same time at which they had to deal with the
much more immediate and serious problems of reconstructing the physical
basis of their very existence!

The amazing thing is that they seem to have mastered all these tasks.
Their economy expands faster than those of France and Britain and
the government of the Federal Republic has been much stabler than was
that of the Fourth French Republic. Between the general elections of
1953 and 1961, one of the parties, the Christian Democratic Union, controlled an absolute majority of the seats in the Bundestag and a two-party
system seemed for a time to be in the offing; both neo-Nazis and Communists made very poor showings at the polls. The competing regime in
the Soviet Zone of Germany would collapse immediately upon the withdrawal of the military and police forces on which it alone rests. If the
outside observer did not know that West German political institutions
and processes were created virtually out of nothing, he might think that
the present order and stability must have been preceded by a long, slow,
gradual, and peaceful evolution. But he knows that this was not the case,
and this leads him to ask: Is the present appearance of stability a mere

illusion? Or is there after all something in German politics that has provided a thread of continuity through all the changing tides of disunity, absolutism, wars, totalitarianism, and economic and political catastrophe? How effective is government in West Germany, both in terms of its capacity to put its policies into effect, and in terms of the likely longevity of the constitutional regime?

The Jagged Curve of Modern German History

Politics has been stable so far during the young life of the Federal Republic of Germany. But twelve years is hardly enough to permit a sound judgment about the endurance of this political stability. For such a judgment, a longer period would have to be considered. The longest period available starts in 1871. Since the German states were not unified until that year, one cannot properly speak of "German" politics before then, but only of the politics of such states as Prussia, Bavaria, Baden, and Hamburg, and of the external relations of these states. German politics since 1871, if viewed in terms of its scope and goals, its structure and policies, has been anything but a paragon of stability. Thus, if we were to picture in a graph the evolution of each of the four political systems considered in this book, the British curve would undoubtedly be the smoothest. The German curve would probably be the most jagged—more jagged, that is, than even the Russian, because Germany achieved national unity so much later than Russia. Since 1871, at least seven major changes have affected Germany. Each of these was bound to be, and was in fact, reflected in German politics, so that there was little opportunity for a stable pattern to evolve.

Of these seven changes, the first and the last were perhaps the most radical, because the first created a unified German political system, and the last destroyed it by division. Bismarck's founding of the Second Empire, at the end of the Franco-Prussian War in 1871, brought together into one state the many diverse political units of the member states, to the exclusion of Austria. The division of the country, formalized by proclamation of the constitutions of the Federal Republic and the German Democratic Republic in 1949, in effect created two German states, of which the Eastern has less continuity than the Western with their common predecessors. In terms of effects on German politics, the first change was probably more important than each of the subsequent ones before the last. The other changes were brought about by rapid industrialization, abolition of monarchy, inflation and depression, establishment of Nazi totalitarianism, and the consequences of defeat in World War II.

NATIONAL UNIFICATION

Before the unification of Germany under Prussian leadership, nothing that could be called a German political system had been in existence.

There was, to be sure, an area of German culture where the German language was spoken and where German literature and thought were predominant. But this area had little political significance, because it was crisscrossed by many barriers of different kinds, some of them insuperable for the forces of political unification. Thus the area of German culture included the German-speaking territories of the Austro-Hungarian Empire, which were to become a part of the German state only for the brief period of the last seven years of Hitler's Third Reich. It included also more than half of Switzerland, among whose German-speaking population there was never much sentiment in favor of political unity with any state outside the Swiss Confederation. Nevertheless, ever since the French Revolution and the elimination of many smaller German principalities under Napoleonic occupation, the goal of national unification of as many of their compatriots as possible under one crown had inspired many Germans, especially the liberal-minded among them. During the revolutionary year of 1848, a national assembly met in Frankfurt and was dominated by such liberals, among them many academic professionals. It offered the German crown to the King of Prussia, Frederick William IV, who rather contemptuously turned it down. During the next two decades, Prussia built up the North German Customs Federation, but it was not until Prussia's victory over Austria in the War of 1866 that the political unification of the German states "from above"—on the initiative of their rulers and under Prussian leadership—became a real possibility. Their common military effort against Louis Napoleon's Second Empire finally gave Bismarck, the Prussian Chancellor and Foreign Minister, the opportunity to bring into being the German Empire as a federation of princes presided over by the King of Prussia, William I, as German Emperor.

Before this happened, one could only speak of several diverse political systems existing in the member states. Their diversity can hardly be exaggerated. Little, for example, was shared in common by people from the eastern provinces of Prussia, dominated by the Junker aristocracy with their large landed estates and their ethics and outlook molded by Protestantism and traditions of military service, and people from the southern parts of the Kingdom of Bavaria, ruled by the Roman Catholic dynasty of the Wittelsbachs, which was much more ancient and "cultured" than the Calvinist Prussian Hohenzollerns. The lower classes did not even share an easily understandable language. Again, there were great differences between the Catholic peasantry and coal miners of Westphalia, a Prussian province, and the trading population of the Hanseatic city-states of Hamburg, Lübeck, and Bremen, with their centuries-old traditions of patrician republicanism and world-wide commercial contacts. Yet all this diversity was merged in one national state and given central representation in the first effective national German parliament in history.

Before 1871, there had been no occasion for setting up political parties or procedures national in scope. Unification thus resulted not only in the establishment of a new structure of government, wider in its scope than any previously set up in the German area, but also in the creation of a need for political practices and parties of similarly unprecedented scope. It also created a single economy. And all of this set in train developments that led toward *one* German society, with less diversity than before and with fairly general agreement on this new German nation as the proper unit of political authority.

INDUSTRIALIZATION

In 1871, the Third French Republic was also born, though under less auspicious circumstances than the Reich, and without any agreement on its republican character. In France by this time, however, national unification was an achievement of the dim past, and a useful stock of procedures of self-government had been built up since the Revolution. Even though this was not the case in Germany, political developments there might have taken much the same course as in France. That they did not is due in large part to the compression into a relatively short period of time of the radical social changes that followed unification. Of these, industrialization came first, belatedly and rapidly, and accompanied by urbanization. Without the founding of the Reich, industrialization would not have come about in the way in which it did. In Britain and France, industrialization took place earlier than in Germany: in Britain, after both national unification and the constitution had ceased to be controversial; in France long after national unification had been achieved, though at the same time as the establishment of her modern constitution. In Germany, on the other hand, the spacing in time of these three problems was much closer: national unification, establishment of a constitution, and industrialization. Moreover, the solutions to all three problems, which were made in the second half of the nineteenth century, were pushed forward under the leadership of the Prussian government. Even industrialization received much more support from the government in Germany than in either of the other two countries. One reason for this was precisely the Germans' conviction that they had to catch up with their neighbors' head-start in this field, and that they could do so only by means of a deliberate national effort. One result of this was the close alliance from the outset between the rising class of industrialists and the old Junker aristocracy, often strengthened through intermarriage. Partly because of this, and partly because of the increasing size and importance of the military establishment during the period that culminated in World War I, it continued to be the Prussian Junkers who largely "set the tone" for the newly industrialized German society. Among other things, this made the orientation of industrialist employers toward their workers much more paternalistic than that of their French or British counterparts. This was to have a lasting influence on the organization and aims of the industrial working class, whose growth was itself an important consequence of industrialization. The longer life, in Germany, of preindustrial and prenational ways of doing things, of forms of organization, and of habits of thought, combined with the need to modernize these radically and rapidly, was later to cast German politics in its own mold, and to introduce some of its more peculiar characteristics. Among these are the desire to revamp in a thoroughgoing way institutions regarded as inadequate and, therefore, to blueprint the reforms beforehand with the help, and in the manner, of academic scholars; the persistence or frequent revival of corporate habits of thought and action, and the desire on the part of corporate groups to be aided and legally regulated by the state; and the lack of a procedural conception of political authority either fully developed or generally agreed upon.

ABOLITION OF MONARCHY

The second great change had primarily economic effects. The third was once more due to political action. Abolition of such monarchies as Imperial German, royal Prussian, and Bavarian, and of the duchies and principalities, was one of the first acts of the new revolutionary regimes that took over power in Berlin and other German capitals when defeat ended World War I in November 1918. This abolition of monarchy was formalized the following year in the republican constitution adopted by the National Assembly at Weimar. It was designed to do away with the many remnants of feudalism still contained in the previous system, and especially with the continued social and political predominance of the old Prussian aristocracy. Though the former ruling families were not deprived of their often vast land holdings, they lost their political power and prerogatives. But some groups had to replace them in their functions of leadership. The make-up of one of these groups is suggested by the article of the Weimar Constitution, which, in its first paragraph, abolishes all titles and, in its final paragraph, specifically exempts academic titles from this prohibition. In any case, though the social revolution that was involved in this abolition of monarchy was nowhere near as radical as had been the revolution of 1789 in France, it did change German society and had strong repercussions on German politics.

ECONOMIC CRISES

This third major change had hardly been consummated and the new Weimar Republic was just beginning to get on its feet, when another change, of economic origin, began to weaken the very social groups that had taken over from the aristocracy. First, the great inflation wiped out most of the savings of the middle class. Then, beginning in 1929, the great depression made millions of workers unemployed and dependent upon relief for their livelihood. The effects on the social structure of these two economic catastrophes were reflected, almost as in a fever chart, in politics in general, and in voting behavior in particular, as will be seen later.

TOTALITARIANISM

In the society that had been ravaged in this way, Hitler established his totalitarian dictatorship, starting in January 1933, when President von Hindenburg appointed him Chancellor. Hitler and his henchmen deliberately engineered the fifth change. It consisted of the attempt to break down all the varied articulation of society, so that nothing would stand between themselves and the vast mass of individuals they sought to control absolutely. The Nazis' attempt was largely successful, though only for the time being, i.e., until their disappearance from the scene in the *Götterdämmerung* of 1945. Virtually all private and public associations and organizations not dependent upon the National Socialist Party were destroyed; so also were other political parties, trade unions, professional, sports, trade, and cultural associations, masonic orders, private clubs, and so forth. Only the Protestant and Roman Catholic churches withstood this onslaught, and they often at the cost of confining their activities completely to the realm of the spirit. Before millions of Germans were killed on the battlefront or homefront of World War II, Germany's 600,000 Jewish citizens—about one per cent of the population—were either forced to emigrate or were exterminated.

DEFEAT

We will never be able to gauge the independent effects of twelve years of totalitarianism on the social structure, because these effects were intermingled with the consequences of total, unconditional defeat in World War II. The society the Nazis had tried to level completely was now subjected to three years of hunger and privation. It had to absorb ten million German expellees and refugees, having harbored, just previously during the War, almost that many foreign slave laborers and prisoners of war. Moreover, all this happened under the stern watchfulness of the victorious Occupation Powers, who were themselves intent upon remaking German society by means of the so-called "four D's"—denazification, demilitarization, decartelization, and democratization. The economic consequences of defeat also made necessary another wiping out of small savings, effected through a currency reform in 1948.

DIVISION

The seventh major change—the division of the country—has brought into being two German economies, two social structures, and two German states. It means that each of the contemporary German governments controls a territory, a population, and an economy that are completely new units and never before had an independent existence. For Western Germany, in particular, this has created a social structure different from any in previous German history. Moreover, it is not only different, but it differs in ways that could not have been foreseen by projecting earlier developmental trends. For example, while the population of Germany before World War II was made up of Protestants and Roman Catholics roughly in the ratio of 2:1, the two denominations are of fairly equal strength in the Federal Republic of today. Its territory contains a relatively higher proportion of the total German population than before division, but it also has to get along without the food traditionally supplied by Germany's eastern breadbasket, which is now located in the eastern Democratic Republic and under Polish and Soviet Russian administration.

Thus runs the jagged curve of modern German history. The character of society in the Federal Republic is very different from that of society under the Weimar Republic, again very different from that of the 1870's. Therefore, we may expect a similar lack of likeness as concerns the main problems faced in each of these three periods, the cleavages running through society, and the party systems, by means of which the controversies arising out of these problems have been fought. In the 1870's, the main problems consisted of consolidating the new nation, industrializing the economy, expanding the military establishment, and generally strengthening Germany's international position. In the 1920's, they consisted of consolidating the new democratic constitutionalism, keeping the economy on an even keel despite reparation payments under the Treaty of Versailles and despite the effects of an erratic world economy, and making the best of military defeat and the consequent loss of territory and restriction of military strength to 100,000 men. And in the 1950's, the main problems concerned constitutional reconstruction in the aftermath of totalitarianism and occupation and rebuilding the destroyed and divided economy. In the 1960's, they concern seeking reunification of a Germany that was split in two by the division of the whole world into two hostile camps, or finding a peaceful accommodation to the continued existence of two German states.

Two Germanys

This brings us back to the questions about stability, continuity, and effectiveness. An approach to some answers may lie by way of comparing the politics of West Germany and East Germany. These two systems are radically opposed to each other in virtually every respect: genesis, goals, popular support, political organization, and procedures. If they nevertheless have some outstanding characteristics in common, this may cast light on the stable elements in German politics, the more so because both regimes were established in the wake of the great catastrophe of 1945. At first glance, this common point of departure and the strong revulsion against anything that smacks of the abhorred Nazi regime seem to be all that the Federal Republic of Germany (*Bundesrepublik Deutschland*) and the German Democratic Republic (*Deutsche Demokratische Republik*) share. Otherwise, they are true opposites and indeed prototypical of all the differences between politics inside and outside the Soviet orbit, because they came into being at one of the main focal points of the Cold War.

The Democratic Republic was established under the aegis of Soviet occupation authorities and the leadership of German Communists who had been specially trained for this task in the Soviet Union. Its evolution has followed a pattern very similar to that of the other Soviet satellites in Central and Eastern Europe. Its leaders have been wholly dependent on the support of the Red Army for their survival in power. In the Federal Republic, on the other hand, a constitution had to be written before the Western Occupation Powers would permit the establishment of a German government for the territory of their three zones. This "Basic Law" was designed to measure up to the highest standards of democratic constitutionalism as practiced in France, Britain, the United States, and elsewhere in the Western world. Its first nineteen articles contain a bill of rights that was meant to be really effective. Many free state-wide and four federal elections have been held under this Constitution. These elections produced stable and efficient coalitions of parliamentary majorities. Peace, prosperity, and good government prevail in West Germany. The population supports its political leaders, who enjoy respect throughout the world, even in Moscow.

A greater contrast than that between the governments of East and West Germany could hardly be imagined. It is so great that all those situational barriers that are usually believed to stand in the way of reaching collective goals by means of deliberately "engineered" political institutions seem to have been overcome. After all, the raw materials with which politicians started in the Eastern and Western Zones, in 1945, were fairly similar. And yet, the two governments are radically different not only from those that preceded them in Germany, but even more from one another. In this sense, contemporary Germany could serve as a superb example of the feasibility of "constitutional engineering."

There is, however, at least one belief on which both systems are based— a faith in precisely this feasibility of constitutional engineering, or in the capacity of men to shape their common fate in a rational way through the deliberate construction of political institutions. Some such faith can be found in all modern societies. The American founding fathers certainly held it. So did the authors of the first and all subsequent French constitutions, and the creators of such international organizations as the League of Nations and the United Nations. This faith is one aspect of the rationalism that has pervaded Western culture, especially since the eighteenth century. And it seems quite natural that it should be stronger in a country like Germany, where the need to create a whole new set of political institutions and procedures arose after both World Wars—just as it seems natural that it should be weaker in Great Britain, where no urgent need to make sudden and vast changes in ancient procedures and institutions has arisen in the course of many centuries. Nevertheless, there are two unusual aspects to the strength of this belief in contemporary Germany: first, its adherents might well have been disillusioned by the failure of the Weimar Constitution, which did not survive although it was written by some of the best legal, political, and social scientists of the time. And second, the intense legalism that accompanies this conviction as to the feasibility of constitutional engineering is not a necessary concomitant, i.e., the conviction could be held just as well with a less legalistic view of politics. In West Germany hardly anyone in any sphere of public life is willing to experiment with new institutions or processes by a method of trial and error unless explicit, detailed, comprehensive, and constitutionally sanctioned legal authority can be established beforehand.

Some sound explanations for this legal formalism can be found in recent German history. One is the absence of anything resembling the rule of law in the Soviet Zone. This has made the West Germans want to put on a blameless performance on this score. Another is the flagrant flouting of the Weimar Constitution and laws by the Nazis, which was obvious to everyone despite the Nazis' effort to maintain a façade of constititutionality and legalism. The present legalism is in part a reaction against that lawlessness. A third reason is the historical sequence, Weimar Republic–National Socialism, which led many to view the one as the "cause" of the other. This turned some Germans against constitutional democracy in general, but they were barred from participation in politics by Occupation fiat during the first few postwar years. Those who were licensed for politics during this period concentrated on the construction of a system of government that would be foolproof against another Hitler, by correcting the alleged short-comings of the Weimar system. All the novel constitutional provisions of the Basic Law are such corrections. The constitutional fathers of Bonn were able to go about this work of constitutional reconstruction in a fairly objective way because the Occupation Powers had at that time not yet returned much political responsibility to the Germans. As a result, political disagreements did not distort their constitutional deliberations to any great extent. They were not forced simultaneously to forge both new policies *and* the new methods by which such policies were to be compromised out of the divergent views of the parties. The constitutional authors at Bonn had to produce only the procedures of compromise, not policies. They were able to rebuild the constitutional system, starting at the state level, some time before they were put on their own politically by the Occupation Powers.

As the Occupation Powers slowly took the lid off West German politics, numerous previously dormant disagreements made themselves felt. Many of these were the common garden variety of political issues that exist in most modern industrial societies and that have existed in Germany ever since industrialization: economic organization, distribution of income, social security, the role of organized labor, relations between the state and the churches, educational opportunities, and the like. Other issues were of a potentially more explosive and divisive nature because they arose out of the National Socialist experience, out of the war and its aftermath, occupation and division of the country. The positions that people took on these issues were determined largely by their attitudes toward the Weimar Republic and the Hitler regime. As a result, additional cleavages were created in German society. Just as politics is complicated in France by the fact that the social, religious, and constitutional cleavages have usually not coincided, so it is in Germany today, because there, too, the social, religious, and constitutional cleavages present a crisscross pattern.

There is another resemblance between the politics of France and Germany: the tendency to justify one's stand on any issue in ideological terms, that is, by reference to a comprehensive, closed, consistent system of knowledge. The two tendencies—toward ideologism and toward legal formalism—mutually reinforce each other. The ideologists believe that *the* truth exist, that it can be known, that they themselves know it and therefore have the answers to all questions and solutions to all problems. Legal formalism persuades them that the inconsistencies, irregularities, and vicissitudes of politics can be replaced by a consistency, regularity, and certainty provided by law and administration. Both orientations, the legalistic and the ideological, lead to a high esteem for the powers of knowledge and for its possessors, the academically trained intellectuals.

In these attitudes toward politics, held almost subconsciously, and mutually related to and reinforcing each other, lies a thread of stability that does run through the discontinuity and institutional and constitutional instability of German politics. Legal formalism, faith in the feasibility of constitutional engineering, ideologism, and faith in the powers of knowledge— all these are marked in the political culture of all of contemporary Germany. They have been manifest in German politics since even before the time when such a thing as German politics can properly be said to have existed—for example, during the Liberal "Revolution" of 1848 and the National Assembly of Frankfurt. Under the Empire, the values and beliefs on which these attitudes were based were further elaborated. At the birth and during the short life of the Weimar Republic they bloomed forth fully. And under the Bonn Republic, one of them, legal formalism, has become more marked than ever before, in reaction to both the previous Nazi, and the present East German Communist totalitarianism.

Political and Constitutional Stability

The stability of politics in the Federal Republic since its establishment in 1949 is outranked as a "miracle" only by the West German "economic miracle." But it is of such recent vintage that it may well be deceptive, especially since it has followed a historical development in which the constitutional pendulum oscillated from one extreme to the other, while the political pendulum—when it was permitted to oscillate freely at all, i.e., under the Weimar Republic—had a most irregular beat. How can we tell how long political stability will last? Will it survive Chancellor Adenauer? More important, will we be able to speak of continued constitutional stability in the 1960's? Does the one stable thread we have found, at the semiconscious procedural level, augur well for constitutional stability?

The fourteen years of the Weimar Republic were a period of political instability. The average life of cabinets was but little longer than under the Third French Republic. Out of the many parties represented in the Reichstag, majority coalitions capable of agreeing on positive policies were hard to forge. The "Weimar Coalition," consisting of the Marxist Social Democrats, the Roman Catholic Center, and the liberal Democratic Party, agreed only on the need for the defense of the Republic, but not on social, economic, or cultural policies. This situation was made even more tenuous by the anti-republican attitudes and the anti-constitutional activities of the conservatives, monarchists, nationalist, and Nazis on the right, and the Communists on the left. For opposed reasons, these two extremes of the German political spectrum wanted to destroy the Republic—and in the end they did. Before that, they sought to sabotage political stability in order to put an end to the temporary constitutional stability the country was enjoying. In the process, they often restored to open violence, the very antithesis of legal formalism. Violence and terror finally won out and, behind the thin veil of feigned legality, they reigned supreme during the period of Hitler's Third Reich.

The very strong contemporary legalism of German political cultures arises out of the desire to ensure permanent stability, both constitutional and (to some extent) political. But by an ironical twist of logic, results are the very opposite of the intentions. To the legalistically oriented, there seems to be no better way to ensure constitutional stability than to include a great many provisions in the Constitution, and then to make this Constitution hard to amend. And there seems to be no better way to straighten out the complexity, and to contain the potential violence, of politics than to divert as much as possible of the raw material of politics into the administrative and judicial machinery. This has been attempted in West Germany.

Meanwhile, however, economic, social, cultural, and foreign-relations problems continue to change in a world that is anything but static. These changes then call for political and constitutional adjustments. Most political processes and institutions have been crystallized by explicit and detailed legislation, or even by inclusion in the Basic Law. The need for change, which could be satisfied by informal adjustment in a less legalistically oriented society, in Germany often requires legislation or even constitutional amendment. It follows that both those who favor and those who oppose some change frequently call on the constitutional courts for legal interpretations of issues that are really political. The courts, however, have neither a tradition of constitutional interpretation nor great popular respect to fall back on in exercising this function. The Basic Law is hard to amend. Therefore, those who are involved in constitutional controversies —of which there are more than would be the case without legal formalism —feel cramped politically, and the intensity of their conflicts is thereby increased. The courts are overloaded with constitutional cases. Politicians who are dissatisfied with a verdict vent their spleen on the judges and seek to ensure having their way in the future through revamping the court system and judicial powers. Any minor issue is easily raised to the level of a constitutional conflict, and thus some of the most fundamental institutions of the Federal Republic are potentially less stable than they might be if their life were not anchored in the Constitution itself.

Other institutions, which were kept out of the Basic Law precisely in order to keep them more flexible even though they are by nature basic, fundamental, or organic, are subject to easier revision. This has been true especially of electoral laws, through which the parties believe they can engineer more advantageous representation for themselves in parliament. It applies also to the territorial organization of the states, which can be changed without constitutional amendment. The drive for constitutional change, enhanced by the scope of the Basic Law, is thus deflected to institutions, not included in this Constitution, which are just as basic but are as a result brought into a condition of potential flux.

This situation is further aggravated by the explicitly tentative status of the Basic Law. Its authors at Bonn were afraid that the title "Constitution" implied permanency to such an extent that it might be viewed as an acceptance of the division of Germany. The document consequently provides that it is to be superseded by an all-German constitution once the country is reunited. Thus the Federal Republic denied itself the kind of permanent constitutional stability for which most of its citizens yearn. Of course, it is considered less reprehensible to criticize or attack a constitution of which one may legitimately hope that it will be short-lived. Moreover, anticipation of the eventual reunification of the Soviet and Western Zones stimulates theoretical speculation about the all-German constitution that will then have to be drafted. Widespread public discussion of these "iffy" constitutional problems of the future further enhances constitutional consciousness and constitutional litigiousness, without at the same time furthering the cementing of a "constitutional myth."

The outcome of all this is a high degree of potential constitutional instability. All that seems stable and well-established is the pervasive legal formalism, which determines the manner in which issues are perceived, stated, and fought over. This means also that the political leadership is made up of people who by education and background fit into this way of doing things. In this respect there is often more resemblance between the leaders of politically hostile organizations than between leaders and followers on each side of the fence. Dr. Eckstein detected a similar resemblance between Socialist and Tory leaders in Great Britain. But there the resemblance—and the consensus—is more on the rules of the game, on procedure, than on the substance of advocated policies. In Germany, leaders of opposing groups are more likely to be in agreement on basic substantive attitudes, like intellectual elitism. And even the procedures on which there is consensus among these leaders have a more substantive, less constitutional orientation than their British counterparts, because of the content of higher education, especially in the law.[1]

West German society is still rent by many divisions, based on present interest, traditional ideological convictions, and recriminations about the past. The one need concerning which there is the most general agreement is the need for the rule of law and order, and this agreement arises out of the revulsion against the experience of lawlessness. Political order has been

---

[1] Herbert J. Spiro, *Government by Constitution* (New York, 1959), chap. 18.

ensured so far through constitutional engineering. For this reason and because of the importance of legal formalism, we will examine the structure
of the Constitution and the procedures for which it provides before we
look at the parties and interest groups that operate within it, the policies
they espouse, the scope of the policies the Government actually puts into
effect, and the effectiveness of government itself.

[18]

The Formal Structure
of Government

By and large, the structure and process of government in West Germany
are what the Basic Law says they are. This is the case neither in Great
Britain nor even in the United States, with its written constitution. An
American professor of government can tell his students not to bother reading the Constitution, because it does not describe the actual operation of
American politics today and might therefore confuse them. His German
colleague often has his students read nothing but the Basic Law and
learned commentaries on it, and from such a study they can actually get
a fair idea of the operation of their political system. Britain, of course,
has neither a written constitution nor even its functional equivalent, partly
because the need to construct a whole system of government, or even parts
of one, never arose. This need did arise in the United States, but only
once, and that before the nineteenth century. In Germany, by contrast,
the repeated need for complete reconstruction, combined with the recent
frequency with which this has occurred, means that the Basic Law does
give a description of government in the Federal Republic that is both accurate and adequate. Another reason for this is the high value placed on
strict observance of constitutional and legal provisions, and the high expectations Germans generally hold of political stability as the necessary
consequence.

As a result, it would be difficult to get an understanding of parties and
pressure groups and their functioning without prior acquaintance with
the constitutional framework within which they operate. This is true even

of such organizations as the Social Democratic Party and the German Trade Union Federation, which are older than the German national state and can pride themselves on their traditions and ideologies. Since they, too, have shared the prevalent faith in the feasibility of constitutional engineering, they have adjusted their modes of operating to the demands of the new constitutional order, to the shaping of which they contributed at least as much as their less democratically inclined political opponents.

The Lapse of Politics

This new constitutional order was built from the bottom up. In this respect it is in contrast with the work of constitutional reconstruction undertaken by the French during and after World War II. That is one of the reasons why there are more differences between the Bonn Basic Law and the Weimar Constitution than between the Constitutions of the last three French republics. There is, however, a more important reason: while republican *government* lapsed in France during the years of the Vichy regime, republican *politics* in one form or another continued throughout the period between the death of the Third Republic and the birth of the Fourth. Thus, while the new constitution was being drafted the very men who were doing the drafting were interested not only in creating a sound set of institutions, but also in their own more or less immediate political aims. In other words, even if there had been agreement in France on long-run constitutional goals—and there was not—disagreement on short-run political goals would have affected the drafting labors. In West Germany, on the other hand, there was not only a lack of weighty and acute disagreement about long-range constitutional objectives—simply because the Occupation Powers did not let anti-constitutional elements participate in public life at this time—but also little short-range political disagreement that could to any very important extent influence the work of constitutional reconstruction—simply because there was relatively little German politics going on at the time.

German politics, as carried on during the four years from the end of the war to the founding of the Federal Republic, was severely restricted by the occupiers in almost every respect. The enumeration of the several functions of government given in the Preamble to the Constitution of the United States may serve as a convenient check list for finding out just what the Germans were allowed to do on their own.

First of all, the Germans were not able to do anything at all toward "forming a more perfect union." On the contrary the country was not only divided into four Zones of Occupation, but two of these were governed by powers that, for different reasons, were intent upon further decentralization inside their territories: the French because of fears of a German revival and hopes of encouraging separatist leanings on the part of some Germans; the United States because of convictions about the virtues of grass-roots democracy and a necessary connection between democracy and federalism. Since the British held neither of these prejudices, their Military Government was the first among the three Western ones to permit the organization of political parties and trade unions with zonal scope. The Americans, by contrast, kept German politics confined to the local and state levels for much longer.

"To establish justice" was a task assumed by Military Government. For a while, German courts were not permitted to function at all and were replaced by Military Government courts. Even after German jurisdiction had been largely restored, the Occupation Powers continued to control such important areas of judicial activity as denazification. The courts also applied much new law that was made by Military Government.

"To ensure domestic tranquillity" was the job of the Armies of Occupation, and when the German police did begin to reappear on the scene it was reorganized, retrained, supervised, and controlled by Military Government.

"The common defense," down to 1957 was provided by the armies of the Western victors of the war, though the Germans were able to contribute to maintaining this defense establishment by bearing some of the costs of the Occupation and making, after 1955, an equivalent contribution to the North Atlantic Treaty Organization.

"The general welfare" was the one thing the Germans were allowed to help promote, through clearing away the debris and rebuilding their towns and industries. But even on this score they received a great deal of Allied help, especially from the United States; and all the important policy decisions—economic, fiscal, with regard to public health, and otherwise— were made or at least supervised by Military Government.

Finally, the Occupation Powers, since they had just defeated the Nazi regime, saw *themselves* as bringing "the blessings of liberty" to the Germans and, presumably, their posterity. That was why one of them, the United States, soon "ordained" that the several states, newly organized as units of government in the American Zone, should "establish" constitutions for themselves.

The basic functions of government were thus not being taken care of by the Germans themselves. They could address their collective efforts to the pressing problems of their immediate material needs, and this they had to do at the level of the grass roots, whether they wanted to or not. The needs were such that not much disagreement arose as to the best ways of meeting them. Those men and women who, as former Nazis, were now considered accountable for contributing to bringing about these disastrous conditions in the first place, were either in Allied concentration camps or else kept out of public affairs. As a consequence of all this, on a zonal or national scale politics was lacking.

Constitutional Reconstruction

When the task of constitutional reconstruction was taken up in earnest, the builders were able to ask themselves what sort of institutions would best serve the public interest, without too much concern for narrow partisan considerations, because concrete partisan interests were not yet as clearly evident as later and partisan conflict had not yet generated among them strong mutual antagonisms or mistrust. On the contrary, in some cases bitter enemies of earlier and later periods were firm collaborators during the first three or four postwar years. Many of them had learned to know and respect one another as common opponents of the National Socialist regime, despite different class, party, or religious backgrounds; others learned about each other in the course of the reconstruction labors; still others had co-operated in resisting some of the more unpopular Occupation measures, such as the dismantling of industrial plants for demilitarization or reparations purposes. All of them, except for the minute minority of Communists, were tied by the further bond of opposition to the Sovietization of the eastern part of their country.

Their task began at the level of the states, in the United States Zone, on American prodding to write constitutions. The men who drafted these first state constitutions had sufficient perspective to realize that their work would influence, and perhaps set the pattern for, the constitution that, they hoped, would sooner or later be written for the whole of Germany. They were deeply and fully conscious of the historical importance of their task. They went about it by asking themselves what constitutional flaws had brought about the failure of the Weimar Republic. To correct these flaws, they produced many ingenious devices. There were, of course, many different and often mutually exclusive interpretations of the life and death of Germany's first experiment with constitutional democracy. But despite this fact they turned out constitutions that were generally sound when judged in terms of internal consistency.

The Occupation Powers had their theories too. Of these, the American were particularly important for their influence on German federalism. After the Americans, the British and French permitted the establishment of state governments in their zones as well, even though some states in the British Zone did not get constitutions until after their delegates had helped to write the Federal Basic Law and their parliaments had ratified it. As a result of this American-initiated reconstruction at the level of the states, the first postwar German representative organ was also established. This was the Economic Council (*Wirtschaftsrat*), which was composed of 52 representatives elected by the state legislatures. The Occupation Powers gave it some jurisdiction over the combined zones of the United States and Great Britain—the so-called "Bi-Zonia"—and later also the French Zone. Later, the Parliamentary Council (*Parlamentarischer Rat*) was created to draft a Federal Constitution. It consisted of 63 members who were elected by the state parliaments and then appointed by the Ministers-President (*Ministerpräsidenten*), who were and are the chief executive officers of the states. It was these same Ministers-President to whom the Military Governors addressed their instructions about the constitution.

Federalism

As a result, the Basic Law had a truly federal genesis. The several member states (*Land*, pl. *Länder*) were in being before the Federal Republic. Its Constitution was drafted by delegates from the states and ratified by all the state legislatures, except that of Bavaria. The degree of federalism to be written into the Constitution was one of the major bones of contention in the debates of the Parliamentary Council. And since the Basic Law has come into effect, one of the most persistent issues of West German politics has been the balance of powers between the states and the Federal government. Besides the circumstances surrounding the birth of the Basic Law, there are good reasons for the persistence of this issue in German history. The Bismarckian Constitution was federal. In 1871 it unified, under Prussian leadership, eighteen grand-duchies, duchies, and principalities, three Hanseatic republican city-states, and four kingdoms. The Weimar Republic, too, was a federal state. But federalism had been one of the obstacles in the path of the centralizing ambitions of Hitler's totalitarianism, so that the governmental wreck that was left on the hands of the Germans at the end of the war was that of a unitary non-federal state. The Soviets would have preferred to leave it that way, judging by the scrapping, in 1952, of the federal structure provided by the Constitution of the Democratic Republic in their zone. British preference also tended toward a non-federal setup. But American and French leanings and advice in the other direction fell upon sympathetic ears with those Germans who believed that a more federalistic Weimar Republic could have better withstood its enemies, and/or that the Nazis' centralism was both against German constitutional tradition and a principal tool of totalitarian control.

They therefore designed each of the Federal provisions of the Basic Law as an improvement on the Weimar Constitution. This is true of the territorial structure of the new federalism, the provisions for reform of the federal structure, the Bundesrat as the federal house of parliament, the distribution of legislative powers, federal emergency powers against the states, the Federal Constitutional Court, and the symbolism of the new Republic.

Territorial Structure

Many interpreters of German history have seen its major blemishes in Prussia, the dominant state both before and after unification in 1871. Under the Imperial Constitution, the Prussian government had 17 of 58 votes in the upper, Federal chamber of Parliament, and could command a majority by exerting pressure on her smaller neighbor states. The Prussian government in turn was responsible to its king—who was also German emperor (*Kaiser*)—and nominally also to the Prussian state Diet (*Landtag*). In this Prussian parliament, representatives of the poorest class of the population had only one-third of the seats, so that it was always controlled by the representatives of the other two-thirds, a conservative or reactionary minority of the people. Under the Weimar Republic, this Prussian class-franchise was abolished, and Prussia's predominance in the Reichsrat, the new Federal chamber of Parliament, was reduced. Prussia now had 25 of 66 votes. But some half of these 25 were not cast by the Prussian state government, but by the governments of the provinces into which Prussia was divided. Nevertheless, after the Nazi experience there were still people who blamed the failure of the Weimar Republic on Prussia's relative predominance. They did this despite the fact that the Prussian state government had, throughout the years between 1919 and 1933, been controlled by the pro-republican parties of the Weimar Coalition. The Allied Powers, too, were so convinced by this argument that the breakup of the Prussian state was one of their war aims, which was restated in the Potsdam Declaration of the Big Four in 1945. Prussia was officially dissolved by an Allied Control Council Law of February 25, 1947.

The constitutional fathers at Bonn were generally agreed on the need for a reasonable balance of territorial size and population among the member states of their new Republic. Since much of the old Prussia was under Soviet or Polish administration, or located in the Soviet Zone of Germany, and because the breakup of the rest had been made mandatory upon them, they were able to achieve such a balance without much trouble. The boundaries of the states did, however, present a problem. As these existed at the time of writing the Constitution, they were partly the result of zonal boundaries between the Occupation Powers, drawn by the latter without much regard for German tradition, or administrative and economic efficiency. There was some doubt as to the viability, in the long run, of a federalism whose member states had as weak a basis in traditional attachment and utilitarian rationale as, for instance, North-Rhine-Westphalia, the largest of them. Considerable sentiment existed in favor of immediate boundary revisions. On the other hand, the states had already been operating long enough for the formation of groups that had a vested interest in their continued existence and in maintenance of the Federal *status quo.*

A compromise was born out of these conflicting considerations. For the time being, the territorial *status quo* was to be kept, but Article 29 of the Basic Law made provision for a general Federal reorganization. This was to be concluded within three years after promulgation of the Basic Law. But since the Allied High Commission withheld permission for initiating this procedure, the deadline had to be postponed. Only in the fall of 1955 did the Federal Government receive the report of a commission, headed by one of the surviving Chancellors of the Weimar Republic, which made recommendations concerning this problem. No action was to be taken on this report. Article 29 also contains a provision for the use of initiatives and plebiscites, but for the purpose of Federal reorganization only. The contrast with the Weimar Constitution on this score is marked, because it characteristically permitted use of these two ultra-democratic devices for all but budgetary purposes. Anti-republicans several times abused the provision in order to launch publicity campaigns against such measures as the Dawes Plan and the building of naval vessels. The men at Bonn did not want to give enemies of their Constitution a similar opportunity.

In the southwest corner of the Federal Republic, the effect of Occupation zoning on state boundaries was particularly noticeable, and clearly went against both tradition and efficiency. Therefore, Article 118 provided that the territorial reorganization in that area should be accomplished by means of a special procedure involving negotiations among the three state governments concerned, federal legislation, and a subsequent plebiscite. This procedure was actually followed and, after a great deal of controversy —including litigation in the Federal Constitutional Court—the three states combined into one, Baden-Württemberg. It adopted a new constitution in 1953.

On January 1, 1957, the Saar was added as the tenth state of the Federal Republic. After the War, it had been placed under French administration, mainly for economic reasons, since its population is wholly German. In 1954, West Germany and France concluded a number of treaties, under which the Saar territory would have been "Europeanized," but continue to remain part of the French economy. But this was overwhelmingly rejected by the Saar voters in a referendum held in October 1955. Subsequently, France and the Federal Republic agreed on a three-year transition period for the complete re-integration of the Saarland into Germany.

Thus some of the states that established the new German "federation" had not existed for long and had little reason for existence. It was partly in order to emphasize this temporary character that the name "Basic Law" (*Grundgesetz*) was given instead of "Constitution" (*Verfassung*). It provided for Federal reorganization, including the possibility of absorption of one state by another, and this actually happened within the first three years of the life of the Federal Republic. Considering this along with the foreign forces that encouraged the Germans to build a Federal structure, one may well ask whether their federalism is not a pretty artificial affair—especially when compared with the federalism of, say, the United States or Canada. If this is true of the federalism of the Federal Republic, is it not likely to be true of contemporary German constitutionalism as a whole? And does not this Constitution itself, by provisions such as those for Federal reform, encourage institutional instability?

The answers are: "Yes, but. . . ." The "yes" is suggested by the tremendous self-consciousness with which the Germans attacked the whole problem of constitutional reconstruction. Having been unused to political responsibility for such a long time and having not yet assumed its full burdens, they were able to approach their task almost as an academic exercise. If political institutions that were conceived and built up in this spirit failed to live up to expectations, this could easily lead to disillusionment.

"Yes, but. . . ." The "but" is required as a qualification because new institutions need people to run them, and these people may develop both sentimental attachment to, and material interest in, them. As a result, they will fight more or less fiercely against any attempts at change or abolition. If enough time is given for the development of such attachments and interests, advocates of reform may become aware of the potential explosiveness of their schemes, and therefore desist from proposing them in the first place. Under favorable conditions, German federalism may lose its present potential fluidity, the more so because there are real economic and cultural differences among the populations of the various parts of the country and because the new arrangements did not do complete injustice to these differences by any means.

The states served an important purpose as the proving ground not only for the rebuilding of German constitutionalism, but also for the revival of German politics. Nevertheless, partly because of their somewhat artificial character, some prophets of the doom of German federalism predicted that state politics would lose all vitality once the Federal Government really got going. Able and energetic politicians would leave for its greener pastures, the attention of the parties would be completely concentrated on capturing control of the Federal Government, and the states would become mere administrative branches of the central bureaucracy.

But these predictions have turned out to be wrong. The main reason for this is the make-up, the position, and the role given to the Bundesrat by the Basic Law.

Bundesrat

The government of each state is represented by three, four, or five members in the Bundesrat, the upper chamber of the Federal Parliament, depending on the size of the state's population (see Table 11). Its votes there must be cast as a unit; that is, even though the state is governed by a coalition of parties that take opposed stands on an issue in the Bundestag, the lower house, all the state's votes must be cast together in the Bundesrat. This has forced the representatives of state governments in the Bundesrat to behave much more like the state delegates they are than like representatives of the political parties to which they happen to belong. Largely as a result of this constitutional provision, the deliberations of the Bundesrat have been structured around true issues of federalism, such as the perennial question of the distribution of revenue between Federal and state governments and among the several states. Of course, this might have happened even without the requirement for bloc voting, since the states have "natural" common interests. But without the requirement party discipline would probably have overcome these considerations. As things actually stand, the state governments have developed so much interest in their common problems, as distinguished from those of the Federal Parliament, that their Ministers-President hold regular conferences very similar to the Governors' Conferences held annually in the United States.

Because of the continued vitality of government at the state level, neither the Bundestag nor the Federal Government can afford to treat the Bundesrat as either a silent or a minor partner. If the Weimar tradition had been followed, the upper house would have performed a useful function as a body of expert civil servants for the revision of technical details of bills and regulations. Under the Basic Law, the states participate in Federal legislation through the Bundesrat. All bills that deal with matters on which the states have the right of concurrent legislation, as well as regulations that implement laws, must be passed by the upper house before they become law. If the Bundesrat rejects a bill by a simple majority, the Bundestag can override this veto by a simply majority of its votes. A two-thirds veto of the upper house requires a two-thirds vote of the lower house to be overridden. Disagreements between the two houses may be resolved by a standing committee consisting of eleven members of each. Since the range of items listed under the concurrent category is wide, and because of the relative independence of the state governments, this committee has often been busy. Members of state governments have made a point of attending meetings of the Bundesrat personally and regularly. Its presidency rotates annually among the Ministers-President. As a result of all this, the Bundesrat has become more important than the Reichsrat, its predecessor of Weimar days.

TABLE 11   Representation in the German Parliament 1961

STATE	POPULATION	VOTES IN BUNDESRAT	SEATS IN BUNDESTAG
Schleswig-Holstein	2,289,900	4	24
Hamburg	1,823,600	3	18
Lower Saxony	6,583,400	5	60
Bremen	691,600	3	5
North-Rhine-Westphalia	15,653,600	5	155
Hesse	4,702,800	4	45
Rhineland-Palatinate	3,367,800	4	31
Baden-Württemberg	7,560,700	5	66
Bavaria	9,278,000	5	86
Saarland	1,040,100	3	9
TOTAL	52,991,500	41	499
West Berlin	2,208,000	4*	22*

* Non-voting deputies. (From *Statistisches Jahrbuch für die Bundesrepublik Deutschland,* 1960, and election returns of 1961.)

Federal Emergency Powers

The strength of the new German federalism is also due in part to the allocation of legislative powers. This allocation was revised for two reasons: to correct the shortcomings of the Weimar Constitution, as interpreted by the members of the Parliamentary Council at Bonn, and to compensate for the evils of centralization under the Nazis. The Basic Law does not reserve any legislative powers exclusively to the states. But it does contain a long list of twenty-three fields subject to concurrent state and Federal legislation.[1] On these matters, the Federal Government has juris-

---

[1] Following is the list of legislative powers of the Federation and the states. It is of interest also because it gives an idea of the considerable scope of governmental functions, a matter to which we will return in Chapter 20.

Basic Law, Article 70:
(1) The States have the power to legislate insofar as this Basic Law does not vest legislative powers in the Federation (*Bund*).

    Article 71:
In the field of exclusive legislation of the Federation, the States have the power to legislate only if, and insofar as, they are expressly so empowered by federal law.

    Article 73:
The Federation has exclusive legislation on:
    1. foreign affairs as well as defence, including service duty (*Wehrpflicht*) for men having completed their eighteenth year and the protection of the civilian population;
    2. citizenship in the Federation;
    3. freedom of movement, passports, immigration and emigration and extradition;

diction when individual states cannot effectively regulate them, when regulation by one state might be prejudicial to the interests of others, or when the requirements of legal or economic unity call for it. The Federal Government has exclusive powers of legislation in eleven fields.

---

4. currency, money and coinage, weights and measures and regulation of time and calendar;

5. the unity of the territory as regards customs and commercial purposes, commercial and navigation agreements, the freedom of traffic in goods, and the exchanges of goods and payments with foreign countries, including customs and border control;

6. federal railways and air traffic;

7. postal services and telecommunications;

8. the legal status of persons in the service of the Federation and of public law corporations directly controlled by the Federal Government;

9. industrial property rights (including patents and trade marks), author's copyrights and publisher's copyrights;

10. co-operation of the Federation and the States in the field of criminal police and in matters concerning the protection of the Constitution, the establishment of a Federal Office of Criminal Police, as well as international prevention and repression of crime;

11. statistics for federal purposes.

Article 74:

Concurrent legislation extends over the following fields:

1. civil law, criminal law and execution of sentence, the constitution of courts and their procedure, the Bar, notaries and legal advice;

2. census and registry matters;

3. law pertaining to associations and assemblies;

4. the right to sojourn and of settlement of aliens;

5. the protection of German works of art and of cultural (historic) significance against removal abroad;

6. matters relating to refugees and expellees;

7. public welfare;

8. citizenship in the States;

9. war damage and compensation;

10. assistance to war-disabled persons and to surviving dependents, the care of former prisoners of war and the care of war graves;

11. law relating to the economy (mining, industry, power supply, crafts, trades, commerce, banking and stock exchange, insurance to which civil and not public law applies);

11a. the production and use of nuclear energy for peaceful purposes, the erection and operation of institutions serving these purposes, protection against dangers resulting from the liberation of nuclear energy ionizing radiation, and the removal of radioactive materials;

12. labor law, including the constitution of enterprises, the protection of workers and provision of employment, as well as social insurance, including unemployment insurance;

13. the furtherance of scientific research;

14. law regarding expropriation insofar as it is concerned with the matters enumerated in Articles 73 and 74;

15. transfer of land and real estate, natural resources and means of production to public ownership or to other forms of publicly controlled economy;

16. prevention of the abuse of economic power;

17. furtherance of agricultural and forestry production, safeguarding of food supply, import and export of agricultural and forestry products, deep-sea and coastal fishing and the guarding and preservation of the coasts;

18. transactions in real estate, law concerning land and matters concerning agricultural leases, housing, settlements and homesteads;

19. measures against epidemics and infectious diseases affecting human beings and

The Federal Government can force a state to fulfill its obligations to the Federation, but only with Bundesrat approval. This provision for Federal interference in state affairs is similar to the one contained in Article 48 of the Weimar Constitution, which some have considered one of the main contributors to the end of the Weimar Republic. Under Article 48, the Reich President could use Federal troops against a state and/or suspend civil rights. Such measures had to be reported at once to the Reichstag and could be rescinded at its request. In the 1920's, Article 48 was used several times with success against states in which extremists were using violence. But during the last three years of the Republic, and especially under the chancellorships of Brüning, von Papen, and von Schleicher, these powers were abused, both by circumvention of the need for parliamentary approval and by their exercise while the Reichstag was either in recess or dissolved. It was also under Article 48 that the Reich Government could issue decrees having the force of law, as it did continually during the years of parliamentary deadlock starting in 1930. The Basic Law, through its Article 67, discussed below, was designed to safeguard against a repetition of the abuse of similar powers, but even more against the possibility of parliamentary deadlock. If such a stalemated situation should nevertheless arise, the approval of the Bundesrat is once more required (under Article 81) for decrees issued by the Federal Government. So long as the representatives of the state governments in the Bundesrat retain the independence of viewpoint that the constitutional position of that body has virtually forced upon them, and that they have displayed so far, these safeguards should be adequate.

However, in 1948 and 1949, while the Basic Law was being drafted, the maintenance of public order was still mainly a task of the Occupation Powers, and it was then anticipated that that state of affairs would prevail for fairly long, the more so since the demilitarization of Germany had been one of the victors' primary war and occupation aims. These hopes were shattered when, after the outbreak of the Korean War in 1950, the Western powers called for German rearmament. After the treaties on Western European Union came into force and the Federal Republic was admitted to the North Atlantic Treaty Organization, the Parliament had

---

animals, the admission of medical and other healing professions and healing practices and the traffic in drugs, medicines, narcotics and poisons;

20. protection concerning traffic in food and stimulants as well as in necessities of life, in fodder, in agricultural and forestry seeds and seedlings, and protection of trees and plants against diseases and pests;

21. ocean and coastal shipping and aids to navigation, inland shipping, meteorological services, sea waterways, and inland waterways used for general traffic;

22. road traffic, motorized transport and the construction and maintenance of highways used for long-distance traffic;

23. railroads other than federal railroads, except mountain railroads.

to consider the constitutional position of the armed forces that were to be brought into being. On this issue, some extreme federalists, especially from Bavaria, advocated the establishment of separate militias, if not armies, in the several states, but they lost out in the face of the exigencies of modern defense requirements. The Basic Law was amended in March 1956 to permit the creation of Federal Defense Forces. In peacetime, these are to be under the supreme command of the Federal Defense Minister. This command is transferred to the Federal Chancellor once a "state of defense" (*Verteidigungsfall*) has been proclaimed, normally as the result of action to that effect by the Bundestag. Legislation concerning the organization and administration of the defense forces requires Bundesrat concurrence.

Umpire of Federalism

Sooner or later, however, this and other questions of constitutional revision will come up again. When this occurs, parliamentarians are likely to ask the Federal Constitutional Court (*Bundesverfassungsgericht*) to give opinions on the most controversial questions. Some of the functions of this Court, especially judicial review of the constitutionality of parliamentary legislation, are among the new constitution's most daring innovations in German practice. But this is not true of its function as umpire of the Federal system. This function was also exercised by the State Court (*Staatsgerichtshof*), the supreme Federal tribunal of the Weimar Republic. To cite the most important example: after Chancellor von Papen abused Article 48 in order to oust the pro-constitutional state government of Prussia in 1932, the ousted state government brought suit against the Reich Government in the State Court. The Court found von Papen's action partly unconstitutional, but, by the time it did so, it was already too late. The authors of the Basic Law consequently tried to strengthen the position and increase the prestige of the highest court in several ways.

First, they raised it one level in the governmental hierarchy in order to make it the equal of the highest legislative and executive organs. They accomplished this goal by reinstituting the equivalent of the old State Court, in the form of the Supreme Federal Court, but then creating the new Federal Constitutional Court and placing it at the apex of the judicial hierarchy. Second, they provided for the election of its judges by the Federal Parliament, half of them to be elected by each House from among the Federal judges and other qualified persons, such as professors of jurisprudence. By contrast, the old State Court had been manned by career judges appointed by the Ministry of Justice. And third, they made it in effect the guardian of the Constitution by giving it the power of judicial review. Thereby they both enhanced its prestige and made its role more

controversial, as will be shown later. Although the Court has had to decide several cases of a mainly Federal character, these have not so far made
up the most important part of its work. This has consisted rather of interpreting basic rights and reviewing legislation for constitutionality.

Finally, under the general heading of federalism, there is the matter of
federalistic symbolism. The title of the country is, of course, *Federal*
Republic of Germany (*Bundesrepublik Deutschland*). Its principal officers
are officially—and are almost always referred to as—*Federal* President,
Federal Chancellor, and *Federal* Ministers, in the *Federal* Government.
Parliament consists of the *Federal* Diet and the *Federal* Council and meets
in the *Federal* House. The new defense establishment is called the *Federal*
Armed Forces. In each case, the word *Bund* has been substituted for the
word *Reich*, used in the Weimar constitutional vocabulary. This terminology has helped create a general awareness of living in a federal
system. At the same time, it has also led some politicians to suggest that
the Bund is merely a temporary organization, to be replaced once more,
after reunification, by the Reich. Revival of the state of Prussia is being
advocated by some in the same connection.

The Federal President

Preoccupation with titles and formal positions has strongly influenced
the constitutional role assigned to the head of state of the Federal Republic, the Federal President (*Bundespräsident*). In the Weimar Constitution, an attempt had been made to combine in the presidency both
power and restraints—power, in order to provide an adequate substitute
for the monarch; and restraints, in order to prevent irresponsible conduct
of the kind in which the last Kaiser, Wilhelm II, used to indulge. The
Reich President was popularly and directly elected, and served for a term
of seven years. His functions were those commonly assigned to Continental heads of state: he was commander in chief of the armed forces,
signed laws and decrees, convened and dissolved Parliament, but always
with the counter-signature of the Reich Chancellor or a Reich Minister,
and these last were to be subject to parliamentary control.

The first President of the Weimar Republic, Friedrich Ebert, a Social
Democrat, performed his duties in a solid if colorless manner. His successor, Field Marshal von Hindenburg, Germany's great commander of
World War I, turned out to be more colorful throughout, but during the
last years of the Republic either unwilling, or—because of senility—unable to live up to the spirit of the Constitution. He dissolved the Reichstag
on the request of Chancellor von Papen, who was supported by a minute
parliamentary minority and should for that reason never have been appointed in the first place. Then, von Hindenburg permitted use of the

emergency powers of Article 48 without parliamentary approval. Ultimately, he was to preside over the establishment of Hitler's dictatorship, remaining President until his death in 1934.

The authors of the Bonn Constitution clearly believed that the President's constitutional position facilitated or even accelerated the downfall of the Weimar Republic. As a result, the powers of the Federal President are but a pale shadow of those of his Reich predecessor. To begin with, his plebiscitary base was removed. He is now elected by the Federal Convention (*Bundesversammlung*), a body that is convened solely for this purpose. It consists of the members of the Bundestag, joined by an equal number of electors, who are elected by and are representative of the political make-up of the state parliaments. His term now runs for only five years, i.e., only one year longer than that of a full-term Bundestag. Most of the discretionary powers that had previously led to abuse have either been abolished completely or severely curtailed. In effect, the main constitutional functions remaining to the President are the symbolic and ceremonial ones and the giving of counsel and advice to the Federal Chancellor and other parliamentary politicians. The soldiers of the new German military establishment no longer take an oath to obey the President. He has the power to find that a "state of defense" exists, but only when the Bundestag is prevented from doing so, and even then only with the Federal Chancellor's counter-signature and after consulting with the presiding officers of both Houses of Parliament. He is no longer supreme commander of the defense forces.

The Federal Chancellor

The fathers of the Bonn Constitution thus weakened the presidency because of their retrospective orientation. But they clearly had to place somewhere the powers they took away from the President. Portions of them ended up with the Bundesrat, as has already been noted. Most of them, however, were lodged in the chancellorship, which was clearly intended to become the keystone of the whole constitutional edifice. However, to make it that, the concentration of powers in the hands of the Federal Chancellor (*Bundeskanzler*) would not suffice unless at the same time something was done to stabilize his tenure in office. The Weimar chancellorship did not compare unfavorably in strength with the premiership in the Third Republic. The trouble was not its lack of strength, but its instability. And this in turn was due to the political fragmentation of the Reichstag and the difficulties connected with producing positive parliamentary majorities, ready and able to support coalition cabinets. Under the Weimar Republic, as under the Third and Fourth French Republics, it seemed easier to obtain a parliamentary majority that would vote lack of confidence in a ministry than to find one that could agree on its successor.

To remedy this situation, the constitutional engineers of Bonn invented an ingenious device—or rather they applied it, because it had previously been patented in the state constitution of Württemberg-Baden. Article 67 of the Basic Law provides that the Chancellor, who is to be elected by a majority of the members of the Bundestag, cannot be forced out of office simply because a majority of the deputies vote against him on a question of confidence. On the contrary, the

> Bundestag may express its lack of confidence in the Federal Chancellor only by electing, by the majority of its members, a successor, and by submitting a request to the Federal President for the dismissal of the Federal Chancellor. The Federal President must comply with the request and appoint the person elected.

One might have asked what effect a similar provision would have had on French politics, had one been included in the last French Constitution. But the question would have been purely academic, because the French politicians who drafted the Constitution of the Fourth Republic could never have agreed on its inclusion. It was precisely the main advantage of the drafters at Bonn over those at Paris that they were not yet involved in the full-blown battles of everyday politics and were, therefore, able to function more as engineering consultants to their public, which had ordered a blueprint for a stable structure, than as self-service builders of their own edifice, who, like the French drafters, were at odds as to the purpose of the building. By contrast, De Gaulle was able to include the French equivalent of Article 67 in his Constitution, in its Article 49, which ensures survival of the government, or adoption of a text proposed by it, unless defeated by a majority of the members of the National Assembly.

Another question concerning this "constructive vote of lack of confidence" makes better sense: Can such a constitutional device, by itself, result in the harnessing of divisive social and political forces? If there are deep cleavages in the society, these are likely also to find their reflection in Parliament. There they may perhaps not result in the overthrow of a ministry, because of Article 67, but nevertheless cause refusal to pass the ministry's legislative program. Then the old problem of negative majorities would be revived, further aggravated by the frustrations caused by the artificially continued life of an unwanted ministry.

But the founding fathers at Bonn thought of this eventuality, too. First, they provided for Presidential dissolution of the Bundestag if it fails to give the Chancellor a requested vote of confidence, and if the Chancellor makes a demand for dissolution within three weeks. But suppose that the subsequent election returns a Bundestag similarly incapable of producing a positive majority? This situation was also anticipated. For, if the Bundestag refuses to pass a bill the Government has declared to be urgent, "the Federal President may, at the request of the Federal Government and with Bundesrat approval, declare a state of legislative emergency with respect to a bill." Then, according to Article 81,

> If the Bundestag, after a state of legislative emergency has been declared, again rejects the Bill or passes it in a version declared to be unacceptable to the Federal Government, the law shall be deemed passed provided that the Bundesrat approves it.

The same procedure may then be applied to any other Bill within one period of six months—and one such period only—during one Chancellor's tenure of office. But, in contrast with Article 48 of the Weimar Constitution, the Bonn Basic Law explicitly forbids use of these provisions for the purpose of amending, repealing, or suspending the Basic Law or any part of it.

This scheme seems to be foolproof, and the life of the Federal Republic so far suggests that it actually is. In 1949, Adenauer was elected Chancellor for the first time by a bare majority—202 of 402 votes. Some bills were passed with the votes of the Social Democratic opposition against those of some members of the Government coalition. But this did not break up the coalition, as was usually the case in similar circumstances in France under the Fourth Republic. In 1953, after the election of the second Bundestag, these provisions appeared to be less important, because Adenauer's own party, the Christian Democratic Union, controlled a majority of the seats by itself and was allied with other parties in a coalition that for some time held two thirds of the seats. Since then, no occasion for their use has arisen. However, when Dr. Adenauer changed his mind in 1959 and decided not to become a candidate for the Federal Presidency, he slyly suggested to his followers in the Bundestag that they could always use Article 67 if they objected to his remaining Federal Chancellor. When the CDU lost its parliamentary majority in the election of 1961, it took almost two months to negotiate a coalition agreement with the Free Democratic Party, so that Dr. Adenauer could be re-elected as Federal Chancellor by a majority of nine votes. The coalition of CDU/CSU and FDP actually held 309 votes out of a total of 499, but only 258 cast their secret ballots for Adenauer.

These patterns, in turn, suggest that the explanation for recent West German political stability must be sought in electoral conditions as well as in constitutional provisions. If the voters had been very much divided, chances are that their parliamentary deputies would have been just as much divided. And in that case, the six months' grace provided by the constitutional article dealing with legislative emergency might have been of little and only temporary help. Still, the problem is not quite as simple as all that. The first Adenauer coalition and, to an even greater extent, the second and third were representative of a "natural" stable popular majority of what may be described as the lowest common denominator of non-socialist middle-of-the-road opinion. The point is that the second coalition, which emerged out of the election of 1953, would not have been as large as it turned out to be, and the CDU itself would not have received 45 per cent of the popular vote, if the politics of the first Bundestag had not clearly been conducted between *the* Government facing *the* Opposition. And this continual confrontation of two alternative programs was largely forced upon the parliamentarians—especially those of the minor parties—by Article 67. If something resembling a two-party system had indeed been evolving in West Germany between 1949 and 1961, the inventors of this clever constitutional gadget were entitled to a good deal of the credit for having brought it about.

The Federal Government

According to Article 62, "The Federal Government (*Bundesregierung*) consists of the Federal Chancellor and the Federal Ministers." According to Article 64, "The Federal Ministers are appointed and dismissed by the Federal President upon the proposal of the Federal Chancellor." And according to Article 65, "The Federal Chancellor determines, and assumes responsibility for, general policy. . . ." The cumulative effect of these provisions, combined with those of Article 67, has been to make the Chancellor much more than *primus inter pares*.

Adenauer did in fact run his Cabinet in a much less collegial fashion than British prime ministers usually do. It was partly out of resentment over the one-man show the Chancellor was running that his first Minister of Interior resigned, even though disagreement over rearmament policy probably played a more important role. (The ex-minister eventually was reelected to the Bundestag on the Social Democratic ticket.) But while the first Chancellor did not always consult his Cabinet colleagues before making policy pronouncements, he usually backed them against attacks in the Bundestag. This happened, for instance, when the Bundestag voted to continue a bread subsidy in opposition to the policy of the Finance and Economics Ministers, and passed a vote of censure against the former. In this case, the government was able to make use of the provisions of Articles 112 and 113 of the Basic Law, which make increases in budgetary expenditures dependent on cabinet approval in a manner reminiscent of the rule of the House of Commons, which restricts initiative in increases in expenditure to Ministers. On the other hand, during the life of the third Adenauer Cabinet, from 1957 to 1961, open rivalry between the

Chancellor and his Minister of Economics cropped up. Adenauer wanted Professor Erhard to become the Christian Democratic candidate for the Federal Presidency. Erhard, who had generally been regarded as Adenauer's most likely successor, did not want to be "kicked upstairs" and refused. When Adenauer announced his own intention to become President, he also indicated that Erhard was not his favorite to succeed him as Chancellor. But when it became clear that the Bundestag would not elect Adenauer's hand-picked choice, he solved his problem by remaining Federal Chancellor. Throughout this "presidential comedy," relations between the two principal actors were understandably strained.

The relative lack of collegiality in the Cabinet was due not only to the constitutional and personal dominance of Chancellor Adenauer, but also to the fact that each of his four Cabinets was a coalition. The first of these, during the period of the first Bundestag (1949-53), was made up of eight members of the CDU/CSU, three of the FDP, and two of the German Party. After Adenauer's victory of 1953, he created two new ministries, one for Expellees and another for Questions Concerning the Family and Youth. He also added four Ministers without Portfolio to his Cabinet, in order to assure himself of a smoothly functioning two-thirds' majority, sufficient to pass the constitutional amendments required for the European Defense Community. This Cabinet was composed of ten members of the CDU/CSU, four of the FDP, two of the Refugee League, and two of the German Party. The Minister for Postal and Telecommunications originally was a member of neither the Bundestag nor a party. After the breakup of both the Refugee League and the FDP, and because of dissatisfaction with the Minister of Defense, Adenauer again reorganized his Cabinet late in 1956. It was especially during the two years preceding this shakeup that disagreements among the members of the Cabinet occasionally received public airing. When the Government was considering the stand it should take on the Saar Agreements, for example, even the results of a vote taken in the Cabinet were publicized.

The third Adenauer Cabinet contained two Ministers representing the German Party until the latter broke up in 1960, and these two men joined the CDU/CSU. The following seventeen ministries were represented in the Cabinet: Foreign Affairs; Interior; Justice; Finance; Economic Affairs; Food, Agriculture, and Forestry; Labor and Social Order; Defense; Traffic; Postal and Telecommunications; Home Construction; Expellees, Refugees, and Persons Damaged by War; Affairs Concerning the Whole of Germany; Family and Youth Questions; Atomic Energy and Water Economics; Economic Property of the Federation; and Bundestag Affairs and *Länder*. When forming his fourth Cabinet after the prolonged coalition negotiations that followed the election of 1961, Chancellor Adenauer added a new Ministry for Economic Cooperation. It and four other ministries were assigned to members of the FDP. The Free Democrats, with 66 deputies as against the Christian Democrats' 243, thus were represented by 5 Ministers in a cabinet of 19.

The Bureaucracy

Both the provisions of the Basic Law and the composition of the first, second, and third Bundestag have enabled the Cabinet to dominate the Bundestag. Seating arrangements symbolized its position of leadership. It had at its disposal a tier of benches to the right of the presiding officer and facing the deputies. Here, Federal Ministers were usually joined by the chief civil servants (*Beamte*), the so-called *Ministerialbürokratie*. These men are even permitted to address the Bundestag and, as representatives of their Ministers, to participate in meetings of the Bundesrat and of committees of the Bundestag. Members of the Bundestag sometimes resent this. On one occasion, a Social Democratic deputy complained about the fact that some civil servants were making faces at the Bundestag, in order to demonstrate their reactions to members' speeches. He claimed that the Minister of Labor had promised that he would bring the bad parliamentary manners of the *Ministerialbürokraten* to the Cabinet's attention, but in the end Adenauer denounced the Social Democrat for trying to be a "censor of manners." The presiding officer of the Bundestag, under its rules of procedure, could not call Ministers to order for unparliamentary remarks, so long as they did not occupy their seats as deputies—below the "angels' choir," as the Government bench has been called.

This kind of outburst against bureaucrats does not arise from any deep hostility between the "administrative" and "representative" traditions, as in France. No such opposition exists. Many—roughly about a quarter—of the ministers and deputies have themselves had administrative careers and the status of the *Beamte*. Many are on the inactive list as civil servants for the duration of their parliamentary service and expect to return to active duty at a later date. Because of the almost identical educational prerequisites for legal, judicial, and administrative careers, parliamentarians and bureaucrats generally "speak the same language." People in West Germany are, as a result, not so aware of the problems of parliamentary control of the bureaucracy as in France or Britain. And this, in turn, makes it hard to estimate the actual power of the bureaucracy in German politics. Moreover, because the CDU dominated the Federal Government during the first twelve years of the life of the Bonn Republic, one cannot tell whether the civil service would loyally serve a Government headed by the present opposition. However, ministry changes at the level of the states indicate that the bureaucracy is loyal and neutral in this respect. And these state turnovers should be adequate test cases, since the state bureaucracies, in most instances, come under the ultimate jurisdiction of the relevant Federal ministry.

With some exceptions under the Nazis, the German civil services have had a long tradition of political neutrality and of loyalty to the incumbent regime. This tradition goes back to the seventeenth century, when the Great Elector brought into being the Prussian bureaucracy, which was to serve as the model for most other bureaucracies for more than three centuries. Next to military service, civil service for the king was looked upon as the highest calling. This administrative tradition is so much older in Germany than either constitutionalism or parliamentary democracy that it still carries great prestige. In many respects it serves as the model profession. For example, the ranks and grades of the bureaucracy are often used to classify the exact status of ordinary citizens. In part, this is due to the great scope of public services, which include, among other branches, the Federal railroads and all public school teachers and university professors. However, not all of these civil servants are *Beamte*. A majority have the lower status of public employees, which is broken down further into salaried and wage-earning groups (*öffentliche Angestellte* and *öffentliche Arbeiter*). Questions about the class basis and bias of civil servants have not played nearly so important a role in Germany as in Britain. Because of the assumed neutrality of both the State and its officials, these officials themselves form an estate, according to their own opinion and that of the public. The assumption is that once an individual takes the civil servant's oath to the State, he leaves behind his previous class or corporate interest.

These traditions, taken together with the presence of many *Beamte* in Parliament, must in part account for the general preference for administration or adjudication over politics. Orderliness is of the very essence of administration. To anyone brought up to become an administrator, parliamentary politics would naturally appear disorderly if not chaotic. Hence the defensive attitude, even on the part of its strongest backers, toward the Weimar Republic. The stability, on the other hand, that has so far prevailed in the Bonn Republic has made this defensive attitude unnecessary. That is why the authors of Article 67 are entitled to so much credit.

Three rival claimants for the plaudits due the authors of political stability might also speak up: those whose efforts were concentrated upon electoral laws; those who made constitutional amendments more difficult to pass than had been the case under the Weimar Constitution; and those who gave a firm constitutional anchor to basic rights by establishing the Federal Constitutional Court as the protector of these rights. Election law is not properly a part of the Constitution, except in a negative sense. The Weimar Constitution provided for proportional representation, whereas the Basic Law contains no such requirement, thus leaving to the legislature greater discretion as to the kind of electoral system they wish to devise. For this reason elections will be discussed later, together with another non-constitutional subject, parliamentary procedure.

Basic Rights

Not only are citizens' rights included in the Constitution, but its entire first Chapter, consisting of nineteen Articles, is devoted to them. Article One sets the tone for the rest:

> The dignity of man is inviolable. To respect and protect it is the duty of all state authority.
> The German people therefore acknowledges inviolable and inalienable human rights as the basis of every human community, of peace and of justice in the world.
> The following basic rights are binding on the legislature, on the executive power, and on the judiciary as directly valid law.

The catalog of rights is long and detailed. Particularly interesting here are the authors' efforts to prevent the abuse of these civil and political rights to subvert or overthrow the constitutional order. This desire was again due to their retrospective orientation. They asked themselves, in effect, "Why did the Weimar Constitution fail?" One answer they found in the abuse of the rights of free speech, free press, and free assembly by partisans of both the Nazi and Communist extremes of the political spectrum—abuses that finally led to the outbreak of open violence and then to the end of the Weimar Republic. Consequently, a right such as that of forming associations and societies carries with it a qualification:

> Associations, the objects or activities of which conflict with the criminal laws or which are directed against the constitutional order or the concept of international understanding, are prohibited. (Article 9)

Article 18 is even more explicit on this score:

> Whoever abuses freedom of expression of opinion, in particular freedom of the press, freedom of teaching, freedom of assembly, freedom of association, the secrecy of the mail, of the postal services and of telecommunications, the right of property, or the rights of asylum, in order to attack the free democratic basic order, forfeits these basic rights. The forfeiture and its extent shall be pronounced by the Federal Constitutional Court.

And Article 21 makes a similar provision with respect to political parties. Moreover, Article 20 proclaims the Federal Republic to be a "democratic and social federal state," in which "Legislation is subject to the Constitution; the executive power and the administration of justice are subject to the Law." Finally, in order to make these "basic principles laid down in Articles 1 and 20" as fixed, fundamental, permanent, and unalterable as humanly possible, an amendment to the Basic Law affecting them is "inadmissible," according to Article 79.

Constitutional Amendments

The amending procedure is set down in Article 79. Here the constitutional fathers were again intent upon correcting their forerunners. The Weimar Constitution could be amended by a two-thirds' majority of a two-thirds' quorum of the members of the Reichstag, i.e., actually by four-ninths, or less than one-half, of the deputies. This made the passage of constitutional amendments relatively easy, at least before the Reichstag was completely fragmented. The procedure was used fairly often. The resultant constitutional instability was, moreover, further aggravated. A bill that was passed by an amending majority did not have to specify whether or not it was in fact intended as a constitutional amendment. And if it was so intended, it did not have to specify just which provisions of the Constitution were to be affected by it. It therefore soon got to be quite difficult if not impossible to tell just what the Constitution consisted of.

In contrast, the Basic Law, according to its Article 79,

may be amended only by a law expressly amending or amplifying the text of the Basic Law.
Such a law requires the approval of two-thirds of the Bundestag members and two-thirds of the Bundesrat votes.

In the Federal Republic, there can thus be no doubt as to the content of the Constitution. An amendment to it can be passed only on matters about which there is substantial consensus. One result has been that relatively few important amendments have been passed so far. One of these dealt with a technical matter assigning jurisdiction over administration of a law designed to equalize the burdens of the war; this was not a matter of controversy. Another made provision for the conduct of foreign affairs and defense and was otherwise meant to give effect to the contractual agreements connected with the abortive European Defense Community. The Allied High Commission used its suspensive veto against this amendment. As things turned out, since these agreements never entered into force, because of French failure to ratify them, the amendment was not then needed. After the Western European Union came into being as a substitute for E.D.C., however, a whole series of amendments was required to fit the new defense establishment into the framework of the Constitution.

These defense amendments were promulgated in March 1956. They established permanent committees of the Bundestag to deal with foreign affairs and defense. They gave the Bundestag the power to find that a "state of defense" exists. They also created the position of Defense Commissioner (*Verteidigungsbeauftragter*) of the Bundestag, copied from a similar Swedish model. The Defense Commissioner resembles the Inspector General of the United States Army, with the important difference that he is not a member of the military establishment itself but is instead responsible to Parliament. It took the Bundestag almost two years to agree on the first incumbent, whose service came to an abrupt end in 1961, when this ex-general attempted suicide because the public prosecutor charged him with a homosexual affair. He was succeeded by an ex-admiral, who had just been defeated for re-election to the Bundestag as a candidate of the CDU. The strong desire of the Bundestag to insure civilian control over the military is reflected throughout this series of amendments. This is largely due to the fact that they could be passed only with the support of the Social Democratic Opposition, which drove a hard bargain. The SPD, like other constitutional engineers involved in these efforts, was once more haunted by its interpretation of the fall of the Weimar Republic and the role of the military in that catastrophe. That is why it insisted on an addition to the Basic Law according to which the individual's "freedom of conscientious decision" may not be limited if he has conscientious objections to war service. In that case, opportunities for substitute service must be provided for him. This addition was also made necessary by the original version of Article 4, according to which "No one may be forced against his conscience to perform war service." And in order to make quite certain that these basic rights would be considered binding upon the now strengthened executive, Article 1, which originally declared them to be binding as directly valid law "on the administration," was amended to read "on the executive power."

The Federal Constitutional Court

The difficulty of the amending procedure has thus contributed substantially toward the stability of the institutions anchored in the Basic Law and of the fundamental rights the Basic Law protects. This is one of several reasons why the Federal Constitutional Court has been assuming an increasingly important role. For, if there is disagreement in Parliament on the proper meaning of a constitutional provision, clarity can no longer be produced by simply elaborating the controversial paragraph by means of a bill passed by a majority of four-ninths, as was the practice in the Weimar period. In most cases, the constitutional passage has to be left unchanged and an interpretation of its meaning obtained from the Constitutional Court. Going to the Court for this purpose is futher encouraged by Article 93. This Article as applied until 1956 obligates the Court to render interpretative opinions having the force of law on questions of constitutionality if it is requested to do so by the Federal or a state government, or by one-third of the Bundestag members. (This of course contrasts sharply with the Supreme Court of the United States, which early in its existence refused to render verdicts on anything but actual controversies at law.) In the Federal Republic, where the latent tendency towards litigiousness is already strong, this contributed to the Court's docket being initially overcrowded. Its wide and varied jurisdiction further complicated its task. The Court is not only the final interpreter of the Constitution and the guardian of citizens' rights, as already mentioned. It also has the final say on Bundestag election controversies. Impeachment trials of the Federal President would take place before it. It has also had the burdensome task of deciding the constitutionality, not merely of contemporary legislation, but also of laws still on the statute books from the days of the Nazis, the Weimar Republic, and earlier periods. Besides that, it is the umpire of the Federal system and the interpreter of Article 31, according to which "Federal law overrides state (*Land*) law."

Although the Basic Law provided for the Court, the law establishing it was not passed by the Bundestag until February 1951, a year and a half after the first Bundestag convened. This law provided for a Court consisting of two chambers (*Senate*) of twelve judges each, which are elected half by the Bundestag and half by the Bundesrat. The procedure for electing the judges is quite complicated. The political parties have had a hard time arriving at compromises as to the composition of the Court, so that the appointment of the first slate of judges, and the filling of vacancies that have arisen since, was delayed, often many months at a time. Originally, the two chambers were assigned jurisdiction over different types of cases. One of them was believed to favor the political outlook of the Government, the other that of the Opposition. They were popularly referred to as the "black chamber" and the "red chamber." Since the Court does not publish dissenting opinions there was no way of gauging the accuracy of this widespread belief. As a result, when parliamentary delegations of political parties had occasion to request an opinion from the Court, they tried to frame their case so as to have it decided by the "friendly" chamber. Needless to say, these practices did not tend to promote the prestige of the Court.

The Court's effectiveness as guardian of the Constitution and of citizens' basic rights is very hard to gauge. For one thing, it has been in operation for only about a decade. For another, many of its non-Federal functions were such innovations for German government that they were bound not to find general acceptance right away. For the first two years of its life the Federal Republic functioned without a supreme constitutional court. But this gap in the constitutional structure was not a serious handicap. The Occupation authorities, under the Occupation Statute, had retained the power to disapprove legislation that "in their opinion . . . is inconsistent with the Basic Law, a state constitution, legislation, or other directives of the Occupation authorities themselves or the provisions" of the Occupation Statute. In this sense, the Allied High Commission served as the ultimate guardian of the Constitution, and the Occupation Statute as a sort of super-constitution, until the abolition of both and the attainment of sovereignty by the Federal Republic in 1955.

Among the major early cases of the Court was one that found the neo-Nazi Socialist Reich Party anti-constitutional and resulted in that party's dissolution; another—a very prolonged one, decided in 1956—that had the same effect for the Communist Party of Germany; a case that found unconstitutional all those parts of the German Civil Law Code dealing with family law that violated the constitutional provision guaranteeing equal rights to the sexes; and others that settled the claims of military personnel and civil servants of the former Reich. The two last-mentioned types of opinions have generated the greatest amount of controversy, because they forced the judges to use wide discretion and to come very close to "judicial legislation." In the decision on family law, for example, the Constitutional Court instructed lower courts to judge in terms of the equal-rights provision of the Basic Law until such time as the Federal Parliament passed legislation replacing those parts of the Civil Code that it found no longer valid. This opinion produced sharp criticism from German jurists and others who believe that the judicial function should properly be confined to the impartial, mechanical, automatically rigid application of existing law. The cases dealing with former civil and military servants of the Nazi regime were controversial, not only because of the highly charged concrete political interests at stake—the treatment to be accorded to men, some of whom had been Nazis—but also because it pronounced on the question of legal continuity between the Nazi Reich and the Federal Republic. Its critics again considered this an excursion beyond the Court's proper sphere of jurisdiction. Verdicts on the continued validity of a Concordat with the Vatican, concluded by Hitler's Reich, and on the unconstitutionality of referenda on atomic armament and establishment of a second television network by the Federal Government were similarly received by the losers in each case.

Thus the Federal Constitutional Court has had to contend with hostility toward the substance of its decisions, as well as with criticism of its procedure, organization, and the method by which its members are selected. Some of this criticism came from the Court itself, which in 1955 worked out proposals for its own reorganization, and submitted these to Parliament. The Bundestag did pass a bill reforming the Court's setup in 1956, and took into account some of the Court's own proposals. The division of labor between the two chambers, with their unequal work loads, was redistributed, and at the same time the number of judges reduced. The three-fourths' majority of the Bundestag committee that had previously been required for the election of the Court's judges was reduced to two-thirds. However, these reforms received a mixed reception from the political public, and some have urged further reforms—or even the Court's abolition. It seems only natural that an institution involving so many novelties should need some reform after a period of experimentation. But if it were not for the tendency toward legalism, many of these reforms might have been accomplished in an informal way. As things actually stand in Germany, however, these requirements could be met only by deliberate legislative reform. In the course of the debates on the reform bill, politicians naturally raised political issues. As a result, the reformed Court—which has continued to get much of its business because of the general preference for adjudication over politics—has enjoyed less prestige than required for the adequate performance of its task.

The Periphery of the Constitution

The organization of the Court, as distinguished from its powers, is one of those matters that fall into the border area between the Constitution and mere legislation, the no man's land between what Oliver Cromwell distinguished as "fundamentals" and "circumstantials," between those matters that it generally requires some kind of extraordinary majority to change and those that can be passed by an ordinary majority. Besides the organization of the Court, two other important questions are to be found in this same ill-defined periphery of the Constitution: parliamentary procedure and the electoral system. In Great Britain, as Dr. Eckstein has shown, the scope of things considered constitutional and fundamental is very wide indeed. The fact that so many institutions are ancient, and accepted as virtually unalterable precisely because of this antiquity, has lent great constitutional stability to British government. On the other hand, the absence of a written constitution actually places no institution beyond Parliament's power to change or even abolish by a majority of only one vote. Nevertheless, it is to the credit of British parliamentary procedure that such changes are made but rarely, and that, when they are made, they usually do not serve only the immediate political advantage of the majority of the day. The British electoral system is as stable as parliamentary procedure with respect to its most important features—elec-

tion by plurality vote and in single-member constituencies. The extent of
the franchise, however, has been subject to occasional parliamentary
changes, which governments felt free to push through since they could
claim a "mandate." This relative constitutional stability in both these
fields has gone along with a widespread unquestioning consensus among
politicians and public alike on the propriety and fairness of these very
important "rules of the game."

Parliamentary Procedure

Nothing approaching this degree of consensus exists in either France
or Germany, though parliamentary procedure has been more stable than
electoral systems. Thus the Bundestag at Bonn initially adopted the Rules
of Procedure of the Reichstag of Weimar days, at the same time adapting them to the constitutional changes that had occurred. It was able to
get along on this basis for two years after its first meeting, until it passed
a new set of rules in December 1951—and these did not differ very much
from the older ones. The rules are long—132 paragraphs and close to
10,000 words—detailed, and comprehensive. They take account of the
strong constitutional positions of both Cabinet and Bundesrat by providing that members of either, or their deputies, must be listened to by the
Bundestag on their request. The Cabinet, on the other hand, does not
have to accede to demands for a major interpellation (*grosse Anfrage*),
though its refusal may be debated in the House if at least 30 members so
request.

The Bundestag, voting by secret ballot, elects its own president by a
majority of votes cast. But if the first two ballots do not produce a majority, a plurality choice is made between the two top contenders on the
second ballot. The three men who have so far served in this capacity have
all been members of the CDU, and have for the most part tried to preside
over the business of the Bundestag in an impartial manner. The third
holder of the presidency was elected by only a plurality of its votes to his
first term, but by a large majority to his second. The President, his
deputies, and representatives of the officially recognized party delegations
(*Fraktionen*) together form the Council of Elders (*Ältestenrat*), which
fixes the agenda of the Bundestag. For this reason, and also because
party representation on committees is proportioned to the strength of
these groups, the rules governing their recognition are important. The
Rules of Procedure themselves, however, do not specify the minimum
number of members required for purposes of recognition as a *Fraktion*.
Rather they state that this minimum is to be fixed by a resolution of the
House. This provision was designed to provide maximum flexibility on
this point, in order to facilitate discrimination against minor parties—

especially the anti-constitutional ones. In the Reichstag, the minimum used to be 15 members, but the Bundestag at first fixed it at 10. Then, in January 1952, it raised it to 15, so as to exclude the Communist deputies from the Council of Elders and the committees. This was made possible by the fact that the Communist *Fraktion*, though originally 15 strong, usually had a smaller number of deputies in the Bundestag, since some of them were frequently barred from the House because of disorderly conduct.

Unparliamentary behavior was quite a problem during the life of the first Bundestag, from 1949 to 1953. At one point, the President even excluded the late leader of the Social Democratic opposition, Dr. Schumacher, from the chamber. The Communists occasionally started near-riots. But since none of them was returned in the general election of 1953, things have gotten relatively quiet and restrained. During the first year of the second Bundestag's tenure, not a single reprimand was issued to members by their presiding officer. After that, reprimands had to be issued occasionally for insulting interjections, especially about deputies' alleged Nazi affiliations. Still, many of the debates have been so orderly as to bore some people—and this despite the fact that deputies must attend sessions and are not allowed to vote by proxy. When the Social Democrats have really wanted to show their disapproval of parliamentary proceedings, they have walked out of the chamber as a group, instead of resorting to the more rowdy tactics that were often used on such occasions in Paris.

One reason for this orderly parliamentary atmosphere is the fact that the function of the Bundestag is more propagandistic than deliberative. Speakers for the various parties usually do not try to convince one another of the merits of their several antagonistic programs—quite a hopeless task for anyone who would attempt it. Nor do they really try to hammer out policies based on reasonable contributions from all those capable of making them. They rather use the forum of Parliament to get publicity for their party's position. The speeches they deliver sound more like the policy declarations delegates of sovereign states make before certain international assemblies, such as the General Assembly of the United Nations, than like attempts to persuade. And although parliamentary reporting in the West German press has not yet reached the same high level as in Great Britain, the publicity value of debates is high. Some of the more important debates are reported verbatim in the better newspapers, some debates are broadcast, and a few are even televised.

The Rules of Procedure themselves conduce to this non-deliberative, propagandistic character of the debates. They do this by providing that speeches are to be delivered from the rostrum, which was located below the President's high pedestal. A speech should last not less than five minutes nor more than one hour, and should not be read but delivered extemporaneously, with occasional reference to written notes permitted. However, this latter rule is often broken. Parliamentary leaders have been quite conscious of the resultant lack of liveliness of Bundestag proceedings. Because of their general wish to "bring Parliament closer to the people," they instituted some formal changes designed to further this aim. One of these affected the question period, by permitting the use of floor microphones by deputies who wished to ask supplementary questions. But this did not reduce the formal atmosphere of the debates in any marked degree. Another change, intended to increase respect for the Bundestag and the dignity of its business, enhanced the prestige of its presiding officer. He is now attired in white tie and tails, and members rise as he enters the chamber. To some observers of contemporary German parliamentarism, this has seemed merely to add to its artificiality. After all, white tie and tails are but a pale image of Mr. Speaker's wig and knee breeches. It is true that some presidents of the French National Assembly have also affected this attire. But the National Assembly at least meets, and has been meeting since the Third Republic, in the Palais Bourbon, which was built in the eighteenth century. By contrast, the modernistic Bundeshaus does make a somewhat artificial, untraditional, and even temporary, provisional, rootless, and unstable impression.

Many members and officers of the Bundestag have been painfully aware of these shortcomings, and repeated efforts have been made to overcome them. For example, during the third Bundestag, the rules governing the question period were further "deformalized," but this was again done in a very formal manner. The result was intended to reproduce the question period of the House of Commons, down to provisions for supplementary questions, but the attempt was not very successful. One reason for this may have been the frequency with which top civil servants replied to questions on behalf of their ministers. Finally, in 1960, the parliamentary leadership of the two major parties frankly admitted what it was that they had been trying to emulate all along. That year the budget contained an item for the reconstruction of the chamber of the Bundestag, so that in the future Government and Opposition would face each other across the center aisle, exactly as at Westminster, except that deputies would have assigned seats with desks (as at Ottawa). Government benches were to be brought "down to the same level" as the benches of the deputies, so that "the difference in altitude" would be removed, as one dissatisfied deputy put it. The change was apparently initiated by the President of the lower house, Dr. Gerstenmaier, who spoke freely of the British model. He regretted the fact that no true discussion had really ever taken place in the Bundestag, that he had been incapable of enforcing the rule concerning extemporaneity, and that the Bundestag had in effect provided only "quasi-notarized acts through official decree." FDP deputies opposed the change, because it assumed the British two-party system, which architectural changes could not introduce into Germany—only the voters could, and they apparently did not want to. One FDP member asked what seating arrangement would be made in case a "great coalition" should be formed. Professor Carlo Schmid, a Vice-President of the Bundestag and leading Social Democrat, replied that he would leave that to the flexibility and capacity for self-transformation of the Free Democrats, an answer that was received with "hilarity." This debate again illustrated that West Germany's revived parliamentarism still had not found its own style or gained much self-confidence after twelve years of operation.

If the plenary sessions of the Bundestag do not in the main have a deliberative function, where in the West German Parliament does deliberation take place? Partly in caucuses of the parties, discussed in the next chapter, and partly in specialized parliamentary committees (*Ausschüsse*). The Rules of Procedure provide that each bill must have three readings before it can be sent on to the Bundesrat and/or the Federal President for his assent. Debate for the first and third readings is about the general principles of the bill only, except that on the third reading detailed consideration is permitted of those parts of a bill that have been amended in the course of the second-reading debate. After the first reading, the bill is normally sent to one or more committees, whose report is then considered in the course of the detailed discussion on its second reading.

The first Bundestag had as many as 39 committees, whose membership varied, some having 27, others 21, 15, or 7 members. The most important committees (e.g., the one on questions of European security) were kept down to the minimum number of seven, so that only the three largest parties were represented on them. In this way, the minor *Fraktionen*—especially the Communists, while they were still recognized officially as a delegation—could be kept away from these frequently secret deliberations. Manipulation of the rules of the parliamentary game, in this case of the size of committees, thus served as means of discriminating against particular parties. Since none of the extremist parties returned any deputies to the second Bundestag, this particular concern ceased to play a role. The second Bundestag established 36 committees (as of November 1953). Their memberships were 17, 19, 23, 29, or 31. Those with 17 members were made up of party members in the following proportion: CDU 9, SPD 5, Free Democratic Party (FDP), Refugee League (GB/BHE), and German Party (DP) one each; those with 29 members: CDU 15, SPD 9, FDP 3, and GB/BHE and DP one each. The third Bundestag worked with less than 30 committees, consisting of 17, 23, or 29 members each. Party membership on a committee with 23 members was distributed as follows: CDU 12, SPD 8, FDP 2, and DP one. (The one member from the German Party lost his vote and became a consultant only after the exodus of its leading members to the CDU left it far below the strength required for recognition as a *Fraktion*.) Committee chairmen are selected by the Council of Elders. They are not necessarily members of the governing party or coalition.

Committee members are often noted experts in the committee's special field, so that they can accomplish a good deal of quiet and businesslike legislative work. The work is quiet, because committee meetings are not normally open to the public or the press, and committee reports do not contain full transcripts of the proceedings, but only the committee's legislative recommendations to the Bundestag. However, while the meetings are closed to the public, members of the Cabinet or the Bundesrat, or their representatives, have access to all committee meetings, according to Article 43 of the Basic Law, which is reinforced further by the Rules of Procedure. As a result, committees are neither able secretly to hatch bills in order to compete with the Cabinet's legislative initiative, nor likely to become strong centers of parliamentary power, as in the case of their counterparts in the French National Assembly or the United States Congress. The best opportunity for this to occur in the Federal Republic would seem to exist in the case of the newly created Defense Committee, and its constitutional position has, for this very reason, been criticized a good deal.

The Committee for Petitions is an interesting innovation, based on citizens' right to petition or complain in writing to Parliament, anchored in Article 17 of the Basic Law. Of course, the Bill of Rights of the United States Constitution contains a similar provision, though the Congress has not thought it necessary to establish a special committee on petitions. That the Bundestag should nevertheless have done so, and made formal provision for its operation in the Rules of Procedure, is another expression of the tendency toward legal formalism: the constitutional right exists; therefore, there must be a legally sanctioned institution designed to make the right effective. German citizens are not likely to exert informal pressure on the deputy from their district or to use other informal contacts. During the four-year life of the second Bundestag, the Committee on Petitions actually had submitted to it, and dealt with, some 30,000 petitions. By April 1961, a total of 328,624 petitions had been received. Some of these came in the form of identical petitions from large organized masses of people; for example, more than 1,800 persons sent in the same petition against passage of an emergency service bill.

On the whole, the Rules of Procedure and character of proceedings of

the Bundestag do not differ very much from those of the Reichstag during
the less troubled years of the Weimar Republic in the mid-1920's. The
extreme kind of disorderliness that marked Reichstag debates after 1930,
while it may at times have been approached in the first Bundestag, has
been inconceivable since 1953. But this was due to the absence of anti-
constitutional elements in the Bonn Parliament and has little to do with
changes in its rules. The largely non-deliberative, declaratory character
of the debates has changed very little, and could be noted before in the
Bismarckian Reichstag, the Prussian and other German parliaments of
the nineteenth century, and such conventions as the National Assembly
of 1848. The intellectual level of the debates was usually very high, the
historical self-consciousness and seriousness of the speakers intense, and
their general learnedness admirable. All this is still true. The President
of the Bundestag, in the course of the debate of the reconstruction of its
chamber, noted that the hall looked too much like a lecture room of the
kind that members had been used to from kindergarten through elementary
and high school through the university. We might add that identification
of Parliament with any of these educational environments contributed to
the non-deliberative character of debates, especially in view of the exemption from any criticism of German teachers and professors—always, but
particularly in the decades when most Bundestag members received their
education. But the Bundestag, in contrast with its predecessors before
1918, and even in comparison with the Reichstag of the Weimar Republic,
is constitutionally endowed with considerable legislative powers, and politically with many real opportunities for making contributions to shaping
the material fortunes of the German people. But debates are still carried
on, to a large degree, in the same old rather abstract and theoretical
manner. Mention of material interest is still avoided in favor of learned
historical and ideological justifications. And as before, the Bundestag
often tampers with important provisions of the not-quite-fundamental
periphery of the Constitution, in order to achieve immediate political
objectives. All that really seems to stay stable at the bottom of this often
deliberately created condition of potential flux is the way of doing things—
the retrospective orientation, the legalistic manner of discourse, the desire
to formalize. These habits are not written down in any document. Those
who have them are not even conscious of being dominated by them. And
yet they seem to be just about the only factors of relatively continuous
stability in German politics.

The Electoral System

The electoral system, by contrast, is one of the most unstable institutions in Germany as in France. In the Weimar Republic, the Constitution itself provided for proportional representation. The scheme had al-

ready been prepared by an election law passed during the last year of World War I, which brought to fruition one of the Social Democrats' principal constitutional demands of the Imperial era. It was designed to make the Reichstag an exact mirror of political opinion in Germany. It divided the whole country into thirty-odd large constituencies. In each of these, the several parties submitted lists of candidates, whose names then appeared on the ballot in the order determined by the party bosses. Votes were cast for a party's list, not for individual candidates. Once the votes were counted in each constituency, each party was given one seat in the Reichstag for every 60,000 votes cast for its ticket. The seats were assigned to candidates in the order in which they appeared on the party's list. After all the votes cast for the several parties in each of these large districts had been divided by 60,000, the remainders, if greater than 30,000, were pooled in electoral district-unions, which consisted of two or three separate constituencies. Here the same process of dividing by 60,000 was repeated, and then remainders were dealt with once more in another pool at the Reich level. As a result, the membership of the Reichstag varied in size from one general election to the next, depending on the number of votes cast.

But this was by no means the most important consequence of the system. It placed the possibility of parliamentary representation within reach of minor groups whose support was geographically scattered rather than concentrated. Consequently, organizations that resembled interest groups more than parties were encouraged to put up candidates and able to get them elected. The system also tended to prevent much real contact between individual deputies and their constituents, since candidates were dependent upon their party bosses for the all-important position assigned to them on the party's list, rather than on the personal good will of the voters of their district. If placed at the top of the constituency list, or even better, of the Reich list, a candidate was virtually assured of election. The system was also believed by some to have contributed to the splintering of the party system. This seems to be a questionable allegation, since the Weimar Reichstag contained almost the same number of significantly represented parties as the Imperial Reichstag before it, and that body had been elected from single-member constituencies.

In any case, whatever may have been the effects of the system of almost perfect electoral justice under the Weimar Republic, most of the men who had the task of reconstructing constitutional democracy in West Germany had very definite theories as to what these effects were—and their theories were not all in agreement. Some went so far as to assert that proportional representation was the principal cause of the failure of the Weimar Constitution. They tried to prove that without proportional representation the Nazis would always have remained a minute minority in the Reichstag, if indeed they could ever have succeeded in getting any candidates elected to that body at all, and that perhaps they would never have entered politics at all, because they could have entertained little hope of electing candidates in single-member districts. Moreover, if more personalized candidatures had been encouraged instead of the list system, it was said, people in the Weimar Republic might have felt greater loyalty to the constitutional regime as such, and been less easily swayed by demagogic denunciations of the futility of parliamentarism.

Most of these views are, at best, debatable. And debated they were in the Parliamentary Council at Bonn, which, having drafted the Basic Law, next drafted the first Federal election law. It did not have to concern itself with provisions for the election of the Federal President, since the plebiscitary selection of the head of state had been eliminated by the Basic Law. Under the Weimar Constitution, the Reich President was elected by a majority of those voting on the first ballot and, this failing, by a plurality on the second. The additional general elections made necessary by this provision had further contributed to the intensity of political excitement during the last years of the Weimar Republic. In 1932, von Hindenburg, as the candidate for re-election, failed to get a majority on the first ballot, so that a run-off had to be held. In addition to these two elections there were three for the Reichstag between September 1930 and November 1932, which followed three dissolutions. Under the Bonn Constitution, this kind of piling national elections one on top of the other was not going to be repeated.

But what kind of electoral system would be used? The CDU favored single-member districts and election by a simple plurality. This position was based not only on relatively "objective" retrospective interpretations of the Weimar setup, but also on a fairly accurate estimate of the party's electoral strength in the country. The Social Democrats, on the other hand, were ideologically committed to proportional representation, since they believed it to be the only scheme embodying true democratic justice. And they, too, had reasons of interest, because of the heavy concentration of their supporters in urban industrial centers.

The outcome of this struggle between divergent views was a compromise. The basis for this compromise came, like so many other parts of the Federal constitutional machinery, from experimentation carried on in the laboratories provided by the member states. The first election held in the British Zone of Occupation was conducted on the basis of single-member plurality constituencies, as used in Britain and the United States. The results strongly favored the CDU over the SPD. Consequently, the "sixty-forty" system—to be explained below—was later introduced. The Parliamentary Council had first agreed on using a "fifty-fifty" system, having half the seats allocated to single-member districts and half to state lists. The Military Governors, however, insisted on having this proportion changed to one of sixty-forty, as used in the British Zone.

The trouble was that the Occupation Powers, too, had theories about the failure of the Weimar Constitution and about the necessary institutional prerequisites for the survival of constitutional and democratic government. These theories were expressed in different ways, for example, the influence on the election law, just cited. Then there was the Military Governors' refusal to permit that part of the draft election law to stand which allowed civil servants who were elected to the Bundestag to go on the inactive list instead of permanently retiring from the service. The Military Governors insisted on permanent retirement, partly because of the suspicious view they took of the bureaucracy that served the Weimar Republic—not in fact much different from that which had served the Empire before—and partly because of American notions about the separation of powers. In practice, this provision tended to discriminate against the Social Democrats. Many of their potential candidates for parliamentary office have traditionally come from the bureaucracy, having no independent income, and would consequently hesitate to run for office unless they had the insurance of being able to return to the security of their career if defeated. In any case, as soon as the Occupation Powers put the Germans on their own in this respect, they proceeded to legislate as they would have in the first place.

Under the first Federal election law, 60 per cent of Bundestag seats were assigned to single-member constituencies in the several states, to be won by the individual candidates who got the largest number of votes. The remaining 40 per cent were assigned to state-wide party lists on the basis of proportional representation (using the d'Hondt maximum figure procedure.)[2] In order to benefit from the proportional representation pro-

---

[2] Example of the d'Hondt procedure: Assume that 460,000 voters have cast ballots and there are 10 seats at stake, the votes being distributed among four parties as follows:

PARTY	VOTES
A	210,000
B	140,000
C	80,000
D	30,000

These figures are successively divided by 1, 2, 3, etc., i.e., by the number of seats already assigned to the party plus one.

÷1	÷2	÷3	÷4	÷5
A 210,000(I)	105,000(III)	70,000(V)	52,500(VII)	42,000(IX)
B 140,000(II)	70,000(VI)	46,666(VIII)	35,000	28,000
C 80,000 (IV)	40,000(X)	26,666	20,000	16,000
D 30,000	15,000	10,000	7,500	6,000

visions, a party had to win either at least one single-member district in the particular state, or 5 per cent of the total vote cast in the state. This provision was clearly designed to discourage minor parties. The election returns on August 14, 1949, showed both the CDU and the SPD to have been right in advancing their respective schemes. The CDU won 114 constituency seats and only 24 from state lists. The SPD won 96 from state lists and only 35 constituency seats. But the Free Democrats, which joined the CDU in Adenauer's first coalition, won 40 of its 52 seats from state lists. In other words, the CDU was able to form a majority coalition in the first Bundestag as a result of the proportional representation provisions that it had opposed. (Of course, if proportional representation had not been provided for at all, the seats that actually went to the FDP might instead have gone to the CDU in the first place.)

The law under which this first Bundestag was elected was not meant to be permanent. An independent citizens organization, the Voters' Union, early expressed the hope that Parliament would soon replace it with a permanent measure. However, the Bundestag did not get around to this task until just before the end of its term. Then another makeshift compromise was passed after rather heated debate, this time by a voting coalition, consisting of both the Social Democrats and the Government parties, against the votes of the Bavarian branch of the CDU, called the Christian Social Union (CSU), and the German Party. This law provided for the election of 484 deputies, in contrast with the first law's 400. Half of these were to be elected in single-member districts as before. To elect the other half, who were put on state lists nominated by the parties, each voter was given a second ballot, on which he voted for one of the party lists. With his first vote, he voted for an individual candidate running in his district. The second votes were counted on a state-wide basis, again using the d'Hondt procedure. From the number of seats thus allocated to each party in a state, there was deducted the number of seats already won on the basis of the first ballots in the individual constituencies. But this time, in order to benefit from the proportional representation provisions, a party had to win either one single-member seat, or 5 per cent of the total votes cast in the whole Federal Republic (instead of just the state involved, as previously).

First, the figures in column ($\div$1) are divided by 1. A has the highest quotient and gets seat I. A's votes are therefore divided by 2 the next time around, giving it 105,000, less than B's 140,000 in the first round; hence B gets seat II. In the end, the seats are distributed as follows:

PARTY	SEATS
A	5
B	3
C	2
D	0

From Hans Trossmann, *Der zweite deutsche Bundestag* (Bonn, 1954), p. 90 f.

Stimmzettel

für die Bundestagswahl im Wahlkreis Nr. 22 Hamburg VIII am 17. September 1961

Jeder Wähler hat

| eine **Erststimme** für die Wahl des Wahlkreisabgeordneten | und | eine **Zweitstimme** für die Wahl nach Landeslisten |

1	Schmidt, Helmut Dipl.-Volkswirt Hmb.-Gr. Flottbek 1 Zickzackweg 6b	Sozialdemo- kratische Partei Deutsch- lands **SPD**	◯	1	Sozialdemokratische Partei Deutschlands Dr. Brauer, Wehner, Frau Keilhack, Schmidt, Kalbitzer **SPD**	◯
2	Gewandt, Heinrich Drogist Hamburg 39 Sierichstraße 20	Christlich- Demokratische Union **CDU**	◯	2	Christlich-Demokratische Union Blumenfeld, Dr. Bucerius, Dr. Seffrin, Gewandt, Frau Blohm **CDU**	◯
3	Rademacher, Willy Max Sped.-Kaufmann Hamburg 39 Sierichstraße 90	Freie Demokratische Partei **FDP**	◯	3	Freie Demokratische Partei Rademacher, Dr. Dahlgrün, Frau Dr. Kiep-Altenloh, Dr. Frankenfeld, Dr. Naumann zu Königsbrück **FDP**	◯
4	Dr. Bialas, Rolf Arzt Hmb.-Fuhlsbüttel 1 Fehrsweg 12	Gesamtdeutsche Partei (DP-BHE) **GDP**	◯	4	Gesamtdeutsche Partei (DP-BHE) Dr. Behn, Radtke, Frau Kayser, Baass, Glabbatz **GDP**	◯
5	Bethge, Horst Lehrer Hamburg 22 Petkumstraße 7	Deutsche Friedens- Union **DFU**	◯	5	Deutsche Friedens-Union Prof. Dr. Gröbe, Frau Dr. Beck, Berg, Lippold, Dr. Colpe **DFU**	◯
6	Dr. Nielsen, Ernst Baurat Hamburg 19 Eichenstraße 50	Deutsche Reichs- Partei **DRP**	◯	6	Deutsche Reichs-Partei Prof. Dr. Kunstmann, Kupka, Hobinder, Bister, Trute **DRP**	◯

BALLOT

For the Federal Election of September 17, 1961
Electoral District No. 22 Hamburg District VIII

Each Voter Has

| One **First Vote** for the election of his district deputy | and | One **Second Vote** for the election from Land lists |

| 1 | NAME of Candidate   Party Occupation Address | ◯ | 1 | NAME of Party Names of Candidates | ◯ |

The result was that the minor parties either elected no deputies at all to the second Bundestag, or suffered substantial losses. The German Reich Party, the Communist Party, the Party of the Bavarians, and some other small groups, which had placed 5, 15, 17, and 12 deputies, respectively, in the first Bundestag, received fewer popular votes and won no representation at all in the second Bundestag. On the other hand, the Refugee Union (GB/BHE), which had run no candidates in the Federal election of 1949, won 27 seats, all from state lists and by means of proportional representation. The CDU/CSU won 243 seats, of which 71 were from state lists. The SPD got 150, of which 105 were by proportional representation. Of the FDP's 48 deputies, only 14 were elected in single-member districts, in contrast with 10 of the German Party's total of 15. Since Adenauer's coalition, as of 1953, consisted of the CDU/CSU, FDP, GB/BHE, and DP, supplemented by the Center Party, its majority in the Bundestag consisted of 198 deputies elected in single-member constituencies and 140 elected by proportional representation from state lists. The surprising thing was that, despite the complicated voting procedure employed, only 3.3 per cent of the ballots cast had to be rejected as spoiled.

During the debate that produced the second electoral law, several speakers said that they hoped for passage of a more permanent electoral law early in the term of the next Bundestag—before political considerations motivated by an imminent election would outweigh "objective" considerations. These hopes turned out to be in vain once more. In the spring of 1956, the CDU threatened to push a still less proportional election law through the Bundestag. This move was largely responsible for causing the FDP's branch in the state of North-Rhine-Westphalia to leave the state coalition in which they had been with the CDU. Using the constructive vote of lack of confidence, for which that state constitution provides, they formed a new coalition government together with their erstwhile opposition, the Social Democrats. Other branches of the FDP threatened to execute similar maneuvers in other state parliaments. Partly because of these threats, the Adenauer Government reneged on its plan to reform the electoral system. The Federal elections that were held on September 15, 1957, were governed by a law that differed from its forerunner in only one important point: this time, a party that did not receive at least 5 per cent of the total popular vote cast in the whole Federal Republic had to elect three single-member seats instead of one, as previously, in order to benefit from proportional representation. As a result, the Refugee League, which received 4.6 per cent of the popular vote but elected no candidate in a district, was not represented in the third Bundestag. In contrast, the German Party, which received only 3.4 per cent of the popular vote but elected six constituency candidates, placed 17 deputies in the Bundestag. The Free Democrats and allied splinter groups got 7.7 per cent of the total vote, elected one district candidate, and were represented by 41 deputies. The Social Democrats (31.8 per cent and 169 seats) and the Christian Democrats (50.2 per cent and 270 seats) now had more than four-fifths of the electorate supporting them and controlled almost nine-tenths of the seats in parliament.

But in 1961, under the same election law, the Free Democrats were able to make more than a comeback, securing 12.7 per cent of the votes and 66 seats, none of them for a district candidate. The Social Democrats for the first time broke out of their 32 per cent "reservation," with 36.3 per cent of the popular vote. More significant was the fact that almost half of the Social Democratic deputies—91 out of 190—had won plurality or majority victories in district election contests. In other words, in 1961 the Social Democrats fell only one man short of electing twice as many district representatives as in 1957. The Christian Democrats' popular vote dropped back to 45.3 per cent, and, of their 243 deputies, 156 were elected directly, and 87 from Land lists.

Election systems in the member states have, in most cases, not been stabilized either, so far. Often a state legislature passes an election law just before the next election, sometimes by a small majority. Occasionally, the constitutionality of provisions of these laws is challenged in state courts or in the Federal Constitutional Court, and the general institutional instability is thereby intensified. Basically, however, this instability is the result of two factors: first, the difficulties involved in, and the fear of, including detailed electoral provisions in the Constitution, which is so much harder to amend than its Weimar predecessor; and, second, the prevalent belief in the feasibility of constitutional engineering, whether its ultimate purpose be immediate partisan advantage or the presumed long-run public interest of the whole country. Because of the first, election laws can be changed by mere parliamentary, rather than amending, majorities. Because of the second, the parties encourage such changes, hoping to gain thereby. As a matter of fact, however, the causal relation between a specific election law and the results of the election governed by it can never be demonstrated with accuracy. This is so because the electorate might have behaved differently with a different law. But if the Germans become aware of this truth, the instability of electoral systems may only be increased.

Politics versus Government

In any case, the relatively unpolitical period of German constitutional reconstruction has now definitely gone, with the same wind that blew out Allied eagerness for German "demilitarization." No longer can the West Germans enjoy the luxury of academically discussing the merits and demerits of various constitutional provisions, in assemblies that are necessarily in general agreement on the authority of constitutionalism as such, and unconcerned with the purposes for which political power is exercised, simply because they have little influence on its exercise. Since 1955 at the latest, constitutional and policy issues—issues of authority and issues of purpose—have been inextricably intertwined. Each issue of predominantly one kind is likely to generate its counterpart, predominantly of the other kind. The belief in the feasibility of constitutional engineering, far from waning, has waxed—and that in both parts of the divided country. For both systems seem to have accomplished the goals they set themselves, largely as a result of the governmental machineries that they deliberately and rationally engineered into existence. The intentional seems to have shaped the situational, rather than the other way around. This is true especially in the Federal Republic. One of the main objectives of its constitutional fathers was political stability—the opposite of the situation that prevailed under the Weimar Republic. They got political stability, marked by its contrast with the rapid succession of cabinets and the end of the Fourth Republic in neighboring France. There is, of course, no proof positive that this is the result of constitutional provisions, such as the one for the constructive vote of lack of confidence. But since nothing succeeds like success, people easily jump to the conclusion that they are the architects of their own current state of relative political bliss.

Moreover, constitutional re-engineering is likely to continue. Changes in the political situation of the Federal Republic—such as change in the status of Berlin, or election to the U.N.—would call for making readjustments even without the existing predilection in favor of making them. At the same time, the increasing urgency with which demands for the reunification of the country were being voiced tended to strengthen the public's awareness of the provisional character of their Constitution. The value of the prizes at stake for the different political groupings constantly increases, together with their awareness of the possibility of having one's way by means of changing fundamental institutions of government. Consequently, the potential explosiveness of both constitutional and policy issues increases as well, and so, therefore, does the desire to avoid friction by the old method of substituting adjudication or administration for politics. We have suggested that this desire is more likely to produce the reverse, namely the politicization of everything constitutional instead of the constitutionalization of everything political. In any case, politics—the resolution of conflicts of interest—has become increasingly more important than government—the framework within which conflict takes place—in the Federal Republic. And it is in the way in which politics is conducted that we can best search for that stability which we have so far failed to find to our satisfaction in those very institutions that were designed to ensure stability.

[19]

Parties, Issues, and
Political Style

"The parties participate in the forming of the political will of the people."
This sentence is not a quotation from a textbook on comparative government, but from Article 21 of the Basic Law of the Federal Republic
of Germany. It illustrates once more the extent to which the formal
constitution in West Germany includes matters that in other countries
would come under the heading of "informal political processes." Even in
Germany, we must admit, much of what the parties do is not explicitly
regulated by law. However, this legal gap is regretted by many Germans
and was not intended by the authors of the constitution, which in this
same Article provides for passage of a "party law." By 1961, no such law
had yet been passed, but the debate of a Government bill on the subject
was the occasion for much recrimination between the parties on such
matters as Big Industry's financial contributions to Hitler and the Federal
Interior Minister's admitted short "candidacy" for the Nazi Storm
Troopers. One reason for failure to adopt a party law was the reluctance
of party managers to make public party finances, as would be required
by such legislation. Only the Social Democratic Party has regularly published its accounts.

The sentence is interesting for another reason: its emphasis on "political will" and the parties' relation to this. British political vocabulary does
not assign an important role to the notion of political will. That the reverse is true on the Continent may be connected with the crucial character
of the concept of sovereignty in Continental political theory, and the fact

that "will" has generally been viewed as the main function of the sovereign, e.g., by Rousseau. Of course, any government has to produce a will in the sense that it must make decisions. This is just as true of British as of French and German government, but the English-speaking peoples have never been as self-conscious about the problem. This in turn may be because of the historical fact that they have never had as much trouble finding and expressing their political will as most of the Continentals.

While this criticism cannot be leveled at contemporary West German government, the explicit linking of parties with forming the political will has created some difficulties. Only parties—not interest groups—have been assigned this role among non-state organizations. In other words, the parties have a constitutional monopoly in this participation. Politics, however, is a continuous and comprehensive process and does not admit of this kind of compartmentalization. Interest groups in many cases have to become involved in politics. Indeed, politics would often not work without such involvement. But formalism leads many Germans to condemn "political" activity by organizations other than parties. The Basic Law itself enables them to make a constitutional issue out of such cases. On the other hand, the parties' constitutional monopoly of this role often leads them to differentiate their function excessively, or unrealistically, from the function of other organizations that are also a part of the structure of effective power. This self-differentiation has a further consequence in that it enables party politicians to claim that they are really not concerned with material interests, since such a concern belongs in the proper sphere of the interest groups. Since they thus exclude material interests from their domain, that leaves ideal interests. And ideals in turn—for reasons already mentioned—often tend to be ideologized in Germany.

In this chapter, we are interested in the structure of effective power, and for that purpose the constitutional statement about the forming of the political will of the people provides a useful focus. After all, the Basic Law and the other laws described in the last chapter cannot really subsume all that we would want to know. Nor would we expect that the ideologies of the various parties really tell us enough about the aims and methods of their members and supporters. There must be other factors that go into making the German political will. This is likely especially because of the radical novelty of the contemporary West German political situation. Many of the problems and issues the West Germans have been facing since the end of World War II differ fundamentally from those that Germans have ever faced before and from those that Britons, Frenchmen, or Russians are facing today. Political parties are among the instruments by which issues are formulated, solutions for them advanced, and controversies about them fought out. Changes in problems and issues, therefore, should result in changes in parties and in the party system. Has this been true of the Federal Republic?

The Changing Party System

In Chapter 17, we saw how often and how profoundly German society has been subjected to changes since national unification in 1871. Of the last three of these changes—totalitarianism, defeat, and division— we would expect that the cumulative effects must have been so revolutionary that there could be little, if any, continuity between the present party system and its predecessors. National Socialist totalitarianism might have had this effect by itself. The Nazis started out as just another member of the multi-party system of the Weimar Republic. Officially, theirs was the National Socialist German Workers' Party (N.S.D.A.P.). By 1933, they had become the strongest single party, though they were still short of having a majority in the Reichstag. Nevertheless, President von Hindenburg was finally persuaded that Hitler might be able to bring order out of the political and economic chaos that reigned in Germany during the last years of the Weimar Republic. On January 30, 1933, he appointed him Reich Chancellor, and Hitler proceeded to form a cabinet of National Socialists and Nationalists. He outlawed the Communist Party on the pretext that alleged Communist arson had caused the fire in the Reichstag building. In the election of March 5, 1933, the Nazis had won 288 seats, the Nationalists 53, and the Communists 81, out of a total of 647. Since the Communist deputies were excluded from participating, this meant that the Nazi coalition held 341 of 566 seats, a majority, though somewhat short of an amending majority. Nevertheless, and partly as the result of violent intimidation, the other parties in the Reichstag, except for the Social Democrats, joined the Nazis in passing the so-called Enabling Act, which transferred full legislative powers to the Reich Government. Thus Hitler could claim with some justification to have attained full power by constitutional means. He proceeded to use this power to outlaw all parties but his own, and eventually, upon von Hindenburg's death, to combine the office of President with those of Chancellor and Führer (leader) of the Party.

The history of Nazi totalitarianism lies beyond the scope of this book. For our immediate interest here, it suffices to state that most anti-Nazi politicians were silenced, often by being killed, imprisoned, or exiled. The Nazis attempted to revolutionize German society completely; the war and its aftermath brought about further changes. Hence, though some men who had been active in politics before 1933 returned to it after the war—the SPD, for example, had maintained a headquarters in exile—there was little cause for them to return to the methods and goals that they had pursued during the Weimar period. There were many reasons for this. The bankruptcy of the old methods and goals had been clearly demonstrated by Hitler's success. He evidently offered things to the German electorate that the other parties did not offer, or that the voters did not believe them capable of achieving. The Germans had by now passed through the crucible of Nazi totalitarianism, which had deeply affected their values, their beliefs, and their expressive symbols, either because Nazi ideological indoctrination had succeeded, or—in the majority of cases— because of their negative reaction to this indoctrination. Half of one generation had died during the twelve years of the Nazi regime, and half another generation had reached voting age. And these reasons for the expediency of devising new political methods and goals could be further multiplied.

The ravages wrought by the war, and the subsequent division of Germany, point at least as strongly to the likelihood of discontinuity in the German party system. As a result of the war, millions died in addition to those who met their end by natural causes between 1933 and 1945. Allied bombings of German cities resulted in tremendous material destruction. The expulsion of ethnic Germans from Eastern Europe, and from formerly German territories that were taken over by such countries as Poland and the Soviet Union, resulted in the influx into the now smaller Germany of somewhere between eight and ten million people, many of whom had not been German citizens under the Weimar Republic—e.g., the Sudeten Germans from Czechoslovakia. Establishment of the totalitarian Soviet regime in the eastern part of the country further added to this migration. The occupation of the country by Allied military forces acquainted the Germans with new political and administrative methods, especially in consequence of the Western effort to "educate" the Germans for democracy. Incidentally the Occupation also provided an outside enemy, in opposition to which the Germans could wish to unite, or with regard to which the issue of opposition or support could further divide the German population.

Thus, as the outcome of these largely intentional efforts on the part of the Nazis, and the largely situational effects of defeat and division, the social structure of West Germany today is certainly not the social structure of the Weimar Republic; neither are the party system and the pattern of interests in general. And this can hardly come as a surprise to anyone who recognizes any connection between social structure and political structure—and in order to do that one need not be a Marxist but simply a realist. The connection may not be very evident in a country such as the United States, where class-consciousness has been weak. But in most European countries, where class-consciousness has been quite strong, this relation between social structure and political structure is correspondingly marked. There, even Roman Catholic parties, which have the avowed aim of surmounting the class-struggle or of denying its reality, are affected in their strength, aims, and methods by changes in the social structure. Nevertheless—and this should come as a surprise—there does seem to be a high degree of continuity about the West German party system. At least this is true so far as the subjective feelings of the leaders and members of most of the contemporary parties are concerned. Most of them think of themselves as carrying on with an old political tradition that goes back at least to 1871, and often beyond that. Of all the parties operating at the Federal level, there was only one of which this was not true—the Refugee League (GB/BHE), and understandably so. The masses of refugees and expellees living in the Federal Republic were a novel phenomenon, the direct consequence of the colossal defeat of 1945 and the division of the country. Nor is it true of the Christian Democratic Union to the extent that it is of the remaining Federal parties, and again for evident reasons: the changes in the denominational make-up of the Federal Republic, along with other factors, made possible the organization of a Christian rather than a merely Roman Catholic party. Nevertheless, the predominantly Roman Catholic element of the CDU, and even more its Bavarian branch, the Christian Social Union, usually make them sound as though they were the legitimate heirs and continuators of the Roman Catholic Center of Weimar and Imperial days, and of the Bavarian People's Party of the Weimar period, respectively.

Traditional Parties

The remaining Federal parties were, if one took their self-estimates at face value, virtually identical in long-range aims with their predecessors. The contemporary Center, reduced though it was to 10 deputies in the first Bundestag, 4 in the second, and none in the third, claimed to be the true residuary legatee of the old Center, though it was farther to the left on social and economic issues. Similarly, the German Party, usually represented by about 17 members, until a majority of these joined the CDU in 1960, considered itself the true heir both of the Hanoverians of the two previous German political systems and of other Conservatives outside of the area of the former kingdom of Hanover, which Prussia annexed in 1866. The Free Democratic Party looks back on what is probably the oldest tradition, that of German national liberalism. This liberalism dominated the abortive Frankfurt Assembly of 1848, split into National Liberals and Left Liberals under the Empire, and continued this bifurcated existence as the German People's Party and the Democrats in the Weimar Republic.

The then Chairman of the FDP, Dr. Thomas Dehler, who was Federal

Minister of Justice in Adenauer's first Cabinet, demonstrated this traditionalist orientation at a congress of the Party in March 1955. Shortly after the Social Democrats and other opponents of German rearmament had held a symbolic rally in St. Paul's Church in Frankfurt, he denounced this use by Socialists of the birthplace of German liberalism as "blasphemy." "We are the heirs of the Paul's Church," he said. He called the Free Democrats "guardians of the heritage of the Frankfurt Parliament, which had sought unity and freedom." A socialist economy could never be combined with liberty. All the attempts of socialism had not led to liberty, and this was true of any form of socialism, including the Ahlen Program of the CDU (which was directed against the excesses of capitalism). Then he denounced denominational parties and said, "German democracy can become healthy only when the last Socialist recognizes that only the free economy can be social, and when the last Christian refrains from carrying on the political battle in the name of Christ. . . . We consciously created parliamentary democracy, but we know how threatened this democracy is today, because there are only a few free men and women in Parliament." This was meant as an attack on parliamentary party discipline, which was followed by an attack on the two-party system as unsuitable for countries with socialist and denominational parties.[1]

The Social Democratic Party has not even changed its name since 1871, when it placed one deputy in the Reichstag. By 1912, it had become the strongest single party in Parliament, which it continued to be until 1932, with one brief exception in 1924. The Social Democrats until recently considered themselves the Party of Marx and Engels, Lassalle, Bebel, and the other Socialist "saints." As late as November 1953, Erich Ollenhauer, Chairman of the SPD, wrote that it was the task of the Social Democrats to analyze the present social structure in the spirit and with the method of Karl Marx, and to draw from the results of these investigations consequences for political work. A Social Democratic party without the Red Flag would be a party without heart. "A party without the *Lieder* and fighting songs, which have grown close to our hearts in the course of ninety years and which . . . may be supplemented by newer timely ones; without the comradely '*Du*' or the binding and obligating form of address, '*fellow*' (*ohne die verbindende und verpflichtende Anrede 'Genosse'*)— that would be a party without blood." At the same time, he denied that the SPD was an ideological party (*Weltanschauungspartei*), because it did not compete with the great religious currents. But the socialist labor movement had released great ethical power among millions of human beings, who had previously been a stolid mass because of the unscrupulous-

---

[1] *Frankfurter Allgemeine Zeitung*, March 26, 1955.

ness of capitalist society and the failure of Christianity in the face of the practical tasks of neighborly love. Ollenhauer admitted that Marx had erred in his prognosis of future social development, but added that Marx had never proclaimed his theory to be a dogma of faith. Only the Communists and reactionary opponents of Social Democracy had done that.[2] And the Communist Party, even though it appeared in strength in the Reichstag under that name for the first time in 1924, and has not been represented since 1953, claims to have even purer ideological blood in its veins.

The Social Democrats and the Communists, as also the other self-styled traditional contemporary West German political parties, use many of the slogans and symbols of their predecessors of Weimar and Imperial times. Much of their appeal to the electorate is couched in terms of the vocabulary of these older ideologies. Leaders, members, and supporters are often thoroughly conscious of their own and others' political and intellectual pedigrees. In some cases, specific solutions to concrete problems are justified by them by reference to statements made by the party's ideological forebears, as illustrated in the excerpts from the debate on movie censorship at the beginning of this section.

Now, if we are at all right about the tremendous difference between the problems facing the Federal Republic today and those that faced its predecessor regimes, then contemporary German politicians must be deceiving themselves and their public with their claims of traditionalistic affiliation. Mendès-France may claim to be the legitimate heir of Gambetta—though he would hardly stress the point—and Churchill of Disraeli. But did Adenauer have anything concretely in common with Windthorst, Ollenhauer with Lassalle, or President Heuss with the men of Frankfurt in 1848? Perhaps this subjective feeling of continuity served merely as subconscious window-dressing, which hid the real discontinuity of German politics and parties. Or perhaps it was the result of the reappearance in Bonn, in 1948 and 1949, of some of the men who had served in the Weimar Reichstag for many years. In any case, it did seem to cover up the relative newness and rootlessness of politics in the Federal Republic, while at the same time exploiting the considerable residue of sentimental and traditional attachments to the political symbolism of older days, which may be remembered by some voters as the good old days.

The Decrease in the Number of Parties

Some answers to these questions about the artificiality of such claims to continuity may be found by taking a look at the evolution of the German party system and by examining the aims of individual parties since

---

[2] *Frankfurter Allgemeine Zeitung*, November 13, 1953.

national unification. Table 12 shows the relative stability of the Center throughout the Imperial and Weimar periods, but a great increase in the percentage of votes garnered by the CDU/CSU, whose Catholic members claim descent from the Center. The Social Democratic vote and representation in the Reichstag, once it had reached the level of 1912, is also very stable. But it seems more continuous than the CDU/CSU in the Bonn Republic, even though some of its former strongholds are now in the Soviet Zone, whereas the old Center owed very little of its support to those areas that are not now part of the Federal Republic. This would suggest that, in order to maintain its Weimar level of strength, the SPD must have obtained additional electoral support, some of it possibly from former Communist voters.

The Conservatives (later the German National People's Party) also present a fairly stable curve from 1871 to 1933, with occasional oscillations. But it would be hard to tell which of the contemporary parties is receiving the support of its surviving former supporters or similar social groups today. This difficulty arises mainly from the absence from present-day German politics of a party of conservatives or primarily nationalist voters. Some of these people may have been voting for the German Party, since it had more deputies than the Hanoverians ever had under either Empire or Weimar Republic. But most of them probably vote for the CDU or the FDP. The FDP also gets some of the votes of both the former Liberals and Left Liberals, whose fortunes suffered a steady decline in the years before 1933.

It is, of course, hard to tell just how the German electorate has redistributed its party allegiance, for several reasons. First among these is the decrease in the number of federally active parties. Under the Empire, there were as many as thirteen represented in the Reichstag—and that was before the introduction of proportional representation. The number was about the same under the Weimar Republic. In the first Bundestag at Bonn, there were nine parties; in the second, only six; in the third only four; and since 1961 only three. Above all, the two extremes of the political spectrum have been eliminated from the Federal Parliament, and, when one considers the combined strength of Communists and National Socialists in the four Reichstage elected after 1929, the difficulties inherent in any attempt to estimate the electorate's reallocation of votes among the remaining parties will be evident. Nor can one do more than guess on this question for all those areas of the Federal Republic in which many newcomers have settled from other parts of the country, or from Central and Eastern Europe. And since the present election districts do not coincide with those of the Weimar Republic, the task is made still more difficult.

Nevertheless, an over-all impression does emerge right away: whether for constitutional or other reasons, the party system has changed drasti-

TABLE 12　Party Strength in the German Parliament*

	EMPIRE												
	MAR. 1871	JAN. 1874	JAN. 1877	JULY 1878	OCT. 1881	OCT. 1884	FEB. 1887	FEB. 1890	JUNE 1893	JUNE 1898	JUNE 1903	JAN. 1907	JAN. 1912
National Socialist													
Conservative	54	21	40	59	50	78	80	73	72	56	52	60	45
Free Conservative	38	33	38	57	27	28	41	21	28	23	20	25	13
Hanoverians	7	4	4	10	10	11	4	11	7	9	5	2	5
National Liberals	119	152	127	99	45	51	99	42	53	47	52	56	44
Other Liberals	30					47							
Left Liberals (Democrats)	47	50	39	26	67	74	32	77	48	50	36	50	42
Middle Estate													
Peasants										6	1	7	3
Bavarian Peasants									3	5	6	1	3
Bavarian People's Party													
Center	58	91	93	93	98	99	98	106	96	102	100	104	90
SPD	1	9	12	9	12	24	11	35	44	56	82	43	110
KPD (Independent Socialists)													
Others	28	37	44	44	41	32	32	32	46	43	43	49	42
Total	382	397	←	–	–	–	–	–	–	–	–	→	397

* The important points to note are: the relative stability of the Center's strength throughout the Empire and Weimar periods; the waning of Liberal strength under the Weimar Republic; the relative stability of the Conservatives; the fixed number of deputies under the Empire, and its fluctuations under the Republic; the decrease of the number of parties from 1949 to 1961.

Under the Empire and the Weimar Republic, there were actually more parties than the table indicates. The category "Others" includes Alsatians, Poles, Danes, and Independents,

cally, simply in terms of the smaller number of parties with parliamentary representation, and the fact that the CDU and SPD together have held more than three-fourths of all the seats since 1953. This means that the relative strength of the remaining parties has also changed radically. From this it follows, finally, that each of the parties must have a clientele that differs a good deal from that of the particular Weimar party from which it claims to be descended. If we add to this the further fact that a whole new generation of voters grew up and reached voting age during the sixteen to twenty-eight years that separate the first and fourth Bundestag elections from the last Reichstag election, then we must recognize how different from their predecessors the present parties are bound to be.

The Parties' Goals

REFUGEE LEAGUE

To begin with the youngest of the West German parties, the "Refugee League" (literally "All-German Bloc/League of the Homeless and Those

	WEIMAR								BONN				
JAN. 1919	JUNE 1920	MAY 1924	DEC. 1924	MAY 1928	SEPT. 1930	JULY 1932	NOV. 1932	MAR. 1933	AUG. 1949	SEPT. 1953	SEPT. 1957	SEPT. 1961	
		32	14	12	107	230	196	288					
42	66	106	111	76	44	39	54	53					
									—	27	—	—	Refugee League
3	4	5	4	3	3	—	1		17	15	17	—	German Party
22	62	44	51	45	30	7	11	2					
									52	48	41	66	FDP
74	45	28	32	25	20	4	2	5					
		7	11	23	23	2	2						
				10	19	1							
5	4	3	6	8	6	2	3	2	17	—	—	—	Bavarian Party
	20	16	19	16	19	22	19	19					
									139	243	270	243	CDU/CSU
89	69	65	69	62	68	75	70	73	10	4	—	—	Center
165	113	100	131	153	143	133	121	120	131	151	169	190	SPD
22	83	62	45	54	77	89	100	81	15	—	—	—	KPD (Communists)
1	4			4	18	4	5	4	21	—	—	—	Others
423	466	472	493	491	577	608	584	647	402	488	497**	499	

who, in 1878, a fairly representative year, placed 14, 14, 1, and 14 deputies, respectively. It also includes "Anti-Semites," also known as the German Reform Party, who in the last seven elections under the Empire elected between one and 17 deputies.

The election of January 1919 was that of the National Assembly at Weimar, which adopted the Weimar Constitution.

** By 1961, internal changes in the Third Bundestag left the CDU with 279, the SPD with 170, the FDP with 42, and the DP with 6 seats.

Who Have Lost Their Rights"—*Gesamtdeutscher Block/Bund der Heimatlosen und Entrechteten*—abbreviated as GB/BHE) could not claim legitimate descent from any predecessor organization. Since there is no precedent for the expulsion into Germany of millions of ethnic Germans (*Volksdeutsche*) or for the division of the country, there is also no precedent for the existence of this kind of political clientele. No previous group of people has faced the same problems as these displaced persons—unless it be the vertically displaced victims of the economic crises of the twenties and thirties, whose lot bore some resemblance to that of the vertically *and* horizontally displaced Germans of the forties and fifties. Consequently, the political aims of the League were also novel. It was first formed in the state of Schleswig-Holstein, which had been flooded by the heaviest concentration of expellees. The Occupation Authorities—the British, for this state—would not license it as a political party. This refusal was prompted by their desire to prevent the direct participation in politics of organizations that seemed to them to be nothing more than economic interest groups. This, therefore, is another instance of the importance of political theory and of interpretations of the fall of the Weimar Republic for post-war German politics. Not only the Germans in their Basic Law, but also the Occupation Authorities in their licensing policies, made a distinction between political parties and interest groups. In the case of the British and the Americans, this distinction was derived from the experience of the two-party system. Superficial views of this kind of party system generally assume that interest groups apply pressure on the parties or representatives, while parties are concerned mainly with capturing control of personnel and policies of the government. People with a background of a multi-party system, such as the French or the Swedes, would be less inclined to exclude interest groups from political activity for this reason. The Germans would not have refused to license the Refugee League on these grounds, either, though they were anxious to prevent the kind of parliamentary fragmentation into splinter groups that had occurred under the Weimar regime.

In any case, the Refugee League was not able to participate in the first Federal election of 1949. After being licensed in Schleswig-Holstein and subsequently in other states as well, it had at the outset some remarkable electoral successes. Its professed goals were directed mainly toward the improvement of the lot of the potentially large segment of society toward which its appeal was aimed. It wanted to make it possible for refugees to move out of the squalid camps, in which hundreds of thousands of them were living, and into new housing units, to be constructed with government subsidies, or onto farms to be provided by government aid. The League also favored revisions in the Law to Equalize the Burdens of the War, in order to favor expellees and refugees. At the same time, it also sought to appeal to groups of socially displaced people by urging legislation favorable to former soldiers and civil servants. It established close contacts with the geographically based organizations of expellees, many of which favored revisions in Germany's present eastern boundaries. In this connection, the party's policies sometimes appeared to be informed by strongly nationalistic strands with an ideological tinge.

After the first electoral victory of the League, several of its leaders became ministers of a coalition government in Schleswig-Holstein. In these positions, they made themselves unusually accessible—by German standards—to their constituents, by having regular open-house office hours. As a result of such tactics, the League won 27 seats in the Bundestag elected in 1953—all of them via state lists and proportional representation. They joined the Adenauer Coalition Government, and two of the leaders became Federal Ministers, one of them in charge of the Ministry for Displaced Persons (*Vertriebene*). Gradually, however, the special public to which the Refugee League had appealed began to lose its identity and to be absorbed into the West German society and economy as these recovered their stability and prosperity. With that, the League began to lose votes in state elections and to show internal rifts. By 1955, these tendencies brought about a split in the party and in its parliamentary delegation. More than half the delegation, led by the two Federal Ministers, joined the Christian Democrats. The rest usually voted with the Opposition. In the 1957 election, the Refugee League failed to elect any deputies. And, in 1960, Professor Oberländer, a former leader of the League, who had joined the CDU, resigned as Minister for Expellees in response to criticism of his Nazi past and connections with Nazi policies in occupied Russia during World War II.

Thus the Refugee League was brought into being by the existence in society of new groups with new problems, which led it to advocate new policies and even to employ novel political methods. But with the gradual disappearance of these groups and their problems, the party began to disappear, too, except at the state level, where it continued to participate in Cabinet coalitions. All of this speaks for the greater absorptive capacities of the major parties, and especially the two largest of them, CDU and SPD. In the Weimar Republic, there were no political procedures that forced people to think in terms of the dichotomy, Government *versus* Opposition. This encouraged each of the parties to retain the purity and consistency of its ideological and material appeal. In the Bonn Republic, this is no longer true. Consequently, its party politics is not only a horse of a different color, but a new kind of animal in German experience. And this, in turn, means that it has had to evolve new codes of conduct and is still doing so all the time. While this has so far made for political stability, it has also made for political unpredictability.

CENTER

The Center (*Zentrum*), smallest of the parties represented in the second Bundestag, appealed to a potential electorate that has not changed appreciably since the 1870's, when Roman Catholicism first organized politically in order to fight the *Kulturkampf* in defense against Bismarck's attacks on the Church. Among the voters who traditionally supported the Center in Imperial Weimar days, there were always many Roman Catholic workers of the industrial Rhineland and the Ruhr area. But because the dominant wing of postwar political Roman Catholicism was willing to join with other Christian groups in the "Democratic Union," and therefore had to dilute its denominationalism and to accept middle-of-the-road social and economic policies, only those former Centrists who were unwilling to accept dilution stayed out of the Union. This was true especially of those who were unhappy about dilution of social and economic policies. On cultural questions, the Center took an orthodox Roman Catholic line, but on social and economic issues it was usually quite close to the Social Democrats. As a result, the Center lost so much support that the Second Bundestag elections would have left them completely out in the cold if the CDU had not agreed to be unopposed to the Center's strongest constituency candidate. He was thereupon elected, so that the party's land-list in the state of North-Rhine-Westphalia could benefit from the second votes it received in that state. It gained these benefits despite the fact that its total for the Federal Republic was far below the minimum of 5 per cent—actually only 0.8 per cent—which was required for that purpose of parties that failed to elect a district representative. Even in North-Rhine-Westphalia, the Center received only 2.7 per cent of the votes cast in 1953. But as a result of this satellite type of alliance, the Center lost both independence and support, mainly because it alone among these parties tried to resist the prevailing trend, which is toward dilution of appeal to a lower common denominator, by further distilling its doctrine to a purer elixir than even that of its predecessor, the Center of the Weimar Republic and earlier days. It, too, disappeared from the Bundestag as a result of the election of 1957 despite an electoral alliance with the Party of the Bavarians, and the Social Democrats' agreement not to run its candidates in three constituencies to assure the alliance's victory.

German Party

The German Party (*Deutsche Partei*) suffered a somewhat similar fate. But its support was numerically stronger and geographically more concentrated than that of the Center. Consequently, its Bundestag representation fluctuated between 17 and 15 in the first three Federal elections. Between 5 and 10 of these were elected in single-member constituencies in the states of Lower Saxony, Hamburg, and Hesse. This suggests some similarity between the electorates appealed to by the German Party and the pre-Nazi Hanoverians, Conservatives, and National Liberals in Northern Germany. This amalgam gave the party a program that made identification with any one of these alleged predecessors somewhat spurious. The Hanoverian Party, for example, arose out of opposition to Prussia on the part of supporters of the Guelph dynasty, which had ruled the kingdom of Hanover until its annexation by Prussia. Yet the German Party, much of whose present strength draws upon these traditional Hanoverian loyalties, nowadays favors the colors black-white-red over the Republic's official black-red-gold—and black-white-red are precisely the national colors that symbolized the unification of the German states under Prussian leadership. Since the German Party's strength was thus highly localized, its aims were too. They focused mainly on the needs of the agricultural population of Lower Saxony, and the commercial interests of the port city-states of Hamburg and Bremen. One of the Party's leaders fittingly headed the Federal Ministry for Traffic. Another was Federal Minister for Bundesrat Affairs until he left the Cabinet in order to head a coalition government in the state of Lower Saxony. In 1960, all but six of the Party's Federal deputies, including its two Ministers, left it to join the majority CDU (except for one who joined the FDP). It has played no role in Federal politics since then.

Free Democratic Party

The aims of the FDP (*Freie Demokratische Partei*), third strongest party at the Federal level, are pitched so as to suit the interests of industrialists, businessmen, shopkeepers, professionals, and white-collar people, and more especially those among them who have qualms about casting their votes for the CDU because of its Roman Catholic majority component. Its platform and campaign appeals have emphasized the virtues of free enterprise in its post-1948 West German version, the "social market economy." With regard to the "cultural" issue, the FDP has opposed denominational schools. In the field of foreign policy, it has tried to work out an independent West German policy, sufficiently differentiated from that of the CDU to make it distinguishable, but not so much as to make it coincide with that of the SPD, or to leave the CDU without the support of its coalition partner when foreign affairs come up for votes in the Bundestag. This latter aim was held to at least until part of the FDP left the coalition. On the whole, the FDP has tried to combine programs somewhat reminiscent of those of two earlier liberal parties: the right-wing nationalists and the left-wing democrats. It also gets much of its support, especially financial, from the type of big industrialists that occasionally provided leadership and funds for the conservative German National People's Party of the Weimar Republic. The two wings of German liberalism never held more than 107 out of 466 seats, the high of the Reichstag elected in 1920, and they sank to a low of 7 out of 647 in the last election of 1933. In the first three Bundestag elections, the Free Democrats received 11.9, 9.5, and 7.7 per cent of the total vote, respectively. The loss appeared to have redounded to the benefit of its former senior coalition partner, the CDU. For a time, the FDP thus also suffered from those institutional pressures that make for the dilution of party programs, and its own platform bears no direct resemblance to any one of those of its claimed predecessors.

In the early part of 1956, the FDP split in two. The first step in this process took place when its branch in North-Rhine-Westphalia brought down its own CDU-dominated coalition government by joining the Social

Democrats in a constructive lack-of-confidence vote. As already mentioned, this was done partly in protest against the threatened new electoral law. Soon thereafter, the Bundestag delegation of the FDP split into two wings, the majority withdrawing support from the Adenauer coalition, while the minority, led by the four FDP Ministers in Adenauer's Cabinet, stayed loyal to it. The minority subsequently founded its own party under the title Free People's Party (*Freie Volkspartei*), which later merged with the German Party. By the end of 1956, its Ministers had withdrawn from the Federal Cabinet, which the Chancellor revised so as to give his own CDU greater strength. Meanwhile, the fight of the FDP for a continued independent existence was rewarded with success in the election of 1961. The Party was reorganized under the leadership of its new Chairman, Dr. Erich Mende, who had been awarded Germany's highest military decoration for bravery during World War II, and who represented the younger, more aggressive wing of the FDP. On letterheads of its campaign literature, the Party listed "The Federal Chairman of the FDP—1948, Prof. Dr. Theodor Heuss—1961, Dr. Erich Mende." In this way, the FDP sought to capitalize on the popularity of the retired Federal President. Dr. Mende, incidentally, lists "*Dozent*," or university instructor, as his profession. In 1961, he tried to cash in on dissatisfaction with both the CDU/CSU—because it was the majority party—and the SPD—because it had been continuously in opposition. This pitch of the FDP's campaign is suggested by a postcard mailed to all voters in one constituency of Hamburg. The card carried a vigorous looking photograph of Dr. Mende, superimposed upon a larger picture of ex-president Heuss' almost spiritlike head, with the inscription, "In his spirit with new power—FDP." The message on the reverse side of the postcard read:

> Dear Voter:
>   My friend Dr. Erich Mende has opened the election campaign in Hamburg with a great speech of objectivity and serious love of the fatherland.
>   Hamburg citizens liked this a great deal—better than partisan political quarrels and strife. With this attitude we are living in the spirit of the first President of the Federal Republic of Germany, Prof. Dr. Theodor Heuss.
>   Therefore follow the reminder of Erich Mende on September 17th:
>   HE WHO THINKS FURTHER VOTES FDP LIST 3.
>   Yours,
>   Ferdinand Ewerwahn.

Mr. Ewerwahn himself was too low on the FDP's state list in Hamburg to get elected, but three of his "friends" did get into the Bundestag from Hamburg through proportional representation. A total of 66 FDP deputies

were elected to the fourth Bundestag in this way, with 12.7 per cent of
the popular votes cast. This enabled the Free Democrats to exert decisive
influence upon the formation of the new cabinet, since neither CDU/CSU
nor SPD had the majority of votes required for the confirmation of a
candidate for the chancellorship by Article 67 of the Basic Law.

Social Democratic Party

Of the SPD (*Sozialdemokratische Partei Deutschlands*), we might
legitimately expect that it would have changed its goals less than the
other parties. It started out as a class party with a definite ideology. It
maintained a headquarters organization in exile during the Nazi and war
years. And there is, after all, still an industrial and working class in West
Germany today. For these reasons, the SPD more than the others could
afford to behave very much as it used to behave in earlier times. And on
the whole, this was true. Nevertheless, considerable changes have occurred.
One of the most noticeable has been the Socialists' stronger tendency
toward nationalism, which was particularly marked before Schumacher's
death in 1952. This emphasis on nationalism can be explained partly again
in terms of a retrospective interpretation of the SPD's history in the Weimar Republic. If it had been more nationalist then, its leaders were thinking after the war, Hitler might have been less successful in his efforts to
exploit nationalist aspirations among the masses. Also, the SPD figures
that it stands to gain more than the CDU from reunification, at least in
terms of electoral support in the predominantly Protestant eastern part
of the country. Again, the SPD has feared the domination of a United
Europe of six states (the Federal Republic, Italy, France, and the three
Benelux countries) by Christian parties, and has therefore sometimes
opposed Adenauer's European integration policy with rather nationalist-
sounding arguments. In part this has undoubtedly been simply because
of the SPD's oppositional role, which encouraged it to take a different if
not wholly opposite stand from that of the less nationalist, more Catholic,
and "little-European" CDU. The SPD has become less doctrinaire about
its Marxism, partly in order to try to win back electoral strength lost as a
result of partition, and partly in response to the more obnoxious manifes-
tations of East German Communist Marxism. The Party has more than
flirted with Protestant theology, and its theorists have written a good deal
about the compatibility of Marxism with Christianity, especially Protestant.
This has led to a lowering of emphasis on socialization and nationalization
as major Social Democratic goals, which they had always been in the Weimar years, and even more so before 1919. Officially, the SPD today insists
on the transfer to public corporations like the British National Coal Board
of the coal industry and certain other branches of the fuel industry. Many

Social Democrats are relatively satisfied with such "social" but hardly Socialist measures as co-determination, which tend to improve the atmosphere in which workers live and their relations with their superiors, without, however, changing the structure of the economy by affecting property rights.

In 1959, the SPD issued a new Program of Principles that did not even mention the names of Marx, Engels, or other Socialist "saints." Explanations for this toning down of ideology and abandoning of earlier goals on the part of the SPD are not hard to come by. Loss of its strongest concentration of electoral support in the present Soviet Zone seems to be the most important factor. The SPD of the Soviet Zone was forcibly merged with the Communist Party there to form the Socialist Unity Party. In West Germany, some of this loss was made up by the weakening of the Communist Party, which was a direct result of the reign of terror conducted by the East Zone Communists, as well as their obvious dependence upon the Russians. When the Federal Constitutional Court outlawed the West German Communist Party as anti-constitutional in 1956, it was expected that some of its votes would switch to the SPD, but, in the Federal election of 1953, this had been a mere 2.2 per cent of the total. The changes in the SPD's program have, however, been far greater than this change in its situation would by itself have called for. The main reason for this seems to lie in the fully oppositional role the SPD is playing today. In the Weimar Republic, the SPD could never hope to obtain a majority of Reichstag seats. It could participate in a government only as one member in a coalition with at least two other parties. It therefore never had occasion to formulate a comprehensive program both consistent and realistic, because it knew that it would never have sole responsibility for putting such a program into effect. Under the Basic Law, however, the institutional pressures —especially because of Article 67—are such that there is not only the tendency to conduct political debate in terms of the dichotomy, Government *versus* Opposition, but also the possibility of an SPD government or at least one dominated by the Social Democrats. Moreover, the SPD has governed in several of the states, so that it had to test its ideology against the requirements of concrete responsibility.

In the first two postwar Federal elections, the SPD was within 0.2 per cent of getting 29 per cent of the vote cast. Despite the truncation of the country, the party thus got a higher proportion of the vote than at any time since the Reichstag election of 1928-30, in which it held just over 31 percent of the seats, a percentage it topped slightly in 1957, and considerably in 1961, when it gained 36.3 per cent of the popular vote. On the programmatic side, the SPD achieved this success by pitching its appeal to wider circles than merely the working class, i.e, really to all those who are for almost any reason (excluding subversive reasons) opposed to the policies of the governing coalition at Bonn. As in the case of the other successful party, this has meant a dilution of its goals, a reduction of the ideological content of its program, and a general attempt to find the lowest common denominator of the predominantly material aspirations of its potential supporters. Again, as for these other parties, this has had the effect of changing the character of the SPD, despite its relatively high degree of continuity with the past, so that its future strength, goals, and possible political allies can hardly be projected.

The new "image" of the SPD comes out in the following letter that was mailed to every household in the Federal Republic during the campaign of 1961:

Berlin, August 1961

WILLY BRANDT
Governing Mayor
Dear Fellow Citizen,

I hesitated for a long time before turning personally to you in this letter. As respect for the voter demands, my friends and I have said very clearly what we will do in detail during the four years lying ahead of us in the government. Above all we will provide more justice. I give you my word that I shall be guided by this as Federal Chancellor.

We will raise prosperity and energetically attack neglected community tasks for the welfare of everyone. Our Federal Republic must be expanded into a socially and culturally exemplary state; the goal is, as my friend Professor Carlo Schmid recently said: "To master tasks and not human beings."

In the past weeks I have travelled about 50,000 kilometers through the cities and villages of the Federal Republic. I know the worries that many have to bear. I also know how much moral force and decency exists in our nation. There are still many forces lying fallow, for which a free path must be opened up.

Our foreign political situation has become more serious. No one must underestimate the threat to which Berlin is exposed, and with it all of us. This situation must not be worsened through quarreling and slander. As a *Gymnasiast** in my Hanseatic home town of Lübeck I learned and never forgot the inscription on our Holsten Gate: *concordia domi—foris pax*, i.e., concord internally, peace externally.

Please think of the morrow and let us go forward full of confidence. To keep that which has proved itself and to do that which is necessary —for this I ask your support.

If you want to help me with this, elect the SPD, the SPD candidate in your election district. Your vote is weighty. You may rest assured that I am not one of those who forget this after the election.

With friendly regard,
Your
(signature)
Willy Brandt

---

* Student in a *Gymnasium*, a highly selective classical high school.

CHRISTIAN DEMOCRATIC UNION

No party is as novel as the Christian Democratic Union (*Christlich Demokratische Union*). In the first Federal election (1949), it received 31 per cent of the vote. In the second Bundestag, it held a majority of the seats after receiving 45.2 per cent of the popular vote. In the third, its strength rose to 50.2 per cent, but, in 1961, it fell back down to 45.3. Some of its leaders make no claim to direct descent from any party of Weimar or Imperial days, although many of its outstanding founders came from the old Center. But their desire to surmount the Center's narrowly Catholic orientation was precisely the leading motive for founding the CDU. "The Union"—as, characteristically, it is usually referred to, rather than as a party—was born out of the desire of men who had been opponents of Nazi totalitarianism to reconstruct German society on the basis of general Christian ideals, both Catholic and Protestant. Their success was immediate in the state elections in which they entered. The bi-denominational nature of the CDU's electoral appeal was demonstrated by the fact that its support was just as strong (within 0.7 per cent) in predominantly Catholic Bavaria as in predominantly Protestant Schleswig-Holstein. The composition of its parliamentary delegation shows that it contains both industrialists and trade union officials, both small farmers or peasants and aristocratic estate owners (such as Prince Bismarck), both descendants of ancient Rhenish families and displaced persons from the Sudetenland. Naturally, in order to attract all of these diverse elements, with their different interests, the CDU has had to formulate a very general sort of program. And whenever the program has been couched in more specific terms on controversial points, actual policy has tended to deviate to that level at which a compromise among all of these often antagonistic interests could be found. This has been true, e.g., of its social and economic policy, which originally opposed capitalism in favor of a "social" economy, but ended up by establishing the "social market economy," which blends free enterprise with social security and well-placed subsidies. Similarly, on the issue of centralism *versus* federalism, where the Union leadership in the Federal Government has leaned toward centralism, some of its state organizations, such as the autonomous Christian Social Union (*Christlich Soziale Union* or CSU) in Bavaria, have espoused the cause of states' rights. The same is true of foreign policy, with regard to which the Western, Catholic, wing tends to be more preoccupied with the priority of European integration, while the Eastern wing, including refugee leaders and former heads of the CDU of the Soviet Zone, is more concerned with reunification.

However, the goals of the CDU are such that it gets support from all these sectors of West German society. Consequently, its clientele is a completely new entity in German politics, and its future behavior one big question mark. Thus some students of German politics believe that this conglomerate coalition of a party has no cement of its own, being held together by nothing but the firm and grandfatherly personality of its leader, the Federal Chancellor, Dr. Adenauer. When he passes from the political scene, they say, his creation will crumble to bits—an event for which they claim to be witnessing previews whenever Adenauer leaves the country for a while, occasions that are often used by his lieutenants for quarreling among themselves. But others had opposite fears, ill-founded though these seem. They claimed that their compatriots have retained so strong an aversion to parliamentary politics because of the failure of the Weimar Republic and because of the Nazis' anti-parliamentary propaganda that they hunger for strong leadership and wish to submerge themselves in one great party and, eventually, another one-party system. In any case, the make-up and the goals of the CDU make it a novelty for German politics. In part this is the result of radical changes in social structure and consequent changes in political values that have taken place in Germany. To a greater extent, however, this novelty seems to be the effect of constitutional provisions, which set off a chain reaction that seemed to be evolving in the direction of something resembling a two-party system. The CDU has been the political anchor of the amazing political stability that has prevailed in the Federal Republic during the twelve years since its founding. All the novel aspects of this party once more underline the tentative character of this stability: If the anchor should crack, the crew of politicians would almost certainly grow panicky, and the whole ship of state might either be put in dry dock for a radical overhauling or redesigning, or just be abandoned to sink, as earlier German models have been.

Political Methods

Germany's changed social and economic problems have thus generated new and different political issues. These new issues have brought into being potential cleavages within the electorate that neither existed before, nor had any counterpart in earlier cleavages. Nevertheless, the effects of the Constitution have been to contain these potential divisions and not to permit them to fragmentize the electorate or Parliament. Consequently, the contemporary party system bears little resemblance to its forerunners. There is, nevertheless, the tendency to preserve continuity with the past in at least one respect, the manner of political discourse. Here we have noted especially the traditionalist and ideological verbiage with which the voters' favor is sought. This suggests that there may be a higher degree of stability in the methods by which politics has been conducted in Germany. Speechmaking, platform-writing, and pamphleteering are, after all, an important part of politics. This relative stability in political methods must be traced partly to the continuity of political personnel, both inside and outside of Parliament. The continuity may be of two kinds: return to politics of the same persons who were active in it before 1933; and service by men with educational and professional backgrounds similar to those of German politicians of the past.

Political parties were organized, or reorganized, in West Germany before there was a great deal of politics in which they could engage, as already mentioned. This was so because most of the really important decisions were still being made by the Occupation Authorities, at least until 1949. The Occupation Powers also controlled most of the material means by which policies could be put into effect. This situation partly explains the attempt of the parties to put on traditionalist clothes. There were few concrete contemporary issues on the basis of which they could effectively differentiate themselves from one another. All of them had to be *for* constitutional democracy and *against* Nazi totalitarianism. If they were not, they would not be licensed by the Occupation Powers. They could exert but very little influence on current domestic events, had hardly any patronage to give away, and could not at all affect Germany's relations with foreign states other than the four that occupied their country. And even those they could not influence to any great extent. To achieve any noticeable degree of differentiation at all, therefore, they had to project their programs into either the past or the future, and they proceeded to do both. The parties' attempted self-identification with their predecessors of the Weimar period thus made good sense, at least until the revival of German politics in 1949. Both leaders and followers during this period actually wanted to take attitudes that were fairly identical with those of their traditional forerunners. Only when the parties began to be effective instruments of self-government did this cease to be so. Then these old and in the main ideological outlooks became obsolete, simply because they were largely irrelevant to the novel problems with which the Federal Republic had to come to grips. By this time, however, the new or revived political organizations had already been identified, and their leaders had identified themselves, with the earlier approach. As a result, this approach was retained for a while, at least on the surface. The uninformed observer might, therefore, have gotten the impression—even in 1958—that West German politics revolved in the main around ideological, legalistic, and "scientific" issues, when it was in fact quite as much concerned with concrete conflicts of material interests as politics in the United States or the United Kingdom. And even the informed German participant might have labored under the same illusion, because he mistook the style of his own political discourse for the substance of his political goals.

The relatively lengthy and non-political incubation period through which the parties had to pass has had an important long-run effect on the way in which issues are formulated, and this in turn naturally affected the methods by which politics in general was carried on in the Federal Republic. Of course, political issues are not formulated by parties alone. Interest groups also play a role, and sometimes a large one, in this first stage of the political process. Since interest groups are supposed to be in the game for the sake of their more or less immediate material interests—regardless of whether these be of an economic or cultural character—we might reasonably expect interest groups at least to see to it that issues are formulated in more concrete and pragmatic, less abstract and ideological-legalistic terms. This expectation would be disappointed in most cases. Relatively little difference is to be found between the way in which parties on the one hand, and interest groups on the other, formulate political issues. Indeed, it almost seems as though everyone in German politics was afraid that he would get no hearing for his cause unless he garbed his goals in ideological, legalistic, and scientific verbiage.

If this were mere façade, and if everyone were aware of this fact, it would not be very important. After all, in other systems politicians also profess the idealism of their motives, point to the superior legal or constitutional validity of their own claims, and occasionally support these with the learned opinions of lawyers, economists, historians, and other men of science. In Germany, however, these practices are not mere façade, but rather part and parcel of the political style. This means that when essentially the same problem arises in Great Britain and Germany—for instance, trade union demands for a higher real income for their members—it is treated very differently in the two countries. In some cases it means that issues of a purely ideological or legalistic nature take on great independent importance in German politics, even though they seem to the outsider to be purely artificial and to have no relevance to any real or concrete problems the society actually confronts.

Ideologism, Legalism, Scientism

The demand of trade unions for higher wages shows the effects of the ideological, legalistic, and scientistic orientation. In Germany, as elsewhere, many different means are at the unions' disposal for pressing such a demand: direct negotiations with employers or their organizations; direct or indirect pressure on Parliament for passage of such measures as food subsidies, rent control, a more favorable tax law, or wage legislation; support of or affiliation with a party; and ultimately the strike. Before the

Nazis outlawed free trade unions and supplanted them with their own National Socialist German Labor Front, there had been three trade union organizations in Germany: a Liberal, a Christian, and a Marxist, affiliated respectively with the Democratic, Center, and Social Democratic party. The Marxist union had been by far the strongest. After the war, former leaders of these organizations came together and decided to found one German Trade Union Federation (*Deutscher Gewerkschaftsbund*, or DGB). It was to be neutral in partisan politics, even though Social Democrats outweighed "Christians" among both leaders and members by a ratio of about four to one. They thus ruled out the Labour Party path. This increased the DGB's bargaining power, since it could in any case count on the support of the SPD, and would on some issues also get the support of the CDU, whenever that party could be swayed by its labor-friendly left wing.

Until 1954, no major strikes for better wages, hours, or working conditions took place. The DGB concentrated rather on getting the Bundestag to pass pro-labor legislation. It made a special effort on behalf of a set of laws granting labor the right of codetermination. This involves participation by labor representatives jointly with stockholders' representatives in the supervision and management of privately owned industrial and business corporations. The practice of codetermination had first evolved for very concrete and practical reasons in steel corporations that were being reorganized under supervision of British occupation authorities. Nevertheless, a systematic ideology was soon built around this institution, lengthy legal arguments were elaborated both for and against it, and learned legal, economic, sociological, and other scientific treatises were produced in its defense and denigration. Practically everybody involved in these controversies was convinced that these pragmatically evolved practices needed nothing more than a solid legislative foundation—and this would not be an unusual thing to provide after a period of trial and error. But these people believed firmly that it would have been better if such legislation had preceded experimentation in the first place, and that no further experimentation in other industries could be carried out without prior legislation in detail. Given a similar situation in Great Britain, chances are that many years would have passed before passage of a law designed to recognize the existence of something that had grown up by the method of trial and error. And once labor had adopted some such goal, it would hardly have justified it in such elaborate ideological terms.

In Germany, this controversy involved the threat of a strike by the Metal Workers and Miners Unions. As a result of this threat, Chancellor Adenauer pushed the demanded legislation through the Bundestag. It was passed by an unusual coalition of his own CDU/CSU and the SPD. More interesting here is the immediate and violent denunciation of the unions by all those who were opposed to the substance of the legislation, and by many others. On the occasion of this and almost every strike or threat to strike since then, the opponents of labor have attacked what they termed political action by economic interest organizations.

Such arguments are based on the generally accepted assumption that public life consists of a number of watertight compartments, and that different public organizations should confine their activities to their respective spheres. German parlance refers to *Staatspolitik, Wirtschaftspolitik, Kulturpolitik,* and so forth, and most Germans would assign parties to the first compartment, trade unions and employers' associations to the second, the churches to the third, and so forth. Any overflow from one compartment to another is frowned upon. That all such questions can ultimately become issues of partisan politics in any modern representative democracy—that it is indeed entirely normal and healthy for the political system for them to do so—is something many Germans would deny. And when such an overflowing occurs, this fact itself rather than the substantive disagreement at hand often becomes the primary issue of the controversy. Thus, in the case of strikes, those opposed to them raise the question whether the stoppage of work is not meant in some way to apply pressure to Parliament and, if so, whether this is not anti-constitutional. If it is not, they ask, "Why not? It should be made anti-constitutional," —whereupon a constitutional issue has been more or less artificially created out of a disagreement over material interests. Similarly, when opponents of rearmament held a protest convention in the same St. Paul's Church in which the first German National Convention of 1848 had held its fruitless meetings, proponents of rearmament argued that this kind of extra-parliamentary consideration of a question that was then before the Bundestag was designed to undermine the constitution, if it was not outright unconstitutional. When the Social Democratic Governments of Hamburg and Bremen had their legislatures pass bills to authorize referenda on the desirability of atomic armaments for the Federal Defence Force, the Federal Constitutional Court held the proposed referenda unconstitutional. "The Basic Law does not provide for them," the Court reasoned, and this state action violated the principle of "federally loyal" (*bundesfreundlich*) conduct. When Chancellor Adenauer had founded a federally owned public corporation to operate a second television network, the Social Democrats, afraid this network would be used against them during the 1961 campaign, got SPD-controlled state governments to sue the Federal government in the Constitutional Court, which this time found that the latter had been "federally disloyal" and ordered the new TV company disestablished. When a newspaper supporting the CDU/CSU charged Mayor Willy

Brandt of Berlin, the Social Democratic candidate for the Chancellorship in 1961, with having fought against the Third Reich in Norwegian uniform during World War II, he sued the paper, which was ordered by a court to pay substantial damages.

Political Recourse to the Courts

Frequently, issues that in France, Great Britain, or the United States would be initiated and fought out in the legislative forum are, in Germany, initiated, fought out, and settled in the courts. This is true of matters of a wide variety of importance, from the sublime to the ridiculous. Two mutually hostile politicians often try to get even with each other by means of libel and slander suits on the basis of campaign statements that, in most other countries, would probably do little more than draw laughs from the other fellow and the public. Seemingly harmless jokes about a "monopoly of divine support" allegedly enjoyed by the Christian delegation in the Bundestag led an outsider to initiate proceedings by the state prosecutor to ascertain whether blasphemy had not been committed. When Federal Ministers think that they have been insulted by a newspaper or magazine, they often sue and have the offensive issue confiscated on court orders. When the Social Democrats were obviously going to be outvoted on the question of ratifying the abortive agreements on the European Defense Community, they tried to stop their promulgation on constitutional grounds through the instrumentality of the Federal Constitutional Court. When the state government of Bavaria threatened to unbalance the budgetary equilibrium of the Federal Minister of Finance, himself a Bavarian, by paying civil servants under its jurisdiction a Christmas bonus that was higher than he deemed defensible, the Federal Government tried to get an injunction against Bavaria from the Federal Constitutional Court—in vain, as it turned out.

Political Issues

The problems that give rise to issues in West Germany are, on the whole, very similar to those that give rise to issues in other European constitutional democracies, especially those on the Continent. This is only natural, since all of them share more or less similar backgrounds, so far as their economies are concerned, their social structures, their cultures, and their foreign relations. German political issues differ to any significant extent only where the German problems are unique. This has been true of all the issues arising out of the National Socialist experience, the Occupation, and the division of Germany. Beyond that, the principal distinctiveness of German politics lies in the methods by which these largely similar issues are dealt with, i.e., the style of politics, and in the predomi-

nance of different kinds of issues at different levels of politics, attributable
to the constitutional structure of the Federal Republic.

ECONOMIC AND SOCIAL ISSUES

We may classify issues under the main headings, social and economic,
cultural, historical, foreign relations, and constitutional. Of these, all but
historical and constitutional issues are mainly of a substantive nature, i.e.,
they deal with the substance of interests that are in conflict. The other
two types of issues are more concerned with the means by which substantive conflicts are being or have been dealt with. Until the Occupation
Powers surrendered their last political controls to the Germans in 1955,
historical and foreign policy issues played a minor role in German politics.
The main concern of the parties was to push through their demands concerning such questions as the distribution of income, social security, relief
for economic victims of the war, reconstruction of productive capacity and
of housing, the educational system, relations between schools and churches,
and the like. And these are roughly the same issues as those that matter
in the politics of other Continental countries, such as France or the Neth-
erlands, or even in insular Great Britain.

During the initial period of postwar reconstruction, economic and social
issues were generally dealt with at the lowest level, mainly because the
Occupation Powers did not permit any higher levels of government to come
into existence for some time. After the founding of the Federal Republic,
this ceased to be true. There was virtual unanimity on the desirability of
a fairly even economic development for the whole country, despite Federalism and the selfishness of the better-off states. Consequently, many of
the early political battles of the Federal Republic dealt with the abolition
of those inequalities that had been created by differences in the aims of
the three Western Occupation Powers. Economic and social legislation
that had been passed in the several states before 1949, e.g., concerning
pensions or labor relations, was superseded by Federal laws. Since 1949,
Federal politics has been the main arena for economic and social issues in
German politics.

CULTURAL ISSUES

German politics differs from that of neighboring countries as a result
of the Federal character of the German constitution. Because of this Federalism, some issues are important mainly at the state level, others mainly
at the Federal level. Cultural questions, for example, have to be settled at
the state level, in the absence of Federal authority in this field. There is
no Federal Minister for Education or Culture. The issue of whether to
have secular schools, "Christian community" schools, or denominational

Protestant and Roman Catholic schools, all of them state-financed, has been an explosive one in the Federal Republic. But given the provisions of the Basic Law, themselves prompted by revulsions against Nazi practices in this field, this issue has had to be settled in each of the member states. As a result, the denominational issue, and such related questions as anti-clericalism, which have always made for the existence of multi-party systems in Continental countries, have been relatively unimportant at the Federal level, except for constitutional litigation. For example, the Federal Government sued governments headed by Social Democrats of predominantly Protestant states for violation, through school legislation, of the Concordat concluded between Hitler's Reich and the Vatican. The Federal Constitutional Court, in what has been called a "Solomonic" verdict, decided that the Concordat was still in force, but that the states could not be forced to comply with it, since cultural affairs are under their jurisdiction according to the Basic Law. In other respects, however, if it were not for the deflection of this potentially divisive set of issues to the state level, the cohesiveness of the bi-denominational CDU probably would not have lasted as long as it in fact has. And friction between the strongly Catholic CDU and its strongly Protestant coalition partners in the first and second Federal coalition governments would probably have been greater.

This situation also explains the different composition of governing coalitions at the Federal and state levels. During the life of the first and second Bundestag, while in Bonn the CDU was allied with the FDP, the DP, and the Center, against the oppositional SPD, practically all the possible combinations existed in the various state cabinets: the "Great Coalition" of CDU and SPD; an even greater coalition including all the parties from SPD on the left to the DP on the right; another of SPD and Refugee League; another of SPD-FDP-DP; and several other types. This also casts light on the existence of parties whose electoral support is confined to one state only. Of this, the Party of the Bavarians is a good example. It was represented in the first Bundestag, but failed to win a place in the second because of the Federal five per cent provision. In Bavaria, for a while, it joined the SPD, FDP, and minor groups in a government whose opposition consisted of the CSU. Table 13 indicates the great variety of coalitions that were in office at the Federal and state levels on January 1, 1960.

HISTORICAL ISSUES

Historical and foreign policy issues were not permitted to figure overtly in West German politics until the Occupation Powers restored sovereignty to the Federal Republic in 1955. By historical issues we mean those that arise out of a nation's past, in Germany's case, especially the recent Nazi

TABLE 13   German Federal and State Coalition Governments 1960

GOVERNMENT	PARTY OF HEAD OF GOVERNMENT	PARTIES OF OTHER VOTING* GOVERNMENT MEMBERS				
		CDU/CSU	SPD	FDP	GB/BHE	DP
Federal	CDU	15				2
Schleswig-Holstein	CDU	4*				
Hamburg	SPD		9	3		
Lower Saxony	SPD		4	2	2	
Bremen	SPD		6	3		
North-Rhine-Westphalia	CDU	9				
Hesse	SPD		4		2	
Rhineland-Palatinate	CDU	4		1		
Baden-Württemberg	CDU	5	3	2	1	
Bavaria	CSU	10		1	3	
Saarland	CDU	3	2			
West Berlin	SPD	5	7			
TOTAL		55	35	12	8	2

* Only those Cabinet Ministers are listed who have the right to vote in Cabinet deliberations. In Schleswig-Holstein at this time, the Minister of Justice and other important Ministers did not enjoy this right, another illustration of the procedural formalism of German governments. (From *Statistisches Jahrbuch für die Bundesrepublik Deutschland*, 1960, p. 139.)

past. Since denazification was controlled by the Occupation—administered at first by its officials, later by Germans on their instructions—and because of the licensing requirements for political parties, recriminatory controversies of this type could not bubble up seriously until former Nazis regained their civil and political liberties. As soon as this did happen, they were able to try to revive their discredited ideology and to denounce their opponents as unpatriotic, un-German, or traitorous. This some of them did, for instance, with regard to the executed and surviving participants in the plot on Hitler's life of July 20, 1944. Ex-Nazis also tried to identify constitutionalist enemies of totalitarianism with the Occupation Powers and hold them responsible for such events as the division of Germany.

Recriminatory historical issues of this kind also play a role in French politics, e.g., in connection with the Resistance movement, as Dr. Wahl shows. Some of these issues have been petrified into ideologies, which often no longer bear any direct relevance to concrete problems of real current significance. This is true of issues of such old vintage as those arising out of antagonism between supporters of the French Revolution and defenders of the *ancien régime,* or critics of clericalism and supporters of the Church. In Germany, issues of this type played a role in earlier periods, too. Their political manifestation, however, differed from that of similar issues in France, because they often had an ideological character *before* the parties were able to do anything about them. And it was precisely because of their lack of power to influence the position the German state would take toward them that their attitudes on these issues became parts of rigid ideologies in the first place. This reversed sequence, in turn, tends to make historical recriminatory issues more divisive in contemporary German politics than in France. This situation is, moreover, further complicated by two facts: The latest experience giving rise to one such issue, Nazi totalitarianism, happened so recently and with such vehemence as to be very much a part of German political memories—more so than the Vichy experience in France. And the policies of the Occupation Powers on this issue during the early postwar years of German political impotence postponed its settlement, and for that very reason stimulated ideologism on this score.

This happened to both neo-Nazism and its opposite, and to anti-Semitism and its opposite, as well as to other recriminatory issues. Active opponents of National Socialism often seek to identify their current political opponents as Nazis. For example, Chancellor Adenauer's chief administrative assistant, State Secretary Dr. Hans Globke, was criticized for his connection with drafting the anti-Semitic Nuremberg racial laws. On the other hand, some refugee and veterans organizations objected to the mammoth indemnification and restitution payments of the Federal Government to the State of Israel and to individual Jewish victims of the Nazis, asserting that former Nazis had suffered just as much from Allied air raids and from the denazification program. By 1961, those opponents of Willy Brandt who accused him of having fought against Hitler's *Wehrmacht* went so far that their statements could be interpreted to mean Germany lost World War II only as a result of this kind of traitorous opposition. We have already indicated how these ideologically conceived issues are then converted into litigation, often before the Federal Constitutional Court.

Foreign Policy Issues

These conditions similarly affected the treatment of foreign policy issues. Politicians who were expressly opposed to the Occupation regime were at first simply not admitted to renascent German politics. The Military Governors and, later, their successors, the High Commissioners, were in full charge of Germany's relations with other countries, even to the extent of representing Germany on international bodies, such as the Office of European Economic Co-operation. When control over her foreign policy was given to the Federal Republic, this was done as the Western Allies' part of the bargain, by which the West Germans were to contribute to the defense of Western Europe and the "Free World" against Soviet Communism. Under this bargain, the Federal Republic, having just been subjected to five years of Allied propaganda and re-education on the evils of German (or Prussian) militarism, was required to rearm and to become a member of the North Atlantic Treaty Organization. But meanwhile Germany had been divided into the Western Federal Republic and the Eastern Democratic Republic. Every question of foreign policy consequently became entangled with the problem of division and the means for bringing about reunification. To some of the related questions the parties had already given much thought and study during the period of their relative impotence. The Social Democrats, for example, had always viewed themselves as the most anti-militarist party. They were therefore quite in sympathy with the earlier Allied demilitarization policy. At the same time, they also evolved theories about collaboration with other European countries, especially those in which their sister Socialist parties, members of the Second International, were strong, such as the United Kingdom and the Scandinavian countries. During the first Bundestag, and particularly before the death of the SPD's postwar leader, Dr. Schumacher, they saw tactical advantage in identifying the Adenauer government with the Occupation Powers. Schumacher at one point even referred to Adenauer as "the Chancellor of the Allies"—for which the President of the Bundestag excluded him from the chamber for using unparliamentary language. The Socialists also believed that they had better reasons than the CDU for actively pushing a policy of reunification, because of the strong electoral support the Party had traditionally received in the areas now in the Soviet Zone. In addition to this, the new, constitutionally encouraged, tendency to conduct politics along the pattern of government *versus* opposition led the SPD to oppose both of the main facets of the CDU's foreign policy, rearmament and European integration in the predominantly Catholic "little Europe," by contrast with the predominantly Protestant "great Europe."

By 1961, the Social Democrats had become loyal participants in the various "little Europe" schemes in which the Federal Republic had become a leading member. They had also reconciled themselves to the need for West German rearmament and universal military service, after the CDU conceded important constitutional safeguards against renewed militarism to the SPD. However, they opposed atomic weapons for the *Bundeswehr* —as already indicated by the judicially thwarted referenda that Hamburg and Bremen wanted to hold on that issue—and criticized Dr. Adenauer's "rigidity" on the question of Berlin. The SPD dramatized its assignment of priority to the problem of reunification by nominating Willy Brandt, the Mayor of Communist-surrounded West Berlin, as its candidate for the Federal Chancellorship. The beginning of the 1961 campaign coincided with Premier Khrushchev's renewal of his earlier threat to conclude a separate peace treaty with the German Democratic Republic. While Chancellor Adenauer, together with the Western Allies, simply wanted to condemn this threat as illegal under the terms of the Potsdam Agreement, Mayor Brandt suggested that the West take the initiative away from the Soviets by convening a peace conference of the fifty-two states that had been—and technically still were—at war with Hitler's Germany. Characteristically, however, Brandt said that he was speaking only as Mayor of Berlin, because it would be presumptuous of him to speak upon questions of international relations.

Constitutional Issues

Constitutional issues may arise in a political system, when it has no constitution; for example, when it is a newly founded system, such as the United States during the Independence period; when there is lack of consensus on the "rules of the game"; or when there is lack of consensus on substantive issues of material interests, in the fighting over which parties find that they can use constitutional issues to their advantage—as has often been the case with filibusters in the United States Senate. The dividing line between the last two cases is hard to draw, although one can usually tell whether the emphasis of consensus, or its lack, tends more toward the substantive or the procedural side. In the Federal Republic, constitutional issues arose for each of these reasons, which is one explanation for the extraordinarily important role they have played.

To begin with, West Germany had no constitution, so that constitutional issues were the only ones that were taken up at one level of politics, that of the constitution-drafting Parliamentary Council. After the Basic Law was adopted, its novelty made for a relatively weak consensus on these new rules of the game, so that new constitutional issues were likely to be raised frequently. Moreover, for both of the preceding reasons, virtually any substantive issue was likely to be converted into a constitutional issue, whenever an opportunity for such a conversion appeared. This happened when Professor Heuss, the popular first Federal President, decided that it would be unwise to have the Basic Law amended to enable him to serve a third term. As already mentioned, Dr. Adenauer, when he failed to persuade Professor Erhard to stand for the Presidency, announced his own candidacy. At the same time, he indicated that he would interpret the Basic Law so as to strengthen the President's political role, especially in foreign affairs. Immediately the issue of succession was converted into a debate on the constitution, which also involved an argument over the Chancellor's or the parties' right to control the votes of their delegates to the Federal Convention that elects the President by secret ballot.

In 1960, the Minister of Interior (whose Ministry is often referred to as the "Constitution Ministry") introduced a bill to amend the Basic Law, designed to give the Bundestag or, in case of its incapacity to act, the President and Chancellor together, emergency powers to deal with internal or external threats to order. By the end of the life of the third Bundestag, this bill had not been passed, but it had engendered prolonged and acrimonious debate, in the course of which treatises and lectures by professors of law and judges of the Federal Constitutional Court were used; all the experience with Article 48 of the Weimar Constitution was exhumed; and questions of the basic loyalty to the constitution of most debaters were raised.

Foreign policy issues have also been frequently debated in constitutional terms. This process began with the hesitancy to constitutionalize the division of the country, a hesitancy that produced the title of Basic Law instead of constitution. It was easy to make this conversion in the case of the treaties on the European Defense Community. On this issue, the Social Democrats insisted that they contained constitutional amendments and should therefore be passed by a two-thirds' majority of Parliament. They also insisted on this with regard to the contractual agreements that brought the Federal Republic into the substitute Western European Union, but by this time, after the election of 1953, Adenauer had the support of two-thirds of the Bundestag. However, he also needed the support of two-thirds of the Bundesrat, whose votes are cast, it will be remembered, by representatives of the state governments.

Issues in State Politics

The requirements for passing constitutional amendments and the Federal make-up of the upper house then had the curious effect of making foreign policy the principal issue in campaigns preceding the elections of state parliaments. Normally, problems within the jurisdiction of these state legislatures, such as cultural, educational and administrative ones, would present the main issues for these campaigns. As things actually turned out, however, both Government and Opposition sent their chief leaders from Bonn into the state campaigns in order to get some kind of mandate on foreign policy. During the Federal election of 1953, the restoration of German self-government had not yet gone far enough on this score to make foreign policy the one overshadowing issue. In that campaign, it was just one issue among several. During the next few years, however, foreign policy did become the main issue, both because of its intimate connection with the question of reunification and because of the relative satisfaction that prevailed regarding most other potential issues. Since the Adenauer coalition could not claim to have a mandate on the conduct of foreign policy, and because W.E.U. and rearmament required constitutional amendments, it sought to get temporary mandates in the state campaigns. Moreover, something similar happened even between such campaigns, as the case of the use of the constructive vote of lack of confidence in North-Rhine-Westphalia, in early 1956, illustrates. The FDP had been restive in its Federal coalition with the CDU, felt itself threatened by the draft of a new electoral law, and also disagreed with Adenauer's foreign policy, preferring more active negotiations with the Russians and even with some East Germans. On all these grounds, it left its coalition with the CDU at the state level in North-Rhine-Westphalia, joining instead in a coalition government dominated by the SPD. All of this happened, not because there was dissatisfaction with the administration of the incumbent Minister President, Karl Arnold, or even because SPD or FDP parliamentarians in Düsseldorf, the state capital, "lacked confidence" in this CDU politician. On the contrary, the SPD had been his coalition partner during early postwar years. Arnold himself, who has a "Christian" trade union background, would have preferred to continue this kind of "Great Coalition," since he distrusted the state's FDP organization, with its industrialist, capitalist leanings. He entered into the coalition with the FDP only under pressure from Adenauer as Federal Chairman of the Christian Democratic Union. On the other hand, having lost his Minister-Presidency, he was able to "get even" with Adenauer: At the next Federal party convention of the CDU, Arnold was elected one of four deputy chairmen of the party, even though Adenauer told the convention that he wanted to continue with only two deputies, in which case Arnold would not have been one of them. We have already seen how state governments unsuccessfully sought to open the question of atomic armaments at their level through referenda.

In any case, the over-all outcome of this situation has been to make the Bundesrat more immediately responsive to public opinion than the Bundestag, since elections of the nine state parliaments take place at irregular intervals during the life of one and the same Bundestag. Some German constitutional experts consider this an anomaly. Partly in order to give state-wide issues their rightful place in state politics, and partly in order to simplify politics in general, they have urged synchronization of Federal and state elections. In other respects, too, some of them have advocated similar measures of defederalization, e.g., by doing away with differences among school curricula and admissions requirements in the various states and establishing uniformity throughout the whole Federal Republic.

Vocabulary of Politics

Campaign speeches and pamphlets, and parliamentary debates, are, of course, not couched solely in terms of constitutional or legal arguments. Nor are they by any means always learned historical, legal, economic, sociological, or ideological treatises. Often they are designed to appeal to the material interests of the voters quite as much as, say, in the United States. In the Bundestag campaign of 1953, for example, CDU speakers emphasized many concrete achievements of their government: the "economic miracle" of recovery under the free "social market economy" since the currency conversion of 1948, the building of homes, the absorption of refugees and expellees, and the return to a position of respect and influence in international politics, so shortly after defeat. Similarly, the SPD, on the other side of the fence, pointed to economic inequalities created in the course of recovery, promised greater government subsidies for home construction and better social security schemes, and blamed the continued division of Germany on Adenauer's foreign policy. The SPD continued this approach in the next two Federal election campaigns, adding its opposition to atomic arms for the *Bundeswehr* in the 1957 campaign. In that year, CDU-sponsored social security raises and stability of the cost of living, along with the planned return to private management of the Volkswagen company (through the sale of stock to the public), were among the main campaign issues. In 1961, means of reunification and the personality of the Social Democratic candidate for Chancellor, Willy Brandt, figured prominently alongside the usual economic issues. Brandt was accused of his illegitimate birth, which he publicly admitted. Afterwards, his opponents, including Chancellor Adenauer, occasionally referred to him as though Brandt were his alias and he should really be using his mother's maiden name. The Social Democrats under Brandt's leadership, on the other hand, had veered around to advocating an apparently stiffer stand by the West against Soviet threats to Berlin than did the CDU. They claimed that President Kennedy dispatched Vice-President Johnson to Berlin in response to a letter from Mayor Brandt, who benefited from the television coverage of Lyndon Johnson's visit.

Dr. Adenauer replied, in part, in his campaign letter that was mailed to every household in the Federal Republic:

Bonn, August 1961

CHRISTIAN DEMOCRATIC UNION
OF GERMANY
  The Chairman
Dear Voter:
 On September 17th the election of the fourth Bundestag will take place.

On September 7, 1949, the first Bundestag convened. The results of twelve years of parliamentary labor by the CDU/CSU lie in front of you, as you go to the election in September.

It was twelve years' hard work: Germany was bleeding in the beginning out of a thousand wounds made by the war; trade and traffic were idle, millions of homes destroyed, many industrial plants had been destroyed or were being dismantled. The Germans were hated and despised in foreign countries. In the world, tensions between the bloc of free nations and the Communist bloc were rising from year to year. At the same time, we were occupied, we had no right to speak up in foreign political questions.

How is it today? The Federal Republic is esteemed and respected in the world; her former enemies among the free nations have become her friends and partners. Trade and traffic are booming, we have full employment. Six million homes have been built. We have an exemplary social order and pension legislation. Millions of expellees have been absorbed with the help of equalization of burdens. Total savings accounts amount to 58 billion D-marks. The German mark is one of the best currencies in the world. Our Europe policy and our NATO policy are bearing rich fruits. In the crisis over Berlin, the free nations, especially the United States, France, and England, stand firmly by our side; just as we, so they also ask for the restoration of the unity of Germany.

Who has achieved all this in only twelve years?

The C D U and the C S U !

Who in the Bundestag voted against everything that led to these successes? The SPD and in part the FDP!

As late as March 15, 1961, the SPD in the Bundestag, in a vote by individual ballot, unanimously rejected the budget for the Federal Defense Force. What a decision in a year as full of crisis as the year 1961!

In increasing measure the voters have presented us with their confidence in every Bundestag election, one proof for the fact that we have not disappointed their confidence. This steady, constantly growing confidence of the voters has been and remains an essential prerequisite for our successes. It has provided the possibility to pursue a *steady* policy through twelve years, so that the force and will to work of the German nation could develop fully. The coming years bear great dangers because of the Communist will to conquer. In such dangerous times, the steady, consequential continuation of previous policy is the basic condition of success. This continuation is vitally necessary for the German nation. Then we shall reach our goal: By way of controlled disarmament an enduring peace in the world.

For *each* enfranchised person exercise of his franchise is a *serious duty!* The voter decides about the future of the German nation and thereby about his own future.

And now, esteemed voters: Before you vote on September 17th, think of what was twelve years ago and what exists today. Think that especially in the case of parties achievements count and not words. Think that a party which has achieved this much in 12 years also bears within itself the warranty for future achievement. Remember which party has created in the Bundestag the foundation for our successes and which party was forever saying nothing but NO.

Election day is payday!

Think of our motto: No experiments!

Vote in such a way that German politics will continue to be led as until now.

Therefore: Elect CDU/CSU!

With best regards
(signature)
Adenauer

Studies made of voting behavior in various parts of the Federal Republic suggest that material considerations influence German voters almost as much as American voters. But even when the core of German political campaigning is concerned with material interests, this is more often than not camouflaged by the trappings of learnedness, historical traditionalism, ideologism, and legalism. This is noticeable in the setting of campaign rallies. The halls are usually decked out with national flags. There is of course nothing distinctively German about that, but each of the parties has its own flag, which is also much in evidence. Rightist and leftist parties often begin and end their rallies with trumpet fanfares, blown by a band belonging to the party's youth organization. CDU rallies are sometimes preceded by a brief concert of classical music; SPD meetings, by marches played by a band of "Falcons," the party's youth organization. Usually, half a dozen or so members of the party's local executive committee are seated at a table on the speaker's platform or stage, facing the audience. But even though the local candidates are among them, it is not the normal practice to have them speak before the main speaker. In most cases, they are not even introduced, an indication of the high degree of centralization and discipline of the parties. Since discipline and control are usually exercised by the party's state rather than its Federal organization, this relative lack of direct contact between local candidates and their constituents is the more remarkable. The speaker, especially when he is the party's state or Federal leader, rarely speaks for less than an hour and often for more than two. He rarely indulges in "local color" oratory, designed to warm up his audience to him. As in the Bundestag, his speech may be punctuated by hostile interruptions from listeners. These he may ignore or respond to. Sometimes there are counterattacks upon the interruptor—occasionally physical and to the point of violence—from loyal members of the audience. At the conclusion of the meeting, the singing of the *Deutschlandlied* is standard operating procedure for all parties but the Social Democrats, who sing the Socialist anthem. At CDU rallies, the official third stanza of the *Deutschlandlied* is the standard, while parties further to the Right prefer the more nationalist first stanza. But even Christian Democrats can often be heard singing the first stanza, probably less for reasons of nationalism than because of their ignorance of any part of their national anthem other than it.

Just as in the parliaments, so in campaigns, the intellectual level of speeches is usually quite elevated (if not elevating), at least when compared with equivalent American political addresses. In fact, to an American observer, some of them would seem very much like university lectures, if it were not for the fact that many of them exceeded the standard fifty-minute duration. Similarly, some political pamphlets resemble scientific monographs in both thoroughness and dullness. When they deal with material interests, both speeches and pamphlets often recite lengthy statistics—a practice, incidentally, of which Hitler, too, used to be fond in his harangues, which sometimes lasted for four hours. When concerned with economic questions, SPD speeches especially seem to assume a level of economic knowledge for the acquisition of which the equivalent of at least a college freshman course in economics would be needed. Since the Social Democrats have always stressed training in Marxist theory, and offer courses in economics in their party schools, their speakers are probably wise to pitch their appeal at this level. Campaign speeches often—almost regularly—delve back into the history of the problem with which they are concerned, to demonstrate the consistency of the party's "right," and its opposition's "wrong" attitude toward it. The practice of citing supporting opinions by professors of jurisprudence, economics, sociology, history, and others is often observed by campaign orators. The dead "saints" of the parties, both of the recent and the dim past, are often with them in spirit. In the campaign of 1953, both the SPD and the CDU used dicta of the late Socialist leader, Dr. Schumacher, in their campaign slogans. While SPD speakers do not directly quote Marx or Engels—in line with their general policy of toning down overt evidence of Marxism—their whole approach to current problems, at least until 1957, was heavily informed by Marxist theory. Such phrases as "class struggle," "imperialist domination," "capitalist exploitation," "proletarian solidarity," and the like figured prominently in their speeches, and were understood in terms of a sort of vulgar Marxism by the audiences.

Door-to-door canvassing is not a common campaign practice in West Germany. But often meetings are held by local organizations of interest groups, at which candidates most sympathetic to the group make speeches. Voters are registered automatically and receive the card they have to present at the polling place through the mails. Since German law has traditionally required individuals to register their residence with the police, this method of automatic voters' registration does not present any organizational problems and is handled with great efficiency. It also offers one explanation for the relatively high participation in elections, despite the early fears of some who expected apathy or revulsion because of the enforced voting under the Nazi terror. And even though most Germans, both academic types and others, usually display an inferiority complex with regard to the average German voter's interest in and information about political questions, most American observers would give them a higher grade in both subjects than their counterparts in the United States.

In the election of 1957, and again in 1961, voters who were away from their district were allowed to mail in their ballots, and five per cent of the electorate did so. A typically legalistic objection to this provision of the electoral law was raised by quibblers who worried about voters who had died between the time they mailed their ballot and the time of the count. But this argument was refuted by others who, just as legalistically, pointed out that the law did not specify that voters had to be alive on polling day![3]

Education for Politics

Where do the voters get their political education, and what is its nature? Answers to these questions may also help to explain the formalistic peculiarities of German politics which have already been noted. In the United States, people get what is probably the most important part of their political training at a very early age, during their school years. While they are getting it, neither the children nor, very often, the teachers are aware of the experience in the processes of American democracy that is being provided. Americans become familiar with these methods in a very informal way, for example, by electing class officers, collecting and spending class dues, or deciding with a minimum of adult interference or guidance where and when to hold the class picnic or which orchestra to hire for the school dance. In the course of all this, they virtually have to acquire familiarity with the kind of procedures contained in Robert's *Rules of Order*, even without being exposed to a course in "civics." The unconsciousness of this process of political education is one of its most important aspects and largely responsible for its effectiveness. On this score, the contrast presented by German education for politics is most marked. Even at this early stage, the whole thing is a very self-conscious, deliberate, planned, and, for these very reasons, formalistic affair. Given the German historical background, and especially the recent Nazi experience, no other approach may have been feasible on a large scale. No one in Germany who reached political maturity after Hitler's access to power in 1933 had any experience with even the most elementary democratic practices. This meant, among other

---

[3] Uwe Kitzinger, *German Electoral Politics* (Oxford, 1960), pp. 32 f.

things, that hardly anyone knew how to work on a committee, or how to arrive at common decisions on the basis of more or less rational contributions made by individuals who were initially in disagreement. The "leader principle" (*Führerprinzip*), one of the ideological hallmarks of National Socialism, made committee work rare and difficult to conduct under the Nazi regime. Compromise was not recognized as a virtue and therefore not openly practiced. The same was generally true of most of the other means by which disagreements are resolved and common policies arrived at in democratic societies.

To this, we must add the Occupation Powers' express desire to "educate the Germans for democracy" and the prevailing traditionally formalistic atmosphere, in order to understand the formalistic approach to political education in West Germany. Since the war, German high schools have also given civics courses to their students, but—to exaggerate the contrast between them and their American counterparts—there students are made to memorize the Basic Law and state constitutions, while here they are taught how government actually works by means that include mock "youth legislatures." In most German classrooms, a strong teachers' paternalism prevails regarding concrete decisions that, in the United States, would be made by the students. The consequence of this is that Germans are usually more familiar with the law than with the practice of the political process. This has its effects on adult politics. For example, in German committee meetings—in politics, business, and elsewhere—several copies of pocket-book editions of the relevant laws and by-laws are prominently displayed on the board table and frequently referred to, so that much time is often spent in parliamentary squabbles. And these quarrels arise, not because different committee members are necessarily in disagreement about policy, but because they feel a yearning to use the right legal procedures in formulating their agreement, while they are at the same time unsure of themselves in the use of these procedures. Even at this low level, as a result, substantive issues or "non-issues" are often transformed without need into procedural, constitutional issues.

Academic Political Personnel

All of this means that the equivalent of the "parliamentarian" plays a very important role. Given the civil and code law tradition, it further reinforces the crucial role of the jurist as one who is learned in these political procedures, which are in most cases reduced to "made" and systematized law. The jurists in turn—and not necessarily out of selfish motives —often encourage this tendency to enhance their prestige by demonstrating their own indispensability to the political process. Moreover, this situation has implications that reach even farther and operate more subtly: It also encourages ideological thought and action. Perhaps because of the methods of legal education used at the universities, and the influence of these methods on pedagogy in general, there is a general tendency toward systematic, comprehensive, codified teaching and learning in other disciplines, some of them far removed from the law itself. With this goes a very high degree of respect for, and deference to, those men and women who are officially certified, by their academic degrees, as having acquired all—literally "all"—this knowledge in a field.

Significant also is the comparatively high proportion of academically trained persons in the Federal Cabinet, the Bundestag, executive committees of the several parties, and politics in general. Adenauer's second Cabinet, for instance, consisted of nineteen Ministers, of whom eleven were listed as holding a doctorate (two as professors) with only eight without an academic degree. The first Federal President was officially listed as "Professor Doktor Heuss," and generally referred to as "Professor Heuss." In the first Bundestage, 114 of 402 deputies were listed as holding doctorates, three of them as holding two doctor's degrees each. These last, incidentally, are often addressed as *"Herr Abgeordneter* (deputy) *Doktor Doktor* Schmidt." In a later Bundestag, the proportion of academic members was about the same. The committee that drafted the new Program of Principles for the Social Democratic Party consisted of thirty-one members, of whom eleven were listed as "Prof. Dr.," including one "Prof. Dr. Dr.," and another eight as plain "Dr." Of course, people with some kind of university education predominate in other modern parliaments as well. For example, the predominance of lawyers in the United States Congress has often been noted. The difference here is, however, twofold: In the first place, these men are trained in the Common Law, which discourages a codified view of the world; secondly, they are not in politics primarily because they advertise themselves as academic men. On the contrary, an American candidate for elective office would probably find an exclusively academic background a great campaign handicap. In Germany, it is the other way around: The case of Chancellor Adenauer illustrates this. Though always referred to and addressed as *"Doktor* Adenauer," his doctorate is actually honorary, and postwar at that. Similarly, the late leader of the Trade Union Federation, Hans Böckler, after having been awarded a doctorate *honoris causa,* was generally referred to as "Dr. h.c. Hans Böckler." Just think of the many honorary degrees conferred on President Truman (and most other Presidents of the United States and British Prime Ministers), or the case of Woodrow Wilson, and how ridiculous it would have sounded to Americans had they made use of these titles. But in Germany since politics at all levels is conducted to such an important extent by men who are supremely conscious of their academic training, to which they often owe their political status in the first place, politics is cast in an academic mold.

Stability of Political Style

This has been true of parliamentary politics in Germany at least since the National Assembly of Frankfurt in 1848, as we have already seen. And this seems to be the one constant and stable factor throughout all the different regimes that have succeeded one another since then. The academic cast of mind and tone was not sloughed off when the parties obtained political responsibilities after 1918, or when self-government was restored to the Germans after 1945. Continuity in the political style after World War II was due in some measure to continuity in political personnel. Most of the leading figures had received their training in the Weimar Republic. But even those who reached political consciousness under the Nazis were then exposed at least to the trappings of a similar atmosphere. Some of the Nazi leaders, despite the generally anti-intellectual orientation of the regime, also boasted of their academic background. The most striking case in point is the Minister of Propaganda and Popular Enlightenment, who was always referred to as "*Doktor* Goebbels." The National Socialists always claimed that their ideology—which they considered as important as the Communists theirs—was based on scientific reasoning and the facts of race, blood, soil, and so forth. The façade of legalism that they tried frantically to preserve through the twelve years of their rule of lawlessness has already been mentioned.

Are these three aspects of the style of German politics, scientism, ideologism, legalism, still equally noticeable in the Federal Republic today? That scientism and legalism are as strong if not stronger should have become evident by now. With regard to ideologism, however, some weakening may be detected. In part this is again the result of the general revulsion against all things connected in German memories with the National Socialist period, and especially those of them that are once more also characteristic of the hated Soviet German dictatorship. Both under the Nazis and the Soviets, courses in political *Weltanschauung* were and are a regular part of the school curriculum. This by itself would provide sufficient reason for many Germans for turning away from an ideological approach to politics. Beyond that, there is the dis-ideologizing effect of politics that is conducted along the pattern of government *versus* opposition, although the weakening of party ideologies may have strengthened the ideologies of interest groups, with which we deal in the next chapter. Increased contacts with the predominantly unideological Anglo-Saxon Occupation Powers may also have had their effects in this direction. And, finally, the realization has dawned upon many Germans that their comprehensive systems of knowledge are not of very much help in solving the concrete problems with which they have had to come to grips. In some cases this has not yet reached the level of full consciousness, and the ideological vocabulary of politics has been retained, even though it often merely hides material interest politics. Other people, however, have such a high degree of awareness of the vicious consequences of ideological politics on Germany's past that they execute a complete about-face, to the point at which they openly advocate pure interest politics. When this position stops short of actual advocacy, it is reflected in a kind of detached cynicism about politics, which sees in it or behind it nothing but naked struggles for power and influence among interest groups, no matter how idealistic or ideological parties and politicians may sound in their protestations. Party campaign managers sometimes seem to be operating on some such assumptions. Their reliance upon the results of public opinion polls suggests this, as a kind of combination of cynicism about the "common man" and scientism about the polls. The almost "subliminal" design of campaign posters makes Madison Avenue appear naive by comparison. Kitzinger, in his excellent study of the election of 1957, reports that Professor Aigner, an Austrian painter, was commissioned by the CDU to "adapt" Chancellor Adenauer's face from a photograph:

> . . . Professor Aigner depicted him in deep earnestness, sun-bronzed, fair-haired, and with penetrating bright blue eyes that appeared to follow the voter. "The electorate," as Heck [*Dr. Bruno Heck, Secretary-General of the CDU*] explained, "wants a ruler type," and excitement ran high in the whole CDU organization when the "Big Brother" poster was released.[4]

All this suggests that the German attitude toward politics is dominated by a curious ambivalence between extremes, as is German political history. People either believe that politics should be thoroughly subjected to the restraining regulation of laws and constitution; or they believe that might makes right. Similarly the Empire is followed by the Weimar Republic, the Republic by Hitler's Third Reich, and that once more by the Bonn Republic. It may be that the experience with violence and the consequent fear of violence has made people want to abolish anything that resembles violence even only slightly, as politics undoubtedly does. So they try to substitute administration and adjudication for politics. But, when they subsequently discover that politics is with them inescapably, they throw up their hands in despair or disgust, and say, "We might as well be honest instead of hypocritical about this. It's all just a matter of power and manipulation of the masses." And while the individual or the

---

[4] Kitzinger, *op. cit.*, p. 113.

whole nation is passing through one stage, there is the fear of reversion to the other, so that the characteristics of the present stage are exaggerated even more in order to prevent this regression.

We have seen that the parties do "participate in the forming of the political will of the people," as the Basic Law provides. They help to formulate the issues, to marshal support for alternative solutions, and to make the resultant policies. But in order to see whether they are doing this in ways that are more or less ideological than formerly, and whether or not somewhere underneath naked power is the final determinant of policy, we shall have to take a look at the content and the scope of policy in the Federal Republic. To this we turn next.

[20]

The Pattern of Policy

The main difficulty facing the student of contemporary German government is the lack of firmly established traditions, institutions, and procedures. Since the Germans themselves are painfully aware of this shortcoming, they display a sort of conscious yearning for tradition. This yearning would be both weaker and less conscious if more real traditions actually did exist. In other constitutional democracies, where institutional and political continuity is quite real, politicians do not need to make such contrived efforts to appear as authentic representatives of ancient traditions as in Germany. We have seen in our study of the German parties how unrealistic these claims to represent tradition necessarily are, in view of the fact that most of the problems the country faces today are radically different from those it confronted when modern parties and their ideologies first grew up. Besides, the constitutional framework within which these problems are dealt with differs just as much. Their lack of tradition thus produces this very yearning for traditionalism, which they seek to satisfy by adopting the old ideologies and the old ideological style of conducting politics. They lack a generally accepted conception of authority, or, to put it differently, they lack constitutional consensus, except on two levels: There is agreement on Germany, the geographic and national entity, as the unit of authority, and there is agreement on the style of politics. But there is no equal degree of agreement on the all-important rules of the political game, because the rules have been switched on the players too many times, and usually to the advantage of the most powerful group, whether it existed inside or outside German society. Consequently, anyone who wants either to justify the present constitution or to impose another set of rules upon his compatriots must try to do this by appealing to the nation, and legalism, ideologism, and scientism. But this raises all sorts of stumbling blocks for the student, for it means that much of what the Germans say about their own politics cannot be taken at face value.

This is what makes it so hard to find a sound answer to questions about power in Germany: How effective is government? What stability is there in this effectiveness? How much can it do? For how long are its policies likely to be accepted? Since their accepted concept of authority is not fully "filled in," it is even more difficult to find out the extent to which there is an accepted conception of purpose, that is, substantive consensus. This is so because two antagonists may claim to be disagreeing about the purpose of government, when actually the same substantive policies would be acceptable to both; they are actually only trying to fight out their conflicts about conceptions of authority. To put it differently, the trouble is that the present "constitution" is only of the vintage of 1949. Many Germans prefer to see it as the direct continuation of the serial, whose first installment ran from 1919 to 1933, under the title of "Weimar Republic." This interpretation sees the twelve years of Nazi rule as a foreign and extraneous interlude. Thereby it unduly minimizes both the causes and the effects of those twelve years on present politics. If those who hold this view were right, there would be much more material on which to base answers to these questions about effectiveness. There is more in the case of the three other governments dealt with in this book. For Germany, we have so far only been able to show how government is organized, why "constitutional engineering" organized it this way, and how the parties operate within the framework of government. In the course of all this, we have been looking for those factors that really do seem to be stable and not merely superficial, but that, because they are firmly rooted in German history, have the backing of a sufficient consensus so that they may be expected to survive any future changes, such as the reunification of West Germany and East Germany.

It would seem that the best way to find out how effective government can be in Germany would be to ask how effective it has been since the founding of the Federal Republic. Why not just ask: How much does government do? How does it do these things? Does the population readily accept government policies? We are going to deal with these questions presently, but we should not expect them to answer the basic questions about effectiveness, because these questions also contain the dimension of time, and this brings us back to our earlier difficulty. Government may have been extremely effective during the years between 1949 and 1962, and the scope of its policies very wide. However, because of the lack of stability and continuity in the past, and because of its tentative present make-up, our answers, too, must be very tentative.

The Scope of Concrete Policy

How much does government do in the Federal Republic? What sort of things does it do? Governments can try to control virtually all spheres of life, as we shall see in the case of the Soviet Union. Even in Great Britain, the scope of policy is and has been wide, especially since the years of World War II and the Labour Government which followed it. In the Federal Republic, it is certainly not as wide as in the Soviet Union. One reason for this is again most Germans' revulsion against the Nazi and East Zone totalitarianisms. They have wanted not only to restore the rule of law, which those regimes destroyed, but also to make government less total and all-engulfing. Furthermore, the Federal Republic only recently emerged from the control of the Occupation Powers, under which—as we have seen—many of the normal functions of government were performed by these non-German authorities. But how does the scope of government policy in the Federal Republic compare with that in Great Britain and France? This comparison cannot be as clear-cut as that with the Soviet Union. The scope of policy is at the same time both wider and narrower. There are some matters handled by the national government in those two countries that in Germany are not taken care of by the Federal Government or any government at all. But in other areas the reverse is true.

Here, as with regard to constitutional provisions, present arrangements are to a large extent the product of deliberate efforts to improve previous arrangements, whether of the Nazi or the Weimar period. This applies, for instance, to the West German economy. The official label describes it as a "social market economy" (*soziale Marktwirtschaft*). That is, it is an economy of the market or of free enterprise, which at the same time also aims toward the goal of social justice. This kind of economic policy is attractive both to the Christian elements in the CDU, because of its social justice component, and to the "liberal" elements in the CDU and its coalition partners, by virtue of its economic liberalism. At the same time, it is not as offensive to many Social Democrats as would be a policy of purely capitalist private free enterprise. Moreover, we have already seen how the SPD itself has considerably toned down its socialism. It wants only the fuel industries to be "de-privatized," and even those to be controlled by public corporations, on whose boards the Government would have only one-third of the seats, the other two-thirds going to consumers and labor. The SPD has come out in favor of competition wherever "feasible," including competition between privately owned monopolistic firms and public enterprises. But even this toned-down socialism has not so far been attractive to any more of the electorate than that portion that supported it in the Weimar Republic.

Statism

Does this relative lack of Socialist enthusiasm in the Federal Republic —when compared, e.g., with Britain even after the Conservatives returned to power—mean that government stays out of the economy altogether? It does not, but rather that government legally regulates even its own non-interference. In this respect, the Federal Republic is, of course, not unique by any means. Even before the advent of what has been called the "mixed economy" in the United States, there were a good many regulatory agencies in the Federal Government. It seems safe to say, however, that the proliferation of codified governmental regulation of most spheres of life has not gone as far in either the United States or Great Britain as it has in Germany. Of neither of those countries could one say, "The people abhor a legal vacuum." And yet this statement seems to characterize the West German situation. Moreover, the fact that the German electorate has given no mandate to socialize the steel or coal industry— as did the British—does not imply that it is in any way "anti-statist." On the contrary, the tradition of economic statism is fairly old in Germany, as was noted in the discussion of the country's rapid industrialization. Thus railroads, which were nationalized in Britain only after World War II, were in Prussia built by the state in the beginning. And Bismarck introduced a social insurance scheme that was the most advanced of its time, partly because it was designed to take the wind out of the Socialists' sails. Also, the close and friendly relations prevailing between the old *Junker* and the new industrialist aristocracies eliminated from the outset the kind of hostility between the state and captains of industry that has played such an important role at various stages of the political evolution of Britain, the United States, and France. Finally, private enterprise without state help and direction would not have been capable of undertaking the enormous task of physical reconstruction that lay ahead at the end of World War II.

The Social Market Economy

The Germans thus have no tradition of principled opposition to state interference in the economy, or to state ownership of industry. Nor do they share the Americans' belief in the virtues of free economic competition. And yet the Federal Republic is today described officially as having an economy of the market. Just what does this mean with respect to the role of government and the scope of its policies? It can be understood only if projected against the background of the first three postwar years, when the parties, because of their lack of real power or influence, were still mainly ideologizing. Because of the destruction, dislocation, disorganization, shortages, and hunger of those years, practically all of the physical wartime controls were retained. Food, fuel, housing, just about everything was subjected to strict rationing and equally strict price controls. All of this further increased the shortages, by encouraging a flourishing black market. Then in 1948, largely on the initiative of American Military Government, and against Russian objections that were connected with the subsequent beginning of the Berlin Blockade, the great currency reform was engineered. Overnight, the show windows of stores were filled to overflowing with goods, and a great burst of economic activity was unleashed. The CDU and the FDP rode to electoral victories on this wave, while the SPD, because of many economic injustices allegedly involved in the currency conversion, recriminated and favored a return to physical controls. The Government parties tried to meet these criticisms by labeling their market economy as "social." By this they meant that the underprivileged would be helped and cared for. Thus one of the major legislative products of the first Bundestag was the unique Law on the Equalization of the Burdens (*Lastenausgleich*) arising out of the war and its aftermath. Out of the proceeds of a capital tax levied over several decades, victims of the war or expulsions are being compensated for their losses. Others receive pensions, and the whole social insurance and social security system, whose beginnings go back at least to Bismarck, has been retained and in many respects expanded. For example, a Children's Allowance Law, which especially benefits families with many children, and is reminiscent of Nazi policies in this respect, was passed by the second Bundestag—incidentally by the votes of the CDU alone, unsupported by any of the other parties. There is also a comprehensive system of subsidies to various sectors of the economy, such as agriculture. The price of coal as a home fuel has been kept artificially low by means of such a subsidy. The initial phases of the housing reconstruction program were financed mainly out of public funds and achieved remarkable results. A system of tariffs complements these arrangements.

There were other measures designed to ensure that the market economy should provide not only prosperity but also social justice. Outstanding among them is the scheme known as codetermination, which has already been mentioned. Under it, representatives of labor have an equal share with stockholders' representatives in the management of privately owned corporations in the iron-, steel-, and coal-producing industries. Its main avowed purpose was to improve labor relations in these industries and to give labor a check on irresponsible industrialists who might finance extremist political groups, as some of them did Hitler before 1933. Codetermination first came into being about 1947, in the steel industry in the Ruhr, which the Occupation Powers wanted to get back into produc-

tion and to decartelize at the same time. In 1950, both CDU and SPD
voted for the bill that provided the legal basis for retention of this scheme
in the steel industry, and its extension to coal. The CDU supported codetermination because it could easily be considered an application of the
modern social doctrines of the Catholic Church. Two years later, a milder
version of codetermination was voted for the rest of the economy, this
time against the votes of the SPD. Under its provisions, employees furnish
one-third of the members of the supervisory boards of directors of private
corporations. The Adenauer coalition parties support such measures as
part of their effort to temper the free enterprise economy with what they
consider to be social justice. And this comes with particular ease to the
CDU, which, according to its official program, is opposed to unrestrained
capitalism because it fails to do full justice to the human qualities and
human needs of human beings. The CDU has also been opposed to "state
capitalism" and has, therefore, "re-privatized" Government-owned enterprises to which the Federal Republic had fallen heir by accident, like the
Volkswagen company. Members of lower and middle income groups were
given opportunities to buy a limited number of shares in this company.
This "reprivatization" scheme was, incidentally, opposed by the Social
Democrats.

Government Regulation

The Government's interference in the economy does not end with these
measures that are designed to ensure social justice. On the contrary, there
is a vast volume of regulatory legislation covering all aspects of economic
activity, regulating competition to such an extent that one can hardly
consider it competition any more, setting standards for vocational and professional qualifications, and much more. Nor is all this regulation in any
sense imposed by government upon an economy that resists it or is restive
under it. In the majority of cases, it is rather given to the various trades,
industries, and professions at their own request to be regulated. The attempt on the part of United States Military Government to introduce
professional and vocational freedom (*Gewerbefreiheit*) in the American
Zone of Occupation may serve as an example. Under the American policy,
licensing requirements for such trades as baker, butcher, barber, and
grocer were reduced to a minimum. The first thing the Germans did, when
given sufficient "sovereignty" to do so, was to restore the whole network
of old regulations, which in many ways resembles the medieval guild system. In fact, many of the regulatory practices are hangovers from the age
of feudalism and, for this reason, by no means confined to Germany alone,
but to be encountered all over Europe, where their most notable effect is
a much lower degree of social and economic mobility than prevails in the

United States. But there are differences in this respect from one European country to the next. Thus, the French Revolution tried radically to abolish all organizations of the guild type by means of the *Loi le Chapelier,* so that the vocational, trade, and labor organizations that do exist in France today have a less traditional and more rational and interest-oriented appearance than their German counterparts. In Britain, there remain a few such associations—such as the City of London Companies—which are of very ancient vintage indeed, but these perform "dignified" rather than "efficient" functions. In Germany, many associations have kept both sorts of functions, but they are not really efficient in any contemporary sense. They have not been fully assimilated to industrial capitalism, as it were, and still have about them much of the aura of the *Ständestaat,* the hierarchical state organized in functional estates, each of which is in turn hierarchically organized within itself.

In this way, even saleswomen in department stores and business secretaries are affected by patterns of corporatist thought. There is much less switching from one job to another than there would be in the absence of so much comprehensive and detailed regulation. The tendency to view life in general and politics in particular in a compartmentalized fashion is also due in part to these institutions. Individuals prefer to do only those things, and to be active in only those fields, to which their "role," their "station and its duties," entitle them. And because, both in their schooling and their economic activity, they are accustomed to having a clear course prescribed for them, they expect to have the same kind of order in politics, too. So far as making a living is concerned, this setup provides a great deal of security and—at least as important—a *feeling* of security, which is highly prized, especially after the several catastrophes through which the Germans have passed in the twentieth century. The fact that they value security more and freedom of opportunity less than Americans is both a cause and an effect of this organization of the economy.

For the younger generations, especially of workers, who do not remember the political battles for more social security, or the period of vast unemployment before Hitler came to power, there is a general tendency to turn as a matter of course to the state for security and help. This attitude also received stimulus from the Nazi regime. The older generation, on the other hand, frequently complain that the youngsters "go to sleep in the ready-made bed" of material comfort which their fathers, fighting for their ideals, prepared for them. The oldsters recall the ideological—or, as they would have it, idealistic—struggles of the past and criticize the alleged "materialism" of their sons and grandsons. Because these did not have to fight for either their freedom or their security, older men often raise doubts as to whether they would be willing to fight to defend them, if the need should ever arise.

This is another form taken by the criticism of contemporary German politics on the ground of its materialistic orientation. To the extent that it points to the fact that the younger generation of Germans did not have to make a great effort in order to bring about the present political and economic stability, it points to an important truth, one of the great differences between contemporary Germany and France. The French fought for their freedom, against both the Nazi German occupation and the Nazi-supported Vichy regime. Dr. Wahl describes the great impetus given to the French reform movement by this experience of the Resistance. The Germans, with minor exceptions, have not fought for freedom for a very long time. They never had an equivalent of the French Revolution. The "revolution" that established the Weimar Republic, at the time of defeat in World War I, was so much a part of that defeat and otherwise so limited in its consequences, that many have denied that it was a revolution at all. There was no effective violent resistance against the Nazi system, which was after all a German, not a foreign, regime. The attempt on Hitler's life of July 20, 1944, failed and had the result of eliminating thousands of the most convinced fighters for freedom from later participation in German politics, since the Nazis executed them. There was no overt, violent resistance worth mentioning against the Occupation Powers after the war. In many ways, the heroic and tragic uprising of the East German workers against the Soviet regime of the Democratic Republic in Berlin and elsewhere, on June 17, 1953, was unique in German experience for over a century. In France, in contrast, there was not only the revolutionary tradition, but also the memory of successful violence used on behalf of freedom, recently enough to be remembered by all. France has made "progress on the barricades," most recently in 1958. Progress in Germany has come through orderly action, usually from above, or from the outside. National unification was achieved largely by Bismarck and sealed as a compact among the German princes. Social insurance, too, was introduced from above, by Bismarck. The first constitutional republican regime was introduced in the wake of defeat and under foreign influence. The same was true of the present second Republic. In Germany, legality, not violence, has paid off.

Interest Groups

But is German politics today really material-interest politics? We have seen that government does a great deal that affects and even controls citizens' material interests. We have yet to see how the policies are made that determine whose interests are to be served, and to what extent. The last chapter showed the role of the parties in the process of policy-making. Different parties appeal to different parts of the electorate in their professed and/or actual goals. Given the present electoral systems in the Federal Republic and its member states, no party that wants to survive, and certainly none that wants to grow in power, can afford to appeal to only one interest, whether it be economic, social, denominational, sectional, or other. Under the election law of the Reichstag of the Weimar Republic, this was not so. There was at least one party that managed to seat twenty-three deputies on the basis of a rather narrow interest-group appeal, in the elections of 1928 and 1930. It called itself the Reich Party of the Middle Estate (not middle class, characteristically). And there was a Peasants Party, and even a Bavarian Peasants Party. In other words, under the Weimar system, interest groups could and did go directly into parliament, in order to participate directly in policy-making there. Present institutions make this virtually impossible. The interests, however, still exist, and they are still organized. How do they try to get for their members what these want?

Bonn became the capital of the Federal Republic in 1949. By 1952, at least 270 interest groups of various kinds had established offices there. The variety represented among them is exceedingly great and ranges from industrial and scientific research groups, labor unions, and employers' organizations, to refugee groups and taxpayers' leagues. They have their offices in Bonn in order to influence both the making and the implementation of policy. The latter can best be done through contacts of "lobbyists" with members of the "ministerial bureaucracy," i.e., civil servants in the Federal ministries concerned. Such contacts are facilitated by the fact that many organizers and representatives of interest groups are themselves former civil servants on leave of absence, who may intend to return to their government jobs at a later date. Most members of the civil service at these upper levels have a background of university juristic training. So do many representatives of interest organizations. After studying law at a German university, and passing a series of state-administered examinations, a student has a legal right to government employment. He may opt for a career in the judiciary or public administration, or for a private career, either as a practicing lawyer or in business or organizational work. If he chooses an administrative career, he can usually leave it for private business or politics but still retain grade and seniority for a later return to the civil service. This opportunity is often used. It not only facilitates communication between the interest groups and the Federal ministries, but also makes it possible for the interest groups to have as their representatives in the Bundestag men with a background of public administrative experience. Furthermore, it provides some politicians with a safe civil service berth to which they can always return in case they are defeated at the polls or fired from their private or organizational jobs.

United States Occupation Authorities objected to those provisions of the Basic Law and the first election law that kept civil servants from having to resign from the service upon accepting elective office. But in the long run the Germans had their way, on this as on other matters. For the first Bundestag, this meant that about one quarter of its members had a civil service background. In many instances, these deputies are also officers of professional civil service organizations. The political parties, in order to obtain the support of these associations or interest groups, nominate such men as their candidates. The same thing happens with representatives of other types of interest organizations, sometimes with their presiding officers. These have many opportunities for influencing policy, both in their party caucus and in committee meetings. The committee meetings are especially useful for this purpose. In contrast with Congressional committees, they hardly ever take testimony from representatives of groups that are particularly interested in legislation under the committees' consideration; nor do they hold public hearings. But because these groups often have leading officers on the committee as members, they are represented perhaps even more effectively in the Federal Republic than in the United States, although—and because—there is less accompanying publicity. For example, in the second Bundestag 20 of the 29 members of the Committee on Nutrition, Agriculture, and Forestry were agriculturalists or officers of interest organizations active in these fields. In the third Bundestag, at least 21 of the 29 members of the Labor Committee were connected with labor organizations. More than 20 of the 29 members of the Committee on Civil Service Law (*Ausschuss für Beamtenrecht*) were civil servants in the second Bundestag. Of the 23 members of the Committee on Questions of War Victims and Returnees, only 7 were born in the territory of the Federal Republic, the remainder having "come home" from places as far apart as the present Democratic Republic and South Africa, East Prussia (now Russia), and Yugoslavia. Some of the lobbies have recently begun to operate in a very modern, "American" way. They have run great publicity campaigns, promoting their cause by means of advertisements in the press and short films in movie theaters. This was done, for example, in relation to legislation on transportation, the automotive, oil, and rubber industries wishing to keep transportation taxes low and to expand the road network. (The close connection between these German industries and their counterparts in the United States may account for this largely unprecedented use of American methods of public and legislative relations.)

Modern methods do not characterize the majority of interest organizations, however, but in the main only those that really are modern simply because they do not have a long life to look back on. Many of the organizations that have offices in Bonn do have long traditions and are rather proud of them. This is true, for instance, of the German Trade Union Federation. Even though this is the first time that there has been one unified and politically neutral labor movement in Germany, the members of the DGB like to trace their origins back at least to the beginnings of both Socialist and Christian trade unions in the middle of the last century. Similarly, the various trade, craft, and professional organizations have traditions that they consider to be both ancient and honorable. Membership in some of them is compulsory for the practice of a trade or profession. This is true, for example, of the chambers of commerce and industry (*Industrie-und Handelskammern*), which carry out some of the state's regulatory activities, such as supervision of apprentices and their training, administering apprentices' examinations, setting fair trade practices, and the like. Commercial and industrial businesses have to belong to these local chambers, which in turn belong to a hierarchy of state chambers, topped by the German Diet of Industry and Commerce. The interests the chambers represent often bring them into conflict with the trade unions, membership in which is not compulsory for workers, and which themselves are not admitted to membership in the chambers of commerce and industry. Now, we might expect that the unions would therefore advocate that the chambers be stripped of their semi-governmental character and their governmental functions. However, the reverse has been true. The unions have advocated that they themselves be made compulsory members of the chambers, by Federal legislation. In addition, some of the trade unionists would like to have membership in the unions made compulsory for employees and to have governmental functions assigned to the unions as well.

The Desire to Be Regulated

This points to one characteristic that most of the German interest groups seem to share in common: the desire not for less government regulation but for more, both of their own affairs and interests, and of their relations with others. Another reflection of this desire may be found in the several systems of specialized courts that exist alongside the regular courts and the administrative courts (*Verwaltungsgerichte*). There are labor courts (*Arbeitsgerichte*), which deal with relations between employees and employers; and "social" courts (*Sozialgerichte*), which handle cases arising out of the administration of the social security system. These specialized courts have the virtues that go with speedy proceedings and judges who are technically informed. At the same time, these very virtues also encourage litigation.

Thus, even though the scope of material policy in the Federal Republic today may not be as great as in Great Britain—e.g., the coal industry is not government owned or operated—the scope of regulatory policy is very great indeed. In Britain, there is less demand on the part of interest groups to be formally regulated by government than in Germany. There is not so widespread and powerful a conviction as in West Germany that the creation of "social peace" is an urgent task for government, which could best be fulfilled by having government organize and regulate most social relations.

One explanation of this desire for comprehensive formal regulation may once more lie in the lack of any long German democratic and parliamentary tradition. In Britain people generally know how to conduct negotiations, say, in collective bargaining or at a meeting of a parent-teacher association. This is less often the case in Germany, and hence the yearning to have procedural rules for such and any occasion laid down once and for all in explicit legislation. Because agreement on authority is incomplete, the attempt is made to engineer it into existence. Because there is no procedural consensus, one has to be created artificially. But this yearning goes even further. People are reluctant to have relations with others that are not part and parcel of the status their vocational or political standing gives them. Therefore, many of them would prefer to have their contacts with other social, economic, and cultural groups formalized as well.

The most overt manifestation of this line of thought is advocacy of a revival of the Reich Economic Council (*Reichswirtschaftsrat*). This was the third, functional, economic house of the Parliament of the Weimar Republic. It was not particularly effective. Nevertheless, today many trade unionists, both Social Democrats and Christian Democrats, are convinced that a series of economic councils, topped by one at the Federal level, would serve the cause of social justice by extending labor's rights of co-determination above the level of the individual business corporation. It would also ease "social tensions" by defining clearly mutual rights and obligations between the "social partners," i.e., employers and employees. Constant contact and exchange of views between representatives of divergent economic interests is going on all the time, of course, in the Bundestag among other places. But because of their tendency to compartmentalize public life, the advocates of a re-established economic council tend to overlook this fact. Parliament, so they argue, deals exclusively with *Staatspolitik*. *Wirtschaftspolitik* therefore requires a separate, functionally specialized, deliberative body. Existing informal contacts between different economic groups do not suffice to promote "social peace," mainly because they are informal. Therefore, they should be formalized.

Are parties more ideological than interest groups? In West Germany, the reverse may well be true. The parties can no longer afford to remain as ideological as they used to be, because of the institutional pressures toward something resembling a two-party system, especially the pattern of government *versus* opposition. Unless they conform to this pattern, they are likely to be snowed under by the two great parties that are conforming to it. Now, this seems to have the consequence of deflecting ideological patterns of conduct "down" to the level of interest organizations. This need surprise us only if we think of interest organizations in British or American terms, i.e., as being concerned mainly with obtaining material gains for their clients. If that were their chief concern, then they would have to operate in a rational manner, applying pressure wherever it is likely to bring results, compromising, log-rolling, making alliances with other groups regardless of the convictions of these groups, and so forth. In other words, such interest organizations could not afford to be ideological, nor would there be any incentive for them to be ideological. But this does not apply to German interest organizations, except for the very modern ones. The older organizations, since they have good reason to think of themselves as bearers of ancient corporatist traditions, already have the ready-made ideology of their estate or guild to fall back upon. This has also been true of the various refugee organizations, whose membership is based upon geographical origins. In this connection, it is significant that even the SPD, for which class has always been the most important social phenomenon, has referred in many an official party program throughout its history, not only to the working class, but also to the workers' estate (*Arbeiterstand*). And the Nazis, when they spoke of the social leveling that would be carried out in order to establish the true national community, attacked "*Klassen und Stände.*" If we combine the ready-made ideologies of the old estates with the deflection of ideologies from the party level, we can understand why the interest groups may be becoming more ideologized. Moreover, since ideological habits of thought and action are direct and obvious obstacles to bargaining and compromise, we can also understand why the interest groups may have more of a stake in explicit government regulation than the less ideological parties. They are afraid of the lack of consensus, the possible outbreak of violence, and therefore want to engineer consensus into existence by constitutional means.

Policy and the Constitution

In Germany as elsewhere most trade unionists are interested above all in improving their standard of living. But in order to get an increase in economic influence or power, they demand a change in the Constitution through creation of the Federal Economic Council. In making this demand, they are also inviting an increasing amount of government regulation of their own affairs. The situation is further complicated by their additional desire to get the prestige that would go with membership in a federal economic council or the chambers of commerce and industry. In this sense, they want to return to something resembling the corporative *Ständestaat*, the state in which the different functional estates were represented, in which the guilds largely regulated themselves with power delegated to them for that purpose by the state, and in which no one had to worry very much about competition. The preference today is for regulation over competition. On this point, American Occupation policy also clashed with German traditions and desires, and the Germans by and large restored the restraints on competition that Military Government had earlier abolished. Later, the High Authority of the European Common Market provided a new source of regulation; or, for those big businessmen who opposed it, the Common Market offered a framework within which they sought to overcome the irregularities of competition through self-regulation with public authority from a new, more broadly legitimized source.

A further explanation for this preference may be found in the important role in politics played by civil servants, officials, bureaucrats (*Beamte*). We know that many members of the Bundestag are of this professional background, which generally involves legal training. These people tend to bring into politics in general and parliament in particular the legalistic, bureaucratic habits of their profession. The same is also true of many of the officials of large organizations, such as trade unions and large business corporations, who enter politics. Moreover, since the civil servants are assured of being able to return to the service in case of need, they are likely to retain a high degree of self-identification with "the state" (*der Staat*), which is certainly one of the most formidable terms in the German vocabulary. This is quite as true of the "progressive," lately revolutionary, Social Democratic Party as of the more conservative FDP. The image many German Socialists have of a Socialist society is that of the State of Civil Servants (*Beamtenstaat*), in which everything will be orderly, regulated, and legalized. A functional, hierarchic organization would be indicated for such a state, and in it conflict, bargaining, competition and compromise would have no legitimate place. Ideally, there would be no politics. In any case, whether they are hopeful for the Socialist state of the future, or nostalgic about the corporatist state of the past, the Germans generally state their aspirations in legal or constitutional form.

Because government regulation is actually desired to such a great extent, the actions of government are respected, that is, effective. If a policy has been arrived at by the prescribed legal and administrative procedures, very few Germans would resist it in any way. There have been many illustrations of this. When the victorious Allies first began to occupy Germany at the end of the war, they expected resistance of the type the French had offered the Germans before the Liberation. There turned out to be virtually no German resistance—not even to the denazification policies, at least overtly. Part of the explanation undoubtedly lies in the sheer exhaustion of the German population, but part of it also in the fact that the Germans realized that the Allies were wielding "sovereignty" over German territory, that they were the source of law, and that they therefore had to be obeyed. The law always has to be obeyed—even in a revolution. The best illustration of this is Professor Sigmund Neumann's delightful story about SPD "revolutionaries" in Leipzig, in November 1918. Following sound revolutionary tactics, they wanted to take over the railroad station. But they did not take it by storm, as the French might have in a similar situation. They knew—as what German does not?—that the law requires that one buy an admission card to the platform, for ten pfennig, and get this card punched at the turnstile before going out on the platform. And that is exactly what they did in order to "seize" the railroad station!

In the recent history of the Federal Republic, even the most controversial policies of the Federal Government were accepted readily after they had been passed by Parliament and/or found constitutional by the Constitutional Court. This was true, for example, for the several acts on codetermination. It was true of the European Defense Community and Western European Union treaties, and of the rearmament and conscription policies. So far, at least, Government policies have been respected regardless of their substantive purpose, so long as they are backed by the authority derived from legal origins. The authoritative origins of policies are considered more important than their concrete consequences. This means that the best way to attack a proposed policy is through criticism of its legal source, and, ultimately, by questioning its constitutional basis. This route of argument makes for potential constitutional instability.

We may now return to our original question about the comparative scope of policy in Germany and Great Britain. In some substantive respects, government does more in Britain. But, if a Social Democratic majority should ever come into power in Germany and pass socialization legislation, there would be little fear that anyone would resist any more than the Tories resisted after 1945. As a matter of fact, Socialism might be accepted more readily in Germany than in Britain. The tradition of state regulation of the economy might have this result, as also the high prestige of the civil service. After all, if major industries were socialized, then practically everybody would be a *Beamter*. About one-ninth of the total labor force, incidentally, is already in the public services. On the other hand, the effective scope of regulatory government policy is much greater in Germany than in Britain. In Germany, almost any substantive issue is likely to be raised to the constitutional level. Many issues arise on the constitutional level in the first place. Many constitutional changes are also likely to be accepted by the population as authoritative, so long as they are arrived at in a legal way. Many others may be of such potential explosiveness that the discussion of them would have very divisive effects on German politics. This would seem to be likely in the case of issues dealing with that part of the concept of authority that has not yet been fully filled in, i.e., the basic rules of the political game. Certainly future years are going to present many opportunities for conducting such debates.

In looking for something stable and continuous we have had to go beyond the institutions of government, beyond parties and their programs, to attitudes toward politics. These are expressed in the ways in which people see their problems and formulate the issues arising out of them. In this respect, we have found elements that seem not to have changed very much over the decades. People are still unhappy rather than cheerful about the necessity of politics. Order is considered a virtue. Politics is disorderly. By substituting adjudication and administration for politics, order may be established. Knowledge alone can provide those principles, by means of which order can be established. Complete knowledge is available to those who devote themselves to study. Social order can be established through application of their knowledge by students of society and law. "The Law" is one of the several, often competing, comprehensive systems of knowledge, on the basis of which politics can be transcended—to the extent that this is at all possible.

These attitudes of legalism, scientism, and ideologism, and the desire to get away from politics altogether, are reflected in the pervasive wish to foreorder all possible future disputes by means of detailed institutional engineering, and in optimism about the likelihood of reaching desired objectives through this instrument. This in turn tends to aggravate further the leanings toward constitutional instability. And it is strengthened even more by the understandable anti-totalitarian desire to establish the true *Rechtsstaat*. As a result, consciousness of the provisions of both constitutional and ordinary law is widespread. Preoccupation with constitutional problems is frequent. Many ordinary disagreements about substantive interests, which elsewhere would be handled within the constitutional framework, tend to become in the Federal Republic issues about the constitutional framework itself.

The tendency to make constitutional issues out of questions of interest might not be too important, so long as the questions of interest themselves are not of a very divisive nature. This was the case in West Germany until full self-government was returned to its citizens by the Western Occupation Powers. The Allied High Commission continued to function as the supreme guardian of the constitution against anti-constitutionalist forces, and some of the most important policies were imposed upon the Germans from the outside. Since then, however, the Germans have no longer been able to blame things on the Occupation—nothing, that is, except the aftereffects of older policies. Rearmament and reunification policy, each directly dependent upon the other, have become the principal current issues in West German politics, as of 1961. Political battles about these two main issues will often be carried on at fever heat. Politicians will make use of many tactics in order to have their way or to obstruct the opposed majority from having its way. One of the best established and most promising tactics is constitutional controversy. Much of this may be expected. Much of this controversy and politics in general will be carried on by men of academic status in positions of leadership. Political discourse will abound with the vocabulary of old, and perhaps some new, ideologies. Even if the worst should happen and violence breaks out between East and West Germany, legalistic arguments and considerations will play an important role. These attitudes are likely to continue to be expressed— that much seems sure. But the specific problems about which policies will have to be made will depend upon the course of world politics, in which Germany has so often been the focal point of war.

[21]

Prospects

The Iron Curtain was first lowered in the middle of this "land of the middle," as some Germans have called it. Chances are that, when and if it is raised again, the most important act of the drama of the Cold War will have come to an end. When the Iron Curtain was first lowered after the end of World War II, the German stage had been set for two gigantic experiments in institutional engineering. In each of the two parts of the divided country, each of the two opposing political theories of the modern West had free play to realize its particular goals through the particular institutions it deemed best designed for that purpose. We say "theories of the modern West," because both democratic constitutionalism and Soviet Communism belong to the modern West, as it is distinguished from the pre-modern West and the East and Africa. These political theories were first forged in response to the needs of modernizing, industrializing, and urbanizing incipient "mass" societies, and they were elaborated in an environment that was more advanced in most respects one hundred years ago than many states of South East Asia and Africa are today. Germans—who called themselves by this name before they had a national home state—contributed much to both streams of thought that are opposing each other in thought and action in the world today.

Fortunately the most influential German contributions were made in the sphere of political theory, not in the design of political institutions or programs of political action. Figures like Pufendorf and Kant, Hegel and Marx became objects of more eager study than Frederick the Great and Baron vom Stein, Bismarck and Ferdinand Lassalle. But it is important to remember that Karl Marx was born, raised, and educated under Prussian sovereignty; that he grew up in Trier, which is in the Federal

Republic today; that he learned about the historical dialectic in Berlin, today the divided capital city of the former *Reich* and the present German Democratic Republic; and that he obtained his degree as a doctor of philosophy in Jena, which is now in the Soviet Zone. In a sense, Marx's thought and the later division of his disciples into Social Democrats and Soviet Communists foretold not only the division of his homeland, but also the ambivalence of the West Germans of our time, between legalistic constitutionalism and pragmatic interest politics, between historical ideologism and here-and-now oriented power manipulations.

Karl Marx asserted the primacy of economic factors and at the same time exhorted the workers of the world to unite in their several national states. He proclaimed that the course of history toward inevitable Socialism was predetermined, and at the same time he urged his followers to engage in a more disciplined and better planned form of massive political action than had ever been attempted by human beings anywhere upon the globe. Both his assertion and his exhortation turned out to be more widely and more deeply influential than anything similar, written either before or since, especially in Germany and elsewhere in Continental Europe. In Germany, even avowed anti-Marxists soon began to base their policies upon more or less Marxian assumptions, upon the Marxian "belief system." In Germany and elsewhere[1]—but first in Germany—even anti-Marxists like Chancellor Bismarck developed partly Marxian and partly nationalist conceptions of substantive purpose, e.g., in pioneering the system of social insurance. Whatever the goal they were pursuing, they understood the reality around themselves by means of categories of economic power, and they proceeded to reshape this reality to their better liking in the belief that deliberately organized human endeavor will bring the intended results. Unfortunately for themselves—as it turned out—this belief was often justified during the first half of the last one hundred years.

First, a massive political effort involving the military defeat of France brought about national unification. And then, another centrally directed political drive enabled Germany to catch up with and surpass the industrial might of her European neighbors. These two successes set the German pattern, in which political authority flows from substantive achievements of the kind won in military and economic battles. When World War I, and later inflation and depression, destroyed the great gains of the Second *Reich*, both causes and remedies were sought and found in economics and power politics. Political authority continued to flow from substantive sources, like great wealth and economic expertise, military decorations and the organized support of millions, religious identification or racial hatred.

---

[1] See below, p. 597.

In Great Britain, by contrast, political authority has usually come from identification with the ancient procedures of politics, and political advancement has more often than not preceded attainment of prominence in substantive endeavors, in the career patterns of political leaders.

This difference—which has had such tragic consequences for Germany and, to the extent that Germany again is at the center of troubles that threaten to lead to another World War, for mankind—cannot be explained in terms of any weakness of German as compared with British consensus. In some respects, German consensus is stronger, e.g., on the nation as the proper unit of politics, perhaps because national unification came too recently and lasted for only three quarters of a century. Even the divided Germany of today has no equivalent of the Scottish nationalists or the Welsh nationalist party that polls close to one-fifth of the votes cast in many Welsh constituencies. On economic policy, too, there has been much stronger consensus in West Germany since the war than in the United Kingdom; otherwise the "economic miracle" would never have taken place and the Federal Republic would not have outstripped Great Britain despite defeat and division. Even culturally the population of the Federal Republic, including all the expellees and refugees from the East, impresses some observers as more homogeneous than that of the United Kingdom, where persons from adjoining counties often have difficulty communicating with one another—not to speak of members of different classes!

Nor has German consensus been weakened by a conflict such as that between the administrative and representative traditions, which, according to Dr. Wahl, divide all the French into two parts. Most Germans might agree that the most representative of what they consider best in the German tradition have been some of the great German administrators. And yet the sources of political authority in Germany tend to be more substantive and less procedural than they are even in France. No two Frenchmen would prefer immediate recourse to the courts to direct and preferably public negotiation according to widely familiar rules of debate; and both rebels and government supporters in the uprisings of 1958, 1960, and 1961 were conducting their conflicts according to fairly old "rules of French civil warfare," to which considerable authority still continues to attach. In other words, the Germans have not needed the substantive authority of power in order to hold together a community so weakened by internal disagreements that nothing else could keep it from breaking apart. On the contrary, their consensus on matters of substance has on occasion been so profound that it brought their greatest glory when focused in expressions of national will. In Britain and France, on the other hand, great national achievements were more often the result, not of single-minded will power and resolution, but of prolonged deliberation among people of divided mind who, because of their divisions, needed, elaborated, and cherished their home-grown procedures of compromise. In Germany, substantive success was achieved without any need of previous compromise. As a result, when catastrophe befell the Germans—or when they brought it upon themselves—they had no home-grown rules for the settlement of quarrels that are always more numerous in adversity than in good fortune. On such occasions, they have sought to achieve constitutional success through the same kind of single-minded and deliberate exercise of will power that had previously brought them military, economic, and cultural victories. This effort failed in the Weimar Republic. Is it likely to fail once more?

If the Federal Republic were France, we could use the French saying, according to which nothing lasts like the provisional, in arriving at an answer. Some Germans have used this saying themselves, but the fact that they have to resort to French lore to express this thought is almost as revealing as the fact, often noted by Germans with some pathos, that their language has no equivalent for the English "fair" or "fair play." Perhaps we can best illustrate the difference between political authority in Germany and England through exaggeration: English sports fans recognize authority in players who observe the rules of the game, though they may lose. German sports fans see authority in players who win. In the German sport of politics, whenever the principal players on one team managed to persuade the public of disadvantages in the current set of rules—which was regarded as provisional because of its newness—they produced a completely new set through a great effort of national will. In England, it has never occurred to either players or fans that the fundamental rules could be changed, and when they were in fact changed—which has to be done from time to time to keep up with technological innovation in sports, e.g., the invention of a new type of ball—all sorts of pretenses were made to deny the reality of the modification and to assert continuity if not identity between present, former, and original rules.

Even political scientists, and especially psephologists (students of voting behavior), are affected, in the esteem with which they are regarded in the two countries, by this difference in sources of authority. In West Germany, the institutes of public opinion are expected to predict with certainty and are for that reason greatly respected by party managers, politicians, and the general public. Not so in the United Kingdom, where the scholar who first gave wide usage to the word wrote:

> A psephologist, like a cricket correspondent, should be judged by his success in enhancing his readers' knowledge and understanding of the game far more than by the accuracy of any forecasts he may

make. Election majorities are not exactly predictable; and there is no likelihood of their becoming so.[2]

Perhaps we, in the English-speaking United States of America, where procedural sources of authority also outweigh substantive ones, should extend Mr. Butler's standards to our estimate of the broad possibilities of German political development.

France lies somewhere between England and Germany with respect to continuity of basic procedures of politics, upon which there is consensus both widely popular and deeply generational. But then politics is not a team sport in France.

In Germany today, both West and East, the main sources of political authority continue to be substantive ones. Immediately after the war, identification with the anti-Nazi resistance and victimization by the Nazis gave great authority, and this remains important today, e.g., in the case of Willy Brandt and other Social Democratic leaders. Substantive achievement during the period of reconstruction and resistance to East German Communism also contribute to Mr. Brandt's authority. Heroism on the German side during World War II can also be considered a valid claim for political fame. Several holders of the German equivalent of the Congressional Medal of Honor (the Knight's Cross of the Iron Cross) are members of the Bundestag. Among them is Dr. Erich Mende, who was leader of the Free Democratic Party in the campaign of 1961. Professor Dr. Erhard has been a leading contender for the succession to the chancellorship, because he is credited with having engineered the "economic miracle" in his capacity as Minister for Economic Affairs. His main competitor within the CDU/CSU is the Minister for Defense, Dr. h. c. Franz-Josef Strauss, who is respected and considered "powerful," because he has been presiding over the rearmament of the Federal Republic. These are the leading figures of the two generations to which, sooner or later, Dr. Adenauer will have to turn over the reins. None of them gained political prominence primarily as a parliamentary politician, though all but Brandt have been members of the Bundestag since its beginning in 1949. This substantive bias of the leadership, of consensus and the sources of authority, warrants the fear that attachment to the procedures of compromise—i.e., to constitutionalism—would be weakened disastrously in West Germany in case of another great catastrophe in the fields of economics or foreign relations.

To be sure, the work of the founding fathers of Bonn has so far been much more successful than that of their predecessors of Weimar, although

---

[2] David E. Butler and Richard Rose, *The British General Election of 1959* (New York, 1960), p. 4.

the problems of 1948 looked more difficult in most respects than those of 1919.[3] As we have seen, the younger generation of constitutional engineers tried very seriously to benefit from the presumed mistakes of their elders. We have also seen that they did indeed learn a great deal—perhaps too much, in the sense that the Basic Law of Bonn might have been a fool-proof safeguard against the economic and international causes of the fall of the Weimar Republic but offers much less help in solving the problems of the Bonn Republic. Constitutional experts, like generals and other strategists, often make the mistake of anticipating the last instead of the next crisis. Germans, for whom history and its philosophy has often become a fetish—witness Hegel, Marx, and Spengler, among others—have been especially prone to this error. Perhaps a future group of German constitution makers will conclude that the Federal Republic needed cabinet stability, a "two-party system," and judicial review less than widespread popular familiarity with informal procedures of compromise, capable of helping its people overcome whatever novel conflicts might arise among themselves and between West Germany and its neighbors, primarily East Germany. Perhaps this later generation of constitutional renovators will wish that their forerunners had made greater efforts to overcome the compartmentalization of politics into a number of segregated containers, each of which was believed to dispense a different policy liquid— *Kulturpolitik, Sozialpolitik, Wirtschaftspolitik*, and, finally, *Staatspolitik*. If this kind of recrimination should take place while the present generation is still alive, so that the two can confront each other—in an exchange that would, no doubt, be declaratory rather than deliberative—then, the men with whose work we have been concerned may well reject these criticisms by saying that Germany's international power situation kept them from following their own wiser insights, and by quoting Prince Bismarck's dictum, according to which politics is the art of the possible.

A great deal was possible in West Germany in and after 1948. While the West Germans did not, of course, start out with a blank slate then, they were working in and on a political system that was—and continues to be today—like a protected laboratory. The protection was provided by the Western Allies and, paradoxically, by the Soviet Russians, who kept their East German Communists firmly "leashed." The Federal Republic could be described as a hothouse for experimentation with political flora, but, because of the rather mechanical view that its constitutional reformers took of their task, the analogy with a physics laboratory seems more apt. No very divisive issues arose in West German politics. Right after the war there was agreement on the need for reconstruction. The Nazi ex-

---

[3] For a comparison of these two efforts in constitution-making, see Herbert J. Spiro, *Government by Constitution*. (New York, 1959), pp. 418-427.

perience and the changed demography of West Germany as a new political system had reduced denominational disagreements. The existence of the Democratic Republic on the other side of the Curtain deflected many previously internal divisions to the higher plane of the East-West conflict. West Germany therefore really did not need its new political machinery for the urgent processing of current issues that were dividing its population. This made it easier for the Federal Republic to innovate, for example, by announcing its readiness in the Basic Law to renounce rights of sovereignty in order to contribute to "a peaceful and enduring order in Europe and among the nations of the world" (Article 24). It also encouraged individual politicians like the President of the Bundestag, in the citation at the beginning of this section, to theorize about the obsolescence of conventional political concepts and institutions. At the same time, the laboratory atmosphere in no way prevented men like Defense Minister Strauss from pursuing the new substance of the old attributes of sovereignty: nuclear weapons for the *Bundeswehr* in its role as the strongest European member of NATO. When a group of distinguished German nuclear scientists called upon the Federal Republic to renounce the possession of atomic weapons, Chancellor Adenauer questioned their competence in the field of politics, for which he bore responsibility. The State continued to be separate from *Kultur* and Economy, and the individual continued to play separate and different roles as a citizen of each. The achievement of power in any one of these spheres is still valued more highly than efforts to bring about compromise of conflicts that inevitably arise out of their different claims, or efforts to integrate these compartments by means of something less than distilled national will power.

Most Germans would ascribe Germany's two greatest achievements of power of the last one hundred years to gigantic exertions of national political will: Bismarck's construction of the Second *Reich* and Hitler's spread of the Third *Reich* over most of Europe. They would explain the national disasters of the same century by way of some determined mechanism of history. After the "catastrophe" of World War II, the Germans were not called upon to exercise their political will. Indeed, it was forbidden them to try to do so. And they were disillusioned with politics. After all, it was Hitler who had said, in a motto inscribed on a special "*Führer's* birthday" issue of postage stamps, "I, however, decided to become a politician," and, "He who is determined to save a nation, can think only heroically." The West Germans, in rebuilding the foundations of their existence, exercised economic will power. To this and to Allied help, given because of the international power configuration that was increasingly focused on their own country as a result of the Korean War, they ascribe their present prosperity and the respect they are enjoying in the world—not to the reformation of West German politics. In other words, even if the authors of the new constitutional order had been better artists of the politically possible, most Germans today would deny the primacy of politics. The British, while they have never had to assert it in an explicit or theoretical fashion, would not deny this primacy. The French, no matter how passionately rational or coldly cynical they may be, are receiving lessons every day on the primacy of politics from that most fascinating master of the art, General de Gaulle.

The Germans, who are said to be fond of paradoxes, remain as plagued today as was the German Karl Marx by the paradox between the situational and the intentional. In the Federal Republic, this paradox will remain unresolved for as long as the different compartments in which its citizens perceive the processes of their common existence remain unintegrated in their perception. What makes this even more worrisome for the rest of mankind is the division of the industrialized, most powerful states of the world into two hostile camps, a division that is most dramatically visible in the middle of Germany. The constitutional states on the whole are not perturbed by the paradox. Their constitutions are *intended* to make possible the shaping of their *situation* toward achievement of common *purposes* and, as Professor Beer pointed out in the Introduction, the more constitutionalist they are, the higher is the priority given to the procedural content of these purposes.[4] The Soviet systems, on the other hand, and especially the Soviet Union—to which Germany provides the logical "port of entry" from France and Great Britain—are wholly dedicated to the pursuit of substantive goals and have in the past not shrunk from the use of any or all methods considered useful to this purpose. Their belief system includes—indeed, it is based upon—Marx's paradox. They believe that they can achieve any end through disciplined and massive political action. But they also interpret the domestic and foreign policies of the Federal Republic in Marxian terms. The German Communist Party in the Weimar Republic did the same thing, on orders from Moscow, which led it indirectly to support Hitler's rise to power, because Fascism was the last stage of monopoly capitalism, after which the Communist revolution would inevitably follow. This of course turned out to be a tragic misunderstanding. In their German policy, the Soviets today are trying to prevent the rise of another Hitler as much as were the founders at Bonn. Both efforts seem equally irrelevant in the age of intercontinental ballistic missiles with nuclear warheads and of manned space flight. President Gerstenmaier of the Bundestag was right in quoting Judge Leibholz of the Federal Constitutional Court: The ethically essential and the

---

[4] See above, p. 38.

existentially decisive does take precedence today over demands coming from the national state. But the Federal Republic is no national state, and he was wrong in calling for spiritual and cultural achievements with which to supplement West Germany's economic and organizational ones in order to save the country from dependent insignificance.

What Germany needs rather is achievement in constitutional politics through the fashioning of a pattern of authority that looks upon the politics of compromise as a higher vocation than the economics of prosperity, the strategy of victory, or the profession of science. Only the Germans themselves can effect this transformation, and they only if they can rid their minds of the "brooding omnipresence" of Karl Marx's and similar theoretical contradictions. This is the German problem. If Premier Khrushchev had had this in mind when he identified solution of the German problem as the key to world peace, he would have been right. But if he, and others on both sides of the Iron Curtain, persist in perceiving the problem of Germany as an equation in domestic and international power politics, then it is possible that the Marxian paradox will be resolved through a kind of violence far worse than that of the revolution which Dr. Karl Marx used to resolve the theoretical contradictions he perceived in the history "of all hitherto existing society."

Part Five

THE RUSSIAN POLITICAL SYSTEM

by Adam B. Ulam

"Accounting and control—that is the *main* thing required for the 'setting up' and correct functioning of the *first phase* of Communist society. *All* citizens are transformed into the salaried employees of the state, which consists of the armed workers. *All* citizens become employees and workers of a *single* national state 'syndicate.' All that is required is that they should work equally—do their proper share of work—and get paid equally. . . . The whole of society will have become a single office and a single factory, with equality of labour and equality of pay." Lenin, *The State and Revolution*, August 1917.[1]

"In every branch of industry, in every factory, in every department of a factory, there is a leading group of more or less skilled workers who must be first and foremost attached to production if we want to make sure of having a permanent staff of workers. . . . And how can we manage to attach them to the factory? It can be done by advancing them, by raising their wages, by introducing such a system of payment as will give the skilled worker his due. . . . *And so our task is to put an end to the instability of labour power, to abolish equalitarianism, to organize wages properly, and to improve the living conditions of the workers.*" J. V. Stalin, speech delivered in June 1931.[2]

---

[1] V. I. Lenin, *Selected Works*, Moscow, 1947, vol. II, p. 210.
[2] J. V. Stalin, *Leninism*, vol. II, pp. 430-431, New York, 1933.

[22]

The Origins of Soviet
Political Culture

When we speak of Soviet Russia (for it takes too long to say or write The Union of Soviet Socialist Republics), we underline the twofold character of the history and government of the communist state. There is Russia the builder and dominant part of the empire: "An unbreakable union of free republics was forged forever by the great Rus" proclaimed the first words of the Soviet national anthem adopted during the second World War.[1] The earlier ideological scruples were then fully displaced by proud glorification of Russia's past and the *Internationale* was no longer deemed suitable for the national anthem. And there is "Soviet," the term that brings to mind the complex of ideas and institutions having to do with Marx, Engels, and Lenin, with the Revolution of 1917, and with a movement that claims to be universal and supranational and has an ideology that claims to present a picture of the future of all of mankind.

Thus the political culture of the U.S.S.R. contains elements of the history of the state and nation that trace their beginnings to the tenth century A.D., yet at the same time it has the imprint of an ideology that has developed within the last century. The history of the Russian people and of Marxism-Leninism are the two major foundations of the Soviet political system.

How to assess their relative importance has been the major point of dispute among the commentators on Russian affairs and Russian historians

---

[1] The word *Rus* has been used traditionally to describe the medieval Russian state in contrast to its modern form: *Rossiya*.

themselves. Is Marxism merely a thin veneer for the latest manifestation of forces apparent throughout the course of Russian history, or is the communist regime a definite break with the historical tradition of Russia? The proponents of the first view have stressed the parallel between Soviet totalitarianism epitomized in Stalin and the high points of despotism and reform in Russian history found under Ivan the Terrible (1533-84) and Peter the Great (1682-1725). Even such characteristic institutions of Soviet Russia as the *kolkhoz* (the collective farm) are for them but a continuation of the old system of peasant tenancy—the *mir* of old Russia. The proponents of basic continuity of Russian history have not infrequently characterized the dictatorship of the Communist Party as the up-to-date expression of the traditional organization of Russian society where the sense of community and social union, often with religious undertones, has assertedly been prized above the "Western" values of personal freedom and individualism.

It has been pointed out with equal force that there is but a faint resemblance between modern totalitarianism and old despotism; that the *kolkhoz*, which is an attempt to apply the factory system to agriculture, has nothing to do with the *mir*; and that it is a gross oversimplification to take the relative absence of liberal and representative institutions in Russian history as an indication of something inherently undemocratic or collectivistic in the Russian national character. And indeed, though no revolution can destroy the accumulated weight of ten centuries of history, both Marxism and totalitarianism are modern phenomena. Russian history explains why they came to Russia, and the modifications they have undergone there. But neither Marxism nor totalitarianism are "typically" Russian. To understand them we must look at the social and economic forces that gave birth to the doctrine and have guided its growth and that of the most influential socialist movement.

Marxism

There has always been a feeling in some circles, both Marxist and non-Marxist, that the victory of a Marxist party in Russia was something of a historical "mistake." Marxism was born in the West. It is the product of political and economic conditions of Western society in the nineteenth century. By its own premises the doctrine of Karl Marx (1818-83) and Friedrich Engels (1820-95) was supposed to triumph in a fully industrialized society. How can one explain, then, the popularity of Marxism in pre-1917 Russia, and finally the victory of a Marxist party in a largely peasant economy undergoing but the intermediate stages of industrialization? Does it make any sense to talk about historical forces and the role of ideologies, or should we consider the prevalence of Marxism in pre-1917

Russia an intellectual fad, and the victory of the Bolsheviks in 1917 a historical accident?

What characterized Marxism in its beginning both as a theory and a political movement were three main elements: (1) an economic theory; (2) a philosophy of history; (3) a philosophy of revolution.

The economic doctrine is based on the famous labor theory of value. Capitalism, resting as it does upon private ownership of the means of production, is not only, or mainly, unjust, but primarily self-destructive. The capitalist's profit is considered an unjust extortion from the worker, who has the right to the total product, since labor is the only source of value. But far more important than the ethical aspect of the problem are its economic consequences: the inevitable exploitation of capitalism creates periodic and successively more severe crises of overproduction. Mature capitalism cannot but lead to increasing unemployment, increasing poverty of the masses, since in order to retain their profits the capitalists must keep depressing the level of wages. At the other end of the social scale this leads to increasing monopoly and concentration of the means of production in fewer and fewer hands. It was the economic aspect of their doctrine that led Marx and Engels to differentiate sharply between their own and other brands of socialism. The others, they held, pleaded for socialism on ethical or political grounds, while only Marxism saw that, quite apart from moral postulates and political conditions, socialism—the ownership of the means of production by the community—is the *inevitable* sequel of fully developed capitalism.

Marx and Engels produced their work at a period when it was widely believed, and not only among socialists, that the social sciences could have the validity and predictability of the natural sciences, and that the laws governing the development of society could be laid down with the rigor of physical laws. That conviction was likewise the basis of their philosophy of history and politics. "Scientific socialism" was built on the broad framework of economic determinism, which provided the main clue to the workings of history. Material factors, and more specifically the character and ownership of the principal means of production, constitute for the Marxist the master key of the social development of mankind. Hegelian dialectic and nineteenth-century materialism are joined in Marxism to provide the gigantic framework of history where, as their economic underpinnings change, civilizations develop, mature, and then collapse. The economic forces determining the content of history are then, themselves, triggered off by changes in science and technology. The industrial use of steam spells the final end of feudal society, where land was the principal means of production. Further inventions and the adoption of industrial techniques bring about the triumph of a new civilization and economic organization—capitalism. Yet *when fully developed,* capitalism is doomed by the same technological and economic forces that had predestined its success, and it must yield to a new way of life—socialism. Whatever its philosophical and political postulates, Marxism is unusually sensitive to and conscious of the development of science and technology. Its frame of mind is both historical and scientific.

The forces of history find their tangible embodiment in the social classes. Hence "the history of all hitherto existing society is the history of class struggles."[2] For the dominant class does not capitulate once its economic basis becomes less important and its political role obsolete. In Marx's lifetime the middle class in Western Europe, and especially in England and France, was winning political concessions from the landowning aristocracy and became the dominant political class in the state. The struggles for parliamentary and social reforms, for the ending of aristocratic privileges, and for civil rights were viewed by Marxism as mere reflections of the basic and immemorial class struggle—itself echoing the evolution of the forces of production. To Marx, the triumph of the middle class (which he witnessed and in a way applauded as rendered inevitable by the forces of history) was but a prelude to the ultimate class struggle between the bourgeoisie and the new class produced by the Industrial Revolution: the working proletariat.

The intricate combination of philosophical, historical, and economic arguments culminated in Marxism in a plea for political action. Even before its theoretical structure was fully complete, Marxism appeared in the *Communist Manifesto* (1848) as a philosophy of revolution. Though Marx considered as inevitable the eventual destruction of the capitalist system by the forces of history, he worked for and at times expected the imminent overthrow of capitalism by the workers. The language of the economist and philosopher is often subdued by the language of the politician and revolutionary who wants to give history a push. If the theoretical part of Marx's writings is flavored by one word: *inevitability*—the inevitability of the Marxian scheme of history, of forces dwarfing human efforts and making the downfall of capitalism certain—then the political side of his argument is colored by the word *exploitation:* the capitalists and industrialists are not mere agents of historical forces, but also malevolent oppressors and exploiters of the workers. The latter, once they gain the consciousness of their real situation, will smash decaying capitalism and its props, the state and organized religion.

Throughout his life the need for a revolution in which the working classes would seize the reins of the state remained for Marx an article of

---

[2] *The Communist Manifesto.*

faith. As to the character and methods of this revolution he did not remain of one mind. When the revolutionary excitement in Western Europe
began to subside after the forties and fifties of the nineteenth century,
Marx's revolutionary optimism subsided with it. At one point he was ready
to grant that in some highly industrialized countries with parliamentary
institutions revolution might come through non-violent and parliamentary
means; i.e., the working classes securing a majority in the parliaments of
their countries. After his death, his *alter ego*, Engels, was to go even
farther in the expectation of a peaceful transition to socialism. But the
most persistent element in original Marxism is its appeal for revolution
and its diffidence toward the institutions of the modern state, whether
parliamentary or judicial, as being based not on impartiality but on the
vested interests of the economically dominant class. Only when the workers capture the state will democracy and equality become a reality. Until
then they are for Marx but hypocritical phrases used by the bourgeoisie
to strengthen its political and economic oppression.

Any large-scale social doctrine is open to many interpretations. Translated into political action, it becomes, of necessity, detached from the
mere opinions of its author and his immediate disciples. Marxist parties,
and not only in Russia, have justified actions most inconsistent with one
another in the name of the same theory and the same body of writings.
Already in Marx's life economic and political facts were impinging upon
some of his principal theories and prophecies. It was a cardinal point of
Marx's theory that the growth of capitalism brings with it the inevitable
lowering of the standard of living and increasing unemployment for the
workers. Yet the second half of the nineteenth century, which saw the
flourishing of capitalism and industrialism in Western Europe, witnessed
also an undeniable increase in the material well-being of the masses. Along
with it came the widening of the parliamentary franchise, rudimentary
measures of social security, and the legalization of labor unions—measures
that Marx had held unlikely to be allowed by the bourgeois state. Socialist
parties, even when they adopted the "orthodox" Marxist program (as in
Germany) and refused to dilute it with liberalism, tacitly discarded Marx's
more revolutionary and undemocratic prescriptions. Marxism in Western
Europe appeared toward the end of the nineteenth century as merely a
radical expression of the cosmopolitan, democratic, and egalitarian tendencies of the era, capable of being absorbed into the mechanics of a constitutional state. It was as such, clothed in democratic and constitutional
phraseology, that it traveled into the economically and politically backward
regions of Eastern Europe.

Even a summary account of Marxism provides some clues as to what
made it so important to Russia, then a predominantly agrarian country,

and what caused Marxism *as a political movement* to be born in the context, not of a fully industrialized society and of democratic institutions, but of the initial stages of industrialization and of semi-feudal political institutions. Its revolutionary appeal echoed the discontent of the former peasant or artisan whom mysterious economic forces had deprived of his previous livelihood and had compelled to seek employment in industry. Here he found himself, even if better paid, without the security of his previous occupation, usually unprotected against sickness and accident, unprovided for in old age, and prohibited by the state and his employer from joining a labor union. Politically, the industrial worker was then without the right to vote, and it is logical that parliamentary institutions must have appeared to him merely as an arena of struggle between the middle and the upper classes. By the end of the neneteenth century the status and material conditions of the working class *in the West* presented a considerably different picture, and precluded a ready response to the revolutionary appeal of Marxism. But the Russia of 1900 was similar in some respects to the West of the 1840's and 1850's, so that Marxism, in its original revolutionary and conspiratorial form, could well take root in Russian soil.

A critical analysis of Marxism and of the validity of its postulates is not needed to perceive its twofold significance as a political movement: In a society undergoing the transition from the agricultural to the industrial order, Marxism offers the lower classes an effective and appealing exposition of their grievances and frustrations. It shares this characteristic with many other socialist and anarchist movements. But unlike the latter, Marxism does not urge blind opposition to the necessary phenomena of modern life: the state and industry. On the contrary, while it advocates the destruction of capitalism and the bourgeoisie by revolution, it also speaks of the inevitability and benevolent effects of both industrialism and the state after capitalism has been destroyed.[3] Marx's qualifications about the withering away of the state and about complete economic equality, both of them inconsistent with modern industrial society, were to provide a useful rationalization to Stalin when he was building his totalitarian state and grossly inegalitarian society. But without burdening Marxism with the full responsibility for totalitarianism, it is clear that

---

[3] Though Marx believes, as do the Anarchists, that the state should wither away, the practical consequences of this notion are nullified by his admission that victorious socialism will need the state, for a while, and a powerful centralized state at that, owner of all the means of production. A similar admission takes most of the strength out of Marxism's message of egalitarianism: complete equality cannot be achieved immediately after the victory of socialism and destruction of capitalism. Only communism, the final stage of socialism—the time schedule is again not specified—will realize the slogan "from each according to his ability, to each according to his needs."

Marxism has considerable tactical advantages over other forms of socialism and radicalism. In a society where the mass of inhabitants are denied the right of participation in politics, and where the birth pangs of industrialism are in evidence, Marxism appeals both to the past, in denouncing the evils of factory discipline and the wage system, and to the future, in promising that in a socialist society industrialism will bring with it democracy and abundance.

Russian Traditions

That Russian history is in some sense "different," that it does not fit into the categories employed for other countries, has been the assumption of many writers, Russian and non-Russian, conservative and socialist. To the nineteenth-century historian with a liberal bias, history meant steady progress from despotism and superstition to democracy and enlightenment. Since Russia did not appear to conform to the pattern, Russian history had to be qualitatively different from that of the West. Today we no longer share the optimism that made such overgeneralizations possible. Nor do we believe in the notion that every country has its own "genius" and historical mission imprinted in the unique character of its political institutions. That Russian history *is* different from that of the West is due not to the "Russian soul" or to the presence of factors absent elsewhere, but to the same social and economic forces found in the West, but appearing in Russia at different times and with different intensity.

We should not minimize the importance of the most obvious differences: a religion accepted from Constantinople rather than Rome, and a Church and society that had undergone neither the Renaissance nor the Reformation; a social system in which the mass of the peasants was not emancipated from serfdom until 1861, long after Western Europe; and the relative absence or fragility of representative institutions and of an independent judiciary. But we need not resort to mysticism or the exaggerated theory of the uniqueness of the Russian national character to explain the heritage of Russian history that the Soviets took over in 1917. The analytical apparatus of the social sciences is quite adequate for that purpose.

The most striking characteristics of Russian society on the eve of the revolutions of the twentieth century were: centralization and the autocratic character of political authority; a social structure in which the mass of the freshly emancipated peasantry was still under severe economic and political restrictions and the middle class far weaker than and different in character from its Western European counterpart; and the rudimentary character of institutions of political and economic representation. The sources of these "peculiarities" that leave an undeniable imprint on today's Soviet institutions can be found in Russian history. Let us therefore spotlight some problems in the development of Russia and examine how the social and political forces that agitated the rest of Europe made their appearance in Russia.

CENTRALIZATION OF POLITICAL AUTHORITY AND THE AUTOCRATIC TRADITION

In the West the principal beginnings of the modern state date from the Renaissance. Every student of history knows how the Tudor monarchy in England and figures such as Louis XI and Richelieu in France strove to overcome the heritage of feudalism and dispersion. The necessary elements of a modern state—a sense of national unity and centralization of political authority with the attendant institutions of the bureaucracy and the standing army—began to emerge only slowly and painfully toward the end of the Middle Ages. Roughly at the same time the task of state- and nation-building also confronted Russia but under vastly different conditions.

Ever since its recorded beginnings in the tenth century, the Russian state struggled for survival and expansion against its neighboring Finnish- and Turkish-speaking tribes and states. After the Mongol invasions, the most notable setback in this struggle resulted in the subjugation of most of the country to the Tartars. For two centuries (from the middle of the thirteenth to the middle of the fifteenth century) most of Russia was isolated from the rest of Europe, with her previous and quite extensive commercial and cultural intercourse almost entirely interrupted, and her princes reduced to Tartar vassals and tribute collectors. Only in the fifteenth and sixteenth centuries did modern Russia begin to take shape, around the nucleus of the Grand Duchy of Moscow. This building of a state took place under conditions that, much more than in the West, facilitated, if not demanded, the erection of a strong and despotic monarchical authority. There was continuous warfare with the Tartars and sporadic wars with Russia's northern and western neighbors: Sweden and the kingdom of Poland-Lithuania, which contained extensive Russian-speaking lands. It is no wonder that even in sixteenth-century Europe, where absolute monarchy was the rule, the government of the Russian tsars epitomized in the reign of Ivan the Terrible became the byword for despotism.

In the West the Middle Ages had bequeathed to the Renaissance states social and political institutions that, centuries later, became the bases on which constitutionalism and representative institutions could, and did, grow. Such institutions were not unknown in medieval Russia. The monarchy was counterpoised by the Church with the Metropolitan of Moscow, later on the Patriarch, as its head. The Estates and Diets of the rest of Europe were paralleled by the Russian Assembly of the Land, and the Council of the Magnates. Even the rising middle class, in Western Europe the fermenting element of the social and political change, found its counterpart in the merchant republics of Novgorod and Pskov, which acknowledged but nominal sovereignty of the prince. But in Russia these institutions were considerably weaker and lacked a wide enough social basis. They were eliminated (as in the loss of autonomy by Novgorod and Pskov), or subjugated through terror and economic sanctions by Ivan III (1462-1505) and Ivan the Terrible (1533-84). The latter's reign is not atypical of certain other great periods of Russian history: though he was a great social and political reformer and the military leader who finally destroyed the Tartar power, his reign abounds in instances of violent and systematic terror. It is a pattern to be found again in Peter the Great and Stalin, and one that is not entirely absent from the reigns of the great state builders in the West—Louis XI in France and Henry VIII in England.

Ivan's reign, with its centralization and despotism, was followed, again not atypically, by a period of reassertion by the nobles, internal anarchy, and foreign invasions. Early in the seventeenth century it appeared as if Russia were to be joined to her western neighbor, the Polish-Lithuanian state. It was at that point that something approaching modern nationalism was born in Russia. A wave of popular feeling, largely religious in its foundations, since the rival Polish monarchy was Catholic, established the Romanov dynasty in Russia and preserved the independence of the country. The inheritance of a prolonged national or religious struggle is likely to be an exaggerated and parochial sense of nationalism. The struggle against the Poles erected the autocracy and Orthodoxy into national symbols, and strengthened the isolation from the political and cultural currents from the West.

It fell to Peter the Great (1682-1725) to modernize the Russian monarchy, but also to clamp tighter the shackles of absolutism. One aspect of his reforms was to impose the externals of Western civilization upon his subjects, symbolic of which was the enforced shaving of beards by the nobility. Modern industry and technology were imported into Russia, not through the action of private citizens, but by the state. In one reign, Russia, a backward and ignored country, became a major power and a member of the European community of states—a historical development unparalleled until the rise of Japan in the late nineteenth century. Peter's reforms, however, also resulted in the destruction of the still existing social and political particularisms, and, consequently, in the strengthening of the principle of autocracy. The Church was deprived of the Patriarch and subjected to a lay official appointed by the emperor. Noblemen's privileges were made dependent on their direct service to the state, and the nobility, as a class, was amalgamated with a bureaucratic caste. Violent repression followed the slightest sign of semi-feudal or religious (one is tempted to say "counterrevolutionary") reaction against the reforms. Serfdom remained the main prop of the economy, and the gap between the upper classes, forcibly westernized and educated, and the mass of the people, became wider.

In a sense the pattern established under Peter has characterized Russian history during the past two centuries and its traces are evident under the Soviet regime: the state became the main planner and executor of social and economic policy. In the West a similar situation prevailed during the heyday of mercantilism in the seventeenth and eighteenth centuries, but it was drastically changed in the nineteenth century when the social classes developed stronger viewpoints and pressures of their own. As compared with western European countries, a sharp contrast marks Russia's development down to our own times. Russia was now in the forefront of the European community of nations. From Peter's time onward her upper classes participated in the most advanced European intellectual and political currents. Yet the mass of the people were left far behind. Revolutionary outbreaks, in which seventeenth- and eighteenth-century Russia abounds, are like medieval risings and *jacqueries*, sporadic outbreaks of disgruntled nobles or oppressed peasants or Cossacks, rather than modern revolutionary movements with their specific political and economic postulates.

The principle of autocracy, now embellished with the latest bureaucratic techniques, remained unimpaired throughout the reign of Catherine the Great (1762-96). Contacts with Europe increased and indeed the partitions of Poland brought Russia much farther West. But if Catherine and her advisers thought of modernizing the state, they thought so in terms of the enlightened absolutism of the century, which sought to increase education and efficiency but neither decentralization nor the subjects' rights. The French-speaking and Westernized nobility was tied more firmly to the throne by economic and social concessions, but any half-hearted attempts at basic social reforms were defeated by the fears arising from the outbreak of the French Revolution.

Only at the beginning of the nineteenth century was the possibility of modern representative assemblies first discussed by the Russian government. This brief era of liberalism under Alexander I and his minister, Speransky, was succeeded by a period of reaction and the fundamental parts of the latter's constitutional proposals were shelved. At the end of the Napoleonic wars the empire was increased by the addition of Finland

and a part of Poland. In these areas the tsar was a constitutional monarch and representative institutions functioned while he remained the Autocrat of a Russia that did not possess anything remotely resembling a parliament!

The reign of Nicholas I (1825-55) began with the first modern revolutionary attempt. The Decembrists of 1825, who failed in an armed *putsch*, were composed mostly of young aristocrats and army officers. They had some constitutional and reformist notions gathered from the West and they stand at the beginning of the great Russian revolutionary tradition. Their abortive attempt provided the justification for a new technique and routine of repression. The Russia of Nicholas I became an autocracy in which the passivity of the citizen was no longer taken for granted. The police state, with its administrative judgments, its secret police, and its all-embracing censorship, became the means through which the tsarist bureaucracy strove to preserve the *status quo* and to repress the social and intellectual ferment. The tsarist state under Nicholas considered itself, and was so considered by Europe, as the bulwark of absolutism. The Polish uprising of 1830-31 was put down by arms and Poland's constitutional privileges abrogated. A Russian army helped the Austrian emperor to put down the Hungarian rebellion of 1848-49. In contrast with a Europe bustling with democratic movements and liberal reforms, Russia stood as the fortress of militarism and of national and social oppression, a seeming exception to all the rules of historical development as propounded by liberalism.

A cursory look at Russian history reinforces one's first impression of the passivity of the population and the consequent ability of the government to exercise absolute and at times tyrannical power. The revolutionary movement of the second half of the nineteenth century, though now almost continuous and punctuated by violent incidents, such as the assassination of Alexander II in 1881, was the work of small groups drawn for the most part from the thin layer of the educated and upper classes. At the end of the nineteenth century, just as at its beginning, Russia was an autocracy. The reforms of Alexander II supplied the rudiments of local government and judicial independence, but they did not affect the reality of the police state and the absence of civil rights. Into this society, politically static but in an economic and social revolution, came Marxism.

The Social Structure and Representative Institutions

Russia's political development becomes intelligible only in terms of her social history, the main characteristics of which are familiar in the history of the West, though the parallel development stops at a certain point. Social classes and their status became frozen in Russia and it was only the coming of the Industrial Revolution in the second half of the nineteenth century that propelled society forward at a feverish speed, ultimately creating a political crisis. An oversimplified explanation, not without elements of truth, would run in a circle: society was weak in Russia because the government was strong; the government could be so strong and oppressive because society was so weak. The actual story is more complicated.

Economic conditions peculiar to eastern Europe made Russia lag in her commercial and industrial development. By the same token, the structure of Russian agrarian society relied on serfdom. A great majority of the cultivators of the soil—hence a majority of the population—were unfree: they belonged to the state or to the landlords. These serfs, besides working their own land, had to work for their masters. The latter had a variety of powers over their peasants amounting almost to that of life and death. In direct opposition to what happened in the West, the legal status of the Russian peasant had deteriorated since the Middle Ages. The building of modern Russia that took place in the eighteenth century did not lead, as one might have expected, to the destruction or alleviation of serfdom. On the contrary, the submission of the nobility to the new autocratic system was won not only through force but also through concessions, at the expense of the peasants. The alliance of the government and the nobility made serfdom far more rigid and the powers of the landlords more extensive. A Russian landowner of the eighteenth century, and indeed until 1861, could whip his serfs, send them into the army (where until 1874 the term of service was twenty-five years) or, in extreme cases, into exile to Siberia. He was not allowed, at least in theory, to ruin them economically or to evict them from their land, as could be done to the tenant farmers in England or Ireland. In short, the lack of rights was mitigated by an extremely low but still real form of economic security, a situation that was to recur in Russian history.

Serfdom and its consequences were the central facts of tsarist Russia's politics and economics, just as the collectivized agriculture of the U.S.S.R. constitutes the main dilemma of the Communist regime. Largely because of serfdom, the nobility remained an obedient tool of the government and could not assume an independent posture toward the throne. It made social mobility almost impossible and hampered commercial and industrial progress. Last but not least, in an age of nationalism as well as liberalism, serfdom was felt to be, and was, a derogation of human dignity, an institution that set a majority of Russians apart from the national community. Yet the government could not bring itself to abolish the institution on which the whole social order was grounded, and the destruction of which might threaten the survival of autocracy.

It was as much the pressure of economic forces as a deliberate decision of the government that led to the Emancipation Edict of 1861. The action of the government of Alexander II was greeted at first with enthusiasm, and was considered, even by some of the political exiles, as a rebirth of Russia. Yet the manner of emancipation was to have grave results for Russian society.

Economically, the result of emancipation was far from being satisfactory to the peasant. The government took all too great care to protect the landlords. The peasants were given land, but in many places not even all the land that they had held as serfs. The government paid off the landlords, while the peasants were to be weighed down for years with redemption dues to the state. But the main point of grievance was to remain the scarcity of land and the peasants' feeling that somehow they had been cheated because so much land remained in the hands of the landlords. The impact of the industrial age was already felt in Russia through a prodigious growth in population. Even with the growth of industry, and with mass migrations to the new lands in Asiatic Russia, the need and hunger for land was deeply felt among the peasant masses.

Politically and socially, the Act of 1861 preserved some of the features of the old village system: a decision endowed with far-reaching consequences. We may be justified in using a twentieth-century term and speak of "nationalization" of the peasants rather than of "emancipation." For the reform of 1861 did not give them full civic and social rights but made them more directly wards of the government. Equally important, the old form of village organization, the *mir*, was preserved and even strengthened. The *mir* was a form of communal self-government that exercised a variety of economic as well as judicial decisions although in tsarist Russia its more important decisions were naturally guided, first by the landlord and then by the government agent. The *mir* collected taxes, sent recruits to the army, judged minor disputes, etc. But in addition it periodically redistributed the land of the peasants, decided on the character and methods of cultivation, and in general acted as the joint possessor of both the land and labor of its members. To a conservative the *mir* appeared as the bulwark of old Russia, which preserved the peasant in his "native" customs and allegiances and saved him from the contamination of modern ideas. But even some of the revolutionaries thought of the institution as a Russian form of socialism and democracy that should be preserved. Karl Marx said in a weak moment that the *mir* could enable Russia to pass into socialism without undergoing the full rigors of capitalism.

The truth is that the *mir* had nothing to do with democracy or socialism, certainly Marxian socialism, as the terms are properly understood. It was an institution at once egalitarian and conservative, but in both senses running against the tendencies of modern times. It was certainly different from the *kolkhoz*, the collective farm, imposed by Stalin, which is based on the application of industrial factory methods to agriculture. The *mir* prevented the application of better agricultural methods and inhibited the development of enterprise among its members. It hampered social mobility and the growth of an enlightened farmer class. It was, in brief, a powerful anti-industrial influence and hence not only anti-capitalist but also anti-socialist in spirit. Its preservation in 1861 for reasons of expediency and conservative ideology did not help the regime but was bound to prevent the rise of a strong middle class such as both enlightened conservatism and liberalism require. It was only a few years before the first World War that the tsarist regime made a resolute attempt to remedy the mistakes of 1861. On the initiative of Peter Stolypin, the ablest social statesman of prewar Russia, the peasants were enabled and encouraged to break up the *mir* and to develop into individual farmers. But the war interrupted what would have been the building of a peasant middle class.

The imperfect emancipation of 1861 was but one of the measures by which the government belatedly recognized that an economic and social revolution was going on in Europe and that Russia could not escape its effects. The lament of a provincial governor is characteristic: the building of railways is dangerous to established institutions, because railways enable people to travel and travel in turn exposes them to subversive ideas! Railways, however, had to be built, and with them came manufacturing and banking and other disturbing paraphernalia of progress. The growth of the middle class never caught up with the advances in industry and commerce. Russia entered the Industrial Revolution during its more advanced stage. The average size of a manufacturing or commercial unit was much greater than during a corresponding period of the industrial development of the West. Hence there was very little in the country in the way of the self-made small and medium manufacturers of France and England. Rather, the Russian middle class of the late nineteenth century had an educational and intellectual status and was composed mainly of members of the liberal professions and of the middle and lower bureaucracy. The intelligentsia was unusually susceptible to the intellectual currents and political ideas of the West. Their frustrated thirst for political activity often found its expression in literature and journalism, which flourished both at home and in exile.

To the growing social aspirations of its educated classes the tsarist government, even in the reforming period of Alexander II, offered but half measures of reform. The jury system and a very limited scheme of local self-government, in the country (*zemstvos*) and cities, heavily weighted in favor of the propertied classes, were substantial advances over the past but insignificant when compared even with recent reforms in the former fellow autocracies of Austria-Hungary and Prussia. Instead of becoming a safety valve, Alexander's reforms stimulated the pressure for more basic reforms. The latter half of his reign (from the late sixties to 1881) was full of revolutionary activity and violent repression. The revolutionary movement was as yet the work of small groups, but it reflected the discontent of several sections of society. Western anarchist and socialist ideas, which in the West had become tamed or insignificant, were being adopted in Russia in their original revolutionary and violent character. When Alexander II fell to the last of several attempts on his life by the revolutionary group called the People's Will, his assassins included a man of peasant antecedents, the daughter of a high tsarist official, a scientist, a Pole, and a Jew. The composition of the group symbolized the diversity of revolutionary premises within the Russian Empire.

It is useful to insert a note of caution: Because the Revolution came in 1917 we tend to think of many preceding years as being years solely of oppression on one side and of revolutionary strivings on the other. A more balanced view would take into account the strength of the nationalist and conservative tradition in nineteenth-century Russia, and popular attachment to the tsar and the Orthodox Church as the symbols of Russian nationhood. The century was also the period of the great flowering of Russian culture, which, in literature, music, and even the sciences, made imperishable contributions to European civilization.

Once Russia entered the industrial race the growth of her economy was rapid indeed. The *rate of growth* of Russia's industry between 1890 and 1914 does not compare unfavorably with that of the U.S.A. for the same period. Perhaps the total picture points up one of the "contradictions" of which the Marxists love to speak: a vigorous and growing society and economy shackled by obsolete political forms. But even in politics the picture is not of one color. After 1905 Russia had a degree of constitutionalism. Her parliament (*Duma*) was neither democratically elected nor very effective, but it provided the promise of political progress. Censorship was relaxed. The lot of political prisoners, while still grim, was considerably better after 1905 than it was to be in Stalin's Russia. In the Constitutional Democrats (*Kadets*) liberalism was the most potent influence among Russia's educated classes.

In brief, the coming and popularity of Marxism in Russia are explicable in terms of historical and social forces, but the Revolution of 1917 and the triumph of the Bolsheviks are as much if not more the result of a fortuitous arrangement of events and personalities.

[23]

The Origins of the Soviet
Pattern of Power

The history of the Soviet state begins, paradoxically, nineteen years before the Revolution. For it was in 1898 at a meeting in Minsk that a handful of delegates organized the Russian Social-Democratic Party, out of which grew the Bolsheviks—the Communist Party of our day. The years of clandestine activity, of conspiracy against tsarism, and of internal strife that characterized the growth of Bolshevism left their indelible imprint on the state the Party created. Hence the "prenatal" period of the U.S.S.R. and with it the habits of thought and action the Bolsheviks acquired before their coming to power, are of much more than academic interest. The Marxism that has stamped its imprint upon the minds of millions of Soviet citizens is not the Marxism of Marx. Much as Soviet ideology today owes to Marx, it owes perhaps even more to the powerful genius of Lenin, who boldly interpreted, altered, and distorted the original doctrine. In so doing he not only dictated the tactics of the revolutionary movement in Russia, but also formulated the political values and beliefs upon which the Soviet dictatorship was founded and in large measure still rests. To follow the fortunes of the tiny handful of conspirators that he led is to witness the emergence in embryo of most of the essential ideals, structures, and practices of the massive Soviet state of today.

Marxism in Russia

The genealogy of Russian Marxism runs back at least to the small groups of revolutionaries who fought and conspired against tsarism during the last decade of Alexander II's reign. In 1879 the most notable of these groups, the People's Will, split into two factions. One of them conducted a campaign of terror that culminated in the assassination of the tsar in 1881. The other, the so-called Black Partition, under the leadership of George Plekhanov, abandoned terrorism and became the nucleus of the Marxist movement in Russia. The original People's Will, like its predecessor the Land and Freedom group, had but a vague populistic ideology that did not go much beyond a plea to summon a constitutional assembly for Russia. Though socialistic in character, the ideology of the group centered upon the peasant and paid but scant attention to the rising industrial proletariat. The People's Will perished in the wave of repression that followed the assassination of the tsar, though some of its ideas and terrorist tendencies were reborn shortly after the turn of the century in the Social Revolutionary Party. Black Partition, on the other hand, became the progenitor of Liberation of Labor, the first Russian Marxist group, formed in 1883 by Plekhanov, Paul Axelrod, and Leo Deutsch. In a series of books Plekhanov laid the foundations of theoretical Marxism in Russia. Thus from the beginning the attitude of the Marxists toward populism, indeed toward the peasant, was an ambivalent one. Marxism in Russia sprang up from a *narodnik* (populist) movement, and inherited some of the latter's conspiratorial flavor as well as a preoccupation with the peasant. On the other hand, the separation from Black Partition meant that Plekhanov and some others felt that conspiring was not enough and that the vague, partly sentimental and partly utopian, philosophy of populism had to be replaced with the systematic philosophy of history and economics of Marxism. While recognizing the revolutionary potentialities of the peasant problem, the Marxists came to feel that the *active element* in a revolution would be provided by the rising working class, and not by the discontented but dispersed and basically conservative peasantry. As we have seen, Russia in the eighties and nineties of the last century was a rapidly industrializing country. Since Russia had entered the industrial race later, her industry was of the new large-unit type, which created large conglomerations of workers in the main cities of the empire. Thus Moscow, St. Petersburg (today's Leningrad), Warsaw, and Lodz in Russian Poland, Baku in the Caucasus, and others became highly industrialized, and these large concentrations of workers of many nationalities provided fruitful ground for revolutionary propaganda.

Little circles of mostly young intellectuals, some of them university and high-school students, were the first to absorb, and then spread, Marxian propaganda. The oppressive intellectual atmosphere of Russia in the nineties, with its censorship and suppression of all political activity on the part of students, merely increased resentment among young people and led them to search for a revolutionary solution. Marx's doctrine, with its intellectual intricacies, its comprehensive scope and theological flavor, was the very thing to appeal to young intellectuals living in revolt against their society. They in turn carried a simplified version of Marxism to the workers, who, scantily protected by the state and forbidden to form unions, were equally responsive to the revolutionary call. In contrast to populism Russian Marxism did not rely on terrorism nor did it expect a sudden and dramatic reversal in the government and society. Its propaganda was of a long-range nature. It worked through discussion and persuasion; it stressed the need of organization, teaching that the struggle, though it would be long and arduous, was bound to end in victory, because the forces of history were on its side. Economic distress and political persecution combined to create a wave of strikes in 1895-98 and they in turn increased the influence of the socialists among the workers.

The foundation of the Social-Democratic Party in 1898 was an attempt to unite the different strains of Marxism within the Russian Empire. The new party was to house not only the various shades of socialism but the Marxist groups based on nationality associations such as the Jewish Bund and various socialist groups in Russian Poland, the Caucasus, etc. The very diversity of the elements the Party was attempting to hold together augured from the outset that its internal life was to be one of ideological and tactical quarrels, of schisms, divisions, and expulsions. There arose a situation quite paradoxical at first glance, and yet common among ideological and revolutionary parties: a group of conspirators pitted against a powerful state was so rent by discords and quarrels that the various factions at times tended to make their struggle against the autocracy secondary to their internecine quarrels. What became known as Bolshevism emerged from two such struggles within the Party: one over the issue of the meaning of Marxism in Russian society; the other over the character and organization of the Marxist party.

Orthodox Marxist doctrine held that as capitalism progresses the working class will organize itself *spontaneously* and the workers will acquire the class viewpoint, that is, will realize the necessity and inevitability of putting an end to capitalism. Drawing upon this interpretation of Marxism, a group of Russian socialists, who were to become known as "Economists," held that the primary task of the socialist party in Russia should be to operate not on the political but on the economic plane. Trade unions, not conspiracies, should be the weapons with which to fight for the immediate *material* interests of the workers: better pay, shorter working hours, the legal right to organize, and social security. Inherent in the position of the Economists were two assumptions: First, that Russia was as yet unprepared for socialism, as she was just entering the capitalist stage of development.

They interpreted Marxism as meaning that a fairly long capitalist development, with the state dominated by the middle class and parliamentarianism, must precede any successful attempt to set up socialism.

The second assumption of the Economists was equally repugnant to revolutionary socialists. In line with the ideas then prevailing among Western socialists,[1] they appeared to hold that the very logic of economic and social development would bring about democracy and then socialism, and that revolutionary activity was consequently unnecessary, if not harmful. Industrialization and social pressures would first temper, and ultimately abolish, the barbarities of Russian tsarism. The road to socialism lay through peaceful organization and education and not through coups d'état.

Had the ideas of the Economists prevailed and become basic to Russian socialism, it would have followed the democratic and evolutionary path of many socialist parties in western Europe and elsewhere. But as a matter of fact, the Economists, though influential among the intelligentsia, were soon to find themselves outside the pale of the Social-Democratic Party, and their subsequent story belongs to the history of Russian liberalism rather than to that of socialism. The reasons for their defeat were fairly obvious. In the first place Russian autocracy was not willing, at least not until after the Revolution of 1905, to allow any political activity even of the most moderate kind. The tsarist bureaucracy was also blind enough to prohibit independent labor unions, and to hesitate long before extending the most rudimentary type of protection to the worker. The soil of parliamentarianism, social legislation, and progress in which democratic socialism could grow, simply did not exist in Russia at the time, and even after 1905 there was to be but little opportunity for free political and professional life.

The answer of the revolutionary wing of the Party to the Economists was uncompromisingly hostile. The great authority of the founder of Russian Marxism, Plekhanov, was thrown against them. The future Bolsheviks and Mensheviks combined in denouncing the Economists as traitors to Marxism. And it was in this polemic that Vladimir Ilich Lenin laid the theoretical foundations of the Soviet version of Marxism.

In 1902 Lenin was but thirty-two, already a veteran revolutionary, his membership in the socialist circles dating from the early 1890's, and his career having included a period of exile in Siberia. Since he came from an intellectual middle-class family one of whose members (his elder brother) was executed for participation in a plot against Tsar Alexander III, his choice of the life of a revolutionary was neither atypical nor dif-

---

[1] Best illustrated in the writings of the Fabians in England, and of Eduard Bernstein and other Revisionists in Germany.

ficult to understand. It was the reading of Plekhanov that had drawn him toward Marxism. He had already established himself as a theoretician, and in 1900, with Plekhanov and others, he began to edit in exile the Social-Democratic paper *Iskra* (Spark). In 1902 Lenin came out with *What Is To Be Done?*, probably his most important work, fundamental to the understanding of the history of the Bolshevik Party and the Communist state.

What Is To Be Done? was a pamphlet addressed to the current problems of the Social-Democratic Party, which was at that time, we must repeat, a small group of revolutionaries, partly in Russia, partly in exile. Neither their most pessimistic enemies nor they themselves would have dreamed that this group would grow in the course of one generation into a party of millions and into the absolute master of a vast state. Yet the argument and the flavor of *What Is To Be Done?* have remained imbedded in the values and beliefs of the Soviet system. They are evident in the pronouncements of Khrushchev as they were in those of Stalin and Lenin.

First, the flavor and tone of the book. We are struck by its *dogmatism*. The theory of Marxism is not to be trifled with. The use of Marx's writings as if they were infallible scriptures, the heavy pedantic tone, and the vituperation of those who would dilute or modify Marx (i.e., those who disagreed with Lenin's interpretation of the master) are already in evidence. We can already see in the book the *undemocratic* temperament that Lenin was to implant in the movement. When he wrote it Lenin was officially and by conviction a Social-Democrat, i.e., his socialism was coupled with the belief in and postulates of democratic institutions. But temperamentally he was opposed to the premises of democracy: in particular its rationalism, which teaches that the mass of people are capable of seeing and resolving the main issues of politics; and its humanitarianism, which holds that human values and feelings should not be sacrificed too readily even at the altar of social and economic progress.

The argument of the book revolves about the concept and the role of the Party. In a remarkable passage in which he attacks the main theses of the Economists, Lenin lays the foundations of Bolshevism. The masses, if left to themselves, he argues, cannot acquire the proper class consciousness or work out a revolution. They must be led by a body of professional revolutionaries. In fact, Lenin is quite ready to reinterpret Marx, while claiming, of course, that he is merely following the letter of the doctrine. Marx had assumed that class consciousness comes to the workers in the course of their economic struggle with the capitalists. But, says Lenin, *spontaneously* the workers will develop only *trade union consciousness*, i.e., the desire to improve their economic conditions, to legalize their organizations, and to secure other material and status concessions. To rely on the spontaneous growth of class feeling among workers, as the Economists would have done, is to abandon the hope for revolution, the hope for socialism, and to resign oneself—though Lenin does not say it in so many words—to a slow *evolutionary* development toward something which, though an improvement on autocracy, will be neither socialism nor Marxism. The first task of revolutionary socialism, therefore, must be the creation of a disciplined party of professional revolutionaries who will instill revolutionary consciousness into the masses. This party cannot be a debating society or a party on the Western model, but must possess a conspiratorial as well as legal organization. Lenin's concept of the Party—that of a quasi-religious order of conspirators devoted to revolution—harks back to the traditions of revolutionary groups of Russian populists. Thus the tradition of a conspiratorial group ready to undertake a coup d'état was linked with the doctrine of Marx—the mixture that constitutes Bolshevism.

What Lenin had to say about the composition of his ideal revolutionary party has likewise been imprinted on the history of the Communist movement, not only in Russia but elsewhere. The workers constitute the best material for the membership, not only because of the reasons Marxism traditionally gives, but also because their very mode of life—the routine of the factory—accustoms them to discipline and organization. Thus they make good soldiers of revolution. Yet the class origin, Lenin implies, is of secondary importance as a qualification for the revolutionary. A socialist party devoted to the cause of revolution must send its detachments into every segment and class of society. Intellectuals as a rule may be too individualistic and opportunistic to submerge themselves in a group, but, by the same token, they have the necessary intellectual tools for conducting revolutionary propaganda. In a sense a revolutionary party must disregard the class origin of its members and must look to the qualities of mind and will, and the capacity for obedience.

In short, the recipe is for a centralized hierarchical and conspiratorial organization whose highest organs will lay down not only organizational directives, but the doctrine as well. To repeat: this is not a political party in the Western sense of the word, not even in the sense in which the contemporary German and French Socialists were parties, but a quasi-religious, almost military, order of revolutionaries. The notion of *elitism*, of subordination of the mass of members to a small directorate, is clearly here. Marxism, born in the era of rationalism, receives in Lenin's hands a definitely irrationalist twist. If the majority of the people cannot see clearly their real interest, i.e., the necessity of revolution, but have to be propagandized and shown the path, does it not follow that the mass of mankind will always have to listen to the dictates of a few? Such a conclusion is not spelled out by Lenin but it is inherent in the argument of *What Is To Be Done?*

In its totalitarian intolerance of differences of opinion, in its anti-democratic contempt for the capacities of the masses and its stress on disciplined obedience to an elite, Lenin's pamphlet formulated the conception of authority that was to triumph in the Soviet dictatorship. This conception defined the role of the Communist Party in relation to the rest of society, endowing it with the unquestioned right to govern. At the same time it also set the movement on its way to a centralization of authority in the top leadership of the Party itself, unchecked by any effective participation from below. This is not to say that Lenin had already conceived the dictatorship of Stalin. There were still traces of democracy and freedom within the Party, if not in the Party's relation to the masses. In time these remnants of liberalism were eliminated from the structure of Soviet absolutism. Still, for the house that Stalin built, Lenin laid the foundation well.

The Bolsheviks before November

The Second Congress of the Russian Social-Democratic Party, which met in 1903 in Brussels and then in London (after the Belgian police drove the delegates out), was the decisive turning point in the history of Russian Marxism. The Economists had for the most part been defeated or had left the Party. The splits that appeared at the Brussels Congress were, thus, between various branches of *revolutionary socialists*. The most notable among them was the controversy and the division between the Mensheviks and the Bolsheviks. These names, meaning respectively "Minoritarians" and "Majoritarians," do not convey accurately what happened at the Congress, for on some issues the Bolsheviks, led by Lenin, were in a minority. So, for example, the definition of a Party member followed the Menshevik draft rather than that of the Bolsheviks. Lenin wanted the Party membership restricted to those who were *actively* participating in the political and conspiratorial work. His Menshevik opponent, Martov, sponsored a slightly different phrase that would have allowed sympathizers as well as activists to enroll in the organization, and he carried the day. On some other issues, notably on the personnel of the Central Committee and the Party organ (*Iskra*), the Bolsheviks, supported by Plekhanov, prevailed, but only after some of their opponents had walked out and refused to participate in the balloting.

It should be kept in mind that in view of conditions then prevalent in Russia, it had not been possible for the delegates to the Party Congress to be elected in any regular and orderly fashion. The Congress that produced the Party program and crystallized the two main tendencies of

Russian Marxism was composed of the revolutionaries who happened to be abroad at the time or who had been able to smuggle themselves out of the country. The basic split in the Party between the Bolsheviks and the Mensheviks was to persist until 1912 when the former declared themselves a separate Party.[2] It is difficult to give a simple reason for the split: the causes are not exhausted either by the ideological differences or by the personalities involved. Thus it would be erroneous to assume that the Mensheviks were, as a body and on every issue, less radical than the Bolsheviks, or less prone to a revolutionary action. It is by and large correct to say that the Bolshevik faction was Lenin's group and that he dominated it to an extent not even approximated by any single leader within the Menshevik group. Thus Lenin's dictatorial ways led to an early split with Plekhanov, who soon joined the Mensheviks, thereby isolating Lenin on the editorial board of the *Iskra*. Many other prominent socialists, some of whom were to rejoin the Bolsheviks in 1917, became estranged from them in the pre-Revolution days simply because they felt that the Party was unduly dominated by one man.[3] In fact, it was being said among the European socialists that Lenin was ruining the cause of Russian Marxism, and that his personal ambition and vindictiveness would destroy Social Democracy in the empire. Yet it should be kept in mind that *prior* to the victory of Bolshevism in November 1917 Lenin did not have at his disposal any instruments of coercive power, and if a sizable body of Marxists followed him both inside Russia and in exile, it must have been because his arguments appealed to them. It would not be far wrong to discern two opposing temperaments in the camp of pre-Revolution Russian Marxism: on the one hand, the Bolsheviks, more akin to the old populist groups in their revolutionary impatience, less democratically minded and more prone to divest Marxism of its elements of humanism and rationalism; on the other hand the Mensheviks, who were closer in spirit to their Western colleagues—revolution in their minds did not take an absolute priority over democracy.

We have to keep in mind that such judgments are really based on hindsight. It was in 1917 and afterward that the full extent of anti-democratic tendencies lurking in Bolshevism was exposed. Prior to the Revolution neither of the two Marxist groups appeared as dangerous and radical, either to the government or to the upper classes, as did the Social Revolutionary party, the inheritor of the populist tradition. One branch of the Social Revolutionary Party conducted a systematic terroristic campaign against

---

[2] Though on many issues, especially within Russia, the two factions continued to collaborate until the Revolution.
[3] The outstanding example is Leon Trotsky.

the government and several high officials fell prey to assassination.[4] The Social Revolutionaries, though led by intellectuals, were mainly a peasant-oriented party and their influence on the peasants, still a decided majority of the population, was a matter of profound concern to both Marxist groups.

The revolution of 1905 was a sign that revolutionary feeling was endemic in Russian society. That revolution was a preview of the conditions that were to destroy tsarism in 1917. First, a wave of peasant unrest, reaching its crest in lootings, land seizures, etc. As usual the peasant rising was unco-ordinated, elemental, and ineffective in its character. Nationalist stirrings of revolutionary character came into the open in Russian Poland. Other non-Russian parts of the empire also experienced trouble. The defeat of Russia in the war with Japan became the catalyst of tension. Peasant unrest proved to be merely the broader canvas against which the decisive revolutionary action took place in the cities, especially in the two capitals, St. Petersburg and Moscow. It was among the workers that the revolutionary movement that had permeated all classes of society took the most drastic expression. The striking workers of St. Petersburg formed a *soviet*. The word is merely Russian for *council*, but its more specific meaning illustrated in 1905 and 1917 could be loosely translated as "a workers' council of action"—a revolutionary body elected *ad hoc* in a time of crisis from among the delegates of factory workers.[5] The soviet in a revolutionary situation was elected with but little attention to democratic safeguards. It tended to be a fluid group in its composition, not unlikely to be dominated by a party that possessed the advantages of strict discipline and superior techniques of agitation. The latter characteristics were to be fully evident only in 1917. In 1905 the almost spontaneous growth of soviets astonished the Russian Marxists and especially the Bolsheviks. The latter could not be expected to be too friendly to the new phenomenon. Didn't Lenin distrust "spontaneity"? Yet they joined in the movement. In the St. Petersburg soviet the leadership was assumed by the Mensheviks but soon a brilliant newcomer, Leon Trotsky, then only twenty-six and temporarily estranged from both factions, became its moving spirit. For a time St. Petersburg was ruled by the soviet, the authorities being fearful of moving against it. The general strike, followed by an insurrection, broke out in Moscow.

---

[4] The attitude of the Bolsheviks toward terror was not without ambiguities. Thus Lenin evidently countenanced terroristic activity in some areas, e.g., in the Caucasus, which was designed to secure funds for the Party. Sporadic acts of terror against government officials were held by Lenin, along with other Marxists, to be harmful to the revolutionary cause. Even before the Revolution some of the Bolsheviks indicated that they were not opposed to *preventive terror*, i.e., the use of extralegal and drastic punishments against political opponents once the socialists were in power.
[5] In 1917 delegates of soldiers were to join the workers in the soviets.

The revolution failed for several reasons. In the first place the government disarmed the more moderate of its opponents by promising constitutional concessions. Secondly, the armed forces had not been demoralized as they were to be in 1917 by three years of a sanguinary war, and remained, with a few notable exceptions, disciplined and obedient to the government.[6] In the third place, the process of social dissolution had not reached the level of 1917. With its opponents divided, the government proceeded to arrest the soviet of St. Petersburg and to suppress in blood the Moscow uprising. The revolution of 1905 had proved to be a great rehearsal.

Viewed as such, it is difficult to overestimate its influence on the Bolsheviks. For Lenin and his followers it was an eye-opening revelation that in a revolutionary situation one has to transcend Marxist formulas and employ flexible and daring tactics. One must swim with the revolutionary current and seize its direction. The discontent of the peasant masses (and peasants furnished the majority of soldiers) could not be channeled into Marxist slogans. Hence, when an opportunity arises the Bolsheviks must forget Marx for a while and appeal to the peasant with a slogan that will assure them of, at least, his benevolent neutrality. The middle classes showed themselves ready to abandon the revolution when promised parliamentarianism. But bourgeois parliamentarianism is less suitable as an arena for revolutionary action that the flexible and volatile system of representation embodied in the soviets. The idea of an alliance with the progressive part of the middle class became for the Bolsheviks entirely secondary to the need of winning the support of *workers and poorer peasants*. Unlike the Mensheviks they decided that liberalism was *not* a natural ally of socialism.

The period of 1906 to 1917 is the only period in the history of modern Russia when something resembling constitutionalism and free political life was in existence. The tsarist government did not have the slightest intention of introducing democracy, nor even a constitutional and parliamentary system in our own sense of the word. The *Duma*, or parliament, convoked in 1906 had very limited powers. Since there was no ministerial responsibility, executive powers continued to reside in the tsar and his advisers. Even in legislative and budgetary fields, the government could still by-pass the parliament. Most important of all, the complicated electoral law was rigged in favor of the more conservative classes, and when the first two parliaments proved unduly radical and obstreperous, the law was still further changed so that the Third and Fourth Dumas were dominated by moderate conservatives. But if Russia in the period immediately preced-

---

[6] That revolutionary stirrings were particularly potent in the Russian navy was already demonstrated in 1905. Thus there was a mutiny in the naval fortress of Kronstadt, and the famous revolt of the battleship *Potemkin*.

ing the War and Revolution did not become a democracy or shed the vestiges of despotism, it must be kept in mind that for the first and only time in the twentieth century (excluding the short period between March and November 1917) political parties could operate in the open and literature critical of the government could be distributed legally. In the Duma there was at least the germ of genuine national representation and a platform for voicing social and political demands. Those who hold that the Bolshevik regime, while repressive, freed Russia from unrestrained monarchical absolutism forget that between 1906 and 1917 the civic freedoms, while not sufficient or considerable, were infinitely more extensive than they were ever to become in the Soviet period.

The fortunes of the Bolsheviks during the period illustrate the axiom that the party was already so constructed both ideologically and organizationally that it was bound to prosper in periods of acute revolutionary excitement and decline in periods of political and economic progress. Like the Mensheviks and the Social Revolutionaries the Bolsheviks finally agreed to participate in the work of the Duma, though, with their radical colleagues, they considered the emasculated parliament as a platform for propaganda rather than a genuine parliamentary forum. It is significant—bearing in mind that the franchise was far from being democratic and the elections could not portray accurately the division of political sentiment in the country—that in the elections to the Second Duma the Bolsheviks obtained half as many deputies as the Mensheviks, and that in the subsequent elections they never topped the number of deputies elected by their socialist rivals. Both Marxist parties were outdistanced by the Social Revolutionaries and their allies, who had what amounted to a monopoly of political influence among the radically-minded peasants. The middle class followed the "Kadets" (the Constitutional Democrats), the leading party in the first two Dumas, who professed liberal ideas and who would have been content to transform Russia into a constitutional monarchy on the English pattern. Even in the freest and most democratic elections, the Bolsheviks would never have got more than a small minority of votes, and they and their sympathizers were a minority even among those who saw a drastic revolutionary change as the only solution.

This fact in itself never bothered the Bolsheviks, who considered the parliamentary struggle as entirely secondary to clandestine revolutionary activity. Lenin reproved some Bolsheviks who would have boycotted the Duma elections, but he was much more severe with those who would have liquidated illegal activities and concentrated on open political life. What was profoundly more disturbing to the Bolsheviks than their numerical weakness or the government's tampering with the electoral law was the possibility that revolutionary feeling would abate and that reform, whether put into effect by the government or forced by the moderates, would relegate them to a small uninfluential group.

Such prospects were quite real in Russia in 1906-17. For once, the tsarist government adopted the policy of intelligent reform in addition to repression to deal with the revolutionary situation. The new premier, Peter Stolypin (1906-11), while a man of the most conservative and reactionary ideas, saw clearly that the police, the Cossacks, and the *agents-provocateurs* would not by themselves preserve the monarchy and the social order. He realized that the source, if not the active carrier, of the lingering revolutionary feeling was the peasant imprisoned in the *mir*, denied more land, and kept under all sorts of social and political disqualifications. The solution was to free the more enterprising peasants from the *mir*, to give them some semblance of civic rights, and, most important of all, to transform them into farmers, with land of their own and opportunities of acquiring more. The peasant would then have a stake in the political and social order, and Russia would have a rural middle class antagonistic to revolutionary changes. A series of laws enabled and encouraged the peasants to break up the *mirs* and to set themselves up as individual proprietors. The peasants' remaining financial obligations to the state (dating from the time of the emancipation) were canceled, and the government now extended credit facilities to the peasants so that they could buy up the nobles' lands. The peasants' land hunger was being at least partly satisfied, and a new peasant class, more conservative in its outlook, was rising in the villages.

Had Stolypin's social engineering been accompanied by a willingness on the part of the regime to introduce genuine constitutionalism and to invite the moderates into the government, there is little doubt that Russia would have been launched on a period of peaceful liberal reform. There was an undoubted decline of revolutionary feeling beginning with 1907. Membership in the revolutionary organizations, especially among the Bolsheviks, declined. Some Party leaders turned to other pursuits. Even though there was a renewal of radical feeling in 1912 and Lenin reorganized his faction into a separate party in the same year, it appeared as if no major chance, on the order of 1905, for a dramatic overthrow of the regime would ever recur. Lenin himself, while not abandoning Bolshevism, more than once indicated that he did not expect an overthrow of tsarism in his lifetime.

All such calculations were completely upset by the outbreak of the war in 1914. The war brought for Bolshevism the sense of final and complete separation from the main current of Western socialism. It had been fondly imagined prior to the summer of 1914 that the working masses in every country would make a world war impossible, and that, under the leadership of the socialists, they would refuse to fight in the quarrels of their capitalist masters. The war demonstrated, on the contrary, that the Marxist notion of the workers' solidarity transcending national boundaries was largely a dream and that the appeal of nationalism was infinitely greater than that of any other social or political idea. The majority of socialists in France, England, and Germany followed their country's policy, some of them entering the war governments. Especially painful and disillusioning to Lenin was the "defection" of the German Social Democracy, until 1917 the leading Marxist party in Europe, whose spokesmen now vied with the bourgeois and conservative parties in the intensity of their chauvinism. Nor was Russian socialism free of the same influence: many radicals, including Plekhanov, urged that the political struggles be postponed until the war was brought to a victorious conclusion.

To Lenin and his followers the war marked the end of a stage in the development of socialism. Marxian socialism had to be reborn in a more radical and revolutionary form. The body uniting all the socialist parties, the Second International, had to be replaced by a new international uniting the "true Marxists." In neutral Switzerland, where he spent the first three years of the war, Lenin held conferences with other socialists who opposed the war. His position, a radical one even within the context of a radical assembly, was that pacifism and prevention of war was not enough, and that the world war should be utilized for the purposes of a socialist revolution. More and more he considered the world-wide struggle as the final and suicidal convulsion of world capitalism—an opportunity for revolution and socialism.[7] During the early stages of the war there was little to justify his hopes. It was socialism and not the old order that seemed to be disintegrating. But the collapse of tsarism in Russia provided a new and unexpected opportunity for Bolshevism and, as it seemed then, for a world-wide socialist revolution.

The Revolution

The first Russian revolution of March 1917 was in no sense the work of the Bolsheviks nor of any organized political movement. Exhausted by its military defeats, its corruption and inefficiency, the tsarist regime simply collapsed in the face of some riots and strikes in Petrograd that at another time could have been easily suppressed. The blood baths of the war, in which after the initial successes Russian armies were being continuously

---

[7] During the war years Lenin wrote his *Imperialism*. The main thesis of the book—that imperial expansion and hence wars are a direct result of the search for investment markets and sources of raw materials by the capitalists of advanced industrial countries—was taken verbatim from the book of the same title by an English radical, J. A. Hobson (with Lenin barely acknowledging his debt). But in Lenin's formulation, Hobson's argument was to serve the Marxist cause: imperialism is the last critical stage of capitalism: the quarrels and wars of rival imperialist powers present a wonderful opportunity to revolutionary socialism, which in backward colonial territories should exploit local nationalism and anti-colonialism.

beaten, had deprived the regime of the army's support. The soldier's disgust with his leaders and the scandalously inefficient and corrupt system communicated itself to the villages. The moderates and even conservatives now saw tsarism as an obstacle to a military victory and a barrier to a reform that would save them from a revolution. Hence it fell easily after a slight push.

What was to take its place? The Duma formed a Provisional Government composed of liberals (the *Kadets*) and moderate conservatives. The war, it was thought, would continue and in due time Russia would have a constitution and a democratic state. Yet revolutionary pressures soon gave the lie to such hopes and pushed toward a more radical solution. A war period is not the time for successful constitutional experimentation. The Provisional Government was from the beginning but a shadow authority, political power having become fragmented and distributed among the *soviets*, which sprang up all over the country. This time the soviets extended to the army, being called the Soviets of the Workers' and Soldiers' Delegates, and even into the front lines. In the villages the *mirs* received a new lease on life, the peasants who under the Stolypin reforms had become "separators" being in many cases forced by their less progressive and less prosperous brethren to come back to the traditional organization. In retrospect it is easy to see that Russia between March and November of 1917 was in a state of anarchy, and that only a very determined action on the part of the democratically minded politicians could have prevented a dictatorship of the right or the left. Yet the democratically minded politicians both in the Provisional Government and in the Soviets were of divided counsel and separated by ideological differences. Popular sentiment was in favor of an end to the war, but the liberals and some socialists felt that they were bound to their allies, and were now fighting in the cause of liberalism against Germany. The peasants as usual wanted land, but the Provisional Government was unwilling to carry out an agricultural reform during the war. The leading person of the "Government" was a moderate Social Revolutionary, Alexander Kerensky, who in July became Prime Minister and who secured for a while the collaboration of the leading Mensheviks and Social Revolutionaries. But the temper of the times was revolutionary and the most extreme suggestions were likely to become most popular. The Bolshevik Party, which in the beginning of the Revolution was a tiny element in the political picture, was to become within a few months, through revolutionary audacity and unabated demagoguery, the state.

Before March the Bolsheviks' numbers are estimated as between 20,000 and 25,000. Its leaders were in exile (like Lenin and Zinoviev), or in Siberia (like Kamenev and Stalin), or in jail. In the first elections to the

Soviets they ran a rather poor third behind the Mensheviks and the Social Revolutionaries. In the villages the latter still overwhelmed both the Marxist groups. Until Lenin's arrival in April, the Bolsheviks were in a quandary as to what their policy should be. According to the Marxist scheme, here was the bourgeois-democratic revolution. Presumably the socialist revolution was to come, but not in the immediate future. Should not the Bolsheviks in the meantime collaborate with the Mensheviks and other radical groups? The first Bolshevik leaders to reach the capital were Kamenev and Stalin, who as members of the Central Committee assumed temporary command and pursued a rather hesitant and ambiguous policy both on the issue of collaboration and on the continuance of the war.[8]

In the middle of April Lenin arrived in Petrograd (formerly St. Petersburg) and in his very first words at the railway station indicated the new tactics. No compromise with the Provisional Government, "all power to the Soviets"; and immediate peace, confiscation of privately owned land, and abolition of the coercive organs of the state. It was clear that to Lenin the Bolsheviks should, Marx or no Marx, try to seize power at the first propitious moment, and for that purpose should not hesitate to outbid everybody else with the most demagogic and anarchist slogans. Lenin's postulates were, at first, greeted with amusement by his enemies and with incomprehension and protests by the Bolsheviks. The "old man" seemed to have lost touch with reality and once again his fanaticism was going to doom Russian Marxism. By the force of his personality Lenin gained the majority among the Bolsheviks, though tactical and ideological scruples lingered on among his closest associates until and after November.

The ridiculous dream of a fanatic who thought that he and his small group could conquer and rule Russia soon became a real threat. The Provisional Government was losing what little power and prestige it had; the armed forces, demoralized by the bloodletting of an unsuccessful offensive and undermined by the revolutionary agitators, were in a mutinous mood. The Bolsheviks' peace agitation was especially effective in gaining converts among the garrison of Petrograd and among the sailors. The moderate leaders of the Social Revolutionaries who in May joined the Provisional Government were being undermined in their own party because of their failure to carry out a land reform. The Bolsheviks in the summer of 1917

---

[8] Joseph Vissarionovich Stalin was at the time neither an obscure Party hack, as he has been pictured by some, nor the leading collaborator of Lenin, as he has been presented in servile official biographies. Since 1912 he had been a member of the Bolshevik Central Committee and one of the leading Bolsheviks. In the over-all hierarchy of Bolshevik leaders he occupied an intermediate position. Certainly people like Kamenev, Zinoviev, and Trotsky were much more prominent during and immediately after the Revolution, and the first two had been much closer to Lenin.

received an accession of strength from a group of socialists who had previously oscillated between the Bolsheviks and the Mensheviks and who now brought into their ranks a group of brilliant leaders, the outstanding among whom, Trotsky, was to be, along with Lenin, the moving spirit of the Bolshevik Revolution and of the first few years of the new regime. The Bolsheviks gained vastly in membership. On the eve of the second revolution, they were still a decided minority in the country. But they were now a sizable and strategically located minority that enjoyed the advantages of almost military discipline while their enemies were divided and confused.

The Government, composed of people with democratic doubts and hesitations, was unwilling, even if it had been able, to proceed resolutely against the Bolsheviks, who made no secret of their intentions. Only in July after an unsuccessful Bolshevik rising were some Bolsheviks imprisoned and was Lenin forced to go into hiding. The structure of the Party was left undamaged. An attempted rightist rising by General Kornilov in September forced Kerensky to relax his half-hearted attempts against the Bolsheviks. The unsuccessful insurrection showed the weakness of the army as a political instrument, but also the hopeless position of Kerensky's Provisional Government and the moderates. Russia was in the throes of anarchy. By late September the Bolsheviks obtained the majority in the Petrograd and Moscow Soviets. On October 23, 1917, the Bolshevik Central Committee decided upon an uprising. The plans for the uprising became a public secret since they were revealed by Zinoviev and Kamenev, who had opposed them within the Central Committee. Still, the Government was powerless to prevent it. On November 7, 1917, the "Government," which by this time meant the city of Petrograd and the control of some arsenals and offices, fell to the Bolsheviks, who had presumed to act in the name of the Petrograd Soviet. The struggle was brief and almost bloodless. Kerensky's Government fled the city, and the Bolsheviks could appear before the All-Russian Congress of Soviets as victors. The Congress, in which the Bolsheviks and their temporary allies, the left wing of the Social Revolutionaries, had a majority, proclaimed the transfer of power to Soviets throughout Russia, in fact to the Bolsheviks. The new Government, the Council of Commissars, was purely Bolshevik in its composition, with Lenin as chairman. The opposition—the Mensheviks, the moderate Social Revolutionaries—left the Congress. The Bolsheviks had "power." At the end of 1917 power meant a strategic position in the civil war that was to engulf Russia for the next three years and that began while the German armies were advancing deeper into Russian territory. The new regime had no army to speak of and no administrative machinery. In the country as a whole the Bolsheviks, at the end of 1917, when they were more popular than ever before or after, were still a decided minority. The proof came in the elections to the Constituent Assembly held before the Bolsheviks established their monopoly of power. The elections produced a majority for the Social Revolutionaries, with the Bolsheviks getting about 25 per cent of the vote. Thus the only free and democratic election held in the twentieth century in Russia produced a decided anti-Bolshevik majority. In January 1918 the Assembly met for its only session and was promptly dissolved and driven out by the Bolshevik Government. January 1918 marks the demise of the last lingering democratic impulses in Bolshevism. No more *free* and *multi-party* elections were to be allowed, and the Party self-professedly assumed an absolue dictatorship.

The rise of the Bolsheviks to power and final stage of victory offer certain lessons that are of importance in understanding the Soviet Union and the Communist movement of today. Lenin had succeeded in creating a party that, unlike so many socialist and radical parties, managed to preserve discipline and to follow its leaders in all their tactical and ideological shifts and maneuvers. The price paid for the achievement was to give up what was left of the democratic element in Marxism. But the Party *itself*, though run dictatorially, had not as yet achieved the totalitarian spirit characteristic of the Stalin period. Zinoviev and Kamenev, although they had disagreed with Lenin on the eve of the revolution, were immediately after the November coup again his closest collaborators. A few weeks after the November Revolution some Bolshevik leaders still felt that the Government should include representatives of the other socialist parties and they felt so strongly about it that they resigned, temporarily, from the Council of Commissars. It would take several more years before the Party, now the instrument of dictatorship, would in itself become so monolithically totalitarian that honest disagreement with the dictator would be branded as treason. But the foundations of totalitarianism were already there.

Another point to be stressed is that the Party did not win power and relative popularity under the banner of Marxism but with anarchist slogans that appealed to the war-weary and demoralized nation. Lenin had preached defeatism and desertion; the taking over of the land and factories by the peasants and the workers; abolition of the bureaucracy and the standing army; and complete economic egalitarianism. Once in power the stark realities confronted the Bolsheviks. Like any Government, they had to defend the country against the enemy, keep the national economy going, and reconstruct the machinery of the state—all tasks that would have been made impossible by literal fulfillment of their own slogans. Powerful brakes had to be applied, and the manner of their application is the history of the decades that followed the November coup, until from the most thoroughgoing, most anarchical, of all revolutions, was born the most dominating and exacting state of modern times.

[24]

The Development of
Soviet Policy

The Struggle with the Peasant

The Bolsheviks seized power in November 1917 with the idea of instituting a new type of society in Russia and eventually in the world. The
basis of that society was to be Marxian socialism and its eventual aim
communism. We have already seen[1] why Marxian socialism should have
won in a society that Marx and Engels thought unlikely to be among the
first seized by socialism. But whatever doubts, conflicting schemes and
theories the Bolsheviks might have had before November 1917 as to
whether Russia was ripe for a socialist revolution or not, whether the bourgeois revolution should not be prolonged, whether they should share power
with liberal and other socialist parties, and whether the Russian Revolution could survive in the absence of a world-wide revolution, etc., they were
faced in November with the fact of having power and of being called on
to build a socialist society from the ruins of what they regarded as having
been, not a fully developed capitalist society, but a mixture of feudal and
capitalist elements.

Now there was precious little in their own ideology to facilitate the task
or to guide them through the first step. Marx and Engels had been socialists but they had written mostly about capitalism. There is very little in
Marx to indicate *concrete* steps that a socialist party should undertake
upon seizing power in a predominantly agricultural country. There is no

---

[1] In Chapter 22.

discussion in the scriptures of Marxism as to how a *socialist country* should *industrialize,* how the mass of small peasant holdings can be brought into large-scale units run by the state, or what kind of price system a socialist administration would evolve. And beyond the vague and contradictory hints in those same scriptures there is but little to indicate, economics aside, what kind of society the dictatorship of the proletariat would bring about. What about the family under socialism? What kind of arts and amusements would the new society have? Of bourgeois ideas and institutions under those headings Marx had written voluminously and scathingly. But he offered no blueprints for the future except to assert that socialism would free man from all his bonds and release his highest creative powers.

All this, understandably, did not help the Communists, who inherited a government and society in complete ruin, had civil and foreign wars on their hands, with industry and agriculture producing at a fraction of their pre-World War I level. As to all revolutionary leaders, so it fell to Lenin and his colleagues to restrain the revolutionary impatience of his followers; to point out that first things come first, that reconstruction and victory in the war must precede social experimentation and the building of a new life. Yet, at first, the broad sweep of the revolution poured past all the cautions and restraints. The peasants seized the landlords' lands, and in effect reinstituted the communal organization of the villages. The workers drove out their employers and directors and attempted to run factories on an ideological rather than technical *expertise.* The more militant among the Communists pushed the official policy of repression of the church to the point of severe persecution of religious cults and their faithful. Wars, famines, and the collapse of established social values led to the decline of the family, to drastic experimentation in the arts, education, etc. In the midst of all the troubles the most stringent measures had to be resorted to, and sometimes they gave the impression that the regime, prompted by the crisis, as well as by its ideological scruples, was drawn despite its better judgment to install socialism and communism right away, skipping several historical periods. Thus in agriculture all land was legally nationalized and the heavy grain requisitions imposed upon the peasant gave the impression that he was to be communized by compulsion. Agricultural communes with land, implements and dwellings held in common were encouraged. In industry a high degree of egalitarianism was in fashion, with any disparity in pay, or difference in status, even if justified by function, considered unproletarian if not outright counterrevolutionary. This was the period (1917-21) of "War Communism," when the inexperience of the new rulers, their ideological premises, and most of all the social and economic chaos, gave rise to the impression that the Communists were impractical fanatics determined to establish the final stage of communism without having industrialized their country, without having gone through the stage of socialism.

A halt was called in 1921 with the institution of the New Economic Policy, the period of 1921-28 taking consequently the name of the Nep. Aside from the need for an economic reconstruction, Lenin and his associates were motivated in establishing the Nep by the anarchistic tendencies they saw in the Party (the Workers' Opposition) and the Kronstadt Revolt. Hence their decision to eschew the most radical policies for the moment. The peasants were to be appeased by being required to pay to the state only a specified portion of their crops, rather than an arbitrary quota to be met regardless of the size of their crop. Trade, and even small-scale industry, run by private operators was legalized. In brief, the state reserved for its ownership banking, transportation, and heavy industry, and allowed free enterprise elsewhere. The march toward socialism was not given up but merely suspended until the country could catch its breath and fully recover from the ravages of the preceding years.

The Nep represented a strategic retreat, during which the forces of socialism in Russia would retrench, recuperate, and then resume their march. Yet both within Russia and abroad the adoption of moderate economic policies was often condemned or praised as indicating that the Bolsheviks had realized the "impracticability" of socialism and were content to establish a mixed economy or state capitalism. Such judgments were based on a gross misunderstanding of the basic ideological premises of the Soviet leaders, or—in the case of those who argued the point in Russia—on purely political motivations. Being by temperament as well as by conviction Marxists, the Soviet leaders, whether led by Stalin, Trotsky, or Zinoviev, were bound in the long run to insist on a full-scale industrialization and socialization of the country. The reasons for their determination were found not only in their ideology and their economic views but also in their most deeply held *social* and *political* opinions. It is almost axiomatic for a Marxist to hold that socialism can come only in an *industrialized* country. It was equally axiomatic for Russian Marxists to have held that the power of any socialist party must be based on a mass of industrial proletarians, and that in a country where the mass of the population was composed of petty landholders, no matter how strong the dictatorship of the Party, no matter how exclusive its monopoly of political power, the forces of history would act against socialism and would eventually bring about the downfall of the Soviet regime. This obsession of the Communists against the individual peasant holder was held with the tenacity of a religious dogma, the strength of which no one who does not share it can fully appreciate. The Communists of all factions held this belief: in the long run Russia must be industrialized, and private ownership in agriculture must be abolished. If not, Soviet power would collapse, either before an external enemy, for a non-industrialized state is weak; or before the internal one, for peasants, no matter how poor, if they have land, are against socialism and have all the instincts and aspirations of the petty bourgeois.

Thus the Nep, during its short duration, 1921-28, was obviously an expedient. Yet even as such it was bitterly assailed by various factions of the Communist Party, especially when to their ideological scruples was joined the resentment of the ruling clique. First Trotsky and then Kamenev and Zinoviev attacked the ruling group and its policy as favoring the peasant and especially the rich peasant, the *kulak*, while neglecting the industrial worker. Stalin and his then ally, Bukharin, were accused in 1924-25 of encouraging the growth of rich peasants by their policy which legalized the leasing of land and the hiring of help by peasants who could afford it. This was decried as the legalization of exploitation of man by man, a fine state of affairs for the first socialist country in the world!

The reasons that brought the Nep to an end and that determined the regime to proceed full speed with collectivization and industrialization are manifold and complex. The ensuing period, 1928-33, has been called with a great deal of justice the "Third Russian Revolution" (the first one being in March, the second in November, 1917). In the space of five years individual ownership of land was practically eliminated, collective farms and state farms taking its place; and Russia was launched on a gigantic industrialization drive that was to make her over from a mainly agricultural country into one of the two leading industrial countries of the world. The scope of this program and the speed with which it was to be accomplished involved tremendous dangers. The regime declared an open war on the majority of the population—the peasants. Industrialization was financed by lowering the standard of living of the masses and thus imperiling the Soviet regime. Why should a power-conscious regime embark on such a perilous course? And if so, why the feverish and reckless pace?

There are three *groups* of reasons behind the decisions reached in 1927 and 1928. *Economically*, by 1927 Russia had recovered from the ravages of war and her production, both agricultural and industrial, had reached the prewar level. Further advance could, the Soviet government became convinced, proceed only on the basis of thorough industrialization. Furthermore the type of economy that became stabilized during the Nep did not allow the Soviet government that *full control over the economic life of the country that every Communist government craves*. The tempo of economic development was dependent not only on the government but on the peasant. If the peasant felt that he was getting enough money for his crops, and if with that money he could purchase some goods, then he would sell his grain. If not, he could consume it on the farm or feed it to his animals rather than sell it at the government-fixed price. In 1927 and 1928 on the basis of such reasons the peasants were reluctant to sell. The socialist government in bondage to the peasant! The Communists forced to appease the peasant economically, and if he is appeased economically, won't he tomorrow demand political concessions as the price for his grain? It is no wonder that Stalin's regime fell upon the peasant with the same fury that it displayed in fighting its opponents within the Party.

Politically, then, the decision to industrialize and *collectivize* was based on the natural aversion of Communism against any independent source of economic or political power in the state. Instead of millions of individual farmers with all their anti-socialist instincts there would be fewer but more efficient collective and state farms. Labor would be released to industry; the government would, so it was hoped, be able to control the production and distribution of food; and, most important of all, the Soviet regime would not be dependent upon the good will of millions of peasants.

General power and international considerations were also not lacking behind the resolution. Stalin's dictatorship was firmly established. But it was a dictatorship over a relatively weak and backward country. Until Russia was industrialized, until she had reached the industrial level of the West, she would be, so ran the thinking of the Communists, at the mercy of the capitalist world. Hence Stalin's slogan that the U.S.S.R. had "to catch up and to leave behind" the leading capitalist countries in the industrial race. Hence his appeal to national pride in evoking the memory of Russia's past defeats because of her weakness, and the pledge that a powerful industrialized and socialized U.S.S.R. would never have to endure a similar fate.

Thus economic, military, and politico-social reasons, as well as the natural impulse of a totalitarian system to grow stronger and vaster, all played their part. In view of the weak position of agriculture and the lack of capital the decision to industrialize rapidly and to telescope into ten years what in the West took generations undoubtedly represented a vast gamble. But the gamble was undertaken by the regime confident of its ideological premises and conscious of its great resources, among which not the least important was coercive power almost, but not quite, unlimited, as the resistance of the peasants was to show.

The decision to industrialize a country involves a choice not unlike that before an individual who decides to buy a house or a car. He will finance it out of a loan, his savings if he has any, or simply by curtailing his expenditures by reducing his standard of living. To the Soviet government beginning its industrialization in 1928 the last choice was the only feasible one. The sinews of industrialization—mainly heavy industry—had to come out of the internal resources of the U.S.S.R., a country that in 1928 already enjoyed, if that is the phrase, one of the lowest standards of living in Europe. From then on the Soviet workers had to work harder and longer. For a time, and it turned out to be quite a long time, fewer among them would be producing commodities to feed, clothe, and shelter people, and more of them would be producing heavy machinery, and the commodities that could be sold abroad, and for which the Soviets would acquire foreign machines and foreign experts. To repeat, none but a totalitarian system enjoying vast powers of compulsion would have attempted to squeeze the wherewithal of industrialization out of the already pitiful standard of living of its people.

The First Five Year Plan was authorized by the Fifteenth Party Congress in 1927 and was to cover the years 1928-33. Many of the delegates to the Congress believed that they were sanctioning a cautious progress toward collectivization and industrialization. The mechanics of planning were theoretically to be worked out by the planning organs, and especially the Gosplan, or the State Planning Commission, an organ staffed mainly by economists, cautious beings aware of resources, rates of growth and other economic realities. But the actual planning and supervision of the plan was soon snatched out of the economists' hands. Decisions as to the goals of economic planning, the pace of industrialization and collectivization, the means to be employed, came to be arrived at—and still are—in the Politburo of the Communist Party, with the planning experts just filling in the details. Thus sometime in 1929 the dictator and his entourage reached the conclusion that the original pace of collectivization prescribed in the First Five Year Plan was too slow. It was decided to accomplish the major part of collectivization before 1933. The ostensible slogan was to exterminate the *kulaks* as a class. But the fury of the Party and the state fell not only upon the rich (by Russian standards) peasant, but upon the broad masses of peasantry. In his incredible tenacity for his land, the peasant refused to be propagandized or "educated" into the collective, where his land and his livestock would be pooled. The government increased its compulsion and the peasant resisted by the only means he knew: by refusing his grain to the state, by slaughtering his animals. In 1929 and 1930 the conflict became violent. Wholesale deportations tranferred to Siberia and elsewhere hundreds of thousands, if not millions, of *kulaks*, now a catchall term for any peasants who resisted collectivization. Famine gripped the Ukraine. The losses of livestock endured during those terrible years have not, in some categories, been made up even today.

The war against the peasant was not merely an incident in Russia's industrialization, and the problem requires a few words. Deeply ingrained in the Marxists has been the habit of thought that socialism cannot be achieved, nor can the power of the Communist Party be secure, if there is in society a considerable element that owns one of the means of production. Thus the millions of peasant households, each tilling its small plot, were not only a bar to rapid industrialization but the breeder of anti-socialist attitudes. The collective farms, on the contrary, Communism believes, are not only more efficient, as they can produce more with less labor, and can be profitably worked with mechanical appliances because of their larger size, but they give the peasant the psychology of the worker rather than that of the small property owner—deadly enemy of socialism. But complete elimination of the private element from agriculture proved beyond the means of even the Soviet regime. True, by 1936 more than 90 per cent of the land in Russia was in the collective and state farms, and as of today there are, practically speaking, no individual farmers in the U.S.S.R. But the government and the Party had to make two important concessions to the peasant.

In the first place, the bulk of arable land is in collective farms rather than in state farms. The latter, the Communists believed early in the first Five Year Plan, would play a more important role than they have actually assumed. A state farm, where the peasants are just hired hands, is the closest thing in agriculture to an industrial factory, hence preferable to the Marxist, and disliked by the peasant. The dominant role of the collectives over the state farms, or *sovkhozes*, is thus a concession.

In the second place the structure of the collective farm has been modified so as somewhat to appease the peasant. True, the collective farm is not a co-operative farm in our sense of the word. Though theoretically it is run by an assembly of its members, it is subject to the most centralized direction. Its manager in many cases comes from outside the *kolkhoz*. Insofar as the nature of its crop, the norm of work and its organziation are concerned, the *kolkhoz* is most stringently subject to regulations that emanate, in the last instance, from Moscow. As the medieval baron's castle stood overawing his serfs in the vicinity, so does the local Machine Tractor Station stand guard over several *kolkhozes*. The M.T.S. not only provides machinery for the *kolkhoz* but supervises its plans and performance. Attached to it are special Party workers who carry on propaganda and ideological indoctrination among the villagers. "Collectivization," then, is a euphemism for land nationalization and direction from above. But in the collective the devil—to the Communists the element of private ownership —has not been entirely chased away. In the prevailing type of the *kolkhoz*, the so-called *artel*, though most of the land is pooled together the peasants still retain their dwellings and little garden plots where they grow fruit and vegetables, which they can sell in the open market, and—faced with the implacable resistance of that powerful personage, the peasant woman

—even Stalin had to yield and grant that peasant households might own fowl and even a cow. Yet, in the main, the *kolkhoz*, in its structure and principle, reminds one of the factory. Peasants work in teams and brigades according to an assignment by the chairman. Their remuneration is adjusted according to the type of the job and their individual performance. The net income of the *kolkhoz* is divided among the members both in cash and in kind. Special bonuses are allotted to the workers and teams that surpass their output quota, and corresponding deductions penalize those who fail to meet the plan. Jobs that require some technical skill, e.g., that of the tractor driver, may have a base pay several times that of an unskilled laborer. In brief, insofar as his collective work is concerned, the peasant is simply in the position of a hired hand rather than a member of a co-operative.

Ridiculous as it may seem to us, the peasant's garden plot and the few pitiful remaining elements of private property in agriculture have been a source of major worry to the Soviet leaders and a matter of major concern to the Soviet economy. For one thing, peasants have spent disproportionately large amounts of time in working their own plots as against working on communal land. For another, the remaining plot, smaller than one acre, and its few appurtenances, stand as a link with the past and with the peasant's nostalgia for individual ownership. Soviet agriculture has not shared in the prodigious growth of the rest of Soviet economy. While Russian industry (and especially heavy industry) has increased its production many fold over its pre-1928 level many sectors of agriculture have not advanced substantially beyond that year. Collectivization has centralized Soviet agriculture at the disposal of the Government, it has released labor for industry, but it has not solved the problem of agricultural production in a country with a growing population, and it has not eradicated the peasant's longing for his own land.

Confronted with this problem, the Soviet regime has pursued the familiar zigzag course between compulsion and concession to the popular feeling. Thus at times the government would limit more sharply the size of the garden plot, tax its produce more heavily, and tighten the discipline of the collective farm. At other times the peasants would be granted tax benefits and encouraged to grow more on their plots. A major debate on the future of Soviet agriculture must have divided the inner circle in 1949-50. One Soviet leader, Andreyev, came out publicly for a loosening of the *kolkhoz* structure in a direction that might transform it into a genuine co-operative farm rather than a government grain factory. But Andreyev was publicly denounced and the opposite tendency prevailed for a time. A great movement to merge collective farms into larger units combining perhaps several villages was initiated and carried through. The main objective was clear: in a gigantic *kolkhoz* the peasants working in brigades some miles away from their homestead would find it impossible to devote much time to their individual plots. Nikita Khrushchev in 1950 formulated an even more drastic remedy. He advocated *agrogorods, or agro-cities,* in which the collectives would be combined into still larger units, peasants would live in apartment houses and be taken out to cultivate the outlying fields. The garden plot and its appurtenances would now completely disappear, and the Communists' dream would be realized: the peasant would be assimilated in his habits, way of living, and psychology to the city dweller. But Khrushchev's plan was in turn repudiated.

The post-Stalin era inherited the dilemma of agriculture. Again a variety of remedies has been tried: tax concessions, promises of more consumers' goods under Malenkov's primacy, reduced requisitions from the *kolkhozes* to the government so that the rest of their produce could be sold in the open market, etc. To increase total agricultural yield, the regime, and especially Khrushchev, who identified himself with the project, has sponsored the settlement and cultivation of "virgin land"—lands in Kazakhstan and elsewhere that were previously thought unsuitable because of their climate and soil for agricultural production.

In a country where the ordinary political processes are denied or are meaningless, people will often express their satisfaction or dissatisfaction with the regime by their economic performance. In that sense the Soviet peasant has "voted" up to now against the government. It remains to be seen whether any structural changes in Soviet agriculture, or a greater flow of consumers' goods, or a greater liberality of the regime, would change their vote. In Russian history up to now the peasant has been the central, though passive, figure. Most of the social and political problems, though often fought out by others, had their source in the status and feelings of the preponderant majority of the nation who dwelt in the villages. Today, with industrialization, the peasants no longer constitute that majority. Yet with their status not entirely satisfactory to the regime and unsatisfactory to them, they constitute a vast social segment that has not quite fitted into socialism and hence a question mark in the uncertain future of the Soviet regime.

How were the Soviet leaders able to win their long and bitter struggle with the vast majority of the population? What was the source of their power? Their principal instrument was the Communist Party, whose weapons and techniques of control we shall examine in detail in Chapter 26. But how did the leadership hold together this huge organization and win from it the emotional commitment and the disciplined devotion necessary to carry out their grandiose plans? We can understand this only if we look at the drive for industrialization, which, under Stalin, became for millions in and outside the Party a compelling national purpose, inspiring fanatic loyalty and legitimizing privation, terror, and rigid conformism.

Industrialization

The appeal of Soviet Communism to people in other countries has often reflected not so much the attraction of the ideas of Communism, but the admiration for a country that in the space of one generation has raised itself from a backward agricultural community to a great industrial power. Though the achievement of the Soviets has undoubtedly been great, it should be kept in mind that it was not created from nothing. Pre-Revolutionary Russia, backward as she was in *absolute* terms in comparison with the West, was in *relative* terms a rapidly growing industrial country. Entering the industrial race very late in the nineteenth century, Russia progressed very fast; her industrial production in some years prior to World War I grew at a faster pace than that of the most advanced Western countries, including the United States. It is reasonable to assume that with some industrial base and with her scientific talent post-World War I Russia under any social and economic system would have become a major industrial power. Still the achievement of the Bolsheviks in absolute terms, and in view of the two devastating wars that have intervened, is very great—as great as their ability to squeeze the sinews of industrialization out of the already pitiful standard of living of the Russian masses. The price in human terms has been enormous but in one respect the fondest expectations of the authors of the November Revolution have been fulfilled: Russia is an industrial power, one of the two greatest in the world.

The original impulse to industrialize was for the Bolsheviks grounded in their Marxist ideology but also in something else. By and large the Communist leaders hated—and their hatred was shared by many non-Communist intellectuals—pre-Revolutionary Russia with its backwardness, its social torpor, and the majority of its population sunk in passivity and superstition. Those exotic social traits that charm many a Western reader of nineteenth-century Russian novels were exactly the ones that the Bolsheviks detested. From the intelligentsia, which, as the saying went, "knew about everything, but could do nothing," to the peasant masses clinging to their immemorial habits, the Russian Marxists saw nothing but backwardness and apathy. Their view, as we have seen, may have been exaggerated, but they were impatient to "give history a push," to establish a modern scientifically organized society. Though they detested the capitalist West, they looked with admiration upon its industry, and its scientific spirit. Years after the Revolution, when the pendulum had swung back and when Russian history was again being glorified, Stalin could still speak with approval of the American spirit of enterprise and wish for its presence in the Russians—together, to be sure, with socialist consciousness.

It is no wonder then that the first years of rapid industrialization after 1928, the years of great suffering, of the persecution of the peasantry, were also years of great ideological fervor and élan, especially among the Communist young. If it had not aroused strong enthusiasm among at least part of its supporters, the regime, cruel and in many ways inefficient, would undoubtedly have collapsed. But the Communists, for all their transgressions and inefficiencies, managed at the time to convey the impression that they were doing something—lifting Russia by its bootstraps. And from the despot himself came the slogans that underlined the grandiose task: "To catch up and to overcome" the West; the U.S.S.R. must within a decade perform the work of industrialization that elsewhere took generations. And since every struggle needs a visible, tangible enemy to justify the privations and sacrifices, Stalin proclaimed the thesis that as socialism progresses the class struggle becomes sharper, the "enemy" becomes more desperate and unscrupulous—the "enemy" being whoever it was convenient to brand as such at the moment: the rich peasant in Russia, the capitalist powers, etc. Hence the great question was, in Stalin's words: "Who will get whom?" Shall "we," the Communists, succeed in building a modern industrial state, or shall "they" defeat our attempts to collectivize, to industrialize, and to destroy the hostile classes and forces? "They" were then not only the *kulak*, or a foreign paid saboteur, but those Communists of little faith who pitied the peasant, who felt that industrialization was proceeding too fast or too inhumanly, "they" were all the traditional forces of apathy and backwardness in Russian society.

The drive toward industrialization proceeded then at a high pitch and, initially, with a kind of religious fervor. But beyond the initial fervor the campaign to industrialize rapidly and at a high cost in human freedom and comfort obviously requires other things. If you want a whole nation to strain everything to produce more and more, to measure success in life and national well-being by production figures, then you must adjust the whole mentality of the nation to the task. Thus industrialization cannot be performed rapidly in a society that is permeated by ascetic values. Nor can it come easily where people believe that equality is the highest social good, and that it is ignoble for a man to strive to have more in goods and services than his neighbor; or that comfort and leisure are more important than production. The Soviet leaders accordingly set about creating a system of sanctions and incentives that had as its main objective the maximization of production. At the altar of industrialization there had to be sacrificed those parts of the Marxist dogma that proclaimed equality, and the protection of the worker against the employer, for industrialization demands incentives based on performance, and a very rapid industrialization demands at times the sacrifice of the worker's health and comfort to the demands of production.

The first to go overboard was the remaining autonomy of the trade unions vis-à-vis the state. In 1930 the Stalinists acquired complete control of the Soviet trade unions. From then on they became but an auxiliary branch of the government with their main function not the protection of the worker against the employer, i.e., the state, but the maximization of production and the indoctrination of the workers in attitudes appropriate to rapid industrialization. The right to strike, though legally not abolished, in fact disappeared, and we hear of no strikes until the post-Stalin era. In 1931 Stalin spelled out a few more of the consequences of the drive for industrialization: workers must be subject to some discipline; they cannot be allowed to flounder from one job to another, and their pay must correspond to their performance at work. Thus arose the institution of labor passports, which limit the worker's freedom of choice of work, and the institution of work norms, which the worker has to meet to earn his full pay, and the excess over which is rewarded by a bonus. Both these devices have always been resisted by the trade unions in every country on the ground that, unless in a real emergency such as wartime, they make the worker into a beast of burden and are likely to limit his freedom and injure his health. But in the socialist state they became the basis of labor relations, and evolution away from them began only two years after Stalin's death. Indeed, they were soon supplemented by a rigorous labor code that subjected the worker to fines for absenteeism or lateness to work, and, for repetition of these offenses, to imprisonment. It goes without saying that the length of the working day was extended. Since the thirties filled the Soviet forced labor camps with a mass of inmates, the government could utilize millions of slave laborers for particularly hazardous tasks such as mining and construction in unfavorable climatic conditions, and could rely upon prison labor for a large part of its scheduled production.[2]

In 1934 Stalin summarized the whole trend in theoretical terms. Marxism, he proclaimed at the Seventeenth Party Congress, has nothing to do with egalitarianism in wages. This is a petty-bourgeois prejudice. Nor had Marxism anything to do, according to the same authority, with the

---

[2] The number of people in forced labor camps has always been a matter of dispute among foreign experts. Some have given fantastic estimates like 20 million, but the most modest guesses for any year between 1932 and 1941 have never gone below 3 million. Authentic Soviet documents, like the secret economic plan for 1941, which was captured by the Germans and then found its way to the West, authorize the assumption that the inmates of the forced labor camps constitute a sizeable proportion of the Soviet labor force. Partial dissolution of the camps began with the amnesties following Stalin's death.

workers' interfering with management. There had already been proclaimed
the dissolution of the "trio" (*troika*) that had used to run the factory,
i.e., the manager, trade union secretary, and the local Party secretary: the
manager assumed full authority with the latter two becoming his helpers
in the task of expanding production. The Soviets have used extensively
that bane of the working class in the West—the speed-up system. The
middle thirties were full of well-publicized workers who would suddenly
break the working norm. The heroes would be properly rewarded and the
average norm would then be raised for all the workers in the given occupation. The shock workers became known after one of the first as the Sta-
khanovites—and they became the aristocracy of Soviet labor, rewarded by
higher pay, bonuses, orders, etc. "Socialist competition," or factories and
industrial regions as well as individuals "spontaneously" challenging each
to a race in production, became a regular feature of the Soviet labor scene,
both in industry and in agriculture. Thus those two proverbial methods of
driving the labor force in a capitalist state, the carrot and the stick, found
their fullest application in the socialist state. Gone in the process was even
the pretense of building a classless society in the real sense of the word. For
now a huge difference in the economic status and in the opportunity to
obtain the amenities of life separated the common worker from a Sta-
khanovite, not to mention an industrial director, a successful engineer, or a
popular author. The disparities in income grew and they were fully authorized by the changes in the Soviet tax structure. The change was symbolized by the quiet disregard of the old principle, operative until the
late twenties, that a Party member should not be paid more than the
equivalent of the wages of an *average industrial worker*. The visible symptoms included the restoration of ranks, orders and more colorful uniform in
the army and navy; and soon, during the second World War, certain
branches of the civil service were put in uniform.

In 1936 Stalin proclaimed that socialism had been achieved in the
U.S.S.R., and that now, instead of the exploiters and the exploited, there
were left only two friendly classes: working peasants and workers, and the
Soviet intelligentsia, not a class, but sprung from the other two. The statement was true insofar as it referred to the abolition of private ownership of
the means of production. But it was emphatically untrue insofar as it implied that the Soviet Union had achieved a society in which the difference
in income and status had narrowed down or even that it was moving in
that direction. It was true that hereditary distinctions had been largely
obliterated, and that careers were now open to talent on a scale unimagi-
nable in pre-Revolutionary Russia. But it was and is emphatically untrue
that the exploitation of man by man—and its source, the exploitation of
man by the state—has been abolished in the U.S.S.R.

The sociologists have noticed that very often a given stage in the economic development of society is accompanied by very specific social customs. Marx and Engels in writing of their contemporary bourgeois societies decried the "philistinism" of their social and moral values. The emphasis on the family tie and on religion; the horror of illicit love and unconventional behavior, even the optimistic and moralistic tone of the literature of Victorian England—they all appeared to the makers of Marxism as hypocritical devices through which the exploiting classes kept the workers content with their miserable lot. Yet all those symptoms appeared, and with official encouragement, during the period of socialist industrialization in the thirties. There was one exception: a Marxist regime could never encourage religion. Yet even so the struggle against the Orthodox Church was relaxed, and militant propagation of atheism was discouraged.

Prior to the thirties divorce was extremely easy to obtain, and abortion was legalized. No sanctions were invoked against unconventional sexual relations. Again the change is drastic in the decade of Great Industrialization. Divorce was still legal but the courts discouraged it and it became expensive. Abortion for reasons other than health was declared illegal. Heavy penalties were prescribed for homosexual acts. The sanctity of the family tie was invoked both in official pronouncements and in Soviet literature. It would be too simple to assume that at a certain point the regime had suddenly decided that the grandiose task at hand required social stability and moral orthodoxy. But certainly in comparison with the immediate post-Revolutionary era, the "line" officially sponsored in the thirties and up to now has been extremely conventional and moralistic. It is as if the individual were told that this is no time to indulge personal whim and life: the state and society expect everyone to have a stable and decorous life and to devote his energies to the important social tasks.

The early Bolsheviks included among themselves, or attracted, experimenters in art, literature, and the theater. Every social revolution breeds and brings the desire for the new in the arts. But as in the case of morals, the arts, and literature and even science became increasingly subject to the authority of the Party. And in the thirties and forties the official line turned heavily toward traditionalism and conventionality. Soviet writers were told, then ordered, to depict the problems and successes of socialist construction. The depiction of the unusual or the morbid, stress on individual problems unconnected with the building of socialism or the defense of the socialist fatherland, became in effect prohibited. The arts and literature became subjugated to the Party, to the extent that distinguished authors were forced to rewrite their works if they did not meet with the Party's approval. The prevailing line became *socialist realism*. Its principal motif in contemporary novels and even poetry was the striving by the

new Soviet man toward—and eventually his attainment of—collectivization and industrialization and the subordination of individual life to society.
In Plato's *Republic* the author anticipates totalitarianism by prescribing
what music a well-ordered state should allow. The rulers of Russia followed by prescribing or banning various styles of musical composition
and by requiring the artists to celebrate patriotic or social motifs in their
music, e.g., Shostakovich's composition celebrating Stalin's afforestation
plan. The Party's control over the artistic and scientific life of the country
duplicated its control over every other aspect of life of the population.
Scientific and artistic disputes would be settled not by the judgment of the
public but by the dictum of a Party authority, with the dictator himself
making pronouncements on the most unexpected subjects.[3]

The main import of the change during the thirties, quite apart from
the strictness of totalitarian controls, was the emphasis on stability, conventionality, and optimism, in the arts and literature. The question must be
posed whether this tendency can be ascribed solely to the dictates of the
Party, or whether the artistic fashions of the period—which is not yet
ended in the U.S.S.R.—are not also due to the natural reactions of a
society undergoing industrialization, and acquiring thereby, for all the
Marxian phraseology, middle-class values reminiscent of Victorian England. The paradox is hard to stomach if we look at Russia as a socialist
state and a totalitarian society. And yet the effect of great changes that
were imposed upon a Soviet society beginning with the first Five Year Plan
was to inculcate in a considerable part of society the good bourgeois
values of the nineteenth-century West: the importance of hard work, of
saving, of measuring one's station in life, among other things, by one's income and the quantity of one's material goods, etc. True, all these things
have been drilled into the Soviet people in the name of socialism, and,
true, no one in the Soviet Union may own a bank or a factory. But otherwise the logic of modernization and industrialization has played a strange
joke on Marxism: Decades of socialism and of the "dictatorship of the
proletariat" have instilled the attitudes and aspirations of a middle-class
society. "Become prosperous," said Stalin to the peasants in 1934. Soviet
literature and newspapers are full of moralistic stories—really the Soviet
version of the Horatio Alger stories—of poor working or peasant boys who,
through hard work and study, advance in life, becoming engineers, doctors, or "shock workers," i.e., reaching the status where they have a car of

---

[3] Thus in 1950 Stalin all of a sudden delivered himself of a judgment condemning
the then leading linguistic theory in the U.S.S.R. and coming out for another one. The
baffled sycophants, not quite knowing why, what, and to whom Stalin was addressing
his pronouncement, declared his commonplace views to be one of the most important
philosophical and scientific documents of the era!

their own, a television set, and enjoy, as the phrase goes, "all the amenities of a rich and cultural life." Such is the ideal set before the youth of Russia by the Communist Party of the U.S.S.R.!

The return to the traditional values[4] has been accompanied by a *qualified* rehabilitation of Russian history. Soviet historians in the immediate post-Revolutionary era and up to the middle thirties depicted pre-November Russia as a barbarous country, sunk in despotism, poverty, and obscurantism. Except for the revolutionary tradition reaching to the beginning of the nineteenth century nothing was presented in a positive light. Tsarist Russia was an oppressor of nations, her population groaned under poverty and superstition, whatever was good and progressive, whether in ideas or technology, came from the West. In this respect a fundamental change was ordered in the mid-thirties. The history of the Russian people was to be extolled. Even some of the imperial rulers were classified as having been "progressive" for their period. Thus, Peter the Great, for all his despotism, was now a man who reformed Russia and made her a world power (and a Soviet reader could not be unmindful of a contemporary parallel). Even Ivan the Terrible, it was discovered, was terrible and terroristic always toward the nobles, but solicitous of Russia and her people. The dangerous international situation and the imminence of war was the major but not the only reason for this rewriting of the past. In a period of great reconstruction and of great purges, the regime was also instinctively reaching for all the elements of stability it could find, and one of the most important ones was Russian patriotism. It seemed to be saying to the dominant nation of the Soviet Union: "The regime may be tyrannical, and it may be subjecting you to all kinds of sufferings and privations, but it is your government, and it is doing it for the greatness of your country."

This note was, of course, sounded even more loudly during the war. During its first, and for the Russians most catastrophic, phase, all the invocations and appeals to stand against the invader were made in the name of *Russian* patriotism, rather than of socialism, Marxism, or even of the more inclusive *Soviet* patriotism. And at the end, at a victory banquet at the Kremlin, Stalin pronounced a famous eulogy of the *Russian* people, again assigning them major credit for the victory, and acknowledging their tolerance toward their government, which, the despot stated—an unusual modesty in Stalin—had made mistakes. Russian patriotism was then rediscovered by the Soviet regime to be their major asset, and the natural instinct of the people to fight for their government, no matter how oppressive, against a foreign foe, to be a surer basis of their power than even Marxism-Leninism.

---

[4] Or rather to the traditional values of the West, since, as we have seen, these values were not shared very widely in pre-Revolutionary and pre-industrial Russia.

Following the war the Russian nationalist motif was not muted but on the contrary intensified. The damages of the war had to be made good in a feverish haste. Instead of easier living and greater liberties, the Soviet people were subjected after 1945 to continuing deprivations, and the continuation of the totalitarian rigor was no longer masked or rationalized by the war effort. As if to offset and justify the disappointed illusions and continued hardships a violent propaganda of Russian nationalism was launched. The non-Russian nationalities of the Bolshevik empire were reminded that the Russian nation even in tsarist times not only did not oppress them, as the earlier Communist "line" had proclaimed, but even then had brought them civilization and progress. Some of their national heroes previously extolled by the Communists as "progressive" fighters against Russian and tsarist oppression now were declared to have been reactionaries and traitors. The past traditions of the Russian people in the arts, science, literature—in a word, in everything but pre-Revolutionary politics—were extolled and declared to have been in advance of those of other nations. A violent campaign was conducted against "cosmopolitanism," by which for a time was meant any feeling that there was anything in the outside world worthy of admiration or emulation. And, an invariable element of extreme chauvinism and xenophobia in any society, an anti-Semitic note crept into even official pronouncements. It is clear from the admissions made by Soviet officials since the Twentieth Party Congress that discrimination was practiced against people of Jewish origin.

The tightening of totalitarian curbs and the officially sponsored chauvinism appear in retrospect to have been prompted by two major reasons. The first one was the recollection of the war, in which Russian nationalism proved to be intense, even on behalf of a tyrannical regime, while in the non-Russian areas of the U.S.S.R., especially the Ukraine during the first stage of the war, capitulation and even collaboration with the invader occurred on a fairly large scale.[5] But above and beyond the experience of the war, its end signified the end of the hopes for more liberal policies and for a more abundant life. Barely pausing for a period of reconstruction, the march toward more complete industrialization was resumed, and with it the continuation of a low living standard for the masses. The victory of the state, which made it one of the two superpowers in the world, which expanded its territory, gave it satellites in Eastern Europe, and won a Communist ally and protégé in Asia, brought no benefits to the people, save the freedom from the invader. It is not inconceivable that to allay and redirect the popular grievances, the Communist authorities sponsored the

---

[5] Though German brutality and exactions soon dissuaded the Ukrainians from the notion that the Nazis were a lesser evil.

nationalist campaign with its distinctly anti-Semitic undertones.[6] The movement that has always boasted of its international orientation and that had vowed unyielding struggle against all national and social prej-udices thus lent itself to a campaign of chauvinism.

The story of Soviet society between 1945 and 1953 is that of a society that had largely matured economically and socially, leaving behind the backwardness of old Russia, and showing both in its resistance to the in-vader and in the economic recovery and progress its great adaptability and strength. But against this social and economic picture the political system still remained geared to the task of running a primitive society that needed the whiplash of totalitarianism to make it into a modern industrial state. Totalitarianism, fastened on Russian society in the name of social and economic reconstruction, has remained and become intensified even though the major task of reconstruction has been accomplished.[7]

Policy Trends since Stalin's Death

Two extreme opinions have been voiced in the West about Soviet policies since Stalin's death. One view would attach extreme importance to the alleged process of liberalization which has gone on in Russia since 1953 and see a gradual though admittedly slow and uneven erosion of totali-tarianism. The other group of commentators points out that the essential features of totalitarianism in the U.S.S.R. have remained unchanged and that the measures liquidating or moderating the worst aspects of the police state, the campaign against the cult of personality, and the "thaw" in the cultural field were but incidents in the struggle for power which occupied the period 1953-1957, and that the years since then have seen a reversal both to undoubted personal dictatorship and to some of the most oppressive features of Stalinism. It would be unenlightening to resolve the problem by the lame truism that the truth lies somewhere in the middle. What exactly has changed in the Soviet system, and which features of totali-tarianism remain unaltered?

As mentioned above, what undoubtedly has changed in the Soviet pic-ture has been society at large. It has been greatly modernized and indus-trialized and the extremes of terror and suppression, as applied in the

---

[6] Another reason is found in the fact that the propaganda authorities had to overcome the effects of their own *wartime* efforts, when, of course, friendliness toward and appreciation of the U.S.S.R.'s Western allies was the officially sponsored line.

[7] The other and the major justification for the stringency of police controls and the continued sacrifices in the standard of living, as given by the regime, has always been the alleged "capitalist encirclement" and the hostility of the outside world to the U.S.S.R. That argument has lost much of its propaganda value after World War II and especially since the Russians' acquisition of nuclear and hydrogen weapons in 1949 and 1953 and the subsequent realization that a *major* war would involve universal and unprecedented destruction.

thirties and between 1948 and 1953, have in the post-Stalin period appeared
not only inhuman but even unnecessary for the preservation of the totalitarian system and further advances in industrialization. The so-called
liberalization of 1953-57 has rested upon two closely interwoven facts.
One has been a recognition, probably unanimous in the highest Party
circles, that terror and suppression in the Stalinist manner was no longer
necessary and that in fact it was interfering with the objectives of totalitarianism itself. The other has been the struggle for succession in which
each of the contenders for supreme power was anxious to appear as a pro-
ponent of liberalization and to ascribe the odium of the defense of the most
oppressive features of Stalinism to his opponents or rivals. As a result, the
extremes of terror and controls over the citizens' lives have been chopped
off. Successive amnesties have largely emptied the forced labor camps.
The well-advertised stress on *socialist legality* has narrowed (though not
entirely abolished, for in a totalitarian state terror can never be abolished
entirely) the range of cases in which penalties are dispensed administratively without juridical procedure. The special panels of the secret police
that dealt out summary justice were officially abolished, and the powers and
role of the secret police curtailed. Greater latitude of views and fashions
has been allowed in the arts, science, and literature. In brief, the regime,
while still totalitarian in its controls and attitudes, has sought to impose
a sane pattern of totalitarianism, in contrast with the extreme of Stalin's
despotism, which undoubtedly imparted something of the psychopathic
to the whole society.

It is well to keep in mind that the period 1953-57 represented also
something in the nature of a controlled experiment in which the regime
probed (if not entirely voluntarily) how far the controls could be relaxed
and terror minimized without damaging the essentials of its totalitarian
power. Beginning in 1957 and coinciding with Khrushchev's undoubted
assumption of primacy, the pace of liberalization first slackened and then
stopped and the regime left no doubt that the campaign against Stalinism
was in no wise intended to begin even to challenge the monopoly of power
of the Communist Party or its absolute control of every aspect of social and
political life.

The same mixture of causes—a common-sense response to a changed
situation, political maneuverings in the struggle for succession, and the
conviction that no measures or concessions must injure the framework of
totalitarianism—has characterized the regime's policy toward the economic
aspirations of its citizens. Under Malenkov (roughly from Stalin's death
to the end of 1954) the government promised and in some ways began to
furnish more in the way of consumers' goods. The fantastically grandiose
plans of capital construction initiated or planned under Stalin, uneconomi-

cally expensive in manpower and capital, have been largely modified or abandoned. The Plenum of the Central Committee held in September 1953 changed drastically the policy of merciless exploitation of the peasantry and instituted added material incentives to restore faltering Soviet agriculture. Malenkov's demotion in 1955 was accompanied by admonitions that heavy industry still has the priority over the consumer's needs. Yet in the long run the demand for a rise in the standards of living cannot be ignored as insistently as it was under Stalin; and barring war this demand must be appeased by the Communist Party, for such is the logic of the social and economic situation of the U.S.S.R.[8] In 1957 Khrushchev threw in the slogan of surpassing the United States within a few years in the production of meat, butter, and milk. The stress on catching up with and overcoming America was now launched in the field of consumers' goods as well as in heavy industry and linked with the promise of the realization of communism as the final stage of socialist society.

The same elements have played a decisive role in the reduction of working time in industry and the increase of the wages of the lower-paid workers. Not unconnected with the yearning for a higher standard of living is the permitting of legal abortions for other than reasons of health.

The crucial element in the campaign for a higher standard of living— indeed, in the long run, in the success or failure of the Soviet economy and system—has been and remains Soviet agriculture. More than five years after Stalin's death the Soviet leaders themselves revealed the dangerous state in which agriculture found itself in the early fifties. Speaking at the Plenum of the Central Committee in December 1958, Khrushchev revealed that the statistics for the grain production in Stalin's last year were falsified, the actual figure being lower by one third than that alleged.[9] The real figures indicated, Khrushchev admitted, that no real advance was made either in average productivity or in total production in Stalin's last year over the harvest in pre-revolutionary Russia in 1913!

The effort to bring Soviet agriculture more in step with the growth of industry has involved several lines of approach. As mentioned above, beginning in 1953 the collective peasant was offered added material incentives to increase his output. In 1957-58 the regime announced the policy of selling the Machine Tractor Stations, traditionally the key in the centralized control of agriculture, to the collective farms—a reform designed to give the collective farmers the feeling of a greater degree of freedom in planning and executing their work.

---

[8] This problem is elaborated in Chapter 26.
[9] The main and favorite method of falsification prior to 1953 was the identification of the so-called biological yield, i.e., of the grains and produce still in the field, with production for consumption.

Another line of attack upon the vexing problem of agriculture has consisted in the attempt to raise its technical level and to extend acreage. Under the first heading the regime, with Khrushchev taking personal leadership, pushed for the extension of the cultivation of corn and other crops previously not very popular with the Soviet peasant, nor assumed to be peculiarly appropriate to the soil conditions of large parts of Russia. Equally connected with the present leader's name has been the campaign to open up the virgin lands, i.e., to increase the area of cultivation by new vast lands (mostly in Kazakhstan and southeast Russia) previously deemed unsuitable for agriculture.

Both avenues of approach illuminate again the nature of the current Soviet regime and the inherent contradictions which still beset Communist policies in agriculture. The policy of concessions and added incentives to the peasant has stopped short of loosening the structure of the kolkhoz. And in a manner reminiscent of Stalin's days the policy of concessions and appealing to the profit motivation of the peasant was inevitably bound to be followed by a period of ideological hardening of the position on agriculture. In 1958-59 the regime again initiated a campaign against the remaining elements of private property in farming. This time the target was the cattle still left in the hands of individual peasants, and considerable pressure was exerted to have this property socialized, i.e., absorbed in the collectively owned herds. At the same time the movement toward the amalgamation of the kolkhozes was given a new spur, thus testifying to the regime's continuing unhappiness with the garden plot of the peasant household. Thus even the economic objectives of the regime are not permitted to assume a priority over its aim of complete control, which in agriculture it identifies with the restructuring of collective farming so as to strip it of the remaining elements of private property.

The extension of acreage and the introduction of new cultures was met both in Russia and abroad with the objection that it was essentially an uneconomic use of resources and that in the long run many of the "virgin territories" would lapse into dust bowls, etc.[10] But in the *short run* the tremendous resources devoted to the new areas certainly increased agricultural production and, incidentally, enabled Khrushchev to confound his opponents in the Central Committee. If in the *long run* the experiment proves less than successful then the blame will be laid not upon the First Secretary but upon the subordinate officials. Thus already a bad crop in Kazakhstan in 1959 was blamed on the highest Party officials of the republic rather than on the economic soundness of the experiment.

---

[10] One of the items of accusation brought out by Khrushchev against the "anti-Party group" of Molotov, Malenkov, and Kaganovich was their alleged opposition to the scheme.

In agriculture we find the most characteristic interplay of the forces which act upon Soviet totalitarianism: its ideology, the frantic drive for expanded production, the tremendous power of control and of concentration of resources which enables it to achieve seeming successes even through policies which are unsound in the long run, and finally the only sense in which the public opinion persists under the circumstances, i.e., the people's ability and willingness to work well or badly depending on the official policies.

The over-all character of the new policies reminds one of the deep-rooted continuity of Soviet totalitarianism. After all, in his social and economic policy Stalin also moved in a zigzag course: once the limit of compulsion was reached, a relaxation was ordered for a time. Thus compulsory and brutal collectivization was arrested in 1930 to be resumed after a breathing spell, and the Second Five Year Plan was kinder to the consumer than the First. We have traced similar zigzags in the post-Stalin era in agriculture, and similar phenomena could be observed in other fields. But while the main characteristic of the Stalin era was the reliance on compulsion and terror with an occasional recourse to incentives and more "liberal" policies, the post-Stalin regimes have reversed this priority: they rely on the general persuasiveness and concrete appeal of their internal policies, but do not shy away from compulsion. It is unlikely that the combination of personality and circumstances that created Stalinism could be reproduced in today's U.S.S.R. One is reminded of the fable of the sorcerer and his apprentice. The sorcerer could evoke a giant of enormous strength but could also render him harmless at will. Lenin and the Bolsheviks activated the masses of the Russian people and carried through a revolution. The task accomplished, they fastened on the people a bureaucratic and oligarchic regime. Stalin poured the enthusiasm and energies of the Communist Party into the task of industrializing and collectivizing the countryside. The foundations of a new industrial society having been laid, he decimated the Party. The sorcerer's assistant, it will be remembered, could evoke the monster but forgot how to control him and the giant threatened his maker with destruction. The fable should not be taken too literally, but it suggests the difficulty of reimposing the full weight of past despotism upon a society that has changed so much in the past generation.

Politically there is nothing to indicate that there can arise in the U.S.S.R. a nucleus of political power to compete with the Communist Party. The weakness of Communism in the satellites, the events in Yugoslavia, Poland, and Hungary—all these phenomena have appeared in countries where Communism is of recent domination and where the powerful force of nationalism have opposed it, and especially its Soviet connection. In the U.S.S.R. *Russian* nationalism has been exploited by the Communist regime, while the nationalisms of other peoples inhabiting the U.S.S.R. have yet to begin to play their full role. Communism and the Communist Party have been fastened on the country for forty years, and it is reasonable to assume that no Soviet citizen has a clear-cut idea of an alternative political and social system. It is possible that the regime may be subjected to increasing social strains, and that the immediate future will not see a violent revolution or upheaval (save probably changes within the ruling hierarchy), but that the pressure of economic and social forces will relatively weaken the Party and its unlimited powers of compulsion toward the people. In time perhaps something like semi-autonomous status might be won by institutions like the *state* bureaucracy, the trade unions, and the armed forces. The prospect, always keeping in mind the possibility of a *temporary* attempt to return to Stalinism, is of an evolution of the regime toward a greater responsiveness to the people's needs and aspirations. But there is no prospect in the foreseeable future of the U.S.S.R.'s evolving into a democracy, or achieving the rule of law rather than that of men and a doctrine.

[25]

The Pattern of Power:
Formal Structure

Soviet Constitutionalism

The constitutional structure of the Soviet Union has always been an elaborate façade behind which one-party rule and totalitarianism have occupied the political scene. No meeting of the Supreme Soviet has ever even faintly approached in importance a Party congress. Neither the Council of Commissars nor the Council of Ministers has ever rivaled the role of the Central Committee or the Presidium-Politburo of the Party as the supreme maker of policies. It is almost superfluous to add that Stalin, during much of the period of his dictatorial power (1925-41), never held a high state position. Lenin's function as the leader of the Soviet state was predicated on his personal and Party stature rather than only on the fact that he was Chairman of the Council of People's Commissars. Malenkov's brief primacy after Stalin's death was again based on a number of factors, only one of which was that he headed the government as the Chairman of the Council of Ministers. If the formal aspect of Soviet politics is to be studied, then the Statute of the Communist Party is a more important document than the Constitution of the U.S.S.R. From the top to the bottom of the Soviet structure the Party has played a more important role than the corresponding state organs.

The question that occurs right away is: why have an elaborate constitutional structure in a totalitarian regime? Is the Soviet constitution, the whole apparatus of elections, representative bodies, etc., merely "propaganda" of no significance whatsoever in the total picture of Soviet politics? And if so, why study the Soviet constitution and its appurtenances?

TABLE 14   The Formal Structure of the Soviet Government

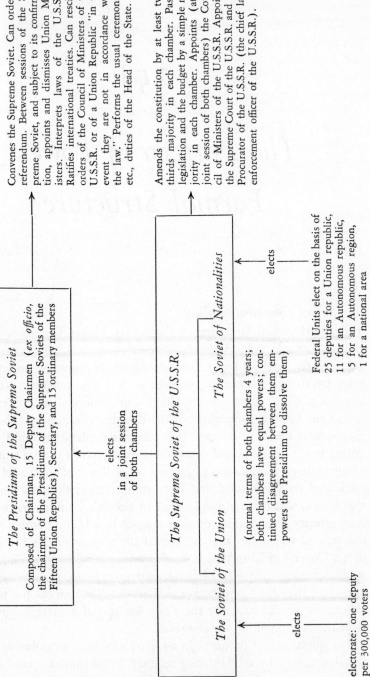

COMPETENCE

THE ORGANS

The Presidium of the Supreme Soviet

Composed of Chairman, 15 Deputy Chairmen (*ex officio*, the chairmen of the Presidiums of the Supreme Soviets of the Fifteen Union Republics), Secretary, and 15 ordinary members

Convenes the Supreme Soviet. Can order a referendum. Between sessions of the Supreme Soviet, and subject to its confirmation, appoints and dismisses Union Ministers. Interprets laws of the U.S.S.R. Ratifies international treaties. Can rescind orders of the Council of Ministers of the U.S.S.R. or of a Union Republic "in the event they are not in accordance with the law." Performs the usual ceremonial, etc., duties of the Head of the State.

Amends the constitution by at least two-thirds majority in each chamber. Passes legislation and the budget by a simple majority in each chamber. Appoints (at a joint session of both chambers) the Council of Ministers of the U.S.S.R. Appoints the Supreme Court of the U.S.S.R. and the Procurator of the U.S.S.R. (the chief law-enforcement officer of the U.S.S.R.).

elects
in a joint session
of both chambers

The Supreme Soviet of the U.S.S.R.

The Soviet of the Union   *The Soviet of Nationalities*

(normal terms of both chambers 4 years; both chambers have equal powers; continued disagreement between them empowers the Presidium to dissolve them)

elects

Federal Units elect on the basis of
25 deputies for a Union republic,
11 for an Autonomous republic,
5 for an Autonomous region,
1 for a national area

electorate: one deputy
per 300,000 voters

elects

There can be no simple answer. The evolution of Soviet constitutional institutions has reflected an important evolution in the thinking of the Bolsheviks about the state and its organization. Although, in practical terms, the state institutions have usually been subordinate to those of the Party and the representative bodies have usually had functions of a declamatory rather than politcal or deliberative character, the over-all significance of the representative institutions has transcended the "propaganda" aspect that is usually stressed by the outside commentators on the Soviet system. Soviet representative institutions as well as Soviet constitutionalism as a whole have several aspects of usefulness for the Communist regime, and by the same token several points of interest for those who want to understand the spirit and mechanics of Russian totalitarianism.

CONSTITUTIONALISM AND THE SOVIET PHILOSOPHY OF THE STATE

The Soviet regime has inherited the ambivalent attitude of Marxism toward the state and bourgeois constitutionalism. As for some Christian philosophers the state was a necessary evil and a consequence of our sins, so for Marx and Engels nineteenth-century Western constitutionalism, if not the state itself, was the product of the specific conditions of the class struggle. Economic exploitation by the possessing classes was protected by the state, while constitutionalism with its fictions of civic equality and legality was designed to appease the non-propertied masses. Yet Marxism, unlike anarchism, never maintained that victorious socialism would be able to dispense with the machinery of the bourgeois state right away. Presumably constitutions, elections, and the administrative machinery of the state would continue until socialism turned into communism, i.e., until production, liberated from the fetters of capitalism, became able to provide abundance for everybody, and thus dissolve classes and make the state, even the democratic state, superfluous. The (presumably) long transition from socialism to communism would be characterized by real—as opposed to bourgeois-fake—democracy; in contrast to the conditions of bourgeois democracy, elections, civil liberties, etc., would flower under the conditions of "proletarian dictatorship," which Marx somewhat paradoxically specifies as the dictatorship of a vast majority of the people.

Marxism, then, offered very little by way of concrete prescription for constitutional experimenting under the conditions of Russia of 1918 or, for that matter, of 1958. It offered several paradoxes: the distrust of Western parliamentarianism, and yet the conviction that under socialism "real" parliamentary institutions and "real" democracy should flourish; the final aim of the withering away of the state, and yet the transitional period during which the socialist state would be extremely powerful, since it would run the economy of the country as well as exercise the usual functions of the state. Within the thinking of Bolshevik leaders, these paradoxes were reflected both before and after the Revolution, in a variety of ideas running the whole gamut from the "abolition" of the state to the most centralized and authoritarian structure. Some problems resolved themselves. Like most secular religions, Bolshevism was for freedom but the "right" kind of freedom, for democratic elections but elections that would end in the "right" side's, i.e., their own, winning. Thus one-party rule became both the reality and the theory of the Bolshevik government a few months after the November Revolution, though at first a few Bolsheviks grumbled and objected that other bona fide revolutionary parties should be allowed to share in the government. The issue was determined when the Bolsheviks drove out the Constituent Assembly in January 1918. Within a few months the temporary alliance of the Bolsheviks and the Left Social Revolutionaries was ended. Up to about 1920 there were still a few stray Mensheviks and Social Revolutionaries in the representative organs (soviets). In effect, however, the two years after the Revolution witnessed the repression and liquidation of *all* other parties including even those elements in the Social Revolutionary and Menshevik parties that offered qualified submission to Soviet power.

While building the one-party state Lenin and his associates, even in the midst of a civil war, still considered it supremely important to settle the constitutional framework. No idea of a revolutionary directorate or complete absence of constitutional forms entered their minds. They set about devising a structure of government in which the Party dictatorship would operate within the context of democratic institutions. Their own form of democracy, it was felt, should represent something new and different from Western parliamentary institutions. Yet for all the nomenclature and all the pyramidal arrangement involved, the network of representative institutions evolved in the Constitutions of 1918 and 1924 bore more than a superficial resemblance to the Western pattern. Though the electoral appurtenances favored the workers over the peasants, and members of the former possessing classes and clergy were banned from voting, the base for elections was the mass of people. The Bolshevik leaders thus felt themselves to be heirs of the Western republican tradition. They early rejected the notion that professional representative institutions, i.e., trade-union councils, should replace wider popular assemblies. The new nomenclature, *soviets*, for representative institutions, "commissars" for ministers, had the revolutionary flavor about it, but the structure of assemblies, provisions for amending the constitution, and parliamentary practices, indicated the link that, on paper and in theory, existed with the main current of Western constitutionalism.

The first two Soviet constitutions, prepared in the early days of the regime and considered as transitional documents until the final triumph of Communism in Russia, illustrate, then, one of the uses of studying the formal side of the government of the U.S.S.R.: Soviet constitutions reflect the basic philosophy of the state of the actual rulers of the Soviet Union— the leaders of the Party and the state—and their estimate of the people's aspirations. Soviet politics is like a vast painted canvas: Action and movement take place on the first plane but they are balanced by a serene background. Thus the actuality of Party politics, of the real pattern of power, is balanced by the background of constitutionalism.

The trend toward "normalcy" in constitutional institutions was emphasized even more in the Soviet Constitution of 1936. The Stalin Constitution, as it was then called, abandoned the unwieldy network of elections of its predecessors. Instead of a huge Congress of Soviets that seldom met, its also overlarge Executive Committee of two chambers, and the Presidium—the only steadily functioning representative organ—the new Constitution returned to the bourgeois simplicity of two normal-sized parliamentary chambers: the Council (Soviet) of the Union and the Council of Nationalities, which designate the Presidium, the collective president of the U.S.S.R. Under this Constitution suffrage is direct, and equal, and the former disqualification from voting of certain classes is abandoned. The Constitution of 1936, adopted incidentally in the period of Popular Front, and the drawing together of the Western democracies and the U.S.S.R. in the face of the threat from the Axis, reflected the conviction of the regime that the Soviet Union should receive a "normal" constitution with the echoes of the early revolutionary struggles and revolutionary romanticism muted. As Stalin proclaimed, socialism had been achieved in Russia. There were no longer any exploiting but only two friendly classes: workers and peasants. Hence there was no longer any need to discriminate against the former landowners, the clergy, etc., nor to weigh the worker's vote more than that of the peasant. The Constitution, which acknowledged the leading role of the Communist Party, proclaimed an impressive list of civil rights guaranteed to the citizens, in which the "bourgeois" freedoms of press, speech, inviolability of the person, were joined by the socialist rights, the state guaranteeing every citizen the right to work and leisure. Again, the value of the Constitution as a beautiful background to the stark political reality is enhanced if we keep in mind that the Stalin Constitution came into effect during the most intense period of terror in the history of the U.S.S.R., when the holocaust, not only within the Party and the state apparatus, but also among the population at large, made a mockery of the civil rights and liberties so emphatically guaranteed in the Constitution.

The background is not without its uses. The regime, unlike the Fascist and Nazi philosophies, does not in theory repudiate the democratic and humanitarian tradition of European political thought. It does not explicitly base its claims on an irrationalist philosophy, or elitism. It claims that political democracy *does* exist in the U.S.S.R. When it becomes necessary or convenient to repudiate a particularly sordid period of Soviet history, it can put the blame on wanton behavior of individuals and their lack of respect for Soviet legality and constitutionalism. None other than the head of the police forces and presumably one of the main supervisors of terror, Lavrenti Beria, blossomed out after Stalin's death (though not for long) as the advocate of legality. In the campaign against the cult of personality and in the general repudiation of the excesses of the Stalinist era, the Soviet leaders led by Khrushchev again based their emphasis on the illegality and unconstitutionality of Stalin's actions and the system of terror from 1934 on. Thus the Constitution and the legal underpinnings of the system enable the regime to have their cake and to eat it too, and to present all the hard political facts that are, in reality, of the essence of the Soviet political system, as temporary and transient aberrations arising out of the willful and illegal acts of individuals, rather than as being imposed by the logic of totalitarianism.

Does not Soviet constitutionalism work against the regime in the sense that the rights proclaimed in the Constitution are belied every day by the facts of Soviet politics? Does not the average citizen resent the gap, say, between the provisions of the Constitution as to free elections and the reality, in which the Communist Party nominates a single list of candidates who are then elected without opposition? Up to now the Soviet regime has not betrayed any apprehension that the gap between the theory and the reality of Soviet politics will undermine the foundations of the dictatorship. Throughout the worst periods of the totalitarian terror under Stalin, the Constitution of 1936 was proudly extolled as the most democratic in the world. Western constitutionalism has been proclaimed as a sham and Soviet liberties have been exalted. Elections to the national representative bodies have always been celebrated as holidays and the foregone results, with over 90 per cent of the electorate voting for the official and unopposed lists, have been hailed as demonstrating the strength and popularity of the regime. Seen from one point of view, Soviet representative institutions and constitutionalism as a whole are a tribute that totalitarianism plays to universal human aspirations for freedom and democratic institutions. Though in practice they are limited by the requirements of the dictatorship, and even in theory they are expounded as consistent with the superior requirements of the ideology and the one-party state, Soviet constitutional institutions are not negligible in the spectrum of Soviet politics, and, under certain circumstances, as will be discussed below, they may acquire a real as distinguished from symbolical importance.

Soviet Constitutionalism as a Unifying and Educational Factor

In their origins Western representative and constitutional institutions had but little to do with any abstract theories of democracy or with the practical necessities of giving the people an opportunity of expressing their preferences as to the system of government. They existed to provide a framework of national or state unity. The monarchs of the Middle Ages summoned parliaments in order to consult their subjects on the most expeditious ways of obtaining money, and to give a select body of their subjects an opportunity of acquainting themselves with the complexity of the problems facing the state. This rudimentary function of constitutional institutions is of great importance in assessing the working of the constitutional framework of the U.S.S.R. In the Supreme Soviet of the U.S.S.R. the delegates from Uzbekistan and the Soviet Far East sit alongside Russians and Ukrainians; factory workers and collective farm peasants who have distinguished themselves in their work are fellow delegates with the highest Party leaders, marshals of the Soviet Union, and academicians. Thus unity and cohesiveness of the Soviet state finds its tangible expression in the constitution and its organs.

The Supreme Soviet serves as a platform for the announcement and demonstration of national policies. Once a motif is thrown out by a leader, the other delegates, in a fashion common to all totalitarian parliaments, join in a chorus expounding and intensifying the official pronouncement, be it a warning to the "warmongers of the West," or, contrariwise, a profession of Soviet friendship and wish for collaboration with the U.S.A.; the need for further development of the Soviet consumer industries, or the reassertion of the superior needs and requirements of heavy industry. In an "activist" totalitarian regime, in which the citizen is expected to be not merely a passive subject and observer but a convinced and enthusiastic participant in the official policies and sentiments, the tribune of the national legislature is one more instrument for enmeshing the common man with the machine of the state, of expounding and amplifying the policies that come from above. The same holds for the Soviet courtroom: the dictator, whether an individual or a group, reserves for himself alone the right to proceed extralegally, while the mass of the citizens in their dealings with one another are bound by general rules and regulations. Thus in a highly developed totalitarian regime constitutionalism and legality become themselves handmaidens of the dictatorship.

In the same vein in a country of the vastness of Russia, of the complexity and ubiquity of the Soviet state machinery, the network of representative and legal institutions serves as one of the most useful devices through which the rulers check both on the behavior of their subordinates and on the sentiments of their subjects. A deputy from Odessa will not criticize Stalin, or, at different times, Malenkov, or Khrushchev, or any of the main figures of the regime, but he will not be restrained but on the contrary encouraged to speak of the administrative deficiencies or shortcomings in his city, or the failure of some ministry to provide an adequate volume or quality of goods. Legal remedies will not avail against officially sponsored terror, but a worker persecuted by his manager or trade-union secretary will have his day in court. Beyond the rigid frame of the dictatorship itself, and beyond the wide scope of official policies, the grievances and aspirations of the people can be aired and redress can be sought.

Soviet Constitutionalism as a Political Factor

We come to the third major consideration of Soviet constitutionalism: its use as a *major* political factor. Admittedly, as implied here throughout, in a stable totalitarian situation, the legal and constitutional framework is secondary to the real complex of political, police, and social forces upon which the regime rests. Yet examples are not lacking in which in a situation of crisis an institution that has existed on paper without interfering with the essence of political power has suddenly become endowed with importance. Throughout many years of the Fascist regime in Italy, it would have been inconceivable for the Grand Fascist Council to have repudiated Mussolini or for the figurehead king to have dismissed the dictator. Yet following Italy's defeats in Sicily in 1943, the constitutional and legal fictions became endowed with temporary reality and the Fascist regime crumbled at the bidding of those institutions it had so long and so readily commanded.

It is rather far-fetched to draw any possible parallels with the Soviet Union. Throughout the long years of the consolidated Bolshevik reign the representative institutions have never registered any but a unanimous vote, the courts have never rendered a political verdict but in accordance with the desires of those in power. When the great struggle for power rocked the Communist Party and the country in the middle twenties, no reflection of it penetrated the All-Union Congress of Soviets or its Executive Committee, so unimportant were they in the over-all political picture. Legal institutions were used during the purges of the thirties as convenient places in which to publicize and denounce the alleged crimes of the former and potential opponents to Stalin. Nor has the use of such extralegal devices died with Stalin. Beria and his henchmen were tried and sent to death without observing any of the constitutional provisions about guarantees against arbitrary arrest and trial in open court. It is not too much to assume that many a humbler citizen has met with an arbitrary arrest since

March 1953, though the frequency of such incidents must have diminished considerably since Stalin's death.

Yet when all is said, the importance of Soviet constitutional devices has increased since the despot died. Essentially the dictatorship has been in transition and constitutional offices are endowed with *potential* political significance. On the morrow of Stalin's death a group of senior Communist Party officials, after (it is reasonable to assume) some bargaining, rearranged the highest offices in the Party and the state. The new arrangements were in obvious violation of both the Party statute and the Soviet Constitution, though *post facto* they were ratified by the competent body. One office that changed hands was that of the chairman of the Presidium of the Supreme Soviet, i.e., the titular head of the Soviet state. Now, that post was never of any political significance, having been held during Stalin's last years by a faithful but indistinguished Stalinist, Nicolai Shvernik. It is significant that with the opening of a new era it was thought important by the highest Party leaders to change the incumbent, and to entrust the presidency to the senior member of the Party Presidium; a man who, it was assumed (and, as the events of 1957 were to show, not quite correctly), because of his age and past role would not be directly involved in the coming struggle for power, Marshal of the Soviet Union Kliment Voroshilov. In an unstable situation the post of the titular head of the state became of consequence.

Totalitarian systems are unable to endow their constitutional systems with vitality, not only because of the unwillingness of the rulers, but also because of their real inability to conceive how free representative and legal institutions can operate. Political struggle thus *has* to assume the aspect of intrigue, of matching physical and organizational forces at the disposal of the factions, rather than of a free interplay of ideas and a test of strength within the constitutional framework. It is not too much to say of the rulers of the Soviet Union that they do not wish to grant the real prerequisites of democracy to their people; that they could not afford to grant them if they wished; and, most important of all, that they would not know how to go about instituting *real* constitutionalism and a *really* independent judiciary even if they could afford to. By the same token, the habits of mind and action, and the social and political settting that enable constitutional and democratic institutions to operate, have at present no root among the peoples of the U.S.S.R., having been extirpated by four decades of dictatorship and having had but a rudimentary development before. Yet history teaches that as the most intensive form of absolutism recedes, social and economic aspirations become translated into political demands. Representative institutions, as asserted by one of their most famous theorists, are a tender growth and it may take a very complicated pattern of events and conditions to bring them to maturity. But the seeds of demo-cratic ideas and institutions possess a vitality that makes them begin their growth even within the freshly opened cracks of totalitarianism.

Federalism

The Constitution of 1936 guarantees each of the fifteen[1] Union repub-lics that constitute the Soviet state the right "freely to secede from the U.S.S.R." More realistic on the subject is the Soviet national anthem when it speaks of "an *unbreakable* union of free republics." The most poignant illustration of both the freedom and the right to secession is seen in the fact that no more serious charge could be preferred against a real or alleged enemy of the regime, whether under or after Stalin, than that of plotting to separate one of the national republics from the U.S.S.R. As for tsarist Russia, so for the U.S.S.R., the problem of the non-Russian nationalities remains a master factor of its politics. The mosaic of nationalities is re-flected by the gradations of legal status from the Union Republic, to the Autonomous Republic, to the Autonomous Region and the National Dis-trict. The intracacies of formal federalism are counterbalanced by the fact of political centralization assured by the totalitarian system. As is the case with other political institutions the nationality problem is an example of the peculiar dialectic of Soviet politics: the theory grounded in the demo-cratic side of Marxism and embodied in the constitution confronts the antithesis of totalitarian reality. The interplay of the two will provide one of the keys to the future of the Union of Soviet Socialist Republics.

This dialectic confronted the Bolsheviks at the time of the Revolution, when the Russian empire was in a state of dissolution and when the Soviet leaders by their own declaration had been committed to the principle of self-determination. Though the discussion about the nationality problems had in the past divided the Russian Social-Democratic Party, Lenin and his partisans had firmly embraced the principle of a free option by each nation as to its remaining within a multi-national state or separating from it. Definitely repudiated was the view of Rosa Luxemburg that national independence is a problem of secondary importance to the working class, and that the triumph of socialism will render superfluous the national ques-tion. The official view enunciated, under Lenin's supervision, by young Joseph Stalin had clung to the territorial principle and independence of nations. Yet power brought with it the immediate posing of concrete questions: Should the Bolsheviks sit idly by and see large parts of the Rus-sian empire slip from their grasp? Should self-determination extend to cases in which "reactionary" (i.e., non-Bolshevik) elements would form states out of the former territories of the Russian empire? At first, in view

---

[1] The number was reduced in 1956 to fifteen through the absorption of the Karelo-Finnish S.S.R. in the Russian S.S.R.

of its weakness, the Bolshevik regime could not but find it good politics to adhere to its announced principles, and to agree to the independence of various nationalities of the old empire. The defeat of Germany freed the Soviets from the oppressive conditions of the Treaty of Brest-Litovsk, which, among other things, would have detached the Ukraine, and have made her in effect a German satellite. Soviet successes in the Civil War infused the regime with more self-confidence and made it solicitous of restoring to the government most of the old empire's territory. There were still in 1919-20 expectations of a Europe-wide revolution, and hence the independence of Poland, of Finland, and of other Baltic states would presumably be but an interlude to their reintegration as Soviet republics. The 1920-21 period saw the end of such hopes. The task was now to reconstruct the Soviet state on a new federal basis, and to implement in practice the Soviet nationality principle.

This principle was to be enunciated later on by Stalin, the first Commissar of Nationalities and one of the architects of Soviet federalism, as requiring a state "proletarian in content and national in form." The expression "proletarian in content" signified in effect that the various "union" and "autonomous" republics could not expect bona fide political self-determination once they found themselves within the spectrum of Soviet power. The Ukrainians, Georgians, Armenians, the Turkic nations of Central Asia, etc., would no longer—this is speaking from the perspective of the early twenties—be submitted to forcible russification and denial of cultural rights, but they would be subject, together with the Great Russians, to the political and economic monolith of the Soviet system.

In the early days of the regime, when the foundations of Soviet federalism and their theoretical underpinnings were being laid, ideological considerations still possessed a vitality that only much later gave way to power considerations. Lenin, the supreme revolutionary pragmatist, was anxious that the practical task of consolidation of the Soviet state and its centralistic organization should not be combined with an underestimation of the potent force of nationalism. Before, as a leader of a handful of revolutionaries, he had adhere to a nationality policy that would avoid a disintegration of the revolutionary movement into its national segments while at the same time it endorsed the spirit of nationalism. Now, as the leader of a multi-national state, he sanctioned forcible incorporation of the Ukraine and Georgia by the Bolsheviks, while at the same time he warned against the excesses of Great-Russian chauvinism. At the Eighth Party Congress in 1919, angered by the arguments of Bukharin and Pyatakov who disparaged self-determination as being strictly secondary to the dictatorship of the proletariat, he exclaimed: "Scratch some Communists and you will find Great-Russian chauvinists." Practically on his deathbed in 1923 Lenin denounced Stalin's and Dzherzinski's repressive policies in Georgia with the observation that people of non-Russian ethnic origin sometimes became the most intense Russian chauvinists, a remark particularly suitable in view of Stalin's subsequent career.

The theoretical disagreement thus paralleled the differences among personalities of Soviet leaders. Dzherzinski, the Pole, and Stalin, the Georgian, could be the warmest advocates of political centralization and, in effect, of Russian predominance in the Soviet Union. Others, like the veteran Ukrainian Communist, Skrypnik, and the Georgian, Budu Mdivani, professed their native nationalism no less intensely than their Communism. Out of the ideological crosscurrents, out of the specifically Russian conditions following the end of World War I and the Civil War, was born both the theory and the practice of Soviet federalism.

The theory was militantly nationalistic insofar as the cultural rights of each, even the tiniest, nationality, were concerned. Not only were the great and ancient non-Russian nations to be given the fullest autonomy in the use of their language, free development of their culture, etc., but similar rights were to be extended to the Chuvash and the Ostyaks, primitive Asian tribes. Siberian tribes barely emerged from the Stone Age were to be encouraged to have their own written language and literature, and to have some form of national organization. The early most ideologically tinged days of the Soviet state were the days of enthusiastic nation-building, when federalism was to join in a harmonious union nationalities at most disparate stages of development and to guide them in a joint socialist experiment. The Bolsheviks went out of their way to provoke and establish the feeling of national separateness, even in such cases as that of the Byelorussians, where this feeling was not very strongly developed. If socialism was eventually (and "eventually" in the early twenties was thought to mean rather soon) to unite all nations of the world in one great union, why be afraid of Ukrainian, Armenian, or Kazakh nationalism? Remove economic exploitation, proclaimed Marxism, and the state becomes an instrument of progress and of social justice, the progress that will gradually make the state itself superfluous. By the same token, remove national oppression, which is but one form of economic exploitation, and various nationalities will abide peacefully together, and through their free development will hasten the day when the triumph of socialism will secure one supranational socialist culture and language. Russia, the jailer of nations under the tsarist regime, would become a Soviet federation, a prototype of the future universal union of socialist states.[2]

---

[2] It is a highly academic question, but one that has occasioned some debate, whether Marxism postulates that the final stage of socialism-communism will see not only the withering away of the state but also of national differences. Certainly Stalin in one of his speeches once forecast the development of a universal language superseding the national one. Late in life, as in his famous article on linguistics, he repudiated the

The practice of Soviet federalism saw at the end of the Civil War several state units nominally independent of each other, but in fact already united, or about to be united through the agency of the Communist Party and the Red Army. By the end of 1922 the process of consolidation, either peaceful or forceful, by the Bolsheviks transformed their empire into four units. The giant among them was the Russian Socialist Federated Soviet Republic, which received its constitution in July 1918. The R.S.F.S.R. contained several autonomous republics and districts, many of them created out of the Turkic-inhabited territories of Central Asia. United in fact, but nominally entirely independent, were the Ukrainian, the Byelorussian, and the Transcaucasian Soviet Socialist Republics. The last one was composed of three previously separate and really independent states, which the Bolsheviks conquered once the Civil and Polish wars were over. The edifice was crowned by a formal union, and as of January 31, 1924, the Soviet state became the Union of Soviet Socialist Republics.

The formal pattern of Soviet federalism has changed but little between 1924 and 1962. The number of Union republics had grown from four to eleven on the eve of World War II, and is now fifteen. The sources of accession have been: "promotion" of autonomous republics to the status of Union republics, as in the case of the Central Asiatic republics; subdivision of existing republics, as in the case of the Transcaucasian republic, resolved into its historic components Azerbaijan, Georgia, and Armenia; and conquest, as in the case of the Moldavian republic (part of which had been in the Ukrainian S.S.R. before 1939) and the three Baltic states annexed to the U.S.S.R. in 1940. Some changes of status have taken place among the lesser gradations within the federal structure. The most noteworthy has been the dissolution during and after the war of some autonomous republics and national regions, the inhabitants of which allegedly collaborated with the Germans. This fate befell, among others, the Volga German and the Crimean Tatar autonomous republics, and was accompanied by a wholesale deportation and dispersal of the surviving population throughout Russia.

Within the framework of the constitution the federal principle is represented in one of the two representative chambers, the Council (Soviet) of Nationalities. Within this Council each of the Union republics is represented by twenty-five members, autonomous republics by eleven members, autonomous regions by five, and each national district sends one member. The 1936 Constitution thus enthrones the federal principle in a more clear-

---

view that the progress of socialism would erase cultural separateness of nations or construct one nation. Like all the more extreme and utopian prognoses of Marxism, the notion of the "withering away" of the state and of national differences has been allowed in the Soviet Union to fall into desuetude.

cut form than its predecessor of 1923-24, in which the Council of Nationalities was one of the two branches of the Executive Committee of the unwieldy Congress of Soviets. The council of Nationalities has coequal powers with the Council of the Union, which is elected on the basis of population. The attractiveness of Soviet federalism was enhanced during the discussion of the 1936 Constitution by Stalin's pointed references to the right of secession of the Union republics, and the need, therefore, of their being fairly large and homogeneous units.

The division of competence between the All-Union and the republic authorities was sketched again in an atmosphere of unreality that has pervaded the whole history of Soviet constitution-making. The administrative organs are divided into three large classes: the All-Union ministries (e.g., heavy industry[3]) reserved to the competence of the central organs; the Union-republic ministries (e.g., agriculture), in which the administrative organs in the republics report to the corresponding ministries in Moscow; and finally republican ministries (e.g., education), where authority is theoretically vested exclusively in the hands of the republics. The Union-republic governments parallel the central organs with their single-chamber Supreme Council, and the Council of Ministers. More or less the same arrangement prevails in the case of the autonomous republics.

Political literature has been rich in discussion occasioned by problems of federalism. Thus the American, Swiss, Canadian, and German systems have since their beginnings been characterized by conflicts and debate as to the extent of federal vs. state or province powers. Within the Soviet Union the secondary character of the constitutional arrangements has prevented any possibility of such conflicts and has rendered almost superfluous a serious discussion of the division of authority between the center and the Union republics. It is still appropriate to make some remarks concerning the problem. Even within the letter of the Constitution the autonomy of the constituent units appears shaky. The Union republics have the right to secede from the Union (Article 17), but the Presidium of the Supreme Soviet of the U.S.S.R. has the power to rescind decisions of the Councils of Ministers of the Union Republics (Article 49-e), and similar powers belong to the Council of Ministers of the U.S.S.R. (Article 69). The Procurator of the U.S.S.R., the chief law-enforcing official of the state, *appoints* the procurators of the Union and autonomous republics (Article 115). The amount of centralization envisaged in the Constitution is so considerable that an argument could be advanced that, even if one takes

---

[3] Some heavy-industry ministries have recently become Union-republic ones, others from Union-republic have become republican, and thus the trend toward greater decentralization of economic organization still continues in the U.S.S.R.

into account the strict letter of law and disregards everything else, the Soviet Union is more of a unitary than a bona fide federal state.

The federal aspect of the Constitution is largely a backdrop against which is played the real and vital problem of nationalities. Whenever foreign or domestic exigencies require it, Soviet federalism is dramatically exhibited to the world as proof that the nationality problem has been solved in the Soviet Union. It is difficult to interpret otherwise the amendment of the Constitution in 1944 whereby the Union republics were granted the right to coduct foreign relations and to possess military forces, and the ministries of defense and foreign affairs were transformed into Union-republic agencies. No federation in the world grants its federal units the right to conduct independent foreign and defense policies. Behind the amendment were obvious political reasons: Soviet Russia was soon to claim seats in the United Nations for each of her sixteen constituent republics, and was actually to obtain two additional seats, one for the Ukraine and one for Byelorussia.[4] Stalin's ingenious reasoning at the Yalta conference, that he might have political trouble in the Ukraine if that war-devastated republic did not become one of the charter members of the world organization, illustrates one of the uses to which the regime has put its federal pretensions. Nobody in his right mind, either in the U.S.S.R. or abroad, is today willing to believe that Kiev or Minsk have policies, or even agencies, capable of conducting policies independent of Moscow.

Even more mysterious has been the fate of the Union-republic defense ministries. The inextricable combination of fiction, propaganda, and potential importance that is Russian federalism was given yet another illustration in 1954. On that date, in celebration of the three-hundredth anniversary of the first union of the Ukraine and Muscovy, the Crimea, which is geographically part of the Ukraine, but which until then had been a district of the Russian Socialist Federated Soviet Republic, was ceremoniously transferred to the Ukrainian S.S.R. The practical political consequence was somewhat parallel to the gesture of a man transferring some change from one pocket to another, but it served as a reminder that the nationality-federal problem remains of great significance for the Soviet state.

The problem of non-Russian nationalities has three main foci in the Soviet Union. The most important non-Russian ethnic group is the Ukrainian. Numbering more than forty million and closely related to the Russians in speech and culture, the Ukrainians are still a separate nation-

---

[4] The U.S.S.R. is thus represented in the United Nations by three member states: the federation and the two republics. The paradox, which escaped comment at the time, is that the largest federal unit, the R.S.F.S.R., was not pushed for admission, while two smaller ones were.

ality with national consciousness and national aspirations that originated at least a century ago.

The two main nations of Transcaucasia, the Armenians and the Georgians, though much less numerous, have memories of a national existence and culture dating back to the first centuries of the Christian era. And both in the Caucasus and in Central Asia there are several Turkic-speaking nationalities: the Uzbeks, Azerbaijanis, Kazakhs, Turkmens, and others, all closely related and with a common background of Moslem culture.

In all three cases local nationalisms have been watched eagerly by the Soviet regime to detect and inhibit any signs of a desire for separate statehood or even a real, as distinguished from a paper, autonomy. This supervision has reached deeply even into a cultural life of the non-Russian nationalities, with anything suggesting past as well as present incompatibility of interests between the given nation and the Russians being declared treason. The process of russification of national cultures and of the indoctrination of the youth in the primacy of and the indissoluble union with the Russian nation has been especially pronounced since World War II. Yet while these means can be effective in the case of small, until recently primitive tribes, or smaller nations like the three small Baltic countries annexed during the war, they cannot be entirely efficacious when dealing with multi-million national groups like the Ukrainians and the Turkic peoples.

In some cases the Soviet regime has resorted to or allowed demographic changes to strengthen the preponderance of the Russian element. Thus in the enormous Kazakh republic, the Texas of the U.S.S.R., the Kazakhs are now in a minority with more than half of the population being relatively recent settlers from the Ukraine and Russia, and this process is likely to go on with the progress of industrialization and the settlement of the "virgin lands." The Russian element seems to predominate also in the larger industrial cities of the Ukraine. Yet in the age of nationalism even the most powerful totalitarian regime cannot resettle, extirpate, or completely eradicate the national feelings of a group of twenty or forty million people.

Here it is necessary to pause once again to observe the use of Soviet "constitutional formalism." The letter of the law stands in stark contrast with the reality of politics. Whether in Uzbekistan, the Ukraine, or Georgia, political authority proceeds from Moscow. But at times the grant, on paper, of national sovereignty has served to relieve the fissiparous tendencies of non-Russian nationalisms, and even to gain enthusiastic adherents for Communism from among the more backward nationality groups, for whom even a paper sovereignty represented an advance and promise over their pre-Revolution status. By the same token, the institutions and liberties that exist on paper sometimes have the knack of becoming transformed into live and menacing demands. No other aspect of the Soviet system is a likelier candidate for this role of Frankenstein monster than its national and federal problem.

Administration

The Soviet state has been, because of the size and complexity of its administrative structure, *the* administrative state of recent times. Modern technology and the consequently enormously involved economic and political systems under which we live have everywhere increased the importance of administration: the art and procedures of doing things political and economic. Some have argued that the very focus of politics has shifted from the public forums and halls of legislatures, where politicians discuss principles and enact laws, to the offices and institutions, where administrators devise the ways and means of keeping going the complex economic and political machinery of the modern state. This development in the pattern of policy has been noticeable even in the democracies. It has reached its highest point in the Soviet Union. The totalitarian state is also the administrative state: a hierarchy of administrators—whether they be Party bureaucrats, officials charged with the planning and development of the economy, army and police officers, etc.—rules Russia. They are accountable, in the last resort, to the highest group of administrators. In the Presidium of the Communist Party the old revolutionary leaders (who themselves had served as Stalin's deputies over a large administrative domain) now play a secondary role to the new generation, whose whole career had been within the administrative apparatus of the state and the Party until their ability or the whim of the dictator, or both, endowed them with a political significance as well.

It was not as a charismatic leader or a victorious general that Stalin ascended the pinnacle of power. Though most accounts of his rise neglect his considerable political ability, it is generally true that his main avenue was his skill as an *"apparatchik,"* a man of the "apparatus" (of the Party) who through his ability at running the routine business of the Party gained an upper hand over his competitors, who shone more brilliantly as theoreticians or orators. Several years of anonymous work in Stalin's secretariat preceded Malenkov's emergence as a major Party figure. Khrushchev had been an obscure Party worker before he was selected by the dictator, at the height of the purges in the thirties, to be the head of the Ukrainian Party organization. Bulganin's career prior to his disgrace in 1958 may serve as a prototype of the *curriculum vitae* of a successful politician in the Soviet Union: a stint with the Secret Service, work at the managerial level, director of the State Bank, chairman of the Moscow

City Soviet, and finally national prominence as a political general and minister of war, accompanied, of course, by membership in the highest Party councils. The new generation of the highest Soviet leaders, the Kozlovs, Kosygins, Kirichenkos, and Suslovs, are for the most part people who have arrived at prominence through long years of administrative work and whose political prominence was a prize for their technical (in the broad sense of the word) usefulness. To be sure, the ability to advance or even to survive within the Soviet administrative system cannot have been unconnected, especially during the period of the Great Purge of the thirties, with political ability, at least in the sense of choosing the right protectors, special usefulness and docility to the dictator, etc. But the fact remains that the ascent to high posts has been apolitical in the Western sense of the word "political": no struggle for votes, no interplay of political ideas, has enabled a man in the Soviet Union to achieve prominence during the last generation. Politics in our sense of the word has atrophied during the Stalin era. Administration has become preeminent.

That this should be so, is one of the poignant ironies of the history of the Soviet state. For, along with the conviction that, under Socialism, the repressive and military tasks of government should wither away, the early Bolsheviks have inherited the notion that there is nothing specialized or special in the task of governing. Lenin's dictum that a kitchen servant can easily be transformed into a political expert is well known. That amateurs could perform the most involved functions of government was clearly expressed in Lenin's *State and Revolution*. Administration would wither away before the state. Popularly elected councils would run the whole complex of governmental functions, executive and legislative, and even judges would be elected. Thus members of the local city soviet (i.e., city councilmen) would give part of their time freely to the task of administering various branches of the city administration. The principle of separation of powers, *at any level*, was felt by the Bolshevik to be obsolete and smacking of fraudulent, bourgeois parliamentarianism. The highest administrative organ could not be dispensed with even in the early beginnings. But no bourgeois-sounding title of "minister" for the land of the soviets. The official appellation was at first the "Provisional Workers' and Peasants' Government." Branches of the central government were called Commissariats, presided over by the People's Commissars, each assisted by a council-collegium. The Soviet of People's Commissars soon became in effect a council of ministers, and the fact was officially recognized when in March 1946 the name itself was changed to conform to the accepted world-wide usage. About the same time uniforms were introduced for members of various branches of administration including those the most "bourgeois" countries are content to leave ununiformed. The symbolism of titles and uniforms has reflected the great change both in actuality and in official thinking on the subject of administrations.[5]

Russia is, then, a much-administered country. It is proposed here to examine the structure of state administration, leaving for the subsequent chapter the structure of the Party. The interrelationship of the Party and state machinery is one of those topics in politics that cannot be described by laying down a set of rules. The Party leads and controls the government. All the state officials, even of the middling rank, are its members. The highest officers of the state are important Party officials (though the converse is not always so). Yet the exact way in which the two machines intermesh and react upon each other varies with each important change in the political atmosphere, the personality of the incumbents of the given positions, etc. A few examples will illustrate the problem. Though they are chosen from the highest ranks of the Party and state administration, they find their parallels at all levels of the hierarchy.

The Chairman of the Council of Commissars, i.e., the prime minister, following Lenin's death, was Alexei Rykov. As early as 1928 Rykov disagreed with Stalin, then already in complete ascendance, over questions of agricultural policy, and fell into disgrace. Yet Rykov retained his chairmanship until December 1930. The head of the executive branch of the government was powerless when confronted with the hostility of the Secretary-General of the Party. While still in office, the former had no alternative but to carry out policies and instructions of which he disapproved. Rykov was succeeded by Molotov, a faithful pupil and follower of Stalin. It was not until May 1941 that the dictator himself assumed the chairmanship. It is possible that the general European situation—Russia was to be plunged into war within a few weeks—may have persuaded Stalin that he should assume immediate and overt leadership of the government. But in terms of real power, the chairmanship was in fact insignificant. No one would argue that Stalin was more powerful on May 6, 1941, when he assumed the office, than he had been on May 5.

In February 1950 an article in *Pravda* attacked A. A. Andreyev for his views on the organization of the collective farms. Andreyev was then a member of the Politburo but, what is more important from our point of view, he was also Chairman of the Council on Kolkhoz Affairs, then the highest governmental organ dealing with collectivized agriculture. A simple notice in the Party organ was a sufficient indication that Andreyev's

---

[5] That the first generation of Bolsheviks should have believed the problems of governing to be relatively simple at the same time that they espoused the notion of a *professional* and *centralized* revolutionary party, is one of those paradoxes that illuminate the twofold character of their Marxist heritage.

views no longer had the support of the very highest Party circles. Andreyev promptly recanted his views and was replaced as the chief spokesman for the regime on agricultural affairs by N. S. Khrushchev. The latter in turn was criticized within a year by a Party official much inferior to him in status, but who was obviously acting on instructions from higher quarters. The incident, which is discussed in another chapter, illuminates not only Soviet politics in the last years of the Stalin era, but also the atmosphere in which policies are formulated and executed under the Soviet system. Neither the ministry of agriculture nor the Council on Kolkhoz Affairs is an independent policy-formulating organization. They go along formulating and supervising policies, until at a crucial point the highest Party organ, or the dictator himself, steps in. Here a matter of great economic and, incidentally, ideological, importance was settled by a decision of one, or at most a few, persons. The Party then lays down the policies and provides the "tone" in which they are administered. What is true at the top is also true lower down. The secretary of a local Party committee is likely to be a more important person than the chairman of the given city's council. The former attends, not only to Party matters in the strict sense of the word, but economic, educational, and other problems of the city or district are also within his responsibilities.

The enormous growth of administration in the Soviet Union is a logical consequence of the concept of the state, which controls and administers every aspect of the national economy. If the state strives at the same time to direct all forms of its citizens' activities from their beliefs to chess playing, then it cannot dispense with a vast army of officials. The logic of totalitarianism as well as that of socialism makes the U.S.S.R. a bureaucratic state.

The administrative history of the Soviet state has exhibited one of those "inherent contradictions" of which Marxists love to talk when they discuss non-socialist countries. Socialism, in the Soviet concept of it, means "doing things": increasing production, expanding the industrial plant, training scientists, athletes, soldiers. Action rather than deliberation, construction rather than the reconciliation of conflicting interests, has been the desired characteristic of the Soviet administrator. The emphasis on quantitative achievement has characterized not only economic administration. It would be comical, if it did not involve so huge a number of human tragedies, to relate how at the height of the Great Purge, 1936-38, Party and security officials set themselves regular quotas of "enemies of the people" and "wreckers" they "had" to discover and liquidate to gain the approval of their superiors. The emphasis on production, in the widest sense of the word, that has characterized Soviet society in the last generation has necessitated the institution of one-man direction in most administrative institutions and the discarding of many devices designed to prevent administrative abuse of powers and corruption. Gone or diminished in importance are the collegial arrangements in ministries whereby the minister was merely a chairman of a collegium of senior officials. The same has happened to the famous *troika*, the arrangement under which major industrial enterprises were run by a committee composed of the director, the secretary of the Party cell, and the trade-union representative. One-man management was prescribed in a famous speech of Stalin's in 1931 as an imperative in the struggle for rapid industrialization, and it has been a rule ever since.

But vesting of complete authority for a certain area of administration in one man is an excellent incentive for efficiency *only up to a certain point*. After that point has been reached the lack of institutionalized restraints is liable to breed complacency, corruption, and, a cardinal sin in a totalitarian regime, a feeling of independence vis-à-vis the central organs. The story of Soviet official utterances on public administration and administrators has consisted in the interplay of two ostensibly contrasting *motifs*. One has been the harping on the need of one-man management, and the inadmissibility of diluting authority, whether in a ministry or in a plant. The other insistent note has been the complaint of officials' "losing touch with the masses," of nepotism and high living among Party and state officials, of their arbitrary behavior, contempt for the rank and file of their subordinates, etc. In place of normal administrative restraints, a system of controls peculiar to a totalitarian state had to be constructed. Officially, the task of control lies in an institution, like the Ministry of State Control, which checks administrative performances of various agencies and has the right of auditing their books; and the Procuracy of the U.S.S.R., which checks on the legality of administrative actions and ordinances. But in fact the most, if not the only, effective way of controlling high officials has been the fear of political disgrace and liquidation that could befall them upon discovery of an administrative failure. Failure, under Soviet totalitarianism, has often been equated with political heresy and treason. A high official—say a Party Secretary of a sizable region or a minister controlling an important segment of the economy—was, especially in Stalin's era, like the proverbial Oriental vizier. While in favor he enjoyed unlimited power over his subordinates, and, if he so desired, the appurtenances of luxurious living. An incautious utterance, an administrative mistake or bad luck that could be seized upon by the envious or by his rivals, could bring his instant downfall, followed by imprisonment or worse.

The system under Stalin, as his successors who had sweated it out were perceptive enough to realize, did not really *control* the administrators, it *terrorized* them. It was not the control agencies and regulations that exercised restraints over the body of bureaucrats, but the secret police and the fear of denunciation. Thus in the last resort the system often defeated itself. For an administrator endowed with the power to make a prompt decision in an economic or other matter would yet be so terrified of making a miscalculation, which might cost him not only his job but also his head, that he would refer the matter to his superior, he to his, etc., until relatively trivial decisions would have to be decided by the Politburo or the dictator himself. The secret police spread its network of informers over all administrative institutions. From a less dramatic viewpoint the obsession with fulfilling and overfulfilling production quotas—the main avenue of success for an ambitious manager and director—often resulted in falsifying statistics, shoddy quality of the product, and corrupt practices in the struggle to obtain scarce raw materials. Soviet administration worked in an atmosphere of nervous tension, conducive to success over shorter periods and emergencies, like the War, but insufferable and self-defeating as a long-run practice.

It is this fact, among others, that persuaded Stalin's successors to carry out their campaign against the "cult of personality," i.e., to spell out and to publicize the crimes and abuses of their great predecessor. Their objective has *not* been to change the totalitarian character of the regime, but to reintroduce a degree of "normalcy" and legality into the Soviet system. Some German political theorists of many years ago formulated the concept of *Rechtsstaat*, i.e, of a state that, while not democratic in character, would yet be ruled by laws, and whose bureaucracy would have its powers and competence strictly defined. The objective of the new masters of the Soviet Union has been to have a form of Communist *Rechtsstaat*. The campaign against Stalin's ghost had the concrete result of exposing thousands of little Stalins who in their spheres acted arbitrarily and corruptly. The relaxation of terror and the imposition of stricter controls on the power of the organs of state security has served to relieve the tension and to assure the rank and file of Soviet administrators that they could now work with at least a modicum of physical security. The new regime has grasped the dangers and inefficiencies of overcentralization. While not for a moment relaxing the totality of political centralization, the bosses of the country—members of the Presidium of the Communist Party of the U.S.S.R.—have allowed and encouraged a degree of economic and administrative decentralization. More emphasis on the quality of work and production, and the restoration of the morale of the administration—these have been the aims of the new leaders, and, as we shall see, behind the new policy there has been not only the desire for administrative efficiency but political considerations as well.

In brief, the objective of the rulers has been what might be called sane Stalinism: policies oriented to preserve the totalitarian character of the state and to assure its economic growth but stripped of the aberrations and excesses that emanated from the despot's personality. It is legitimate to pose the question whether it is in the nature of things political to have a halfway house between unbridled totalitarianism and government of laws; and a related question: what effect have the new policies had up to now? No simple answer will suffice. It is reasonable to assume that in the administrative sphere as elsewhere, Soviet totalitarianism is in a fluid condition and capable of retrogressing into some of the excesses of the Stalin era as well as progressing to a pattern more closely approximating bureaucracies of the West. The lessened fear of the secret police, greater freedom of criticism, and the encouragement of more initiative and decision-making at the lower and local levels of administration: all these reforms cannot but improve the morale and efficiency of Soviet administration. But the Khrushchev era has also seen a rapid turnover of high Party and administrative officials, some of them within the highest circle of power. The bad harvest in 1959 in Kazakhstan was blamed directly on the First Party Secretary of the Republic; a member of the Presidium, Belyayev, was subsequently dismissed from his high posts. 1960 witnessed the disgrace and demotion of a yet higher official: A. Kirichenko, Secretary of the Central Committee, member of the Presidium, and a long time associate of Khrushchev, was, for reasons not fully divulged, removed to a post of lesser importance and dismissed from the Presidium. In the wake of unsatisfactory agricultural performance and of the revelations of a widespread falsification of statistics, a wholesale removal of local Party officials took place in the spring of 1961. The most drastic illustration is provided by the case of the Party boss of Tadjikistan, Uldzhabayev. Accused of systematic falsification of the figures relating to the harvesting and production of cotton, Uldzhabayev and some of his subordinates were stripped of their Party and government posts and faced with criminal prosecution.

The Soviet official, especially in a crucial economic sphere, is still expected to perform at a feverish pace. The analogy of an Oriental potentate may no longer be suitable, but insofar as his security and peace of mind are concerned, he may not unfairly be compared to an American baseball manager or football coach. Failure to produce may not always be excused by references to the poor material available or to the hard schedule. He may find himself accused of an improper attitude or the inability to work with people, and no civil service regulations will protect him from a curt dismissal. And the element of terror has not of course been entirely eliminated. The main subordinates of Beria were hunted down and eliminated with the same thoroughness that in Stalin's times characterized the persecution of real and alleged Trotskyites and Bukharinites. Malenkov's replacement as the top man of the regime by Khrushchev was followed by a shakeup in several important Party and state positions. Should Khrushchev be replaced or removed, the change would reverberate throughout the Soviet administrative machinery.

MINISTERS AND MINISTRIES

The structure of the Soviet administration bears witness to the complexity of functions assumed by the state and to the undercurrents of totalitarian politics. Thus, since the state controls *directly all* the spheres of economic life, the Soviet administrative apparatus includes all the agencies of production and consumption. Every store and every factory in the U.S.S.R. is owned and administered by the state. Every acre of land is under control of the state, while most cultivated soil and forest is owned and run either by state agencies or by collective enterprises like the collective farms, which for all purposes are units in the state economic administration.

To supervise this vast network of enterprises the Soviets until recently resorted to centralized economic administration as well as planning. The number of ministries both of the U.S.S.R. and the Union republics was consequently large, for they included in addition to departments common to all states, such as finance, war, interior, and commerce, ministries covering every region of economic activity, such as ministries of chemical and heavy industry, of the automobile industry, etc. The total roster of central ministries (i.e., both All-Union and Union-republic) has oscillated between twenty-five and fifty and the number would be considerably larger if we included a number of special commissions and committees whose heads have ministerial status (e.g., the Gosplan—the committee to plan national economy; the committee for state security, etc.). Some of the ministries used to be, and a few still are, not administrative agencies in the Western sense of the word, but headquarters of gigantic economic enterprises that cover all of the Soviet Union.[6] Others are great preserves of political power, and their heads are, by virtue of their position, among the leading men of the regime. Thus, at the height of his power in the late forties and again for a few months after Stalin's death, Lavrenti Beria was clearly more than just a deputy prime minister and minister in charge of security matters. He was a man who controlled a vital segment of power in a totalitarian state. The police and the special armed forces of his min-

---

[6] Something like the Atomic Energy Commission in the U.S.A., which is charged with the production of atomic products as well as the extraction of fission-producing materials, comes close to the *type* of economic agency in the U.S.S.R.

istry were at his disposal. Some of his closest subordinates were his personal protégés and friends. It is only gradually and cautiously that Stalin himself moved to diminish the enormous concentration of power in Beria's hands, and the security chief's ultimate downfall evidently required a concerted action of all other major leaders of the regime. In a somewhat similar sense the Ministry of Defense, for so long jealously preserved by Stalin against any potential Bonaparte, enjoys, under currently fluid conditions of Soviet totalitarianism, a special status. Its head had been for a long time Stalin's crony, Voroshilov, followed by ministers who were either technicians or political generals. That the ministry of armed forces has now become a preserve of political power and its incumbent a figure of great influence has been demonstrated in both the political rise and downfall of Zhukov. Elected an alternate member of the Presidium at the Twentieth Congress, he was promoted to a full member in the July 1957 crisis and removed as well as dismissed as Minister a few months later. While the reasons for his dismissal are not clear, the Party bosses obviously did not enjoy the presence in the highest organ of a man who was primarily a general and only secondarily a Party man, and who, worst of all, enjoyed a wide popularity in the country.

The problem of co-ordination and of relative competence of various ministries is again posed in a sharper focus in a totalitarian society than it is in the framework of democratic administration. In England a war minister who feels that he is being imposed upon by the Treasury will carry his case to the Prime Minister and the Cabinet or, as a last resort, he can resign and explain his case to Parliament. In the U.S.S.R. the major decisions are reached outside the context of the ministerial council, and the given ministers participate in them only insofar as they are important members of the Presidium of the Communist Party. Thus in the middle thirties when Russian transportation was in a deplorable state and was proving to be a major obstacle in rapid industrialization of the country, Lazar Kaganovich was appointed Commissar of Transportation. Kaganovich had the reputation of a capable administrator, but what is more important, he was then a person of enormous political importance: a member of the Politburo and right hand of Stalin in economic affairs. He had thus the ability to make decisions and commandeer resources far beyond the reach of an "ordinary" minister of transport.

The Council of Ministers even from a mechanical point of view is not the proper body to debate and determine policies. Even in the post-Stalin days it remains a large body to perform the functions, say, of the British Cabinet, which, though only between one-third and one-half of its size, has been accused of being too large for efficient policy formulation. It may be assumed that insofar as *administrative* policies are concerned they are

~~determined by a smaller group, composed of the Chairman, first deputy chairmen, and deputy chairmen.~~[7] This in October 1956 gave a group of fourteen, of whom seven were until June 1957 members of the Presidium of the Communist Party, and all of whom were members of the Party Central Committee. The Chairman of the Council is traditionally, though as we have seen not always, one of the highest men in the regime. The Premier until March 1958, Bulganin, was for the most part of his tenure considered second man in the Soviet hierarchy. Khrushchev's assumption of the office is significant, not for its own sake but simply because it shows a considerable deviation from the current theory of collective leadership, in so far as the highest positions both in the Party and in the administration are for the moment combined as they were during the latter part of the Stalin era.[8]

The administrative reforms and the party crisis of 1957 have affected the structure of the Council of Ministers. Most of the deputy chairmen happened to be in a group opposed to Khrushchev and lost their ministerial positions as well as their party posts. Thus, the two senior first deputy chairmen, Molotov and Kaganovich, were dismissed, as well as deputy chairmen Malenkov, Saburov, and Pervukhin. Previous reforms had added to the All-Union Council of Ministers (not inconceivably to increase Khrushchev's influence) chairmen of Councils of Ministers of the Union Republics. Again, the years from 1957 have demonstrated the constriction-expansion pattern of Soviet administration. The number of deputy chairmen at first dropped to four and the title "first deputy chairman" disappeared. Since then the number has been expanded and two of them as of 1961, Kosygin and the durable Mikoyan, have reverted to the title of first deputy chairmen. The over-all number of ministers, diminished by the disbanding of many economic ministries and the handing over of their functions to the Union republics or to the economic councils (sovnarkhozy), has been raised again by bringing into the Council of Ministers the chairmen of various state councils and commissions and subdivisions of the Gosplan, many of which fill the functions of the old All-Union ministries disbanded in 1957-58. The current set-up is not likely to remain fixed. For one thing, if the Council of Ministers meets frequently, it is

---

[7] The Chairman and first deputy chairmen constitute the Presidium of the Council.
[8] The relative ranking of the Soviet oligarchs was for a long time easy to assess by simply following the official order of names at a function as given in the Soviet press. Thus in the thirties the names of Molotov, Voroshilov, and L. Kaganovich invariably followed that of the dictator. Stalin's death brought about the ranking (1) Malenkov, (2) Beria, (3) Molotov. Sometime after Beria's imprisonment in the summer of 1953, the pattern was set whereby members of the Presidium of the Party are listed first and alphabetically, then members of the Party Secretariat, then deputy chairmen of the Council of Ministers who are not members of the preceding bodies, etc. Official etiquette thus conforms to "collective leadership."

difficult to see how the chairmen of the Council of Ministers of the Union Republics can be in regular attendance. Also, in view of the vastness of the Soviet administrative machinery, it is quite likely that the number of deputy chairmen of the All-Union Council of Ministers will be expanded still further. Each of the deputies is likely to wear several hats: some are still heads of ministries or committees; all of them are high Party officials. Multiplication of offices in one person is not as pronounced as in Stalin's time. Jealous though he was of his subordinates' becoming too prominent, the dictator, himself a man of enormous energy and industry, required his lieutenants to imitate his working habits. L. Kaganovich, for instance, was at one time in the thirties Secretary of the Moscow Party organization and member of the Central Party Secretariat, in addition to being in over-all supervision of heavy industry. But Soviet administrators still are, as a rule, overworked.

There have been but a few glimpses of the decision-forming process at the highest levels of Soviet administration. We know, for instance, that important decisions used to be reached under Stalin (and there is no reason to believe that the procedure is now greatly different) at a meeting of either the plenum or a committee of the Politburo. The specialists, i.e., the ministers in charge, would report or recommend, and the Politburo would decide. In his "secret" speech denigrating Stalin at the Twentieth Congress, Khrushchev criticized his erstwhile boss for, among other things, his completely chaotic way of assigning responsibility for various matters or of simply by-passing even the Politburo and settling vital decisions on his own. Yet there is little to indicate that, administratively, things have changed very much. There is no more Stalin to act completely arbitrarily but there has not been and there cannot be in a totalitarian system a nice division of functions between the government and the Party. Khrushchev has not found it inconsistent to address himself to matters of administration as well as policy. Thus, he spelled out the way in which new areas are to be brought under cultivation and prescribed the main crops for them, etc. He has upbraided the Soviet construction industry for not using enough structural steel and cement. And so it will be as long as the Soviet system continues; the Party will not leave any branch of administration to its own devices, whether its head is Khrushchev or anyone else.

The same confused line of authority runs through the ministries and through the councils of ministers of Union and autonomous republics. One might imagine that the improvement of dairy cultivation in the Ukraine is the primary responsibility of the Minister of Agriculture of the Ukrainian S.S.R. But it will be the First Secretary of the Ukrainian Party who will make the authoritative statement on the subject. Somewhat in the manner of a dog chasing its tail the regime is forever trying to estab-

lish clearer lines of authority and to free its administrative machinery
from the insufferable amount of red tape the system entails. Ministries
are merged into larger units to assure greater flexibility and more scope of
action, then it is found that the unit is too large and unwieldy, or that,
for political reasons, it is unwise to concentrate so much authority under
one minister. It is useless to recount how many times light industry has
been split and then reunited into one ministry, or how, for different reasons, the Ministry of the Interior has fissioned into Internal Affairs and
State Security, only to regroup again.[9] In 1957 *administrative* decentralization again became the order of the day in the U.S.S.R. The ground had
been prepared previously by the transformation of several Union-republic
ministries into republican ones, i.e., by putting them within the full
administrative competence of the Union republics. The decisive step
prescribed in the spring of 1957 abolished most of the central economic
ministries, such as those of the chemical industry, food products, and
textile industry. Most of the functions of the former industrial and
economic ministries were split up among a number of economic councils
corresponding to the major industrial and production regions of the
country—the *sovnarkhozes*. Each territorial council administers multiple
economic enterprises within the region. The original plan envisaged in
1957 ninety-two sovnarkhozes, sixty-eight within the Russian S.S.R., eleven
within the Ukrainian S.S.R. and one for each of the remaining federal
republics. By the spring of 1961 the number had grown to 104. Thus huge
industrial complexes like Moscow or Leningrad as well as some of the
smaller Union republics like Estonia or Moldavia constitute an economic
unit within the new structure.

The reform was prompted by several factors. Economically it was felt
desirable to bring administration closer to the units of production. Under
it a chemical plant, say in Minsk, no longer is directly administered by a
ministry in Moscow but is run by a department of the Byelorussian Economic Council with its seat right in Minsk. Savings in personnel, the

---

[9] The Ministry of Internal Affairs was re-created on the morrow of Stalin's death
out of the ministries of Internal Affairs (N.K.V.D.) and of State Security (M.G.B.).
The former had specialized in the more routine functions of the Ministry of the
Interior; the latter's functions were devoted to the more political tasks: the tracking
down of espionage and subversion, the supervision of the forced-labor camps, and so
on. Their reunification in the hands of Beria indicated his reassertion of power, just
as their previous separation reflected the realization that complete and immediate
control over *all* the security apparatus made its incumbent dangerously powerful. Following Beria's downfall the political importance of the security apparatus was decisively
reduced and the still important segment of police and security powers again split up.
Thus there was the Ministry of Internal Affairs, with its usual tasks and supervision
of ordinary police, and the Committee of State Security (K.G.B.), which has inherited the function of the old M.G.B. More recently the functions of the Ministry
of Internal Affairs were brought within the competence of the Union republics and
the Ministry dissolved.

avoidance of wasteful duplication of production facilities, and greater powers of initiative for the people on the spot are among the gains of the new system. Like everything about Soviet administration, the decision to decentralize was also motivated by political reasons. When it was formulated in 1957 it meant a weakening of the central administrative apparatus then not firmly in Khrushchev's control and an appeal for political support among the local interests, especially among the local Party secretaries, whose help during the June 1957 crisis did in fact enable Khrushchev to swing the majority of the Central Committee against the Malenkov-Molotov group.[10] Economic reasons combined with administrative and political ones to make the reform desirable.

From the perspective of five years, the administrative restructuring of 1957 appears as a fairly durable arrangement. It has to be kept in mind that since a totalitarian system lives by centralization, while there may be *administrative* decentralization, there is no room in the Soviet system for a bona fide decentralization of economic policy planning. Overall economic plans are still worked out by the highest councils of the Communist Party and the Gosplan, and the Ukrainian or the Kazakh economic administration is not allowed to develop the economy of its region according to its own ideas. It is clear that even in its inception the decentralization was not conceived of as being synonymous with local autonomy in any extensive way. Khrushchev's speech on the reorganization made this quite clear:

> The U.S.S.R. State Planning Commission (Gosplan) will have in addition to its general departments for over-all planning, specialized agencies, divisions and specialists for various branches of industry, thus co-ordinating and directing the development of specialization and cooperation in separate branches of the national economy in coordination with the plans for economic development on a national scale. These specialized agencies and divisions will have to work out plans for the development of different industries and *supervise their implementation.* [My italics.]

Many of the abolished economic ministries have reappeared in effect as subdivisions of the Gosplan or as special state committees whose chairmen are ex officio ministers of the U.S.S.R.—for example, the state committees and councils on chemistry, radio-electronics, and ship building. In a sense, every modern industrial state has confronted the problems of how far the centralization of vast industrial enterprises can be reconciled

---

[10] Disgraced or demoted were not only the old Party leaders like Malenkov, Molotov, and Kaganovich, but also the principal administrative leaders, Pervukhin, until June in overall control of economic administration, Saburov, and finally Bulganin himself. The latter three, it was announced in December 1958, had during the crisis supported the Molotov-Malenkov group.

with efficiency and of how effective economic planning can be made compatible with the autonomy of individual industrial units. These problems are not irrelevant to the discussion of nationalized industries in Great Britain and of huge private corporations in the United States and England. But in the absence of democratic institutions and of private enterprise, the problem is much more fundamental and much more political in the U.S.S.R.

For all the qualifications stated above, the new organization of Soviet industry has conferred enhanced powers and responsibilities upon the organs of local government, the Union republics and the local Party organs. Behind the apparent decentralization there is always the centralizing and unifying apparatus of the Communist Party. Yet it is not entirely out of the question that a decentralization of management may sometime lead to claims for partial economic autonomy on the part of various national regions of the U.S.S.R. Administrative decentralization thus increases the importance of the national and regional problem in the U.S.S.R. To repeat, the reorganization took place in the name of efficiency, with its authors not unmindful of its favorable reception among the local Party and state leaders. But like many other transformations of the post-Stalin era, the administrative reforms may in the future, should the political situation allow it, affect the crucial fact of totalitarian controls by the Party of all aspects of Soviet life. For the time being, the pattern is still one of administrative decentralization combined with centralized economic planning and control. Above the network of territorial economic councils is the Gosplan,[11] as well as the ministers' councils of the Union republics and ultimately the Council of Ministers of the U.S.S.R. and the Presidium of the Central Committee of the Communist Party.

Behind the problem of Soviet administration stands the larger issue of the Soviet administrator. In the early days of the regime they were of two varieties—the specialist taken over from the tsarist or pre-November days, indispensable because of his technical qualifications but watched and suspected by the regime; or a professional revolutionary, well-versed in Marx and Plekhanov but not necessarily competent to run a ministry or factory. Both types are now extinct, either through natural attrition or through the Great Purge of the thirties. In their place has arisen the new Soviet bureaucrat, a product of the Stalin era. He is a man almost equally distant from pre-Revolutionary society and from the struggles and ideological excitement of the Revolution and the first years after it. His training, often even in the non-economic and non-technical branches of the admin-

---

[11] Actually intermediate bodies between the Gosplan and the sovnarkhozes were set up in the case of Russia, the Ukraine, and Kazakhstan in the form of super–economic councils combining the supervision of several economic councils in each republic.

istration, is likely to have been scientific, or in the social sciences. Questions of ideology, the great doctrinal disputes of the past, are for him matters of, at most, historical interest. He is, in brief, not terribly dissimilar from a bureaucrat, business executive, or army officer in the West *insofar as his training* and his *objectives* in life are concerned. If he belongs to the Party, it is more often than not a consequence of his job and the desire to advance, rather than of a deeply thought-out ideological preference. Communism in Russia has managed to produce in its officialdom a new middle class not startlingly different in its aspirations and viewpoint from the middle classes elsewhere, though it is superficial to speak of a managerial revolution and unwise to consider this new class as a monolithic whole in its attitudes and interests.

Soviet administration is thus an important factor in the changing social scene of the U.S.S.R. Here, as in other aspects of the Soviet political scene, the relentless terror of the Stalin era has obscured but has not stopped the growth of new social forces and aspirations. Russia's industrialization and growth as a great world power would have been inconceivable without the creation of the enormous and intricate administrative machinery. For all its shortcomings, for all the tenseness and insecurity in which the Soviet administrator has worked, this machinery has performed the day-to-day tasks of administration and planning. It has served the state well, and the Soviet administrator may soon feel and demand that his rewards should go beyond the enhanced social status and relative physical security accorded to him by the post-Stalin regime. His technical ability and his vital function in the system give him a base of power from which to press such a demand.

[26]

The Communist Party
of the U.S.S.R.

The Character and Function of the Party

In the years that have passed since Lenin wrote his *What Is To Be Done?* the Bolsheviks have grown from a handful of conspirators partly in exile abroad and partly in the underground in Russia into a huge party of several million members. No longer fugitives and in the background, the Communists rule Russia, control or guide other Communist parties that have sprung up in all countries of the world and some of which have since World War II achieved power in their own countries. It is certainly no longer the party of the hunted, of the Marxian intellectual and the revolutionary worker. Its resources are in effect the resources of the largest country of the world and for its funds it no longer has to beg from rich sympathizers or to stage "expropriation" raids on banks like the ones in which young Dzugashvili–Stalin first achieved revolutionary renown. Over the years the Party has grown and changed until it is today the party of business managers, ministers, generals; of the elite of skilled workers and collective farm officials; of professors and engineers. Membership in the Party has become almost synonymous with achieving success and status in Soviet society. The symbolism that the Party retains, of being the representative of the oppressed, of the "prisoners of starvation," as the *Internationale*, the Party hymn, still proclaims, is clearly obsolete and paradoxical.[1]

---

[1] The evolution of the name of the Party is an interesting story. Until 1918 the Bolsheviks remained the "Social-Democratic Workers Party–Bolshevik faction." To demon-

And yet if the Party's composition and its function have changed, the spirit of its organization and its professed aims still remain based on the principles postulated by Lenin in 1902, fought for and evolved by him in 1903 and in the succeeding years. Democratic centralism: i.e., strict discipline and unquestioned and absolute authority of the central organs of the Party, remain the official dogma for the six to seven million Party members, just as they were for a few thousands before the Revolution. The Party is still officially the vanguard of the working class, and as such it cannot be content just to express and execute what the masses want: its official aim is to propel them to what they *"really"* want (i.e., what they *ought to* want), and as such it is the teacher and censor of the people. Officially, again, socialism in Russia has been achieved, but the final goal of the Party remains as it was in 1903—further expansion, and strengthening of socialism, and, eventually, its transformation into communism where "from each according to his ability, to each according to his needs" will become the basis of social relations. Thus the split personality of the Communist Party—the party of conspiracy—in power; the champion of the oppressed, now an organization thoroughly bureaucratized, its high officials enjoying the privileges and perquisites of good living; the party aiming to bring about the most absolute and perfect democracy, which is yet organized with the strictest discipline and lack of inner democracy surpassing that of the most rigorous military organizations and religious orders.

The Communist Party of the U.S.S.R. is, then, many things. It is certainly not a political party in the American, English, or French sense of the word. It does not seek and solicit members the way a democratic party does. To gain membership in the Party is an achievement and privilege. There is a period of probation, and any member who fails to live up to the standard of behavior set for the Party member, whether in his public or private life, faces expulsion. In theory, even the rank-and-file member is an "activist"—a man who takes a leading part in public activities of his city, town, or village, who on any job is an example to his fellow workers in industry and diligence, who has at least a rudimentary knowledge of Marxism-Leninism and hence is capable of explaining political situations in his country and the world at large. The Bolshevik is, then, expected to

strate the Bolsheviks' drastic break with the "reformist" Socialists of the West as well as with the Mensheviks, Lenin prevailed at the Seventh Party Congress (not without protests from some Bolsheviks) in having the name changed to the "Communist Party (of Bolsheviks)." The change was designed to emphasize that while the Bolsheviks remained Socialists and Marxists, they repudiated the name allegedly stolen by "opportunistic" and non-Marxist socialist parties, and by their new name emphasized *revolutionary* and non-reformist Marxism and socialism. At the Nineteenth Party Congress the parenthesis "(of Bolsheviks)," so full of history, disappeared from the Party's name, which is now officially the "Communist Party of the U.S.S.R."

be a *superior citizen*, if not a superior type of human being. There are many descriptions of this idealized version of Party member in Soviet literature. In Sholokhov's *Upturned Virgin Soil*[2] the author describes the struggle for collectivization in a small Cossack village. The period is that of the great collectivization drive of the late twenties and early thirties. The Party representatives encounter all sorts of opposition in their attempt to persuade the peasants to join in a collective: sabotage by the rich peasants, "wrecking" activities of the emissaries of counterrevolution, and simply ignorance and attachment to their own land on the part of the mass of peasants. One *non*-Party man stands out in helping the Party officials to overcome these obstacles and to make the peasants see the justice and wisdom of pooling their land and cattle in a communal organization. At the end of the book this patriotic Soviet citizen is invited, as a reward, to join the Party. He begs off for the moment, saying that he is still not worthy of membership in the Party of Lenin and Stalin, because whenever he sees his cow, now a part of the communal herd, he still has a twinge of regret that his property has been "communalized." The old Adam of bourgeois mentality is not entirely dead and until he is laid to rest, the new Communist man cannot take his place!

The process of indoctrination begins not too long after the cradle, with the organization of the Little Octobrists following which Soviet children may at nine (!) join the Young Pioneers. But the burden of indoctrination of the young falls upon the *Komsomol*, the League of Communist Youth, with its membership ranging from the age of fourteen to twenty-six. An organization patterned in its structure upon the Party itself, and strictly controlled by it, the Komsomol is even more numerous, having over fifteen million members. The organization has its congresses and central committee. Though, as their relative size indicates, by no means all of the Komsomol graduates join the Party, the former is the main recruiting ground for the ruling group.

Totalitarianism is especially watchful in indoctrinating the young. And the young are perhaps less convinced by paper theories than by the romanticism of action, of working and playing together. Hence to the Komsomol have been addressed the special calls for action, as during the First Five Year Plan, during the War, when the membership in it grew by leaps and bounds in the Armed Forces, and most recently when the call went out to settle and cultivate "virgin land" in Kazakhstan and elsewhere. Physical culture and paramilitary training emphasize the "activist" character of the Komsomol. It is definitely *not* merely a discussion group, or an assembly of

---

[2] Published in the U.S. under the title *Seeds of Tomorrow*.

political sympathizers of a "grown-up" party like the Young Conservatives or the Young Republicans.

In brief, the mystique of Communism is propagated from the earliest days. It is a mystique of an active and devoted life—devoted to the service of the Party and the Soviet Fatherland. The young Komsomol member is supposed to be a junior replica of the image of the Communist: enthusiastic, eternally watchful (against the enemies of the Party and the state), and joyfully creative and enterprising at whatever post he finds himself in.

This mystique of Communism, again strange in an ideology claiming its descent from the most rationalistic and materialistic creed of the nineteenth century, is very deeply ingrained in the official myth. The Communists, as the popular saying had it about the Seabees in this country, are supposed to be able to do the impossible in only a little longer while than it takes them to do the difficult! The Communist is a dedicated builder of a new society and a new life. He is a man whose mind is free of superstitions about private property and religion, a perfect repository of the scientific truths inherent in Marxism-Leninism. So much for the official picture, the picture the Party presents especially to its ancillary youth organizations, the Pioneers and the Komsomol, which are designed to train young devotees for its membership. The actual picture is more complicated.

The concept of the Communist Party emphasizes that it is the party of workers. In the early days before the Revolution, while most of the leaders came from the intelligentsia, the bulk of membership was in fact found among the factory workers. After the Revolution, when the Party was in power, it still put a premium upon recruitment among workers. The Party was now governing a predominantly rural country yet it shrank from admitting too many peasants into its ranks. They were a "hostile class element." The Bolsheviks in order to govern had to employ tens of thousands of former tsarist officials, engineers, officers, etc. Yet these also as a group were debarred from membership. In the rules about admission to Party membership until the middle thirties one finds inherent the theory of what might be called hereditary and occupational taint: except in unusual circumstances, no one who had been born into a middle-class environment, or who had at one time possessed real property, even if only a few acres, could be expected to become as trustworthy a Communist as a *real worker*, himself a son of a worker or of a landless peasant.[3] The more the prospective candidate was removed from the worker, the more difficult

---

[3] The injunction did not apply of course to the old Bolsheviks themselves, among whom could be found: Lenin sprung from a family of tsarist bureaucrats; Trotsky, son of a *kulak*, i.e., a prosperous farmer; Leonid Krassin, who had before World War I been an engineer and industrial manager; and even somebody like V. V. Ossinsky, whose real name was Obolensky, and who came from the famous princely family.

were the conditions for admission and the longer was the probationary period before full membership. Already in the early days there were voices on both sides of the question: The Workers' Opposition[4] cried as early as 1921 and 1922 that the Party and the country were run not by workers but by bureaucrats. Zinoviev and Kamenev in 1924 and 1925 exclaimed that the rich peasants were penetrating the Party. On the other side Leonid Krassin, an early Commissar of Trade, an old Bolshevik but an engineer by profession, protested that a country like Russia could not be run without the help of a technical intelligentsia, and that the Party should not scorn the administrators, industrialists, and engineers. Yet the Party's attitude on qualifications for membership continued substantially unchanged into the thirties. The beginning of the great drive for industrialization and collectivization and the first Five Year Plan were bound to have an effect on the problem. In 1936 Stalin proclaimed that exploitation of man by man was extinguished in Russia. Socialism had been achieved and instead of *antagonistic* classes, two friendly classes now existed—the peasants and workers—and the intelligentsia was not like the old intelligentsia, the product of a class society, but came out of the working classes and hence was entirely trustworthy. The change in the attitude of diffidence toward the non-worker was coming about slowly even amidst the tremendous revolution that was transforming Soviet society and the vast purge that was decimating the old revolutionaries among the Bolsheviks.[5] The watershed was represented by the Eighteenth Party Congress, held in 1939. The discriminatory regulations about accepting new Party members from among the non-workers were abolished, and the attitude of diffidence toward the intellectuals, engineers, etc., was proclaimed to be non-Soviet.

The Party has thus abandoned both in practice and in theory social discrimination when it comes to accepting new members. With industrial growth and the passage of years, the Communists no longer feel as they most certainly did in the 1920's, that they are a garrison in a country peopled either by the class enemy or the ignorant and that consequently it is courting disaster to let the enemy or wavering elements into the ruling group. What does remain is the conviction that the broad basis of the Party must still remain the worker. Even amidst the most total terror and

---

[4] See below, p. 704.
[5] The late twenties and the early thirties thus witnessed quite a series of trials of engineers accused of "wrecking" the growing industry of the Soviet Union. Quite apart from the substance of the accusations, the trials represented a propaganda effort to picture the failures and privations of the First Five Year Plan as being largely caused by the "class enemy" rather than by its inherent defects. In the purges of the thirties, including the trials of the old Bolsheviks, a subsidiary charge leveled against the accused was the concealment of their class origin upon joining the Party. X joined the Party pretending to be the son of a poor peasant while in reality his father was an exploiting *kulak*. Not surprisingly, X, several years later while a high official, turned out to be a "wrecker" bent upon sabotaging the Soviet people's victorious march toward socialism!

most absolute one-man dictatorship, the Bolsheviks paid more than lip service to this principle. Stalin expressed it when in a speech he compared the Communists to Antaeus of Greek mythology: Antaeus was invincible when he was in contact with Mother Earth; only by lifting him up and depriving him of this strength-giving connection could Hercules defeat him. And so this thoroughly totalitarian and oligarchically run organization is forever seeking to have its contacts with the masses of the population. Clearly an elite body, it still sees it supremely important to have the workers and the collective farmers as the bulk of its membership. In his report to the Twentieth Party Congress Khrushchev again pointed out that unless the Party penetrates every sphere of national life, and unless it has its members everywhere, both Soviet power and Russia's economic progress will be endangered. The standard complaint reappears in Khrushchev's remarks: The Party is becoming too bureaucratized, too distant from the common worker: "It is an abnormal state of affairs that in a number of branches of national economy a considerable number of Communists working in these branches are doing work which is not directly connected with the decisive sectors of production. For instance, at coal industry enterprises there are nearly 90,000 Communists, but *only* 38,000 are employed underground. Over three million Party members and candidate members live in rural areas, *but less than half of them are working directly on collective farms, M.T.S.,[6] and state farms.*"[7] And in an attempt to revivify the Party that still recalls the terrible sufferings and oppression of the Stalin era, the Party boss once again emphasized the cardinal point of the Communist creed: nothing can go well in Russia unless the Party is directly connected with it and unless every Party member has a sense of mission and responsibility: "The C.P.S.U. is a governing party, and what is done in our Soviet land is of vital interest for the Party as a whole and for every Communist. A *Communist has no right to be an onlooker.*"[8] The attempt to spread its membership widely in the occupational sense is emphasized in the renewed attempt to strengthen the Party organization in the villages. Traditionally, and still distrustful of the peasant and peasant mentality, the Party believes that the performance of the agricultural sector of Russian economy, which still lags behind the industrial, would improve if there were more Communists and more Party activity in the countryside. The Twentieth Party Congress approved that every machine tractor station—the focal point of a rural region's economy— should have a Party organization. Again, the problem and proposed solution are nothing new. The beginning of the great collectivization drive of

---

[6] Machine Tractor Stations.
[7] The italics are mine.
[8] My italics.

1928-29 was signalized by thousands of Party activists and agitators being sent out from the cities to the villages to explain to, to cajole, and, as it turned out in most cases, to coerce the peasants into pooling their land and cattle in collective farms.

The injection of the Party into the most crucial sectors of the nation's economy has been paralleled by saturation with Party members of the most important segments of the power structure. It goes without saying now that a vast majority of high-ranking officers in the Army are now card-carrying Communists. The situation is thus drastically different from the days of the Civil War and the twenties, when a majority of officers were still outside the Party circle, many of them still veterans of the tsarist army, and when the institution of the political commissar was created largely to watch over the apolitical officer. The security organs have always been the part of the state apparatus most heavily saturated with Party members, and in the early days of the regime they were, at the higher level, a special preserve for the old Bolsheviks.

The story of the changing national composition of the Bolsheviks is another interesting sidelight of the changing function of the Communist Party. Along with other revolutionary movements in pre-World War I Russia, the Bolsheviks drew heavily, especially within their leading circles, on the national minorities within the tsarist empire. It is not surprising that disproportionate numbers of Jews, Poles, Letts, Georgians, and Armenians flowed into the ranks of the revolutionary movement.[9] The national character of the Party immediately after the Revolution and throughout the twenties continued to reflect the numerically disproportionate contribution that the erstwhile persecuted minorities and nations had brought into the Bolshevik Party. The trend began to be reversed with the growing ascendance of Stalin. A Georgian by birth who to his death spoke Russian with an accent, Stalin became in effect an exponent of Great-Russian chauvinism within the Party. In the struggle for leadership, first against Trotsky and then against the so-called Left Opposition,[10] the Stalinist faction was not above using anti-Semitic arguments capitalizing on the fact that the "left" leaders, Trotsky, Kamenev, Zinoviev, and many of their supporters were Jews. The purges of the thirties fell with particular vehemence upon non-Russian Communists. The Party had now clearly embraced Great-Russian nationalism, and what was implicit in Communism before now became explicit: the continuation and intensification both within the country and externally of Russian imperialism.

---

[9] If any generalization is possible then it could be stated that the Bolsheviks were more "Russian" in their leadership and composition than their rivals the Mensheviks and, insofar as the leadership was concerned, than the Social Revolutionaries, the representatives *par excellence* of the peasants.

[10] See below, p. 706 ff.

In the early days of Soviet power a fugitive Hungarian or Polish Communist would be welcomed in the Soviet Union and quite often pass into a high Party or even state position. In the mid and late thirties the majority of these honored guests were liquidated, often after an absurd charge that they were spies for the very governments from which they had fled. While the purge hit the Party hard as a whole, it was particularly ferocious in the Ukraine and the Central Asian republics. By the end of the thirties the Party was overwhelmingly and disproportionately Great-Russian in its composition. One expert concludes that numerically the Party was especially strong in Russia proper and in Transcaucasia, weaker in the Ukraine, and especially in Byelorussia and in the Central Asian republics, and presumably even in these last Great Russians accounted for a considerable proportion of its membership.[11] The trend continued unabated until Stalin's death. While victory over the Germans was officially the triumph of all nationalities of the Soviet Union, it was to the Russian nation in particular that Stalin raised his toast at the famous victory celebration at the Kremlin in 1945. The last years of the tyrant's life witnessed a renewed campaign against the alleged nationalist aberrations among the non-Russian nationalities, and a clearly officially sponsored anti-Semitic campaign.

A fuller story of these events belongs to a discussion of social changes in Russia. What should be stressed is that the Communist Party has become predominantly Russian. It is an ironic fact that the Party that claims to represent the proletariat of the whole world, and in its ideology the humanistic tradition of all mankind, conducted in the late 1940's a deliberate campaign against cosmopolitanism and for, in effect, Russian chauvinism. The years that have passed since Stalin's death have brought some changes in the nationality policy of the Party. Russian chauvinism has become muted. In the local Party organizations, especially in the Ukraine, more prominence is given to the natives. It is impossible to say how far this policy has been reflected in the national distribution of Party members. It is clear, however, that the Russian predominance within the Communist Party as a whole is here to stay. One factor that worked against Beria in his struggle for Party leadership was undoubtedly his non-Russian origin. And Russian nationalism, as well as its broader version, Soviet patriotism, remains one of the leitmotifs of the Party.

The evolution of the character of the Communist Party and the distribution of its membership among various social and national groups already throw a considerable light on the role of the Party in Soviet society.

---

[11] Merle Fainsod, *How Russia Is Ruled,* Cambridge, 1953, p. 229.

But in what sense are its some seven million members the "governing party," as phrased by Khrushchev? To be sure, *all office holders in Russia in every branch at every level of government are either Party members or in fact nominees of the Party*. To be sure, *all political and economic decisions in Russia are made either by the Party directly*, or indirectly through the state organs staffed and led by Party members. But, as distinguished from the small group at the top, be it the Politburo, the Presidium, or the Central Committee, how do the millions of individual members "govern"? And what is the basis of their power as a party?

We have seen the idealized concept of the Party member, and we shall see in the next section how an individual Party member fits into the machine of Party organization. Here we want to define the personality and the role of the Party member in Soviet society. For all the machinery of terror and police, for all the armed might of the state, political power rests in Russia, in some sense, upon these some seven million members. If their sense of identification with the Party weakens or disappears, if the Party member who is a trade unionist thinks of himself mostly as a unionist, the one who is an officer mostly as an army man, and so on, then the structure of monolithic totalitarianism will be weakened beyond recovery. History is full of examples of revolutionary parties that carried through victorious revolutions and ruled for a while until their revolutionary élan weakened or degenerated and they themselves atrophied, eventually yielding to new social or political forces. The regime has always boasted and boasts today, forty years after the November coup d'état, that in the Communist Party there is still enshrined the *Revolution;* that the revolutionary regime has not given way to a military dictatorship or a bureaucratic clique, that the Communist Party—the spirit of Revolution—not only reigns but rules.[12] An impartial observer will not accept the regime's self-estimation. He will point out that Russia is in fact ruled by a clique, or, today, by several cliques, of Party bureaucrats and that the high idealism of the Revolution has often given way to disenchantment, cynicism, and, in the high places, cynical enjoyment of the fruits of victory and power. But he will also be forced to admit that there has been some truth in the regime's boast: the Party's composition has changed, its rule has become vested in dictators and oligarchies, but the Communist Party, even during the worst periods

---

[12] It is interesting to note how the Communists have clung to the democratic and progressivistic symbolism. Their periodical organs have traditionally borne names like *Forward, Truth,* and *Worker's Cause.* Their propaganda, even at times of the greatest terror in the Soviet Union, has always been couched in terms of democratic and humanitarian trends bringing to mind the dynamic, forward-moving character of the movement. And those who are, or who are alleged to be, opposed to the Soviet regime are branded not as revolutionaries, but as *counterrevolutionaries,* implying that they are not only traitors but people who stupidly and vainly oppose the inevitable march of history.

of oppression and terror, has remained the catalyst of the vital forces in Russian society. It has led the Soviet Union through enormous economic growth and to the position of a great world power. The Party has often succumbed to corruption and terror, but never to lassitude. And if the Party is to continue to be the vital force in Russia, then the rank-and-file members must continue to see in their Party card something meaningful beyond an acknowledgment of status and an open door to personal success.

"A Communist has no right to be an onlooker." The individual member must have a sense of mission. Is this as true today as it was in the days of the Revolution, and in the days following it? The average member of the Party throughout the twenties was still very much of a revolutionary. Any party in power will attract careerists, and even pure opportunists, but in its general tone the Communist Party of the earlier years was still very much like a religious order with a special mission. An average member, even if a laborer with no formal education, was still assumed to be something of an intellectual, with a knowledge of the principles of Marxism and an acquaintance with the politics and economy not only of Russia but of the capitalist world as well. In theory no Communist, no matter what his official position or formal salary, was supposed to live on a scale surpassing the income of the average skilled worker. Marxism in its most theoretical aspect was still very much a live force in Party life. The great struggle for power that took place following Lenin's death was accompanied by the protagonists' tossing citations from Marx, Engels, and Lenin at each other. Not only Party congresses but small Communist cells debated the theoretical as well as practical aspects of such problems as whether socialism could be fully realized in Russia before a proletarian revolution took place in the West; whether a social revolution could succeed a national one in China and what the role of the Communists should be in it, etc. Of freedom of discussion, in the wide sense of the word, there was always very little in the Communist Party, but there was certainly a lot of *ideological* excitement, which must have seeped down to the humblest member. The Party, then, in the earliest days of the regime was bound by the cohesive force of ideology and the sense of mission both in Russia and in the world at large. This embryonic political culture enabled the Communists to preserve their power, while still weak numerically, first against their Civil War foes, and then in a country beginning to recover from the ravages of the wars, and still weak and rather primitive in its economy.

The ascendancy of Stalin, which must be marked as definitive from the Fourteenth Party Congress in 1925 and as absolute from the Sixteenth Congress in 1930, brought a different emphasis. The age of discussion, of ideological fervor, was over. What replaced it was the fascination of concrete tasks, the gigantic enterprise of collectivizing Russian agriculture and industrializing Russia. The average Party member in 1930 already felt the tightening of Party discipline and the beginning of relentless terror, which was directed against anybody who opposed the dictator. In the country at large terroristic measures were in full swing against the recalcitrant peasants. But for all the sufferings and famines and privations the Party had a new and concrete task to uphold its élan: the vision of a Russia full of factories, of manufactured goods, with all the major means of production really socialized—a gigantic step in the realization of socialism. It is doubtful that any society in modern times has undergone such a shock of privation, of a lowered standard of living, and of oppression as did Russia during the years 1928 to 1933 without overthrowing the regime that was causing the sufferings. The tightness of police controls does not provide the entire explanation. Part of it must be found in the fact that throughout the terrible years the ruling order—the Communist Party—could still operate with zeal and cohesion inspired by the awesome task.

The ability of Stalin to push the country and the Party close to the brink of disaster and yet to avoid a catastrophe was vividly demonstrated again in the middle and late thirties when, while the economic situation was considerably improved (over the conditions of the early thirties) and industrialization was gathering momentum, terror of unprecedented proportions gripped the party and society.[13] But aside from terror, the Communist Party was kept as a functioning organism by the magnitude of the task still at hand and by the knowledge that to slacken in the effort toward economic power would be to risk defeat in a war that was clearly approaching. To the incentive of socialist construction the regime added the note of Soviet—and even plain Russian—patriotism. Russia's past was rehabilitated. No longer was Russia's history to be presented, as it had been in the twenties by official Marxist historians, as a story of backwardness and oppression. The Bolsheviks were now cast in the role of the continuators of the great figures of Russia's past, like Peter the Great. The Russian nation was allowed to have had a great history, with some of the most tyrannical tsars being presented as having played a "progressive" role for their time. In other words, through the most trying times the Communist Party

---

[13] Incidents illustrating the extent of terror were given by Stalin's right-hand man Zhdanov at the Eighteenth Party Congress in 1939 when the most acute phase of terror had been concluded, and the regime had piously denounced its excesses. In some Party organizations regular quotas were set for the percentage of "wreckers" and "spies" that had to be discovered in the Party membership. In one district hysterical Communists would provide themselves with medical certificates testifying that Comrade X, because of the poor state of his physical and mental health, could not conceivably become a tool of the class enemy! Stalin himself acknowledged that some errors had been made.

could still play a leading role, and through its existence assure the regime and the state of a degree of cohesion. The second World War and its immediate aftermath recharged the Party with patriotic élan. The struggle against the invader and then the reconstruction of the ravaged country were again the kind of aims to spur the Communists, to give them some feeling that they were still a "governing party" and not onlookers.

In some sense the Communist Party through its long years in power has been like an athletic team that preserves its morale throughout all the privation of training, and despite all the bullying by the coach or manager, as long as the aim is concrete and visible, and the performance of the team satisfactory. But if there is no game in sight, or the discipline and privations are obviously excessive for the desired purpose, the spirit of rebellion or sullen apathy replaces that of purpose. That in some way was the story of the Communist Party in the last years of Stalin's rule. The Party had long before ceased to be a revolutionary corps, a handpicked elite of activists. It was, and it is now, composed mostly of people who have grown up under the Soviet regime and for whom the old ideological struggles and issues have no meaning. The asceticism of old days and the feeling of a special mission are also gone. Russia has been modernized and industrialized, and an average Russian does not have to be a fervent Communist or a reader of Marx to feel that it is a good thing for his country to produce more steel or to have more institutions of higher learning. During the last generation Russia has leaped into the front rank of modern industrial states. But this success of Communism has by the same token created its greatest problem: What is the rationale for the iron discipline within the Party, or for privations in terms of the standard of living, if the main struggle has been won?

The fondest dream of the Communist leaders of a generation ago was to create an administrative and technical elite that should not yield anything in terms of competence and skill to its Western counterpart. That elite has now been created and its members comprise a large part of the Communist Party membership. But by the same token, why should an engineer or an administrator or a factory manager who is also a Communist have aspirations different from those of his Western confrere? In what sense is he different *because he is a Communist?* To be sure, though socialism has been realized in Russia the officially proclaimed goal still remains ahead: communism. But how realistic or how desirable is it to an average number of the Party to conceive a society where the state will "wither away" and where "from each according to his ability, to each according to his needs" will be the fundamental law? What does Communism have to offer now to justify further privations, the continuance of the police state, the stringent duties inherent in being a member of the

Party? The desirable achievements of Communism from the point of view of a convinced Communist—public ownership of the means of production, the widespread system of social security, modernization and industrialization of Russia—do not have to be fought for any more. They exist, and they will go on of their own momentum even if the Communist Party disappears tomorrow.

The problem that faces the Communist Party is, then, the problem of preserving cohesion and the sense of purpose without which the Party, though it would continue to exist, would degenerate in importance and would ultimately yield as the ruling organ to some other force—the bureaucracy, the army, or something else—with incalculable consequences for the whole Soviet system. The problem is not new. What marked its existence in Stalin's last years was the reign of terror exerted by the dictator. By the same token the degree of suppression exerted by the despot, while it masked the crisis, deepened its nature, and it was inevitable that with Stalin gone and a more fluid situation confronting the leadership in the country and in the Communist Party, the crisis would appear with full force.

Another part describes in some detail how the late dictator appraised the nature of the crisis in the party and the means that he proposed to undertake in order to deal with it. To his successors it appeared imperative to lift, as the first step, the excessive amount of terror exerted within and without the Party by Stalin and to demonstrate to the rank and file of the members that while the Party would continue to be run according to "democratic centralism," i.e., from the top, a certain degree of latitude and freedom would be allowed in intra-Party relationships. When the Presidium of the Party took their seats on the opening day of the Twentieth Party Congress in February 1956 they were greeted as during the Stalin days by the servile applause of the delegates, but Nikita Khrushchev admonished the members to act with more dignity and restraint since they were masters and not servants of the Presidium! Nothing could be more symbolical of the changed times. Under Stalin a frenetic applause for the Leader was the prescribed form at a Party Congress, and his closest subordinates would receive ovations, the intensity of which was proportionate to the official's closeness to the dictator.[14] Apart from the official etiquette the charted course of the new leaders of the Party became obvious from

---

[14] Thus at the Sixteenth Party Congress in 1930 Stalin was greeted according to the official transcript by "loud, long lasting applause turning into a long ovation; shouts 'Hurrah'; the whole Congress greeting him standing up." Molotov and Kaganovich and a few others received "long applause," while a mere member of the Central Committee in good standing (with Stalin) had to be content with "applause." In the subsequent Congresses the art and nuances of "spontaneous ovations" become considerably more developed.

two speeches by Khrushchev, first his official report as the First Secretary of the Party and then his speech to the closed session of the Congress in which he berated the late Joseph Stalin and attacked the "cult of personality," a euphemism for the craven worship of the despot in which Khrushchev along with all other Communists had to engage for more than a generation. The same leitmotif appeared in other speeches at the Congress.

By hacking at the Stalin legend the leaders were in effect undermining their own position, for had they not been the most servile helpers of the despot, and did they not reveal the abject terror in which the Party, along with the whole society, had lived for more than twenty years? Why? Part of the reason must be sought in the developments in the Party leadership just before and after Stalin's death. But beyond those reasons it is clear that the partial denigration of Stalin had a wider and more profound reason. Because of the developments we shall discuss later, it is no longer possible to exert, either in Russia or among the foreign Communists, the degree of terror with which the late dictator had ruled. If the Communist Party, the Soviet state, indeed the whole Communist world, is to be held together, then a new spirit, a new sense of mission, a new conception of purpose has to be poured into the Communists. What Khrushchev and other leaders attempted to say could be translated as follows: "Look, Communism is not terror, forced labor camps, and the whole nation prostrate before one man. Those things were just an accident traceable to the personality of one man. Communism is a live, creative doctrine; it requires discipline and privations to be sure, but not servility and complete negation of legal and rational processes. We as Communists still have great tasks to perform, and we can perform them best if we return to the Leninist purity of our Party and its doctrine." In other words, in place of terror, though its *moderate* use can never be abandoned by a totalitarian regime, the Soviet leaders are trying to revive ideological fervor and a sense of mission. Khrushchev quoted approvingly the criticism of Party officials by the great Soviet poet, Mayakovsky. Though written many years ago, it has become particularly applicable to the Stalin and post-Stalin era: "They have rooted themselves in their own spot and see nothing beyond their own nose. Having passed his exams on Communism according to the book, having learned 'the isms' by heart, he has finished forever with thoughts about Communism. What is the use of looking further? Sit and wait for the circular. You and I do not have to think if the leaders think." It might be added that under Stalin it was not always safe "to look further." The current line is to encourage initiative of Party members and to appeal especially to the youth. Great tasks like the settlement and agricultural development of new virgin lands are designed, quite apart from their economic desirability, to rekindle the sense of mission among young Communists.

It might be objected that the post-Stalin leaders want to have their cake and to eat it too. They do not dream of abandoning the substance of the police state or of replacing oligarchical rule by real Party democracy. At the same time they want all the advantages that in a democratic system accrue from free discussion and individual initiative. In a sense this has been a perennial dilemma of the Soviet system, hence the alternative periods, even under Stalin, of relative liberalization and of extreme terror. What makes the present system different is that there have been economic and social changes in Russia that impinge upon the Party and that make a return to full-fledged Stalinism impractical.

The role of the Party as the guiding force of the Soviet state and society is, then, in a state of flux. There is in the foreseeable future no alternative but the rule of the Communist Party. But to repeat, if the Party does not recover its vitality and *esprit de corps*, it will lose ground to other social forces, and other institutions, like the army, and eventually the point will be reached when it will be "a governing party" only in name and its members will feel a prior loyalty to other social and political groups with which they are associated. It is often said that the monopoly of education and propaganda enjoyed by the regime can ward off such dangers, and can continue to bring up generations of Communist fanatics. But the most powerful and penetrating propaganda machinery in the world will still be ineffective if social and economic conditions make its postulates unrealistic and distant from the circumstances of life of the persons being propagandized. The regime is quite explicit in its concept of the Communist Party. It wants an active and ideologically motivated elite, or, as Mikhail Suslov, member of the Presidium, stated at the Twentieth Party Congress: "The Party does not admit all who declare their wish to join its ranks. It selects for itself the most advanced and active people; it regulates admission in conformity with the tasks facing it at one or another stage of its work. During the industrialization and collectivization of agriculture, the Party admitted mainly workers and peasants; during the years of war preferential admittance to the Party was given to those who were at the front line. It is hardly necessary to prove that at present, when the problem of a steep improvement of material benefits is being solved, it is wise to lay stress primarily on the admittance of the direct producers of these benefits —workers and peasants." But will the new members, under changed social and economic conditions, respond as readily as of old to indoctrination and the old appeals of Communism? Suslov himself—and it is well worth noting that for many years he had been in charge of propaganda and agitation for the Party—gives examples of how boring the old stock in trade of

Communist propaganda is to the average member. Thus he quotes approvingly the criticism of a rank-and-file member: "I am now in my thirteenth year of study of the history of the Party, and for the thirteenth time propagandists are talking about the Bund. Have we no more important problems than the criticism of the Bund? We are interested in the problems of our MTS, *rayon*, and *oblast*. *We want to live in the present and future*.[15] Yet our propagandists are so stuck in the bog of the affairs of the Narodniki and Bund that they cannot get out of it." But if Party members are bored by the stories of what was after all the heroic period of the Party, are they likely to be more interested in the intricate theories of Marx and Engels? If they begrudge the time spent at countless educational and propaganda meetings are they likely to remain attached to the Party that forces them to go through what are now largely meaningless motions? They want to live in the present and the future as engineers, students, workers, men with concrete needs and aspirations, and they will remain attached to the Party only if the Party shows that it responds to those needs and aspirations.

The future of the Communist Party is thus bound up with the changes the whole Soviet society is undergoing. And in turn this future is bound up with the wider question whether Communism has still something to offer to Soviet society or whether it, instead of the state, will "wither away." By relaxing one of the traditional levers of power in a totalitarian society, terror, the regime hopes to use more effectively the supplementary mechanism of propaganda and indoctrination. It explains to the millions of Party members that Communism is not blind obedience or bureaucratic self-satisfaction or learning by rote, but healthy self-criticism and accomplishment of great tasks of socialist construction. The success or failure of the new campaign will go a long way in determining the future of politics in the U.S.S.R.

The Power Structure

In its structure and the spirit of its organization the Communist Party bears an indelible stamp of having been born as the party of conspiracy, pitted against the resources of a powerful state, and forced to operate in secrecy and illegality. Today it is the ruling party, a body of several million members that monopolizes all political power in the Soviet Union, and yet its organization preserves the tone inherited from the years of illegality, of the struggle against overwhelming odds, of the years when the Party, in power but still a small group, was transforming the social and economic character of the vast country. The character of the struggle many years

---

[15] My italics.

ago imposed upon the Party the need of deliberating in secret. Today, though the Party is no longer a group of hunted conspirators but the ruler, still, insofar as the deliberations of its highest bodies are concerned, the Presidium or the Central Committee, it reaches its decisions in secret, the mass of the membership and the world outside learning only the final conclusions—and not always even that. The conditions of the revolutionary struggle were presented by Lenin in 1902 and 1903 as necessitating iron discipline and firm control of the central organs. But the victory of the Bolsheviks and then, by their own account, of socialism in Russia, has not weakened the discipline nor relaxed, up to now, the iron grip of the central organs over the whole organization. The early Bolsheviks could not have bothered, even if they had wanted to, about the niceties of the democratic process. Terror, though not considered by them as a major means of reaching their objectives, was still held to be legitimate and useful under certain circumstances. And terror both within and without the Party was never used as extensively as during the period when the Communist rule was unchallenged in the 1930's, and, though relaxed, it was not abandoned either in theory or in practice by Stalin's successors.[16]

Thus the early pattern has perpetuated itself, and though in recent years it has begun to give way under the pressure of new social forces being generated in Russia, the "ruling party" is still the party of conspiracy.

The statements above cover the general behavior of the Communist Party in the forty years that it has been in power. Yet within the general pattern there have been considerable variations in detail: periods when there was savage struggle for power within the ruling oligarchy; times when the hand of one man lay heavily upon the whole organization; times when there was, at least, a semblance of inner party democracy; other times when terror and intimidation restrained a member of the Politburo as well as a rank-and-file worker.

---

[16] In his speech to the Twentieth Congress denouncing Stalin, Khrushchev contrasted the circumstances justifying terror as practiced by Lenin with Stalin's illegitimate use of the technique: ". . . Lenin without hesitation used the most extreme methods against the enemies. Lenin used such methods, however, only against actual class enemies and not against those who blunder, who err, and whom it was possible to lead through ideological influences and even retain in the leadership. Lenin used severe methods only in the most necessary cases, when the exploiting classes were still in existence and were vigorously opposing the Revolution, when the struggle for survival was decidedly assuming the sharpest forms, even including a civil war. Stalin, on the other hand, used extreme methods and mass repressions at a time when the Revolution was already victorious, when the Soviet state was strengthened, when the exploiting classes were already liquidated and socialist relations were rooted solidly in all phases of national economy, when our party was ideologically consolidated and had strengthened itself both numerically and ideologically. It is clear that here Stalin showed in a whole series of cases his intolerance, his brutality, and his abuse of power." Yet the speaker himself and his colleagues, despite the fact that "the Revolution was already victorious" applied methods not much different from Stalin's against Lavrenti Beria and his associates. Beria and his real or alleged associates were denounced as guilty the day after their arrest, tried in secret, and executed.

Like the Soviet state institutions, so also the Party institutions and laws exhibit a twofold character. The language of the statute, the concept of organization, is, more often than not, democratic. The reality behind very often limits or negates the democratic phraseology. Thus the cardinal organizational principle of the Party is "democratic centralism." As defined in the Party statutes its meaning is: "a) Election of all Party governing bodies from bottom to top. b) Periodic accountability of Party bodies to their Party organizations. c) Strict Party discipline and subordination of the minority to the majority. d) The decisions of higher bodies are unconditionally binding upon lower ones."[17] There is nothing in the bald statement of the principle with which a democratically minded person would quarrel. But the crucial word is "election." Here our usage of the term and its meaning within the Communist Party differ sharply. Just as in the election to the Supreme Soviet, or for that matter to any legislative body in the Soviet Union, there is only one list; thus the pattern of election to any Party office is monotonously simple: one candidate, or one list, and a unanimous election. It is likely that a small Party cell of a few members would be free to elect any one of them to be the secretary of the cell, but—and in this "but" there is the whole story of the Party structure—his election would not be binding until and unless it received the sanction of a higher Party organ. When we reach the upper levels of the Party organization the picture becomes even clearer. Nobody in the Soviet Union, at least for a generation, could have imagined the election of a secretary of a sizable Party unit, be it territorial or a great factory, as the result of a free play of sentiments and interests of the members of the given organization. The secretary of the Party, say in the city of Krasnodar, will be selected by a higher Party organization, most likely by the central secretariat of the Communist Party of the U.S.S.R. At the time of his selection, he will not necessarily be a resident of the area. Quite likely he will be doing Party work thousands of miles away from Krasnodar, which he may have never visited in his life. An emissary of the central organs will appear before the Party committee of Krasnodar with the "suggestion" that Comrade X be elected, and elected he will be unanimously! The same procedure applies with variations to the bureaus, committees and other organs of the Party at the local and national levels. To be pedantic, those officials are *elected* by members of the given organization, but *selected* by somebody else, the somebody else being in the last resort the dictator, or the ruling oligarchy.

If the word "election" is a euphemism for something else, then the next principle of democratic centralism, "periodic accountability of Party bodies to their Party organizations," also requires an appraisal. Again, there is no

---

[17] Quoted in *Current Soviet Policies,* ed. Leo Gruliow, New York, 1953, p. 29.

doubt that members of a small Party cell would ordinarily feel no compunction about criticizing or removing their secretary or their bureau (i.e.,
the executive committee) for inefficiency or corruption. When, however, it
comes to a "higher up"—an official who is a considerable Party functionary
—criticism or removal will have to come from above. An institution of
which the Soviets are very proud and which they cite very often as a proof
of their superiority over the Western forms of democracy throws a glaring
light on democratic centralism. This is the famous "samokritika," or self-
criticism. As applied to Party organization, a typical example would be a
letter by a worker to a local or national newspaper pointing out that the
Party secretary in the factory is falling down on his job, or is a person of
low moral standards, and inquiring why *the regional or central Party
committee does not undertake a corrective action*. The letter will be published or spoken criticism allowed, but not before the responsible Party
officials determine that there is enough substance in the accusation. What
is most characteristic is the fact that the call is always for *superior* Party
organization to take action. Our worker will seldom or never start agitating
against the official within the Party organization and call for a free vote of
members to remove or chastise the culprit. Again, it is an emissary of the
higher Party organs who is to investigate and chastise. It hardly needs to
be added that this form of self-criticism is not infrequently a put-up job
to remove for political reasons somebody who has become suspect or in-
convenient to the higher-ups. And if the person concerned is really in the
upper levels of the Party hierarchy, say a regional or republic secretary,
the chances are overwhelming that his liquidation, through self-criticism,
is at the orders of the ruling hierarchy.

Democratic centralism has, thus, meant in practice centralism and domination of the Party by a small group at the top, which, *as long as it is
united*, can and has been able to exercise an absolute sway over the whole
vast body of the membership and hence over the U.S.S.R. The qualification is important, for as we shall see, the pattern might be altered only
during periods when a serious breach occurred within the very top group—
this group usually being smaller than the membership of the Central Committee and usually identical with the Politburo (renamed "Presidium" at
the Nineteenth Congress in 1952). Then politics, or rather politicking,
could take place within the Party, and various factions reflecting the views
of the leaders would try to gain adherents at the Central Committee and
local levels, offering in effect competing ideological and political platforms,
with the consequence that, as in earlier times, heated debates and conferences would take place at the Party Conferences and Congresses. Some
writers in referring to such periods, especially the years following the November Revolution and up to the beginning of Stalin's dictatorship (usually

dated from the Fourteenth Party Congress in 1925), have seen in them an intra-Party democracy, which was then restrained and finally destroyed only by the iron hand of the dictator. Yet it is stretching the term a great deal to see in disagreements and struggles within a narrow elite an essential part of the democratic process. It is true that under Lenin those Party members who disagreed with the leader and the majority group in the Central Committee were not physically liquidated or instantly imprisoned, or forced to degrade themselves by humiliating recantations. Yet in most cases they were demoted from their Party posts and sent to diplomatic posts abroad, or to do Party work in remote parts of the U.S.S.R. What Stalin often accomplished through terror and arrest, his great predecessor often did through lesser chicanery and through persuasion. The return to Lenin's ways as advertised by Stalin's successors is a return to more humane, more rational ways of ruling the Party, but still ruling it undemocratically.

The problem of power in the structure of the Communist Party is then a subject of considerable fascination. How was it that a group of revolutionaries—people who, we are always told by social psychologists, are unstable, liable to be quarrelsome, and, as history always has shown, liable to fall out among themselves once the victory is secure—managed to preserve an organizational unity and over so vast a country? To pose the question thus is partly to answer it, for the magnitude of the task as well as of the danger held the Bolsheviks together. And before the instruments of terror and bureaucratic controls could be perfected by his successor, the Party had been held together by the extraordinary personality of Lenin. He had held his flock together not only during the wanderings in the wilderness of exile, the Revolution, and the Civil War, but also, what was even more difficult, during the first years in the promised land of absolute power and the beginnings of the recasting of Russia's economy and society. By his very success in being a moderate dictator, he laid the foundations for a thorough despotism.

The development of the power structure in the Party and the shifting role of the Party organs can best be studied in the light of the major crises that have shaken the Communist Party ever since its victory and the latest of which, a crisis of ideology, as well as a struggle for power, is still continuing as this is being written.

The first crisis, for all its undramatic resolution, and in spite of the fact that among the Bolsheviks it claimed no human sacrifices, was in a sense the most important one in the forty years that the Communist Party has been in power. For in breaking, though through fairly humane methods, the various factions and opposition groups in the Party, and reaffirming the organizational principles postulated in 1902 and 1903, Lenin cut off all the

possibility that a different, democratic spirit might begin to grow in the
Party. The methods employed had none of the perfidy that Stalin exhibited
in outmaneuvering the "Left Opposition" in 1924-25 and the Right Opposition in the late twenties. Certainly they had none of the bloodthirsti-
ness and sadism of Stalin when he sent the old Bolsheviks, then already
discredited and impotent, to their death by the thousands during the
Great Purge. Yet the latter phenomena would not have been possible except for the developments in 1920-22 which determined that there could
be no "loyal opposition" within the Communist Party; that any disagreement on political or ideological grounds would be branded by the prevailing group in the leadership as heresy, and then treason, and that the
defeated faction would be forced to recant or face expulsion or worse. The
crisis had as a far-reaching side effect Lenin's sanctioning the erection of
an elaborate apparatus of Party bureaucracy that would help prevent the
recurrence of dissidence and of his entrusting the leadership of it to Joseph
Stalin, who in 1922 became the Secretary-General of the Communist Party.

The arena of the struggle was twofold: the Party Congress and the
Central Committee. The Party Congress was then, as it is now officially,
the sovereign organ of the Communist Party. During the first post-Revolutionary era the Congress was no longer the motley assembly it had been
before, of a few exiles and revolutionaries who managed to get out of Russia to hold a conclave on foreign soil, nor was it yet the assembly of delegates summoned to worship and applaud the great man and his lieutenants
that it was to become under Stalin. It was still a live and reasonably democratically elected body. Under Lenin it met every year, and, for all the
dissonances and bitterness of debate, the magic personality and enormous
prestige of Lenin was still sufficient to secure a majority for the leader's
postulates and policies. But increasingly the focus of power was shifting to
a much smaller group, the Central Committee elected by the Congress
but liable to be more subservient to Lenin than the parent body. Those
organs of the Party that were to be manipulated so skillfully by Stalin to
secure his predominance—the Secretariat, the Organizational Bureau, and
the Party Control Commission—were during the period 1919-23 thought of
as mainly of administrative importance, inferior to the Central Committee
in fact as well as in theory. The Congress as the sovereign policy-determin-
ing body, and the Central Committee as the executive and policy-formulating organ, enjoyed real importance during Lenin's postwar leadership.
Beginning with Lenin's incapacitating illness in 1922, their real political
importance declined, until they eventually were to serve as additional
tools of personal dictatorship of Stalin or of the oligarchy that succeeded
him.

The issue of the struggle was nothing else than the character of the

Soviet state being born, and consequently of the Communist Party that was guiding it. The Communist Party, as we observed before, inherited from Marxism its twofold character. It was the Party of revolution, of opposition to the state, the party that embraced the anarchistic slogans of complete equality, of abolition of all social distinction and rank and of the standing army. At the same time, and paradoxically, it was the party that believed in the creation of a modern industrialized state as a prerequisite to socialism. Such a state, especially under the conditions of Russia of 1920, required many things directly opposed to the anarchistic side of the postulates of Bolshevism, the postulates under which it won the Revolution and the Civil War. Instead of weakening the state and hence the central organs of the Party, the vision of an industrialized and socialist Russia required a strong state, hence the unchallengeable authority of the central Party organs. Instead of economic equality and socialism right away, it required economic stability and reconstruction and incentives for hard work. Instead of the dissolution of bureaucracy and the standing army, it required the erection of an administrative and planning machinery. Lenin very early perceived the necessity of abandoning the "campaign oratory" in which the Bolsheviks indulged during the Revolution and of facing the facts. When the Kronstadt sailors, who in the crucial days of the fall of 1917 had been the staunchest supporters of the Bolsheviks, revolted in 1921 and tossed in the face of the Bolsheviks the very same anarchistic slogans they themselves had employed, their uprising was mercilessly suppressed. In 1921 Lenin had sanctioned the New Economic Policy, which was premised on the belief that before Russia could advance toward socialism her economy must be reconstructed and hence private trade and private ownership in agriculture must be tolerated for an indefinite period of time. The same line of reasoning persuaded Lenin and, especially, Trotsky that the Red Army could not become a revolutionary mob but had to have officers and discipline, and that the factories had to have skilled workers and engineers and they in turn had to have salaries above the wages of a common laborer.

These common-sense conclusions were opposed by a number of Bolshevik leaders, not only because of the persistence in the Bolshevik ranks of anarchistic and egalitarian sentiments, but also because of their more reasonable belief that the ruling group among the Communists was already settling down in the enjoyment of power and its appurtenances, and was inclined to defer the realization of socialism to an indefinite future. As in all dissensions within the Communist Party, we find in those early struggles an inextricable mixture of the power drive and ideological and temperamental dissonances. It would take too long to give a reasonably full story of the early Party schisms. The most characteristic and important

were those of the Workers' Opposition, which provides the best opportunity for study of the early structure of the Party and the ways then
employed in managing it.

At the Eighth and Ninth Party Congresses in 1919 and 1920 there were
already voices decrying bureaucratization of the Party, admission of former
tsarist officers into the Red Army, etc. With the end of the Civil War the
discontent within the Party found an expression in a new movement sponsored by some Party leaders. The two most prominent names were those
of Alexandra Kollontai, an upper-class intellectual who had joined the
Bolsheviks,[18] and Alexander Shlyapnikov, a true proletarian in origin and
a member of the Central Committee. The Workers' Opposition had as its
first and most important postulate the plea that the trade unions should
be fairly independent of the state and the Party, that they should run the
economy of the country. As secondary postulates they advocated scaling
down the wage differential,[19] and democratization of the Party. Repeated
in the Worker's Opposition's propaganda was the charge that the Party
was run by an oligarchy and that the country freshly freed from the rule
of landlords and tsarist officials was in the process of getting a new official
caste of Communist functionaries.

Their position was condemned by Lenin, not unjustifiably, as being
anarchist-syndicalist rather than Marxian. At the Tenth Party Congress,
which met in 1921 in the shadow of the Kronstadt revolt, Lenin's position
that the trade unions should be autonomous but not independent of the
Party received overwhelming approval. Lenin's motion prevailed not only
against the Workers' Opposition, but also against the views of Trotsky,
who would have made explicit what was implicit in Lenin's motion and
what became an accepted maxim in Stalin's period, namely that the trade
unions are strictly subordinate to the Party and are to help carry out the
government's economic policies rather than to have any policies of their
own. Sentiments akin to those reflected by the opposition were strong
among the rank and file of the Party. Yet characteristically the Workers'
Opposition could muster only a handful of votes at the Congress when
the great prestige of Lenin was thrown against them, and they had almost
no support within the Central Committee. The Tenth Congress condemned the Workers' Opposition as a "syndicalist and anarchist" deviation
and forbade further propaganda of their ideas.

The dispute had its most concrete application in the adoption by the
Congress of a provision still in the Party statute in a revised form, stating

[18] Mme. Kollontai gained notoriety also by her strenuous advocacy of free love, and
literary efforts dedicated to the same theme.
[19] Though from our point of view, or from that of the U.S.S.R. since the thirties,
Russia in the period under discussion was economically as close to an egalitarian society
as you can get.

that a joint plenum of the Central Committee of the Party and its Control Commission could by a majority of two-thirds expel a member of the Central Committee from his post or even from the Party. Thus was formalized a provision that enabled the Party oligarchy, without recourse to the Congress, to deal summarily even with Party notables should they set themselves in opposition to the dominant fashion. This weapon was to be used frequently by Stalin. The Tenth and Eleventh Congresses sanctioned an extended purge of the Party and of its "anarchist and syndicalist" deviationists. Thus, what began as a common-sense position of Lenin's against extreme radicalism ended as the negation of any democratic opportunities in the Party, the consolidation of the position of the Central Committee, and the forging of the weapon of the Party purge, by which the leaders could always rid the Party of elements they did not desire. It is not accidental that at the same time Lenin entrusted the direction of the Party apparatus to a man he did not particularly like, but who among the top Party leaders showed the least propensity for ideological quarrels and the most for quiet organizational work. In 1922 Joseph Stalin, already a member of the Political and Organizational Bureaus, became the Secretary-General. The expectation was that he would bring order out of the chaos into which routine administrative affairs of the Party had fallen, and also that he would help curtail the factional strife the Tenth and Eleventh Congresses had demonstrated.

Stalin's emergence as the top administrator of the Party was the culmination of an organizational career. Before 1922 he already belonged to the Party's Organization Bureau and had held various important political posts, chief among them the Commissariats of Nationalities and of the Workers' and Peasants' Inspection, the latter devised as a control organ to check the performance of Soviet administration. His rise to power coincided with and was partly based on the growing importance of the administrative and control organs within the Party and the state. An indefatigable worker, master of detail and routine, Stalin struck a vivid contrast with the rest of the first-rank Communist leaders, who were much more impressive as speakers or writers but lacked the patience or temperament to attend to dull administrative work. Within a short time the Secretariat of the Communist Party ceased to be a simple organization where a few people received provincial delegations and attended to the grievances and problems of various local Party organizations, and became the veritable nerve center of the Party. The Secretariat assumed the responsibility for instructional and propaganda work, it sent out emissaries to check on the performance of Party organizations. The Secretary-General was in a position to determine who was to head Party work in various organizations (except, during the first few years, for the capitals of Moscow and Leningrad), and his work gave him an enhanced opportunity to make wide contacts and recruit partisans among the important Communist activists. If, in addition to Stalin's supremacy in the Secretariat and the Organizational Bureau, is added his considerable influence in the Party Control Commission, the body charged with standing watch over the activities and performance of the Party members, then it becomes understandable how an ambitious and able man was capable of building a tremendous power base and the foundations for an absolute dictatorship.

But the explanation cannot be given entirely in terms of Stalin's mastery of the apparatus. At any time between 1922 and 1925 the Central Committee or the Party Congress could have dismissed Stalin from his powerful position as Secretary-General. None of those bodies was dominated as yet by Stalin. Shortly before his death, Lenin, irked by Stalin's rudeness to his wife, Nadezhda Krupskaya, and alarmed by the reports that Stalin was building a personal machine, did in fact propose the replacement of the Secretary-General in a letter that was certainly known to the Central Committee.[20] But none of the aspirants for Lenin's mantle could be enticed to take on the strenuous job of day-to-day administration of the Party. Among the Party leaders of secondary importance, Stalin did at the time enjoy a certain popularity. In the light of what was to happen later this reputation of Stalin in the years 1922-25 may appear incredible. But his views and activities were, as a matter of fact, of the kind to appeal to a Communist administrator. He appeared then as a man of moderate views, desirous of rebuilding the Russian economy before taking drastic steps, such as the expropriation of the peasants. In brief, he was the advocate of moderate social policies. While the others were planning grandiose foreign revolutions, Stalin, while all for the support of foreign Communists, directed attention primarily to the tasks of socialist construction in Russia.[21] In terms of personality, Stalin, for all his scheming propensities, had, so it seemed at the time, none of Trotsky's intellectual arrogance, or Zinoviev's and Kamenev's vacillation. He stood—and it is not surprising that so many Communists were taken in—as an advocate of

---

[20] The new generation of Communists heard of it for the first time in Khrushchev's indictment of Stalin at the Twentieth Party Congress.

[21] Stalin's position on this issue, his famous "socialism in one country" plea, is almost invariably misrepresented. It is made to appear as if Stalin, in the period under discussion, was for the abandoning of the revolutionary work abroad, while his antagonist Trotsky believed that a socialist reconstruction of Russia must be postponed until after a world revolution. The position of neither man was that categorical and one-sided, and as a matter of fact there was but little difference between their real views on the subject. Once in opposition Trotsky was maneuvered into arguing that Stalin was betraying the revolution, an argument that further weakened Trotsky's position, for it gave Stalin an opportunity to present Trotsky's followers as adventurists who, instead of attending to concrete tasks at home, wanted to engage in dangerous adventures abroad.

Communist "normalcy," of moderate policies, neither too much to the left nor too much to the right, in brief, for the continuation of Lenin's policies and tactics. It is no accident that after Lenin's death it was mainly Stalin who inaugurated a veritable cult of the dead leader, who for all his faults had detested sycophancy and religious veneration of personalities.

For all its democratic phraseology the Communist Party was then, as it is now, an organization calling for a united leadership. Stalin's management of the problem of succession combined all the elements necessary to the guidance of a totalitarian movement: the seizure of the administrative structure, a degree of acceptance and popularity among the Party activists, and the erection of a quasi-religious cult of the departed leader that would facilitate the acceptance of a new one. Within the highest circles of the Party he skillfully exploited the distrust of the majority of the top Communist leaders toward Leon Trotsky. The latter, the leader of the Red Army and Lenin's right hand during the Revolution and the Civil War, aroused the admiration of certain circles of the Red Army, the Soviet youth and foreign Communists. A brilliant and many-sided man, Trotsky proved to be poorly equipped for the kind of infighting into which Communist Party politics resolves itself at times of transition. To the Party hierarchy he appeared as a potential Bonaparte of the Russian Revolution, a man who was not "really" a Bolshevik, as he had rejoined Lenin only on the eve of the Revolution, and all his enormous services to the cause did not diminish their envy and fear of his brilliant abilities. In contrast with Trotsky, Stalin stood out as a solid but rather drab personality, capable through hard work and attention to administrative detail of warding off the brilliant rhetoric and charismatic personality of the Commissar of War. It was thus that the two senior Communist leaders Kamenev (a brother-in-law of Trotsky) and Zinoviev joined with Stalin to provide the collective leadership of the Party during Lenin's incapacity and after his death. The triumvirate (in Russian *troika*) was the product of the fear of Trotsky and of the assumption that through a division of leadership personal dictatorship could be avoided.

The story has often been told how Stalin maneuvered his allies into committing themselves too far against Trotsky, and how he disposed of them in turn with the help of the right wing of the Party, and how then, in sole possession of power, he crushed his erstwhile right-wing allies in 1929-30.[22] But personalities and personal struggles provide only part of

[22] The discussion of Communist leaders and policies in terms of right and left wings and deviations is likely to appear puzzling. Thus Bukharin, when he opposed Lenin on the signing of the Treaty of Brest-Litovsk in 1918, was described as the leader of the Left Communists. In 1929 and 1930 we find Bukharin denounced by Stalin's faction as a "right opportunist" for his opposition to rapid collectivization. In line with the usual semantic jugglery at which the Communists are so adept, the Party's course,

the story. What is necessary for the understanding of the mechanics of
Party politics is the realization that personal factors, ideological issues, and
administrative controls all play their part and it is impossible neatly to
separate one factor from the others. Thus Stalin's ambition and diabolical
cunning are usually isolated as the key factor in his rise to power. Stalin's
defeated enemies have traced his perfidy and deception throughout his
whole career. Charges have been made, some of which are absurd and
others unverifiable, about Stalin's early career, such as the stories of his
poisoning Lenin or having been a tsarist police agent. But at the crucial
point—to repeat—Stalin stood as morally no better and no worse than
the other would-be successors of Lenin. Far from the future author of
purges that decimated the Old Bolsheviks, it was he who restrained his
allies, Zinoviev and Kamenev, from taking too drastic steps against Trotsky,
whom they wanted to expel from the Party. When in 1925 Zinoviev and
Kamenev turned against Stalin and his new allies, the future right opposition, Stalin the moderate again presented his erstwhile allies as extremists.
In a dramatic moment at the Fourteenth Congress he exclaimed that
Zinoviev and Kamenev wanted the "blood of Bukharin," his then ally
on the Politburo, and having aroused the horror of the Congress at the idea
of a revered Bolshevik leader's being assailed as if he were a counterrevolutionary, he announced that "we will not give you the blood of Bukharin."[23]

But Stalin's personal skill and the equally sordid but less skillful intrigues of his opponents provide just one part of the picture. In 1923-25
the policies embraced by Stalin, his political "platform," were of the kind
to appeal to the great mass of Communists: cautious progress toward
socialism, but certainly no drastic break with the New Economic Policy
designed to set Russia on her feet before a wholesale socialist transformation. When Zinoviev and the Left finally turned on the Secretary-General,
they pictured the country as reverting to a capitalist economy, with rich
peasants becoming stronger and stronger and dictating the pace of Russia's
economy. Stalin imperturbably met the charge by justifying his policies,
as he justified everything he did, in the name of Leninism. Thus in 1925
private property in agriculture, and the allowing of richer peasants to hire
help and lease more land (strange doings under a socialist regime!) was

i.e., the course of the prevailing faction of the Party, is *always* correct and *always* in
the middle. Those Communists who are fearful that the policies are too drastic or
rapid are denounced as the "right opportunists"; those who at other times believe them
to be too cautious are branded as "left-wing adventurists." Most of the proposals
advanced by Trotsky, Kamenev, and Zinoviev in 1924-25 and decried by Stalin as
senselessly "left," were put into effect by him in *much more drastic form* in 1929-30
but as emanating from himself alone. These policies were no longer either "left" or
"right"—they were "correct," and any criticism of them (often in the very words of
the Stalin of 1925) was piously described as "right-wing" opportunism.
[23] In 1938 Bukharin and a whole group of Old Bolshevik leaders were tried and
shot, thus following the fate of Zinoviev and Kamenev.

Leninism, just as in 1929-30 it was Leninism to expropriate the peasants and to force them into collectives. On the previous occasion Stalin informed the assembled Communists that Zinoviev and Kamenev obviously intended to force and rob the peasant, to attempt to coerce him into socialism instead of educating him through example and persuasion as Vladimir Ilich Lenin had taught should be done! And in the spirit of revolutionary pragmastism, answering the opposition's charge that Marx and Engels, were they alive, would be alarmed at what was happening in Russia under an allegedly socialist regime, Stalin maintained that Marx and Engels would say: "May the devil take the old formulas; long live victorious socialism in the U.S.S.R." Quite apart from the administrative and personal intrigues of the Stalinists, the program thus presented and thus stated would always gain some popularity, especially in a country still recovering from the ravages of war, and still mainly peasant in its population.

The struggle for succession reached its peak at the Fourteenth Party Congress, held in December 1925. It repays the effort to examine the proceedings of the Congress, for it was the culminating point in Stalin's rise to power, the most opportune moment when his rise could have been checked by a determined, skillful, and united opposition to him within the Party. For the first and, up to the present day the last, time the division within the Communist ranks spilled out from the Central Committee into the larger body, and, to an extent not approximated in the days of the Workers' Opposition nor in the feeble last movements of opposition of the next few years, threatened to split the victorious Communist Party. The Fourteenth Congress was the last one about which there was still some of the air of a gathering of revolutionaries. Debates were heated, and yet there was some remnant of the free and comradely spirit of the underground and the Revolution. Future Congresses were to prostrate themselves before the dictator, and, like gatherings of Oriental satraps, respond to his slightest whim.

The Communist Party and the world Communist movement were treated to the spectacle of the Central Committee split into two factions. Thus in place of a single report of the Central Committee, traditionally the token of united leadership of the movement delivered by its leading figure, two reports were presented: the majority's by Stalin, and the minority's by Zinoviev. All the negotiations in advance had not been able to prevent the split's becoming public and violent. Zinoviev and Kamenev felt that it was now or never: organizationally and politically they were being surrounded. Their frantic attempts to garner and convert delegates before and during the Congress were not successful. Stalin's machine now assured him of a strong majority. It was only in Leningrad, where Zinoviev had been the Party boss, that the Opposition, through methods similar to those used by Stalin in the Party at large, had secured very strong support —hence its name, the "Leningrad Opposition." Moscow, the other capital, where Kamenev's influence had been strong in the Party organization, at first gravitated somewhat to the Opposition, but just before the Congress the Stalinists obtained the adherence of the Moscow Party boss, Uglanov, and with him went the majority of his delegation. It was thus a struggle of Party bosses, of Party "machines," in which what had once been the Social-Democratic Party of Russia finally surrendered the last vestige of its democracy.

The substance of the debate has already been presented. Ranged with Stalin against the Left or Leningrad Opposition were the Party leaders whom in a few years he would denounce as "right-wing opportunists"— Chairman of the Council of Commissars, Alexei Rykov; leader of the trade unions, Tomsky; and an outstanding Communist writer and theoretician, Bukharin. They joined Stalin, seeing in him the advocate of moderate policy and a believer in collective leadership. Silent throughout the Congress remained Leon Trotsky, who, still a man of influence in the Party, refused to join Kamenev and Zinoviev, his persecutors of only a few months before. The Opposition's fire, at first, was directed mainly at Bukharin, in whom they saw the author of the lenient policy toward the peasant. It was only toward the end that an open attack was made upon the already fearsome figure of the Secretary-General. It was related how the Party's control organs abused their powers in persecuting and ejecting partisans of the Opposition. And the essence of the struggle was revealed when Kamenev proclaimed that the Secretariat of the Party had become *a political organ* and its head had raised himself to a position unheard of in a free revolutionary movement, that of a totalitarian leader. We believe, stated Kamenev, that the party should be run by its senior officials (i.e., the Politburo) and we are against the theory of a Leader. An oligarchy rather than a personal dictatorship was the best that the Opposition could prescribe for the Party, and it was brought out by the Stalinists, not without justification, that Kamenev and Zinoviev were piqued at having had their personal ambitions thwarted, and that Stalin's ascendancy in the Party's councils was largely the product of their own organizational ineptitude and indolence. Stalin himself modestly denied any intention or possibility of dictatorship within the Party.

Five years later, at the Sixteenth Party Congress, the effect of the Fourteenth was fully demonstrated. The old Left Opposition had been fully shattered, its leaders had been stripped of their posts and many of its followers imprisoned. Trotsky was in exile. Russia was in the midst of forced collectivization, which was to lead to a famine in the Ukraine and the deportation of hundreds of thousands, if not millions, of peasant families. No longer the genial compromiser, the middle-of-the-road man who eschewed all extremism, Stalin now appeared as a resolute dictator, a man who would brook no opposition. Throughout his speech lashing out at his recent allies, Rykov, Tomsky, Bukharin, and Uglanov, he kept repeating with terrible intensity the phrase: "If you don't press those people, you don't get anywhere." The obedient delegates responded with jeers and abuse directed at the culprits, all of them at one time trusted lieutenants of Lenin and men of great popularity and influence within the Party.

It is instructive to compare Stalin's destruction of the Left Opposition with another great crisis in the Party, the crisis that took place before and after Stalin's death, and that is, as this is being written, still unresolved. The details of the latest crisis are largely a matter of conjecture. We do not possess, as we do for the period of the twenties, Party Congress speeches, minutes of the Central Committee, and even of the Politburo, with the position of contestants for power and their political moves clearly delineated. The struggle of the late forties and the fifties has been taking place in secrecy, illuminated only occasionally by a public announcement of the removal and execution of a high official. Yet it is possible to reconstruct the general outlines of the struggle for power within the Communist Party during the last years of Stalin and the current period of collective leadership. Like the preceding crisis, the current one has had the ingredients of personal rivalry, political and administrative maneuvering, and an ideological debate.

In the background of the crisis lay the absolute dictatorship of Stalin, which, since 1934, had liquidated physically not only all the members of opposing factions but many of Stalin's closest collaborators, who, for one reason or another, incurred the dictator's distrust or displeasure. To be specific and to list only those leaders who at one time or another had occupied the highest positions in the Party: to their deaths, after trials in which they had to confess to the most improbable crimes, went Zinoviev and Kamenev, as well as Rykov and Bukharin. Liquidated without a trial and in secrecy were Stalin's erstwhile closest collaborators and members of the Politburo: S. V. Kossior, Rudzutak, and Chubar. If we add to the list Kuibyshev and Ordzhonikidze, who assertedly died of natural causes but actually under suspicious circumstances, we get an impressive picture of the decimation of Lenin's and the post-Lenin Politburo.[24] It is superfluous to list all the other high officials of the army, Party, and government who were purged, or to elaborate on what has now been admitted by the Soviets themselves, that the purge not only attacked the big people, but spread

---

[24] Leon Trotsky died in exile, murdered by a hired assassin; Sergei Kirov, whom Stalin had delegated to clean up the Leningrad organization after Zinoviev's deposal, was assassinated allegedly by an anti-Stalinist in 1934.

to all layers of Soviet society. Terror, as a regular philosophy of government, and the secret police and an elaborate system of spying and denunciation as the means of controlling the Party and the state, became the
routine features of Soviet society. Even after the massive purge that ended
in 1939, the dictator continued these practices on a more moderate scale,
and indeed they are the essential ingredients of Soviet totalitarianism.

But apart from terror and concentration camps, and the frightening
reality of the power structure, Soviet society underwent profound changes
during the Stalin era. Social changes continued to exert a mounting pressure on the Communist Party of the U.S.S.R. To use a favorite Marxist
term, an "inherent contradiction" developed between Russian society and
the system of government. As society was modernized and industrialized,
a new pattern of interests emerged. The Russian people, including the
mass of members of the Communist Party, obviously longed to enjoy the
fruits of progress: to acquire a higher standard of living, to achieve a modicum at least of personal security, of "normalcy," and a release from the
continuous dread of terror. Yet this social pressure—which is merely
another name for the needs and aspirations of Soviet citizens of all walks
of life—was simply unavailing against what appeared then as a cast-iron
system of dictatorship, buttressed by the secret police and fortified by the
people's fear and downright inability to conceive of an alternative to
Stalin's personal rule. In the eyes of the dictator and the ruling hierarchy,
the situation, though secure, had two grave contradictions in it. There was,
first of all and quite understandably, a decline of the *esprit de corps* of the
Communist Party, a loss of vitality in the organization almost synonymous
with Soviet power. And how could it be otherwise? The Party was terrorized. Its leading organs almost stopped functioning. In defiance of the
Party statute no Party Congress took place between 1939 and 1952. If the
Central Committee met between the end of the War and Stalin's death,
we have no record of it. Even the Politburo functioned irregularly, with
some members sometimes forbidden to attend because of the dictator's
whim. The most crucial decisions were often taken by Stalin himself with
whoever at the moment was closest to him. The day-to-day task of running the country was evidently in the hands of the secret police, the two
ministries comprising it, the M.V.D. (the Ministry of Internal Affairs),
and the M.G.B. (the Ministry of State Security) rapidly becoming a state
within a state. If the situation bothered Stalin and some of his lieutenants,
it was not because of democratic scruples. It was because of the simple
realization that the economic growth of the country and the development
of stability of Soviet society could not be assured by bayonets, prisons, and
concentration camps, and that somehow the role of the Communist Party
would have to be revived.

Closely connected with the preceding problem was that of leadership of the Party and succession to the despot. At the close of World War II Stalin was sixty-six. Whatever his health, his age would no longer allow him to exercise a continuous and detailed supervision of the many departments of the Party and the state. Authority had to be delegated, and at the same time Stalin, with a true dictator's instinct, lived in constant apprehension of a subordinate's becoming too powerful. His technique had always been to liquidate or demote those closest to him as soon as they became too influential. Thus, the period immediately after the Great Purge, 1939-41, saw reduction in status of those who in the thirties had been closest to him—Kaganovich, Molotov, and Voroshilov—and the emergence of new men in the leading positions: Zhdanov, Malenkov, Beria, and Khrushchev. At the same time, the logic of the situation and the tyrant's advanced age tended necessarily to enable his lieutenants to build strong personal followings. In the immediate postwar years, Lavrenti Beria obtained a powerful hold on the vast machinery of the security forces, as well as on the Party organizations in Transcaucasia, while the Party apparatus was the scene of an undercover struggle between Zhdanov and Malenkov. The competing factions vied for strategic positions as well as for the despot's favor. The latter was always distributed with the object of keeping any one of the powerful aides from becoming too powerful. Thus after Zhdanov's death in 1948 (under circumstances that have not been fully clarified) Malenkov appeared for a while in sole control of the Party apparatus. But not for long, for he was soon joined in the Party Secretariat by Nikita Khrushchev. Beginning in 1949-50, if not before, steps were taken to weaken Lavrenti Beria's hold on the security apparatus, and purges were carried out in his special preserve, the Georgian Communist Party.

The picture of the Party situation in conjunction with social and economic developments in the country at large may have inclined Stalin and whoever were the people who had his ear at the time to give yet another drastic turn to the development of the Communist regime. The reform was to conform to the usual recipes of Stalin's reforms: in part terror, in part an ideological offensive. In 1950-51 we have the reopening of the discussion of the future of Soviet agriculture. Amalgamation of the collective farms was designed to weaken elements of private property that still lingered in agriculture.[25]

At the same time the leadership of the Party was to be changed, and a

---

[25] The rulers were casting about for a solution of a most pressing problem of the Soviet economy *and at the same time were seeking something that would restore the sense of ideological mission and purpose to the Party.* Stalin's *Economic Problems of Socialism in the U.S.S.R.*, a pamphlet written in 1952, was designed to inspire new ideological fervor into the rank and file of the Party.

new wave of terror perhaps on the scale of the Great Purge was to shake the Party. There are several solid pieces of evidence that this was what Stalin had in mind. The Nineteenth Party Congress, convened in the fall of 1952, doubled the size of the top organ, the Politburo, now renamed Presidium of the Central Committee. The old leaders were still there but they were swamped by "new men," mostly younger bureaucrats and regional Party secretaries; the latter were obviously to be given on-the-job training and then to replace the old guard, whose scheming and intrigues may have wearied Stalin.[26] But the purge was not only to be political. In January 1953 a group of leading Soviet medical specialists was "unmasked" and promptly confessed to some successful and some planned assassinations of various leading figures in the Party, army, etc. Judged by the sad precedent of the thirties, the investigation would undoubtedly link the "criminal doctors" to some other currently leading figures. On the eve of Stalin's death in March 1953 a new purge was in the offing, and it was to be accompanied by a redirection of the Party's efforts and leadership.

Stalin's death at one blow cut short both processes. Its immediate consequence was a veritable coup d'état, in which the old leaders, some of them probably intended victims of the purge, proceeded to rearrange the highest state and Party positions. The Presidium was cut down to its old size, most of the newcomers from the Nineteenth Congress being ejected. From the bargaining that must have followed, Malenkov emerged as the head of the government but had to relinquish his seat on the Party Secretariat. Beria once again assumed what appeared to be full control of the security forces; even the position of the titular head of the state, unimportant in a stable totalitarian system, but potentially important in an unstable situation, changed hands and was entrusted to the senior member of the Presidium, Voroshilov. It was clear on the morrow of Stalin's death that none of his successors inherited all or even most of the tyrant's powers. None of them was in a position, as Stalin had been, to consign the majority of his colleagues to political obscurity or liquidation. None of them could, alone and at will, chart the future of the Communist Party and Soviet society. It was obvious that in public the leaders would strive to preserve the appearance of solidarity and unanimity, but at the same time sparring for position and political maneuvering would go on.

It is sometimes assumed in the West that political power in the Soviet

---

[26] From Khrushchev's indictment of Stalin at the Twentieth Congress: "Stalin evidently had plans to finish off the old members of the Political Bureau. He often stated that Political Bureau members should be replaced by new ones. His proposal, after the Nineteenth Congress, concerning the election of twenty-five persons to the Central Committee Presidium, was aimed at the removal of the old Political Bureau members and the bringing in of less experienced persons so that these would extol him in all sorts of ways."

Union is like a concrete object locked in the offices of the Presidium of the Communist Party of the U.S.S.R., and that anybody who seizes it becomes the absolute dictator. But the first effect of Stalin's death was that the arena of political maneuvering in Russia was considerably enlarged. Previously the struggle for influence had gone on in the closest entourage of the dictator. It was relatively unimportant what a Party secretary in Odessa may have felt about the relative virtues of policies advocated by Khrushchev and Malenkov. For one thing, any public disagreement among the Bolshevik leaders on policies reflected only a temporary hesitation on the given issue by the dictator. His closest collaborators had no identifiable ideological personalities. After his death the picture became different. With the situation fluid at the top, it *does* become important to the aspirants for power not only to have their men in the strategic positions in the Party and state apparatus but also to woo the whole mass of officialdom by appealing to their interests and convictions.

The classical case of a "political campaign" in a totalitarian system is the career of Beria between March and the summer of 1953. Like any politician in any country, the Minister of the Interior knew the requirement for success was twofold: strengthen your organization and have an attractive political platform. The widespread agencies of the Ministry of the Interior and the security forces were cleansed (though, as it turned out later, not completely) of the anti-Beria or neutral elements. But, in addition, Beria became both in his public pronouncements and official acts an advocate of "socialist legality" and national equality. He appeared desirous of taking to himself most of the credit for the curbing of the worst abuses of official terrorism—as shown by his repudiation of the doctors' case—and for the greater opportunities offered to non-Russian officials in the state and Party. It is not far-fetched to suggest that he realized the political appeal of measures that held out to the middle ranks of the Soviet hierarchy the promise of a modicum of security for their lives and their positions. And against the background of frantic Russian chauvinism of Stalin's last years, Beria's policies must likewise have suggested greater opportunities for advancement and more freedom from Great-Russian supervision for the non-Russian elements of the officialdom. The dramatic fall of Beria and his associates in June 1953 indicates, paradoxically, the success of those policies. Rehabilitation of the victims of Stalinist terror and greater latitude on the nationality issue have continued under the "collective leadership." It is unnecessary to postulate an attempted coup by Beria as an explanation for his liquidation. He was becoming too well entrenched in his administrative machinery, and was courting popularity too strenuously not to arouse the deepest apprehension of his colleagues. It does not matter that the propaganda machine has managed to picture him as an exponent of terror and the author of the plan to dismember the Soviet Union. The measures he had advocated have proved appealing and have been endorsed as their own by the rest of the leadership.

The elimination of Beria did not bring harmony to the ruling elite. The vacuum created by Stalin's death continues down to our own day, and the impression of harmony that the ruling hierarchy attempts to convey conceals considerable strains.[27] Beria's personal empire was dismantled and his partisans throughout Russia purged.[28] The realization that the leadership of the vast security apparatus conferred enormous power upon an individual, and that the secret police was abhorred by the population, and—what in the context of Russia's politics is much more important—by influential Party and army leaders, has led the regime to weaken the principal arm of terror, to disband some of its armed forces, and to make sure that no single person or organization should have exclusive control over the security apparatus.

If terror is weakened as the principal lever of totalitarian power, then other instrumentalities must take its place. The leaders must have realized that a mixed policy of concessions to the population and the strengthening of the Communist Party was the most fruitful approach. Concessions included a modest attempt to raise the standard of living, the attempt with which Malenkov especially identified himself, and the general relaxation of the most obnoxious features of the police state, including abolition of special police courts which meted out penalties in secret, reduction of the drastic labor discipline, and partial disbanding of forced labor camps. We cannot tell how far those decisions were the result of a united decision of the Politburo-Presidium and how far they reflected maneuvering among the rulers and pressure of outside elements, such as the army. It is characteristic that Malenkov's degradation in February 1955, when he stepped down as chairman of the Council of Ministers though remaining in the government and the Presidium, was justified on the grounds of his alleged preference for the development of consumers' goods over heavy industries.

---

[27] It is interesting to list several instances of both the confusion produced by the lack of a single absolute leader and of the oligarchy's frantic attempts to conceal discords. On the morrow of Stalin's death the official communiqué spoke of the changes in Party and government leadership as having been executed so as to insure prevention of "disorder and panic." In the funeral orations over Stalin's bier delivered by the triumvirs Malenkov, Beria, and Molotov, it was Beria who made warm personal remarks about Malenkov, and it was on Beria's motions in the Supreme Soviet that Malenkov was confirmed as Chairman of the Council of Ministers. One is reminded of Stalin's warm eulogies of Bukharin in the twenties!

[28] The extent to which the secret police had penetrated all aspects of the governmental machinery is best indicated by the fact that among those tried and executed with Beria as his principal aides was one Dekanozov, Beria's personal appointee as Minister of the Interior in Georgia. Dekanozov's previous posts had included that of Ambassador to Germany and Deputy Commissar of Foreign Affairs. He had been, it is not too much to surmise, delegated to operate within the diplomatic corps.

As Stalin's favorite during his last years, and conceivably as the only member of the late dictator's entourage not slated for the purge he had been preparing, Malenkov must have been eyed suspiciously by his colleagues in the "collective leadership." Perhaps in his identification with the masses' desire for greater amenities of life his colleagues saw again a political campaign designed to secure absolute power, very much in the style of Stalin's moderation and middle-of-the-road position of the early 1920's. The mildness of his "punishment" indicates that perhaps, unlike Beria, Malenkov did not attempt to fight back. A wave of changes in Party posts followed the change at the top. In their peregrinations throughout the Soviet Union, it was not unusual for Khrushchev and Bulganin to meet with the Party Committee of a republic or region, the result being very often a new First Secretary of the given organization.

But the main effort of the new leadership, divided and fluctuating as it is, has obviously been to infuse new spirit into the Party. The Twentieth Congress, which met in February 1956, was to chart the new course. For a long time prior to the Congress there had been a silent de-emphasis of Stalin. During the dictator's absolute rule no public speech, no book on any subject, no leading article, failed to refer to Comrade Stalin. Not long after his death the references became scarcer and scarcer and even implied criticism of the late dictator had been allowed. The Twentieth Congress was to mark a definite break with this cautious de-emphasis and criticism by implication. For reasons known only to themselves, the leaders decided to attack Stalin's memory openly. Thus in the public speeches at the Congress Khrushchev and Mikoyan referred scathingly to the personality cult and the atrophy of Party organs that prevailed during the last twenty years of Stalin's reign. Mikoyan assailed Stalin's version of the Party's history, *History of the Communist Party, A Short Course*, published under his name, and filled with adulatory references to himself. Stalin's *Economic Problems of Socialism in the U.S.S.R.*, hailed in 1952 by the same speakers as a work of genius, was now described as containing serious theoretical errors.

These speeches were only a prelude to a special address by Khrushchev about Stalin. Though delivered before a closed session of the Congress, it was circulated to all the Party organizations in the U.S.S.R. and thus became a public secret.[29] Khrushchev's speech was not an unqualified condemnation of Stalin. The great dictator was pictured as a man who, for all his faults, until 1934 performed great services for socialism in the U.S.S.R. But beginning with 1934 and the opening of the Great Purge, Stalin is presented as a tyrant and sadist, dispatching people to death out

[29] All the quotations from the speech are from the version published by the *New Leader* under the title *The Crimes of the Stalin Era*, edited by Boris I. Nicolayevski.

of whim and increasingly thirsty for adulation. In his last years the picture is that of a psychologically sick man contemplating on the eve of his death a wholesale liquidation of his associates.

Khrushchev's account cannot be entirely trusted. It should be borne in mind that those who now denounced Stalin were coauthors, and at times probably instigators, of his purges. Nikita Khrushchev had himself been Stalin's chosen instrument of purge in the Ukraine; Georgi Malenkov, for many years an official of his personal secretariat. Many of the liquidations and executions of the period can be traced not only to Stalin's undoubted sadism, but also to the intense rivalry of those closest to him. Yet some of the facts cited by Khrushchev are supported by other evidence. Thus of the Central Committee elected in 1934 at the Seventeenth Party Congress 70 per cent of the membership was arrested or liquidated within the next five years. The same fate befell 1108 delegates out of 1966 who attended the same Congress. We have a confirmation of the fact that the Central Committee and even the Politburo practically ceased to function during Stalin's last years, and that the despot transacted the most important business by himself, or with whoever enjoyed his confidence at the moment. Thus in 1949 Nicolai Voznesensky, the head of Russia's economic planning and a member of the Politburo, was liquidated along with a number of other high officials at a period when Khrushchev asserts "Stalin became even more capricious, irritable and brutal; in particular his suspicion grew," and when "everything was decided by him alone without any consideration for anyone or anything."[30] In short, out of the mouth of the highest Party functionary, Soviet and foreign Communists heard the confirmation of the worst attacks of their enemies, and an avowal that for a long time the U.S.S.R. and world Communism had been ruled by a bloodthirsty tyrant who had thought nothing of ordering tortures for veteran Bolsheviks.

Some other details of Khrushchev's speech may or may not be confirmed by a future historian. There are two pertinent questions that belong in the study of the Soviet government. First, though we cannot know the exact reasons for the revelations, what lines of reasoning could have persuaded the leaders to admit so much, and thus, as they must have realized, to threaten their own positions as formerly the closest servants of Joseph Vissarionovich Stalin, not to mention the shock they must have imparted to millions of Party activists in telling them authoritatively that all they had been taught about the Party's history during the preceding twenty years was a big lie. As suggested before, the only reasonable explanation is two-

---

[30] The reason why Stalin's "suspicion grew" may have been a fairly rational feeling on his part that as he grew older his closest collaborators were maneuvering for power positions in the eventuality of his death.

fold. First, in condemning the cult of the individual, the collective leadership may have thought that it was acquiring a collective insurance against any one of them trying to emulate the late dictator and to ascend the summit of power in Stalin's fashion. Secondly, the revival of the Party's spirit under conditions that would not allow one absolute dictator, would have indicated the necessity of a dramatic break with the past, a surgical operation on the Party's history, painful and dangerous, no doubt, but, in the long run, it was hoped, to prove salutary.

The other question turns on the hypothetical reasons and how far they have been and are likely to be justified by the events. There is no doubt that the regime gained in popularity through its new policies. The attempt to ascribe most of the repressive and unpleasant things of the preceding twenty years to Stalin's personal foibles has also been a qualified success. The deliberative organs of the Communist Party have revived. We hear of meetings of the Central Committee; there is more of the air of real discussion of issues in the Party press and less of the craven sycophancy that characterized Party speeches and writings in Stalin's time. The new developments have undoubtedly increased the administrative efficiency of the Party machinery and encouraged the development of more initiative and spirit at the lower levels. As a whole the Party is now a healthier organism, the average member less driven by mere compulsion, than was the case five or six years ago.

At the same time the fundamental problem has not been solved. Much has been said and written about a return to the Leninist principles and spirit. But the circumstances of today's Russia make the condition of the Party as it was in Lenin's time simply inapplicable and irrelevant to today's problems. By publicly confirming the terrible excesses of the past, the Party has not only shattered the incredible if not feigned innocence of many foreign Communists, but must have injured itself in the eyes of the younger and more credulous of Soviet Communists. Human gratitude for the removal of the worst type of repression is notoriously short-lived and succeeded by demands for more substantial freedoms.

The latest development in the evolution of Soviet leadership involve the changes brought about by the crisis of the summer of 1957. Characteristically the details of the crisis have been released by Khrushchev and his associates over a period of years with as yet the fullest version being presented at the Twenty-second Party Congress in October 1961, more than four years after the crisis. And equally characteristically the details of the crisis have been presented with an eye to the propaganda points the regime hopes to score rather than with regard to strict historical truth. The incontrovertible facts are that in June 1957 the majority of the Presidium called an extraordinary session at which by a vote of seven to four it elected to remove Khrushchev from the post of the First Secretary. The majority included the older dignitaries who had been associated with Stalin in his struggle for power, i.e., Voroshilov; Molotov; Kaganovich; the then Prime Minister, Bulganin; Stalin's probable intended successor, Malenkov; and the newer generation of leadership, Pervukhin and Saburov, both of them associated mainly with industrial administration and planning. In his speech at the Twenty-second Congress Khrushchev accused the group of having had as its aim the restoration of Stalinist practices and methods. Though outvoted at the Presidium, Khrushchev succeeded in mobilizing the Central Committee members then present in Moscow, called a meeting of the Central Committee which reversed the Presidium's decision, and expelled the anti-Khrushchev faction from the Presidium and the Committee. Bulganin's part in the proceedings was made public in 1959, Voroshilov's not until 1961. That the alleged conspirators attempted to bar the Central Committee members from the Kremlin where their plot was unfolding and that they employed for this purpose Bulganin's bodyguards casts a lurid light on the methods of political selection in the U.S.S.R.

Was it really Stalinism that united the seven dissident leaders? To be sure nothing can more discredit a politician in the Soviet Union in 1957 or in 1962 than the charge that he would bring back the full horrors of the Stalin era. On the face of it Khrushchev's charge contains too many inconsistencies. It has been mentioned before that every faction attempting to seize power in the U.S.S.R. since the despot's death "campaigned" on the platform of liberalization and de-Stalinization. Molotov and Kaganovich might have felt that in his campaign against the cult of personality, Khrushchev was being too rash, and that he was using it as a political weapon against them. The truth lies probably in the fact that the events of 1957 constituted a power struggle pure and simple; that the majority of the Presidium resented Khruschev's increasing power, and his attempts to offer them as sacrificial goats for the horrors of Stalinism. The events of the previous fall in Hungary and in Poland must have reflected some discredit on the First Secretary and encouraged the disgruntled in their plot. Khrushchev's plan in 1957 to decentralize economic administration must have appeared as a direct threat to the top economic administrators on the Presidium, Saburov and Pervukhin. And thus a variety of motivations and apprehensions must have persuaded the conspirators to try to get rid of the impulsive and threatening First Secretary and in a manner more reminiscent of the warfare of the Chicago gangland in the Twenties than of the political arena.

In his speech at the Twenty-second Congress Khrushchev once again, and this time in greater detail, went into the crimes and horrors of Stalin's time. This time the speech and its horrid revelations were made public— Stalin's body was removed from its place of honor next to Lenin's in the Mausoleum. The sins of the despot were also attributed to Voroshilov, Kaganovich, and Malenkov, though the majority of the Congress delegates, and indeed of the Soviet citizens, must have realized that Khrushchev himself was one of the late dictator's closest subordinates and advisors. To a large extent the renewed vigor of the anti-Stalin campaign was designed to obscure the fact that Soviet totalitarianism remains, though stripped of its pathological and terroristic excrescences, fundamentally what it had been in Stalin's day. Twenty-five years ago Stalin, with his purges, was largely successful in persuading the Soviet people that their sufferings and privations had been caused not so much by the system, but by the "wrecking," and treacherous activities of factions like the Trotskyites and the Bukharinites. Now Khrushchev has attempted to repeat the maneuver.

One is struck forcibly by the parallel between this episode of 1956-57 and the story of Stalin's maneuvers in 1923-27. The Khrushchev of 1957, like the Stalin of 1924, is the advocate of "normalcy," of concessions to the peasant, of better life for the citizen. Like his great predecessor, he eschews warlike policies; when his position is undermined in the Presidium he carries the struggle, as Stalin did, from the Politburo to the Central Committee. He improvises freely to keep his grip on power. Stalin, to reinforce his position, established the practice of the Central Committee's meeting with the Control Commission, where his influence was even stronger. The meeting of June 1957 which chastised the dissidents was held by the Central Committee together with the Audit Commission, a body formerly of minor importance and with purely accounting duties but where evidently Khrushchev had additional support. And like Stalin's opponents so did Khrushchev's persist in their divisions until it was too late. Kamenev and Zinoviev, could they have joined with Trotsky in 1924 or 1925, might conceivably have unseated the General Secretary. Malenkov and his supporters did not join with the old guard of Molotov and Kaganovich until the First Secretary's position was too strong, and until "his" policies had gained the support of a majority of the Party bureaucrats and his moderation the support (probably) of the majority of Party members.

Is the parallel to be complete, and will Khrushchev, once his position is invulnerable, revert to terror and to the policies designed to increase production with scant thought for the consumer, as did Stalin once he no longer had to bother about popularity or votes in the Central Committee? This is most unlikely. For, in the first place, Khrushchev's position can never reach the pinnacle of personal dictatorship achieved by Stalin. His predecessor was a man in his forties when he became the absolute ruler;

Khrushchev is in his sixties. But far more important than the biological factor is the new appearance of Soviet society, and the role of the Communist Party in it. The new and industrialized U.S.S.R. cannot be ruled by sheer despotism and terror, as was Russia in the thirties. Nor can the aspirations of the various newly born segments of Soviet society be trampled upon *quite* as ruthlessly as they were in the late twenties and thirties. This changed social picture in turn affects the role of the Party and of its leader.

Within the new Presidium, Khrushchev's position became stronger when the June 1957 Plenum appointed his supporters in place of his opponents. The Presidium now is heavily weighted with Party secretaries both of the central and of the major local organizations. If it is true that in the struggle against Molotov, Malenkov, and Kaganovich, the First Secretary found himself in a minority on the Presidium and had to extricate himself by appealing to the Central Committee, then, as has been indicated since Stalin's death, the latter body will play a more important role than at any time since the twenties. On both the Presidium and the Central Committee Nikita Khrushchev's influence is now paramount but not absolute. The logic of the slogans propounded by the Party boss is in itself a threat to his position. If the Central Committee is to play a more important role, does it not encourage factions in the Party? And if the ejection of the old guard was also a repudiation of the bad old practices of Stalinism, is not Khrushchev one of the few close collaborators of Stalin still in a position of power? In brief, the parallel with Stalin's tactics cannot be complete and it must be assumed that the situation in the highest Party Councils is still fluid.

The Party's position was certainly weakened by the events between March 1953 and June 1957. The gain in vitality resulting from de-Stalinization was balanced by the loss of prestige due to constant splits within its highest councils. The period since 1957 has witnessed the undoubted ascendance of Khrushchev which was demonstrated rather than augmented when in 1958 the First Secretary assumed also the office of the chairman of the Council of Ministers. His leadership and prestige, solidified by his trips abroad and especially to the United States in the fall of 1959, have pushed into the background the formula of collective leadership. Nor has Khrushchev hesitated to remove and disgrace some of his closest collaborators. Such was the fate of Bulganin in 1958, supposedly for his duplicity in the crisis the year before, and of Kirichenko and Belyayev in 1960. The latter two had belonged to the Khrushchev faction and their disgrace (removal from the Presidium and dismissal from their posts) was officially stated to have been the consequence of their failure as administrators.

It would be false at the same time to conclude that the Stalinist pattern has been reimposed. For all of Khrushchev's primacy, for all of the restrictions which since 1957 have been applied to curb the modest "thaw" of 1955, the pre-1953 situation has not recurred either in the Party at large or in its highest circles. The international situation and the Soviet successes in diplomacy and space exploration have overshadowed but have not removed the basic causes of the crisis of Communism and hence of the Communist Party in the U.S.S.R.

The weakening of the secret police has had the natural effect of strengthening the other source of armed power, namely, the Red Army. But it would be a gross exaggeration to speak of the Soviet Army as a homogeneous whole or of its officer corps as a united body of men with a definite viewpoint and a political philosophy of its own. The Red Army has been both a source of pride and an object of apprehension to the Communist leaders. From the very beginning the army has been honeycombed with political commissars, regular Party activists delegated for propaganda and political indoctrination work within the armed forces. Stalin's reign brought with it an increasing penetration of the armed forces by the security apparatus. The Great Purge decimated the officer corps. Three of the then five marshals of the Soviet Union were liquidated: the famous court-martial of 1937 alone claimed the life of the Deputy Commissar of War, Marshal Tukhachevsky, and seven other leading commanders, executed for alleged treason. The regime took every care that the officer corps should be largely composed of Party members, that the rank and file should be strenuously educated in Communist ideology, and that, as in other upper segments of Soviet society, the higher officers should be compensated for their lack of freedom by all sorts of material and status amenities. Military figures were effectively barred from the highest Party councils, the only exceptions being political generals like Stalin's old-time collaborator and Commissar of War, Voroshilov, and Bulganin, who had been transferred from civil to military administration in the thirties. Military commanders who acquired too much national renown were either liquidated or thrust into obscurity, the former having been the fate of Marshals Tukhachevsky and Blucher before 1939, and the latter that of Zhukov after 1945. Thus within the mechanics of Stalin's dictatorship there could be no effective army pressure group either within or outside the Party.

In a divided rather than a united dictatorship, the army's role has changed. It was symptomatic that on the morrow of Stalin's death Marshal Zhukov was brought out from the obscurity of a military district and named a First Deputy Minister of Defense. Military figures, and this time professional soldiers, began to appear in high Party posts. It has become something of a custom for military commanders of certain regions to become ex-officio members of the highest Party organs of the given regions. Thus the Presidium of the Central Committee of the Communist Party of the Ukraine, as of March 27, 1954, listed as its alternate members Marshals V. I. Chuikov and Ivan Konev; General Antonov, Commander of the Transcaucasian Military District, was in 1954 a full member of the Presidium of the Communist Party of Georgia, etc. It is rumored, though it cannot be ascertained, that the army took an active part in the downfall of Lavrenti Beria and in the partial suppression of the security forces that followed his arrest.[31]

On Malenkov's demotion in 1955 Zhukov became Minister of Defense. At the Twentieth Congress a rather large number of military figures, and this time primarily professional soldiers, airmen, and sailors, became members of the Central Committee. And for the first time in Soviet history a man primarily a soldier, Marshal Georgi Konstantinovich Zhukov, became a member of the highest policy-forming body as an alternate member of the Presidium. Neither Zhukov's subsequent advancement to full membership, supposedly for the help he rendered Khrushchev in the summer 1957 crisis, nor his later expulsion affect the fact that the army is now *politically* more important. It is inaccurate to speak of the army as competing with the Party or taking over the Party, but the enhanced status of the army leaders is at least a proof that realizing their weakened-position the Party leaders are more and more constrained to bring into the inner councils of the regime professional military leaders, and are desirous of exploiting their prestige and ready to appease their ambitions. The enhanced status of the generals is emphasized by the small number of the Central Committee members and alternate members who are clearly identifiable with the security forces.

In brief, the post-Stalin reforms have introduced a new era of flux and, this time, more open maneuverings within the Communist Party of the U.S.S.R. Whether the intention of the authors of the reforms will be fulfilled or whether the apprehensions of those who feared too rapid a retreat from Stalinism will be justified will depend on several questions. Casting aside for the moment the international picture, and the turbulent state of the satellites, the principal equation in the answer will be the effect of economic and social changes that within the last generation have transformed the life of the nations of the U.S.S.R.

The Formal Organization

CONGRESSES AND CONFERENCES

Nothing would be more deceptive than to judge the importance and actual role of various organs of the Communist Party on the basis of their

---

[31] At the end of World War II, Beria was created a Marshal of the Soviet Union, a gesture that could not but grate upon even the thoroughly intimidated officer corps of the Red Army. A more substantial grievance must have been the penetration of the army by the security apparatus, which dominated the political administration of the defense forces.

TABLE 15 Formal Organization of the Communist Party at the Time of the Twenty-Second Congress—October 1961

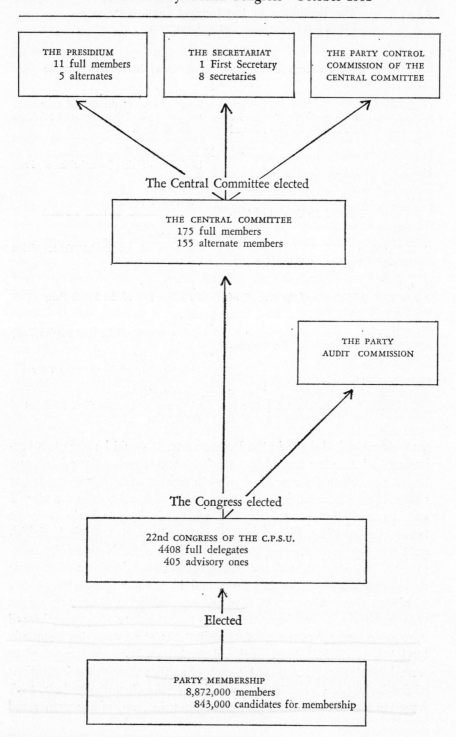

THE PRESIDIUM
11 full members
5 alternates

THE SECRETARIAT
1 First Secretary
8 secretaries

THE PARTY CONTROL
COMMISSION OF THE
CENTRAL COMMITTEE

The Central Committee elected

THE CENTRAL COMMITTEE
175 full members
155 alternate members

THE PARTY
AUDIT COMMISSION

The Congress elected

22nd CONGRESS OF THE C.P.S.U.
4408 full delegates
405 advisory ones

Elected

PARTY MEMBERSHIP
8,872,000 members
843,000 candidates for membership

TABLE 16   The Presidium of the Central Committee after
the Twenty-Second Party Congress

L. I. Brezhnev
Chairman of the Presidium of the Supreme Soviet

G. I. Voronov
First Vice Chairman of the Bureau for
the Affairs of the Russian Soviet Federated
Republic

F. R. Kozlov
Secretary of the Central Committee

A. N. Kosygin
Deputy Chairman of the Council of Ministers

O. V. Kuusinen
Secretary of the Central Committee

A. I. Mikoyan
First Deputy Chairman of the Council of
Ministers

N. V. Podgorny
First Secretary of the Ukrainian Communist Party

D. S. Polyanski
Chairman of the Council of Ministers of
the Russian Soviet Federated Republic

M. K. Suslov
Secretary of the Central Committee

N. S. Khrushchev
First Secretary of the Central Committee
and Chairman of the Council of Ministers
of the U.S.S.R.

N. M. Shvernik
Chairman of the Commission of Party
Control

Alternate Members
_____

V. V. Grishin
Chairman of the Soviet Trade Union
Council

Sh. R. Rashidov
First Secretary of the Uzbek Party

K. T. Mazurov
First Secretary of the Byelorussian Party

V. P. Mzhavanadze
First Secretary of the Georgian Party

V. V. Shcherbitzky
Chairman of the Council of Ministers of
the Ukraine

competence as laid down in the Party statute. It would be almost as misleading to ignore the flux of Soviet politics which makes the role of, say, the Central Committee of the Party—though its official competence has changed but little throughout the years—quite different today from what it was in Lenin's time, or, we may add, what it is likely to be in a year or two. A student of British government may write about the role in British politics of the Cabinet, or the House of Lords, or of the National Executive of the Labour Party, confident that their importance, barring a cataclysmic development, will change but little, and in a quite foreseeable fashion within the immediate future. Students of totalitarian systems would be wise to avoid such confidence. It falls to them to sketch the general trend of the development of the political institutions of a totalitarian state, taking into account both the formal and the informal (i.e., not expressed in formal statutes or constitutions) aspects of politics. As with the institutions of the Soviet state, so with the *institutions of the Communist Party*, their importance cannot be entirely assessed either in terms of the statute and constitutional phraseology or in terms of the role they have actually played in the power struggle of the totalitarian system. As we have seen, the organs that at one point constituted the battle scene of Soviet politics have in many cases become tame and ornamental adjuncts of the dictatorship. And, on the other hand, the paper realities of today may become vital and important factors of Soviet politics tomorrow. Therefore an appraisal of the most important Party institutions both in terms of the Party statute and in terms of their past and present evolution presents a perspective for the future.

The Party Congress, as noted before, is in theory, as it has been from the very beginning, the sovereign organ of the Party. Delegates to the Congress are elected in a specified ratio per number of Party members. Party rules used to specify that the Congress should meet at least once every three years. As amended in the statutes of 1952 they provide that ordinary Congresses are to be convoked every four years. So much for the constitutional provisions. A student of Soviet politics will draw conclusions from the fact that following the Revolution Party Congresses met every year until 1925. Following the Fourteenth Congress, which marks a watershed in the real importance of Congresses, there was a two-year hiatus before the Fifteenth in 1927; then a three-year hiatus until 1930. In defiance of the Party statute no Congress met for four years between the Sixteenth and the Seventeenth, in 1934. Then came a five-year period, coinciding with the Great Purge, until the Eighteenth in 1939, and after that thirteen years until Stalin's last Congress in 1952!

The lengthening and unstatutory interval has an eloquence of its own. For the Congresses until 1925 still were fairly genuine representative assemblies. They had a life of their own, often a lively discussion, and at times a clash of points of view: as between Lenin and the Workers' Opposition at the Ninth and Tenth Congresses (1920 and 1921); between Trotsky's partisans and those of the ruling *troika* in 1923 and 1924; and the decisive clash between Stalin and the Leningrad Opposition led by Zinoviev and Kamenev in 1925. Beginning with the Sixteenth Congress in 1927 the picture changes. Congresses are triumphant reviews by the Stalinist rulers of their subordinates. There is no discussion in the sense of a controversy, but only obedient reports and unanimity on the theses presented by the leader. Former opponents of Stalin as long as they are alive are given the opportunity to recant and to crawl in the dirt to the revilings and amusement of those assembled. At the Eighteenth Congress, held on the morrow of the blood bath, no opposition voices are heard. Veteran Communist leaders, as if incredulous that they are still alive, recite little poems in praise of Stalin, and a delegation of school children intones: "Thank you Comrade Stalin for our happy childhood!"

The mechanics of the Congress stay the same. The Presidium and the Secretariat (the former including the most prominent leaders) having been elected, the central point of the proceedings is the report of the Central Committee delivered by the acknowledged leader of the Party. Thus it was Lenin who reported until his fatal illness; then in 1923 Zinoviev, followed in succeeding Congresses by Stalin. At the Nineteenth Congress the report was presented by Malenkov, Stalin contenting himself with a brief speech at the end. Reasons for this may not be difficult to find. The report requires a not negligible physical effort, which in 1952 might have been beyond the powers of the seventy-three-year-old despot. Thus for example Khrushchev's report at the Twentieth Congress covers 116 pages in English translation. The delivery usually occupies two separate sessions and the speaker reviews both the world situation and domestic politics as well as the state of the Party, usually in some detail and with elaborate statistical data. Following the report a lengthy debate takes place, with scores of delegates participating. Since 1925 the debate increasingly consisted in the speakers' agreeing with the report, praising Stalin, and actually giving reports of their own on conditions in their particular organization and part of the country. Another major speech might be delivered by a Party leader on, say, the directives for a new economic plan, and that in turn would be discussed, i.e., agreed to by numerous speakers. It used to be said of members of Hitler's Reichstag that they were the best paid male chorus in the world, for they met infrequently, heard the Fuehrer speak, sang the national anthem, and went home. The same claim cannot be made for members of the Party Congress, for when one reads the minutes of Stalin's Congresses, and even of the post-Stalin Twentieth Congress, one is struck by the massive monotony and tedium of the proceedings, which must have constituted hard work to the participants.

The mechanics of the Congress include minor routine things such as the report of the Audit and Mandate Commissions, greetings from foreign Communist Parties, factories, army units, etc. In the earlier and spontaneous days these indeed helped give an air of holiday and comradely meeting to the Congress; in Stalin's days they became a travesty. And at the end comes the concluding word of the leader or leaders and then a unanimous agreement on the reports, and unanimous election of the Central Committee and other organs of the Party. The Twentieth Congress, held in 1956, did not change the pattern. Here again was unanimity, which included a unanimous condemnation of the "cult of personality" and thus of Stalin. But though the speeches differed somewhat from the old monotonous pattern, it was still a propaganda show arranged and directed down to the smallest detail by the (this time collective) dictator, and not a Congress, not a deliberation, in the proper sense of the word.

Aside from the Party Congress, an assembly that has played an important role in Bolshevik history has been the *Party Conference*. The Conference was a less formal and smaller version of the Party Congress. Instead of being elected by the body of the membership of the Party, it was a conclave of the Party hierarchy, i.e., its central organs and delegates of the committees and bureaus of regional and territorial organizations. In the twenties, the days of the struggle for power, the Conference was a more pliable and convenient assembly for the Party apparatus to manipulate than the Congress. The latter, as we have seen, still had some vestigial remnants of a democratic gathering, some delegates still could be swung by oratory, while the Party Conference, because of its character, could be relied upon to be more responsive and submissive to the *apparatus* headed by Stalin. That is how it worked at the Fifteenth Party Conference in 1926, when Zinoviev and Kamenev, previously crushed at the Fourteenth Congress, made one last effort at a defiance of Stalin. They were joined this time by Trotsky. But this combination, which two or three years before could have swung any Congress or Conference of the Party, was in 1926 impotent to break the hold that the Stalinist machine had on the majority of Party officials.

But with the dictatorial system fully grown, the Conference became something of a fifth wheel. It was abolished in 1934, restored by the Party Congress in 1939; and finally the Nineteenth Congress in 1952 abolished it again. It is interesting to speculate whether it will ever be restored. The Party Congress, which has thousands of delegates and meets infrequently, obviously cannot function as a deliberate assembly. There would appear to exist a place in the Party structure, assuming that "collective leadership" will prevail for some time, for a body that would bridge the gap between the Congress and the Central Committee. But the rulers of Russia are not bound to take the advice of foreign experts on their government!

The Central Committee

To the Central Committee belongs a more essential and continuous part in the history of the Party. Just as the constitutional fiction of the Party statutes proclaims that the Congress is the supreme body, so in theory the Central Committee is the executive arm of the Party, but in this case the theory has a more substantial link with the reality. The Secretariat, the Politburo, or the Presidium are thus in theory only organs and servants of the Central Committee. When Stalin between 1934 and 1939 imprisoned, dismissed, or sent to death two thirds of the Committee as elected by the Party in 1934, he was in the eyes of the law merely a Secretary of the Central Committee, "removable" by a simple majority of its members!

Again, the genealogy of the institution is an impressive reminder of change in history. The Central Committee of pre-World War I days was a handful of revolutionaries holding its meetings in a shabby room in London or somewhere else outside Russia. Today it is an assembly of potentates; of ministers, marshals, and men who direct vast domains of power in the U.S.S.R. But the growth in splendor and numbers has not always coincided with the growth in real power. The few men who met in a shabby room abroad did really direct the activities of the Party, though their adherents may have been just a few thousands of clandestine revolutionaries. The assemblage of Party bigwigs, marshals, and directors of enterprises often surpassing (in size) the General Motors Corporation has been, at least for a generation, the servant of one man or a handful of men, officially just their colleagues and their executive officers but in truth their masters. That it should have become so will not surprise a student of government who remembers that the British Cabinet, officially the servant and executive committee of Parliament, is in fact the master of the House of Commons. But it is the extent and the character of subjugation of the Central Committee that require some comment.

As organized originally the Committee was a relatively small group that met very frequently. Thus after the Seventh Congress in 1918 it consisted of twenty-three people; fifteen full members, eight alternates. The earlier Party statutes required it to meet, at first twice a month then once every two months, etc. In fact in those early days it met usually more often than statutorily required. If, even in those early days, it was a bit too large to decide and execute really important decisions with speed and secrecy, it was still small enough to decide on most executive matters, and of an ideal size to debate and decide policy issues within the scope defined by the Congress. The Central Committee was then an active powerful body. Elected by the Congress it contained partisans of various viewpoints in the Party, though Lenin's views had almost always enjoyed a majority. Another factor of vital importance, in the years immediately after the Revolution, was that the personnel of the Central Committee was in its vast majority composed of persons domiciled in the capitals of Moscow and Leningrad. Many of its members, certainly more than after 1927, were people with no day-to-day administrative work.

The Stalinist period has profoundly altered the nature of the Central Committee and its work. It is best to look at the end result—the Central Committee of today—though there has already begun an evolution from the most extreme Stalinist pattern. For an executive body the Central Committee is enormous and unwieldy. Already in 1927 it was decreed that it should have seventy-one members and sixty-eight alternates. Since the Twenty-second Congress it has 175 full members and 155 alternates. The rules adopted at the same time specify that it should meet ordinarily once every six months. But even this decrease over the earlier required frequency of meetings gives no idea of the decline of the Central Committee's meetings during the latter Stalin era. As a matter of fact for several years before 1952 there is no authenticated report of the Committee's meetings. It is not too much to say that from the end of World War II to 1952 it existed largely on paper and that various acts announced as having been done by the Committee were simply decrees issued by the dictator and his associates. Stalin's death brought new life to the Central Committee. It now undoubtedly exists and meets fairly frequently and in the era of *collective leadership* its importance is undoubtedly enhanced, though still not what it was in Lenin's time.

This point is underlined if we look at the list of members whether at the time of Stalin's last Congress in 1952 or at the latest one in 1961. They are almost without an exception people who have at least one other full-time job, often at a great distance from Moscow. Once Stalin's rule was firmly planted, membership became a reward for faithful service, whether in the state, the Party, or the armed forces. It was a recognition—though often a fleeting one, for the despot was whimsical and sadistic—that the man "had arrived." Thus a Party secretary six thousand miles away from Moscow, an ambassador to London, and an admiral of the Black Sea Fleet might sit on the Committee, though it is difficult to see how they could have performed their functions if the Committee had been a regularly meeting and active body.

Stalin's death has not changed the occupational pattern of the Committee. There are now perhaps more military and naval personnel among its *full* members.[32] Also, in the Committee elected at the Twentieth Congress secret-service bureaucrats appear in much smaller numbers than before. But the character of the bulk of membership is still very much the same: bureaucrats from the central state and Party organs and most of the important local Party functionaries. While the will and choice of one man is no longer the key to all posts and honors, it is not too much to surmise that most of those on the Committee are there as protégés of one or another of the ruling group.

The Central Committee has undoubtedly gained in importance since Stalin's death. To repeat, as long as the ruling group in the Presidium is united, or dominated by one man, the Central Committee acts as a ratifying body and a sounding board of Soviet notables. Whenever there is

---

[32] In Stalin's days an admiral or marshal of the Soviet Union, unless a special pet of the dictator, had to be content with the status of an alternate member.

factional strife in the Presidium the Central Committee may be called upon to decide. Thus, it is highly probable that the downfall of Beria and the demotion of Malenkov were preceded by discussion in the Committee. The crisis of 1957 was decided in and by the Central Committee. Finding himself outvoted in the Presidium by a vote of 7 to 4 Khrushchev managed to convoke a special session of the Central Committee which reversed the Presidium's decision and ejected instead his main enemies. Khrushchev imitated successfuly Stalin's tactics of the early and middle twenties when, surrounded by rivals in the Politburo, he played against it the larger body, where the majority of the Party bureaucrats were his partisans.

While the June crisis was followed by the official admonition that the Central Committee is the parent body of and superior to the Presidium, it still remains true that the former is too large and too dispersed to function *continually* as the highest policy organ in the intricate Soviet structure. If and when Khrushchev gets a Presidium entirely of his own choosing the Central Committee may revert to its ornamental function. But until then and at each occasion when there is factional strife within the ruling hierarchy, the Central Committee may be called upon to decide and thus become a decisive factor in a crisis of the Soviet system.

The Politburo–Presidium

In justifying his decision in 1916 to run the British war effort with a war cabinet of five to seven members instead of the usual fifteen- to twenty-member Cabinet, Prime Minister Lloyd George stated that you cannot run a war "with a Sanhedrin." This assertion about the relations of arithmetic to the mechanics of a war is equally true of the mechanics of a totalitarian society. The latter, in a sense, lives in a continuous state of emergency. It cannot be "run" by a parliament nor by a many-member committee. It requires a unified direction by one person, or, at most, by a handful of people. Hence it is not surprising that it has been assumed that of all the organs of the Soviet government and the Communist Party of the U.S.S.R., it is in the Politburo-Presidium that the ultimate decision-making power has resided. This small group of people, usually of about ten full members, has been assumed to be the repository of all power, the kingpin of the political structure of the U.S.S.R. Like all generalizations, this one requires some elaboration and correction, though in the main it remains true.

The original Politburo, or, to give it its full name, the Political Bureau of the Central Committee, was set up for a specific purpose. On the eve of the November uprising in 1917 a special committee of seven members was set up by the Central Committee to provide guidance to the insurrection. The Eighth Party Congress in 1919 sanctioned a permanent Politburo, as a subcommittee of the Central Committee, to which it would regularly report and of which it would remain a subordinate organ. But the list of members already indicated then that the new organization could not be thought of as "subordinate" to any other. Elected as full members were Lenin, Kamenev, Trotsky, Stalin, and Krestinsky; as alternates Zinoviev, Bukharin, and Kalinin. All of them were persons of the highest importance, though Krestinsky, then the Party's Secretary, not long afterward dropped from the most important political plane, and Kalinin, long the figurehead president of the Soviet Union, remained content to play a passive role, and received his reward by being the only member of the original group—in addition to Lenin and (probably) Stalin—to die a natural death in his old age.

The personnel of the organization assured it from the beginning of a decisive role in the structure of the Party and government organization. Once united, the Politburo could settle everything, since other members of the Central Committee were for the most part either secondary figures or protégés and friends of the Politburo members. But by the same token, the Politburo could not initially assume absolute power over the Party, since most of its initial members were, except for Lenin, personal rivals and unlikely to agree on the most fundamental questions. The main arenas of struggle were the Party Congresses and the Central Committee meetings. In the struggle for succession after Lenin's stroke, Stalin could not use the Politburo as his instrument of rise, for every other member was his competitor! Hence his policy of working for power through the Secretariat and control organs of the Party. The Party leaders in the Politburo were increasingly "surrounded" as more and more of Stalin's partisans were put in the Central Committee. At the same time it was decreed that on certain important questions the Presidium of the Central Control Commission (then already filled with Stalin's partisans) would sit with the Politburo. At the Fourteenth Congress Kamenev in his attack upon Stalin demanded a "collective leadership" of the Party by the Politburo. Stalin piously denounced the proposal as smacking of oligarchical rule and not consonant with inner-Party democracy. The Politburo was the last of the power positions in the Party conquered by Stalin. It was only in 1925 and 1926, with the ejection from it of Zinoviev, Kamenev, and Trotsky and the addition of Molotov, Voroshilov, Kalinin, and Rudzutak, that he gained a majority on the Politburo, and it was not until 1930, when Bukharin, Rykov, and Tomsky were dismissed, that the Politburo, like everything else in the Party, became solidly Stalinist.

It was natural then that the Politburo would become the focus of all governmental action, arrogating to itself most of the functions belonging to other Party organs such as the Central Committee and the Council of Commissars. The Politburo came to be composed of the leader and his principal lieutenants. We have very little to go on to illustrate the manner of its operation during Stalin's ascendancy. We know, however, that in the previous era in the twenties the Poliburo already functioned as the supreme political and economic organ. It was the supreme decision-making body in political and economic matters; it required reports from the governmental and Party organs; and it supervised as a body or through subcommittees the most important spheres of action. It is natural to surmise that with the dictatorship firmly established after 1930, and with just one faction established in the Politburo, the supreme functions of that body were still further aggrandized. Even the most absolute despot needs advice and help in directing his government, and a small group of intimates, people who had been Stalin's main helps in his rise to power, was the best instrument of despotic government. Membership in the Politburo became the most exalted and powerful position in the Soviet hierarchy and those who achieved it became beings apart from the other, even the highest, Party and state officials. One thing even the highest office in a despotic system cannot bestow and that is physical security and safety from the tyrant's whim or wrath. And thus among the officials destroyed in the great purge of the thirties were Stalin's colleagues on the Politburo—people who had got there because they had been his most faithful and useful servants and creatures. Liquidated in secrecy were Stanislav V. Kossior, Vlas I. Chubar, and Ian E. Rudzutak among the full members. Two other full members, Valerian V. Kuibyshev and Georgi "Sergo" Ordzhonikidze, died in good graces but under suspicious circumstances. Among the alternate members of the Politburo who met their end suddenly, their name one day dropping out of the news and the well-informed simply forgetting that they ever existed, was the main instrument of terror and Commissar of the Interior, the unspeakable Nicolai Yezhov.

From Khrushchev's secret speech we get some occasional, though unverifiable, accounts of the functioning of the highest Party organ under Stalin. Thus, says Khrushchev, Stalin was in 1936 vacationing in the Caucasus with Andrei Zhdanov, then Stalin's favorite, head of the Leningrad Party organization and alternate member of the Politburo. From there they sent a telegram to the Politburo demanding the immediate dismissal of the then Commissar of the Interior, Yagoda, and his replacement by Yezhov. The Politburo complied, and terror was intensified under Yezhov until he, like his predecessor, was sent to his reward. Whether the other members of his Politburo were ever able to restrain or temper Stalin remains unclear, though there are unverified reports that the slackening of the terror in late 1938 and the liquidation of Yezhov were due to the intervention of Molotov and Kaganovich. But the incident, if true, illustrates what was undoubtedly the case most of the time: Stalin could dominate and over-

~~rule even the Politburo,~~ and at times his closest advisers could be chosen from among others than full members of the Politburo. Thus in 1936 Zhdanov was only an alternate.

During the war the supreme function of the Politburo was largely superseded by the State Committee of Defense. As originally composed in June 1941 it comprised Stalin, Molotov, Voroshilov, Beria, and Malenkov, the last two at the time alternate members of the Politburo. With victory, the committee was dissolved and the prewar structure of authority evidently restored. Of the postwar Politburo we know only scraps of information given by Khrushchev. Thus he informs us that the arrest and liquidation of Nikolai Voznesensky was not even brought before his colleagues on the supreme body but was a decision of the dictator himself. Khrushchev also confirms what could be suspected from other sources: a man nominally a member of the Politburo might still be forbidden by Stalin to attend its sessions, or simply ejected from it without any public notice. The latter was the fate of Andreyev in 1950. The former was the fate of Kliment Voroshilov, toward whom the dictator took a dislike just before his death.[33]

The Nineteenth Party Congress took measures that, had they survived Stalin's death, would have drastically changed the nature of the Politburo. Renamed the Presidium, it was now composed of twenty-five full members and eleven alternates. Co-opted into the supreme body were some veteran Communist Party functionaries but also a number of the younger and rising Party and state bureaucrats. As stated above and confirmed by Khrushchev, the warning must have been plain: the dictator contemplated a change of the guard, and most of the surviving members of the pre-1952 Politburo were going to be pushed out. In the enlarged Presidium there was evidently a smaller directing body—the bureau of the Presidium. Who its members were we do not know. Before the new pattern could jell Stalin died, and on the morrow of his death the veteran members threw out most of the newcomers added at the Nineteenth Congress. The Presidium was restored to more or less its previous size: ten full members and four alternates.

The Presidium after the Twentieth Congress remained of a mixed character. Of the Old Bolsheviks who helped Stalin in his rise to power, four remained: Vyacheslav Molotov, erstwhile premier and foreign minister; Lazar Kaganovich, long the chief economic planner and previously Stalin's

---

[33] The career of A. A. Andreyev is one of the proverbial exceptions to the rule. An Old Bolshevik, involved in opposition activities in the early twenties, criticized for administrative incompetence in the thirties, Andreyev not only survived but continued in very important Party positions. Until 1950 he was in the Politburo and head of the Party Control Commission. He incurred disgrace in that year, allegedly for his views on agriculture (he was also the head of the Commission on the Kolkhoz Economy), yet he was merely demoted, and survived!

chief helper in Party affairs; Marshal Kliment Voroshilov, formal head of the Soviet state; and Anastas Mikoyan, expert on trade. In the second group were those who rose to prominence when Stalin's dictatorship was already firmly established during the purges of the thirties: Georgi Malenkov, who had worked long in Stalin's personal secretariat and was probably his intended successor; Nikolai Bulganin, Premier until March 1958; and the head of the Party, Nikita Khrushchev. In the third group were pure products of the Stalin era who climbed the rungs of the Party and state hierarchy to merge into prominence after the war. Here were M. G. Pervukhin and Maxim Saburov, both of whom have been connected with industrial affairs, and Party bureaucrats Mikhail Suslov and Alexei Kirichenko.

This crisis of June 1957 changed the composition of the Presidium. The alleged leaders of the anti-Khrushchev faction, Molotov and Kaganovich, each of whom had served on the powerful council for over a generation, were ejected, as was Georgi Malenkov. Dropped, though without any charges, was Maxim Saburov. Mikhail Pervukhin was demoted to alternate member. Pervukhin and Dimitri Shepilov, who was dismissed as an alternate member, were presumably potential candidates for Khrushchev's job.

The post–June 1957 Presidium has not been, from the point of view of personnel, very stable. Some of "Khrushchev's men" elected in 1957-58 had already managed to incur disgrace prior to the Twenty-second Party Congress and were dismissed. The most prominent of them was A. I. Kirichenko, a long time associate of the dictator in the Ukraine and one of the minority of the Presidium who supported the dictator in the June 1957 crisis. Kirichenko's dismissal in 1960 and demotion to a lower Party position was possibly an outcome of a struggle for the role of the heir apparent to Khrushchev in which Kirichenko might have lost to Kozlov. Marshal Zhukov, raised to full membership in June, was dismissed in October 1957 for his alleged "Bonapartism" and his intention to turn the army into his political preserve. Whatever the truth of the charges, it is not likely that Khrushchev would have tolerated in the highest council of Communism a man whom many Russians regarded as a national hero and who could have become a focus of opposition to the dictator.

Some of the demotions from the Presidium must be ascribed to reasons of efficiency rather than politics. Thus dismissed in 1960 was N. I. Belyayev who was blamed for the disastrous harvest of 1959 in Kazakhstan where he had been First Secretary. Others like Madame Y. A. Furtseva, Minister of Culture, and A. B. Aristov were dropped at the Twenty-second Congress, not in disgrace, but simply because they evidently had not measured up to the stature expected of a member of the highest Party organ.

In the Presidium of 1962, there are still two men who had been most closely associated with Stalin during a long part of his rule: Khrushchev, who joined the body in 1939, and Mikoyan, a member since 1935. Two veterans of the Stalin period but not then or now of the highest importance in the Party councils—Kuusinen, eighty-one years old, and Shvernik, seventy-three years old, are being kept for reasons which are hard to divine, unless they are experience, and, in the case of Kuusinen, a Finn, a long and intimate connection with the international Communist movement. Much younger but already important in Stalin's last years are Party Secretary Suslov and Kosygin, although the latter, throughout his career, has been an economic administrator rather than a politician. The "newer" generation, i.e., the people who have become important during Khrushchev's supremacy, is represented by people like Brezhnev, Polyanski, and Podgorny. Kozlov, whose name among the Party secretaries was listed immediately after Khrushchev and out of the alphabetical order, is clearly the rising power on the Presidium. Among the alternate members some attention is given to the principle of geographic distribution, the Party organizations of Georgia, Byelorussia, and Uzbekistan being represented by their First Secretaries.

It would be unreasonable to expect this Presidium to be more stable than its predecessors. Promotions and demotions to the highest body of Communism take place in an atmosphere of incessant intrigue and strife. Witness Kirichenko, Khrushchev's closest collaborator in 1958, banished to obscurity in 1960, or Marshal Voroshilov, retiring with honors and apparent reverence at great age in 1960, reviled as a Stalinist in 1961. Political strife and reversal of form extend into one's extreme age and even beyond the grave, as in the case of Stalin. Membership in the Presidium is a glittering prize—participation in the world's most powerful political oligarchy—but hardly an assurance of a quiet old age.

THE PARTY CONTROL ORGANS

The Party Control Committee is a continuation in its ostensible function of the Central Control Commission, which existed until 1934. Insofar as its political powers and significance are concerned, it is but a feeble imitation of its predecessor, which in the twenties enjoyed a status almost equal to that of the Central Committee, and members of whose presidium were summoned to the sessions of the Politburo.

It would take too long to recite the full history of both Party and state control organs. But the moral of their evolution is very clear: no machinery of control, however elaborate, can substitute for the element of control that

is provided by the multi-party system and by the give-and-take of democratic politics. The Party control organs were evolved originally to "guard
the guardians," to save the Party from evils of bureaucratism, corruption,
and abuse of power. Yet operating within a totalitarian society the control
organs did not prevent, but hastened, the shackling of the Party and the
rise of absolute personal dictatorship.

The Central Control Commission was organized in 1920. It stood at the
top of a control organization that paralleled the territorial organization of
other Party organs. The personnel and the functions of the Commission
soon expanded. It was given the additional duties of ferreting out anti-
Party activities—in effect of probing into the lives of Party functionaries
and even rank-and-file members in order to see if their behavior as well as
politics were of a kind expected of a Bolshevik. The Commission was to
be independent of other Party institutions. Thus a member of it could
not simultaneously be a member of the Central Committee. The apparatus
and the size of the Commission grew prodigiously. At the Sixteenth Party
Congress in 1930 it reached the size of 187 members, some of them attached to the central organ, others delegated to tasks of local supervision.
In its original concept as envisaged by Lenin, the control organs were to
function so as to curtail and point out various abuses, to act as a check
on the very considerable power of the "political" organs like the Central
Committee. The Central Control Commission was to function as a
restraint on political power, performing some of the role that an independent judiciary performs in democratic states. Lenin's last moments were
occupied in thinking about the ways and means of controlling the inner
Party strife and of erecting a bar both against fatal dissensions that would
split the Party wide open, and against the seizure of power by one man.

Yet in a totalitarian system nothing can be apolitical. From its inception
the Central Control Commission interpreted its task as that of enforcing
the Party "line," i.e., rooting out various oppositionists, beginning with
Lenin's opponents in the very early twenties and ending with Stalin's.
From a censor of Communist morals and guardian of revolutionary morality, the control organs became almost from the beginning an instrument of
political purges.

The Central Control Commission very early came to be dominated by
Stalin's faction. It would be too simple to attribute this only to Stalin's
personal machinations. In the control organs just as in the other branches
of the Party's administration the dominant type became very soon the
apparatchik, "man of the machine," with a bureaucratic mentality, seeing
politics in terms of practical administrative problems and distrustful of
intellectuals in the Party (and Trotsky, Zinoviev, and Kamenev were *par
excellence* revolutionary intellectuals). It was natural for such men to feel

an affinity with Stalin and to see in him a man of practicality and moderation. In the struggle for power in the twenties the control organs regularly supported Stalin, chastised or expelled from the Party his opponents, and overlooked the transgressions of the Secretary-General's partisans. Quite apart from the "control" functions the Commission had an important political role. Certain important political decisions such as demotion of a Central Committee member could be transacted only at a joint meeting of the Central Committee and the Commission. Three members of the presidium of the Commission had the right to sit in with the Politburo. Thus the relative strength of Stalin's opponents in the Central Committee and the Politburo was effectively neutralized or overcome by his domination of the Control Commission.

With the end of all open opposition to dictatorship, the political function of the control organs became superfluous. The control organs could return to their administrative duties, without, however, abandoning the task of rooting out disloyal and would-be disloyal Party members. In connection with the latter, the personnel of the Central Control Commission was increasingly penetrated by high officials of the N.K.V.D. (the Commissariat of the Interior—the security forces). By 1934 the Commission was renamed the Committee of Party Control. The fiction of its independent status was abandoned, and though still elected by the Party Congress, it was now officially inferior to the Central Committee and charged with implementing its directives. The statutes of 1952 make the Party Control Committee fully a creature of the Central Committee. Unlike the Central Auditing Commission, a body of minor importance, the Party Control Committee is no longer elected by the Congress, but organized by the Central Committee of the Communist Party. In the structure of Soviet power the Control Committee no longer has any independent political role. It confines itself to its stated duties, i.e., the preservation of Party discipline and ethics,[34] supervises the fulfillment of the decrees of the central organs, etc. It is not impossible, however, that any deep split within the present leadership and factional strife could again awaken the political role of the control organs, and that the dossiers and files of the Party Control Committee could again become the instrument of factional strife.

THE SECRETARIAT

The nerve center of the Communist Party has been since the beginning of the twenties the Secretariat of the Central Committee. Prior to the Nineteenth Congress of 1952 there existed in addition to the Secretariat the Organizational Bureau (Orgburo) of the Central Committee. But the

---

[34] A violation of Party ethics is defined as "dishonesty and insincerity in relation to the Party, slander, bureaucracy, moral turpitude, etc."

latter body, extremely important during the post-Revolutionary period and again one of the avenues through which Stalin rose to power, was later increasingly superseded in its functions by both the Secretariat and the Politburo, and at the time of its abolition was actually a fifth wheel.

The Secretariat, on the other hand, has preserved its crucial importance. The First Secretary of the Communist Party is in the U.S.S.R. the leading man in the country, whether he holds another office or not. The same pattern prevails in almost all Communist-ruled countries (except occasionally as in China where there is the office of Chairman of the Party). The word "secretary" evokes in our mind a rather clerical person occupied with shuffling papers, etc. Actually the General or First Secretary of the Communist Party is not only the chief administrative officer, but also the man with the dominant voice in formulating the policies of his Party, and, if it be in power, of the country.

The pattern was set in 1922 when Joseph Stalin became the General Secretary of the Central Committee of the Russian Communist Party. The Party, which had inherited so much of the anarchistic contempt for problems of political organization, had given but little thought to its own administration prior to the Revolution. Following November 1917 the functions of the chief administrative officer of the Party were discharged by Jacob Sverdlov, a close collaborator of Lenin. His death in 1919 left the Party without a first-rate figure charged with administration. Lenin had all the cares of the state and policies to be busy with. Trotsky was running the Red Army, and other leading figures of the regime were much more at home in making speeches, writing pamphlets, and preparing revolutions abroad, than in day-to-day administrative routine. Yet the Party was no longer a small conspiratorial organization that could be run informally. One of the central problems was that of liaison between the center and the local organizations. Another was the problem of admission of new members; of ideological education of Party members, their apportionment to the government apparatus, etc. To deal with the broader organizational problems the Eighth Congress created the Orgburo, one of whose original members was Stalin. To deal with immediate administrative problems, a Secretariat of the Central Committee was set up.

Under its first leaders the Secretariat remained very much what it had been intended to be: an administrative and liaison organ. The change came in 1921 when three secretaries were appointed (one of whom was Molotov) who were closely linked to Stalin. And in 1922 he himself became Secretary-General and the office underwent a transition.

The Secretariat rapidly arrogated to itself the function not only of administrative, but also of general, guidance of the Party. The tasks of agitation, propaganda, and ideological education were taken over by the rapidly expanding institution. From a modest office where unassuming secretaries sat ready to counsel and comfort visiting Party officials from the provinces, the Secretariat became a veritable command post, which transferred Party leaders from the Caucasus to the Ukraine, changed ideological instructors, and even disciplined and dismissed Party functionaries. A list of departments of the Secretariat between 1924 and 1930 gives a fair idea of this Frankenstein-like growth of an administrative department that came to engulf the whole Party. The departments included: organization—assignment one, village affairs, statistical, general administration, agitation and propaganda, information, etc.[35] From newspaper articles to the appointment of a Party secretary in a small town; all these affairs—the very lifeblood of a political organism—were regulated by the Secretariat. Complaints of the opposition, cries that the Secretariat should return to a purely administrative role and leave politics to political organs, went unheeded. The Secretariat more and more absorbed the real task of governing Russia as well as the Party.

With the effective elimination of opposition in the Party, the remnants of which task could now be handed over to the secret police, the Secretariat was adjusted largely to propelling the country toward industrialization. Thus the reorganization of 1930 split the organization-instruction section into two, one of which, the assignment department, had several sub-departments dealing with the assignment of Party workers to several major areas of the Russian economy, e.g., heavy industry, light industry, agriculture, sub-departments as well as sections devoted to Soviet administration, foreign Communist activities, etc.[36] Soviet government was thus reduced to the typical bureaucratic model. The main function of the Party organization became to select personnel, and this in turn would be decided in the offices of the Secretariat, which was now running not only the Party, but also almost directly the whole country's administration and economy. Even a more direct functional principle was introduced in 1934, when this time special departments rather than sub-departments were created in the Secretariat paralleling large areas of the Soviet economy, i.e., agriculture, transport, industry, and finance and trade. The Secretariat thus became not merely the power behind the throne, but a body *directly* supervising and staffing all branches of the Soviet government, expanding directly into industry, agriculture, etc. The resulting confusion of authority led to the scheme's being temporarily abandoned in 1939, and most of the departments again corresponded to purely Party affairs. But in 1948 the functional setup was restored, and among the departments there now

---

[35] Fainsod, *op. cit.*, p. 167.
[36] *Ibid.*, p. 168.

appeared a special one devoted to political administration of the armed forces.[37]

The whole development since 1930 again demonstrates the dilemma of a totalitarian regime, even at an administrative level. The regime feels the need of checking and double-checking every sphere of activity. Everything is controlled by the government apparatus, which in turn is supervised by the Party apparatus—and then you have the secret police. It is likely that during Stalin's last years there was a special personal secretariat surrounding the leader and independent of the Party apparatus. The result, however, when you come to concrete tasks of administration and economy, is often inefficiency and confusion. So periodically the cry is raised that the Party should not stick its fingers into the details of running the economic machinery and just as periodically it is exclaimed that things are not going well because the Party does not evidence enough care for economic problems. But the administrative history of the Secretariat shows how a modest administrative office, in a system where there are no effective checks on power, may grow into the kingpin of the whole political and economic system of a vast country.

The actual work of the Secretariat, at the highest level, has been shrouded in something of a mystery. Since the office has been the locus of political power in the Soviet Union for at least thirty years, its innermost operations have been secret, and the only conjectures we can form are on the basis of changes in its personnel. Stalin's ascendancy in the Secretariat was immediate and unqualified. As Secretary-General in 1922 he was assisted by two secretaries, Molotov and V. V. Kuibyshev, both of them members of his faction. From then on the pattern of Secretary-General and two, three, or four "plain" secretaries of the Central Committee persisted. The latter were invariably the closest associates of the dictator, though for reasons that are obvious none of them was allowed to warm up his seat in the Secretariat for more than a few years before being transferred to other work. In the regional and republic party organizations there has often been the pattern of designating a hierarchy of secretaries, one of them being designated as first secretary, another as second, and sometimes there being even an official third secretary. In the central secretariat, except for Stalin, other secretaries were not differentiated in status. Yet with the dictatorship in full swing and Stalin occupied with other vast responsibilities it becomes possible to identify his chief deputy for organizational matters in the Party. In the early thirties that function was performed by Lazar M. Kaganovich. It was Kaganovich who first selected for higher Party posts many of the current leaders like Khrushchev and Ma-

---

[37] Fainsod, *op cit.*, pp. 173 and 195.

lenkov. In the later thirties Andrei Zhdanov succeeded to the post of Stalin's main Party lieutenant. A Party secretary, since 1934 head of the Leningrad organization, he played a large but still unexplained role during the Great Purge of 1936-38 and in the immediate postwar era. During the latter period he was in open (insofar as anything in the Soviet system can be open) rivalry with Georgi Malenkov, Party secretary since 1939, but temporarily dropped from the Secretariat in 1946. Zhdanov died, assertedly of a heart attack, in the summer of 1948, and Malenkov, until Stalin's death, enjoyed the position of the main Party administrator, and presumably Stalin's intended successor. He was soon, however, joined on the Secretariat by another Party figure of importance, Nikita Khrushchev.

The story of the top personnel of the Secretariat preceeding and immediately following Stalin's death has a little bit of the air of a mystery story. At the Nineteenth Congress the number of secretaries was raised to ten, all of them members of the Presidium. On the morrow of Stalin's death the communiqué about the changes in other branches of the government and the Party was quite explicit; but on the reconstruction of the secretariat its language was unclear and confused. Some secretaries were dropped, some were added, but it was impossible to tell whether anyone would occupy the chief position in the Secretariat, and whether Malenkov, just made Prime Minister, was retained on this body or not. The leaders, who evidently agreed after Stalin's death and for the moment on the redistribution of other government and Party positions, were evidently unable to come to a full agreement on the redistribution of power in the most important office of all. Only one week later, on March 14, 1953, it was announced that Comrade Malenkov requested and was granted permission to resign from the Secretariat. One of the secretaries freshly appointed in March, S. D. Ignatiev, was dismissed on April 7.[38]

The office of the General Secretary was not restored. As a matter of fact, for reasons that are difficult to divine, that title was not used by Stalin in the postwar era, he being referred to in his Party capacity as *a* secretary of the Central Committee. Among the secretaries appointed or confirmed after his death none was designated as the chief one. It was only after Beria's liquidation in the summer of 1953, and possibly as a part of another political bargain between the leaders, that Nikita Khrushchev was appointed as First Secretary. The personnel of the Secretariat following the Twentieth Congress confirms the impression that the other secretaries are mostly, but not entirely, Khrushchev's creatures, and that the same situa-

---

[38] S. D. Ignatiev was Minister of State Security at the time of the "Doctors' Plot," and made a member of the Presidium at the Nineteenth Congress. Chastised for political blindness on account of his role in the preparation of a new purge before Stalin's death, he made a modest comeback after Beria's downfall. At the time of the Twentieth Congress he was head of the Party organization in Bashkiria.

tion prevails in the regional and local Communist organizations. It is equally clear that the days of the greatest power of the Secretariat are over and that lacking a Stalin it cannot enjoy the absolute supremacy it had had in the thirties and forties vis-à-vis the Central Committee and the Presidium.

The sketch of the main organs of the Communist Party suggests forcibly the logic of both the development and the potential decline of a totalitarian state. Under one-party government even the deliberative organs atrophy, and the control organs, instead of being checks on absolute despotism, become its tools. Power is withdrawn more and more into a tight administrative clique, and even this clique becomes subject to one man's rule. But the atrophy of the Party in turn weakens the very basis on which despotism rests, and the death of the despot reveals this weakness. For all its divisions and splits, for all of Russia's weaknesses, the Communist Party in the early twenties was a live, vigorous organism, which the powerful and monolithic Party of seven million members at the death of Stalin was not. Bureaucracy and terror have throttled what there was of the comradely spirit, of spontaneity and revolutionary enthusiasm and sense of mission among the Communists. The political and organizational future of the Communist Party is being shaped by its new masters so as to recapture some of the old spirit. This time, however, Russian society, vastly changed in the last thirty years, will have a potent voice in shaping that future.

[27]

Prospects

On July 30, 1961, the program of the Communist Party of the U.S.S.R. was published, which was in turn accepted (with but minor emendations) at the Twenty-second Party Congress in October. This program, a statement of general philosophy, past achievements and future goals, is the third in the history of Russian Socialism. The first was voted by the Second Congress of the Party in 1903, when Russian Marxism was not yet *organizationally* split between the Bolsheviks and the Mensheviks. The second program marked the Bolsheviks' seizure of power and was voted by the Eighth Congress in 1919. The present program is designed to spell out the recent internal and external successes of the Soviet Union and to promise solemnly that the economic and political developments of the next two decades will enable Soviet society by 1980 to find itself in an advanced stage of Communism.

An ideological self-appraisal by any regime or party is of course not only a statement of goals and achievements but also a propaganda document. Certainly nobody but a Communist would accept the statement of the program that democratic socialism had long ago been realized in the U.S.S.R. Nor could any orthodox Marxist accept the definition of Communism to be achieved by 1980, for unlike what Marx and Engels thought on the subject, the state would not have withered away but would still exist and with it the Communist Party. The program speaks enticingly about the development of co-operation, of spontaneous social forms taking over one after another of the state's functions, but the final disappearance of the state is conditioned upon that very iffy formula: "For the final extinction of the state are necessary both internal conditions—construction of fully developed communist society—and external conditions—the final resolution of the contradictions between capitalism and communism on the international scene in favor of Communism."

The concrete importance of the program lies not so much in its rather distant pretensions and promises, but in the light it throws on the current and most immediate problem of Soviet society as seen by the Soviet leaders. As such it mirrors their hopes, their anxieties, and much of the political and psychological atmosphere of the leading Communist circles. The Party leaders do not propose even in the distant perspective of twenty years to concede concrete political liberties, or a change in the present structure of Soviet totalitarianism. The document, needless to say, does not even mention the possibility of toleration of other political parties and views; there is no hint that at any stage of the march toward communism the Party would lose its supreme and omnipresent role. The only *concrete* political admonition is the prohibition of the "cult of personality" and the provision for a periodic renewal of the personnel of the highest Party bodies. Yet as we observed before, that provision is completely ineffectual either in preventing personal dictatorship or in affecting the oligarchic character of Party leadership. Its insertion is largely ornamental and in practice it is not likely to make any difference. One is reminded of the Soviet Constitution of 1936 which established universal, equal, and secret voting for the legislative bodies without in the slightest affecting the despotic character of Stalin's rule. The key to effective democracy is free competition among various ideologies and parties; when that is missing and acknowledged as unthinkable even the most recondite formal conditions of formal democracy must remain meaningless.

The program reminds us forcefully of the production orientation of Soviet Communism. The realization of the stage of communism is both conditioned and premised upon a great increase in industrial and agricultural production. On the industrial side the language of the declaration is fairly specific: industrial production is to increase within a decade two and a half times and within twenty years no less than six times. On agriculture, the Achilles heel of the Soviet economy, the promise is more discreet and modest: its production is to assure an "abundance" of food and other products and to increase three and a half times. In a characteristic admission of the inferior economic status of the peasant as compared with the urban dweller, the program sets as its twenty-year goal the increase of the real wages of the worker by three to three and a half times, of the peasant *more* than four times; for the technical intelligentsia it promises a "considerable" increase.[1] By projecting different rates of increase as con-

---

[1] Two observations are pertinent under this count: even in terms of the propaganda-oriented program the rise in the standard of living proposed at the end of twenty years is considerably smaller than the projected rise in total production—something

ducive to eventual greater equality the document acknowledges serious disparities in real income as between the various social classes in the U.S.S.R. A large part of the increase in the standard of living is to come out of the extension of free services provided by the state, and the program promises that in addition to free education and health services they will come to include eventually free transportation, water, gas, and electricity.

One is struck by the fact that the program even when outlining fairly distant goals reflects the cautions and anxieties of the current Soviet regime. The increase in the standard of living is predicated upon the extension of free communal services, and only secondarily upon the increase in income disposable by the consumer. The current differences in the standard of living by various classes are implicitly acknowledged and the trend toward a greater equality is prescribed, but the Program shies away from the formula which to the fathers of Marxism contained the essence of the stage of Communism: "From each according to his ability, to each according to his needs." Nothing in the document foresees a fundamental change in the present methods of political and social control. Though much space in the document is devoted to the growth of spontaneous social organizations which are to take over various state functions, the implication is clear that at the end of twenty years the Communist Party of the U.S.S.R. will still continue to discharge the functions it does today—and in the Soviet Union it is the Communist Party which is the real state.

The program of the Communist Party of the U.S.S.R. is typical of the propaganda aspect of the social engineering in which the Party has been engaged since its seizure of power. The vision of a better, freer, and more abundant life for the people of the U.S.S.R. is combined with a reminder that the essentials of Party control and ideology must not suffer in the achievement of those goals. Typical of this implicit compromise between the aims of the regime and the aspirations of the people is the treatment of the future of agricultural organization. It has been stated here repeatedly that the ideal solution from the point of view of the Communist Party would have been a gradual transformation of the kolkhozes into sovkhozes and the final obliteration of the former as still containing elements of private property. But the regime has been inhibited by the repeated demonstrations that any move in that direction has aroused the peasants' opposition and threatened agricultural disaster. The program's language on the subject is extremely cautious and ambiguous. It is proposed to retain the collective farm as the major element in agriculture. At the same time

---

which runs against the orthodox Marxist teachings on the subject; and the projected rise in real income would give the Soviet citizen of 1980 the average standard of living of the American in 1961.

it is asserted that the growth of the material well-being of the kolkhozes will *eventually* enable the peasants to dispense with the private plot—the long-time *bête noire* of the regime,—and that by the same token the collective peasants will come to realize the advantages of further combinations and consolidations of individual kolkhozes into larger units (which would, of course, assimilate them more and more to the state farms), something the peasants have always stoutly resisted. Thus, for all the formal promise of the retention of collective farming, the aim and ambition of the regime is as always the ultimate destruction of the peasant household as an economic unit, and the transformation of the peasant into an agricultural worker.

The future evolution of the Soviet government rests upon contingencies both internal and external which cannot be foreseen, or (with all due respect to the authors of the program who forecast confidently the events of the next twenty years) foreordained. The general characteristic of the period since Stalin's death has been the increased awareness of the rulers of Russia of their people's aspirations combined with their determination to meet them only insofar as they do not intrude upon the totalitarian character of the system. In that sense, and if the term is not understood improperly, one may speak of a crisis of the Soviet system, a crisis by which is meant the growing inability of the ideology and formulas to meet the needs and aspirations of a society which has been largely modernized and industrialized. The old formulas and even the main tenets of Marxism-Leninism begin to sound more and more artificial and forced against the background of contemporary Soviet reality.[2] It is precisely because the Soviet leaders realize the lessening relevance of their ideology for their society that they intensify their efforts at ideological indoctrination and propaganda, and that they attempt to persuade their society that the great tasks of construction of communism still lie ahead, and that they require the continued presence and power of the Communist Party.

Considerations of foreign policy may appear to be out of place in a discussion of social and economic factors that shape the Soviet system. Yet no political system has been influenced so much *internally* by its ap-

---

[2] Here is one example taken from January 1961 Plenum of the Central Committee. *Kunayev* (First Secretary of the Communist Party of Kazakhstan): ". . . The working people of Kazakhstan meet with great enthusiasm the news about the calling of the Party Congress for October 1961. The news has everywhere produced political enthusiasm and a spurt of production in the factories, construction sites, kolkhozes and sovkhozes of our republic" (excitement among the participants)—*Kunayev* (continuing) "There is no doubt that . . ." (excitement in the meeting continues)—*Kunayev*: "I don't understand. Have I said anything wrong?" *Khrushchev*: "No, you did not say anything wrong, but you say that the nation of Kazakhstan has greeted the news about the Twenty-second Congress, but you cannot know how the nation did in fact greet the news, because it was announced just today, and you are in Moscow."

any case, would have made the old Stalinist type control of the satellites impractical since there is now in the Communist bloc another world power in addition to the U.S.S.R.

After the initial period of relaxation, 1955-57, the inter-Communist bloc policies, like internal Soviet politics, turned toward a consolidation and a balance between the old and the new. The Hungarian revolt in 1956 demonstrated that insofar as the European satellites were concerned the Soviet Union would still use force as the last resort to prevent any defection from the Communist bloc or even a far-reaching autonomy within it. Thus, while there is no longer any day-to-day supervision of internal politics of the satellites as in Stalin's day, there persists—even in the case of Poland, the most emancipated of all the satellites—a complete subordination to the U.S.S.R. in the fields of foreign policy and defense. Insofar as the general outline of social and economic policies is concerned the fact that, for the present, independence or even a far-reaching autonomy is incompatible with the membership in the European Communist bloc is best illustrated by the history of Soviet-Yugoslav relations. The post-Stalin regime spared no efforts to remove the anomaly of a Communist state aligned with the West and on hostile terms with the U.S.S.R. A period of rapprochement with the Yugoslavs in 1955-57 was followed by the realization that Tito's regime would never willingly return to complete dependence upon the U.S.S.R. At the same time, the example of Yugoslavia, seemingly restored to Communist orthodoxy by Moscow and yet independent in her policies, was proving demoralizing (from the Soviet viewpoint) to the satellites and played a role in the events of the fall of 1956 in Poland and Hungary.

The new policy which was designed to set limits to relaxation and liberalization of the intra-bloc relations was officially formulated in the spring of 1958. It came in the Soviet condemnation, echoed by the Chinese and the satellites, or revisionism and of the Yugoslav Communists as exponents of "revisionism." The word itself comes from the Marxist vocabulary, and it first referred to the views of several German socialists around the turn of the century who sought to bring Marxism in line with the changed conditions of Europe fifty years after its formulation. Some of them, especially Eduard Bernstein, sought to stress the democratic and evolutionary side of Marxism, and to de-emphasize its message of the class war. By resurrecting the term, Soviet propaganda has employed a typical semantic trick. Under "revisionism" are comprised all sorts of theories and tendencies, most of them having no connection with original revisionism, or often with each other, but having one common characteristic: their tendency to question or to weaken the supremacy of the Soviet Union and its monopoly on the correct interpretation of Marxism and Leninism. The Soviet leaders have thus sought to confound any opposition to Soviet

praisals of and attitude toward the world outside it. The November Revolution took place amidst the vivid expectations of the Bolsheviks that it would be but a prelude to a world-wide *socialist* upheaval in which industrialized societies of the West would follow the Russian example. For years afterward the Soviet regime lived in the fond expectation of capitalism crumbling and soviet regimes springing up all over the world, thus fulfilling the promise of its ideology, which holds that socialism is the eventual destiny of all mankind. A visible expression of this hope has been the *Communist (Third) International,* or *Comintern.* With its seat in Moscow the Third International consists of Communist parties in most civilized countries and is dedicated to the overthrow of non-Communist regimes. The Soviet government, though for diplomatic reasons it often insisted that the Third International was an independent organization that just happened to be situated in Moscow, never really made a secret of its own intimate connection with and then domination of the international Communist movement. From the middle twenties on, the International, like political life in the U.S.S.R., came under the very stringent domination of the Stalinist faction. And in turn the devotion to Moscow of the various national Communist parties and their total subjugation reached the point where their internal disputes, problems, and leadership were settled not in their countries but by a decision in Moscow. The Soviet Union has thus been in a very peculiar position insofar as her foreign policy and its instrumentalities have been concerned. For in addition to the usual influence exerted abroad by a great power, her policy has been helped and supported by groups of devoted followers in every country in the world. Soviet foreign policy has thus had two strings to its bow: the Foreign Commissariat or Ministry and the international Communist movement, which even after the dissolution of the Comintern in 1943[3] remained firmly under Moscow's thumb. The Comintern was supposed to be a genuinely international body with equality of the participating parties. Yet quite apart from and beyond the fact that Soviet Russia was the only state in which Communism was in power during the duration of the Comintern, the Soviet regime dominated foreign parties, such as the French Communists over whom it had no physical hold, with almost the same facility with which it could tell the Communists in the Ukraine or the Caucasus what to do.

Two quite different questions are posed by this tie-in between the Soviet state and the international Communist movement. The first touches on the strange phenomenon of the subjugation of the movement to the dictates of the rulers of the U.S.S.R. How could the foreign Communist

---

[3] The gesture was one of courtesy toward Russia's allies and otherwise meaningless, since the habit and mechanism of obedience to Moscow were too much ingrained among the foreign Communists to be disrupted by it.

parties, which often included courageous and intelligent people in their ranks, submit so tamely to summary orders? How have they been able to ignore the excesses and brutalities of the Soviet regime, its frequent violations of its Marxian premises, and its equally frequent sacrifices of international Communism to its own power interests?[4] To answer fully would require an elaborate psychological and political treatise. A very simple explanation would see in the hard-core Communists outside the U.S.S.R. not so much partisans of a political movement, as devotees of a religious cult with Russia its spiritual as well as power center.

A more germane question from our point of view is how far the connection has influenced Russia's policies both externally and internally. Do the Soviet leaders subordinate their policy to the aim of establishing Communism everywhere in the world? Do they look at the world through Marxian spectacles, or simply as rulers of a great and expanding state?

The answer must acknowledge that political motivations, just like personal ones, are a complex business and cannot be explained in single-factor terms. Certainly there has been a vast change from the very earliest days of the Soviet regime, when the Bolsheviks expected a world revolution and when their every policy was discussed with that aim in mind. In the succeeding years the support given to the foreign Communist parties was given increasingly only in return for their absolute obedience, and with the idea that they were a *valuable asset to the Soviet state*. Thus from the middle of the twenties to the present the U.S.S.R., instead of being the servant of international Communism, appeared increasingly as its master. This trend was fully demonstrated following World War II when Communist regimes in eastern European countries (Poland, Hungary, Bulgaria, Czechoslovakia, Rumania, Yugoslavia, and Albania) were established either largely or completely with the help of the Red Army. Quite apart from their ideological character and policies they were treated as appendages of the Russian state, and those Communists who were, or even appeared to be, more nationalistically minded were purged as mercilessly as any opponents of the Communist regime. The defection of Yugoslavia in 1948, which was due to the determination and ability of the ruling Yugoslav Communists not to submit unconditionally to Moscow, opened a new era in international Communism. For it demonstrated that while Communists *out of power* are likely to be fanatical followers of the line laid down by Moscow, once *in power* they like to augment and consolidate their position and to think in their own *national terms*, rather than to continue being humble and ever-ready-to-be-dismissed servants of another state and

---

[4] The Russo-German Pact of 1939, which opened the way for the German invasion of Poland and hence World War II, is of course the most notorious example of the latter.

its leaders. Titoism is then an organic disease of successful Communism rather than a phenomenon making a sporadic appearance in Yugoslavia.

As to the broader question whether the Soviet leaders always see foreign countries and policies through the prism of Marxism, the answer, with qualifications, must be in the affirmative. No matter how cynical or power-oriented a group of people may be, it is likely that they will view an unfamiliar situation in terms that reflect their upbringing, their deeply ingrained habits of thought and speech. Thus it may be impossible for even unusually well-informed Soviet Communists to view Western politics as being run in the main by something other than what Marxism-Leninism teaches them it is being run by: the class interests of the big-business circles. While *their experience* may teach them to be skeptical about their regime's propaganda about the conditions in the U.S.S.R., they are much more likely to believe in it when it "explains" the outside world.

This problem should not be confused with another one: whether the ruling circles in Russia believe in the inevitable armed clash between the U.S.S.R. and the capitalist world, or whether they believe that social (real Communist) revolutions abroad are likely to have a violent rather than evolutionary character. The Soviet leaders' pronouncements on those two subjects ever since the earliest and most ideological phase of the Communist regime was over in the early twenties, exhibit a familiar zigzag pattern. whenever a useful propaganda point could be scored at home or abroad by depicting an armed clash as inevitable, that was done. Thus, the hardships and sacrifices of rapid industrialization were rationalized by Stalin in the late twenties and early thirties on the grounds of an approaching war. During World War II, on the contrary, the virtues of coexistence of the U.S.S.R. and the Western world were extolled, and foreign Communists were told to collaborate even with "progressive" capitalists! Just as the people are being periodically scared by the prospect of the return of the internal enemy, i.e., their erstwhile capitalists and landowners (though it is never explained from where!), so the vision of a foreign aggressor and imperialist is a necessary device in the propaganda armory of the totalitarian regime, one that is periodically exhibited and retired. As far as *actions* are concerned, the foreign policy of the U.S.S.R. has for a long time been characterized by a *determined but cautious* policy of territorial aggrandizement, of expanding its sphere of influence, and yet avoiding the risk of an all-out war with the main power of the West that would undoubtedly be catastrophic to both sides in the present age.

The post-Stalin period has introduced some variations in this pattern. Just as in internal politics so in their policies *within* the Communist bloc the Soviet rulers have de-emphasized sheer coercion and laid more stress on the ideological bonds. The rise of Communist

domination with the betrayal of Marxism. Revisionism in the current Soviet parlance has thus become an omnium-gatherum including such diverse phenomena as the Yugoslav Communists' assertion that the U.S.S.R. as well as the United States is responsible for the world tension, the tendency toward freer cultural life sponsored by some Polish Communists, and the approaches to more objective history writing by some Soviet historians. Revisionism, in brief, has become a synonym for the loosening and evolution of the Communist system both internally and internationally toward a greater freedom and autonomy of the constituent parts.

Not since the very earliest days of the Soviet regime when it expected a world revolution have the problems of foreign policy weighed as heavily on the internal situation as they have since the death of Stalin. Both in their campaign against revisionism and in their pushful policies all over the world, the Soviet leaders testify to the fact that they consider the future of their own totalitarian system and of Communism in the U.S.S.R. firmly bound up with continued Soviet expansion and successes abroad. The reasons are both political and ideological. Politically, success or failure abroad affects the personal fortunes of the present leaders of the Party to a degree inconceivable in Stalin's lifetime. The old dictator's position was so unchallengeable that even a far-reaching defeat or miscalculation of Soviet foreign policy could not affect his internal power. Thus neither the failure of his Chinese policy in the beginning of his rule nor the defection of Yugoslavia toward the end could make the slightest difference in the extent of his despotism. Contrariwise, Khrushchev's position was considerably shaken in the winter of 1956-57 due to the mishaps of the satellite policy with which he was personally associated, and as we know he came close to being removed in the crisis of June 1957. His subsequent recovery and consolidation of personal dictatorship have reflected first, the popularity of his "peaceful coexistence" theme, and then, the undoubted successes of Soviet foreign policy in the wake of weakness and vacillation of Western policies over large areas of the world. The decline of Western influence and especially the hasty pace of decolonialization have undoubtedly created among the Soviet policy-makers an impression of Western impotence in the face of both Soviet power and the social forces stirred up in the underdeveloped areas of the world, and this undoubtedly persuaded them to step up their own pushfulness as exemplified in the Berlin crisis. The current interpretation of "peaceful coexistence" as contained in the program of the Communist Party envisages a peaceful, to be sure, but inevitable evanescence of the Western system, and the continuous growth in power and extent of the Communist one. The language of the program is quite explicit when it comes to the duties of foreign Communist parties: "The success of the working class in its struggle for the victory of revolution will depend on how successfully the working class and its [Communist] party will master all the *forms* of struggle—both peaceful and violent, both parliamentary and non-parliamentary—and how ready they will be to shift rapidly from one form to the other."

The Twenty-second Congress of the C.P.S.U. brought forth new evidence about the differences in the Communist bloc. Khrushchev's attack upon Albania and the Chinese defense of the Communist leaders of this country has dramatized the fact that the Communist bloc now contains two great powers and that the logic of the situation makes the previous unquestioning obedience of *all* Communist governments and all Communist parties to the U.S.S.R. a thing of the past. Thus Soviet Communism has been confronted with a dilemma of its own making, of its own success: the spread of Communism will in the future no longer automatically redound to the advantage of the Soviet Union. The country which, as Khrushchev has boasted, has become the greatest military power in the world and which has first conquered space through the flights of Gagarin and Titov, finds itself challenged by small and primitive Albania with a population of a million and a half. Communism's most spectacular success in the last forty years, the conquest of China, is now seen as something which might have deleterious effects on the interests of the U.S.S.R. Thus the assumption of the identity of interests of the U.S.S.R. and world Communism, the cornerstone of Soviet ideology and politics for so many years, is exposed as an illusion, and Communism which has spoken so glibly about "the inherent contradictions of the capitalist world" and its rival imperialisms is now confronted with the same phenomena in its own midst.

The dilemma of international Communism is thrown into sharper focus by its internal situation. The Twenty-second Congress has brought forth new denunciations of Stalin and the anti-Party groups, culminating in the ejection of his body from the Mausoleum. It is easy to eject Stalin's body and to blame the excesses and sufferings of the past on the dead tyrant and on those of his henchmen who have been defeated politically within the last few years. But it is much harder, in fact, impossible, for the present leaders to remove Stalinism from the system of government, for it has become a part and parcel of Soviet totalitarianism. Despite the reforms instituted by Khrushchev and the undoubted abolition of the worst Stalinist practices, the essential monolithic Party system, with its political and police controls over every form of social and cultural expression, remains very much the way it was before 1953. The anti-Stalin campaign is designed partly as a means to scare off any future opposition to Khrushchev in the Party but also as a propaganda measure to persuade the Soviet people that they now live under a democratic and benevolent system. But the revelations of the past excesses and crimes committed by

Stalin and his closest lieutenants make it even more imperative for the regime to present Communism in the world at large as an irresistible force for progress and peace.

The wager on the further expansion of Communism and Soviet power by the present leaders of the U.S.S.R. has, it is safe to say, a significance which transcends its immediate political consequences for the ruling group. We have suggested before that the very process of industrialization and modernization of Soviet society has evoked social forces which impinge upon the ideology, and indirectly upon the totalitarian character, of the regime. The ideology of Marxism can in the Soviet Union no longer serve the dynamic function it did during the crucial struggle for industrialization. In recent years it has increasingly become an official quasi-religious ortho-doxy designed to serve as the rationale of the totalitarian system. But if *internally* Communism can no longer evoke the enthusiasm of the earlier period and if one meets increasingly among the Soviet people what might be described as ideological agnosticism, then the external successes of So-viet foreign policy and Communism, the fact that in the underdeveloped areas of the world Communism can still evoke missionary zeal and religious enthusiasm, may serve to obscure the growing irrelevance of Marxist-Leninist formulas to everyday problems and politics in Soviet Russia. We have seen that even the most despotic totalitarianism cannot be entirely im-mune to social pressures and that the very successes of Communism in in-dustrializing and modernizing the country have created popular desires and aspirations which press upon the system. It is a commonplace, though sometimes a forgotten one, to say that the internal politics of any country can never be separated from its international situation. And so in the case of Soviet Russia it is not only the evolution of society but successes or defeats of Communism on a world scale which will determine the duration and character of the totalitarian system.

SELECT BIBLIOGRAPHY

I: The Analysis of Political Systems

How political science can be made a more scientific discipline has been discussed a great deal in recent years. The student would do well to begin with Roy C. Macridis' essay, *The Study of Comparative Government*, in which he criticizes traditional approaches and suggests a general scheme for comparative analysis. Also highly critical of the present state of political science, David Easton, in *The Political System*, like the authors in the present volume, takes the position that politics can best be studied as a system and explains the meaning of this approach in comparison with others. Harold Lasswell has probably done more than anyone else to develop the concept of power as a tool of analysis and the student will find his *Power and Society* (co-author, Abraham Kaplan) a rewarding, though difficult, book. Greater stress on the role of purpose will be found in R. M. MacIver, *The Web of Government*. A major work on interest groups in American politics is David Truman's *The Governmental Process*, based on an explicit theoretical scheme that can also be used in the study of the politics of other countries.

The approach followed in the present volume owes a great deal to the sociological theory of Talcott Parsons. From him, for example, we have taken the threefold division of culture into belief systems, values, and expressive symbols. Perhaps the best place to begin the study of his ideas is Part 2 ("Values, Motives, and Systems of Action") of *Toward a General Theory of Action*, a volume edited by Parsons and Edward A. Shils. For greater elaboration see Parsons, *The Social System*. A very helpful discussion of scientific method in both the natural and social sciences will be found in Karl Popper's *Poverty of Historicism*.

Almond, Gabriel, "Comparative Political Systems," *Journal of Politics*, Vol. 18 (1956)

Catlin, G. E. G., *Science and Methods of Politics*. New York, 1927.

————, A *Study of the Principles of Politics*. New York, 1930.

Duverger, Maurice, *Political Parties: Their Organization and Activity in the Modern State*, trans. by B. and R. North. New York, 1954.

Easton, David, *The Political System: An Inquiry into the State of Political Science*. New York, 1953.

Eulau, Heinz, Samuel J. Eldersveld, and Morris Janowitz, eds., *Political Behavior: A Reader in Theory and Research*. Glencoe, Ill., 1956. Includes an extensive bibliography on methodology for political scientists.

Finer, Herman, *The Theory and Practice of Modern Government*, rev. ed. New York, 1949.

Friederich, Carl J., *Constitutional Government and Democracy: Theory and Practice in Europe and America*, rev. ed. Boston, 1950.

Hecksher, Gunnar, *The Study of Comparative Government and Politics*. London, 1957.

Lasswell, Harold D., *Politics: Who Gets What, When, How*. New York, 1936.

———, and Abraham Kaplan, *Power and Society: A Framework for Political Inquiry*. New Haven, Conn., 1950.

Lazarsfeld, Paul F., and Morris Rosenberg, eds., *The Language of Social Research: a Reader in the Methodology of Social Research*. Glencoe, Ill., 1955.

Lipset, Seymour M., *Political Man: The Social Bases of Politics*. New York, 1960.

MacIver, R. M., *The Web of Government*. New York, 1947.

Macridis, Roy C., *The Study of Comparative Government*. New York, 1955.

———, and Bernard E. Brown, eds., *Comparative Politics: Notes and Readings*. Homewood, Ill., 1961.

Merriam, Charles E., *Political Power*. New York, 1934.

———, *Systematic Politics*. Chicago, 1946.

Merton, Robert K., *Social Theory and Social Structure*. Glencoe, Ill., 1949. Ch. II, "The Bearing of Sociological Theory on Empirical Research."

Morgenthau, Hans J., *Scientific Man vs. Power Politics*. Chicago, 1946.

Neumann, Sigmund, ed., *Modern Political Parties*. Chicago, 1955.

Parsons, Talcott, *Essays in Sociological Theory: Pure and Applied*. Glencoe, Ill., 1949. Ch. II, "The Present Position and Prospects of Systematic Theory in Sociology."

———, *The Social System*. Glencoe, Ill., 1951.

———, and Edward Shils, eds., *Toward a General Theory of Social Action*. Cambridge, Mass., 1951.

Popper, Karl, *The Poverty of Historicism*. London, 1957.

———, *The Logic of Scientific Discovery*. London, 1959.

Russell, Bertrand, *Power: A New Social Analysis*. New York, 1938.

Spiro, Herbert J., *Government by Constitution: The Political Systems of Democracy*. New York, 1959.

Truman, David B., *The Governmental Process: Political Interests and Public Opinion*. New York, 1951.

Weber, Max, *The Theory of Social and Economic Organization*, trans. by A. M. Henderson and Talcott Parsons, with an introduction by Talcott Parsons. New York, 1947. Especially Part III, "The Types of Authority and Imperative Coordination."

II: The British Political System

SOURCES: The chief source material for the study of British government is found in the publications of Her Majesty's Stationery Office (especially the Reports of Parliamentary Debates—*Hansard*—annual reports of the administrative departments, and the reports of special committees), publications of the Conservative and Labour Parties, and certain newspapers and journals, notably (for reliability and thoroughness of coverage) *The Times* (of London) and *The Economist*. The standard work on parliamentary procedure is Sir Thomas Erskine May, *A Treatise on the Law, Privileges, Proceedings and Usage of Parliament*, but the beginner will find especially useful L. A. Abraham and S. C. Hawtrey, *A Parliamentary Dictionary* (1956).

IMPORTANT SECONDARY WORKS: The classic interpretation of British government, still valid in many ways, is Walter Bagehot, *The English Constitution*, first published in 1867. More recent interpretations include L. S. Amery's provocative *Thoughts on the Constitution* (2nd ed., 1953), H. R. G. Greaves's socialist interpretation in *The British Constitution* (1948) and Herbert Morrison's *Government and Parliament* (1954), the latter useful chiefly as a view of British government from the inside.

BACKGROUND: Dennis Brogan, *The English People* (1943), is a gay but highly informative work that should be read before such studies as Geoffrey Gorer, *Exploring English Character* (1956), and R. Lewis and A. Maude, *The English Middle Classes* (1949). The best introduction to constitutional history is S. B. Chrimes, *English Constitutional History* (1953), the best work for further study D. L. Keir, *Constitutional History of Modern Britain, 1485–1951*. K. G. Feiling, *History of England to 1918* (1950), is a useful general history.

BIOGRAPHIES AND MEMOIRS: An extensive bibliography of biographies and memoirs of British statesmen may be found in Sir Ivor Jennings, *Cabinet Government* (1951), Appendix V.

THE CABINET: The standard work is Jennings, *Cabinet Government* (2nd ed., 1951). A. B. Keith, *The British Cabinet System* (2nd ed., 1952), and Lord Hankey, *Diplomacy by Conference* (1947), are also widely used.

PARLIAMENT: Sir Ivor Jennings, *Parliament* (2nd ed., 1957), is a thorough and detailed study; A. P. Herbert, *The Ayes Have It* (1937), gives perhaps a more vivid picture of Parliament than any other book; J. F. S. Ross, *Parliamentary Representation* (1944), is an important analysis of the membership of the House. By far the best brief introduction to the subject is Eric Taylor, *The House of Commons at Work* (1951).

ADMINISTRATION: For the beginner, G. A. Campbell, *The Civil Service in Britain* (1955), is excellent. H. E. Dale, *The Higher Civil Service* (1941), is standard on the administrative class; H. R. G. Greaves, *The Civil Service in the Changing State* (1947), deals with problems of administration in the welfare state and E. W. Cohen, *The Growth of the Civil Service* (1941), is a useful historical account.

PARTIES: R. T. McKenzie, *British Political Parties* (1955), is a comprehensive empirical account, making other works on British parties almost superfluous. Students are referred, however, to the excellent studies of British general elections since 1945 published by the Oxford University Press.

ECONOMIC AND SOCIAL POLICY: Much of the British welfare state is based on *The Beveridge Report: Social Insurance and Allied Services* (1942) and

Sir William Henry Beveridge, *Full Employment in a Free Society* (1944).
R. Brady, *Crisis in Britain* (1950), remains the best general account of
the Labour Government's policies. On the nationalized industries see
D. N. Chester, *The Nationalized Industries* and the *Studies in National-
ised Industry* issued in pamphlet form by the Acton Society Trust. On
national insurance services: D. C. Marsh, *National Insurance and Assistance in Great Britain* (1951). On the National Health Service: H. Eckstein, *The English Health Service* (1958). On Planning: S. H. Beer,
Treasury Control (2nd ed., 1957). On Town and Country Planning:
Town and Country Planning 1943–1951, H.M.S.O., Cmd. 8204.

III: The French Political System

The essential primary source of information about official acts of the
French government is the *Journal Officiel de la République Française*.
Laws, ordinances, and decrees, as well as the verbatim record of debates
in all the parliamentary bodies, are to be found in various sections of this
serial publication. Of even greater usefulness for most research is the
annual series, *L'Année Politique*, which contains in each year's volume a
chronological account of all phases of French public life and a selection
of important documents, speeches, and statistics. The best current record
of everyday politics, including a detailed description of party activities, is
to be found in the Paris daily, *Le Monde*. Important, though purely descriptive, monographs on various parts of the governmental structure and
on the content of government policy are published by the government
publications service, *Documentation Française*. Their series of studies
entitled *Notes et Etudes Documentaires* is especially useful. More analytical and scholarly studies are to be found regularly in the two leading
journals of French political science: the *Revue Française de Science Politique*, published quarterly in Paris; and the *Revue du Droit Public
et de la Science Politique*, published in Paris bi-monthly.

The general historical background can best be drawn from: Alfred
Cobban, *A History of Modern France*, 2 vols. (Penguin Books, 1961)
and Gordon Wright, *France in Modern Times* (Chicago, 1960). A useful
history of political institutions since 1789 is: Jean-Jacques Chevallier,
Histoire des Institutions Politiques de la France Moderne (Paris, 2nd ed.
1958). The detailed history of the Third Republic may be found in:
D. W. Brogan, *The Development of Modern France 1870–1940* (London,
1939); François Goguel, *La Politique des Partis sous la Troisième
République* (Paris, 1946); David Thomson, *Democracy in France* (New
York, 3rd ed. 1958); Alexander Werth, *The Twilight of France* (New
York, 1942), which deals with the 1930's. On the Vichy period there is:
Robert Aron, *The Vichy Regime* (New York, 1958); Dorothy Pickles,
France Between the Republics (London, 1946). The best history of
the Fourth Republic is: Jacques Fauvet, *La IVᵉ République* (Paris,

1959). The early years are described in: Dorothy Pickles, *French Politics: The First Years of the Fourth Republic* (London, 1953) and almost the whole span is recounted in: Alexander Werth, *France 1940–1956* (London, 1956). A more analytical account is: Herbert Luethy, *France Against Herself* (New York, 1955).

Any serious study of the French political system must begin with the three outstanding general works in English on the regimes of the recent past: dated, yet still very useful, is J. E. C. Bodley, *France* (London, New and Revised ed. 1902) for the early Third Republic, and Walter Rice Sharp, *The Government of France* (New York, 1938) for the later Third Republic. The most impressive study of the political system of the Fourth Republic is: Philip M. Williams, *Politics in Postwar France* (London, 2nd ed. 1958). Other interesting essays and general studies on the Third Republic are: Robert de Jouvenel, *La République des Camarades* (Paris, 1913); W. L. Middleton, *The French Political System* (New York, 1933); and André Tardieu, *La Révolution à Refaire*, 2 vols. (Paris, 1936, 1937). On the Fourth Republic there are: Maurice Duverger, *Droit Constitutionnel et Institutions Politiques* (Paris, 1955); François Goguel, *France Under the Fourth Republic* (Ithaca, N.Y., 1952) and his *Le Régime Politique Français* (Paris, 1955); Jacques Fauvet, *The Cockpit of France* (London, 1960); Nathan Leites, *On the Game of Politics in France* (Stanford, Cal., 1959), Constantin Melnik and Nathan Leites, *The House Without Windows: France Selects a President* (Evanston, Ill., 1958). For a detailed and purely descriptive work on the evolution of French political institutions see: *Les Institutions Politiques de la France*, Vol. I, in the collection entitled *Le Monde Contemporain*, published by the official government publications office, La Documentation Française (Paris, 1959).

The decline and fall of the Fourth Republic and the crisis in which the Fifth Republic was born are best described and analyzed in: Philip M. Williams and Martin Harrison, *De Gaulle's Republic* (New York, 1960), which also studies the new political institutions; Merry and Serge Bromberger, *Les 13 Complots du 13 Mai* (Paris, 1959); Léo Hamon, *De Gaulle dans la République* (Paris, 1958). Among the many books on the Algerian war and its impact on French politics, the most useful are: Joseph Kraft, *The Struggle for Algeria* (New York, 1961); Germaine Tillon, *Algeria: the Realities* (New York, 1958) and her *France and Algeria: Complementary Enemies* (New York, 1961); Thomas Oppermann, ed., *Le Problème Algérien* (Paris, 1961), which is a collection of documents; Charles-Henri Favrod, *La Révolution Algérienne* (Paris, 1959). The complex relationship between France's recent economic and social development and her political evolution is studied in: Raymond Aron, *France: Steadfast and Changing* (Cambridge, Mass., 1960); Edward R. Tannenbaum, *The New France* (Chicago, 1961); Roger Priouret, *La République des Députés* (Paris, 1959).

On the institutions and politics of the Fifth Republic, the most comprehensive, if partisan (critical) treatment is: Maurice Duverger, *La Cinquième République* (Paris, 2nd ed. 1960). Other general studies are: Dorothy Pickles, *The Fifth French Republic* (New York, 1960); Roy C. Macridis and Bernard E. Brown, *The De Gaulle Republic: Quest for Unity* (Homewood, Ill., 1960). The best translation of the new constitution, along with a brief commentary is: William Pickles, *The French Constitution of October 4th, 1958* (London, 1960). The most complete study of the origins and drafting of the constitution is to be found in a special issue of *La Revue Française de Science Politique* (Paris, Vol. IX, No. 1, March 1959) entitled *La Constitution de la Cinquième République*. The nature of the new form of political instability generated by the Algerian war is best grasped in a study of the third Algiers uprising of 1961: Jacques Fauvet and Jean Planchais, *La Fronde des Généraux* (Paris, 1961). For a highly detailed and purely descriptive work on the administrative and judicial institutions see: *Les Institutions Politiques de la France*, Vol. 2, in the collection entitled *Le Monde Contemporain*, published by the official government publications office, La Documentation Française (Paris, 1961). Interesting suggestions for further reform of French political institutions are to be found in: Maurice Duverger, *La VIe République et le Régime Présidentiel* (Paris, 1961); and in the excellent collective work of the small reform group called Le Club Jean Moulin, *l'Etat et le Citoyen* (Paris, 1961).

Finally, for an insight into the kind of men who founded the Fifth Republic and governed during its early years, there is no better source than their own writings. President de Gaulle has published his *War Memoirs* in three volumes (New York, 1955, 1959, 1960). Prime Minister Michel Debré has described his constitutional and political ideas in: *La Republique et son Pouvoir* (Paris, 1950) and *Ces Princes qui nous Gouvernent* (Paris, 1957).

The following are studies of more specialized subjects:

Association Française de Science Politique, *Le Référendum de Septembre et les Elections de Novembre 1958*. Paris, 1960.

Barthélemy, Joseph, *L'Introduction du Régime Parlementaire en France*. Paris, 1904.

Blum, Léon, *La Réforme Gouvernementale*. Paris, 1936.

Brayance, Alain, *Anatomie du Parti Communiste Français*. Paris, 1953.

Campbell, Peter, *French Electoral Systems and Elections 1789-1957*. London, 1958.

Chapman, Brian, *Introduction to French Local Government*. London, 1953.

————, *The Prefects and Provincial France*. London, 1955.

Clough, Shepard, *France: A History of National Economics 1789-1939*. New York, 1939.

Curtius, Ernst, *The Civilization of France*. London, 1932.

Earle, Edward M., ed., *Modern France: Problems of the Third and Fourth Republics*. Princeton, N.J., 1951.

Ehrmann, Henry W., *French Labor from Popular Front to Liberation*. New York, 1947.

————, *Organized Business in France*. Princeton, N.J., 1957.

Einaudi, Mario, et al., *Communism in Western Europe*. Ithaca, N.Y., 1951.

————, *Christian Democracy in France and Italy*. South Bend, Ind., 1952.

————, *Nationalization in France and Italy*. Ithaca, N.Y., 1955.

Goguel, François, *Géographie des Elections Françaises de 1870 à 1951*. Paris, 1951.

Grosser, Alfred, *La Quatrième République et sa Politique Extérieure*. Paris, 1961.

Lidderdale, D. W. S., *The Parliament of France*. London, 1951.

Lorwin, Val R., *The French Labor Movement*. Cambridge, Mass., 1954.

Meynaud, Jean, *Les Groupes de Pression en France*. Paris, 1958.

Robson, William A., ed., *The Civil Service in Britain and France*. New York, 1956.

Sharp, Walter Rice, *The French Civil Service: Bureaucracy in Transition*. New York, 1931.

Siegfried, André, *France: A Study in Nationality*. New Haven, Conn., 1930.

Soulier, A., *L'Instabilité Ministérielle sous la Troisième République 1871-1938*. Paris, 1939.

Wahl, Nicholas, "The French Constitution of 1958: The Initial Draft and its Origins," in: *The American Political Science Review*. Vol. LIII No. 2, June, 1959.

Wright, Gordon, *The Reshaping of French Democracy*. New York, 1948.

IV: The German Political System

Among basic sources, reports of parliamentary debates are the most important, especially *Verhandlungen des deutschen Bundestages*, and its predecessor of the Weimar period and before, *Verhandlungen des deutschen Reichstages*. For the Bonn Republic, *Sitzungen des deutschen Bundesrates* and *Entscheidungen des Bundesverfassungsgerichtes* are also useful. Many publications of the Office of the United States High Commissioner for Germany contain translations of German documents.

Deutschland-Jahrbuch, an annual edited by Mehnert and Schulte, is full of factual information. Among learned journals, the following are useful: *Archiv des öffentlichen Rechts, Süddeutsche Juristenzeitung, Zeitschrift für Politik, Politische Studien. Frankfurter Allgemeine Zeitung* is one of the best daily newspapers. *Das Parlament* is a weekly devoted to parliamentary affairs in particular and politics in general. *Der Wähler*, published by the German Voters' Association, concentrates on matters electoral. The Trade Union Federation publishes *Gewerkschaftliche Monatshefte. Der Spiegel* is Germany's equivalent of *Time* magazine. *Die Gegenwart* appeals to intellectuals. Among contemporary German publications, the series of the Association for Political Science, edited by Dolf Sternberger, is of special interest. In this series, Breitling's work has been most helpful for our purposes. The series published by the *Kommission für Geschichte des Parlamentarismus und der politischen Parteien* (History of Parliamentarism and Political Parties) (Bonn, 1952-   ) contains a number of useful volumes.

I. GENERAL

Bergsträsser, Ludwig, *Geschichte der politischen Parteien in Deutschland*. 7th ed., Munich, 1952.

Bowen, Ralph H., *German Theories of the Corporative State*. New York, 1947.

Buchheim, Karl, *Geschichte der christlichen Parteien in Deutschland*. Munich, 1953.

Butz, Otto, *Modern German Political Theory*. New York, 1955.

Clapham, J. H., *The Economic Development of France and Germany, 1815-1914*. Cambridge, Mass., 1936.

Glum, Friedrich, *Das parlamentarische Regierungssystem in Deutschland, Grossbritannien und Frankreich*. Munich, 1950.

Krieger, Leonard, *The German Idea of Freedom: History of a Political Tradition*. Boston, Mass., 1957.

Meinecke, Friedrich, *The German Catastrophe*. Cambridge, Mass., 1950.

Neumann, Sigmund, *Die deutschen Parteien*. 2nd ed., Berlin, 1932.

Pollock, James K., and H. Thomas, *Germany in Power and Eclipse*. New York, 1952.

Schorske, Carl, *German Social Democracy*. Cambridge, Mass., 1950.

Taylor, A. J. P., *The Course of German History*. New York, 1946.

Treue, Wolfgang, *Deutsche Parteiprogramme, 1861-1954*. Göttingen, 1954.

Ullmann, R. K., and Sir Stephen King-Hall, *German Parliaments*. London, 1954.

Valentin, Veit, *The German People*. New York, 1946.

Wheeler-Bennett, John W., *The Nemesis of Power*. London, 1953.

II. THE WEIMAR PERIOD

Anschütz, Gerhard, and Richard Thoma, eds., *Handbuch des deutschen Staatsrechts*. 2 vols., Tübingen, 1930-32.

Bracher, Karl D., *Die Auflösung der Weimarer Republik*. Stuttgart, 1955.

Brecht, Arnold, *Federalism and Regionalism in Germany*. New York, 1945.

——, *Prelude to Silence*. New York, 1944.

Epstein, Klaus, *Matthias Erzberger and the Dilemma of German Democracy*. Princeton, N.J., 1959.

Flechtheim, Ossip K., *Die Kommunistische Partei Deutschlands in der Weimarer Republik*. Offenbach, 1948.

Gatzke, Hans, *Stresemann and the Re-Armament of Germany*. Baltimore, Md., 1954.

Halperin, S. William, *Germany Tried Democracy*. New York, 1946.

Heberle, Rudolf, *From Democracy to Nazism*. Baton Rouge, La., 1945.

Heiden, Konrad, *Der Fuehrer*. Boston, Mass., 1944.

Hermens, F. A., *Democracy or Anarchy?* Notre Dame, 1941.

Matthias, Erich, *Sozialdemokratie und Nation*. Stuttgart, 1952.

Rosenberg, Arthur, *The Birth of the German Republic*. London, 1931.

Scheele, Godfrey, *The Weimar Republic*. London, 1946.

Sturmthal, Adolf F., *The Tragedy of European Labor*. New York, 1943.

Watkins, F. M., *The Failure of Constitutional Emergency Powers under the German Republic*. Cambridge, Mass., 1939.

III. NATIONAL SOCIALISM

Bullock, Allan, *Hitler—A Study in Tyranny*. London, 1952.

Fraenkel, Ernst, *The Dual State.* New York, 1941.

Neumann, Franz, *Behemoth.* New York, 1944.

Shirer, William L., *The Rise and Fall of the Third Reich: A History of Nazi Germany.* New York, 1960.

IV. 1945-1961

Amtliches Handbuch des deutschen Bundestages. Bonn, 1949, 1953, 1957, 1961.

Breitling, Rupert, *Die Verbände in der Bundesrepublik,* Dolf Sternberger, ed., Meisenheim, 1955.

Clay, Lucius D., *Decision in Germany.* New York, 1950.

Deschamps, Bruno, *Macht und Arbeit der Ausschüsse,* Dolf Sternberger, ed., Meisenheim, 1954.

Deutsch, Karl W., and Lewis J. Edinger, *Germany Rejoins the Powers.* Stanford, Calif., 1959.

Eschenburg, Theodor, *Staat und Gesellschaft in Deutschland.* Stuttgart, 1956.

Flechtheim, Ossip K., *Die deutschen Parteien seit 1945.* Berlin, 1955.

Friedrich, Carl J., "Rebuilding the German Constitution," *American Political Science Review,* June, August, 1949.

Fromme, Friedrich K., *Von der Weimarer Verfassung zum Bonner Grundgesetz.* Tübingen, 1960.

Gimbel, John, *A German Community under American Occupation.* Stanford, Calif., 1961.

Golay, John Ford, *The Founding of the Federal Republic of Germany.* Chicago, 1958.

Grosser, Alfred, *Die Bonner Demokratie.* Düsseldorf, 1960.

Heidenheimer, Arnold J., *Adenauer and the CDU.* The Hague, 1960.

——, *The Governments of Germany.* New York, 1961.

Heydte, F. A. v. d., and K. Sacherl, *Soziologie der deutschen Parteien.* Munich, 1955.

Hund, H., *Der BHE in Koalition und Opposition.* Heidelberg, 1953.

Institut für Staatslehre und Politik e.V. Mainz, *Der Kampf um den Südweststaat.* Munich, 1952.

Kitzinger, Uwe, *German Electoral Politics.* Oxford, 1960.

Litchfield, Edward H., ed., *Governing Postwar Germany.* Ithaca, N.Y., 1953.

Markmann, Heinz, *Das Abstimmungsverhalten der Parteifraktionen in deutschen Parlamenten* Dolf Sternberger, ed., Meisenheim, 1954.

Morgenthau, Hans J., ed., *Germany and the Future of Europe.* Chicago, 1950.

Plischke, Elmer, *Contemporary Government of Germany.* Boston, Mass., 1961.

Pollock, James K., ed., *German Democracy at Work.* Ann Arbor, Mich., 1955.

Roth, Götz, *Fraktion und Regierungsbildung,* Dolf Sternberger, ed., Meisenheim, 1954.

Sänger, Fritz, *Handbuch des deutschen Bundestages.* Stuttgart, 1954.

Spiro, Herbert J., *The Politics of German Codetermination.* Cambridge, Mass., 1958.

Trossmann, Hans, *Der zweite deutsche Bundestag.* Bonn, 1954.

Wallenberg, Hans, *Report on Democratic Institutions in Germany.* New York, 1956.

Wallich, Henry C., *Mainsprings of German Revival.* New Haven, Conn., 1955.

V: The Russian Political System

The most essential materials toward the study of Soviet government are in Russian. Among them may be mentioned *Sbornik Zakonov S.S.S.R. I Ukazov Prezidiuma Verkhovnogo Soveta S.S.S.R. (Collection of the Laws of the U.S.S.R. and Decrees of the Supreme Soviet of the U.S.S.R.)*, Moscow, 1945; *Vsesoyuznaya Kommunisticheskaya Partiya V Rezolutsiyakh I Resheniyakh S'ezdov, Konferentsii, I Plenumov Tsk 1898–1939 (All-Union Communist Party (B) in Resolutions and Decrees of Congresses, Conferences, and Plenums of the Central Committee 1898–1939)*, Moscow, 1941. Stenographic reports of Congresses and Conferences of the Communist Party of the U.S.S.R. are available in Russian, and they provide the most illuminating guide to the Soviet system.

Among many studies in English Merle Fainsod, *How Russia Is Ruled* and Barrington Moore, Jr., *Soviet Politics—The Dilemma of Power* are the most perceptive and comprehensive treatments of the Soviet government. The already existing volumes of E. H. Carr, *A History of Soviet Russia* provide the most detailed account of the development of Soviet power, though some of Mr. Carr's interpretations, especially in the first volume, are questioned by other authorities. Bertram Wolfe, *Three Who Made a Revolution* is an excellent treatment of the origins of Bolshevism. A valuable tool for the student who does not command Russian is the *Current Digest of the Soviet Press*, which translates the most important articles appearing in the Soviet press. Some of the bibliography available in English is indicated in the list below.

The Anti-Stalin Campaign and International Communism, Russian Institute, Columbia University. New York, 1956.

Arakelian, A., *Industrial Management in the U.S.S.R.* Washington, 1950.

Barghoorn, Frederick C., *The Soviet Image of the United States*. New York, 1950.

Bauer, Raymond A., *The New Man in Soviet Psychology*. Cambridge, Mass., 1952.

Berman, Harold J., *Justice in Russia*. Cambridge, Mass., 1950.

Bienstock, Gregory, Solomon M. Schwarz, and Aaron Yugow, *Management in Russian Industry and Agriculture*. London and New York, 1944.

Burns, Emile, *A Handbook of Marxism*. New York, 1935.

Carew Hunt, R. N., *The Theory and Practice of Communism*. New York, 1951.

Carr, E. H., *A History of Soviet Russia: The Bolshevik Revolution*, Vols. I–III. New York, 1951–53.

———, *A History of Soviet Russia: The Interregnum 1923–24*. New York, 1955.

Chamberlin, W. H., *The Russian Revolution, 1917–1921*. 2 vols. New York, 1935.

Current Soviet Policies: The Documentary Record of XIXth Communist Party Congress and the Reorganization After Stalin's Death. New York, 1953.

Curtiss, J. W., *Church and State in Russia, 1900–1917*. New York, 1939.

Dallin, David J., *The Real Soviet Russia*. New Haven, Conn., 1944.

———, and Boris I. Nicolaevsky, *Forced Labor in Soviet Russia*. New Haven, Conn., 1947.

Deutscher, Isaac, *Soviet Trade Unions*, London and New York, 1950.

———, *Stalin: A Political Biography*. New York, 1949.

Fainsod, Merle, *How Russia Is Ruled*. Cambridge, Mass., 1953.

Fischer, Ruth, *Stalin and German Communism*. Cambridge, Mass., 1948.

Florinsky, Michael T., *The End of the Russian Empire*. New Haven, Conn., 1931.

Gsovski, Vladimir, *Soviet Civil Law*. 2 vols. Ann Arbor, Mich., 1948.

History of the Communist Party of the Soviet Union (Bolsheviks); Short Course. New York, 1939.

Holzman, Franklyn D., *Soviet Taxation*. Cambridge, Mass., 1955.

Inkeles, Alex, *Public Opinion in Soviet Russia*. Cambridge, Mass., 1950.

Kolarz, Walter, *Russia and Her Colonies*. New York, 1952.

Kursky, A., *The Planning of the National Economy of the U.S.S.R.* Moscow, 1949.

Lenin, V. I., *State and Revolution*. New York, 1935.

Lyashchenko, P. I., *History of the National Economy of Russia to the 1917 Revolution*. New York, 1949.

Marx, Karl, *Capital*. 3 vols. Chicago, 1908–09.

———, *The Civil War in France*. London, 1941.

———, *Critique of the Gotha Programme*. London, 1943.

Masaryk, Thomas G., *The Spirit of Russia*. 2 vols. London, 1919.

Mavor, James, *An Economic History of Russia*. 2 vols. London and Toronto, 1914.

Moore, Barrington, Jr., *Soviet Politics—The Dilemma of Power*. Cambridge, Mass., 1950.

———, *Terror and Progress: the U.S.S.R.* Cambridge, Mass., 1955.

Radkey, Oliver H., *The Election to the Russian Constituent Assembly of 1917*. Cambridge, Mass., 1950.

Report of Court Proceedings in the Case of the Anti-Soviet "Bloc of Rights and Trotskyites." Moscow, 1938.

Report of Court Proceedings, the Case of the Trotskyite—Zinovievite Terrorist Centre, Heard before the Military Collegium of the Supreme Court of the USSR, August 19–24, 1936. Moscow, 1936.

Robinson, Geroid T., *Rural Russia under the Old Régime*. New York, 1949.

Schumpeter, Joseph, *Capitalism, Socialism, and Democracy*. New York, 1942.

Schwartz, Harry, *Russia's Soviet Economy*. New York, 1950.

Seton-Watson, Hugh, *From Lenin to Malenkov*. New York, 1953.

Souvarine, Boris, *Staline: Aperçu historique du bolchévisme*. Paris, 1935.

Stalin, Joseph, *Foundations of Leninism*. New York, 1932.

———, *Problems of Leninism*. New York, 1934.

———, *Survey of Russian History*. 2nd ed. London, 1947.

Timasheff, Nicholas S., *The Great Retreat*. New York, 1946.

Towster, Julian, *Political Power in the USSR*. New York, 1948.

Treadgold, Donald W., *Lenin and His Rivals*. New York, 1955.

Trotsky, Leon, *The History of the Russian Revolution*. 3 vols. New York, 1932.

Vernadsky, George, *A History of Russia*. New York, 1944.

Webb, Sidney and Beatrice, *Soviet Communism: A World Civilization?* 2 vols. London, 1936.

White, D. Fedotoff, *The Growth of the Red Army.* Princeton, N.J., 1944.

Wolfe, Bertram D., *Three Who Made a Revolution.* New York, 1948.

Wollenberg, Erich, *The Red Army.* London, 1938.

Index

THE AUTHORS

SAMUEL H. BEER, co-editor of *Patterns of Government* and author of *Part I: The Analysis of Political Systems*, holds an A.B. from the University of Michigan, a B.A. from Oxford University (where he attended Balliol College as a Rhodes Scholar), and a Ph.D. from Harvard University. Before joining the Harvard faculty in 1938, he worked for the Resettlement Administration as a writer, did some writing for the Democratic National Committee, was a reporter on the *New York Post* and, later, a researcher and writer on *Fortune*. Chairman of the Department of Government at Harvard University 1954-58, he is the author of *The City of Reason*, of *Treasury Control*, of the section on Great Britain in *Modern Political Parties* (Sigmund Neumann, ed.), and of numerous articles in scholarly journals. He is an Associate Editor of the *American Political Science Review*.

ADAM B. ULAM, co-editor of *Patterns of Government* and author of *Part V: The Russian Political System*, received his B.A. from Brown University and his Ph.D. from Harvard University. He began teaching at the University of Wisconsin and since 1947 has been on the faculty of Harvard University, where he is a professor of Government. He joined the Russian Research Center there in 1949 as a Research Associate. In 1953-54 he was a Research Associate of the Center for International Studies at the Massachusetts Institute of Technology and in 1956-57 he received the Rockefeller Fellowship in Political Theory. He was granted a Guggenheim Fellowship in 1956-57. He is the author of *Philosophical Foundations of English Socialism*, *Titoism and the Cominform*, and *The Unfinished Revolution*. He has contributed to *Continuity and Change in Russian and Soviet Thought* (Ernest J. Simmons, ed.) and to *Constitutions and Constitutional Trends since World War II* (Arnold J. Zurcher, ed.). In addition, he has published many articles in professional journals.

HARRY H. ECKSTEIN, author of *Part II: The British Political System,* was granted his B.A., M.A., and Ph.D. by Harvard University. He is now an Associate Professor of Politics at Princeton University. Two years of his graduate work were spent at the London School of Economics. He has written widely for academic journals and is the author of *The English Health Service* and *Pressure Group Politics.*

HERBERT J. SPIRO, author of *Part IV: The German Political System,* was graduated from Harvard College and holds a Ph.D. from Harvard University. He was in Europe in 1953-54 on a Sheldon Traveling Fellowship and a Fulbright Grant, doing research for his book on *The Politics of German Codetermination.* In 1955 he returned to Germany to gather material on some aspects of the Soviet occupation of East Germany. He has published many articles in American and foreign journals and has contributed to *Governing Postwar Germany* (E. H. Litchfield, ed.). He is the author of *Government by Constitution,* published by Random House. He is an Associate Professor at Amherst College.

NICHOLAS WAHL, author of *Part III: The French Political System,* was awarded his bachelor's degree by the University of Wisconsin and his master's degree and doctorate by Harvard University, where he has taught from 1953-63. He is now Associate Professor of Politics at Princeton University. He has also studied at the University of Paris and the University of Geneva and has taught at the University of Lyons and the University of Saigon. He is author of *The Fifth Republic,* published by Random House, and is spending 1962-63 at Nuffield College, Oxford, completing a forthcoming book, *De Gaulle and France.*